The Nature of Human Consciousness

The Nature of
Human Consciousness

A BOOK OF READINGS

Edited by

ROBERT E. ORNSTEIN

Institute for the Study of Human Consciousness,
The Langley Porter Neuropsychiatric Institute

THE VIKING PRESS   NEW YORK

By special arrangement, the paperbound educational edition of this book is published and distributed by W. H. Freeman and Company, San Francisco, California, and the hardbound trade edition is published and distributed by The Viking Press, New York, New York.

Copyright © 1973 by Robert E. Ornstein

Published in 1974 by The Viking Press, Inc.
625 Madison Avenue, New York, N.Y. 10022

Published simultaneously in Canada by
The Macmillan Company of Canada Limited

SBN 670-50480-7 (hardbound)
7167-0790-X (paperbound)

Library of Congress catalog card number: 73-7693 (hardbound)
73-4431 (paperbound)
Printed in U.S.A.

To David Sobel (and stress in early infancy)
for those wonderful summer days, sitting in his room,
in Janet's house, editing this book, and playing with the cat.

Contents

Preface

Psychology is, primarily, the science of consciousness. Its researchers deal with consciousness directly when possible, and indirectly, through the study of physiology and behavior, when necessary. Psychologists are now returning to the essential questions of our discipline: How does the mind work? What are the major dimensions of human consciousness? Is consciousness individual or cosmic? What means are there to extend human consciousness? These questions have not yet had a full treatment within academic science, having been ruled out of inquiry by the dominant paradigm of the past 60 or so years.

Yet there is a cultural and scientific evolution, if not revolution, in process. Academic people, being members of their culture, reflect the general interest in "Altered States" of consciousness, meditation, drug states, and new and old religions. The intent of this book is to assist in a small way in regaining a lost perspective in psychology. Often teachers and their students become sidetracked in their study, and wind up investigating One Minor Aspect of One Possible Means of Approaching Psychological Problems. The central aim, the context, the original impetus to study consciousness may become forgotten. There is, therefore, a continuing need to reestablish the basis of psychology and to link current research with that of other students of consciousness, such as William James and Carl Jung, and with the "esoteric" psychologies of other cultures, such as Sufism, Yoga, and Buddhism.

A major thesis of this book is that two major modes of consciousness exist in Man, the intellectual and its complement, the intuitive. Contemporary science (and, indeed, much of Western culture) has predominantly emphasized the intellectual mode, and has filtered out rich sources of evidence: meditation, "mysticism," non-ordinary reality, the influence of "the body" on "the mind." In part, this book is intended to open inquiry into that inelegant, tacit, "other" side of ourselves.

A new focus is developing within psychology. Contemporary research has documented that a person's consciousness is limited by his assumptions or available categories. But we as psychologists have not yet turned this insight fully upon ourselves and our discipline. Our primary need, now, is to reevaluate the premises of our work and to extend once again the boundaries of scientific inquiry and our conception of human capacities. In general, for the past 60 or so years, psychologists have tended to limit their conception of what is possible to what can currently be measured. If a community of fishermen all possess fish-nets with openings three inches in diameter, they run a serious risk of ignoring and even denying the existence of two-inch fish.

Since the psychology of human consciousness is in a period of new formation, a book of readings like this needs to contain a rather rich mixture of sources: "hard" science reports and techniques of meditation, philosophy and anthropology, neurophysiological articles on brain function and the ancient Chinese *I Ching*, linguistic analyses and yoga. In common they point toward an extended and more complete conception of consciousness.

The *process* of editing a book can be a useful teacher. Articles from quite diverse traditions and different specializations can be juxtaposed to allow their essential similarity to show through. The total effect of the articles here, taken together, is far greater than their individual excellences. A major portion of the process of a book is, simply, pointing— to areas of research not yet fully explored and to a new perspective on facts which we already know.

But this perspective, too, is a bias. It requires filtering out those items which do not fit and selecting material to fit one particular design, for space as well as bias limits content. For additional input, I highly recommend Charles Tart's *Altered States of Consciousness* (Wiley, 1969), which includes material on hypnosis, dream and drug states, and other articles which are not included in this book.

Although the articles are divided up into sections, the reader should not consider these sections to be fixed categories. The articles reflect each other in a complex and sometimes unexpected manner, and need not be read in any prescribed order. The selections themselves are part of other wholes. My major hope is that this book will help lead the reader back to those original sources, be they Sufi literature, the *Scientific American*, or the *Bulletin of the Los Angeles Neurological Societies*. In a new area of inquiry, the student needs to be able to consult and to integrate such diverse input.

Again, James, at the turn of the century, best set the spirit of this book:

> Our normal waking consciousness, rational consciousness as we call it, is but one special type of consciousness, whilst all about it, parted from it by the filmiest of screens, there lie potential forms of consciousness entirely different. We may go through life without suspecting their existence; but apply the requisite stimulus, and at a touch they are there in all their completeness, definite types of mentality which probably somewhere have their field of application and adaptation. No account of the universe in its totality can be final which leaves these other forms of consciousness quite disregarded. How to regard them is the question,—for they are so discontinuous with ordinary consciousness. Yet they may determine attitudes though they cannot furnish formulas, and open a region though they fail to give a map. At any rate, they forbid a premature closing of our accounts with reality.

Robert E. Ornstein
San Francisco
February 18, 1972

I.

THE SCOPE
OF PSYCHOLOGY

Introduction

Abraham Maslow once said, "If the only tool you have is a hammer, you tend to treat everything as if it were a nail." Such a one-tool viewpoint has been all too evident for many years in psychology, and has caused certain useful and productive methods, such as behaviorism, to be equated with the extent of all knowledge. Perhaps such an equation is inevitable; being human, we often confuse our tools with reality. But it is important at times to step back from such involvement and look again at the entire situation. Some who have done so recently have realized that psychology, as it has most often been taught, studied, and researched, has been unduly restricted to one special method, one special state of analysis, one special manner, in which human consciousness can operate. As it was for John Watson in 1913, it is time once again to open up the scope of psychology to areas of thought that have not been fully represented in contemporary research, and to return to its primary source, to the analysis of consciousness, but now employing the technological and methodological advances that have been made in the course of the past century.

James's piece, the first chapter in his monumental classic, *The Principles of Psychology*, is a useful introduction to this volume, for it clearly defines psychology as the science of mental life, that is to say, of consciousness, and argues for a psychology with a broad content and a deliberate "vagueness" appropriate to the state of current knowledge. This idea will be very difficult for many to accept, especially for those who might prefer a more limited scope, restricted to phenomena of which we are absolutely sure. But such an approach unduly restricts investigation to "nails," in Maslow's terms, even though it *seems* more "scientific." In contrast, James articulates a concept of psychology as a whole and complete science of mind, a position echoed by the later writers in this section.

The authors of the second paper, Cantril, Ames, Hastorf, and Ittelson, formed the major part of current psychology's most sophisticated view of consciousness. They were called "Transactionalists," a weighty word which reflected their view that human consciousness is largely an interaction, or a "bet," between the organism and the environment.* It is of the utmost importance to apply our knowledge about the nature of human consciousness to scientific psychology *itself*, and this group is one of the few who have attempted to do so. They echo a concept offered by James 60 years earlier, that we must not foreclose the possibilities, must always attempt to maintain a broad and open view of the field and to build science toward the limits, not inward from the "sure and hard facts." They stress that quantification is but one function of science, one that has currently overdominated psychological inquiry to the detriment of a full scope and an open view of the possibilities.

Both James and the transactionalists stress that science, as described in textbooks as a purely quantitative enterprise, is incomplete. Michael Polanyi, a philosophical writer, makes more clear that what we usually term "mind" is but one mode of thought—explicit verbal-logical thinking. He contrasts this mode with the "tacit" mode, a nonverbal mode which he holds to underlie all knowledge. This dichotomy opens a fundamental duality of consciousness as it is manifest in scientific inquiry, psychology, neurophysiology, and personally as it aids in "understanding ourselves."

Polanyi takes us in one direction toward an analysis of consciousness as two complementary modes of thought. Blackburn is more concerned with the problems of science itself (not restricted to psychology), and here employs an analysis like Polanyi's to make a judgment similar to that of James and of Cantril *et al.*: our scientific endeavor in general, not

---

*See also selections 14 and 15 for more explicit statements of their views.

merely the psychology of consciousness, has become overrefined, and in some very real cases out of control; we have developed the explicit-intellectual component of knowledge-seeking, but at the expense of the intuitive or "sensuous" component. This article recalls the great physicist Oppenheimer's comment on the scientific and mystical ways of knowing:

> "These two ways of thinking, the way of time and history, and the way of eternity and timelessness, are both part of man's effort to comprehend the world in which he lives. Neither is comprehended in the other nor reducible to it . . . each supplementing the other, neither telling the whole story."

As a result of many forces, both scientific and cultural, we may be at the brink of an era in which both the intellectual and the intuitive modes can be recognized as performing complementary functions. Instead of science and direct experience being opposed to one another, it may be possible for both to attain a higher perspective of complementarity. A Sufi tale (from Shah, 1971a, p. 67) about the judging function in us makes this clearer:

> Nasrudin was made a judge and listened to his first case. When the prosecution rested its argument, he stood up and said: "I believe you are right!"
> When the defense had finished its summation, Nasrudin again stood up and said: "I believe you are right!"
> The clerk of the court came in front of the judge: "Your honor, they cannot both be right."
> "I believe you are right!" said Nasrudin.

Tart's paper is the first new attempt to take both modes of knowledge into account. He proposes that we must restructure the very method of scientific inquiry itself to account for many phenomena which people experience. In many ways as we consider the esoteric disciplines of Sufism, Buddhism, Yoga, they emerge as *sciences* of inner states, technologies developed to treat these most pressing problems of philosophy, psychiatry, psychology. Conventional science, as it is usually practiced, often neglects the essential component in studying consciousness. Concerning marijuana intoxication, Tart asks whether anyone would be willing to risk going to jail for the sake of having their eyes redden, their performance on complex psychomotor tests decline, etc. These are clearly side-effects, not the *central* components of marijuana intoxication, and an attempt to pass off research on such side-effects as the "hard science" in this area simply misses the point. Tart's approach is one of the very first contemporary attempts to synthesize the two modes of knowledge-seeking; the concrete workings of his new approach will take a while to emerge.

1.

The Scope of Psychology

William James

Psychology is the Science of Mental Life, both of its phenomena and [of] their conditions. The phenomena are such things as we call feelings, desires, cognitions, reasonings, decisions, and the like; and, superficially considered, their variety and complexity is such as to leave a chaotic impression on the observer. The most natural and consequently the earliest way of unifying the material was, first, to classify it as well as might be, and, secondly, to affiliate the diverse mental modes thus found, upon a simple entity, the personal Soul, of which they [were] taken to be so many facultative manifestations. Now, for instance, the Soul manifests its faculty of Memory, now of Reasoning, now of Volition, or again its Imagination or its Appetite. This is the orthodox "spiritualistic" theory of scholasticism and of common-sense. Another and a less obvious way of unifying the chaos is to seek common elements *in* the divers mental facts rather than a common agent behind them, and to

Reprinted from William James, *The Principles of Psychology* (1890), I, 1–8 (New York: Dover, 1950).

explain them constructively by the various forms of arrangement of these elements, as one explains houses by stones and bricks. The "association-ist" schools of Herbart in Germany, and of Hume the Mills and Bain in Britain have thus constructed a *psychology without a soul* by taking dis-crete 'ideas,' faint or vivid, and showing how, by their cohesions, repul-sions, and forms of succession, such things as reminiscences, perceptions, emotions, volitions, passions, theories, and all the other furnishings of an individual's mind may be engendered. The very Self or *ego* of the indi-vidual comes in this way to be viewed no longer as the pre-existing source of the representations, but rather as their last and most compli-cated fruit.

Now, if we strive rigorously to simplify the phenomena in either of these ways, we soon become aware of inadequacies in our method. Any particular cognition, for example, or recollection, is accounted for on the soul-theory by being referred to the spiritual faculties of Cognition or of Memory. These faculties themselves are thought of as absolute prop-erties of the soul; that is, to take the case of memory, no reason is given why we should remember a fact as it happened, except that so to re-member it constitutes the essence of our Recollective Power. We may, as spiritualists, try to explain our memory's failures and blunders by secondary causes. But its *successes* can invoke no factors save the existence of certain objective things to be remembered on the one hand, and of our faculty of memory on the other. When, for instance, I recall my graduation-day, and drag all its incidents and emotions up from death's dateless night, no mechanical cause can explain this process, nor can any analysis reduce it to lower terms or make its nature seem other than an ultimate *datum*, which, whether we rebel or not at its mysteriousness, must simply be taken for granted if we are to psychologize at all. How-ever the associationist may represent the present ideas as thronging and arranging themselves, still, the spiritualist insists, he has in the end to admit that *something*, be it brain, be it 'ideas,' be it 'association,' *knows* past time *as* past, and fills it out with this or that event. And when the spiritualist calls memory an 'irreducible faculty,' he says no more than this admission of the associationist already grants.

And yet the admission is far from being a satisfactory simplification of the concrete facts. For why should this absolute god-given Faculty re-tain so much better the events of yesterday than those of last year, and, best of all, those of an hour ago? Why, again, in old age should its grasp of childhood's events seem firmest? Why should illness and exhaustion enfeeble it? Why should repeating an experience strengthen our recollec-tion of it? Why should drugs, fevers, asphyxia, and excitement resusci-tate things long since forgotten? If we content ourselves with merely affirming that the faculty of memory is so pecularily constituted by nature as to exhibit just these oddities, we seem little the better for having invoked it, for our explanation becomes as complicated as that of the crude facts with which we started. Moreover there is something grotesque and irrational in the supposition that the soul is equipped with elementary powers of such an ingeniously intricate sort. Why *should* our memory cling more easily to the near than the remote? Why should it lose its grasp of proper [names] sooner than of abstract names? Such peculiarities seem quite fantastic; and might, for aught we can see *a priori*, be the precise opposites of what they are. Evidently, then, *the faculty does not exist absolutely, but works under conditions;* and *the quest of the conditions* becomes the psychologist's most interesting task.

However firmly he may hold to the soul and her remembering faculty, he must acknowledge that she never exerts the latter without a *cue*, and that something must always precede and *remind* us of whatever we are to recollect. "An *idea!*" says the associationist, "an idea associated with the remembered thing; and this explains also why things repeatedly met with are more easily recollected, for their associates on the various occasions furnished so many distinct avenues of recall." But this does not explain the effects of fever, exhaustion, hypnotism, old age, and the like. And in general, the pure associationist's account of our mental life is almost as bewildering as that of the pure spiritualist. This multitude of ideas, existing absolutely, yet clinging together, and weaving an endless carpet of themselves, like dominoes in ceaseless change, or the bits of glass in a kaleidoscope—whence do they get their fantastic laws of clinging, and why do they cling in just the shapes they do?

For this the associationist must introduce the order of experience in the outer world. The dance of the ideas is a copy, somewhat mutilated and altered, of the order of phenomena. But the slightest reflection shows that phenomena have absolutely no power to influence our ideas until they have first impressed our senses and our brain. The bare existence of a past fact is no ground for our remembering it. Unless we have seen it, or somehow *undergone* it, we shall never know of its having been. The experiences of the body are thus one of the conditions of the faculty of memory being what it is. And a very small amount of reflection on facts shows that one part of the body, namely, the brain, is the part whose experiences are directly concerned. If the nervous communication be cut off between the brain and other parts, the experiences of those other parts are non-existent for the mind. The eye is blind, the ear deaf, the hand insensible and motionless. And conversely, if the brain be injured, consciousness is abolished or altered, even although every other organ in the body be ready to play its normal part. A blow on the head, a sudden subtraction of blood, the pressure of an apoplectic hemorrhage, may have the first effect; whilst a very few ounces of alcohol or grains of opium or hasheesh, or a whiff of chloroform or nitrous oxide gas, are sure to have the second. The delirium of fever, the altered self of insanity, are all due to foreign matters circulating through the brain, or to patho-logical changes in that organ's substance. The fact that the brain is the one immediate bodily condition of the mental operations is indeed so universally admitted nowadays that I' need spend no more time in illus-trating it, but will simply postulate it and pass on. The whole remainder of [*The Principles of Psychology*] will be more or less of a proof that the postulate was correct.

Bodily experiences, therefore, and more particularly brain-experiences, must take a place amongst those conditions of the mental life of which Psychology need take account. *The spiritualist and the associationist must both be 'cerebralists,'* to the extent at least of admitting that certain peculi-arities in the way of working of their own favorite principles are explic-able only by the fact that the brain laws are a codeterminant of the result.

Our first conclusion, then, is that a certain amount of brain-physiology must be presupposed or included in Psychology.

In still another way the psychologist is forced to be something of a nerve-physiologist. Mental phenomena are not only conditioned *a parte ante* by bodily processes; but . . . lead to them *a parte post.* That they lead to *acts* is of course the most familiar of truths, but I do not merely mean acts in the sense of voluntary and deliberate muscular performances. Mental states occasion also changes in the calibre of blood-vessels, or alteration in the heart-beats, or [in] processes more subtle still, in glands and viscera. If these are taken into account, as well as acts which follow at some *remote period* because the mental state was once there, it will be safe to lay down the general law that *no mental modification ever occurs which is not accompanied or followed by a bodily change.* The ideas and feelings, e.g., which these present printed characters excite in the reader's mind not only occasion movements of his eyes and nascent movements of articu-lation in him, but will some day make him speak, or take sides in a dis-cussion, or give advice, or choose a book to read, differently from what would have been the case had they never impressed his retina. Our psychology must therefore take account not only of the conditions ante-cedent to mental states, but of their resultant consequences as well.

But actions originally prompted by conscious intelligence may grow so automatic by dint of habit as to be apparently unconsciously per-formed. Standing, walking, buttoning and unbuttoning, piano-playing, talking, even saying one's prayers, may be done when the mind is absorbed in other things. The performances of animal *instinct* seem semi-automatic, and the *reflex acts* of self-preservation certainly are so. Yet they resemble intelligent acts in bringing about the *same ends* at which the animals' consciousness, on other occasions, deliberately aims. Shall the study of such machine-like yet purposive acts as these be included in Psychology?

The boundary-line of the mental is certainly vague. It is better not to be pedantic, but to let the science be as vague as its subject, and include such phenomena as these if by so doing we can throw any light on the main business in hand. It will ere long be seen, I trust, that we can; and that we gain much more by a broad than by a narrow conception of our subject. At a certain stage in the development of every science a degree of vagueness is what best consists with fertility. On the whole, few recent formulas have done more real service of a rough sort in psychology than the Spencerian one that the essence of mental life and of bodily life are one, namely, 'the adjustment of inner to outer relations.' Such a formula is vagueness incarnate; but because it takes into account the fact that minds inhabit environments which act on them and on which they in turn react; because, in short, it takes mind in the midst of all its concrete relations, it is immensely more fertile than the old-fashioned 'rational psychology,' which treated the soul as a detached existent, sufficient unto itself, and assumed to consider only its nature and properties. I shall therefore feel free to make any sallies into zoology or into pure nerve-physiology which may seem instructive for our purposes, but otherwise shall leave those sciences to the physiologists.

Can we state more distinctly still the manner in which the mental life seems to intervene between impressions made from without upon the body, and reactions of the body upon the outer world again? Let us look at a few facts.

If some iron filings be sprinkled on a table and a magnet brought near them, they will fly through the air for a certain distance and stick to its surface. A savage seeing the phenomenon explains it as the result of an attraction or love between the magnet and the filings. But let a card cover the poles of the magnet, and the filings will press forever against its surface without its ever occurring to them to pass around its sides and thus come into more direct contact with the object of their love. Blow bubbles through a tube into the bottom of a pail of water, they will rise to the surface and mingle with the air. Their action may again be poetically interpreted as due to a longing to recombine with the mother-atmosphere above the surface. But if you invert a jar full of water over the pail, they will rise and remain lodged beneath its bottom, shut in from the outer air, although a slight deflection from their course at the outset, or a re-descent towards the rim of the jar when they found their upward course impeded, would easily have set them free.

If now we pass from such actions as these to those of living things, we notice a striking difference. Romeo wants Juliet as the filings want the magnet; and if no obstacles intervene he moves towards her by as straight a line as they. But Romeo and Juliet, if a wall be built between them, do not remain idiotically pressing their faces against its opposite sides like the magnet and the filings with the card. Romeo soon finds a circuitous way, by scaling the wall or otherwise, of touching Juliet's lips directly. With the filings the path is fixed; whether it reaches the end depends on accidents. With the lover it is the end which is fixed, the path may be modified indefinitely.

Suppose a living frog in the position in which we placed our bubbles of air, namely, at the bottom of a jar of water. The want of breath will soon make him also long to rejoin the mother-atmosphere, and he will take the shortest path to his end by swimming straight upwards. But if a jar full of water be inverted over him, he will not, like the bubbles, perpetually press his nose against its unyielding roof, but will restlessly explore the neighborhood until by re-descending again he has discovered a path round its brim to the goal of his desires. Again the fixed end, the varying means!

Such contrasts between living and inanimate performances end by leading men to deny that in the physical world final purposes exist at all. Loves and desires are to-day no longer imputed to particles of iron or of air. No one supposes now that the end of any activity which they may display is an ideal purpose presiding over the activity from its out-set and soliciting or drawing it into being by a sort of *vis a fronte*. The end, on the contrary, is deemed a mere passive result, pushed into being *a tergo*, having had, so to speak, no voice in its own production. Alter the pre-existing conditions, and with inorganic materials you bring forth each time a different apparent end. But with intelligent agents, altering the conditions changes the activity displayed, but not the end reached; for here the idea of the yet unrealized end co-operates with the conditions to determine what the activities shall be.

The pursuance of future ends and the choice of means for their attainment are thus the mark and criterion of the presence of mentality in a phenomenon. We all use this test to discriminate between an intelligent and a mechanical per-formance. We impute no mentality to sticks and stones, because they never seem to move for *the sake of* anything, but always when pushed, and then indifferently and with no sign of choice. So we unhesitatingly call them senseless.

Just so we form our decision upon the deepest of all philosophic problems: Is the Kosmos an expression of intelligence rational in its inward nature, or a brute external fact pure and simple? If we find ourselves, in contemplating it, unable to banish the impression that it is a realm of final purposes, that it exists for the sake of something, we place intelligence at the heart of it and have a religion. If, on the contrary, in surveying its irremediable flux, we can think of the present only as so much mere mechanical sprouting from the past, occurring with no reference to the future, we are atheists and materialists.

The traditional code of science—that is, the objectives sought and the methods of investigation—cannot satisfy the requirements of our critical times, and this is why science has failed to measure up to the opportunities and obligations before it. The generally accepted ideas of what natural science is and what it is for are out of date and need radical revision.—C. J. Herrick (1949)

2.

Psychology and Scientific Research

Hadley Cantril, Adelbert Ames, Jr., Albert H. Hastorf, and William H. Ittelson

THE NATURE OF SCIENTIFIC INQUIRY

A feeling of urgency for a more adequate understanding of man and his social relations can be sensed in today's intellectual atmosphere. People are becoming more and more anxious about the ability of psychologists and social scientists to help solve the problems arising from our technological advances and from the swift social transitions they leave in their wake. But, unfortunately, what Herrick has said about the natural sciences applies especially to those sciences which deal with man—psychology and the social sciences in general. Moreover, in these sciences, in contrast to the physical sciences, there seems to be less agreement as to what constitutes significant research.

Reprinted by permission in modified form from *Science*, 110 (1949), 461–464, 491–497, 517–522.

Obviously, an increase in our understanding of man can come about only as we extend our empirical knowledge and improve our formulations through research of demonstrated significance. Before that is possible we must increase our understanding of the scientific process through which discoveries are made. But sometimes the scientist's interest in building up the content of his discipline sidetracks him from a consideration of the scientific process itself and creates a lag in the understanding and improvement of scientific tools. What follows is an attempt to clarify our thinking about the nature of scientific research in those fields which take upon themselves the primary responsibility of accounting for man's thoughts and behavior. Only then will such research accomplish what we have a right to expect of it.

We shall first consider the nature of scientific inquiry, trying to find out why man pursues scientific inquiry, anyway—what function it serves him and what steps seem to be involved. We shall then distinguish between scientific inquiry and scientific method—a distinction which seems necessary to avoid certain pitfalls and to assure a scientific progress. Then we shall try to point out some of the specific implications to be derived for psychology from a better understanding of the nature of scientific inquiry and the role of scientific method, and we shall indicate to what degree science can be "objective." Finally, some suggestions will be made which might accelerate the kind of scientific research that will increase our understanding of man.

The apparent reason for scientific inquiry is essentially the reason for any inquiry—to solve a problem. Scientific inquiry can never be understood if it is somehow put on a pedestal and viewed as something remote and apart from man's everyday activities. "Science," says Conant (1947, p. 24), "emerges from the other progressive activities of man to the extent that new concepts arise from experiments and observations."

These activities of life are carried through in an environment which includes people, artifacts, the phenomena of nature. Man's only contact with this environment is through his senses, and the impressions man's senses give him are cryptograms in the sense that they have no meaning unless and until they become functionally related to man's purposive activities. The world man creates for himself through what Einstein has called the "rabble of the senses" is one that takes on a degree of order, system, and meaning as man builds up through tested experience a pattern of assumptions and expectancies on which he can base action.

What man brings to any concrete event is an accumulation of assumptions, of awarenesses, and of knowledge concerning the relatively determined aspects of his environment as derived from his past experiences.

But since the environment through which man carries out his life transactions is constantly changing, any person is constantly running into hitches and trying to do away with them. The assumptive world a person brings to the "now" of a concrete situation cannot disclose to him the undetermined significances continually emerging; and so we run into hitches in everyday life because of our inadequate understanding of the conditions giving rise to a phenomenon, and our ability to act effectively for a purpose becomes inadequate.

When we try to grasp this inadequacy intellectually and get at the "why" of the ineffectiveness of our purposeful action, we are adopting the attitude of scientific inquiry. Man as scientist tries to understand what aspect of his environment is responsible for a hitch and then calls upon what knowledge he has that is relevant to an understanding of the determined, predictable nature of the particular phenomenon in question. Modern man uses the scientific method as a tool because he has found empirically that he can increase his understanding and act more effectively if his pursuits are guided by some knowledge concerning the determined aspects of the phenomenal world. . . .

The processes involved in scientific inquiry would seem to be somewhat as follows: (1) sensing the inadequacy of the conceptual aspects of our assumptive world, thereby being faced with a problem for which we must seek an answer; (2) deciding on all those aspects of a phenomenon that might have a significant bearing on the problem: deciding on those aspects except for which the functional activities in question would not exist; (3) picking out from the various aspects assumed to be involved those that seem most important in terms of the original hitch we faced and that will serve as bases for standards we can think about and manipulate; (4) working out some method of changing those aspects we have chosen as variables or bases for standards and conducting our empirical investigations accordingly; (5) modifying our assumptive world on the basis of the empirical evidence concerning the validity of formulations that have resolved an immediate problem.

The solving of the immediate problem will automatically give rise to new hitches and the above process constantly repeats itself. *

---

*There seems to be a striking similarity between the processes used in scientific inquiry and the processes man makes use of in building up the assumptive world. Both science and common sense can be regarded as functional activities man uses in carrying out his life transactions. The method of scientific inquiry seems in many ways to be an unconscious imitation of those age-old processes man has employed in his common-sense solutions of problems. In common-sense activity, the assumptions and awarenesses on which man depends for effective action are the hypotheses he has built up from his

Specifically, it seems that scientific inquiry has two major functions for man. First, it provides man with a bundle of what are called "scientific facts." This bundle is composed of his up-to-the-now understandings of the determined, predictable aspects of nature and is used by him for purposes of prediction and control. There are essentially two varieties of these scientific facts: general statements of relationships of determined aspects of nature which we refer to as "scientific laws" and which, in the physical sciences, tend to be expressed in mathematical formulas; second, applications of these general laws to concrete situations for purposes of verification, specific prediction, or control. The characteristic of all these generalized scientific laws is that they disclose predictable aspects of types of phenomena no matter where or when they occur, irrespective of actual concrete situations.

A second function of science is that it provides a conceptual reorganization of the knowledge man has already acquired of the determined aspects of nature. Here we are trying to increase our range of understanding, or, as Dewey and Bentley (1945, p. 225; 1946, p. 645) phrase it, to improve our "specification"; that is, our accuracy in naming. Here, for example, the specifications involved in relativity are more accurate namings of phenomena than are Newton's concepts and, in this sense, Newton's concepts are not to be regarded as "wrong." This function of science includes that of increasing the range of man's conceptual knowledge through the discovery of more and more predictable aspects of nature that up to the present time remain undetermined. . . .

Transactional Observation

Our own philosophical basis for our thinking concerning the nature and function of scientific inquiry and scientific method should be made explicit. We are using as our take-off point what Dewey and Bentley

---

many experiences; weighted averages he unconsciously uses to give him a high prognosis for effective action.

There are, however, certain important differences between the steps involved in pursuing scientific inquiry and the apparent processes that constitute common sense. A most important difference is the fact that, in using scientific inquiry, man is the operator who decides what he is going to operate on and how. In an everyday life situation, however, man is not only the operator but is also being operated on and must carry out his activities in the midst of the situation itself. When we meet hitches in everyday life and try to overcome them with hunches for effective action, we test these hunches by the action itself in a more or less insightful, more or less conscious way. In scientific inquiry, on the other hand, hunches are tested by controlled experiments and a deliberate attempt is made to intellectualize the processes involved (see Dewey, 1948, p. 197).

have referred to in a series of articles as a "transactional approach." What they mean by the term *transactional* can best be gathered by their own words. "Observation of this general (transactional) type sees man-in-action not as something radically set over against an environing world, nor yet as merely action 'in' a world, but as action *of* and *by* the world in which the man belongs as an integral constituent" (1945, p. 228). Under this procedure all of man's behavings, "including his most advanced knowings," are treated as "activities not of himself alone, nor even as primarily his, but as processes of the full situation of organism-environment" (1946, p. 506). "From birth to death every human being is a *Party*, so that neither he nor anything done or suffered can possibly be understood when it is separated from the fact of participation in an extensive body of transactions—to which a given human being may contribute and which he modifies, but only in virtue of being a partaker in them" (Dewey, 1948, p. 198). . . .

While it is easy enough to understand this point of view intellectually, it is not nearly so easy to put it into operation in pursuing actual scientific inquiry. It tends to go against the grain of the psychologist's working procedures to regard any formulation merely as a certain "connection of conditions" (Dewey, 1946, p. 217). It is perhaps particularly difficult for psychologists to understand the full implications of the transactional point of view, because, as Dewey and Bentley (1946, p. 546) have pointed out, "The interactional treatment, as everyone is aware, entered psychological inquiry just about the time it was being removed from basic position by the physical sciences from which it was copied." But we must remember that psychology, by comparison, is still in its infancy, that the transactional approach, which Dewey and Bentley trace to the preface of Clerk Maxwell's *Matter and Motion*, dated 1876, antedated the first psychological laboratory. . . .

THE TRANSACTIONAL VIEW IN PSYCHOLOGICAL RESEARCH

When psychology emancipates itself from dependence on interactionism alone by taking a transactional view of the phenomena which come within its province, we should expect that the division of psychologists into schools would rapidly disappear. Schools (Gestalt, behaviorism, psychoanalysis, etc.) would disappear not because they are "wrong" or "have been overthrown" but because the formulations of each school that meet empirical tests would be encompassed within wider formulations of problems. What are some ways to speed this development?

First of all, the psychologist not only must realize intellectually but must make a part of his functional assumptive world the idea that man's thought and behavior can be understood only as processes of a "full situation of organism-environment." The point has been made by H. A. Murray and collaborators (1948, p. 466) in their contention that "the main body of psychology started its career by putting the wrong foot forward, and it has been out of step with the march of science much of the time. Instead of beginning with studies of the whole person adjusting to a natural environment, it began with studies of a segment of a person responding to a physical stimulus in an unnatural laboratory environment." Brunswik (1949), in his well-known "ecological analysis," has pointed out the need to understand the complete "representativeness of circumstances" operative in any situation under observation. But while an increasing number of psychologists are calling for a revision in traditional psychological procedure, their voices are still those of men crying in the wilderness of the universe which constitutes so much of psychological inquiry today. The psychological investigator, of all people, cannot separate the observer from what is being observed, the process of knowing from what is known, what is "out there" from whatever goes on in the experiencing organism. Psychology must disavow completely any "field theory" which implies that an environmental field acts *on* a person rather than *through* a person.

Because man inevitably builds up for himself an assumptive world in carrying out his purposive activities, the world he is related to, the world he sees, the world he is operating on, and the world that is operating on him is the result of a transactional process in which man himself plays an active role. Man carries out his activities in the midst of concrete events which themselves delimit the significances he must deal with.

In the process man is himself changed in greater or lesser degree by having his own assumptive world changed through confirmation or denial as a result of action. In his immediate activity man abstracts from the immediate situation certain determined aspects according to his assumptive world. This, as we indicated, includes far more than the immediate occasion; it is a continuum which includes the past and the future, a storehouse of both past experience and ideals. As Bentley (1941, p. 485) has pointed out, "Behaviors are present events converging pasts into futures. They cannot be reduced to successions of instants nor to successions of locations. They themselves span extension and duration. The pasts and the the futures are rather phases of behavior than its control." Psychologists must be constantly aware of the effects man's own actions have both on his assumptive world—confirming or denying certain aspects of it—and concurrently on the "environment out there" as it is perceived and experienced. . . .

There is also a tendency in psychology to use catchwords in labeling the fields of social, clinical, educational, or industrial as "applied" fields of psychology, and to separate them from the more traditional "experimental" psychology. Any such division is absurd unless the person who uses it consciously reserves it for rough descriptive purposes. Investigators in these fields must, of course, also rely on experiments. But, beyond that, any such distinction acts as a deterrent in the search for more adequate formulations which will better account for human behavior, whether in the laboratory, the clinic, the factory, or in everyday social life. . . .

We can illustrate the way in which psychological inquiry has been restricted by the use of terms with reference to the field of perception, which has so often been a weather vane in psychology. In working on perception, psychologists early found that certain variations in objective or physiological factors produced marked subjective variations. This naturally led to the idea of correspondence between subjective factors, on the one hand, and objective and physiological factors, on the other hand. Since an alteration of objective and physiological factors could so easily be shown to cause subjective effects, and since the converse could not so easily be demonstrated, the assumption was built up that the subjective aspects of perception had their origin largely in the corresponding objective factors and the accompanying physiological disturbances they caused. Studies of perception have thus concentrated largely on the analysis of objective and physiological factors. Since these objective or physiological factors could be varied quantitatively, scientific methodology in psychology tended to become identified with measurement alone.

This led to a long neglect of those factors not amenable to precise measurement. These neglected factors were, of course, subjective factors described by such symbols as past experience, loyalties, expectancy, and purpose, whether these were operating consciously or unconsciously. This methodological dam has recently been cracked, largely through research in social and clinical psychology, where the effects of subjective factors on perception are especially obvious. More recently, in an attempt to liberate investigators somewhat from correspondence between subjective and objective or physiological factors, demonstrations of perceptual phenomena have been designed which deliberately make use of illusions. By using illusions the investigator gains more freedom to understand the nature of the functional activities involved in the scientific inquiry of perception and thereby gets a better toehold on the function of perception in man's purposive behavior. For example, it can be demonstrated that the perception of *where* a thing is depends upon the perception of *what* a thing is and on *when* it is perceived. Carr (1935, p. 326) has pointed out that "illusions contrasted with correct perceptions are the experimental variants that reveal the common principle involved in both." . . .

VALUE JUDGMENTS AND "OBJECTIVITY"

It is becoming increasingly clear that the process of mentation involved in scientific inquiry is not a simple one of bringing "impartial analysis" to bear on a set of conditions. The scientist's own value judgments are involved in (1) sensing the inadequacy of his conceptual structure— posing a problem for himself; (2) sensing the functional activities or subphenomena which may be involved in the phenomenon that has caused the original hitch; (3) deciding on which aspects of a phenomenon (variables) can fruitfully be used as bases for standards in experimentation; and (4) designing an experimental procedure to test the validity of these bases for standards. Scientific research thus involves an elaborate process of weighing and integrating which may take place largely on an unconscious level.

In this process, all the unconscious assumptions, all the awarenesses, and all the conceptual abstractions of the individual investigator's assumptive world are operative. Whether any scientist likes to admit it or not, any interpretation he makes must be regarded as a value judgment. To be sure, rational thought and the conscious intellectual manipulation of abstracted variables can, often do, and obviously should play a most important role in the process of scientific inquiry. But to assume that rational thought and conscious manipulation alone are the determinants of the judgments involved in scientific research is to go against the overwhelming evidence already obtained from scientific research itself. The dictionary definition of the word "objective," in the sense that it is used in discussions concerning the objectivity of science is: "Emphasizing or expressing the nature of reality as it is apart from self-consciousness; treating events or phenomena as external rather than as affected by one's reflections or feelings." For example, our knowledge of perception, showing that "the nature of reality" as we experience it would not exist *except* for the assumptive world we bring to a concrete situation, flatly contradicts the contention that the scientist can be objective in any such sense.

The objectivity of science can therefore only refer to the use of accepted rules of empirical research *after* the problem, the variables, and the experimental design have been decided upon. Here the scientific investigator takes every precaution he can to see that he does not mis-interpret what he observes by allowing any subjective bias to enter into the actual conduct of the experiment itself.

Not only is objectivity illusory in the sense of eliminating personal bias, it is also undesirable. We cannot improve on the conclusion reached by Herrick (1949, pp. 180f) after a lifetime of productive research in neurology:

> The bias which arises from unrecognized personal attitudes, interests, and pre-conceptions is the most treacherous of all the subversive enemies of sound, scien-tific progress; yet these attitudes and interests are the key factors in all really original scientific investigation. This issue must be faced frankly and courageously. The easy way out is to ignore the troublesome personal ingredients of the problem and say that science has no concern with them. This is now generally regarded as the standard, or normal, scientific method. But actually this cannot be done, and we cannot afford to try to do it; for the interests and the attitudes of the inquirer shape the whole course of the investigation, without which it is meaningless and fruitless. To neglect these components of scientific work and the satisfactions of a successful outcome is to sterilize not only the process but also the results of the inquiry. The vital germ of untrammeled imaginative thinking is thrown into the discard, and too often we seem quite content with the dead husk which is so easily weighed, measured, classified, and then stowed away in the warehouse.

In the social sciences, Robert Lynd (1939) has made the same point in his plea for "outrageous hypotheses."

The myth that "science is objective" may tend to be fostered in most cultures today in an attempt to preserve whatever status quo exists by giving it scientific blessing. But any scientist will resent boundaries placed on his thinking by social, economic, political, religious, or any other ideological barriers and taboos. This danger is especially prevalent in the field of inquiry labeled "social psychology" and in the social sciences, where the data gathered have been largely determined and precondi-tioned by the purposes and conditions within which the investigator has worked.

Psychologists and social scientists who honestly try to bring their most mature value judgments to bear on concrete social problems are all too frequently labeled as biased, crackpot reformers if they even implicitly criticize existing social relationships. Yet it is because scientific inquiry is shot through with value judgments that no scientist can avoid some responsibility for the judgments he makes. Because value judgments play so important a role in scientific thinking, ways and means must be dis-covered of making value judgments themselves the subject matter for scientific inquiry (see Cantril, 1949, p. 363). Value judgments concern the significance of the constant emergents which are not subject to explanation in determined and verifiable terms. Here the scientist has a freedom of choice; here conscience, the "sense of oughtness," must be recognized as the highest standard for effective action. When the subject matter with which the scientist deals consists of human beings trying to act effectively to carry out their purposes, then the social responsibility of anyone who pretends to be an expert obviously becomes very great indeed.

3.

Understanding Ourselves

Michael Polanyi

Man's capacity to think is his most outstanding attribute. Whoever speaks of man will therefore have to speak at some stage of human knowledge. This is a troublesome prospect. For the task seems to be without end: as soon as we had completed one such study, our subject matter would have been extended by this very achievement. We should have now to study the study that we had just completed, since it, too, would be a work of man. And so we should have to go on reflecting ever again on our last reflections, in an endless and futile endeavour to comprise completely the works of man.

This difficulty may appear far-fetched, but it is, in fact, profoundly characteristic both of the nature of man and of the nature of human knowledge. Man must try for ever to discover knowledge that will stand

Reprinted by permission from Michael Polanyi, *The Study of Man* (University of Chicago Press, 1961), pp. 1–6.

up by itself, objectively, but the moment he reflects on his own knowledge he catches himself red-handed in the act of upholding his knowledge. He finds himself asserting it to be true, and this asserting and believing is an action which makes an addition to the world on which his knowledge bears. So every time we acquire knowledge we enlarge the world, the world of man, by something that is not yet incorporated in the object of the knowledge we hold, and in this sense a comprehensive knowledge of man must appear impossible.

The significance which I attribute to this logical oddity will become apparent in the solution suggested for it. Its solution seems to lie in the fact that human knowledge is of two kinds. What is usually described as knowledge, as set out in written words or maps, or mathematical formulae, is only one kind of knowledge; while unformulated knowledge, such as we have of something we are in the act of doing, is another form of knowledge. If we call the first kind explicit knowledge, and the second, tacit knowledge, we may say that *we always know tacitly that we are holding our explicit knowledge to be true*. If, therefore, we are satisfied to hold a part of our knowledge tacitly, the vain pursuit of reflecting ever again on our own reflections no longer arises. The question is whether we *can* be satisfied with this. Tacit knowing appears to be a doing of our own, lacking the public, objective, character of explicit knowledge. It may appear therefore to lack the essential quality of knowledge.

This objection cannot be lightly overruled; but I believe it to be mistaken. I deny that any participation of the knower in the shaping of knowledge must invalidate knowledge, though I admit that it impairs its objectivity.

Tonight I shall try to transmit this conviction to you or at least to familiarize you with this view—for all I have to say may not convince you—by showing that tacit knowing is in fact the dominant principle of all knowledge, and that its rejection would, therefore, automatically involve the rejection of any knowledge whatever. I shall begin by demonstrating that the personal contribution by which the knower shapes his own knowledge manifestly predominates both at the *lowest levels* of knowing and in the *loftiest achievements* of the human intelligence; after which I shall extend my demonstration to the *intermediate zone* forming the bulk of human knowledge, where the decisive role of the tacit coefficient is not so easily recognizable.

I shall speak therefore first of the most primitive forms of human knowing, at which we arrive by descending to those forms of intelligence which man shares with the animals: the kind of intelligence that is situated behind the barrier of language. Animals have no speech, and all the towering superiority of man over the animals is due almost entirely to man's gift of speech. Babies and infants up to the age of eighteen months or so are mentally not much superior to chimpanzees of the same age; only when they start learning to speak do they rapidly out-distance and leave far behind their simian contemporaries. Even adults show no distinctly greater intelligence than animals so long as their minds work unaided by language. In the absence of linguistic clues man sees things, hears things, feels things, moves about, explores his surroundings and gets to know his way about, very much as animals do.

In order to bring out the logical characteristics of such tacit knowledge we must compare it with the articulate knowledge possessed by man. We see then in the first place that, obviously, the kind of knowledge which we share with the animals is incomparably poorer than that of an educated man, or indeed of any normally brought up human being. But while this richness of explicit knowledge is admittedly related to its distinctive logical characteristics, it is not itself a logical property. The essential *logical* difference between the two kinds of knowledge lies in the fact that we can critically reflect on something explicitly stated, in a way in which we cannot reflect on our tacit awareness of an experience.

To make this difference apparent, let me compare an instance of tacit knowledge with a knowledge of the *same subject* given in explicit form. I have mentioned that men can look round and explore their surroundings tacitly and that this propensity is also well developed in animals. It is known from studies of rats running a maze. A great connoisseur of rat behaviour, E. C. Tolman, has written that a rat gets to know its way about a maze as if it had acquired a mental map of it. And observations on human subjects suggest that a man, however intelligent, is no better at maze-running than a rat, unless assisted by notes, whether these are remembered verbally or sketched out in a drawing. But of course a man *can* make such notes or have them made for him. He may be provided with a detailed map of a region through which he is passing. The advantage of a map is obvious, both for the information which it conveys and for the more important reason that it is much easier to trace an itinerary on a map than to plan it without a map. But there is also a new risk involved in travelling by a map: namely that the map may be mistaken. And this is where critical reflection comes in. The peculiar risk that we take in relying on any explicitly formulated knowledge is matched by a peculiar opportunity offered by explicit knowledge for reflecting on it critically. We can check the information embodied in a map, for example, by reading it at some place that we can directly survey and compare the map with the landmarks in front of us.

Such critical examination of the map is possible for two reasons. First, because a map is a thing external to us and not something we are ourselves doing or shaping, and second, because even though it is merely an external object, it can yet speak to us. It tells us something to which we can listen. It does that equally, whether we have drawn up the map ourselves or bought it in a shop, but for the moment it is the former case that we are interested in, namely when the map is in fact a statement of our own. In reading such an utterance we are playing back to ourselves something we have said before so that we may listen to it in a critical manner. A critical process of this kind may go on for hours and indeed for weeks and months. I may go through the manuscript of a whole book and examine the same text sentence by sentence any number of times.

Obviously, nothing quite like this can take place on the pre-articulate level. I can test the kind of mental map I possess of a familiar region only in action, that is, by actually using it as my guide. If I then lose my way, I can correct my ideas accordingly. There is no other way of improving inarticulate knowledge. I can see a thing only in one way at a time, and if I am doubtful of what I see, all I can do is to look again and perhaps see things differently then. Inarticulate intelligence can only grope its way by plunging from one view of things into another. Knowledge acquired and held in this manner may therefore be called *a-critical*.

We can enlarge and greatly deepen this contrast between tacit and articulate knowledge by extending it to the way in which knowledge is acquired. Remember how a map is drawn up by triangulation. Starting from a set of systematically collected observations, we proceed according to strict rules applied to these data. Only explicitly formulated knowledge can be thus derived from specifiable premises according to clear rules of inference. And it is the most important function of critical thought to test such explicit processes of inference, by rehearsing their chain of reasoning in search of some weak link.

The contrast between the two domains should now be sharp enough. Pre-verbal knowledge appears as a small lighted area surrounded by immense darknesses, a small patch illuminated by accepting a-critically the unreasoned conclusions of our senses; while man's articulate knowledge represents a panorama of the whole universe, established under the control of critical reflection.

4.

Sensuous-Intellectual
Complementarity in Science

Thomas R. Blackburn

We live in a technological culture, and that culture is in trouble. Recent essays (White, 1967; Moncrief, 1970; Brown, 1959, chap. 16; Roszak, 1969; Mumford, 1970) that have explored the relationship between modern science and the history and psychology of technological man, have generally concluded that the scientist's quantifying, value-free orientation has left him helpless to avoid (and often a willing partner in) the use of science for exploitative and destructive ends.

The past few years have seen the rapid growth of a counter-technological culture in which science, as we know it, plays no role in the contemplation of nature. The counterculture, because it is still in the process of growth and formulation and because of its very nature, is no single

---

Reprinted by permission from *Science*, 172 (June 11, 1971) 1003–1007. Copyright ©1971 by the American Association for the Advancement of Science.

philosophical system. For our purposes, the salient feature of the counter-culture is its epistemology of direct sensuous experience,* subjectivity, and respect for intuition—especially intuitive knowledge based on a "naive" openness to nature and to other people. Both on its own merits and as a reaction to the abuses of technology, the movement has attracted increasing numbers of intelligent and creative students and professional people. I believe that science as a creative endeavor cannot survive the loss of these people; nor, without them, can science contribute to the solution of the staggering social and ecological problems that we face.

More fundamentally, much of the criticism directed at the current scientific model of nature is quite valid. If society is to begin to enjoy the promise of the "scientific revolution," or even to survive in a tolerable form, science must change. In its own terms, the logical-experimental structure of science that has evolved since Galileo's lifetime is magnificent. It has, in Lewis and Randall's phrase (1923), its cathedrals. To demolish these, to reject what has been achieved, would be barbaric and pointless, since the very amorality of science makes it not wrong, but incomplete. The claims of science as such (as opposed to, say, "defense" research), as well as the claims of its critics, while contradictory, are not incompatible.

Niels Bohr's concept of complementarity arose when apparently conflicting results in elementary particle physics forced an expansion of the frame of reference of classical physics (Heisenberg, 1967). Bohr himself came increasingly to believe that complementarity was a concept that could be applied to far more than just the purely physical systems that had led him to its formulation (1958, pp. 3–22). It is conceivable, then, that the notion of complementarity offers a method of including both sensuous and intellectual knowledge of nature in a common frame of reference. The result, far more than a mere compromise or amalgamation of the two viewpoints, could be a richer science, in which esthetic and quantitative valuations, each retaining its own integrity, would contribute equally to the description of nature that science long ago took for its province. Further, it may produce a scientific ethic that is less destructive toward nature.

---

*To some readers "sensuous" may suggest genital sexuality. Although "unconventional" sexual morality is a feature of the counterculture (as it is of the technological one), I use the word in a more general sense: that is, the response of the whole body, including the senses, to phenomena. Usually, such a response is, of course, not susceptible to quantification. It is also dependent on subjective factors such as mood and attention, but it is undeniably a source of information about the world around us.

COMPLEMENTARITY IN MODERN PHYSICS

Phenomena on the atomic level present the investigator with a wealth of seemingly contradictory observations. Light undergoes diffraction, which can only be explained by adopting the classical wave model. Yet, in the photoelectric effect and in photon-scattering experiments, the predictions of the wave model are not realized, and the actual observations can only be rationalized by postulating quanta of light that carry momentum and have a relatively definite location (subject to the restrictions of the Heisenberg uncertainty principle). Again, negative electricity is first found to be quantized in electrolysis and the oil-drop experiment, and each unit of negative electricity behaves in a cathode-ray tube like a little lump, with a mass of 9 times 10^{-28} gram, and a charge of 4.8 times 10^{-10} electrostatic unit. Yet, direct a stream of these "particles" onto a crystal, and diffraction phenomena take place; to explain these phenomena requires that the "electrons" be treated as a train of waves. Attempts to measure the position and momentum of a particle, or the energy and duration of a state of a dynamic system, may be perfectly successful in separate experiments, but never in the same experiment on the same system.

All of these familar results of quantum physics are given a quantitative expression in the Heisenberg uncertainty principle, and a general philosophical basis in Bohr's principle of complementarity. Viewing these phenomena from the standpoint of deterministic descriptions of events in space and time (the goal of classical physics), Bohr (1963) says that: "Within the scope of classical physics, all characteristic properties of a given object can in principle be ascertained by a single experimental arrangement, though in practice various arrangements are often convenient. . . . In quantum physics, however, evidence about atomic objects obtained by different experimental arrangements exhibits a novel kind of complementary relationship. . . . Far from restricting our efforts to put questions to nature in the form of experiments, the notion of *complementarity* simply characterizes the answers we can receive by such inquiry, whenever the interaction between the measuring instruments and the objects forms an integral part of the phenomena."

And again, "Indeed the ascertaining of the presence of an atomic particle in a limited space-time domain demands an experimental arrangement involving a transfer of momentum and energy to bodies such as fixed scales and synchronized clocks, which cannot be included in the description of their functioning, if these bodies are to fulfill the role of defining the reference frame. Conversely, any strict application of the laws of conservation of momentum and energy [that is, any causality] implies, in principle, a renunciation of detailed space-time coordination of the particles" (Bohr, 1963).

After complementarity in physics had been accepted, it was realized that observations which give conflicting (complementary) views of phenomena cannot, when taken by themselves, be accepted as complete *nor, therefore, as totally correct* descriptions of nature. Electrons behave in ways that can be accounted for by thinking of them as particles; but they are *not* particles, since they also (under different conditions of observation) behave in ways that can be accounted for by thinking of them as waves. Only the complementary description is complete and, to the best of our knowledge, correct. However, to say this is not to impugn the accuracy of the different experimental measurements that give, respectively, the one-sided wave or particle results.

Bohr made it very clear that, in the context of quantum physics, the idea of complementarity had nothing to do with any renunciation of rational objectivity in science. Yet the very idea of an objective description of phenomena (for example, in unambiguously reporting the results of an experiment) requires that macroscopic (that is, classical) equipment and observations be described in ordinary language, no matter how much that language could be refined and specialized for technical usage. The duality of light's behavior arises not from the light "itself" (if such an idea even has any meaning), but from the observation of light as it interacts with experimental equipment and in the description of such observations in language that only contains the classical terms "wave" and "particle" as models for the phenomenon.

Although it was the phenomena of quantum physics that forced Bohr to the idea of complementarity as a mode of knowledge, he quickly realized that other apparent contradictions in the description of nature also admitted of a similar resolution. In a series of essays, he considered its application to biology and psychology (1963) and, finally, to the whole range of human intellectual experience (1958, pp. 67–82). Since the extension to wider problems of an idea that is valid in a clearly limited context is dangerous to the integrity of that idea, the present attempt at even further extension requires a list, as complete as possible, of the characteristics both of the idea of complementarity, and of the situations to which it may be fruitfully applied. It will then remain to discover to what extent the conflict between the analytical and intuitive understandings of nature satisfies those criteria. I intend to use only the physical application of complementarity as a model, since it seems the least ambiguous and is generally accepted as a necessary interpretation of phenomena by workers in the field.

On this basis, then, the following characteristics defining complementary realities may be listed.

1. A single phenomenon (for example, "light" or "matter") manifests itself to an observer in conflicting modes (for example, as "waves" or "particles").

2. The description or model that fits the phenomenon depends on the mode of observation. (In this way, the idea of objectivity is somewhat broadened, but not eliminated.)

3. Each description is "rational"; that is, language (including mathematics if necessary) is used according to the same consistent logic in either description, with no appeal to revealed truth or mystical insight.

4. Neither model can be subsumed into the other. Thus, for example, classical and statistical thermodynamics do not constitute complementary formulations, even though they can be developed from apparently independent axiomatic bases.

5. Because they refer to a (presumably) single reality, complementary descriptions are not independent of each other. For example, the differential equation of wave motion used in the description of an electron in an atom must be "normalized"; that is, its integral over all space must correspond to the quantity of mass and electrical charge carried by one electron (measurable only in experiments in which particle behavior is manifested).

6. Complementarity is not mere contradiction. The alternate modes of description never lead to incompatible predictions for a given experiment, since they arise from different kinds of experience. Thus, Newtonian and relativistic mechanics are not complementarities, since it can be shown experimentally that the former leads to incorrect predictions of phenomena that are correctly predicted by the latter.

7. It follows from number 6 that neither complementary model of a given phenomenon is complete; a full account of the phenomenon is achieved only by enlarging the frame of reference to include both models as alternative truths, however irreconcilable their abstract contradictions may seem.

QUANTITATIVE SCIENCE AND
THE SENSUOUS ALTERNATIVE

The importance of quantitative modeling in the creation of the scientific world view is an old story, and there is no need to belabor it here. Critics and apologists of science alike have recognized that the cyclic coupling of experimental observation with mathematical theorizing has been the driving force behind the huge advances achieved since the time of Descartes in understanding the complex of phenomena that we call nature. Where critics and apologists have parted, however, is on the moral consequences of such an approach to nature. Some, like C. P. Snow (1959) and J. Bronowski (1956), find in the scientist's rigorous adherence to verifiability, and in his humility in the face of evidence contradictory to his theories, the best hope of salvation that mankind has. To others (Roszak, 1969, p. 205), the alleged objective consciousness of the scientist is not only a myth, but a vicious one, behind which men may perpetrate monstrous crimes against nature without acknowledging personal involvement and, therefore, guilt. Most recently, Lewis Mumford (1970) has found in the mechanical world view the fatal metaphor for a society of machine-like repression of human feelings and human freedom. It is not my purpose to evaluate Mumford's critique of science [which is sometimes too condemnatory even for the generally antitechnological *New York Review of Books* (Hobsbawn, 1970)]. It seems to me, however, that some undeniably dangerous attitudes do exist in science's present stance toward nature; and, to the extent that these attitudes exist, they represent dangers to the integrity of human freedom and of the terrestrial environment.

In his everyday experience, man finds the world chaotic and, in the perhaps revealing word of the scientific theorist, "messy." Complex brown and black mixtures prevail over pure substances. It is no wonder, then, that mankind, in reaction to this chaos, is inclined to bring the phenomena indoors to calm, well-lighted laboratories in which they can be studied one at a time, or in well-defined combinations. Nor is it any wonder that he often chooses to understand nature in terms of mental models (which include scientific theories and "laws" as well as pictorial or tactile models) that are understandable just because they are the creation of his own mind. These mental models serve as maps or blueprints of reality. Like maps and blueprints (and like shadows), they simplify complex systems by projecting them onto a simpler space that has a smaller number of dimensions than are required for a complete description of the original system. A complex part of nature (such as a coral reef, a cell, or a city) is, metaphorically, many-dimensional. It is brought under scientific scrutiny by projecting it onto a simpler, under-dimensioned space, within which it can be grasped and quantified.

Then, depending on its appearance within that space, generalizations are drawn according to the logical and mathematical rules appropriate to the quantification space. Physical implications of the mathematical model are subjected to quantitative test under controlled conditions. To the extent that experiment confirms theory and suggests new theoretical steps, science progresses.

The pure intellectual excitement of science, its success in illuminating some of the darkness that threatened to engulf us with the fall of religious world views, and the social benefits of its technological consequences are beyond serious question. There are those who are chafing to get on with the extension of mankind's intellectual hegemony to the understanding and complete control of our natural environment, our societies, our heredity, and our fellow man. Yet the potential and actual evils that have already come from the "ethically neutral" pursuit of knowledge for its own sake, and the alienation of science and scientists from the rest of the culture, are also beyond question. To take credit for the successes of science and the blessings of technology, but to blame the abuses on the incompetence or venality, or both, of planners, politicians, and businessmen, seems fatuous in the extreme. Nor, knowing what we do now of the momentous social consequences of the "purest" science, can we seek forgiveness for the next social or ecological disaster. Our understanding of really complex systems (organisms, societies, ecosystems, the mind) is rudimentary, and our ways of investigating such systems and communicating about them, primitive. The danger of a scientific-technological disaster arises when practitioners of the quantifying art forget about the philosophical foundations of their enterprise. It is easy to ignore the too-messy world outside the laboratory door: to mistake domains and functions in quantification space for nature, and the manipulation of these for the only method of understanding nature. (As a physicist once remarked to me in the course of a seminar on group theory, "The matrices are all there is.")

I realize that the connection I have just made between scientific practice and ethics is a tenuous and controversial one, though Roszak and Mumford make it with great force. In fact, Alfred North Whitehead made just these points over 40 years ago in his widely admired and little heeded series of lectures, *Science and the Modern World* (1925). However, by relying lopsidedly on abstract quantification as a method of knowing, scientists have been looking at the world with one eye closed. There is other knowledge besides quantitative knowledge, and there are other ways of knowing besides reading the position of a pointer on a scale. The human mind and body process information with staggering sophistication and sensitivity by the direct sensuous experience of their surroundings. We have, in fact, in our very selves, "instruments" that are capable of confronting and understanding the blooming, buzzing, messy world outside the laboratory. If that were not so, *Homo sapiens* would never have survived the competitive pressure from predators who are also so equipped. There are three tenets of countercultural thought that, it seems to me, hold great promise for the enrichment of scientific practice and, perhaps, for the improvement of scientific morality.

1. The most reliable and effective knowing follows from direct and open confrontation with phenomena, no matter how complicated they are. Nature can be trusted to behave reliably without suppression of the manifold details of a natural environment, and nature's ways are open to direct, intuitive, sensuous knowledge.

2. It follows from the first point that, to know nature well, the human body is to be trusted, cherished, and made sensitive to its natural and human environment. Since the self and the environment are inextricable (contrary to the philosophical stance of classical science), [man] can understand his surroundings by being sensitive to his own reactions to them.

3. Because knowledge of nature is, in this way, equally open to all, the "expert" is highly suspect. His expertise is likely to be confined to abstractions, and there is a danger that he will project sensitive and complex problems onto some underdimensioned space where he feels less involved and more in control of phenomena. (This threatening aspect is generally confined to the psychological and social sciences, but it can also be seen in the attitude of the ecology movement toward the Army Corps of Engineers.)

In sum, it seems to me that there is much of value in the mind-set that includes these ideas. It is certainly not confined to hippies and "ecofreaks." Thoughtful and respectable writers on educational theory (e.g.: Bruner, 1962; Holt, 1967; Jones, 1967) hold much the same view of learning and have much the same criticism of conventional knowledge, which is based on quantification. Furthermore, for very different reasons, industrial scientists have been telling academic scientists this for years. Industrial scientists have attacked what they see as a ludicrous overemphasis on abstract theory in science education. In fact, it may be just the academic scientist's self-imposed isolation from the complexities of the "real" world that has made him so helpless to curb the ecological abuses of his profit-motivated colleagues.

A COMPLETE NATURAL SCIENCE

I now consider whether abstract-quantitative and direct sensuous information meet the requirements of a complementary description of nature.

1. The language, the epistemology, and the models of the two approaches all present us with conflicting pictures of nature; yet the phenomena are consistent and repeatable in each mode.

2. Which description of nature one gives depends entirely on one's method of knowing. For example, one can predict rain by reading the barometer or by going outdoors and sniffing the air, with about equal reliability. The explanations of the prediction, though, will differ, depending on the manner in which the experiment was performed on the atmosphere.

3. Though it may be difficult to convince partisans of either viewpoint, both approaches are "rational." That is, both use a consistent logic, based clearly on the observation of phenomena, in such a way as to ensure that another observer in the same situation would come to the same conclusion. (Before conventional scientists rush in with cries of "subjectivity" in criticism of the sensuous approach, they might stop to consider whether or not a person selected at random off the street could be asked to repeat their highly sophisticated observations. "With the proper training he could," they reply; and the reply of the sensuous observer of nature would be exactly the same for *his* method.)

4. It goes without saying that neither approach to nature can be subsumed into the other. A number is not an experience, nor is an equation the same thing as intuition. These things are projections of nature into separate (disjunct) mental spaces.

5. Sensuous information is not independent of quantitative knowledge, since they both have their referent in the same system of nature. Of course, abuses of both methods are possible: drug- or wish-induced distortion of the senses, and politically or economically motivated suppression of contrary data for the quantifier. [The controversies in Russia over genetics and those in the United States over the carcinogenicity of smoking have been fought entirely on traditional, theory-experiment grounds. They recall the happiness of Watson and

Crick when a colleague guessed the *wrong* structure for DNA (Watson, 1968).] Yet in the long run, such distortions are corrected or at least forgotten, since both the sensuous and experimental investigator share humility in the face of nature.

6. By the same reasoning, both sensuous and quantitative descriptions of nature may be true; they lead, by the process of continuous self-correction, to reliable models of nature. The woodsman or farmer knows when to expect rain or frost, or where to find a given animal, without quite knowing *how* he knows these things. Reasonably accurate descriptions of weather patterns and animal behavior may also emerge from the tabulation and correlation of quantitative data.

7. Finally, neither sensuous nor quantitative knowledge of nature is complete. In fact, it should be clear from the examples I have chosen that each is really an undernourished view of nature, because each lacks information available through the other mode. Indeed, it is difficult to think of single problems that have been attacked by both modes of knowing, so different are the mind-sets of the two classes of investigators.

The theoretical-experimental mode has built its grand structure by confining the phenomena investigated to the kind that can be brought into a laboratory. Worse, because such laboratories and their operation are very expensive, the phenomena investigated have largely been confined to those in which a source of wealth has a vested interest—however broadly that interest has been expressed, and however apparent has been the freedom of the investigator to follow knowledge for its own sake.

On the other hand, the sensuous investigation of nature has generally been confined to "naturalists." Their undoubted and often sublime understanding of nature, and the integrity they have preserved by being poorly funded, have been undercut by their concomitant (in fact, complementary) weakness in rigorous quantitative formulation of what they know. Competition for funds and recognition has made naturalists and scientists rivals, mutually indulgent at best, contemptuous at worst, rather than colleagues in the process of learning about nature. The two groups are, in fact, comparable to two groups of physicists, one of which insists on regarding light as particles, and the other of which treats light only as waves. Such a situation would be ludicrous in modern physics, yet it is exactly what we now confront in science as a whole.

Having said these things, I am now in the position of having to supply a positive model for science. I will try by suggesting that, just as in quantum physics, the truth about nature is to be found only by expanding the frame of discourse to include both of these complementary models of reality.

Two successful models of complementarity in serious scientific investigation may show what I mean. First, there is what began (and, as far as I know, is still regarded) as a dispute between Goethe and Newton over the nature of color. Both men developed theories of color: Newton's was purely quantitative; Goethe's dealt with the sensuous perception of color, including such phenomena as complementary colors and clashing colors. In a speech before the Society for Cultural Collaboration in Budapest in 1941, the German physicist Werner Heisenberg [who played a central role in the formulation of complementarity in quantum physics (1967)] reviewed these two theories, especially the less familiar one of Goethe. Heisenberg clearly saw that the two are complementary, in that they are addressed to the same phenomenon from entirely different points of view. Yet, even for Heisenberg (1952), Goethe's view had to be seen as in *opposition* to Newton's, and his verdict is rendered in language that is unfortunately characteristic of our approach to complementary realities:

> [The] battle is over. The decision on "right" and "wrong" in all questions of detail has long since been taken. Goethe's color theory has in many ways borne fruit in art, physiology, and esthetics. But victory, and hence influence on the research of the following century, has been Newton's.

Yet, if one asks [oneself] "What is color?" the complete answer to such a question can be found only in the complementary descriptions from physics and art. To insist on projecting the question into one or the other of those separate worlds may be a good way to initiate research, but, at the same time, it distorts the original intention of the question.

The second area of nature in which complementary modes of learning have been applied, this time often by the same investigator, is in the study of animal behavior. Of many examples, the finest of which I am aware is George Schaller's study (1965) of gorillas. Here, in a beautiful whole, are a "serious" and straightforward account of the nature of the gorilla, and an account of Schaller's own presence in the forest—how he interacted with the gorillas and what he learned by observing the effects of this interaction.*

---

*In fact, Schaller's method was so far from the observation, by concealed experimenters, of captive animals in drab and sensuously meaningless mazes, cages, and boxes that it is inconceivable that his understanding of gorilla behavior is at all accessible to the orthodox animal psychologist.

For a single research paper that nicely combines sensuous and mathematical descriptions of a phenomenon, see McCutchen (1970).

IMPLICATIONS FOR THE FUTURE OF SCIENCE

At this writing, it seems beyond dispute that, for at least the next decade, the most important, active, and heavily funded field of science will be ecology—in its broadest sense. Unless we reach a full and effective understanding of human society and its place in the biosphere, there will be no science worth speaking of in the twenty-first century. It is lucky indeed that the generation born since 1950 is, as a group, deeply interested in all aspects of ecology. Yet this group will not use its energy and intelligence to seek scientific approaches to ecological problems until they are convinced that science is not "irrelevant" or, in fact, demonic.

What is urgently needed is a science that can comprehend complex systems without, or with a minimum of, abstractions. To "see" a complex system as an organic whole requires an act of trained intuition, just as seeing order in a welter of numerical data does. The conditions for achieving such perceptions have been discussed at length among scientists (with little discernible impact on the way we train scientists). The consensus, if any, is that they follow only after long periods of total immersion in the problem. The implication for the present discussion is that the intuitive knowledge essential to a full understanding of complex systems can be encouraged and prepared for by: (i) training scientists to be aware of sensuous clues about their surroundings; (ii) insisting on sensuous knowledge as part of the intellectual structure of science, not as an afterthought; and (iii) approaching complex systems openly, respecting their organic complexity before choosing an abstract quantification space into which to project them.

Because of the primitive, and even repressed, attitudes we now have (and pass on to our students) about intuitive knowledge and its transmission from one person to another, it is difficult to be more precise. Perhaps science has much to learn along this line from the disciplines, as distinct from the mystical content, of Oriental religions. If we do learn to know complexities through the complementary modes of sensuous intuition and logical abstraction, and if we can transmit and discuss the former as reliably as we do the latter, then there is hope for a renaissance in science as a whole comparable to that which occurred in physics between 1900 and 1930.

As usual, the bulk of the active and creative work in any such renaissance will fall to younger people: that is, to just those who, as a group, view the present posture of science as most suspect. Because the recruitment of each new generation of scientists takes place in the undergraduate colleges, I believe that the time is far overdue for a thorough restructuring of the way we educate scientists. Because higher education in Europe and the United States flourished along with the scientific revolution, its assumptions are largely those of science: that knowledge abstracted and codified into lectures and textbooks will stand for full knowledge. *

In ex post facto response to the demands of our students (who may be only dimly aware of what is bothering them), we "inject" relevance into our teaching by means of examples that have been wrenched from their organic context and used to exemplify the abstractions that are the real matter of serious courses in science. I have gone so far, in my own teaching, as to sacrifice a few laboratory afternoons for my students to contemplate—without "lab sheets," ill-concealed hints about procedure, or even a demand that they keep and turn in a notebook—the colors, smells, textures, and changes of some substances on which they would do a rigorous and abstractly interpreted experiment the following week. In many instances, students have seen the connection and have become really excited about their dual insights into chemical systems. But even this is only a feeble fluctuation in the normal curriculum. Most of the students who go through it on their way to a degree are, at best, tolerant of my efforts to let them really know something about equilibria in aqueous solutions. At the risk of judging them too harshly, I cannot but feel that, by the time I see them, their natural curiosity about the physical world has been corrupted by too many years of rules, abstractions, and quickie true-false tests. And their fellows, who have awakened to the one-sidedness of the abstract worlds of scholarship in general and of science in particular, and have summarily rejected them, I never see at all.

I might address these remarks primarily to those who teach undergraduates. Yet there is no teacher of science who is not himself a scientist, and science as it is taught is allegedly a representation of science as it is practiced. If the practice of science continues its present one-sided and underdimensioned course, new scientists will be recruited predominately from among those people to whom such a view of the world is most congenial. Yet such people are least fitted, by temperament and training, to hold in mind the complementary truths about nature that our looming

---

*Of course, we know that that isn't really true; we just act as if it were. And it takes no great perception on any teacher's part to see that most of his class don't really understand what they write back to us on examinations; perhaps that's why we are careful to set such examinations as soon as possible after the material is "learned."

tasks will require. Indeed, one may seriously question whether even an underdimensioned science can be maintained as a creative enterprise by scientists recruited from among those of lesser imagination, sympathy, and humanity. Neils Bohr's vision of the unity of human knowledge only echoes, a half-century later, that of Walt Whitman:

> "I swear the earth shall surely be complete to him
> or her who shall be complete.
> The earth remains jagged and broken to him
> or her who remains jagged and broken."

5.

States of Consciousness and State-Specific Sciences

Charles T. Tart

Blackburn [in the selection here preceding] noted that many of our most talented young people are "turned off" to science: as a solution, he proposed that we recognize the validity of a more sensuous-intuitive approach to nature, treating it as complementary to the classical intellectual approach.

I have seen the same rejection of science by many of the brightest students in California, and the problem is indeed serious. Blackburn's analysis is valid, but not deep enough. A more fundamental source of

Reprinted by permission from *Science*, 176 (June 16, 1972), 1203–1210. Copyright ©1972 by the American Association for the Advancement of Science.

I wish to thank Ida Rolf and Seymour Carter for their assistance in writing this paper. Ida is the discoverer of Structural Integration and Seymour gave me my first session. This first session produced an immense release of energy, such that the basic themes of this paper came to me within a few hours after the session, and the paper was finished a few days later. [This footnote appeared in an earlier version of this paper. Ed.]

alienation is the widespread experience of altered states of consciousness (ASC's) by the young, coupled with the almost total rejection of the knowledge gained during the experiencing of ASC's by the scientific establishment. Blackburn himself exemplifies this rejection when he says: "Perhaps science has much to learn along this line from the disciplines, *as distinct from the content*, of Oriental religions" (my italics).

To illustrate, a recent Gallup poll (*Newsweek*, Jan. 25, 1971, p. 52) indicated that approximately half of American college students have tried marijuana, and a large number of them use it fairly regularly. They do this at the risk of having their careers ruined and going to jail for several years. Why? Conventional research on the nature of marijuana intoxication tells us that the primary effects are a slight increase in heart rate, reddening of the eyes, some difficulty with memory, and small decrements in performance on complex psychomotor tests.

Would you risk going to jail to experience these?

A young marijuana smoker who hears a scientist or physician talk about these findings as the basic nature of marijuana intoxication will simply sneer and have his antiscientific attitude further reinforced. It is clear to him that the scientist has no real understanding of what marijuana intoxication is all about. *

More formally, an increasingly significant number of people are experimenting with ASC's in themselves, and finding the experiences thus gained of extreme importance in their philosophy and style of life. The conflict between experiences in these ASC's and the attitudes and intellectual-emotional systems that have evolved in our ordinary state of consciousness (SoC) is a major factor behind the increased alienation of many people from conventional science. Experiences of ecstasy, mystical union, other "dimensions," rapture, beauty, space-and-time transcendence, and transpersonal knowledge, all common in ASC's, are simply not treated adequately in conventional scientific approaches. These experiences will not "go away" if we crack down more on psychedelic drugs, for immense numbers of people now practice various nondrug techniques for producing ASC's, such as meditation (see Naranjo and Ornstein, 1971) and yoga.

The purpose of this article is to show that it is possible to investigate and work with the important phenomena of ASC's in a manner which is perfectly compatible with the essence of scientific method. The conflict discussed above is not necessary.

---

*An attempt to describe the phenomena of marijuana intoxication in terms that make sense to the user, as well as the investigator, has been presented elsewhere. See Tart (1971).

STATES OF CONSCIOUSNESS

An ASC may be defined for the purposes of this article as a qualitative alteration in the over-all pattern of mental functioning, such that the experiencer feels his consciousness is radically different from the way it functions ordinarily. An SoC is thus defined not in terms of any particular content of consciousness, or specific behavior or physiological change, but in terms of the over-all patterning of psychological functioning.

An analogy with computer functioning can clarify this definition. A computer has a complex program of many subroutines. If we reprogram it quite differently, the same sorts of input data may be handled in quite different ways; we will be able to predict very little from our knowledge of the old program about the effects of varying the input, even though old and new programs have some subroutines in common. The new program with its input-output interactions must be studied in and of itself. An ASC is analogous to changing temporarily the program of a computer.

The ASC's experienced by almost all ordinary people are dreaming states and the hypnogogic and hypnopompic states, the transitional states between sleeping and waking. Many other people experience another ASC, alcohol intoxication.

The relatively new (to our culture) ASC's that are now having such an impact are those produced by marijuana, more powerful psychedelic drugs such as LSD, meditative states, so-called possession states, and autohypnotic states.*

STATES OF CONSCIOUSNESS AND PARADIGMS

It is useful to compare this concept of an SoC, a qualitatively distinct organization of the patterning of mental functioning, with Kuhn's (1962) concept of paradigms in science. A paradigm is an intellectrual achievement that underlies normal science and attracts and guides the work of an enduring number of adherents in their scientific activity. It is a kind of "super theory," a formulation of scope wide enough to affect the organization of most or all of the major known phenomena of its field.

---

*Note that an SoC is defined by the stable parameters of the pattern that constitute it, not by the particular technique of inducing that pattern, for some ASC's can be induced by a variety of induction methods. By analogy, to understand the altered computer program you must study what it does, not study the programmer who originally set it up.

Yet it is sufficiently open-ended that there still remain important problems to be solved within that framework. Examples of important paradigms in the history of science have been Copernican astronomy and Newtonian dynamics.

Because of their tremendous success, paradigms undergo a change which, in principle, ordinary scientific theories do not undergo. An ordinary scientific theory is always subject to further questioning and testing as it is extended. A paradigm becomes an implicit framework for most scientists working within it; it is the natural way of looking at things and doing things. It does not seriously occur to the adherents of a paradigm to question it any more (we may ignore, for the moment, the occurrence of scientific revolutions). Theories become referred to as laws: people talk of the law of gravity, not the theory of gravity, for example.

A paradigm serves to concentrate the attention of a researcher on sensible problem areas and to prevent him from wasting his time on what might be trivia. On the other hand, by implicitly defining some lines of research as trivial or nonsensical, a paradigm acts like a blinder. Kuhn has discussed this blinding function as a key factor in the lack of effective communications during paradigm clashes.

The concept of a paradigm and of an SoC are quite similar. Both constitute complex, interlocking sets of rules and theories that enable a person to interact with and interpret experiences within an environment. In both cases, the rules are largely implicit. They are not recognized as tentative working hypotheses; they operate automatically and the person feels he is doing the obvious or natural thing.

PARADIGM CLASH BETWEEN "STRAIGHT" AND "HIP"

Human beings become emotionally attached to the things which give them pleasure, and a scientist making important progress within a particular paradigm becomes emotionally attached to it. When data which make no sense in terms of the (implicit) paradigm are brought to our attention, the usual result is not a reevaluation of the paradigm, but a rejection or misperception of the data. This rejection seems rational to others sharing that paradigm and irrational or rationalizing to others committed to a different paradigm.

The conflict now existing between those who have experienced certain ASC's (whose ranks include many young scientists) and those who have not is very much a paradigmatic conflict. For example, a subject takes

LSD, and tells his investigator that "You and I, we are all one, there are no separate selves." The investigator reports that his subject showed a "confused sense of identity and distorted thinking process." The subject is reporting what is obvious to him, the investigator is reporting what is obvious to him. The investigator's implicit paradigm, based on his scientific training, his cultural background, and his normal SoC, indicates that a literal interpretation of the subject's statement cannot be true, and therefore must be interpreted as mental dysfunction on the part of the subject. The subject, his paradigms radically changed for the moment by being in an ASC, not only reports what is obviously true to him, but perceives the investigator as showing mental dysfunction, by virtue of being incapable of perceiving the obvious!

Historically, paradigm clashes have been characterized by bitter emotional antagonisms, and total rejection of the opponent. Currently we are seeing the same sort of process: the respectable psychiatrist, who would not take any of those "psychotomimetic" drugs himself or sit down and experience that crazy meditation process, carries out research to show that drug takers and those who practice meditation are escapists. The drug taker or meditator views the same investigator as narrow-minded, prejudiced, and repressive, and as a result drops out of the university. Communication between the two factions is almost nil.

Must the experiencers of ASC's continue to see the scientists as concentrating on the irrelevant, and the scientists see the experiencers as confused* or mentally ill? Or can science deal adequately with the experiences of these people? The thesis I shall now present in detail is that we can deal with the important aspects of ASC's using the essence of scientific method, even though a variety of nonessentials, unfortunately identified with current science, hinder such an effort.

THE NATURE OF KNOWLEDGE

Basically, science (from the Latin *scire*, to know) deals with knowledge. Knowledge may be defined as an immediately given experimental feeling of congruence between two different kinds of experience, a matching. One set of experiences may be regarded as perceptions of the external world, of others, of oneself; the second set may be regarded as a theory, a scheme, a system of understanding. The feeling of congruence is some-

---

*Note that states of confusion and impaired functioning are certainly aspects of some drug-induced SoC's, but are not of primary interest here.

thing immediately given in experience, although many refinements have been worked out for judging degrees of congruence.

All knowledge, then, is basically experiential knowledge. Even my knowledge of the physical world can be reduced to this: given certain sets of experiences, which I (by assumption) attribute to the external world activating my sensory apparatus, it may be possible for me to compare them with purely internal experiences (memories, previous knowledge) and predict with a high degree of reliability other kinds of experiences, which I again attribute to the external world.

Because science has been incredibly successful in dealing with the physical world, it has been historically associated with a philosophy of physicalism, the belief that reality is all reducible to certain kinds of physical entities. The vast majority of phenomena of ASC's have no known physical manifestations: thus to physicalistic philosophy they are epiphenomena, not worthy of study. But insofar as science deals with knowledge, it need not restrict itself only to physical kinds of knowledge.

THE ESSENCE OF SCIENTIFIC METHOD

I shall discuss the essence of scientific method, and show that this essence is perfectly compatible with an enlarged study of the important phenomena of ASC's. In particular, I propose that state-specific sciences be developed.

As satisfying as the feeling of knowing can be, we are often wrong: what seems like congruence at first later does not match, or has no generality. Man has learned that his reasoning is often faulty, [that] his observations are often incomplete or mistaken, and that emotional and other nonconscious factors can seriously distort both reasoning and observational processes. His reliance on authorities, "rationality" or "elegance," are no sure criteria for achieving truth. The development of scientific method may be seen as a determined effort to systemize the process of acquiring knowledge in such a way as to minimize the various pitfalls of observation and reasoning.

I shall discuss four basic rules of scientific method to which an investigator is committed: (i) good observation; (ii) the public nature of observation; (iii) the necessity to theorize logically; and (iv) the testing of theory by observable consequences; all these constitute the scientific enterprise. I shall consider the wider application of each rule to ASC's and indicate how unnecessary physicalistic restrictions may be dropped. I will show that all these commitments or rules can be accommodated in the development of state-specific sciences that I propose.

OBSERVATION

The scientist is committed to observe as well as possible the phenomena of interest and to search constantly for better ways of making these observations. But our paradigmatic commitments, our SoC's, make us likely to observe certain parts of reality and to ignore or observe with error certain other parts of it.

Many of the most important phenomena of ASC's have been observed poorly or not at all because of the physicalistic labeling of them as epiphenomena, so that they have been called "subjective," "ephemeral," "unreliable," or "unscientific." Observations of internal processes are probably much more difficult to make than those of external physical processes, because of their inherently greater complexity. The essence of science, however, is that we observe what there is to be observed whether it is difficult or not.

Furthermore, most of what we know about the phenomena of ASC's has been obtained from untrained people, almost none of whom have shared the scientists' commitment to constantly reexamine their observations in greater and greater detail. This should not imply that internal phenomena are inherently unobservable or unstable; we are comparing the first observations of internal phenomena with observations of physical sciences that have undergone centuries of refinement.

We must consider one other problem of observation. One of the traditional idols of science, the "detached observer," has no place in dealing with many internal phenomena of SoCs. Not only are the observer's perceptions selective, he may also affect the things he observes. We must try to understand the characteristics of each individual observer in order to compensate for them.

A recognition of the unreality of the detached observer in the psychological sciences is becoming widespread, under the topics of experimenter bias (Rosenthal, 1966) and demand characteristics (Orne, 1962) A similar recognition long ago occurred in physics, when it was realized that the observed was altered by the process of observation at subatomic levels. When we deal with ASC's where the observer is the experiencer of the ASC, this factor is of paramount importance. Knowing the characteristics of the observer can also confound the process of consensual validation, which I shall now consider.

PUBLIC NATURE OF OBSERVATION

Observations must be public in that they must be replicable by any properly trained observer. The experienced conditions that led to the report of certain experiences must be described in sufficient detail that others may duplicate them and consequently have experiences which meet criteria of identicality. That someone else may set up similar conditions but not have the same experiences proves that the original investigator gave an incorrect description of the conditions and observations, or that he was not aware of certain essential aspects of the conditions.

The physicalistic accretion to this rule of consensual validation is that, physical data being the only "real" data, internal phenomena must be reduced to physiological or behavioral data to become reliable or they will be ignored entirely. I believe most physical observations to be much more readily replicable by any trained observer because they are inherently simpler phenomena than internal ones. In principle, however, consensual validation of internal phenomena by a trained observer is quite possible.

The emphasis on public observations in science has had a misleading quality insofar as it implies that any intelligent man can replicate a scientist's observations. This might have been true early in the history of science, but nowadays only the trained observer can replicate many observations. I cannot go into a modern physicist's laboratory and confirm his observations. Indeed, his talk of what he has found in his experiments (physicists seem to talk about innumerable invisible entities these days) would probably seem mystical to me, just as many descriptions of internal states sound mystical to those with a background in the physical sciences.

Given the high complexity of the phenomena associated with ASC's, the need for replication by trained observers is exceptionally important. Since it generally takes 4 to 10 years of intensive training to produce a scientist in any of our conventional sciences, we should not be surprised that there has been very little reliability of observations by untrained observers of ASC phenomena.

Further, for the state-specific sciences that I propose should be established, we cannot specify the requirements that would constitute adequate training. These would only be determined after considerable trial and error. We should also recognize that very few people might complete the training successfully. Some people do not have the necessary innate characteristics to become physicists, and some probably do not have the innate characteristics to become, say, scientific investigators of meditative states.

Public observation, then, always refers to a limited, specially trained public. It is only by basic agreement among those specially trained people that data become accepted as a foundation for the development of a science. That laymen cannot replicate the observations is of little relevance.

A second problem in consensual validation arises from a phenomenon predicted by my concept of ASC's, but not yet empirically investigated, namely, state-specific communication. Given that an ASC is an overall qualitative and quantitative shift in the complex functioning of consciousness, such that there are new "logics" and perceptions (which would constitute a paradigm shift), it is quite reasonable to hypothesize that communication may take a different pattern. For two observers, both of whom, we assume, are fluent in communicating with each other in a given SoC, communication about some new observations may seem adequate to them, or may be improved or deteriorated in specific ways. To an outside observer, an observer in a different SoC, the communication between these two observers may seem "deteriorated."

Practically all investigations of communication by persons in ASC's have resulted in reports of deterioration of communication abilities. In designing their studies, however, these investigators have not taken into account the fact that the pattern of communication may have changed. If I am listening to two people speaking in English, and they suddenly begin to intersperse words and phrases in Polish, I, as an outside (that is, a non-Polish-speaking) observer, will note a gross deterioration in communication. Adequacy of communication between people in the same SoC and across SoC's must be empirically determined.

Thus consensual validation may be restricted by the fact that only observers in the same ASC are able to communicate adequately with each other, and they may not be able to communicate adequately to someone in a different SoC, say, normal consciousness.*

THEORIZING

A scientist may theorize about his observations as much as he wishes to, but the theory he develops must consistently account for all that he has observed, and should have a logical structure that other scientists can comprehend (but not necessarily accept).

The requirement to theorize logically and consistently with the data is not as simple as it looks, however. Any logic consists of a basic set of

---

*A state-specific scientist might find his own work somewhat incomprehensible when he was not in that SoC because of the phenomenon of state-specific memory—that is, not enough of his work would transfer to his ordinary SoC to make it comprehensible, even though it would make perfect sense when he was again in the ASC in which he did his scientific work.

assumptions and a set of rules for manipulating information, based on these assumptions. Change the assumptions, or change the rules, and there may be entirely different outcomes from the same data. A paradigm, too, is a logic: it has certain assumptions and rules for working within these assumptions. By changing the paradigm, altering the SoC, the nature of theory-building may change radically. Thus a person in SoC 2 might come to very different conclusions about the nature of the same events that he observed in SoC 1. An investigator in SoC 1 may comment on the comprehensibility of the second person's ideas from the point of view (paradigm) of SoC 1, but can say nothing about their inherent validity. A scientist who could enter either SoC 1 or SoC 2, however, could pronounce on the comprehensibility of the other's theory, and the adherence of that theory to the rules and logic of SoC 2. Thus, scientists trained in the same SoC may check on the logical validity of each other's theorizing. We have then the possibility of a state-specific logic underlying theorizing in various SoC's.

OBSERVABLE CONSEQUENCES

Any theory a scientist develops must have observable consequences, and from that theory it must be possible to make predictions that can be verified by observation. If such verification is not possible, the theory must be considered invalid, regardless of its elegance, logic, or other appeal.

Ordinarily we think of empirical validation, of validation in terms of testable consequences that produce physical effects, but this is misleading. Any effect, whether interpreted as physical or nonphysical, is ultimately an experience in the observer's mind. All that is essentially required to validate a theory is that it predict that "When a certain experience (observed condition) has occurred, another (predicted) kind of experience will follow, under specified experiential conditions." Thus a perfectly scientific theory may be based on data that have no physical existence.

STATE-SPECIFIC SCIENCES

We tend to envision the practice of science like this: centered around interest in some particular range of subject matter, a small number of highly selected, talented, and rigorously trained people spend considerable time making detailed observations on the subject matter of interest. They may or may not have special places (laboratories) or instruments or methods to assist them in making finer observations. They speak to one another in a special language which they feel conveys precisely the important facts of their field. Using this language, they confirm and extend each other's knowledge of certain data basic to the field. They theorize about their basic data and construct elaborate systems. They validate these by recourse to further observation. These trained people all have a long-term commitment to the constant refinement of observation and extension of theory. Their activity is frequently incomprehensible to laymen.

This general description is equally applicable to a variety of sciences, or areas that could become sciences, whether we called such areas biology, physics, chemistry, psychology, understanding of mystical states, or drug-induced enhancement of cognitive processes. The particulars of research would look very different, but the basic scientific method running through all is the same.

More formally, I now propose the creation of various state-specific sciences. If such sciences could be created, we would have a group of highly skilled, dedicated, and trained practitioners able to achieve certain SoC's, and able to agree with one another that they have attained a common state. While in that SoC, they might then investigate other areas of interest, whether these be totally internal phenomena of that given state, the interaction of that state with external, physical reality, or people in other SoC's.

The fact that the experimenter should be able to function skillfully in the SoC itself for a state-specific science does not necessarily mean that he would always be the subject. While he might often be the subject, observer, and experimenter simultaneously, it would be quite possible for him to collect data from experimental manipulations of other subjects in the SoC, and either be in that SoC himself at the time of data collection or be in that SoC himself for data reduction and theorizing.

Examples of some observations made and theorizing done by a scientist in a specific ASC would illustrate the nature of a proposed state-specific science. But this is not possible because no state-specific sciences have yet been established.* Also, any example that would make good sense to the readers of this article (who are, presumably, all in a normal

---

*"Ordinary consciousness science" is not a good example of a "pure" state-specific science because many important discoveries have occurred during ASC's, such as reverie, dreaming, and meditative-like states.

SoC) would not really illustrate the uniqueness of a state-specific science. If it did make sense, it would be an example of a problem that could be approached adequately from both the ASC and normal SoC's, and thus it would be too easy to see the entire problem in terms of accepted scientific procedures for normal SoC's and miss the point about the necessity for developing state-specific sciences.

STATE-SPECIFIC SCIENCES AND RELIGION

Some aspects of organized religion appear to resemble state-specific sciences. There are techniques that allow the believer to enter an ASC and then have religious experiences in that ASC which are proof of his religious belief. People who have had such experiences usually describe them as ineffable in important ways—that is, as not fully comprehensible in an ordinary SoC. Conversions at revivalistic meetings are the most common example of religious experiences occurring in various ASC's induced by an intensely emotional atmosphere.

In examining the esoteric training systems of some religions, there seems to be even more resemblance between such mystical ways and state-specific sciences, for here we often have the picture of devoted specialists, complex techniques, and repeated experiencing of the ASC's in order to further religious knowledge.

Nevertheless the proposed state-specific sciences are not simply religion in a new guise. The use of ASC's in religion may involve the kind of commitment to searching for truth that is needed for developing a state-specific science, but practically all the religions we know might be defined as state-specific technologies, operated in the service of a priori belief systems. The experiencers of ASC's in most religious contexts have already been thoroughly indoctrinated in a particular belief system. This belief system may then mold the content of the ASC's to create specific experiences which reinforce or validate the belief system.

The crucial distinction between a religion utilizing ASC's and a state-specific science is the commitment of the scientist to reexamine constantly his own belief system and to question the obvious in spite of its intellectual or emotional appeal to him. Investigators of ASC's would certainly encounter an immense variety of phenomena labeled religious experience or mystical revelation during the development of state-specific sciences, but they would have to remain committed to examining these phenomena more carefully, sharing their observations and techniques. with colleagues, and subjecting the beliefs (hypotheses, theories) that result from such experiences to the requirement of leading to testable

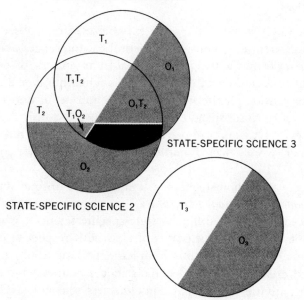

STATE-SPECIFIC SCIENCE 1

T_1

T_1T_2

T_2

T_1O_2

O_1

O_1T_2

STATE-SPECIFIC SCIENCE 3

O_2

STATE-SPECIFIC SCIENCE 2

T_3

O_3

Figure 5.1.   Possible relationships between three state-specific sciences.

predictions. In practice, because we are aware of the immense emotional power of mystical experiences, this would be a difficult task, but it is one that will have to be undertaken by disciplined investigators if we are to understand various ASC's.

RELATIONSHIP BETWEEN STATE-SPECIFIC SCIENCES

Any state-specific science may be considered as consisting of two parts, observations and theorizations. The observations are what can be experienced relatively directly; the theories are the *inferences* about what sort of nonobservable factors account for the observations. For example, the phenomena of synesthesia (seeing colors as a result of hearing sounds) is a theoretical proposition for me in my ordinary SoC: I do not experience it, and can only generate theories about what other people report about it. If I were under the influence of a psychedelic drug such as LSD or marijuana (see Tart, 1971), I could probably experience synesthesia directly, and my descriptions of the experience would become data.

Figure 5.1 demonstrates some possible relationships between three state-specific sciences. State-specific sciences 1 and 2 show considerable overlap.

The area labeled O_1O_2 is subject matter capable of direct observation in both sciences. Area T_1T_2 consists of theoretical inferences about common subject matter from the two perspectives. In area O_1T_2, by contrast, the theoretical propositions of state-specific science number 2 are matters of direct observation for the scientist in SoC number 1, and vice versa for the area T_1O_2. State-specific science number 3 consists of a body of observation and theory exclusive to that science and has no overlap with the other two sciences: it neither confirms, denies, nor complements them.

It would be naively reductionistic to say that the work in one state-specific science *validates* or *invalidates* the work in a second state-specific science; I prefer to say that two different state-specific sciences, where they overlap, provide quite different points of view with respect to certain kinds of theories and data, and thus complement (Bohr, 1963) each other. The proposed creation of state-specific sciences neither validates nor invalidates the activities of normal consciousness sciences (NCS). The possibility of developing certain state-specific sciences means only that certain kinds of phenomena may be handled more adequately within these potential new sciences.

Interrelationships more complex than those that are illustrated in Figure 5.1 are possible.

The possibility of stimulating interactions between different state-specific sciences is very real. Creative breakthroughs in NCS have frequently been made by scientists temporarily going into an ASC (Ghiselin, 1952). In such instances, the scientists concerned saw quite different views of their problems and performed different kinds of reasoning, conscious or nonconscious, which led to results that could be tested within their NCS.

A current example of such interaction is the finding that in Zen meditation (a highly developed discipline in Japan) there are physiological correlates of meditative experiences, such as decreased frequency of alpha-rhythm, which can also be produced by means of instrumentally aided feedback-learning techniques (Green, Green, and Walters, 1970). This finding might elucidate some of the processes peculiar to each discipline.

INDIVIDUAL DIFFERENCES

A widespread and misleading assumption that hinders the development of state-specific sciences and confuses their interrelationships is the assumption that because two people are normal (not certified insane), their ordinary SoC's are essentially the same. In reality I suspect that there are enormous differences between the SoC's of some normal people. Because societies train people to behave and communicate along socially approved lines, these differences are covered up.

For example, some people think in images, others in words. Some can voluntarily anesthetize parts of their body, most cannot. Some recall past events by imaging the scene and looking at the relevant details; others use complex verbal processes with no images.

This means that person A may be able to observe certain kinds of experiential data that person B cannot experience in his ordinary SoC, no matter how hard B tries. There may be several consequences. Person B may think that A is insane, too imaginative, or a liar, or he may feel inferior to A. Person A may also feel himself odd, if he takes B as a standard of normality.

In some cases, B may be able to enter an ASC and there experience the sorts of things that A has reported to him. A realm of knowledge that is ordinary for A is then specific for an ASC for B. Similarly, some of the experiences of B in his ASC may not be available for direct observation by A in his ordinary SoC.

The phenomenon of synesthesia can again serve as an example. Some individuals possess this ability in their ordinary SoC, most do not. Yet 56 percent of a sample of experienced marijuana users experienced synesthesia at least occasionally (Tart, 1971), while they were in the drug-induced ASC.

Thus we may conceive of bits of knowledge that are specific for an ASC for one individual, part of ordinary consciousness for another. Arguments over the usefulness of the concept of states of consciousness may reflect differences in the structure of the ordinary SoC of various investigators.

Another important source of individual differences, little understood at present, is the degree to which an individual may first make a particular observation or form a concept in one SoC and then be able to re-experience or comprehend it in another SoC. That is, many items of information which were state-specific when observed initially may be learned and somehow transferred (fully or partially) to another SoC. Differences across individuals, various combinations of SoC's, and types of experience will probably be enormous.

I have only outlined the complexities created by individual differences in normal SoC's and have used the normal SoC as a baseline for comparison with ASC's; but it is evident that every SoC must eventually be compared against every other SoC.

PROBLEMS, PITFALLS, AND PERSONAL PERILS

If we use the practical experience of Western man with ASC's as a guide, the development of state-specific sciences will be beset by a number of difficulties. These difficulties will be of two kinds: general methodological problems stemming from the inherent nature of some ASC's; and those concerned with personal perils to the investigator. I shall discuss state-related problems first.

The first important problem in the proposed development of state-specific sciences is the obvious perception of truth. In many ASC's, one's experience is that one is obviously and lucidly experiencing truth directly, without question. An immediate result of this may be an extinction of the desire for further questioning. Further, this experience of obvious truth, while not necessarily preventing the individual investigator from further examining his data, may not arouse his desire for consensual validation. Since one of the greatest strengths of science is its insistence on consensual validation of basic data, this can be a serious drawback. Investigators attempting to develop state-specific sciences will have to learn to distrust the obvious.

A second major problem in developing state-specific sciences is that in some ASC's one's abilities to visualize and imagine are immensely enhanced, so that whatever one imagines seems perfectly real. Thus one can imagine that something is being observed and experience it as datum. If one can essentially conjure up anything one wishes, how can we ever get at truth?

One way of looking at this problem is to consider any such vivid imaginings as potential effects: they are data, in the sense that what can be vividly imagined in a given SoC is important to know. It may not be the case that anything can be imagined with equal facility, and the relationships between what can be imagined may show a lawful pattern.

More generally, the way to approach this problem is to realize that it is not unique to ASC's. One can have all sorts of illusions and misperceptions in our ordinary SoC. Before the rise of modern physical science, all sorts of things were imagined about the nature of the physical world that could not be directly refuted. The same techniques that eliminated these illusions in the physical sciences will also eliminate them in state-specific sciences dealing with nonphysical data—that is, all observations will have to be subjected to consensual validation and all their theoretical consequences will have to be examined. Insofar as experiences are purely arbitrary imaginings, those that do not show consistent patterns and cannot be replicated will be distinguished from those phenomena which do show general lawfulness.

The effects of this enhanced vividness of imagination in some ASC's will be complicated further by two other important problems, namely, experimenter bias (Rosenthal, 1966; Orne, 1962), and the fact that one person's illusion in a given ASC can sometimes be communicated to another person in the same ASC so that a kind of false consensual validation results. Again, the only long-term solution to this would be the requirement that predictions based on concepts arising from various experiences be verified experientially.

A third major problem is that state-specific sciences probably cannot be developed for all ASC's: some ASC's may depend on or result from genuine deterioration of observational and reasoning abilities, or a deterioration of volition. Those SoC's for which state-specific sciences might well be developed will be discussed later, but it should be made clear that the development of each science should result from trial and error, and not from a priori decisions based on reasoning in our ordinary SoC's.

A fourth major problem is that of ineffability. Some experiences are ineffable in the sense that: (i) a person may experience them, but be unable to express or conceptualize them adequately to himself; (ii) while a person may be able to conceptualize an experience to himself he may not be able to communicate it adequately to anyone else. Certain phenomena of the first type may simply be inaccessible to scientific investigation. Phenomena of the second type may be accessible to scientific investigation only insofar as we are willing to recognize that a science, in the sense of following most of the basic rules, may exist only for a single person. Insofar as such a solitary science would lack all the advantages gained by consensual validation, we could not expect it to have as much power and rigor as conventional scientific endeavor.

Many phenomena which are now considered ineffable may not be so in reality. This may be a matter of our general lack of experience with ASC's and the lack of an adequate language for communicating about ASC phenomena. In most well-developed languages the major part of the vocabulary was developed primarily in adaptation to survival in the physical world.

Finally, we should recognize that various phenomena of ASC's may be too complex for human beings to understand. The phenomena may depend on or be affected by so many variables that we shall never understand them. In the history of science, however, many phenomena which appeared too complex at first were eventually comprehensible.

PERSONAL PERILS

The personal perils that an investigator will face in attempting to develop a state-specific science are of two kinds, those associated with reactions colloquially called a bad trip and a good trip, respectively.

Bad trips, in which an extremely unpleasant, emotional reaction is experienced in an ASC, and in which there are possible long-term adverse consequences on a person's personal adjustment, often stem from the fact that our upbringing has not prepared us to undergo radical alterations in our ordinary SoC's. We are dependent on stability, we fear the unknown, and we develop personal rigidities and various kinds of personal and social taboos. It is traditional in our society to consider ASC's as signs of insanity; ASC's therefore cause great fears in those who experience them.

In many ASC's, defenses against unacceptable personal impulses may become partially or wholly ineffective, so the person feels flooded with traumatic material that he cannot handle. All these things result in fear and avoidance of ASC's, and make it difficult or impossible for some individuals to function in an ASC in a way that is consistent with the development of a state-specific science. Maslow (1966) has discussed these as pathologies of cognition that seriously interfere with the scientific enterprise in general, as well as ordinary life. In principle, adequate selection and training could minimize these hazards for at least some people.

Good trips may also endanger an investigator. A trip may produce experiences that are so rewarding that they interfere with the scientific activity of the investigator. The perception of obvious truth, and its effect of eliminating the need for further investigation or consensual validation have already been mentioned. Another peril comes from the ability to imagine or create vivid experiences. They may be so highly rewarding that the investigator does not follow the rule of investigating the obvious regardless of his personal satisfaction with results. Similarly, his attachment to good feelings, ecstasy, and the like, and his refusal to consider alternative conceptualizations of these, can seriously stifle the progress of investigation.

These personal perils again emphasize the necessity of developing adequate training programs for scientists who wish to develop state-specific sciences. Although it is difficult to envision such a training program, it is evident that much conventional scientific training is contrary to what would be needed to develop a state-specific science, because it tends to produce rigidity and avoidance of personal involvement with subject matter, rather than open-mindedness and flexibility. Much of the training program would have to be devoted to the scientist's understanding of himself so that the (unconscious) effects of his personal biases will be minimized during his investigations of an ASC.

Many of us know that there have been cases where scientists, after becoming personally involved with ASC's, have subsequently become very poor scientists or have experienced personal psychological crises. It would be premature, however, to conclude that such unfortunate consequences cannot be avoided by proper training and discipline. In the early history of the physical sciences we had many fanatics who were nonobjective about their investigations. Not all experiencers of various ASC's develop pathology as a result: indeed, many seem to become considerably more mature. Only from actual attempts to develop state-specific sciences will we be able to determine the actual SoC's that are suitable for development, and the kinds of people that are best suited to such work. *

PROSPECTS

I believe that an examination of human history and our current situation provides the strongest argument for the necessity of developing state-specific sciences. Throughout history man has been influenced by the spiritual and mystical factors that are expressed (usually in watered-down form) in the religions that attract the masses of people. Spiritual and mystical experiences are primary phenomena of various ASC's: because of such experiences, untold numbers of both the noblest and most horrible acts of which people are capable have been committed. Yet in all the time that Western science has existed, no concerted attempt has been made to understand these ASC phenomena in scientific terms.

It was the hope of many that religions were simply a form of superstition that would be left behind in our "rational" age. Not only has this hope failed, but our own understanding of the nature of reasoning now makes it clear that it can never be fulfilled. Reason is a tool, and a tool that is wielded in the service of assumptions, beliefs, and needs which are not themselves subject to reason. The irrational, or, better yet, the arational, will not disappear from the human situation. Our immense

---

*The ASC's resulting from very dangerous drugs (heroin, for example) may be scientifically interesting, but the risk may be too high to warrant our developing state-specific sciences for them. The personal and social issues involved in evaluating this kind of risk are beyond the scope of this article.

success in the development of the physical sciences has not been particularly successful in formulating better philosophies of life, or increasing our real knowledge of ourselves. The sciences we have developed to date are not very human sciences. They tell us how to do things, but give us no scientific insights on questions of what to do, what not to do, or why to do things.

The youth of today and mature scientists in increasing numbers are turning to meditation, oriental religions, and personal use of psychedelic drugs. The phenomena encountered in these ASC's provide more satisfaction and are more relevant to the formulation of philosophies of life and deciding upon appropriate ways of living, than "pure reason" (see Needleman, 1970). My own impressions are that very large numbers of scientists are now personally exploring ASC's, but few have begun to connect this personal exploration with their scientific activities.

It is difficult to predict what the chances are of developing state-specific sciences. Our knowledge is still too diffuse and dependent on our normal SoC's. Yet I think it is probable that state-specific sciences can be developed for such SoC's as auto-hypnosis, meditative states, lucid dreaming, marijuana intoxication, LSD intoxication, self-remembering, reverie, and biofeedback-induced states (Tart, 1969). In all of these SoC's, volition seems to be retained, so that the observer can indeed carry out experiments on himself or others or both. Some SoC's, in which the volition to experiment during the state may disappear, but in which some experimentation can be carried out if special conditions are prepared before the state is entered, might be alcohol intoxication, ordinary dreaming, hypnogogic and hypnopompic states, and high dreams (Tart, 1969). It is not clear whether other ASC's would be suitable for developing state-specific sciences or whether mental deterioration would be too great. Such questions will only be answered by experiment.

I have nothing against religious and mystical groups. Yet I suspect that the vast majority of them have developed compelling belief systems rather than state-specific sciences. Will scientific method be extended to the development of state-specific sciences so as to improve our human situation? Or will the immense power of ASC's be left in the hands of many cults and sects? I hope that the development of state-specific sciences will be our goal.

II.

TWO MODES
OF CONSCIOUSNESS

Introduction

In 1268, Roger Bacon, one of the founders of modern science, wrote (in his *Opus Maius*, quoted in Shah, 1971b, p. xxvi),

> There are two modes of knowing, through argument and experience. Argument brings conclusions and compels us to concede them, but does not cause certainty nor remove doubts in order that the mind may remain at rest in truth, unless this is provided by experience.

These two modes are complementary (both are "right"), and together form the basis of the complete human consciousness. Many of the selections in this book follow this distinction. We have already encountered Polanyi and Blackburn on this matter. One mode, the articulate or verbal-intellectual, involves reason, language, analysis, and sequence. The "other" mode is tacit, "sensuous," and spatial, and operates in a holistic, relational manner.

This section collects evidence from quite diverse sources on the workings of the two major modes of consciousness. We draw here from psychiatry, psychology, neurosurgery, anthropology, and Chinese mysticism, in addition to the opening philosophical and scientific writings. Taken as a unit, this section covers the two modes as they exist between cultures, within one culture, within science, in mysticism, in an individual's psychological makeup, and even in the organization of the human brain.

The first article in this section is by Arthur Deikman, who is studying consciousness with the perspective of a William James, always attempting to focus on the major questions of the discipline, and employing appropriate methods to these ends. Making use of his broad perspectives, which include psychoanalysis, Zen, and contemporary psychology, Deikman here attempts to delineate the two major modes of consciousness, into the active and receptive modes. His work, along with that of Dorothy Lee, emphasizes that the dominant mode of consciousness of a culture is directly reflected in every activity as well as in social and political organization. Deikman also stresses, as do others in this section (and Polanyi), that the often-devalued "sensuous" or tacit mode (called the Receptive here), far from being "regressive" or in some way inferior, is an essential component of man's highest capabilities.

In their articles, both Gazzaniga and Bogen shift the emphasis to the neurophysiological level, to present the biological basis of two modes of consciousness. They present the findings of a group of researchers, headed by Roger Sperry of the California Institute of Technology, who have investigated the implications of dividing the human cerebral cortex in two by surgery. Gazzaniga's article is a lucid summary of this work, written for a general audience. He treats the two modes conventionally as "major" and "minor," the major of course being the verbal-analytic, which is the function of the left hemisphere. Bogen's work is of great theoretical import, for it is the first paper by a neurologist which runs counter to the social, cultural, philosophical, and even biological bias against the "other" side of ourselves.

Bogen stresses that the right hemisphere of the cortex in man not only subtends different functions from the left, but that its very mode of information-processing is different. It works simultaneously, a mode complementary to that of the ordered sequence of logical thought. The right hemisphere of the brain is primarily responsible for music, art, crafts, orientation in space (and body image), and even perhaps for dreams. These activities, along with phenomena termed "mystical," have been largely devalued in our technological culture. No wonder the portion of the brain responsible for them is termed "minor."

This article was not written for a general audience but for clinical neurologists, and thus differs from most in this book, but it is superbly written. The interested student of consciousness must, in any case, be prepared to work with radically different kinds of material in this unfamiliar area, be they neurosurgical articles or Sufi texts. In Bogen's article, definitions of most unfamiliar terms are provided.

Following Bogen there is a juxtaposition: the *I Ching*. Many ancient traditions have expressed similar bipolar dichotomies of consciousness. In the Chinese *I Ching*, these polarities are named *Ch'ien* (the Creative) and *K'un* (the Receptive). They are explicitly complements, not opposites. This formulation is a striking parallel to the complementarities discussed by Oppenheimer, by Blackburn, and by Polanyi, to the model of Deikman, and to the left-right hemisphere research of Gazzaniga and Bogen of Sperry's group. Note, too, that "The Creative" is in time but not in space, whereas "The Receptive" is in space not in time, just as the functions of the right hemisphere of the brain are predominantly spatial, those of the left linear and sequential.

We often notice in our daily lives that individuals tend to employ one or the other mode predominantly. Dorothy Lee's article indicates that an entire culture may adopt one or the other mode. Since most—if not all—Western cultures are predominately verbal and linear, her study of the Trobrianders, a "right-hemisphere" culture, is especially significant. In conjunction with Benjamin Lee Whorf's work, it is interesting to note that the "nonlinear" mode of the Trobrianders is manifest even in that most linear portion of life, language.

Lee agrees with the Transactionalists that individuals, within a given culture, *construct* their own personal or group reality according to their assumptive world. In her treatment of planning and purposiveness, she clearly demarcates the two modes of consciousness. As Bogen puts it, "the most important distinction between the left and right hemisphere modes; that is, the extent to which a linear concept of time participates in the ordering of thought." She superbly contrasts the linear scientific mode with the "present-centeredness" (see Naranjo's article) of the Trobrianders.

Many aspects of everyday language and consciousness are rooted in our biological duality. Recall, first, that the brain's control of the body is reversed—the left side of the cortex connects with the right side of the body, the right half of the cortex with the left of the body. Thus, referring to the "left" in our body refers to the right hemisphere of the brain. In negating a person, we might say that he is awkward, *gauche*, or perhaps evil, *sinister* (both words derive from "left," in French and Latin), dominated by the devalued right-hemisphere mode. French for the Law, that most linear and language-rooted achievement of man, is *le droit*, the right. When we want to say that a person is correct, we say "You're right." Domhoff, from his perspective as a psychoanalyst, reviews this duality, and notes in addition that the "left" is the unexplored area, the sacred and the unconscious, the domain of the mysterious. Later selections more explicitly treat the nonlinear disciplines of the mysterious.

6.

Bimodal Consciousness

Arthur J. Deikman

When we consider the psychological and physiological variations that occur from day to day and from minute to minute as we work, eat, play, or respond to emergencies or drugs, or to radical shifts in our environment or goals, we are presented with a confusing mass of observations that are difficult to organize. Changes occur in body boundaries, in muscle tension, in sensory vividness, in electroencephalograms, in imagery, in logic, and in self-awareness. Some of these changes are slight, others can be extreme. Discussions of states of consciousness usually do not integrate these many physiological and psychological variables, and,

Reprinted by permission from the *Archives of General Psychiatry*, 25 (Dec. 1971), 481–489. Copyright ©1971, American Medical Association. An earlier version of this paper was read before the Conference on Voluntary Control of Internal States, Council Grove, Kan., April 16, 1970.

This study was supported by research grant MH 16793-02 from the Public Health Service and by the Department of Psychiatry, University of Colorado Medical Center.

Drs. I. Charles Kaufman, David Metcalf, and Robert Emde advised in the preparation of this manuscript.

in addition, it is usually assumed that unusual states of consciousness are pathological or unreal. This paper will present a model in which psychological and physiological variations are viewed as manifestations of two basic organismic states or modes that are coordinated to a particular function. The model will be used to clarify phenomena in the fields of attention, mystical perception, hallucinogenic drugs, and psychosis.

ACTION MODE AND RECEPTIVE MODE

Let us begin by considering the human being to be an organization of components having biological and psychological dimensions. These components are coordinated in two primary modes of organization: an "action" mode and a "receptive" mode.

The action mode is a state organized to manipulate the environment. The striate muscle system and the sympathetic nervous system are the dominant physiological agencies. The EEG shows beta waves and baseline muscle tension is increased. The principal psychological manifestations of this state are focal attention, object-based logic, heightened boundary perception, and the dominance of formal characteristics over the sensory; shapes and meanings have a preference over colors and textures. The action mode is a state of striving, oriented toward achieving personal goals that range from nutrition to defense to obtaining social rewards, plus a variety of symbolic and sensual pleasures, as well as the avoidance of a comparable variety of pain.

The attributes of the action mode develop as the human organism interacts with its environment. For example, very early in life focusing attention is associated not only with the use of the intrinsic muscles of the eyes, but also becomes associated with muscle movements of the neck, head, and body, whereby visual interest is directed toward objects. Likewise, thinking develops in conjunction with the perception and manipulation of objects and, because of this, object-oriented thought becomes intimately associated with the striate muscle effort of voluntary activity, particularly eye muscle activity (Piaget, 1954). Specific qualities of perception, such as sharp boundaries, become key features of the mode, because sharp boundaries are important for the perception and manipulation of objects and for acquiring knowledge of the mechanical properties of objects. Sharp perceptual boundaries are matched by sharp conceptual boundaries, for success in acting on the world requires a clear sense of self-object difference. Thus, a variety of physiological and psychological processes develop together to form an organismic mode, a multidimensional unity adapted to the requirements of manipulating the environment.

In contrast, the receptive mode is a state organized around intake of the environment rather than manipulation. The sensory-perceptual system is the dominant agency rather than the muscle system, and parasympathetic functions tend to be most prominent. The EEG tends toward alpha waves and baseline muscle tension is decreased. Other attributes of the receptive mode are diffuse attending, paralogical thought processes, decreased boundary perception, and the dominance of the sensory over the formal. The receptive mode is aimed at maximizing the intake of the environment, and this mode would appear to originate and function maximally in the infant state. The receptive mode is gradually dominated, if not submerged, however, by the progressive development of striving activity and the action mode.

In the course of development the action mode has priority to insure biological survival. The receptive mode develops also—but it occurs as an interlude between increasingly longer periods of action-mode functioning. This developmental preference for the action mode has led us to regard the action mode as the proper one for adult life, while we have tended to think of the more unusual receptive states as pathological or "regressive."

Within each mode the attributes or components are interrelated to form a system, so that a shift in any one component can affect any of the others. For example, a decrease in muscle tension can decrease anxiety because of a shift in mode. Depending on the relative strength of competing motives and functional orientation, a change in one component of a mode may or may not bring about a noticeable shift to the other mode and with that shift a change in other components. The components are not independent of each other or caused by each other (e.g., lowering muscle tension lowers anxiety; muscle tension, therefore, equals anxiety), but are related through the pattern or mode of organization in which they participate. If the balance of motivational force is very strong in favor of a particular mode, that mode will be quite resistant to change, even if a component is changed.

A very commonplace instance can be given of these two different modes in daily experience. Try thinking about a problem while lying flat on your back, and then . . . thinking about the same problem while sitting upright. You will notice that maintaining a directed, logical stream of thought is much easier in the upright position. This can be understood as a function of two different organismic states, initiated by postural changes, but not determined by postural changes alone. It is possible to think logically while supine but it is more difficult. Our action-mode activities develop in conjunction with an upright posture, while receptivity originated in the reclining, infant state.

Language, it should be noted, is the very essence of the action mode; through it we discriminate, analyze, and divide up the world into pieces or objects which can then be grasped (psychologically and biologically) and acted upon. The richness of our vocabulary reflects the extent to which we apply the action mode to a particular sector of our environment. For example, the average person has only one word for snow, the skier has several, and the Eskimo many. It is not just a matter of how much we detect differences between varieties of snow or any other dimension. Consider the experience of "love." Here again, the average person has only one word for love, yet he has probably experienced a variety of love states. We have not developed words for these states because love is experienced in the receptive mode; indeed, it requires the receptive mode for its occurrence. Color *experience* (rather than color as a sign) requires the receptive mode; colors have only a few names compared to the vast variety of hues to which we are sensitive. [For] the artist, however, who *works* with, *manipulates*, and *makes* color objects, the case is different. An artist's vocabulary is much expanded. The Whorfian hypothesis, that we are unable to think outside of our language structures, has relevance only for the action mode. We manipulate our environment through language-direct strategies.

To illustrate the modes more concretely, consider a cab driver in heavy traffic, struggling to get a passenger to the airport in time. He is in the action mode, contending maximally with his environment, trying to direct and control what happens, and focusing intensely on a goal located in future time. His conscious experience features sharp boundary perception, high field articulation, and verbal, logical thought patterns. His EEG is desynchronized and his baseline muscle tension is high. At the opposite pole is the monk in meditation, who is in a receptive mode with a corresponding state of consciousness that may feature merging of the self with the environment or an ineffable (nonverbal) perception of unity, or both. Muscle relaxation, cortical synchrony, and sensory dominance are principal features of his state. The monk endeavors to adopt an attitude of selflessness and abandonment of personal striving. To this end, he gives up personal choice and material gain. Language and thinking are given low priority and a vow of silence may be taken.

These two modes are not to be equated with activity and passivity. The functional orientation that determines the mode has to do with the *goal* of the organism's activity: whether or not the environment is to be acted upon, or whether stimuli or nutriment are to be taken in. "Letting it" is an activity, but a different activity than "making it." Likewise, it is not the presence or absence of physical activity per se that is the mode determinant. In the pure state of the receptive mode, the organism does seem helpless to act on the environment, as in states of ecstasy or drug intoxication. In most receptive-mode conditions, however, an active relationship with the environment takes place, as in the case of the monk working in the garden or lovers in sexual intercourse. Characteristically, the relationship to the environment in the receptive mode is what Buber (1958) describes as the "I-Thou," in contrast to the "I-It" of the action mode. For example, the monk at work in the garden could have two quite different *experiences* depending on which mode is dominant. Likewise, the lovers may be "screwing" rather than "making love." In most cases, we are talking about·a modal balance or mixture, whose characteristics depend on the extent of dominance of a particular mode. The enlightened monk, working in the garden, operates in the action mode only to the extent needed to conduct his work activity, and the receptive mode can thereby still play a prominent role in his conscious experience.

Just as the action mode and the receptive mode are not the equivalents of activity and passivity, they are also not to be equated with the secondary and primary process of psychoanalytic theory. There is some similarity between aspects of the receptive mode and the cognitive style associated with the primary process. The bimodal model, however, addresses itself to a functional orientation—that of taking in versus acting on the environment. The receptive mode is not a "regressive" ignoring of the world or a retreat from it—although it can be employed for that purpose —but is a different strategy for engaging the world, in pursuit of a different goal.

The choice of mode is determined by the motives of the individual organism. Motivations exist, however, at different levels and with different time scales. It is hard to say much about the specific hierarchy of motives that affect the choice of mode. It is my impression, however, that the baseline of mode choice is set by the general orientation of the individual's culture. In Western civilization, that orientation is toward the individual's exerting direct, voluntary control over all phases of his life. This orientation of control is enhanced by the ideal of the self-made man and by the pursuit of material and social goals—all of which call for manipulation of the environment and of the self. The action mode dominates our consciousness. Men, however, have been concerned for many years with ways to shift to what I have described as the receptive mode. Later on I will discuss an example of a system that was developed to make the receptive mode the dominant orientation.

Although this bimodal analysis of organismic states at first may seem to be quite arbitrary and make little theoretical difference, I will now show how this model is very useful in clarifying a number of problems that otherwise would remain obscure.

Poetzel Effect

Poetzel *et al.* (1960) observed a difference in what happens to stimuli that are perceived in the periphery of awareness as compared to those in the center. A stimulus that is incidental, on the margin of the field of awareness, is "processed" differently [from] stimuli in the center. In the former case, dream processes dominate; in the latter case, rational logic holds sway. This phenomenon can be understood in terms of the two organizational modes. Stimuli at the center of awareness are subject to the organizational mode associated with object manipulation—the action mode. In terms of thought processes, this means object-based logical thought. Stimuli in the periphery are processed according to the more indirect, sensually oriented, intake goals of the receptive mode. This mode of thought uses paralogical strategies.

Silverman's Chronicity Study

Silverman (1967, 1968) and his colleagues (1965) have described changes in the cognitive style of schizophrenic patients as their stay in the hospital increases. They report that with confinement of three years or more the attentional style of schizophrenic patients changes toward diminished field articulation and diminished scanning. Similar results were found in prison inmates. These findings are not easy to explain on the basis of chemical deficits or "deterioration." The mode model does, however, suggest a way of understanding the shift. Diminished field articulation means that an object is less sharply differentiated from its surroundings, and diminished scanning means that fewer objects in the visual field have awareness centered on them. On the other hand, where field articulation is sharp and scanning is wide, the subject is in the best position to encounter and manipulate, to actively engage the object environment. This active striving style, however, is specifically defeated by the hospital environment if the patient must stay in it over several years. Such long-term frustration of active striving would be expected to result in diminished striving and a shift to the receptive mode.

Gaffron Phenomenon

Gaffron (1956) has described different modalities of conscious experience according to where on the object attention is focused. For example, if visual awareness is centered on the near side of an object ("grasping"), the object is perceived "exteriorly" and the dominant qualities of the experience are form, surface, distance, and separateness from the observer. Awareness centered on the far side of an object ("mere looking") features "proprioceptive" qualities of volume, weight, and "interior" feelings of tension and inner movement. The object seems to intrude or extend into the boundaries of the self. The reader can observe this for himself if he stops for a moment and looks at a nearby object in these two ways.

It is most instructive to observe this shift of mode in situations such as eating a pear. In reaching for the pear, the focus is on the near side, in preparation for grasping it. As the pear is brought to the mouth, the focus shifts to the far side and beyond. In the act of eating, the pear is inside the zone of focus and, literally, being incorporated into the organism. The grasping of the pear is associated with the action mode and the intake of the pear with the receptive. The accompanying visual shifts are integral parts of the change in mode, so that a shift of visual activity is accompanied by a shift in other components of the mode involved, for example, muscle relaxation and parasympathetic stimulation. The developmental coordination of the visual focus and body activity persists even though the objects involved may not be ones that can be eaten.

Neurotic Styles

Shapiro has presented evidence that the characteristic way an individual attends to stimuli, his attentive *style*, has important effects on his conscious experience. Shapiro distinguishes between two main groups—sharply focused attention (obsessive-compulsive and paranoid styles) and diffuseness of attention with absence of sharp focus (hysterical styles). His conclusions are as follows:

> "The most conspicuous characteristic of the obsessive-compulsive's attention is its intense, sharp focus. These people are not vague in their attention, they concentrate and particularly do they concentrate on detail . . . (they) seem unable to allow their attention simply to wander or passively permit it to be captured. Thus, they rarely seem to get hunches, they are rarely struck or surprised by anything."

The consequence of such a pervasive style of attention is that

> "he will often miss those aspects of a situation that give it its flavor or its impact; thus, these people often seem quite insensitive to the 'tone' of social situations. . . . Certain kinds of subjective experiences, affect experiences, particularly require, by their nature, an abandonment or at least a relaxation of the attitude of deliberateness and where such relaxation is impossible, as in the obsessive-compulsive style, those areas of psychological life tend to shrink."

Shapiro's conclusions support the concept of different organizational modes. In the case of the obsessive-compulsive, his thought and style [are] focused on object manipulation, an activity at which he is usually quite successful. Hunches or moments of inspiration that come about involuntarily in creative states or moments of mystical revelation are, however, quite absent from the experience of persons rigidly committed to the object-manipulative mode of cognition and perception. Likewise, rich affective experience is not found with that mode because "abandonment" and "relaxation of the attitude of deliberateness" is not compatible with the action mode. In the diffuse, hysterical style, however, we see the counterpart to the receptive-sensory mode. Here, sensory details, inspiration, and affect dominate the experience.

Body Boundaries, Muscle Relaxation, and Perception

Reports of subjects undergoing autogenic training, a European treatment technique of self-suggested relaxation, and reports of subjects undergoing relaxation training by means of feedback devices, indicate the frequent occurrence of body-boundary changes correlated with deep levels of muscle relaxation (Schultz and Luthe, 1959; Kleinsorge and Klumbies, 1964; Stoyva and Budzynski, personal communication). Similar phenomena are noted under conditions of sensory isolation and in the induction phase of hypnosis. These correlations become understandable when we identify fluid boundaries and muscle relaxation as components of the receptive mode, components that tend to vary as a group when a shift in mode takes place. The conditions of autogenic training, sensory isolation, and hypnosis all predispose to a taking in of the environment rather than [to an] acting on the environment. Although the direct influence on muscle tension or sensory input is important, the shift in mode may be due as much to the accompanying shift in the orientation of the subject.

This line of reasoning also suggests an explanation for instances of reduction of anxiety as a consequence of muscle relaxation. Insofar as anxiety is an affect linked to future action (e.g., "If I perform this destructive or forbidden act, I will be destroyed"), the shift to the receptive mode could be expected to decrease anxiety because the state of receptivity is not organized around action to be directed at the environment. In the time dimension, the action mode is the Future and the receptive mode is the Now.

Experimental Studies of Meditation

For many centuries contemplative meditation has been prescribed as a technique for bringing about an altered perception of the world and of the self. This different mode of perception is characterized by a sense of unity of the person with his environment. In some cases, heightened sensory vividness is part of the description as well as timelessness, exultation, strong affect, and a sense that the horizon of awareness has been greatly expanded. In an attempt to study the possible connection between contemplative meditation and mystical experiences, I instructed a group of normal subjects in a basic procedure adapted from the Yoga of Pantanjali (Deikman, 1963, 1966b):

> The purpose of the sessions is to learn about concentration. Your aim is to concentrate on the blue vase. By concentration I do not mean analyzing the different parts of the vase, or thinking a series of thoughts about the vase, or associating ideas to the vase; but rather, trying to see the vase as it exists in itself, without any connections to other things. Exclude all other thoughts or feelings or sounds or body sensations. Do not let them distract you, but keep them out so that you can concentrate all your attention, all your awareness on the vase itself. Let the perception of the vase fill your entire mind.

Each subject performed this exercise for one-half hour at a time, for 40 or more sessions spread over several months. The subjects' perceptions of the vase changed in the following directions: (1) an increase in the vividness and richness of the vase percept (for example, they described it as "luminous," "more vivid"); (2) the vase seemed to acquire a kind of life of its own, to be animated; (3) there was a decrease in the sense of being separate from the vase, occurring in those subjects who continued longest in the experiment (e.g., "I really began to feel, you know, almost as though the blue and I were perhaps merging or that the vase and I were. It was as though everything were sort of merging"); and (4) a fusing and alteration of normal perceptual modes (e.g., "when the vase changes shape, I feel this in my body," "I began to feel this light going back and forth").

As I have discussed in an earlier paper (1963), these data are not easily explained by the usual concepts of suggestion, projection, autohypnosis, or sensory isolation. I interpreted these changes as being a "deautomatization," an undoing of the usual ways of perceiving and thinking due to the special way that attention was being used. The meditation exercise could be seen as withdrawing attention from thinking and reinvesting it in percepts—a reverse of the normal learning sequence. However, the concept of modes serving a particular function clarifies the phenomenon even further. It was required that the subjects adopt a particular *attitude*, that of a passive abandonment. This attitude represented an important shift for the subject away from the action mode and toward the receptive mode. Instead of grasping, manipulating, or analyzing the object in front of him, he was oriented to a different function. Instead of isolating and manipulating the object, he becomes one with it or takes it into his own space. Then sensuous attributes of the object, which are ordinarily of little importance, became enhanced and tend to dominate.

It is of interest that after the experiments subjects tended to report that they had learned something important in that experience but could not specify what it was. "I've experienced . . . new experiences, and I have no vehicle to communicate them to you. I expect that this is probably the way a baby feels when he is full of something to say about an experience or an awareness and he has not learned to use the words yet." The experience was ineffable in the sense of not being suited for verbal communication, not fitting the customary categories of language of the action mode.

Physiological studies of Yogis, Zen masters, and students of transcendental meditation indicate that proficiency in meditation is characterized by a predominance of alpha waves plus such changes as a lowered respiratory rate (Bagchi and Wenger, 1957; Akishige, 1968; Wallace, 1970). Beginning students, intermediate students, and masters could be separated on the basis of their EEG during the meditation state—the further advanced the student, the greater the dominance of alpha waves. These data can be understood if we regard meditation training as developing the receptive mode.

Zen Consciousness

Zen Buddhism aims at changing the experience of a person to that particular view of himself and the world which is called "enlightenment." If one looks closely at the psychosocial system of a Zen monastery, it becomes clear that different aspects of that system are coordinated toward changing the individual's usual orientation of striving for personal goals. The monastery aims at producing a state of acceptance and "nondiscrimination." The principal means by which this is accomplished are meditation, communal living, and an ascetic way of life.

The highest form of Zen meditation is *shikan-taza* or "just sitting." At first it is hard to grasp the literalness of the instruction to "just sit." But it means exactly what it says. A person meditating is "not supposed to do" anything except to *be* sitting. He is not to strive for enlightenment because if he is truly "just sitting," he *is* enlightened. That state of beingness is enlightenment itself. During meditation, thinking and fantasy are treated as intruders or distracting influences, to be patient with until they go away. Pain from the crosslegged sitting posture is regarded as part of the sitting and not to be avoided or categorized or even fought. "Be the pain" might be the instruction given to a student. The "being" that is referred to is essentially a sensory-perceptive experience. The teaching is aimed specifically at doing away with categorizing and classifying, an activity that is felt to intervene between the subject and his experience.

In meditation, the sense of time can change to what might be called timelessness. Again, the urgency to accomplish things is undermined by this timeless orientation. Furthermore, during meditation the subject may experience a sense of total satisfaction with his moment-to-moment experience so that the need to strive for a distant satisfaction is diminished once again.

The sessions of sitting meditation take place three or more times daily within the setting of a communal society. No one accrues profits in that society. There are some status rewards, but these tend to be minimized. The students share in whatever work needs to be done, share the same daily routine, the same daily food, and the same discipline. Every activity is represented as being equally important as any other. Thus, washing dishes is held to be as "good" as an activity as walking in the woods. Once again, such an attitude and structure militates against an orientation toward the future, because the future contains nothing intrinsically more satisfying than what is contained in the present.

I stress the matter of the shift in functional orientation because the concept of an organizational mode is based on the idea that psychological and biological activities are integrated in the service of the total organism and the functional attitude of that organism is the crucial determinant of which mode is adopted. To take another example, the wish for perpetual survival is perhaps the most powerful desire motivating the ordinary person's life. It is very interesting to see how this problem is handled in the Zen system. To begin with, the idea of being dead versus being alive is labeled a fallacious concept based on dualism. The Buddhist cosmology of constant change, of a basic Nothing that takes an endless variety of forms, says that the student is part of a process that does not end but simply changes or flows. Most important of all, the student is taught that his notion of a soul, of an enduring self, is erroneous. Indeed, the concept of a self is held to be the cause of all suffering. During meditation the student may have the concrete experience that his sense of separateness is arbitrary and an illusion.

The principal purpose or goal held out for the students as legitimate and worthwhile is that of the Buddhist vow "to save all sentient beings" from the suffering of delusion. It should be noticed that this is a selfless goal. The student will not be rewarded by having a special place in heaven if he accomplishes this, but rather that purpose is the purpose of the universe of which he is a part. Such an ethic of action directed toward the good of others (the basic ethic of almost all religions) provides a dimension for participation in the world in an active and energetic way, but one that attempts to minimize the mode of consciousness associated with striving for one's own personal goals.

The asceticism of the Zen community is not that of the anchorite who despises sensual pleasure as an enemy, but an asceticism that forms a backdrop against which the student can see clearly the role that his desires play in his suffering. In this connection it should be noted that a contemporary Zen master (Suzuki, 1968) described renunciation as, "We do not give them up, but accept that they go away." This open-handed approach to life means that any sensual pleasure that comes along is to be enjoyed for its own sake, but there is to be no attempt to hang on, to grasp, to strive for, to reach for. If we look at the goals around which we organize many of our activities, we see that they are often oriented toward prolonging or bringing back a particular pleasure that we have had, often at the detriment of the pleasure available at the moment. This lesson of nongrasping is brought home to the student over and over again in the different situations that arise at the monastery.

Thus, the emphasis on experiencing, or enduring, and on being—

rather than on avoiding pain or seeking pleasure—provides the groundwork for a mode of consciousness that Zen texts describe as nondualistic, timeless, and nonverbal. It is part of the mode of organismic being that I have categorized as the receptive mode.

Mystical Psychosis

One of the puzzling phenomena of psychosis is that of the mystical state preceding or marking the onset of many cases of acute schizophrenia. As Bowers and Freedman (1966) have described, the specific configurations of these states vary from case to case but they share basic features: marked heightening of sense perception; a feeling of communion with people, the world, God; intense affective response; and blurring of perceptual and conceptual boundaries. First-person accounts of this type of psychotic experience are strikingly similar to reports of sensate mystical experience and suggest a similar process. In terms of the bimodal model, the experience is one of a sudden, sharp, and extreme shift to the receptive mode: decreased self-object differentiation, heightened sensory intake, and nonverbal, nonlogical thought process.

Both mystical and psychotic states appear to have arisen out of a situation in which the individual has struggled with a desperate problem, has come to a complete impasse, and given up hope, abandoned the struggle in despair (Bowers, 1968). For the mystic, what emerges from the "cloud of unknowing" or the "dark night of the soul" is an ecstatic union with God or Reality. For the psychotic person, the world rushes in but does not become integrated in the harmony of *mystico unio* or *satori*. Instead, he creates a delusion to achieve a partial ordering and control.

As I have discussed earlier, mystical practice can be viewed as a cultivation of the receptive mode by means of a particular functional orientation and control of thought and environment. No such training program precedes the many examples of mystical psychotic episodes cited above. How are we to understand them then? Maternal deprivation in the case of children and loss or rejection by a loved person in the case of adults are frequently reported as precursors or precipitants of psychosis (Mednick and Schulsinger, 1970, pp. 87–88). In my own experience and in that of others, therapeutic investigation reveals intense hatred and destructive fantasies directed toward the loved person but not acknowledged by the patient. The emergence into consciousness of the anger directed towards the appropriate person is usually accompanied by a dramatic improvement in the patient's condition and marks the demise of the psychotic defense. This suggests the possibility that the psychotic alteration in consciousness is a defensive shift to a mode that will preclude destructive action on the other person. If someone is ecstatic, Christlike, overcome with the significance of a thousand details, buffeted by alternate winds of fear, exultation, grief, and rapture, he is in a state that maximizes what comes in and minimizes the possibility of aggressive action on someone else. Not incidentally, maximum sensory intake can be viewed as dealing with the painful emptiness following deprivation of love.

Although such a person may pass to a phase of tightly ordered paranoid delusion in which he can be dangerous, in the mystical, flooded stage he is helpless, like an infant. The shift to the mystical state is a functional shift on the part of an organism desperately concerned over final loss of nutriment. The control gates are thrown down, and the world floods in through the senses and through the inner stores of affect and memory. The action mode is abandoned. When the person begins to drown in the overload, he asserts control in a delusional compromise that to some extent restores order and effectiveness while providing a substitute object.

The mystics' success in achieving a harmonious integration of self and world may be explained by a consideration of the many factors that differentiate the life and practice of the mystic from that of the psychotic. But the similarity of the initial experience that occurs when striving towards the world is abandoned suggests a similar basic organismic shift— the giving up of the action mode in favor of the receptive. In the case of acute mystical psychosis, a crucial rejection or life impasse triggers a collapse of the action mode, and a sudden rush of receptive-mode cognition and perception ensues for which the person is unprepared and unsupported. Delusional reordering then takes place to solve the affective impasse.

Lysergic Acid Diethylamide (LSD)

Accounts of LSD experiences reveal a cluster of characteristics identifying it with the receptive mode: a marked decrease in self-object distinction; a loss of control over attention; the dominance of paralogical thought forms; intense affect and vivid sensory experience; decreased field articulation and increased parasympathetic stimulation; plus a reification of thought and feeling with a corresponding decrease in "reality testing."

As in the case of meditation, I hypothesized that the general effects of LSD and related drugs were those of "deautomatization," an undoing of the automatic psychological structures that organize, limit, select, and interpret perceptual stimuli (Deikman, 1966a). In considering the problem of explaining the perceptual and cognitive phenomena of mystic experience as a regression, I stated, "One might call the direction regressive in a developmental sense, but the actual experience is probably not within the psychological scope of any child. It is a de-automatization occurring in an adult mind, and the experience gains its richness from adult memories and functions now subject to a different mode of consciousness." That mode of consciousness I would now designate as the receptive mode and consider it to be a mature cognitive and perceptual state, one that is not ordinarily dominant, but is an option that has developed in richness and subtlety in parallel with the development of the action mode that is our customary state of consciousness. Reports of the LSD experience show the complex possibilities of thought and perception that can occur in the receptive mode (Masters and Houston, 1967; Harman et al., 1966).

It is noteworthy that one of the effects of widespread use of LSD and other psychedelics has been to stimulate a revival of interest in Eastern religions. This orientation toward Eastern mysticism can be understood if Yoga and Zen are viewed as developments of the receptive mode: a perception and cognition that features the blurring of boundaries; the merging of self and environment, coupled with affective and sensory richness, and marked by a detachment from the object-oriented goals of the action mode.

Physiological Dimensions in Psychosis and LSD

The physiological data pertaining to meditating Yogis and Zen monks are clear and support the mode hypothesis. In the case of acute and chronic schizophrenia, however, the data are ambiguous or contradictory. Chronic schizophrenic patients tend to have EEGs suggesting cortical activation and high anxiety levels (Lindsley, 1944; Venables, 1964, p. 41; Kennard, 1965). A study of hospitalized schizophrenic patients undergoing acute decompensation shows an increase and wide variability of muscle tension, rather than the decreased muscle tension predicted on the basis of the receptive-mode model (Whatmore, 1967). On the other hand, Salamon and Post (1965), using a special method of measuring alpha waves, found increased alpha-wave production in schizophrenic patients as compared to controls. Studies of autonomic function are likewise variable and unclear. Issues of diagnosis, chronicity, and drug effects undoubtably confound the data. [For] LSD states, there is not much data to work with, but the clinical variability of the states and the frequent occurrence of anxiety suggest a situation similar to the psychoses. Although a more detailed and systematic physiological investigation needs to be done to solve this problem, in these instances we are probably dealing with an unintegrated mixture of modes. One way of understanding this is to consider the fact that, in . . . schizophrenia, the shift to the receptive mode may arouse great anxiety and a compensatory attempt to control the receptive-mode experience, an attempt that is an action-mode response. That such a response creates a problem is suggested by the lore of LSD user's, whose standard advice for those about to take LSD is not to fight the experience, but to "go with it," to "float downstream," and abandon oneself to what feels like "ego death." It is said that if one can do this, chances are good that the experience will be beatific. On the other hand, if the subject attempts to control or fight the experience, a "bad trip" is the likely result. Giving oneself up to an unusual experience, abandoning oneself to "ego death," is precisely what Yogis and Zen monks are trained to do, but what schizophrenic persons find most difficult. Perhaps this difference underlies the different physiological portraits accompanying these different situations.

IMPLICATIONS

Control of Psychological and Physiological Dimensions

The concept that dimensions of a state of consciousness are components of organismic modes suggests the possibility of indirect control over specific aspects of each mode. For example, it becomes reasonable to affect the sharpness of perceptual boundaries by increasing muscle tension or to decrease anxiety by lowering it. Similarly, by restricting analytic thinking and attending to a sensory mode, alterations in muscle tension, EEG, and galvanic skin response can be obtained. By delineating other dimensions of the modes we may be able to widen our repertoire of techniques for change along a variety of organismic dimensions.

Strategic Options

The receptive mode seems to be one in which certain *activities* are facilitated. The examples below are assumed to involve instances of the receptive mode, by virtue of their emphasis on relinquishing conscious striving and intellectual control.

Subjects who learn to control functions of the autonomic nervous system, such as alpha-wave production or finger temperature, learn that they must let it happen rather than make it happen. In the case of temperature control, Green *et al.* (1970) have termed this activity "passive volition."

Accounts of the process of creative synthesis show several distinct stages: first a stage of directed intellectual attack on the problem leading to a feeling of impasse, then the stage of "giving up," in which the person stops struggling with the problem and turns his attention to other things. During this unfocused rest period the solution to the problem manifests itself as an "Aha!" or "Eureka!" experience—the answer is suddenly there of itself. The final stage sees a return of directed intellectual activity as the "answer" is worked over to assess its validity or fit with the object world. In terms of the mode model, the first stage is one in which the action mode is used, followed by the receptive mode, in which the creative leap is made, followed by a return to the action mode to integrate the discovery with the object world.

It may be that paranormal phenomena require the development of the receptive mode. Such a possibility fits well with assertions of classical Yogic literature and with contemporary dream research (Ullman and Krippner, 1969).

A prosaic example of the need to switch to the receptive mode to achieve a particular aim is the attempt to recover a forgotten name. Typically, the person struggles with it and then gives up, saying, "It will come to me in a minute"—and it does. What could not be gained by a direct effort was accomplished by relinquishing effort and becoming relatively receptive.

In ordinary life circumstances, the receptive mode probably plays its most important role in sexual intercourse. Erikson (1950, p. 230) describes the psychological importance of the healthy sexual act as "a supreme experience of the mutual regulation of two beings (that) in some way breaks the point off the hostilities and potential rages caused by the oppositeness of male and female, of fact and fancy, of love and hate. Satisfactory sex relations thus make sex less obsessive, overcompensation less necessary, sadistic controls superfluous." Psychotherapeutic investigation shows that an individual's capacity for such a satisfying sexual experience is in proportion to his or her capacity to relinquish control, to allow the other person to "enter in," to adopt what I have termed the receptive-mode orientation. It is of interest to this discussion that sexual climax in persons with such a capacity is associated not only with intensely heightened sensation and diffuse attention, but with a decrease in self-other boundaries that in some cases results in experiences properly classified as mystical (Laski, 1961, pp. 145–153). An inability to shift to the receptive mode, however, results in a serious impairment of the sexual act. Sensation, release, and feelings of closeness become attenuated or absent.

Knowledge

Although this discussion of modes began with a simple dichotomy of action—namely, manipulating the environment versus taking it in—the study of mystical consciousness suggests that the receptive mode may provide a way of "knowing" certain aspects of reality not accessible to the action mode. The "knowing" that takes place is usually a nonverbal experience, although it may later be translated into words in order to be shared with others. Thus, what is taken in is not only those aspects of the environment with which we are familiar but other aspects as well.

Contemporary psychological models, such as primary process theory, view the object world as the standard by which to judge the realism of perception and cognition. The receptive mode and other modes yet to be discerned or utilized can, however, be conceptualized as modes by which the organism addresses itself to reality dimensions other than those of the object world associated with the action mode and logical thinking. The "thinking" of the receptive mode may be organized in terms of a *different* logic in pursuit of aims located along different dimensions of reality than those to which we ordinarily address ourselves.

It may be felt that to talk of other dimensions of reality is to indulge in romantic thinking, but however it may be judged the idea of other dimensions is not illogical. Considerations of developmental psychology provide the basis for the possibility that the organism has exercised a considerable selection over what features of the world it gives the priority of its attention and the structuralization of its language. That the view of the world thus obtained is relative, rather than absolute, and incorrect in certain applications is held by many theoretical physicists. Furthermore, it has been noted that the correspondence between the cosmology of mystics and that of contemporary physicists is striking (LeShan, 1969). Such a correspondence suggests that the receptive mode of mystic consciousness may have validity in terms of the "external world" if the sector of reality being considered is different from that of the biological with which we are familiar and in which we developed.

Values

The crises now facing the human race are technically solvable. Controlling population, reducing pollution, and eliminating racism and war do not require new inventions. Yet these problems may prove fatally insolvable because what is required is a shift in values, in self-definition, and in world view on the part of each person—for it is the individual consciousness that is the problem. Our survival is threatened now because of our great success in manipulating our environment and acting on others. The action mode has ruled our individual lives and our national politics, and the I-It relationship that has provided the base for technical mastery is now the primary obstacle to saving our race. If, however, each person were able to feel an identity with other persons and with his environment, to see himself as part of a larger unity, he would have that sense of oneness that supports the selfless actions necessary to regulate population growth, minimize pollution, and end war. The receptive mode we have been discussing is the mode in which this identification—the I-Thou relationship—exists and it may be needed to provide the experiential base for the values and world view now needed so desperately by our society as a whole.

CONCLUSION

I believe it is important that we recognize the relativity of different modes of consciousness rather than assign an absolute primacy and validity to that mode with which we are familiar. The simple dichotomy of receptive and active modes is undoubtedly not a complete inventory of the options available to the human organism. Whether or not we are successful in adopting a variety of appropriate modes of consciousness may well depend on factors with which psychoanalysis is very familiar: defenses against the unknown, against relinquishing conscious control, against the blurring or loss of self boundaries. Perhaps the first step in awarding ourselves new options is to make them legitimate. The limits of what is thinkable tend to be prescribed by the assumptions that permeate a culture. In our own culture mystical means unreal or "kooky," altered states of consciousness are considered "regressive" or pathological, "spiritual" wishes and intuitions are labeled "omnipotent." There are instances where these cultural assumptions are justified, but the area encompassed by unusual experiences is much larger than that allotted by such pejorative categories. I hope I have been able to indicate how different states of consciousness can be viewed as organismic modes that may have an important reality-based function necessary for our growth, our vitality, and our survival as a species. Instead of "regression" or "unrealistic" or "autistic," we might better term our organismic options "alternative modes" and be receptive to what they have to teach us.

7.

The Split Brain in Man

Michael S. Gazzaniga

The brain of the higher animals, including man, is a double organ, consisting of right and left hemispheres connected by an isthmus of nerve tissue called the corpus callosum. Some 15 years ago Ronald E. Myers and R. W. Sperry, then at the University of Chicago, made a surprising discovery: when this connection between the two halves of the cerebrum was cut, each hemisphere functioned independently as if it were a complete brain. The phenomenon was first investigated in a cat in which not only the brain but also the optic chiasm, the crossover of the optic nerves, was divided, so that visual information from the left eye was dispatched only to the left brain and information from the right eye only to the right brain. Working on a problem with one eye, the animal could respond normally and learn to perform a task; when that eye was covered and the

Reprinted by permission from *Scientific American*, 217, no. 2 pp. 24–29. (Aug. 1967), (Scientific American Offprint 508) Copyright © 1967 by Scientific American, Inc. All rights reserved.

same problem was presented to the other eye, the animal evinced no recognition of the problem and had to learn it again from the beginning with the other half of the brain.

The finding introduced entirely new questions in the study of brain mechanisms. Was the corpus callosum responsible for integration of the operations of the two cerebral hemispheres in the intact brain? Did it serve to keep each hemisphere informed about what was going on in the other? To put the question another way, would cutting the corpus callosum literally result in the right hand not knowing what the left was doing? To what extent were the two half-brains actually independent when they were separated? Could they have separate thoughts, even separate emotions?

Such questions have been pursued by Sperry and his co-workers in a wide-ranging series of animal studies at the California Institute of Technology over the past decade [see Sperry, 1964a]. Recently these questions have been investigated in human patients who underwent the brain-splitting operation for medical reasons. The demonstration in experimental animals that sectioning of the corpus callosum did not seriously impair mental faculties had encouraged surgeons to resort to this operation for people afflicted with uncontrollable epilepsy. The hope was to confine a seizure to one hemisphere. The operation proved to be remarkably successful; curiously there is an almost total elimination of all attacks, including unilateral ones. It is as if the intact callosum had served in these patients to facilitate seizure activity.

This article is a brief survey of investigations Sperry and I have carried out at Cal Tech over the past five years with some of these patients. The operations were performed by P. J. Vogel and J. E. Bogen of the California College of Medicine. Our studies date back to 1961, when the first patient, a 48-year-old war veteran, underwent the operation: cutting of the corpus callosum and other commissure structures connecting the two halves of the cerebral cortex (see Figure 7.1). As of today 10 patients have had the operation, and we have examined four thoroughly over a long period with many tests.

From the beginning one of the most striking observations was that the operation produced no noticeable change in the patients' temperament, personality, or general intelligence. In the first case the patient could not speak for 30 days after the operation, but he then recovered his speech. More typical was the third case: on awaking from the surgery the patient quipped that he had a "splitting headache," and in his still drowsy state he was able to repeat the tongue twister "Peter Piper picked a peck of pickled peppers."

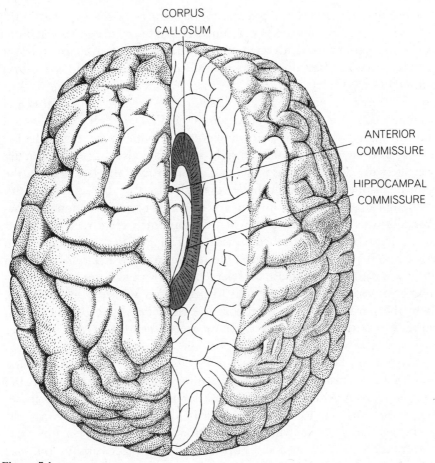

CORPUS
CALLOSUM

ANTERIOR
COMMISSURE

HIPPOCAMPAL
COMMISSURE

Figure 7.1.
Two hemispheres of the human brain are divided by neurosurgeons to control epileptic seizures. In this top view of the brain the right hemisphere is retracted, and the corpus callosum and other commissures, or connectors, that are generally cut are shaded.

Close observation, however, soon revealed some changes in the patients' everyday behavior. For example, it could be seen that in moving about and responding to sensory stimuli the patients favored the right side of the body, which is controlled by the dominant left half of the brain. For a considerable period after the operation the left side of the body rarely showed spontaneous activity, and the patient generally did not respond to stimulation of that side: when he brushed against something with his left side he did not notice that he had done so, and when an object was placed in his left hand he generally denied its presence.

More specific tests identified the main features of the bisected-brain syndrome. One of these tests examined responses to visual stimulation. While the patient fixed his gaze on a central point on a board, spots of light were flashed (for a tenth of a second) in a row across the board that spanned both the left and the right half of his visual field. The patient was asked to tell what he had seen. Each patient reported that lights had been flashed in the right half of the visual field. When lights were flashed only in the left half of the field, however, the patients generally denied having seen any lights. Since the right side of the visual field is normally projected to the left hemisphere of the brain and the left field to the right hemisphere, one might have concluded that in these patients with divided brains the right hemisphere was in effect blind. We found, however, that this was not the case when the patients were directed to point to the lights that had flashed instead of giving a verbal report. With this manual response they were able to indicate when lights had been flashed in the left visual field, and perception with the brain's right hemisphere proved to be almost equal to perception with the left. Clearly, then, the patients' failure to report the right hemisphere's perception verbally was due to the fact that the speech centers of the brain are located in the left hemisphere.

Our tests of the patients' ability to recognize objects by touch at first resulted in the same general finding. When the object was held in the right hand, from which sensory information is sent to the left hemisphere, the patient was able to name and describe the object. When it was held in the left hand (from which information goes primarily to the right hemisphere), the patient could not describe the object verbally but was able to identify it in a nonverbal test—matching it, for example, to the same object in a varied collection of things. We soon realized, however, that each hemisphere receives, in addition to the main input from the opposite side of the body, some input from the same side. This "ipsilateral" input is crude; it is apparently good mainly for "cuing in" the hemisphere as to the presence or absence of stimulation and relaying fairly gross information about the location of a stimulus on the surface of the body. It is unable, as a rule, to relay information concerning the qualitative nature of an object.

Tests of motor control in these split-brain patients revealed that the left hemisphere of the brain exercised normal control over the right hand but had less than full control of the left hand (for instance, it was poor at directing individual movements of the fingers). Similarly, the right hemisphere had full control of the left hand but not of the right hand. When the two hemispheres were in conflict, dictating different movements for the same hand, the hemisphere on the side opposite the hand generally took charge and overruled the orders of the side of the brain with the weaker control. In general the motor findings in the human patients were much the same as those in split-brain monkeys.

We come now to the main question on which we centered our studies, namely how the separation of the hemispheres affects the mental capacities of the human brain. For these psychological tests we used two different devices. One was visual: a picture or written information was flashed (for a tenth of a second) in either the right or the left visual field, so that the information was transmitted only to the left or to the right brain hemisphere (see Figure 7.2). The other type of test was tactile: an object was placed out of view in the patient's right or left hand, again for the purpose of conveying the information to just one hemisphere—the hemisphere on the side opposite the hand.

When the information (visual or tactile) was presented to the dominant left hemisphere, the patients were able to deal with and describe it quite normally, both orally and in writing. For example, when a picture of a spoon was shown in the right visual field or a spoon was placed in the right hand, all the patients readily identified and described it. They were able to read out written messages and to perform problems in calculation that were presented to the left hemisphere.

In contrast, when the same information was presented to the right hemisphere, it failed to elicit such spoken or written responses. A picture transmitted to the right hemisphere evoked either a haphazard guess or no verbal response at all. Similarly, a pencil placed in the left hand (behind a screen that cut off vision) might be called a can opener or a cigarette lighter, or the patient might not even attempt to describe it. The verbal guesses presumably came not from the right hemisphere but from the left, which had no perception of the object but might attempt to identify it from indirect clues.

Did this impotence of the right hemisphere mean that its surgical separation from the left had reduced its mental powers to an imbecilic level? The earlier tests of its nonverbal capacities suggested that this was almost certainly not so. Indeed, when we switched to asking for nonverbal answers to the visual and tactile information presented in our new psychological tests, the right hemisphere in several patients showed considerable capacity for accurate performance. For example, when a picture of a spoon was presented to the right hemisphere, the patients were able to feel around with the left hand among a varied group of objects (screened from sight) and select a spoon as a match for the picture. Furthermore, when they were shown a picture of a cigarette they succeeded in selecting an ashtray, from a group of 10 objects that did not include a cigarette, as the article most closely related to the picture. Oddly enough, however, even after their correct response, and while they were holding the spoon or the ashtray in their left hand, they were unable to name or describe the object or the picture. Evidently the left hemisphere was completely divorced, in perception and knowledge, from the right.

Other tests showed that the right hemisphere did possess a certain amount of language comprehension. For example, when the word "pencil" was flashed to the right hemisphere, the patients were able to pick out a pencil from a group of unseen objects with the left hand. And when a patient held an object in the left hand (out of view), although he could not say its name or describe it, he was later able to point to a card on which the name of the object was written.

In one particularly interesting test the word "heart" was flashed across the center of the visual field, with the "he" portion to the left of the center and "art" to the right. Asked to tell what the word was, the patients would say they had seen "art"—the portion projected to the left brain hemisphere (which is responsible for speech). Curiously when, after "heart" had been flashed in the same way, the patients were asked to point with the left hand to one of two cards—"art" or "he"—to identify the word they had seen, they invariably pointed to "he." The experiment showed clearly that both hemispheres had simultaneously observed the portions of the word available to them and that in this particular case the right hemisphere, when it had had the opportunity to express itself, had prevailed over the left.

Because an auditory input to one ear goes to both sides of the brain, we conducted tests for the comprehension of words presented audibly to the right hemisphere not by trying to limit the original input but by limiting the ability to answer to the right hemisphere. This was done most easily by having a patient use his left hand to retrieve, from a grab bag held out of view, an object named by the examiner. We found that

Figure 7.2.

Visual input to bisected brain was limited to one hemisphere by presenting information only in one visual field. The right and left fields of view are projected, via the optic chiasm, to the left and right hemispheres of the brain, respectively. If a person fixes his gaze on a point, therefore, information to the left of the point goes only to the right hemisphere and information to the right of the point goes to the left hemisphere. Stimuli in the left visual field cannot be described by a split-brain patient because of the disconnection between the right hemisphere and the speech center, which is in the left hemisphere.

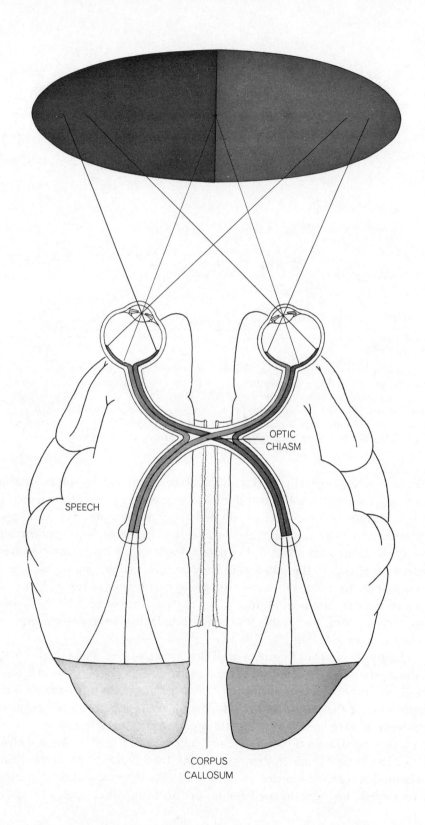

94

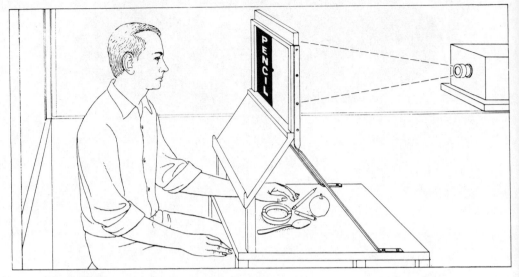

Figure 7.3.

Response to visual stimulus is tested by flashing a word or a picture of an object on a translucent screen. The examiner first checks the subject's gaze to be sure it is fixed on a dot that marks the center of the visual field. The examiner may call for a verbal response—reading the flashed word, for example—or for a nonverbal one, such as picking up the object that is named from among a number of things spread on the table. The objects, hidden from the subject's view, can be identified only by touch.

the patients could easily retrieve such objects as a watch, comb, marble or coin. The object to be retrieved did not even have to be named; it might simply be described or alluded to. For example, the command "Retrieve the fruit monkeys like best" results in the patients' pulling out a banana from a grab bag full of plastic fruit; at the command "Sunkist sells a lot of them" the patients retrieve an orange. We knew that touch information from the left hand was going exclusively to the right hemisphere because moments later, when the patients were asked to name various pieces of fruit placed in the left hand, they were unable to score above a chance level.

The upper limit of linguistic abilities in each hemisphere varies from subject to subject. In one case there was little or no evidence for language abilities in the right hemisphere, whereas in the other three the amount and extent of the capacities varied. The most adept patient showed some evidence of even being able to spell simple words by placing plastic letters on a table with his left hand. The subject was told to spell a word such as "pie," and the examiner then placed the three appropriate letters, one at a time in a random order, in his left hand to be arranged on the table. The patient was able to spell even more abstract words such as "how,"

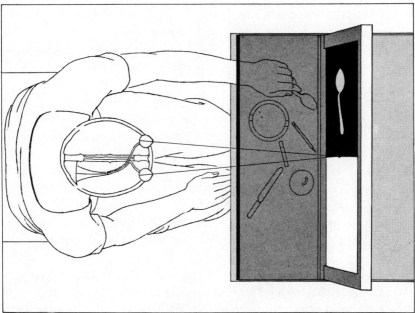

Figure 7.4.
Visual-tactile association is performed by a split-brain patient. A picture of a spoon is flashed to the right hemisphere; with the left hand he retrieves a spoon from behind the screen. The touch information from the left hand returns mainly to the right hemisphere, but a weak "ipsilateral" component goes to the left hemisphere. This is usually not enough to enable him to say (using the left hemisphere) what he has picked up.

"what" and "the." In another test three or four letters were placed in a pile, again out of view, to be felt with the left hand. The letters available in each trial would spell only one word, and the instructions to the subject were "Spell a word." The patient was able to spell such words as "cup" and "love." Yet after he had completed this task, the patient was unable to name the word he had just spelled!

The possibility that the right hemisphere has not only some language but even some speech capabilities cannot be ruled out, although at present there is no firm evidence for this. It would not be surprising to discover that the patients are capable of a few simple exclamatory remarks, particularly when under emotional stress. The possibility also remains, of course, that speech of some type could be trained into the right hemisphere. Tests aimed at this question, however, would have to be closely scrutinized and controlled.

The reason is that here, as in many of the tests, "cross-cuing" from one hemisphere to the other could be held responsible for any positive findings. We had a case of such cross-cuing during a series of tests of whether the right hemisphere could respond verbally to simple red or green stimuli. At first, after either a red or a green light was flashed to the right hemisphere, the patient would guess the color at a chance level, as might be expected if the speech mechanism is solely represented in the left hemisphere. After a few trials, however, the score improved whenever the examiner allowed a second guess.

We soon caught on to the strategy the patient used. If a red light was flashed and the patient by chance guessed red, he would stick with that answer. If the flashed light was red and the patient by chance guessed green, he would frown, shake his head and then say, "Oh no, I meant red." What was happening was that the right hemisphere saw the red light and heard the left hemisphere make the guess "green." Knowing that the answer was wrong, the right hemisphere precipitated a frown and a shake of the head, which in turn cued in the left hemisphere to the fact that the answer was wrong and that it had better correct itself! We have learned that this cross-cuing mechanism can become extremely refined. The realization that the neurological patient has various strategies at his command emphasizes how difficult it is to obtain a clear neurological description of a human being with brain damage.

Is the language comprehension by the right hemisphere that the patients exhibited in these tests a normal capability of that hemisphere or was it acquired by learning after their operation, perhaps during the course of the experiments themselves? The issue is difficult to decide. We must remember that we are examining a half of the human brain, a system easily capable of learning from a single trial in a test. We do know that the right hemisphere is decidedly inferior to the left in its overall command of language. We have established, for instance, that although the right hemisphere can respond to a concrete noun such as "pencil," it cannot do as well with verbs; patients are unable to respond appropriately to simple printed instructions, such as "smile" or "frown," when these words are flashed to the right hemisphere, nor can they point to a picture that corresponds to a flashed verb. Some of our recent studies at the University of California at Santa Barbara also indicate that the right hemisphere has a very poorly developed grammar; it seems to be incapable of forming the plural of a given word, for example.

In general, then, the extent of language present in the adult right hemisphere in no way compares with that present in the left hemisphere or, for that matter, with the extent of language present in the child's right hemisphere. Up to the age of four or so, it would appear from a variety of neurological observations, the right hemisphere is about as proficient in handling language as the left. Moreover, studies of the child's development of language, particularly with respect to grammar, strongly suggest that the foundations of grammar—a ground plan for language, so to speak—are somehow inherent in the human organism and are fully realized between the ages of two and three. In other words, in the young child each hemisphere is about equally developed with respect to language and speech function. We are thus faced with the interesting question of why the right hemisphere at an early age and stage of development possesses substantial language capacity whereas at a more adult stage it possesses a rather poor capacity. It is difficult indeed to conceive of the underlying neurological mechanism that would allow for the establishment of a capacity of a high order in a particular hemisphere on a temporary basis. The implication is that during maturation the processes and systems active in making this capacity manifest are somehow inhibited and dismantled in the right hemisphere and allowed to reside only in the dominant left hemisphere.

Yet the right hemisphere is not in all respects inferior or subordinate to the left. Tests have demonstrated that it excels the left in some specialized functions. As an example, tests by us and by Bogen have shown that in these patients the left hand is capable of arranging blocks to match a pictured design and of drawing a cube in three dimensions, whereas the right hand, deprived of instructions from the right hemisphere, could not perform either of these tasks.

It is of interest to note, however, that although the patients (our first subject in particular) could not execute such tasks with the right hand, they were capable of matching a test stimulus to the correct design when it appeared among five related patterns presented in their right visual field. This showed that the dominant left hemisphere is capable of discriminating between correct and incorrect stimuli. Since it is also true that the patients have no motor problems with their right hand, the patients' inability to perform these tasks must reflect a breakdown of an integrative process somewhere between the sensory system and the motor system.

We found that in certain other mental processes the right hemisphere is on a par with the left. In particular, it can independently generate an emotional reaction. In one of our experiments exploring the matter we would present a series of ordinary objects and then suddenly flash a picture of a nude woman. This evoked an amused reaction regardless of whether the picture was presented to the left hemisphere or to the right. When the picture was flashed to the left hemisphere of a female patient, she laughed and verbally identified the picture as a nude. When it was later presented to the right hemisphere, she said in reply to a question that she saw nothing, but almost immediately a sly smile spread over her face and she began to chuckle. Asked what she was laughing at, she said:

EXAMPLE	LEFT HAND	RIGHT HAND

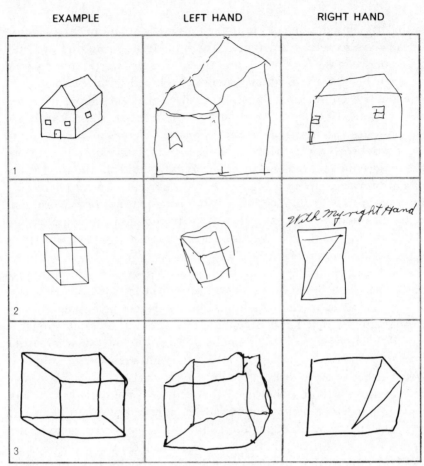

Figure 7.5.

"Visual-constructional" tasks are handled better by the right hemisphere. This was seen most clearly in the first patient, who had poor ispilateral control of his right hand. Although righthanded, he could copy the examples only with his left hand.

"I don't know . . . nothing . . . oh—that funny machine." Although the right hemisphere could not describe what it had seen, the sight nevertheless elicited an emotional response like the one evoked from the left hemisphere.

Taken together, our studies seem to demonstrate conclusively that in a split-brain situation we are really dealing with two brains, each separately capable of mental functions of a high order. This implies that the two brains should have twice as large a span of attention—that is, should be able to handle twice as much information—as a normal whole brain. We have not yet tested this precisely in human patients, but E. D. Young and I have found that a split-brain monkey can indeed deal with nearly

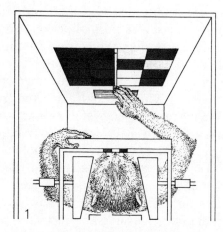

Figure 7.6.
Split-brain monkeys can handle more visual information than normal animals. When the monkey pulls a knob (1), eight of the 16 panels light momentarily. The monkey must then start at the bottom and punch the lights that were lit and no others (2). With the panels lit for 600 milliseconds normal monkeys get up to the third row from the bottom before forgetting which panels were lit (3). Split-brain monkeys complete the entire task with the panels lit only 200 milliseconds. The monkeys look at the panels through filters; since the optic chiasm is cut in these animals, the filters allow each hemisphere to see the panels on one side only.

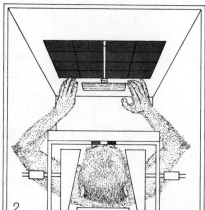

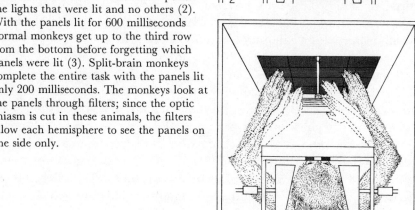

twice as much information as a normal animal (see Figure 7.6). We have so far determined also that brain-bisected patients can carry out two tasks as fast as a normal person can do one.

Just how does the corpus callosum of the intact brain combine and integrate the perceptions and knowledge of the two cerebral hemispheres? This has been investigated recently by Giovanni Berlucchi, Giacomo Rizzolati and me at the Istituto de Fisiologia Umana in Pisa. We made recordings of neural activity in the posterior part of the callosum of the cat with the hope of relating the responses of that structure to stimulation of the animal's visual fields. The kinds of responses recorded turned out to be similar to those observed in the visual cortex of the cat. In other words, the results suggest that visual pattern information can be transmitted through the callosum. This finding militates against the notion that learning and memory are transferred across the callosum, as has usually been suggested. Instead, it looks as though in animals with an intact callosum a copy of the visual world as seen in one hemisphere is sent over to the other, with the result that both hemispheres can learn together a discrimination presented to just one hemisphere. In the split-brain animal this extension of the visual pathway is cut off; this would explain rather simply why no learning proceeds in the visually isolated hemisphere and why it has to learn the discrimination from scratch.

Curiously, however, the neural activity in the callosum came only in response to stimuli at the midline of the visual field. This finding raises difficult questions. How can it be reconciled with the well-established observation that the left hemisphere of a normal person can give a running description of all the visual information presented throughout the entire half-field projected to the right hemisphere? For this reason alone one is wearily driven back to the conclusion that somewhere and somehow all or part of the callosum transmits not only a visual scene but also a complicated neural code of a higher order.

All the evidence indicates that separation of the hemispheres creates two independent spheres of consciousness within a single cranium, that is to say, within a single organism. This conclusion is disturbing to some people who view consciousness as an indivisible property of the human brain. It seems premature to others, who insist that the capacities revealed thus far for the right hemisphere are at the level of an automaton. There is, to be sure, hemispheric inequality in the present cases, but it may well be a characteristic of the individuals we have studied. It is entirely possible that if a human brain were divided in a very young person, both hemispheres could as a result separately and independently develop mental functions of a high order at the level attained only in the left hemisphere of normal individuals.

8.

The Other Side of the Brain:
An Appositional Mind

Joseph E. Bogen

It is here proposed that one way of interpreting the considerable evidence now available is to postulate the existence of two different ways of thinking; and a variety of neurologic findings will be discussed from this point of view. . . .

This article concludes with a few philosophic considerations and has appended an informal discussion of some related opinions of others.

IMPERCEPTION

Hughlings Jackson wrote in 1864: "If, then, it should be proved by wider evidence that the faculty of expression resides in one hemisphere, there

Reprinted by permission from the *Bulletin of the Los Angeles Neurological Societies*, 34, no. 3 (July 1969), 135-162.

is no absurdity in raising the question as to whether perception—its corresponding opposite—may not be seated in the other." (Taylor, 1958, p. 220).

Jackson's proposal was not only reasonable, but was subsequently supported by his observation of a patient with a right hemisphere tumor (Taylor, 1958, p. 148):

> She did not know objects, persons and places . . . there was what I would call 'imperception,' a defect as special as aphasia.*
>
> I think, as Bastian does, that the posterior lobes are the seat of the most intellectual processes. This is in effect saying that they are the seat of visual ideation, for most of our mental operations are carried on in visual ideas. I think too that the right posterior lobe is the 'leading' side, the left the more automatic. This is analogous to the difference I make as regards use of words, the right is the automatic side for words, and the left side for that use of words which is speech.

But the tide was running against Jackson, for most neurologists of the late nineteenth century were increasingly preoccupied with the localization of various functions (or the lack of it) within the left hemisphere. . . .

For at least three decades after 1900, little consideration was given to the special capacities, if any, of the right hemisphere. This was true of the entire spectrum, from the extreme localizers such as Henschen to prominent proponents of the holistic school such as Henry Head. When Henschen specifically considered the right hemisphere in his 1926 review, he allowed it only a compensatory role following left hemisphere lesions. Even then, "in every case the right hemisphere shows a manifest inferiority as compared with the left, and plays an automatic role only." In Henschen's view, the right hemisphere was probably a "regressing organ" although "it is possible that the right hemisphere is a reserve organ." . . .

The most prominent neurologists emphasized the prevailing view. The Lord Brain (1962, p. 81) averred: "The posterior half of the left cerebral hemisphere is thus the site of those neuronic linkages which underlie the elaboration of meanings in response to auditory and verbal stimuli." In their popular textbook, Grinker, Bucy, and Sahs (1959, p. 621) said: "the hemisphere which controls handedness, expression, and comprehension is known as the dominant hemisphere."

And W. Ritchie Russell (1963) wrote: "The processing of past and present information arriving in the dominant hemisphere seems to provide a scaffolding on which thought activity depends." The preoccupa-

---

*Aphasia: defect or loss of the power of expression by speech, writing, or signs, or of comprehending spoken or written language. Ed.

tion of clinical neurologists with the left hemisphere diffused into medical knowledge as a whole; and the overall impression was expressed by Strong and Elwyn (1943, p. 374), "in man the higher cortical functions are vested principally in one cerebral hemisphere, the left one in right-handed individuals . . . the dominant hemisphere . . . lesions of the other hemisphere producing as a rule no recognizable disturbances." . . .

DISORDERS OF SPATIAL THOUGHT

A disorder of spatial thought is often associated with bilateral or diffuse brain disease; but it can also occur when the injury is restricted to one hemisphere. This was the import of Nielsen's best-known article on the subject (1937), although his argument was somewhat alloyed by his tendency to lump object agnosia* and spatial agnosia together. In spite of this, he was able to conclude in a subsequent review (1940), "The right occipital lobe is far more often dominant than would be antici-pated on the basis of left-handedness." . . .

In 1963, Hécaen and Angelergues summarized findings in 415 pa-tients with various lesions in the posterior of the brain. In general, dis-orders of spatial thought were associated with right hemisphere lesions. "The right hemisphere appears to play a special role in the apprecia-tion of space and the recognition of faces." . . .

Neuropsychological studies on patients with tumors are often con-taminated by secondary symptoms and patients with vascular lesions are frequently symptomatic in both hemispheres. . . . Because removals for epilepsy leave relatively clean lesions of known extent, the study of Milner (1958) was of special importance: Patients with left temporal lobectomy had certain verbal disabilities in contrast to right temporal lobectomy patients who had impairment in the comprehension of pic-tures. Changes in brain function consequent to longstanding epilepsy (as well as the not infrequent head injuries) complicate the interpre-tation of these results. However, Milner (1971) and her colleagues have continued on with a variety of studies contributing to an imposing body of evidence for right hemisphere specialization. Most of these tests con-cern "spatial thought," but not all, so that Milner and some others have come to use the term "nonverbal" rather than "spatial" or "per-ceptual." . . .

---

*Agnosia: loss of the power to recognize the import of sensory stimuli. Ed.

MUSIC AND THE RIGHT HEMISPHERE

Suzerainty of the right hemisphere is not restricted to "visuospatial" functions. Over thirty years ago, Dide (1938) espoused a right hemisphere superiority for "kinesthetic" function. There is other evidence for nonspatial abilities special to the right hemisphere. For example, Luria (1966, p. 90) considered "the right hemisphere dominant with respect to certain mental processes [including] music . . . and the awareness of a personal disability"; and he has published a striking case of a composer whose best work was done after he was rendered aphasic by a massive stroke in the left hemisphere (1965).

Survival of musical ability in spite of severe aphasia has long been known. Perhaps the earliest recorded example was the description by Dalin in 1745, quoted by Benton and Joynt (1960):

> he had an attack of a violent illness which resulted in a paralysis of the entire right side of the body and complete loss of speech. . . . He can sing certain hymns, which he had learned before he became ill, as clearly and distinctly as any healthy person. However, it should be noted that at the beginning of the hymn he has to be helped a little by some other person singing with him. Similarly, with the same type of help, he can recite certain prayers without singing, but with a certain rhythm and in a highpitched, shouting tone. Yet this man is dumb, cannot say a single word except 'yes' and has to communicate by making signs with his hand.

Henschen (1926), who considered the right hemisphere "primitive" in almost every other respect, was led by his extensive literature review to admit: "In many cases of motor aphasia the faculty of singing words is conserved, in spite of the inability to speak a single word. In such cases the patient probably sings by means of the right hemisphere."

More recently Critchley (1953, p. 375) mentioned a patient with severe aphasia who conducted his own orchestra. Head (1926, p. 520) wrote: "We know very little of the behavior of auditory images in aphasia; but the direct reproduction of melody and the recognition of time and tune are not affected, apart from the difficulty of forming the words of a song, or reading the notes of the music." . . .

The musical capacity of the right hemisphere is most clearly shown after left hemispherectomy* in the normally developed adult. In the one such patient who survived over a year, the paucity of speech was in marked contrast to his ability to sing a variety of songs learned in early life (Smith, 1966).

Recognition of the lateralization of language to the left hemisphere is based on two observations: language deficit following left hemisphere

---

*Hemispherectomy: surgical removal of cerebral hemisphere. Ed.

lesions, and retention of speech following right hemisphere injury. Similarly, the preservation of musical ability (aside from written music) with left hemisphere lesions is complemented by a loss of musical ability with right hemisphere lesions leaving speech intact. . . . Schlesinger (1962) extensively reviewed the question of amusia,* noting the numerous reported examples of both amusia without aphasia and of aphasia without amusia; and he concluded, "In contrast to propositional language, the psychoneural component of musical ability, more especially the expression of musical aptitude, seems to be mediated by both hemispheres."

When Wertheim (1963) reviewed the literature on amusia, he concluded that a lesion of the left anterior temporal area could cause receptive deficits. We may note that such deficits are usually demonstrated by tests requiring speech or writing by the patient, so there is often a question of contamination by a deficit in language function. On the other hand, musical expression can be tested more readily without recourse to language; and Wertheim found expressive amusia to be associated with lesions of the right frontal lobe. Wertheim concluded: "Actually there is a tendency to consider that the musical functions have a bilateral hemispheric representation and it is to be assumed that musical dysfunctions have a lesional substratum far wider than is generally admitted."

Hécaen (1962) discussed the localization of lesions causing amusia. He considered the problem not yet settled, referred to the opinion of Kleist that hemispheric dominance varies between individuals, and concluded by suggesting that right-sided lesions cause defects in the "recognition of musical sounds" whereas left hemispheric lesions cause a "disorganization of musical understanding."

Hécaen's clinically derived insight has further meaning in the light of the experimental observations of Milner (1962). She gave the Seashore music tests to patients with left and right temporal lobectomy: Those with left lobectomy showed little deficit, whereas those with right lobectomy were impaired particularly as regards timbre and tonal memory. Milner's findings were confirmed by Chase (1966) in a different series of patients. Subsequently Kimura (1964) reported evidence for better recognition of melodies by the right hemisphere; and Shankweiler (1966) found greater impairment of melody recognition following temporal lobectomy on the right.

Assuming that the right hemisphere is well supplied with auditory images or "engrams," including words, but not organized as they are

---

*Amusia: inability to produce (expressive) or to comprehend (receptive) musical sounds. Ed.

on the left side, we can better interpret a variety of clinical observations. For example, as Alajouanine and Lhermitte (1964) say, "There are numerous cases of aphasia with disorders of understanding spoken language without agnosia; on the other hand, cases of pure auditory agnosia without aphasia are quite rare; such a situation results from bilateral temporal lobe lesions."

Indeed, Nielsen and Sult (1939) reported that auditory agnosia without aphasia can sometimes result from a unilateral right hemisphere lesion, subsequently confirmed by Brain (1941). More recently Spreen *et al.* (1965) reported a carefully documented case of auditory agnosia without aphasia, caused by a circumscribed right hemisphere softening.

If the right hemisphere capacity for spatial function, and for the tonal (as opposed to the notational) aspect of music is recognized, we can see in a new light the intriguing observations of Alajouanine (1948) on three patients with artistic creativity who suffered aphasia. One was a famous writer whose memory, judgment, and esthetic sense were unimpaired by a severe expressive aphasia; his loss of creativity was attributed by Alajouanine to a "disturbance of literary technique due to disease which converted that delicate artist and subtle grammarian into an agrammatist." He says of a famous musician (Ravel) who was struck down at the peak of his career that his "analytic recognition" of musical notation, and piano playing at sight were grossly disabled; on the other hand, melodic, rhythmic and stylistic sense were unimpaired, and playing or singing from memory was largely retained: "Although all artistic realization is forbidden . . . his artistic sensibility does not seem to be in the least altered." He says of a prominent painter who suffered a sudden and severe aphasia: "His artistic activity remains undisturbed; indeed, he has even accentuated the intensity and sharpness of his artistic realization and it seems that in him the aphasic and the artist have lived together on two distinct planes."

Cases of left hemisphere lesions interfering with language, but leaving other functions intact, do not as strongly support a belief in special right hemisphere capacity as would similar findings after total left hemispherectomy; but explanation of such cases springs so simply and surely from that belief as to urge its adoption.

THE HYPOTHESIS OF AN APPOSITIONAL MODE OF THOUGHT

If the right hemisphere is dominant for certain higher functions, we may naturally suppose there might be others. This direction of thought could eventually lead us to the view that every higher function is distributed unequally between the hemispheres, and that we might hope to determine the ratio or gradient of distribution for each function. . . . The distribution of functions between the hemispheres involves many difficulties, not the least of which is the variation among individuals. But there is a more serious objection to this approach. As soon as we try to distribute, or to localize in any way a particular function, we are soon faced with the heart of the problem—what is a function? Is recognition of animate objects a faculty separable from recognition of the inanimate, as suggested by Nielsen (1946, pp. 234, 246)? Is love of children a function to be localized in some particular part of the brain as Gall once maintained? It is on such questions as these that all localization of higher function has foundered. Furthermore, if we could solve this fundamental difficulty (rather than ignore it as is so often done), we would have another; our understanding of brain function would consist of a myriad of items without cohesion. *

For the above reasons it may be helpful to take as simple a view as possible by returning to the original and hardly arguable fact: the left hemisphere is better than the right for language and for what has sometimes been called "verbal activity" or "linguistic thought"; in contrast we could say that the right hemisphere excels in "non-language" or "non-verbal" function. The principal difficulty here is not that "non-language" (or "non-verbal") is so non-specific, but moreover it is misleading, because there is a significant right hemisphere capacity (Bogen, 1969, p. 150; Kinsbourne, 1971; Zangwill, 1967).

First of all, the aphasic often utters words or sentences. In fact, as Head pointed out: "When an aphasic cannot employ more abstract terms, he often uses descriptive phrases, similes, and metaphorical expressions in an appropriate manner."

Second, injuries to the right hemisphere produce certain defects in language or verbal activity. It is interesting that, according to Weinstein, the language defects after right hemisphere lesions often are different from those in dysphasia,† the errors being "existential" rather than phonetic or semantic.

Third, a gross defect in understanding speech usually requires, in addition to a left hemisphere lesion, an associated deconnection of the right temporal lobe.

Fourth, ictal‡ utterance more often occurs with an epileptogenic focus

---

*See Luria (1966, pp. 1–16) for a particularly clear and concise consideration of these issues.

†Dysphasia: impairment of speech, consisting of lack of coordination and failure to arrange words in their proper order. Ed.

‡Ictal: pertaining to a stroke. Ed.

in the right temporal lobe than in the left.

Fifth, certain kinds of verbal activity (poetry) may first appear subsequent to an aphasiogenic left hemisphere lesion.

Sixth, vocalization as well as alteration of ongoing speech have been produced by stimulation of the right hemisphere.

Seventh, the right hemisphere of the split-brain patient can read many words as well as understand spoken sentences.

Lastly, two adults having left hemispherectomy could each speak at least a few words; and a third had good comprehension of speech and could articulate long sentences while singing.

Although we now possess many more facts than Hughlings Jackson did, he was fully aware of the need to characterize the hemispheric difference. He repeatedly recognized the presence in the right hemisphere of a verbal capacity. He wrote (Taylor, 1958, pp. 130, 186),

> I think the facts of cases of loss of speech from damage to but one—the left—half, show conclusively that as regards the use of words the brain is double in function. But the very same cases show that the two hemispheres are not mere duplicates in this function. Both halves are alike in so far as each contains processes for words. They are unlike in that the left alone is for the use of words in speech and the right for other processes in which words serve. . . . the speechless patient has lost the memory of the words serving in speech; . . . he has not lost the memory of words serving in other ways. In healthy people every word is in duplicate. The 'experiment' which disease brutally makes on man seems to me to demonstrate this; it takes one set of words away and leaves the other set.

Jackson also pointed out (p. 130m) that the distinguishing feature of the major hemisphere is not its *possession* of words but rather its *use* of them in propositions: "A proposition is not a mere sequence . . . it consists of words referring to one another in a particular manner [so that each] modifies the meaning of the other."

Henry Head (1926, I, 42) summarized Jackson's view neatly: "The words removed are those employed in the formation of propositions; those which remain to the speechless patient are the same words used non-propositionally." . . . As Denny-Brown (1962) put it:

> Nor am I happy about the use of 'symbolic' to describe the lost activity (though we ourselves have used it in the past). . . . The type of defect that is peculiar to the phenomenon of dominance is propositional, its most vulnerable aspect being the proposition 'as if' in relation to some highly particularized situation.

Although we might be satisfied by a characterization of the left brain as "propositional," we can no longer follow Jackson and call the right brain's use of words "automatic." In the first place, such a distinction between voluntary and automatic inevitably implies a certain view of causation or free will. This is an important subject, but for our purposes here it can be divisive and diversionary. We would be better served by a verbal distinction which does not force this issue upon us prematurely.

There is a second objection: Jackson said both sides had a capacity for "automatic" use of words, and that only the left side had a capacity for their propositional use. But we are looking for a way to characterize the right hemisphere so as to emphasize its possession of capacities *not* present on the left. . . .

There is a third and most important objection to Jackson's proposal to call the right hemisphere "automatic"; this was in the main based on the "automatic utterance of aphasics"—it accounts for them well enough but not for the other abilities retained in aphasia.

The preservation of intellect in spite of severe aphasia has been argued for many years, both pro and con (Goldstein, 1960; Zangwill, 1964; Bay, 1964). For the present, without entering into this question at length, we can recall the conclusion of Weisenberg and McBride (1935) mentioned earlier that, "purposeful and effective thinking can be carried through when language is extremely inadequate." Such abilities might perhaps be argued away as dependent upon residual capacity of the left hemisphere. However, this argument cannot apply to the wealth of non-automatic functions elicited in testing of the right hemisphere of the split-brain human or the patient with left hemispherectomy. It is also doubtful that "automatic" adequately describes the capacity of the right hemisphere to respond appropriately at a time when the left hemisphere has been paralyzed by intracarotid amytal (Rosadini and Rossi, 1967).

The right hemisphere recognizes stimuli (including words), apposes or collates this data, compares this with previous data, and, while receiving the very same stimuli as the other hemisphere, is often arriving at different results. As Teuber (1965) wrote, it is a question of "different modes of organization [in the two hemispheres]." This statement reflects the results of Teuber's study together with Semmes, Weinstein, and Ghent in 1960, from which they concluded that organization of somatosensory function in the left hemisphere is relatively discrete as compared with a more diffuse representation in the right hemisphere. In a recent article, Semmes (1968) has extended this conclusion to encompass other functions.

Hécaen, Ajuriaguerra, and Angelergues (1963) had a different approach when they wrote:

> It is indeed remarkable that the apraxias* expressing an impairment of relations between the subject and his body or between the body and the surrounding

---

*Apraxia: inability to carry out purposeful movements in the absence of paralysis or other motor or sensory impairment. Ed.

space are found in connection with lesions of the minor hemisphere. This fact
might lead to the assumption that the paramount importance of language in the
organization of the major hemisphere leaves to the minor hemisphere the task of
organizing the functions arising from, and marked by, the pre-verbal mode of
communication.

This statement clearly resembles the hypothesis being proposed here,
except for their use of the word "pre-verbal."

Humphrey and Zangwill described in 1951 three patients who spontaneously reported cessation of dreaming after a posterior brain injury.
They tentatively suggested:

it may be argued that just as the aphasic is unable to express his thought in
propositional form, so the agnosic patient may fail to express his ideation at the
lower level of phantasy and dream. While not denying that the trend and content
of any given dream, or indeed of any given proposition, cannot be interpreted
without reference to psychological factors, we would like at the same time to suggest that visual thinking, dreaming, and imagination are liable to organic dissolution in a manner directly comparable to the dissolution of symbolic thought in
aphasia.

There is here a clear suggestion of two modes of thought: "symbolic" or
"propositional" predominantly associated with the left hemisphere, and
"visual thinking and imagination" whose lateralization was doubted by
these authors.* . . .

It was Zangwill's superb review of 1961 which first enabled us to relate our dysgraphia-dyscopia† data to the emerging evidence of others.
In that review he tentatively characterized left and right hemisphere
dominance as "symbolic" and "visuo-spatial" respectively. When we
first ventured (Bogen and Gazzaniga, 1965) to suggest that two different
thought processes are lateralized, one in each hemisphere, we attempted
to combine the terminology of Milner and of Zangwill, using the terms
"verbal" and "visuo-spatial." Recognition of a non-automatic verbal
capacity in the right hemisphere has rendered this usage obsolete.

Even when good ipsilateral control obscures the lateralized dissociation of dysgraphia and dyscopia following cerebral commissurotomy,‡
special tests can show a right hemisphere superiority for matching spatial forms. This finding by Levy-Agresti led her with Sperry (1968) to
suggest:

---

*On casual inquiry it seems that cerebral commissurotomy is typically followed by
alteration in dreaming. Several patients (but not all) have specifically denied any
dreams after operation in contrast with frequent, vivid dreams before.

†Dysgraphia: inability to write properly. Dyscopia: inability to copy. Ed.

‡Commissurotomy: surgical incision of the connecting fibers between the two cerebral
hemispheres. Ed.

The data indicate that the mute, minor hemisphere is specialized for Gestalt perception, being primarily a synthesist in dealing with information input. The speaking, major hemisphere, in contrast, seems to operate in a more logical, analytic, computerlike fashion [and] the findings suggest that a possible reason for cerebral lateralization in man is basic incompatibility of language functions on the one hand and synthetic perceptual functions on the other.

The difficulty in characterizing the ability of the right hemisphere (Table 8.1) arises largely from our ignorance—we have barely scratched the surface of a vast unknown. We would do well therefore to choose arbitrarily a word, homologous in structure with the word "propositional" but sufficiently ambiguous to permit provisional use. For example, we can say that the right hemisphere has a highly developed "appositional" capacity. This term implies a capacity for apposing or comparing of perceptions, schemas, engrams, etc., but has in addition the virtue that it implies very little else. If it is correct that the right hemisphere excells in capacities as yet unknown to us, the full meaning of "appositional" will emerge as these capacities are further studied and understood. The word "appositional" has the essential virtue of suggesting a capacity as important as "propositional," reflecting a belief in the importance of right hemisphere function.

TABLE 8.1
Dichotomies with Lateralization Suggested

Suggested by	Right hemisphere	Left hemisphere
Jackson (1864)	Expression	Perception
Jackson (1874)	Audito-articular	Retino-ocular
Jackson (1876)	Propositionizing	Visual imagery
Weisenberg & McBride (1935)	Linguistic	Visual or kinesthetic
Anderson (1951)	Storage	Executive
Humphrey & Zangwill (1951)	Symbolic or propositional	Visual or imaginative
McFie & Piercy (1952)	Education of relations	Education of correlates
Milner (1958)	Verbal	Perceptual or non-verbal
Semmes, Weinstein, Ghent, Teuber (1960)	Discrete	Diffuse
Zangwill (1961)	Symbolic	Visuospatial
Hécaen, Ajuriaguerra, Angelergues (1963)	Linguistic	Pre-verbal
Bogen and Gazzaniga (1965)	Verbal	Visuospatial
Levy-Agresti and Sperry (1968)	Logical or analytic	Synthetic perceptual
Bogen (1969)	Propositional	Appositional

ONTOGENETIC LATERALIZATION OF THE
TWO MODES OF THOUGHT

We recognize that the lateralization of higher function is not invariable. For example, there are cases of right-handers whose right cerebral lesions caused aphasia as well as left hemiplegia*; and in left-handers the situation is much less determinate. More important, there have been reports in which a unilateral lesion disturbs both propositional and appositional functions. But we must not permit the rich diversity of natural phenomena to obscure our recognition of the common and representative types (Bogen, 1969, p. 150).

Zangwill (1964) recently wrote that in earliest infancy, "the two hemispheres are equipotential, or nearly so with regard to the acquisition of speech. . . . Lateralization of speech begins early, almost certainly in the second year, and would appear to proceed *pari passu* with the acquisition of speech." The hypothesis of an appositional mode of thought implies that in this regard, too, the hemispheres are equipotential; and as the ability to propositionize tends to dominate the activity of the left hemisphere, the appositional mode is more free to exploit the intellectual capacities of the other side. The extent to which appositional ability develops must depend on the nature and extent of environmental exposure, just as the development of propositional capacity is highly culture-dependent.†

In the adult, left hemispherectomy may be followed by the partial reappearance of propositional function in the remaining brain (Smith, 1966); and after massive right-sided ablations, we can expect that appositional capacity of the left hemisphere will re-emerge to a degree dependent on the patient's age, intelligence, and completeness of lateralization before the ablation. Even in the young patient, however, there may not be a complete return of the ability proper to the other side. For example, there is some evidence that, even after a long recovery period, patients with left hemispherectomy tend to remain deficient in verbal comprehension while patients with right hemispherectomy remain relatively deficient in block designs.

In the event of congenital cerebral hemiatrophy,‡ one hemisphere must do the work of both. The possibility of two different, parallel modes

---

*Hemiplegia: paralysis of one side of the body. Ed.

†Nature-nurture interaction in language development was recently discussed by Lenneberg (1969).

‡Cerebral hemiatrophy: wasting away of a cerebral hemisphere on one side of the brain. Ed.

of thought going on simultaneously in one hemisphere naturally raises the question as to their structural allocation. That is, do they use the same neural elements simultaneously, or different combinations of them, or are the neural elements of each mode spatially distinct? Even a cursory discussion of these questions must be put off to the future. For the moment we need only to recognize the existence of two types of thinking, and that in the common circumstance they come to dominate the activities of their respective hemispheres.

THE DUALITY OF THE BRAIN

According to Hippocrates (Chadwick and Mann, 1950, p. 183), "The human brain, as in the case of all other animals, is double." This duality is so apparent to the most casual inspection that it has intrigued neurologists for centuries, especially since it occasionally happens that one hemisphere is destroyed with preservation of the personality. It is straightforward to conclude that if possession of a "mind" requires only one hemisphere, having two hemispheres makes possible the possession of two minds. This view was forcibly argued at least as early as 1844 by Dr. A. L. Wigan. He wrote:

> The mind is essentially dual, like the organs by which it is exercised. (p. 4).
> This idea has presented itself to me, and I have dwelt on it for more than a quarter of a century, without being able to find a single valid or even plausible objection. (p. 9).
> I believe myself then able to prove—1. That each cerebrum is a distinct and perfect whole as an organ of thought. 2. That a separate and distinct process of thinking or ratiocination may be carried on in each cerebrum simultaneously. (p. 26).

Wigan defended this position with a variety of reasons, including the many instances of two simultaneous, opposing, concurrent trains of thought; of these he said, "On any other hypothesis they are utterly inexplicable." But the original impetus was his knowledge of some surprising autopsies, beginning with one he observed himself:

> One hemisphere was entirely gone—that was evident to my senses; the patient, a man about 50 years of age, had conversed rationally and even written verses within a few days of his death. (p. 40).
> Dr. Conolly mentions the case of a gentleman who had so serious a disease that it spread through the orbit into the cerebrum, and by very slow degrees destroyed his life. He was a man of family and independence . . . on examining the skull, one brain was entirely destroyed—gone, annihilated—and in its place (in the

narrator's emphatic language) 'a yawning chasm.' All of his mental faculties were apparently quite perfect and his mind was clear and undisturbed to within a few hours of his death. (p. 41).

Dr. James Johnson mentions to me another example of a gentleman under his care, who retained the entire possession of his faculties until the last day of his existence, yet on opening the skull, one cerebrum was reduced by absorption to a thin membrane—the whole solid contents of the one half of the cranium, above the tentorium, absolutely gone. (p. 42). . . .

If, for example, as I have so often stated, and now again repeat, one brain be a perfect instrument of thought—if it be capable of all the emotion, sentiments, and faculties, which we call in the aggregate, mind—then it necessarily follows that Man must have two minds with two brains; and however intimate and perfect their unison in their natural state, they must occasionally be discrepant when influenced by disease, either direct, sympathetic, or reflex. (p. 271).

We will leave to the future an expanded discussion of the implications for psychiatric illness of this conception. For the present, we should stop to inquire: Why was Wigan forgotten? Was he simply overlooked? No—for he was quoted by Brown-Séquard, when the latter wrote in 1877: "I have come to the conclusion that we have two brains, perfectly distinct the one from the other." Brown-Séquard was not alone, for Ferrier wrote in 1886 (p. 426), "The brain as an organ of motion and sensation, or presentative consciousness, is a single organ composed of two halves; the brain as an organ of ideation, or representative consciousness is a dual organ, each hemisphere complete in itself." Several years later, Sir Victor Horsley asserted (Paget, 1919): "We are not single animals: We are really two individuals joined together in the middle line."

The likely explanation of the eclipse of the two-brain view was the emergence of the concept of cerebral dominance. The social disabilities of the dysphasic (especially in a society which emphasizes "rational" thought) were so much more obvious than the defects of the right-brain-injured person that when dysphasia was accepted as a left hemisphere symptom, the right hemisphere was soon forgotten. And the increasing preoccupation of neurologists with the peculiarities of the left hemisphere diverted them from a more comprehensive view. Hughlings Jackson (a student of Brown-Séquard) summarized in 1874 (Taylor, 1958, p. 129) what was soon to be generally accepted:

> Not long ago, few doubted the brain to be double in function as well as physically bilateral; but now that it is certain from the researches of Dax, Broca, and others, that damage to one lateral half can make a man entirely speechless, the former view is disputed. Thus, Broca and Moxon supposed that but one half of the brain—the left in the vast majority of people—is educated in words.

Whatever the eminence of its advocates (Brown-Séquard, Ferrier, Horsley, etc.), an idea may be abandoned because of an accumulation of adverse evidence. In this case, it appears that it was the theoretical suppositions accompanying the concept of "cerebral dominance" that resulted in the loss of the two-brain view; it was not the appearance of any adverse evidence. We should not suppose that the flowering of experimental neuro-physiology, at the same time as the emergence of the concept of dominance, supplied similar information, for animal experiments have repeatedly supported Wigan's view.

The first experimental hemispherectomies were done by Goltz (von Bonin, 1960). He wrote in 1888:

> I will begin by relating an experiment which I hope will be acclaimed by all true friends of science. I succeeded in observing for 15 months an animal in which I had taken away the whole left hemisphere. (p. 118).
>
> We have seen that a dog without a left hemisphere can still move voluntarily all parts of his body and that from all parts of his body, action can be induced which can only be the consequence of conscious sensation. This is incompatible with that construction of centers which assumes that each side of the body can serve only those conscious movements and sensations which concern the opposite half of the body. (p. 130).
>
> Finally, as far as Man is concerned, the fact that a dog after an extirpation of a whole hemisphere shows essentially the same personality with only slightly weakened intelligence might make it possible to take out even very large tumors if they are confined to one half of the brain. (p. 158).

Subsequent experimental hemispherectomy has provided no contradiction of Goltz. . . . But what of the Human for whom the concept of cerebral dominance was invented?

Following Krynauw (1950) the removal of an entire hemisphere from the human as a treatment for certain kinds of epilepsy became relatively common. And it has been noted over and over again, as Glees (1961, p. 486) wrote; "Even the removal of a complete hemisphere (about 400 grams of brain substance) may be said to have little effect on intellectual capacity or social behavior, producing at most a lessened capacity for adaptability and a more rapid mental exhaustion." Furthermore, it is particularly interesting that of the 150 cases reviewed by H. H. White (1961) and the 35 cases reviewed by Basser (1962) approximately half involved the left hemisphere and half the right hemisphere. And following the removal of one hemisphere (or brain, Wigan would say), there remained a "person," no matter which hemisphere was removed.

It can be argued that hemispherectomy for epilepsy is done in a setting of abnormal maturation, and that the crucial test comes with hemispherectomy in a normally developed adult. We recall that Goltz suggested hemispherectomy for tumors; Dandy (1928) carried out such operations, as have a number of subsequent surgeons. Because of the relative rarity of such operations, as well as the progressive nature of the disease, there have been only a few long-term psychometric studies (Smith, 1966, 1969; Rowe, 1957; Bell and Karnosh, 1949; Mensh *et al.*, 1952; Bruell and Albee, 1962). Although the patients have more severe neurological deficit than after hemispherectomy for infantile hemiplegia, they have confirmed the original observation that only one hemisphere is needed to sustain, in Wigan's words, "the emotions, sentiments, and faculties which we call in the aggregate, mind."

THE SPLIT BRAIN

The most reasonable argument may prove incorrect when experimentally tested. Wigan argued that if one hemisphere can sustain a mind, "it necessarily follows" that a man with two hemispheres must have two minds. This conclusion has been tested in part by section of the neocortical commissures, sometimes called "splitting the brain."

When the optic chiasm of a cat or a monkey is divided sagittally, the input into the right eye goes only into the right hemisphere and similarly the left eye informs only the left hemisphere. If an animal with this operation is trained to choose between two symbols while using only one eye, later tests show that it can make the proper choice with the other eye. But if the commissures, especially the corpus callosum, have been severed before training, the initially covered eye and its ipsilateral* hemisphere must be trained from the beginning. That is, the training does not transfer from one hemisphere to the other if the commissures have been cut. This is the fundamental split-brain experiment of Myers and Sperry (1953; Sperry, 1961; Myers, 1965; Sperry, 1967).

The second eye can be trained to choose the opposite member of the pair. Then, the symbol which is considered correct depends on which eye is covered. In other words, one hemisphere is solving the problem one way and one hemisphere solving it the other way.

Subsequent experiments by Trevarthen (1962) showed that the two hemispheres can work not only independently but also simultaneously. More recently Gazzaniga and Young (1967) showed that monkeys whose hemispheres are disconnected can solve independent problems with each hand simultaneously, in contrast to unoperated monkeys whose ability to do these two tests simultaneously is quite limited. The same phenomenon, of independent problem solving by the two hands

---

*Ipsilateral: situated on or pertaining to the same side. Ed.

simultaneously, has also been shown in the human. Indeed, the many studies (Bogen, Sperry, and Vogel, 1969; Sperry, Gazzaniga, and Bogen, 1969; Sperry, 1964c; Gazzaniga, 1970; Sperry, Vogel, and Bogen, 1970) of our patients with cerebral commissurotomy have abundantly supported Dr. Wigan's conclusion. The data are consistent with the interpretation that disconnection of the hemispheres splits not only the brain but also the psychic properties of the brain. As Sperry wrote (1964c), "Everything we have seen so far indicates that the surgery has left each of these people with two separate minds, that is, with two separate spheres of consciousness."

THE ILLUSION OF MENTAL UNITY

Using special tests following a special operation, cerebral commissurotomy, we can regularly elicit a behavioral dissociation from which are inferred two separate, parallel streams of thought. The crucial question is whether these two minds exist with the commissures intact. It may be that an essential function of the corpus callosum is to keep the two hemispheres in exact synchrony, so that only one Mind can exist, that is, until the commissures are cut. This may be stated differently as a question: Does cerebral commissurotomy produce a splitting or doubling of the Mind, or is it more correctly considered a maneuver making possible the demonstration of a duality previously present?

Every experiment involves the introduction of artifice or alteration, so that every experimental result can be explained as attributable more to the technique than to the process under investigation. Ultimately, this question is settled by production of the same result with a different technique. In this particular case, we can choose with certainty between the alternatives only if some other approach illustrates the same duality of mind.

Pending further evidence, I believe (with Wigan) that each of us has two minds in one person. There is a host of detail to be marshalled in this case. But we must eventually confront directly the principal resistance to the Wigan view: that is, the subjective feeling possessed by each of us that we are One. This inner conviction of Oneness is a most cherished opinion of Western Man. It is not only the common sense of the layman but also the usual assumption of the most prominent neurobiologists. Ramon y Cajal (1960) wrote: "it is impossible to understand the architectural plan of the brain if one does not admit as [one of the] guiding principles of this plan the unity of perception." The issue was drawn with surpassing clarity by Sir Charles Sherrington (1947, p. xvii):

> This self is a unity . . . it regards itself as one, others treat it as one. It is addressed as one, by a name to which it answers. The Law and the State schedule it as one. It and they identify it with a body which is considered by it and them to belong to it integrally. In short, unchallenged and unargued conviction assumes it to be one. The logic of grammar endorses this by a pronoun in the singular. All its diversity is merged in oneness.

The strength of this conviction is no assurance of its truth. An unarguable certainty in men's minds was no guarantee of the flatness of the World, the geocentricity of the Universe, spontaneous generation, the inheritance of acquired characteristics, the Vital nature of organic compounds, the conservation of mass, etc. Commonsensical (at one time) were all of these, self-evident—and all eventually recognized as wrong.

In the last resort, Common Sense has often been defended by the misuse of theological arguments. In this case, for example, some might appeal to St. Augustine's dictum, that whatever its multiplicity of manifestations, there is but one Soul—"Quoniam omnia ista una anima est, proprietates quidem diversae." But the hypothesis advanced here does not concern the Soul (Anima). The Soul is indeed the proper concern and authority of the theologian. *

But we are concerned here with the Mind, an entity created in their own subjective image by certain pre-Christian philosophers of the ancient world (Plato, Cicero) and concretized by a mathematician (Descartes) long before the availability of physiological or even any precise anatomical knowledge of the brain. Bartemeier† wrote:

> The Platonic-Augustinian idea was that man was essentially a soul, dwelling temporarily in the body. This was also the heart of Descartes' theory, and is often confused with Christian doctrine (it is called the 'official dogma' by Gilbert Ryle, 1950). St. Thomas Aquinas would have none of this: 'Passio proprie decta non potest competere animae nisi per accidens, inquantum scilicet compositum patitur.'

---

*Although the hypothesis presented here does not concern the Soul, the reader may feel entitled to some indication of my personal position. Such convictions are not easily capsulized; but I do believe that while it is not necessary to cerebrate in order to be aware, it is necessary to be aware in order to think. Everyday clinical experience has led me to believe, that in so far as an escape of the Soul from the body can be correlated with anatomico-physiological events, that most likely such event is irreversible damage to the reticular core of the central cephalid brain stem (as is commonly seen in advanced tentorial herniation). At this crucial inner level, there is no duplication of either function or structure (Magoun, 1958).

†There is an especially clear and concise discussion by Rather (1965) of the views of Plato, Cicero, St. Augustine, and Descartes. See particularly pages 7, 8, 45, and 125.

(S. T. 1a 2 ae, QXXII a1). (Trans.: Emotion in the strict sense cannot apply to the soul, except incidentally, in so far, in other words, as it affects the psycho-physical composite.) This implies a clear distinction between soul and psyche.

Modern psychologists have occasionally taken exception to the unitary concept of mind; one such was Lashley (1958) who wrote, "Psychologists, however, at least in recent times, have seen no reason to keep mind unitary." Lashley was in truth an exceptional psychologist; most of his contemporaries and successors have continued to discuss Mind in the singular. So it was with Hebb (1954), when he suggested that we abandon the idea altogether. In the same paper, Hebb emphasized the unrecognized influence of out-dated psychology on the subsequent thinking of physiologists. Surely one of the most outstanding examples must be the practically universal acceptance in Western scientific thought of this venerable belief in the singularity of the Mind.

SUMMARY OF THE HYPOTHESIS

The hypothesis which is the main burden of this paper may be summarized as follows:

One of the most obvious and fundamental features of the cerebrum is that it is double. Various kinds of evidence, especially from hemispherectomy, have made it clear that one hemisphere is sufficient to sustain a personality or mind. We may then conclude that the individual with two intact hemispheres has the capacity for two distinct minds. This conclusion finds its experimental proof in the split-brain animal whose two hemispheres can be trained to perceive, consider, and act independently. In the human, where *propositional* thought is typically lateralized to one hemisphere, the other hemisphere evidently specializes in a different mode of thought, which may be called *appositional*.

The rules or methods by which propositional thought is elaborated on "this" side of the brain (the side which speaks, reads, and writes) have been subjected to analyses of syntax, semantics, mathematical logic, etc. for many years. The rules by which appositional thought is elaborated on the other side of the brain will need study for many years to come.

A POTPOURRI OF DICHOTOMIES

Having believed for several years in the duality of the minds, I have collected a variety of related opinions from various sources (Table 8.2).

TABLE 8.2
Dichotomies Without Reference to Cerebral Lateralization

Suggested by	Dichotomies	
C. S. Smith	Atomistic	Gross
Price	Analytic or reductionist	Synthetic or concrete
Wilder	Numerical	Geometric
Head	Symbolic or systematic	Perceptual or non-verbal
Goldstein	Abstract	Concrete
Reusch	Digital or discursive	Analogic or eidetic
Bateson & Jackson	Digital	Analogic
J. Z. Young	Abstract	Map-like
Pribram	Digital	Analogic
W. James	Differential	Existential
Spearman	Education of relations	Education of correlates
Hobbes	Directed	Free or unordered
Freud	Secondary process	Primary process
Pavlov	Second signalling	First signalling
Sechenov (Luria)	Successive	Simultaneous
Levi-Strauss	Positive	Mythic
Bruner	Rational	Metaphoric
Akhilananda	Buddhi	Manas
Radhakrishnan	Rational	Integral

They are included here in the hope that they may be of interest, and perhaps a little enlightening, in an appositional sort of way.

The belief that man is possessed of two ways of thought, occasionally conflicting, is common in everyday speech, where it often takes the form of supposing a struggle between "reason" and "emotion," or between "the mind" and "the heart." This is, of course, a mere figure of speech, as pointed out by the Reverend McCleave (1959):

> The matter of heart transplant raises no moral question. Society and our culture have used the heart as a symbol for so long that in the minds of many the symbol has become reality. I do not believe that the heart is life, that it contains love, compassion, or mercy, nor do I believe that it is the dwelling place of the soul. The heart is simply another organ of the body.

Even in olden times it was recognized that "the heart" was a figure of speech and that both of the contending forces exist within the mind. In 1763, Jerome Gaub wrote (Rather, 1965),

> If you yourselves have neither been taught by a certain interior sense to agree with my previous assertion that the mind contains two very different principles of action. . . . I hope that you will believe Pythagoras and Plato, the wisest of the ancient philosophers, who, according to Cicero, divided the mind into two parts, one partaking of reason and the other devoid of it.

Great literature has characteristically concerned itself with this issue. For example, it has been said of Dostoievski that "The anguish arising from the dual nature of man rings forth in great chords throughout his work."

Not all mental duality is anguished: Dr. Samuel Johnson is said to have been much annoyed by dreams in which he found himself in repartée with an antagonist of superior wit. "Had I been awake," said he, "I should have known that I furnished the wit on both sides."

André Gide averred: "There is always a struggle between what is reasonable and what is not." It is perhaps because we live in a society in which rational thought is held in particularly high esteem that the "other" is often considered to be base or undesirable even when it is un-named. More likely this evaluation is not cultural in origin, but arises from the fact that the hemisphere which does the propositioning is also the one having a near monopoly on the capacity for naming. C. S. Smith (1968) recently remarked on "the curious human tendency to laud the more abstract." He went on to suggest that scientists are becoming increasingly aware of the need for a simultaneous and synchronous use of two points of view, "one, intellectual, atomistic, simple and certain, the other based on an enjoyment of grosser forms and qualities." In a recent presidential address to the American Association for the Advancement of Science, D. K. Price (1969) goes so far as to suggest that today's "cosmopolitan rebellion" reflects not so much a generation gap or a racial problem, but rather a confrontation between two "processes of thought" one of which he terms "analytic, reductionist, simple, or provable," and the other he describes variously as as "synthetic, concrete, complex, and disorderly."

When Ruesch and Kees (1956) proposed that Man thinks simultaneously in two different ways, they used the popular terminology of this computer age and called them *digital codification* (discursive, verbal, or logical) and *analogic codification* (non-discursive, non-verbal, or eidetic). The same terminology (digitial and analogic) was urged by Bateson and Jackson (1964).

In a recent discusssion on the duality of the brain, J. Z. Young (1962) supposed the cerebrum to represent reality in two ways, "abstract" and "maplike." In the same conference, Pribram (1962) referred to the distinction made by William James (1890, I, 49) between two types of discrimination: differential and existential. Pribram went on to the usual distinction of "digital" and "analogue." He also suggested that the maintenance of stability in space utilizes a different mechanism than that which provides stability in time.

Although terminology has varied with the times, the notion of two modes of thought has frequently been proposed by psychologists. For example, Hobbes (Murphy, 1951, p. 27) supposed that "mental discourse is of two sorts," free or "unordered" thinking on the one hand and "directed" or purposeful thinking on the other. Similar views have since been advanced by both experimental (for example, reflexologic) and introspective (for example, psychoanalytic) schools. Pre-eminent among experimental psychologists was I. P. Pavlov. He considered human thought to be particularly distinguished by the presence of a second signaling system, differentiated out of the first signaling system of the cerebrum. The first signaling system concerns phenomena immediately connected with real reactions of the external world. The second signaling system depends on language and has a capacity of abstraction. This distinction between two modes of thought was used by Pavlov to explain human neuroses, and he is quoted by Frolov (1937, p. 233) as saying: "thanks to the two signaling systems . . . the mass of human beings can be divided into thinking, artistic, and intermediate types. The last named combines the work of both systems in the requisite degree." Pavlov's view may well have stemmed in part from a knowledge of Sechenov's suggestion, quoted and supported by Luria (1966, p. 74), that the cerebrum has two basic forms of integrative activity: organization into "simultaneous and primarily spatial groups"; and into "temporally organized successive series."*

Probably the most influential proponent of introspective psychology in this century was Sigmund Freud. So well known was the antagonism between Pavlov and Freud that it is quite revealing to find them here in agreement! Freud (1946, IV, 119ff) supposed the brain to have two modes of thought, apparently arriving at this quite independently of Pavlov and on altogether different grounds. He considered "secondary process" thinking to develop with the growth of language. "Primary process" thinking he considered concrete rather than verbal, as well as

---

*Although this distinction (Sechenov-Luria) suggests no lateralization, it implies what may well be the most important distinction between the left and right hemisphere modes; that is, the extent to which a linear concept of time participates in the ordering of thought.

having a more mobile cathexis. Fenichel (1945), a well-known disciple of Freud, described primary process thinking as: "carried out more through pictorial, concrete images, whereas the secondary process is based more on words . . . it is remote from any (sic) logic. But it is thinking nevertheless because it consists of imaginations according to which later actions are performed." Fenichel emphasized that such "pictorial thinking" is "less fitted for objective judgment" because it is: "relatively unorganized, primitive, magical, undifferentiated, based on common motor reactions, ruled by emotions, full of wishful or fearful misconceptions, archaic, vague, regressive, primal." He considered it to lack "lofty intellectual interest" and to be typified by "emotional fantasy" and in general "not in accord with reality." Perhaps Fenichel protests too much! One is reminded of the song from *My Fair Lady*, "Why Can't a Woman be Like a Man?" Perhaps Fenichel's condemnatory tone reflects his own unconscious denial of the value of "non-logical" or pictorial thought. *

Spearman's experience with a variety of "intelligence" tests led him to accept a verbal factor and a spatial factor as well as [his factor "g"] called the "general intelligence." (Supposing verbal and spatial abilities tend to lateralize to left and right hemispheres, one can easily suppose that the factor "g" is distributed, not necessarily equally, between the hemispheres.) Spearman asserted furthermore that intelligence can be considered to consist of two components, a capacity for abstract reasoning which he called the "education of relations" and a capacity for analogical reasoning which he called "education of correlates." In referring to this view, McFie and Piercy (1952) wrote, "Intellectual functions most sensitive to dominant hemisphere lesions appear to be cases of 'education of relations,' while functions sensitive to minor hemisphere lesions may be classified as cases of 'education of correlates.' "

The notable studies of Goldstein (1948, 1960) were characterized by a psychological approach in which anatomic correlations were avoided and the emphasis was given to the nature rather than the origin of symptoms. Throughout Goldstein's work there recurs a division of mental function into two modes of thought: an "abstract attitude" involving discursive reasoning, and a "concrete attitude" which is "un-reflective" and "more realistic." His belief that one of these is a

---

*Some reinterpretation may be afforded by the hypothesis of an appositional mind not only for the primary process, but also for what Fromm (1968) has called the fundamental observations of psychoanalysis: the Unconscious; repression; resistance; and the therapeutic value of conscientiation. [Also see Maslow, 1957.]

"higher" function than the other and his disaffection for anatomical localization are not necessarily bound up with the essential point, that there are two types of thinking generated in the same cerebrum.

It is not only in the Western world that the dual nature of man is recognized. For example, Benedict (1953) studied the Bagobo people of Malaysia:

> Inhabiting every individual, two souls called *Gimokud* are recognized— shadowy, ethereal personalities that dominate the body more or less completely. The right-hand soul, known in Bagobo terminology as the *Gimokud Takawanan* is the so-called 'good soul' that manifests its self as the shadow on the right-hand of one's path. The left-hand soul called *Gimokud Tebang* is said to be a 'bad soul' and shows itself as the shadow on the left side of the path.

There are many examples of various peoples believing that man is dual. In addition to those discussed by Hertz (1960) and Domhoff (1969), Griaule (1950, p. 54) has emphasized the West African belief in the co-existence of two spiritual entities which he translated "soul" and "vital principle." The cultural anthropologist Levi-Strauss (1965) concluded:

> Primitive man is clearly capable of positive thought . . . but it is his myth-creating capacity which plays the vital part in his life . . . I believe that these two ways of thinking have always existed in man, and they go on existing, but the importance they are giving is not the same here and there.

In the East are much more highly developed systems of thought comparable to those of the Western world. I must admit to a vast ignorance of Oriental philosophy; but it seems to me as reasonable to suppose that the pre-Confucian concept of Yang and Yin reflects a projection onto the surroundings, as to suppose that it is forced on thoughtful man by the external world. With respect to Vedanta, or Hindu thought, we are on slightly firmer ground. Akhilananda (1946) distinguishes intellect (*buddhi*) from mind (*manas*); and Professor Huston Smith has informed me (personal communication) that this distinction between buddhi and manas is common among Hindu psychologists. He pointed out further that this was once rendered into English by Radhakrishnan as "rational thought" and "integral thought."

It seems that certain contemporary Western psychologists are con-verging toward the Vedantic view. Bruner (1962, p. 74) recently wrote: "The elegant rationality of science and the metaphoric nonrationality of art operate with deeply different grammars; perhaps they even represent a profound complementarity."

Certain other psychologists are not so converging. K. J. Hayes (1962) argued what may be called a mosaicist view, that intellect is an "accumulation" of a large number of individual skills or faculties. In recent conversation, he has pointed out that the occurrence of so many terminologic dichotomies is not obviously related to the bilateral symmetry of the brain, but that it can be ascribed to a nearly universal predilection for the logical simplicity of a binary system. On the other hand, perhaps this predilection is itself one expression of the duality of the minds [see also Bogen and Bogen, 1969].

9.

I Ching
(The Book of Changes)

1. Ch'ien: The Creative

≡ *above* Ch'ien, The Creative, Heaven
≡ *below* Ch'ien, The Creative, Heaven

The first hexagram is made up of six unbroken lines. These unbroken lines stand for the primal power, which is light-giving, active, strong, and of the spirit. The hexagram is consistently strong in character, and since it is without weakness, its essence is power or energy. Its image is heaven. Its energy is represented as unrestricted by any fixed conditions in space and is therefore conceived as motion. Time is regarded as the basis of this motion. Thus the hexagram includes also the power of time and the power of persisting in time, that is, duration.

Reprinted by permission from *The I Ching: The Book of Changes*, translated into German by Richard Wilhelm, then into English by Cary F. Bayes (copyright © 1950 and 1967 by Princeton University Press, Bollingen Series XIX), pp. 3, 10–11. British copyright is held by Routledge and Kegan Paul.

The power represented by the hexagram is to be interpreted in a dual sense—in terms of its action on the universe and of its action on the world of men. In relation to the universe, the hexagram expresses the strong, creative action of the Deity. In relation to the human world, it denotes the creative action of the holy man or sage, of the ruler or leader of men, who through his power awakens and develops their higher nature.

2. K'un: The Receptive

above K'un, The Receptive, Earth
below K'un, The Receptive, Earth

This hexagram is made up of broken lines only. The broken line represents the dark, yielding, receptive primal power of yin. The attribute of the hexagram is devotion; its image is the earth. It is the perfect complement of THE CREATIVE—the complement, not the opposite, for the Receptive does not combat the Creative but completes it. It represents nature in contrast to spirit, earth in contrast to heaven, space as against time, the female-maternal as against the male-paternal. However, as applied to human affairs, the principle of this complementary relationship is found not only in the relation between man and woman, but also in that between prince and minister and between father and son. Indeed, even in the individual this duality appears in the coexistence of the spiritual world and the world of the senses.

But strictly speaking there is no real dualism here, because there is a clearly defined hierarchic relationship between the two principles. In itself of course the Receptive is just as important as the Creative, but the attribute of devotion defines the place occupied by this primal power in relation to the Creative. For the Receptive must be activated and led by the Creative; then it is productive of good. Only when it abandons this position and tries to stand as an equal side by side with the Creative, does it become evil. The result then is opposition to and struggle against the Creative, which is productive of evil to both.

10.

Codifications of Reality:
Lineal and Nonlineal

Dorothy Lee

The people of the Trobriand Islands codify, and probably apprehend reality, nonlineally in contrast to our own lineal phrasing. Basic to my investigation of the codification of reality in these two societies, is the assumption that a member of a given society not only codifies experienced reality through the use of the specific language and other patterned behavior characteristics of his culture, but that he actually grasps reality only as it is presented to him in this code. The assumption is not that reality itself is relative; rather that it is differently punctuated and categorized, or that different aspects of it are noticed by, or presented to the participants of different cultures. If reality itself were not absolute, then true communication of course would be impossible. My own position is that there is an absolute reality, and that communication

Reprinted by permission from *Psychosomatic Medicine*, 12, no. 2 (1950), 89–97.

is possible. If, then, that which the different codes refer to is ultimately the same, a careful study and analysis of a different code and of the culture to which it belongs, should lead us to concepts which are ultimately comprehensible, when translated into our own code. It may even, eventually, lead us to aspects of reality from which our own code excludes us.

It is a corollary of this assumption that the specific phrasing of reality can be discovered through intensive and detailed analysis of any aspect of culture. My own study was begun with an analysis of linguistic formulation, only because it is in language that I happen to be best able to discover my clues. To show how these clues can be discovered and used as guides to the apprehension of reality, as well as to show what I mean by codification, I shall present at first concrete material from the field of language.

That a word is not the reality, not the thing which it represents, has long been a commonplace to all of us. The thing which I hold in my hand as I write, *is* not a pencil; I *call* it a pencil. And it remains the same whether I call it *pencil, molyvi, Bleistift*, or *siwiqoq*. These words are different sound-complexes applied to the same reality; but is the difference merely one of sound-complex? Do they refer to the same *perceived* reality? *Pencil* originally meant little tail; it delimited and named the reality according to form. *Molyvi* means lead and refers to the writing element. *Bleistift* refers both to the form and to the writing-element. *Siwiqoq* means painting-stick and refers to observed function and form. Each culture has phrased the reality differently. To say that *pencil*, for example, applies primarily to form is no idle etymologic statement. When we use this word metaphorically, we refer neither to writing element nor to function, but to form alone: we speak of a pencil of light, or a styptic pencil.

When I used the four words for this object, we all knew what reality was referred to; we knew the meaning of the word. We could visualize the object in my hand, and the words all delimited it in the same way; for example, none of them implied that it was a continuation of my fist. But the student of ethnography often has to deal with words which punctuate reality into different phrasings from the ones with which he is familiar. Let us take, for instance, the words for "brother" and "sister." We go to the islands of Ontong Java to study the kinship system. We ask our informant what he calls his sister and he says *ave*; he calls his brother *kainga*. So we equate *ave* with "sister" and *kainga* with "brother." By way of checking our information we ask the sister what she calls her brother; it turns out that for her, *ave* is "brother," not "sister" as we were led to expect; and that it is her sister whom she calls *kainga*.

The same reality, the same actual kinship is present there as with us; but we have chosen a different aspect for naming. We are prepared to account for this; we say that both cultures name according to what we would call a certain type of blood relationship; but whereas we make reference to absolute sex, they refer to relative sex. Further inquiry, however, discloses that in this, also, we are wrong. Because in our own culture we name relatives according to formal definition and biologic relationship, we have thought that this formulation represents reality; and we have tried to understand the Ontong Javanese relationship terms according to these distinctions which, we believe, are given in nature. But the Ontong Javanese classifies relatives according to a different aspect of reality, differently punctuated. And because of this, he applies *kainga* as well to a wife's sister and a husband's brother; to a man's brother's wife and a woman's sister's husband, as well as to a number of other individuals.

Neither sex nor blood relationship, then, can be basic to this term. The Ontong Javanese name according to their everyday behavior and experience, not according to formal definition. A man shares the ordinary details of his living with his brothers and their wives for a large part of the year; he sleeps in the same large room; he eats with them, he jokes and works around the house with them; the rest of the year he spends with his wife's sisters and their husbands, in the same easy companionship. All these individuals are *kainga* to one another. The *ave*, on the other hand, names a behavior of great strain and propriety; it is based originally upon the relative sex of siblings, yes, but it does not signify biologic fact alone. It names a social relationship, a behavior, an emotional tone. *Ave* can never spend their adult life together, except on rare and temporary occasions. They can never be under the same roof alone together, cannot chat at ease together, cannot refer even distantly to sex in the presence of each other, not even to one's sweetheart or spouse; more than that, everyone else must be circumspect when the *ave* of someone of the group is present. The *ave* relationship also carries special obligations toward a female *ave* and her children. *Kainga* means a relationship of ease, full of shared living, of informality, gaiety; *ave* names one of formality, prohibition, strain.

These two cultures, theirs and our own, have phrased and formulated social reality in completely different ways, and have given their formulalation different names. The word is merely the name of this specific cultural phrasing. From this one instance we might formulate the hypothesis—a very tentative one—that among the Ontong Javanese names describe emotive experiences, not observed forms or functions. But we cannot accept this as fact, unless further investigation shows it to be implicit in the rest of their patterned behavior, in their vocabulary and the morphology of their language, in their ritual and their other organized activity. . . .

I have discussed at length the diversity of codification of reality in general, because it is the foundation of the specific study which I am about to present. I shall speak of the formulation of experienced reality among the Trobriand Islanders in comparison to our own; I shall speak of the nature of expectancy, of motivation, of satisfaction, as based upon a reality which is differently apprehended and experienced in two different societies; which is, in fact, for each, a different reality. The Trobriand Islanders were studied by the late Bronislaw Malinowski (1923, 1929, 1935), who has given us the rich and circumstantial material about them which has made this study possible. I have given a detailed presentation of some implications of their language elsewhere (1940, 1949); but since it was in their language that I first noticed the absence of lineality, which led me to this study, I shall give here a summary of the implications of the language.

A Trobriand word refers to a self-contained concept. What we consider an attribute of a predicate, is to the Trobriander an ingredient. Where I would say, for example, "A good gardener," or "The gardener is good," the Trobriand word would include both "gardener" and "goodness"; if the gardener loses the goodness, he has lost a defining ingredient, he is something else, and he is named by means of a completely different word. A taytu (a species of yam) contains a certain degree of ripeness, bigness, roundedness, etc.; without one of these defining ingredients, it is something else, perhaps a *bwanawa* or a *yowana*. There are no adjectives in the language; the rare words dealing with qualities are substantivized. The term *to be* does not occur; it is used neither attributively nor existentially, since existence itself is contained; it is an ingredient of being.

Events and objects are self-contained points in another respect; there is a series of beings, but no becoming. There is no temporal connection between objects. The taytu always remains itself; it does not *become* over-ripe; over-ripeness is an ingredient of another, a different being. At some point, the taytu *turns into a yowana*, which contains over-ripeness. And the yowana, over-ripe as it is, does not put forth shoots, does not *become* a sprouting yowana. When sprouts appear, it ceases to be itself; in its place appears a *silasata*. Neither is there a temporal connection made—or, according to our own premises, perceived—between events; in fact, temporality is meaningless. There are no tenses, no linguistic distinction between past or present. There is no arrangement of activities or events into means and ends, no causal or teleologic relationships. What we consider a causal relationship in a sequence of connected events, is to the Trobriander an ingredient of a patterned whole. He names this ingredient *u'ula*.

There is no automatic relating of any kind in the language. Except for the rarely used verbal it-differents and it-sames, there are no terms of comparison whatever. And we find in an analysis of behavior that the standard for behavior and of evaluation is non-comparative.

These implications of the linguistic material suggest to my mind an absence of axiomatic lineal connection between events or objects in the Trobriand apprehension of reality, and this implication, as I shall attempt to show below, is reinforced in their definition of activity. In our own culture, the line is so basic, that we take it for granted, as given in reality. We see it in visible nature, between material points, and we see it between metaphorical points such as days or acts. It underlies not only our thinking, but also our aesthetic apprehension of the given; it is basic to the emotional climax which has so much value for us, and, in fact, to the meaning of life itself. In our thinking about personality and character, we have taken for granted the presence of the line.

In our academic work, we are constantly acting in terms of an implied line. When we speak of *ap*plying an *at*tribute, for example, we visualize the process as lineal, coming from the outside. If I make a picture of an apple on the board, and want to show that one side is green and the other red I connect these attributes with the pictured apple by means of lines, as a matter of course; how else would I do it? When I organize my data, I *draw* conclusions *from* them. I *trace* a relationship between my facts. I describe a pattern as a *web* of relationships. Look at a lecturer who makes use of gestures; he is constantly making lineal connections in the air. And a teacher with chalk in hand will be drawing lines on the board whether he be a psychologist, a historian, or a paleontologist.

Preoccupation with social facts merely as self-contained facts is mere antiquarianism. In my field, a student of this sort would be an amateur or a dilettante, not an anthropologist. To be an anthropologist, he can arrange his facts in an upward slanting line, in a *unilinear* or *multilinear course* of development; or in *parallel lines* or *converging lines*. Or he may arrange them geographically, with *lines* of diffusion connecting them; or schematically, using *concentric circles*. Or at least, he must indicate what his study *leads to*, what new insights we can *draw from* it. To be accorded status, he must use the guiding line as basic.

The line is found or presupposed in most of our scientific work. It is present in the *induction* and the *deduction* of science and logic. It is present in the philosopher's phrasing of means and ends as lineally connected. Our statistical facts are presented lineally as a *graph* or reduced to a normal *curve*. And all of us, I think, would be lost without our *diagrams*. We *trace* a historical development; we *follow the course* of history and evolution *down* to the present and *up from* the ape; and it is interesting to note, in passing, that whereas both evolution and history are lineal, the first goes up the blackboard, the second goes down.

Our psychologists picture motivation as external, connected with the act through a line, or, more recently, entering the organism through a lineal channel and emerging transformed, again lineally, as response. I have seen lineal pictures of nervous impulses and heartbeats, and with them I have seen pictured lineally a second of time. These were photographs, you will say, of existing fact, of reality; a proof that the line is present in reality. But I am not convinced, perhaps due to my ignorance of mechanics, that we have not created our recording instruments in such a way that they have to picture time and motion, light and sound, heartbeats and nerve impulses lineally, on the unquestioned assumption of the line as axiomatic. The line is omnipresent and inescapable, and so we are incapable of questioning the reality of its presence.

When we see a *line* of trees, or a *circle* of stones, we assume the presence of a connecting line which is not actually visible. And we assume it metaphorically when we follow a *line* of thought, a *course* of action or the *direction* of an argument; when we *bridge* a gap in the conversation, or speak of the *span* of life or of teaching a *course*, or lament our *interrupted career*. We make children's embroidery cards and puzzle cards on this assumption; our performance tests and even our tests for sanity often assume that the line is present in nature and, at most, to be discovered or given visual existence.

But is the line present in reality? Malinowski, writing for members of our culture and using idiom which would be comprehensible to them, described the Trobriand village as follows: "Concentrically with the circular row of yam houses there runs a ring of dwelling huts." He saw, or at any rate, he represented the village as two circles. But in the texts which he recorded, we find that the Trobrianders at no time mention circles or rings or even rows when they refer to their villages. Any word which they use to refer to a village, such as *a* or *this*, is prefixed by the substantival element *kway* which means *bump* or *aggregate of bumps*.

This is the element which they use when they refer to a pimple or a bulky rash; or to canoes loaded with yams. In their terms, a village is an aggregate of bumps; are they blind to the circles? Or did Malinowski create the circles himself, out of his cultural axiom?

Again, for us as well as in Malinowski's description of the Trobrianders, which was written necessarily in terms meaningful to us, all effective activity is certainly not a haphazard aggregate of acts, but a lineally planned series of acts leading to an envisioned end. Their gardening with all its specialized activities, both technical and magical, leading to a rich harvest; their *kula* involving the cutting down of trees, the communal dragging of the tree to the beach, the rebuilding or building of large sea-worthy canoes, the provisioning, the magical and ceremonial activities involved—surely all these can be carried through only if they are lineally conceived.

But the Trobrianders do not describe their activity lineally; they do no dynamic relating of acts; they do not use even so innocuous a connective as *and*. Here is part of a description of the planting of coconut: "Thou-approach-there coconut thou-bring-here-we-plant-coconut thou-go thou-plant our coconut. This-here it-emerge sprout. We-push-away this we-push-away this-other coconut-husk-fiber together sprout it-sit together root." We who are accustomed to seek lineal continuity, cannot help supplying it as we read this; but the continuity is not given in the Trobriand text; and all Trobriand speech, according to Malinowski, is "jerky," given in points, not in connecting lines. The only connective I know of in Trobriand is the *pela* which I mentioned above; a kind of preposition which also means "to jump."

I am not maintaining here that the Trobrianders cannot see continuity; rather that lineal connection is not automatically made by them, as a matter of course. At Malinowski's persistent questioning, for example, they did attempt to explain their activities in terms of cause or motivation, by stating possible "results" of uncooperative action. But Malinowski found their answers confused, self-contradictory, inconsistent; their preferred answer was, "It was ordained of old"— pointing to an ingredient value of the act instead of giving an explanation based on lineal connection.

And when they were not trying to find answers to leading questions, the Trobrianders made no such connection in their speech. They assumed, for example, that the validity of a magical spell lay, not in its results, not in proof, but in its very being; in the appropriateness of its inheritance, in its place within the patterned activity, in its being performed by the appropriate person, in its realization of its mythical basis.

To seek validity through proof was foreign to their thinking, yet they attempted to do so at the ethnographer's request. I should add here that their names for constellations imply that here they do see lineal figures; I cannot investigate the significance of this, as I have no contextual material. At any rate, I would like to emphasize that, even if the Trobriander does occasionally supply connecting lines between points, his perception and experience do not automatically fall into a lineal framework.

The fact remains that Trobrianders embark on, what is certainly for us, a series of acts, which "must require" planning and purposiveness. They engage in acts of gift-giving and gift-receiving which we can certainly see as an exchange of gifts if we want to. When we plot their journeys, we find that they do go from point to point, they do navigate a course, whether they say so or not. Do they merely refrain from giving linguistic expression to something which they actually recognize in nature? On the nonlinguistic level, do they act on an assumption of a lineality which is given no place in their linguistic formulation?

I believe that, where valued activity is concerned, the Trobrianders do not act on an assumption of lineality at any level. There is organization or rather coherence in their acts because Trobriand activity is patterned activity. One act within this pattern brings into existence a pre-ordained cluster of acts. Perhaps one might find a parallel in our culture in the making of a sweater. When I embark on knitting one, the ribbing at the bottom does not *cause* the making of the neckline, nor of the sleeves or the armholes; and it is not part of a lineal series of acts. Rather it is an indispensable part of a patterned activity which includes all these other acts. Again, when I choose a dress pattern, the acts involved in the making of the dress are already present for me. They are embedded in the pattern which I have chosen.

In this same way, I believe, can be seen the Trobriand insistence that though intercourse is a necessary preliminary to conception, it is not the cause of conception. There are a number of acts in the pattern of procreating; one is intercourse, another the entrance of the spirit of a dead Trobriander into the womb. However, there is a further point here. The Trobrianders, when pressed by the ethnographer or teased by the neighboring Dobuans, showed signs of intense embarrassment, giving the impression that they were trying to maintain unquestioningly a stand in which they had to believe. This, I think, is because pattern is truth and value for them; in fact, acts and being derive value from the embedding pattern.

So the question of the perception of a line remains. It is because they find value in pattern that the Trobrianders act according to nonlineal pattern; not because they cannot perceive lineality.

But all Trobriand activity does not contain value; and when it does not, it assumes lineality, and is utterly despicable. For example, the pattern of sexual intercourse includes the giving of a gift from the boy to the girl; but if a boy gives a gift so as to win the girl's favor, he is despised. Again, the kula pattern includes the eventual reception of a gift from the original recipient; the pattern is such that it keeps the acts physically and temporally completely disparate. In spite of this, however, some men are accused of giving gifts as an inducement to their kula partner to give them a specially good kula gift. Such men are labeled with the vile phrase: he barters. But this means that, unvalued and despised, lineal behavior does exist. In fact, there are villages in the interior whose inhabitants live mainly by bartering manufactured articles for yams. The inhabitants of Omarakana, about whom Malinowski's work and this study are mainly concerned, will barter with them, but consider them pariahs.

This is to say that it is probable that the Trobrianders experience reality in nonlinear pattern because this is the valued reality; and that they are capable of experiencing lineally, when value is absent or destroyed. It is not to say, however, that this in itself means that lineality is given, is present in nature, and that pattern is not. Our own insistence on the line, such as lineal causality, for example, is also often based on unquestioned belief or value. To return to the subject of procreation, the husband in our culture, who has long hoped, and tried in vain, to beget children, will nevertheless maintain that intercourse causes conception; perhaps with the same stubbornness and embarrassment which the Trobrianders exhibited when maintaining the opposite.

The line in our culture not only connects, but it moves. And as we think of a line as moving from point to point, connecting one to the other, so we conceive of roads as *running from* locality to locality. A Trobriander does not speak of roads either connecting two points, or as *running from* point *to* point. His paths are self-contained, named as independent units; they are not *to* and *from*, they are *at*. And he himself is *at*; he has no equivalent for our *to* or *from*. There is, for instance, the myth of Tudava, who goes—in our view—from village to village and from island to island planting and offering yams. The Trobriand text puts it this way: "Kitava it-shine village already (i.e. completed) he-is-over. 'I-sail I-go Iwa'; Iwa he-anchor he-go ashore . . . He-sail Digumenu . . . They-drive (him off) . . . he-go Kwaywata." Point after point is enumerated, but his sailing from and to is given as a discrete event. In our view, he is actually following a southeasterly course, more or less; but this is not given as course or line, and no directions are even mentioned. In fact, in the several texts referring to journeyings in the Archipelago, no words occur for the cardinal directions. In sailing, the "following" winds are named according to where they are *at*, the place where they strike the canoe, such as wind-striking-the-outrigger-beam; not according to where they *come from*. Otherwise, we find names for the southwest wind (youyo), and the northwest wind (bombatu), but these are merely substantival names which have nothing to do with direction; names for kinds of wind.

When a member of our society gives an unemotional description of a person, he follows an imaginary line, usually downward: from head to foot, from tip to toe, from hair to chin. The Navaho do the opposite, following a line upward. The Trobriander follows no line, at least none that I can see. "My head boils," says a kula spell; and it goes on to enumerate the parts of the head as follows: nose, occiput, tongue, larynx, speech, mouth. Another spell casting a protective fog, runs as follows: "I befog the hand, I befog the foot, I befog the head, I befog the shoulders . . ." There is a magic formula where we do recognize a line, but it is one which Malinowski did not record verbatim at the time, but which he put down later from memory; and it is not improbable that his memory edited the formula according to the lineality of his culture.

When the Trobriander enumerates the parts of a canoe, he does not follow any recognizable lineal order: "Mist . . . surround me my mast . . . the nose of my canoe . . . my sail . . . my steering oar . . . my canoe-gunwale . . . my canoe-bottom . . . my prow . . . my rib . . . my threading-stick . . . my prow-board . . . my transverse stick . . . my canoe-side."

Malinowski diagrams the garden site as a square piece of land sub-divided into squares; the Trobrianders refer to it in the same terms as those which they use in referring to a village—a bulky object or an aggregate of bumps. When the plots in the garden site are apportioned to the gardeners, the named plots are assigned by name, the others by location along each named side of the garden. After this, the inner plots, the "belly" of the garden, are apportioned. Following along a physical rim is a procedure which we find elsewhere also. In a spell naming villages on the main island, there is a long list of villages which lie along the coast northward, then westward around the island, then south. To us, of course, this is lineal order. But we have no indication that the Trobrianders see other than geographical location, point after point, as they move over a physically continuous area; the line as a guide to procedure is not necessarily implied. No terms are used here which might be taken as an implication of continuity; no "along the coast" or "around" or "northward."

When we in our culture deal with events or experiences of the self, we use the line as guide for various reasons, two of which I shall take up here. First, we feel we must arrange events chronologically in a lineal order; how else could our historians discover the causes of a war or a revolution or a defeat? Among the Trobrianders, what corresponds to our history is an aggregate of anecdotes, that is, unconnected points, told without respect to chronological sequence, or development, or causal relationship; with no grammatical distinction made between words referring to past events, or to present or contemplated ones. And in telling an anecdote, they take no care that a temporal sequence should be followed. For instance, they said to Malinowski, "They-eat-taro, they-spew-taro, they-disgusted-taro"; but if time, as we believe, is a moving line, then the revulsion came first in time, the vomiting was the result, coming afterward. Again, they say, "This-here . . . ripes . . . falls-down truly gives-birth . . . sits seed in belly-his"; but certainly the seed is there first, and the birth follows in time, if time is lineal.

Secondly, we arrange events and objects in a sequence which is climactic, in size and intensity, in emotional meaning, or according to some other principle. We often arrange events from earlier to later, not because we are interested in historical causation, but because the present is the climax of our history. But when the Trobriander relates happenings, there is no developmental arrangement, no building up of emotional tone. His stories have no plot, no lineal development, no climax. And when he repeats his garden spell, his list is neither climactic, nor anticlimactic; it sounds merely untidy to us:

> The belly of my garden lifts
> The belly of my garden rises
> The belly of my garden reclines
> The belly of my garden is-a-bushhen's-nest-in-lifting
> The belly of my garden is-an-anthill
> The belly of my garden lifts-bends
> The belly of my garden is-an-ironwood-tree-in-lifting
> The belly of my garden lies-down
> The belly of my garden burgeons.

When the Trobrianders set out on their great ceremonial kula expedition, they follow a pre-established order. First comes the canoe of the Tolab wage, an obscure subclan. Next come the canoes of the great chiefs. But this is not climactic; after the great chiefs come the commoners. The order derives meaning not from lineal sequence, but from correspondence with a present, experienced, meaningful pattern, which is the recreation or realization of the mythical pattern; that which has been ordained of old and is forever. Its meaning does not lie in an item-to-item relationship, but in fitness, in the repetition of an established unit.

An ordering of this sort gives members of our society a certain esthetic dysphoria except when, through deliberate training, we learn to go beyond our cultural expectation; or, when we are too young to have taken on the phrasings of our culture. When we manipulate objects naively, we arrange them on some climactic lineal principle. Think of a college commencement, with the faculty arranged in order of rank or length of tenure or other mark of importance; with the students arranged according to increasing physical height, from shortest to tallest, actually the one absolutely irrelevant principle as regards the completion of their college education, which is the occasion for the celebration. Even when the sophisticated avoid this principle, they are not unconscious of it; they are deliberately avoiding something which is there.

And our arrangement of history, when we ourselves are personally involved, is mainly climactic. My great grandmother sewed by candle light, my grandmother used a kerosene lamp, my mother did her studying by gaslight, I did it by a naked electric ceiling light, and my children have diffused fluorescent lighting. This is progress; this is the meaningful sequence. To the Trobriander, climax in history is abominable, a denial of all good, since it would imply not only the presence of change, but also that change increases the good; but to him value lies in sameness, in repeated pattern, in the incorporation of all time within the same point. What is good in life is exact identity with all past Trobriand experience, and all mythical experience.

There is no boundary between past Trobriand existence and the present; he can indicate that an action is completed, but this does not mean that the action is past; it may be completed and present or timeless. Where we would say "Many years ago" and use the past tense, the Trobriander will say, "In my father's childhood" and use non-temporal verbs; he places the event situationally, not temporally. Past, present, and future are presented linguistically as the same, are present in his existence, and sameness with what we call the past and with myth, represents value to the Trobriander. Where we see a developmental line, the Trobriander sees a point, at most a swelling in value. Where we find pleasure and satisfaction in moving away from the point, in change as variety or progress, the Trobriander finds it in the repetition of the known, in maintaining the point; that is, in what we call monotony.

Esthetic validity, dignity, and value come to the Trobriander not through arrangement into a climactic line, but rather in the undisturbed incorporations of the events within their original, nonlineal order. The only history which has meaning for him is that which evokes the value of the point, or which, in the repetition, swells the value of the point. For example, every occasion in which a kula object participates becomes an ingredient of its being and swells its value; all these occasions are enumerated with great satisfaction, but the lineal course of the traveling kula object is not important.

As we see our history climactically, so do we plan future experiences climactically, leading up to future satisfaction or meaning. Who but a very young child would think of starting a meal with strawberry short cake and ending it with spinach? We have come to identify the end of the meal with the height of satisfaction, and we identify semantically the words dessert and reward, only because of the similarity of their position in a climactic line. The Trobriand meal has no dessert, no line, no climax. The special bit, the relish, is eaten *with* the staple food; it is not something to "look *forward to*," while disposing of a meaningless staple.

None of the Trobriand activities is fitted into a climactic line. There is no job, no labor, no drudgery which finds its reward outside the act. All work contains its own satisfaction. We cannot speak of S—R here, as all action contains its own immanent "stimulus." The present is not a means to future satisfaction, but good in itself, as the future is also good in itself; neither better nor worse, neither climactic nor anticlimatic, in fact, not lineally connected nor removed.

It follows that the present is not evaulated in terms of its place within a course of action leading upward to a worthy end. In our culture, we can rarely evaluate the present in itself. I tell you that Sally is selling notions at Woolworth's, but this in itself means nothing. It acquires some meaning when I add that she has recently graduated from Vassar. However, I go on to tell you that she has been assistant editor of *Vogue*, next a nursemaid, a charwoman, a public school teacher. But this is a mere jumble; it makes no sense and has no meaning, because the series leads to nothing. You cannot relate one job to another, and you are unable to see them discretely simply as part of her being. However, I now add that she is gathering material for a book on the working mother. Now all this falls in line, it makes sense in terms of a career. Now her job is good and it makes her happy, because it is part of a planned climactic line leading to more pay, increased recognition, higher rank. There was a story in a magazine about the college girl who fell in love with the milkman one summer; the reader felt tense until it was discovered that this was just a summer job, that it was only a means for the continuation of the man's education in the Columbia Law School. Our evaluation of happiness and unhappiness is bound with this motion along an envisioned line leading to a desired end. In the fulfillment of this course or career—not in the fulfillment of the self as point—do we find value. Our conception of freedom rests on the principle of non-interference with this moving line, non-interruption of the intended course of action.

It is difficult to tell whether climax is given in experience at all, or whether it is always imposed on the given. At a time when progress and evolution were assumed to be implicit in nature, our musicians and writers gave us climactic works. Nowadays, our more reflective art does not present experience climactically. Then, is emotion itself climactic? Climax, for us, evokes "thrill" or "drama." But we have cultures, like the Tikopia, where life is lived, to our perception, on an even emotive plane without thrill or climax. Experiences which "we know to be" climactic, are described without climax by them. For example, they, as well as the Trobrianders, described intercourse as an aggregate of pleasurable experiences. But Malinowski is disturbed by this; he cannot place the erotic kiss in Triobriand experience, since it has no climactic function.

In our culture, childbearing is climactic. Pregnancy is represented by the usual obstetrician as an uncomfortable means to a dramatic end. For most women, all intensity of natural physical experience is nowadays removed from the actual birth itself; but the approach of birth nevertheless is a period of mounting tension, and drama is supplied by the intensive social recognition of the event, the dramatic accumulation of gifts, flowers, telegrams. A pregnancy is not formally announced since, if it does not eventuate in birth, it has failed to achieve its end; and failure to reach the climax brings shame. In its later stages it may be marked with a shower; but the shower looks forward to the birth, it does not celebrate the pregnancy itself. Among the Trobrianders, pregnancy has meaning in itself, as a state of being. At a first pregnancy, there is a long ceremonial involving "preparatory" work on the part of many people, which merely celebrates the pregnancy. It does not anchor the baby, it does not *have as its purpose* a more comfortable time during the pregnancy, it does not *lead to* an easier birth or a healthy baby. It makes the woman's skin white, and makes her be at her most beautiful; yet this *leads* to nothing, since she must not attract men, not even her own husband.

Are we then right in accepting without question the presence of a line in reality? Are we in a position to say with assurance that the Trobrianders are wrong and we are right? Much of our present-day thinking, and much of our evaluation, are based on the premise of the line and of the line as good. Students have been refused admittance to college because the autobiographic sketch accompanying their application showed absence of the line; they lacked purposefulness and ability to plan; they were inadequate as to character as well as intellectually. Our conception of personality formation, our stress on the significance of success and failure and of frustration in general, is based on the axiomatically postulated line. Yet can there be blocking without presupposed lineal motion or effort? If I walk along a path because I like the country, or if it is not important to get to a particular point at a particular time, then the insuperable puddle from the morning's shower is not frustrating; I throw stones into it and watch the ripples, and then choose another path. If the undertaking is of value in itself, a point good in itself, and not because it leads to something, then failure has no symbolic meaning; it merely results in no cake for supper, or less money in the family budget; it is not personally destructive. But failure is devastating in our culture, because it is not failure of the undertaking alone; it is the moving, becoming, lineally conceived self which has failed.

Ethnographers have occasionally remarked that the people whom they studied showed no annoyance when interrupted. Is this an indication of mild temper, or might it be the case that they were not interrupted at all, as there was no expectation of linear continuity? Such questions are new in anthropology and most ethnographers therefore never thought of recording material which would answer them. However, we do have enough material to make us question the line as basic to all experience; whether it is actually present in given reality or not, it is not always present in experienced reality. We cannot even take it for granted as existing among those members of our society who are not completely or naively steeped in their culture, such as many of our artists, for example. And we should be very careful, in studying other cultures, to avoid the unexamined assumption that their actions are based on the predication of a lineal reality.

11.

But Why Did They Sit on the King's Right in the First Place?

G. William Domhoff

Folklore has it that the "Right" is good and the "Left" bad in Western thinking, particularly political thinking, because of the seating arrangements in the French National Assembly of the eighteenth century—the nobles sitting on the king's right, the then-upstart capitalists sitting on his left.* However, Theodore Thass-Thienemann (1955), an expert on psycholinguistics, has shown that this right–good, left–bad polarization has been present for a very long time in the entire Indo-European language family, as well as in Hungarian, a non-Indo-European language. Further, psychologist Sylvan Tomkins (1964a, b) has shown that the

Reprinted by permission from *Psychoanalytic Review*, 56 (1969–70), 596–596.

*For the "official" version of the origin of left and right as political terms see the unabridged *Oxford English Dictionary*.

underlying assumptions dividing the political Left and Right are also the basis for age-old ideological disputes in mathematics, philosophy, science, and child-rearing. The work of these two men suggests that the real problem is why the nobles supposedly sat on the king's right in the first place.

A simple explanation for the Left–Right dichotomy seems to follow from an inborn bilaterality, for all known cultures are righthanded to varying degrees. It would thus be natural that the less useful hand would be considered "bad" and that "good" and "bad" could by symbolized by Right and Left. However, according to those who have studied handedness, the predominance of righthandedness is not an obvious given to be accounted for genetically. [Hildreth, 1949] concludes from her exhaustive survey that "righthandedness is a cultural and social convention to which most people are trained and find it expedient to conform . . . In an unbiased world, lefthandedness would be as common as righthandedness, for the play of chance factors would be equal for the two sides."

Thus, it may be that the good–bad distinction has contributed to the development of handedness rather than the other way around, which is the usually-assumed relationship. When one reads reports of tribes that bandage left arms so children cannot use them, not to mention reports of the dexterity of both hands in many preschoolers, the psychological explanation for bilaterality takes on a degree of plausibility. Unfortunately, psychological explanations have not gone beyond such static factors as "negativism," "conformity," and "rebelliousness." . . .

The most complete summary of historical and anthropological findings on Left and Right, published in French some 58 or so years ago, has only recently been translated into English (Hertz, 1960). While some of the material is "out of date," it in no way contradicts more recent studies. This admirable survey gives innumerable accounts of left–right dichotomies around the world, from the Australian aborigines who hold the "male" stick in the right hand and the "female" stick in the left hand to the American Indians whose sign language uses the left hand for such concepts as "weak" and "cowardly" to the African natives who fear the poison under their neighbor's left thumbnail. Perhaps the most extreme tribe on the left–right polarization is the Maori of New Zealand, who associate the Left with the bad, the dark, the profane, the feminine, the night, homosexuality, and death, while the polar opposites of these concepts are associated with the Right. Data are equally abundant from this survey to verify the same distinctions in our own history: witches are lefthanded; one of the earliest signs of a saint is that he refuses the left breast; girls come from the semen of the left testicle, boys from the semen of the right testicle; rings are worn on the left hand to protect the "weaker" side.

Recent anthropological research supports the older studies. The Hindus use only the left hand for dirty tasks and calls of nature. The right hand is used to touch any part of the body above the navel, the left hand any part below the navel. American Mohave Indians believe it is bad to be lefthanded because the left hand is used for toilet functions. Furthermore, for the Mohave, the left hand represents the maternal side of the family, the right hand the paternal side. American Chippewa myths portray the Left as bad, the Right as good. Bedouin Arabs have a whole left–right cosmology. Women are bad—they live on the left side of the tent. Men are good—they live on the right side of the tent. Finally, a tribe of African Bantu still equate Left with feminine and other undesirable qualities, the Right with maleness and its wonderful accouterments. *

The evidence presented thus far suggests that many nonliterate peoples, our ancestors, . . . impute similar connotations to the Left and the Right. But, asks the skeptic, is this dichotomy something that is present in the thinking of a majority of healthy, well-educated Americans? There is a technique for answering this question. It is called the semantic differential, and it measures the meaning of a word, concept, or image by having the person rate it on a series of scales of word opposites (Osgood, Suci, and Tannenbaum, 1957). For example, each person taking the test has to mark an X in the space on the following questionnaire that best captures the strength of the relationship between one or the other of the following opposites and the concept at the top of the questionnaire:

Left

Good		:	:	:	:	: X :	Bad
Female	X	:	:	:	:	:	Male
Strong		:	:	:	:	: X	Weak

Using this semantic differential technique, it was a simple matter to have American subjects rate Left and Right on the polarizations sug-

---

*Our "modern-day" anthropological evidence on left and right comes from several different sources. On the Hindus see Berkeley-Hill, (1921), pp. 317–319. On the Mohave see Devereux (1951), pp. 400, 401 and 405. On the Chippewa see Barnouw's reports of his own findings in his textbook (1963). Our knowledge of the extensive left-right mythology of the Arabs comes from personal conversations with our colleague Richard Randolph, an anthropologist who has done considerable original field work with the Arabs. The Bantu tribe referred to is discussed by Beidleman.

gested by the historical and anthropological record. The scales were given to college freshmen and sophomores who did not know the purpose of the study. Eighty rated only the concept "Right," 78 rated only the concept "Left." Details and statistics aside, we can make a long story short by saying the students' ratings were overwhelmingly in agreement with the anthropological and psycholinguistic literature from which the scales derived.

The Left was characterized as bad, dark, profane, female, unclean, night, west, curved, limp, homosexual, weak, mysterious, low, ugly, black, incorrect, and death, while the Right meant just the opposite— good, light, sacred, male, clean, day, east, straight, erect, heterosexual, strong, commonplace, high, beautiful, white, correct, and life. Further, our study of school children from the third through the ninth grades showed similar results for the Right on the eight semantic differential scales utilized, although it was not until the sixth grade that the Left became extremely negative on most dimensions. However, when the question "Does the word 'Left' remind you of Good or Bad?" was asked verbally so the test could be extended to first graders, a significant and age-increasing majority of the children from the first grade through the ninth grade answered that the Left reminded them of Bad. . . .

Let us turn briefly to the problem of the sacred, which is closely related, we believe, to dualism and Left–Right. The Left half of dualism does not return merely in dreams, thinking, and symptoms. Its territory is the "mysterious" and "taboo" that can be found in any tribe or society. Indeed, we believe that "the sacred" and "the unconscious" are practically one and the same, for that which takes place in the sacred world of mysteries and rituals is but an institutionalized "return of the repressed." Thus it is first of all in the study of religions, as both Freud and Norman O. Brown (1959) tell us, that we must stalk the artifacts of the unconscious. The dynamics that create dualistic thinking also create the taboo and the mysterious.

If we now return to our earlier comments on handedness, we can see how possible it is that dichotomous thinking may have fastened on to the slight genetic tendency for right bilaterality and increased that tendency by investing it with the good–bad, active–passive, and potent– castrated polarities that pervade so much of our thinking. Reinforced by the functional need for specialization due to tool use, and embedded in language and mythology, these infantile psychodynamics helped to select for hereditary righthandedness and to convert the ambidextrous and uncommitted. It became a righthanded world, with the percentage of lefthanders increasing only during wars, depressions, and Left (permissive) epochs.*

Perhaps we finally can answer the question of why the nobles sat on the king's right in the first place. They were identified with the King–Father and his rightist values. They were part of the fatherhood—the ruling class. On the other hand, the capitalists and dissident intellectuals were on the left—a brotherly grouping espousing brotherhood and mother-derived values—because they were at that time the rebellious young upstarts who had not developed an identification with the patriarchal trappings of the French monarchy.

---

*The source for the changes in per cent of lefthanders during wars and depressions is the *New York Times*, August 2, 1959: "Lefthanded find handicap grows." We learned about it in one of the few child psychology textbooks that devotes more than a line or two to handedness (Hurlock 1964, pp. 187–188). Only 2.6 per cent of a sample of college graduates born before 1918 were lefthanded, but the percent for those born between 1918 and 1921 was 8.3. In a sample born between 1929 and 1931 the per cent of lefties was back down to 5.7, but it was an astounding 17.64 for the peak depression year of 1932. The average for the depression years was a very high 9.2. We think per cent of lefthanders, along with length of hair, are two good indicators of "left" and "right" historical periods, or "matrist" and "patrist" periods (*see* Taylor, 1954).

III.

THE CONSTRUCTION OF "ORDINARY" CONSCIOUSNESS

Introduction

We often feel that our own personal consciousness *is* the external world, that we are aware of everything that exists "out there." But obviously we are not thus aware, even at the grossest physical level, since our very physiological receptors are evolved to discard information. We have no sense for high-frequency electromagnetic waves, for instance; yet they exist and are present all around us, carrying the information of television and radio. Most who have thought about the question agree: awareness is selective and limited, and is ultimately a construction. Here, William James and Aldous Huxley write in the traditional philosophical manner on these matters, providing useful metaphors for an over-all analysis of consciousness and its limitations. For James we are as sculptors, carving one unique statue out of marble. He also provides a perspective on consciousness which has not been fully researched by more modern scientists: that consciousness is a continuous stream, ever-changing, ever-moving, never the same from moment to moment.

The brief extract from Aldous Huxley's *The Doors of Perception* most elegantly argues why our personal consciousness must be limited—the constraints of individual biological survival have made it so. In the book from which this is taken, Huxley goes on to note that psychedelic drugs, such as mescalin, can alter the selective and restrictive process of personal consciousness. Accounts of drug effects are not included here, but the interested reader can refer to Tart's *Altered States of Consciousness* and to Castaneda's *The Teachings of Don Juan, A Separate Reality*, and *Journey to Ixtlan*. As we will consider later in the book, meditation and other techniques of the esoteric psychologies are attempts to circumvent the reducing valve, which Huxley, most interestingly, identifies with language.

These selections are followed by two papers of the "transactionalists," one of contemporary psychology's most sophisticated analyses of consciousness. The first, by Ittelson and Kilpatrick, contains a set of compelling illusions which indicate that we continuously "bet" on the nature of reality. In some artful situations, this "bet" can be made apparent to us as we make mistakes. We can then directly experience the effects of our assumptions on consciousness.

The thirteenth-century Sufi poet Jallaludin Rumi wrote "What a piece of bread looks like depends upon whether you are hungry or not." The article by Hastorf and Cantril furthers this point. It concerns a life situation in which two psychologists were able to apply their theoretical knowledge to an ordinary event—a football game. This piece is a high-water mark in contemporary psychology. It employs a clear perspective and is grounded in everyday phenomena. The authors' "transactionalist" approach allows them to view the biases which can affect ordinary awareness and to delineate them in a scientific demonstration.

Such demonstrations as these two articles bode well for a return to a science of consciousness that is as much at home in the precision of the laboratory as in the fabric of everyday life. The closing few paragraphs of Hastorf and Cantril deserve careful reading.

Neisser's article makes clear that similar general principles hold at different levels of the analysis of consciousness. Where James presents the metaphor of a man carving his reality out of a block of stone which contains many other possibilities, and Hastorf and Cantril apply a similar principle to the analysis of a social event, showing that each side constructs its own "reality," Neisser applies the same idea to the quantitative analysis of visual experience. There is no "image" on the retina which we "see." Our visual experience (even at the most basic level) is a *constructive* synthesis, based on past experience, expectation, filtering, and tuning. The eye itself is not a camera, but a selective information-gatherer.

12.

The Stream of Consciousness

William James

We now begin our study of the mind from within. Most books start with sensations, as the simplest mental facts, and proceed synthetically, constructing each higher stage from those below it. But this is abandoning the empirical method of investigation. No one ever had a simple sensation by itself. Consciousness, from our natal day, is of a teeming multiplicity of objects and relations, and what we call simple sensations are results of discriminative attention, pushed often to a very high degree. It is astonishing what havoc is wrought in psychology by admitting at the outset apparently innocent suppositions, that nevertheless contain a flaw. The bad consequences develop themselves later on, and are irremediable, being woven through the whole texture of the work. The notion that sensations, being the simplest things, are the first things to take up in psychology is one of these suppositions. The only thing which psychology

Reprinted from William James, *The Principles of Psychology* (1890), I, 224–290 (Dover, 1950).

has a right to postulate at the outset is the fact of thinking itself, and that must first be taken up and analyzed. If sensations then prove to be amongst the elements of the thinking, we shall be no worse off as respects them than if we had taken them for granted at the start.

The first fact for us, then, as psychologists, is that thinking of some sort goes on. I use the word thinking . . . for every form of consciousness indiscriminately. If we could say in English "it thinks," as we say "it rains" or "it blows," we should be stating the fact most simply and with the minimum of assumption. As we cannot, we must simply say that *thought goes on.* . . .

THOUGHT TENDS TO PERSONAL FORM

When I say *every thought is part of a personal consciousness,* "personal consciousness" is one of the terms in question. Its meaning we know so long as no one asks us to define it, but to give an accurate account of it is the most difficult of philosophic tasks. . . .

In this room—this lecture room, say—there are a multitude of thoughts, yours and mine, some of which cohere mutually, and some not. They are as little each-for-itself and reciprocally independent as they are all-belonging-together. They are neither: no one of them is separate, but each belongs with certain others and with none beside. My thought belongs with my other thoughts, and your thought with your other thoughts. Whether anywhere in the room there be a mere thought, which is nobody's thought, we have no means of ascertaining, for we have no experience of its like. The only states of consciousness that we naturally deal with are found in personal consciousness, minds, selves, concrete particular I's and you's.

Each of these minds keeps its own thoughts to itself. There is no giving or bartering between them. No thought even comes into direct *sight* of a thought in another personal consciousness than its own. Absolute insulation, irreducible pluralism, is the law. It seems as if the elementary psychic fact were not *thought* or *this thought* or *that thought,* but *my thought,* every thought being *owned.* Neither contemporaneity, nor proximity in space, nor similarity of quality and content are able to fuse thoughts together which are sundered by this barrier of belonging to different personal minds. The breaches between such thoughts are the most absolute breaches in nature. Everyone will recognize this to be true, so long as the existence of *something* corresponding to the term "personal mind" is all that is insisted on, without any particular view of its nature being implied. On these terms the personal self rather than the thought might be treated as the immediate datum in psychology. The universal conscious fact is not "feelings and thoughts exist," but "I think" and "I feel." No psychology, at any rate, can question the *existence* of personal selves. The worst a psychology can do is so to interpret the nature of these selves as to rob them of their worth. . . .

THOUGHT IS IN CONSTANT CHANGE

I do not mean necessarily that no one state of mind has any duration—even if true, that would be hard to establish. The change which I have more particularly in view is that which takes place in sensible intervals of time; and the result on which I wish to lay stress is this, that *no state once gone can recur and be identical with what it was before.* . . .

We all recognize as different great classes of our conscious states. Now we are seeing, now hearing; now reasoning, now willing; now recollecting, now expecting; now loving, now hating; and in a hundred other ways we know our minds to be alternately engaged. But all these are complex states. The aim of science is always to reduce complexity to simplicity; and in psychological science we have the celebrated "theory of *ideas*" which, admitting the great difference among each other of what may be called concrete conditions of mind, seeks to show how this is all the resultant effect of variations in the *combination* of certain simple elements of consciousness that always remain the same. These mental atoms or molecules are what Locke called "simple ideas." Some of Locke's successors made out that the only simple ideas were the sensations strictly so called. Which ideas the simple ones may be does not, however, now concern us. It is enough that certain philosophers have thought they could see under the dissolving-view-appearance of the mind elementary facts of *any* sort that remained unchanged amid the flow.

And the view of these philosophers has been called little into question, for our common experience seems at first sight to corroborate it entirely. Are not the sensations we get from the same object, for example, always the same? Does not the same piano-key, struck with the same force, make us hear in the same way? Does not the same grass give us the same feeling of green, the same sky the same feeling of blue, and do we not get the same olfactory sensation no matter how many times we put our nose to the same flask of cologne? It seems a piece of metaphysical sophistry to suggest that we do not; and yet a close attention to the matter shows that *there is no proof that the same bodily sensation is ever got by us twice.*

What is got twice is the same OBJECT. We hear the same *note* over and over again; we see the same *quality* of green, or smell the same objective perfume, or experience the same *species* of pain. The realities, concrete and abstract, physical and ideal, whose permanent existence we believe in, seem to be constantly coming up again before our thought, and lead us, in our carelessness, to suppose that our "ideas" of them are the same ideas. [Later], we shall see how inveterate is our habit of not attending to sensations as subjective facts, but of simply using them as stepping-stones to pass over to the recognition of the realities whose presence they reveal. The grass out of the window now looks to me of the same green in the sun as in the shade, and yet a painter would have to paint one part of it dark brown, another part bright yellow, to give its real sensational effect. We take no heed, as a rule, of the different way in which the same things look and sound and smell at different distances and under different circumstances. The sameness of the *things* is what we are concerned to ascertain; and any sensations that assure us of that will probably be considered in a rough way to be the same with each other. This is what makes off-hand testimony about the subjective identity of different sensations well-nigh worthless as a proof of the fact. The entire history of Sensation is a commentary on our inability to tell whether two sensations received apart are exactly alike. What appeals to our attention far more than the absolute quality or quantity of a given sensation is its *ratio* to whatever other sensations we may have at the same time. When everything is dark a somewhat less dark sensation makes us see an object white. Helmholtz calculates that the white marble painted in a picture representing an architectural view by moonlight is, when seen by daylight, from ten to twenty thousand times brighter than the real moonlit marble would be.

Such a difference as this could never have been *sensibly* learned; it had to be inferred from a series of indirect considerations. There are facts which make us believe that our sensibility is altering all the time, so that the same object cannot easily give us the same sensation over again. The eye's sensibility to light is at its maximum when the eye is first exposed, and blunts itself with surprising rapidity. A long night's sleep will make it see things twice as brightly on wakening, as simple rest by closure will make it see them later in the day. We feel things differently according as we are sleepy or awake, hungry or full, fresh or tired; differently at night and in the morning, differently in summer and in winter, and above all things differently in childhood, manhood, and old age. Yet we never doubt that our feelings reveal the same world, with the same sensible qualities and the same sensible things occupying it. The difference of the sensibility is shown best by the difference of our emotion about the things from one age to another, or when we are in different organic moods. What was bright and exciting becomes weary, flat, and unprofitable. The bird's song is tedious, the breeze is mournful, the sky is sad.

To these indirect presumptions that our sensations, following the mutations of our capacity for feeling, are always undergoing an essential change, must be added another presumption, based on what must happen in the brain. Every sensation corresponds to some cerebral action. For an identical sensation to recur it would have to occur the second time *in an unmodified brain*. But as this, strictly speaking, is a physiological impossibility, so is an unmodified feeling an impossibility; for to every brain-modification, however small, must correspond a change of equal amount in the feeling which the brain subserves.

All this would be true if even sensations came to us pure and single and not combined into "things." Even then we should have to confess that, however we might in ordinary conversation speak of getting the same sensation again, we never in strict theoretic accuracy could do so; and that whatever was true of the river of life, of the river of elementary feeling, it would certainly be true to say, like Heraclitus, that we never descend twice into the same stream.

But if the assumption of "simple ideas of sensation" recurring in immutable shape is so easily shown to be baseless, how much more baseless is the assumption of immutability in the larger masses of our thought!

For there it is obvious and palpable that our state of mind is never precisely the same. Every thought we have of a given fact is, strictly speaking, unique, and only bears a resemblance of kind with our other thoughts of the same fact. When the identical fact recurs, we *must* think of it in a fresh manner, see it under a somewhat different angle, apprehend it in different relations from those in which it last appeared. And the thought by which we cognize it is the thought of it-in-those-relations, a thought suffused with the consciousness of all that dim context. Often we are ourselves struck at the strange differences in our successive views of the same thing. We wonder how we ever could have opined as we did last month about a certain matter. We have outgrown the possibility of that state of mind, we know not how. From one year to another we see things in new lights. What was unreal has grown real, and what was exciting is insipid. The friends we used to care the world for are shrunken to shadows; the women, once so divine, the stars, the woods, and the waters, how now so dull and common; the young girls that brought an aura of infinity, at present hardly distinguishable existences; the pictures so empty; and as for the books, what *was* there to find so mysteriously significant in Goethe, or in John Mill so full of weight? Instead of all this, more zestful than ever is the work, the work; and fuller and deeper the import of common duties and of common goods.

But what here strikes us so forcibly on the flagrant scale exists on every scale, down to the imperceptible transition from one hour's outlook to that of the next. Experience is remoulding us every moment, and our mental reaction on every given thing is really a resultant of our experience of the whole world up to that date. The analogies of brain-physiology must again be appealed to to corroborate our view. . . .

Every brain-state is partly determined by the nature of this entire past succession [of experiences]. Alter the latter in any part, and the brain-state must be somewhat different. Each present brain-state is a record in which the eye of Omniscience might read all the foregone history of its owner. It is out of the question, then, that any total brain-state should identically recur. Something like it may recur; but to suppose *it* to recur would be equivalent to the absurd admission that all the states that had intervened between its two appearances had been pure nonentities, and that the organ after their passage was exactly as it was before. And (to consider shorter periods) just as, in the senses, an impression feels very differently according to what has preceded it; as one color succeeding another is modified by the contrast, silence sounds delicious after noise, and a note, when the scale is sung up, sounds unlike itself when the scale is sung down; as the presence of certain lines in a figure changes the apparent form of the other lines, and as in music the whole aesthetic effect comes from the manner in which one set of sounds alters our feeling of another; so, in thought, we must admit that those portions of the brain that have just been maximally excited retain a kind of soreness which is a condition of our present consciousness, a codeterminant of how and what we now shall feel. *

Ever some tracts are waning in tension, some waxing, whilst others actively discharge. The states of tension have as positive an influence as any in determining the total condition, and in deciding what the *psychosis* shall be. All we know of submaximal nerve-irritations, and of the

---

*It need of course not follow, because a total brain-state does not recur, that no *point* of the brain can ever be twice in the same condition. That would be as improbable a consequence as that in the sea a wave-crest should never come twice at the same point of space. What can hardly come twice is an identical *combination* of wave-forms all with their crests and hollows reoccupying identical places. For such a total combination as this is the analogue of the brain-state to which our actual consciousness at any moment is due.

summation of apparently ineffective stimuli, tends to show that *no* changes in the brain are physiologically ineffective, and that presumably none are bare of psychological result. But as the brain-tension shifts from one relative state of equilibrium to another, like the gyrations of a kaleidoscope, now rapid and now slow, is it likely that its faithful psychic concomitant is heavier-footed than itself, and that it cannot match each one of the organ's irradiations by a shifting inward iridescence of its own? But if it can do this, its inward iridescences must be infinite, for the brain-redistributions are in infinite variety. If so coarse a thing as a telephone-plate can be made to thrill for years and never reduplicate its inward condition, how much more must this be the case with the infinitely delicate brain? . . .

What makes it convenient to use . . . mythological formulas is the whole organization of speech, which, as was remarked a while ago, was not made by psychologists, but by men who were as a rule only interested in the facts their mental states revealed. They only spoke of their states as *ideas of this or of that thing*. What wonder, then, that the thought is most easily conceived under the law of the thing whose name it bears! If the thing is composed of parts, then we suppose that the thought of the thing must be composed of the thoughts of the parts. If one part of the thing has appeared in the same thing or in other things on former occasions, why then we must be having even now the very same "idea" of that part which was there on those occasions. If the thing is simple, its thought is simple. If it is multitudinous, it must require a multitude of thoughts to think it. If a succession, only a succession of thoughts can know it. If permanent, its thought is permanent. And so on *ad libitum*. What after all is so natural as to assume that one object, called by one name, should be known by one affection of the mind? But, if language must thus influence us, the agglutinative languages, and even Greek and Latin with their declensions, would be the better guides. Names did not appear in them inalterable, but changed their shape to suit the context in which they lay. It must have been easier then than now to conceive of the same object as being thought of at different times in non-identical conscious states.

This, too, will grow clearer as we proceed. Meanwhile a necessary consequence of the belief in permanent self-indentical psychic facts that absent themselves and recur periodically is the Humian doctrine that our thought is composed of separate independent parts and is not a sensibly continuous stream. That this doctrine entirely misrepresents the natural appearances is what I next shall try to show.

WITHIN EACH PERSONAL CONSCIOUSNESS, THOUGHT IS SENSIBLY CONTINUOUS

I can only define "continuous" as that which is without breach, crack, or division. I have already said that the breach from one mind to another is perhaps the greatest breach in nature. The only breaches that can well be conceived to occur within the limits of a single mind would either be *interruptions*, *time*-gaps during which the consciousness went out altogether to come into existence again at a later moment; or they would be breaks in the *quality*, or content, of the thought, so abrupt that the segment that followed had no connection whatever with the one that went before. The proposition that within each personal consciousness thought feels continuous, means two things:

1. That even where there is a time-gap the consciousness after it feels as if it belonged together with the consciousness before it, as another part of the same self;

2. That the changes from one moment to another in the quality of the consciousness are never absolutely abrupt.

The case of the time-gaps, as the simplest, shall be taken first. And first of all, a word about time-gaps of which the consciousness may not be itself aware. . . . We saw that such time-gaps existed, and that they might be more numerous than is usually supposed. If the consciousness is not aware of them, it cannot feel them as interruptions. In the unconsciousness produced by nitrous oxide and other anaesthetics, in that of epilepsy and fainting, the broken edges of the sentient life may meet and merge over the gap, much as the feelings of space of the opposite margins of the "blind spot" meet and merge over that objective interruption to the sensitiveness of the eye. Such consciousness as this, whatever it be for the onlooking psychologist, is for itself unbroken. It *feels* unbroken; a waking day of it is sensibly a unit as long as that day lasts, in the sense in which the hours themselves are units, as having all their parts next each other, with no intrusive alien substance between. To expect the consciousness to feel the interruptions of its objective continuity as gaps, would be like expecting the eye to feel a gap of silence because it does not hear, or the ear to feel a gap of darkness because it does not see. So much for the gaps that are unfelt.

With the felt gaps the case is different. On waking from sleep, we usually know that we have been unconscious, and we often have an accurate judgment of how long. The judgment here is certainly an inference from sensible signs, and its ease is due to long practice in the particular field. The result of it, however, is that the consciousness is, *for itself*, not what it was in the former case, but interrupted and continuous, in the mere time-sense of the words. But in the other sense of continuity, the sense of the parts being inwardly connected and belonging together because they are parts of a common whole, the consciousness remains sensibly continuous and one. What now is the common whole? The natural name for it is *myself*, *I*, or *me*.

When Paul and Peter wake up in the same bed, and recognize that they have been asleep, each one of them mentally reaches back and makes connection with but *one* of the two streams of throught which were broken by the sleeping hours. As the current of an electrode buried in the ground unerringly finds its way to its own similarly buried mate, across no matter how much intervening earth; so Peter's present instantly finds out Peter's past, and never by mistake knits itself on to that of Paul. Paul's thought in turn is as little liable to go astray. The past thought of Peter is appropriated by the present Peter alone. He may have a *knowledge*, and a correct one too, of what Paul's last drowsy states of mind were as he sank into sleep, but it is an entirely different sort of knowledge from that which he has of his own last states. He *remembers* his own states, whilst he only *conceives* Paul's. Remembrance is like direct feeling; its object is suffused with a warmth and intimacy to which no object of mere conception ever attains. This quality of warmth and intimacy and immediacy is what Peter's *present* thought also possesses for itself. So sure as this present is me, is mine, it says, so sure is anything else that comes with the same warmth and intimacy and immediacy, me and mine. What the qualities called warmth and intimacy may in themselves be will have to be matter for future consideration. But whatever past feelings appear with those qualities must be admitted to receive the greeting of the present mental state, to be owned by it, and accepted as belonging together with it in a common self. This community of self is what the time-gap cannot break in twain, and is why a present thought, although not ignorant of the time-gap, can still regard itself as continuous with certain chosen portions of the past.

Consciousness, then, does not appear to itself chopped up in bits. Such words as "chain" or "train" do not describe it fitly as it presents itself in the first instance. It is nothing jointed; it flows. A "river" or a "stream" are the metaphors by which it is most naturally described. *In talking of it hereafter, let us call it the stream of thought, of consciousness, or of subjective life.*

But now there appears, even within the limits of the same self, and between thoughts all of which alike have this same sense of belonging together, a kind of jointing and separateness among the parts, of which this statement seems to take no account. I refer to the breaks that are produced by sudden *contrasts in the quality* of the successive segments of the stream of thought. If the words "chain" and "train" had no natural fitness in them, how came such words to be used at all? Does not a loud explosion rend the consciousness upon which it abruptly breaks, in twain? Does not every sudden shock, appearance of a new object, or change in a sensation, create a real interruption, sensibly felt as such, which cuts the conscious stream across at the moment at which it appears? Do not such interruptions smite us every hour of our lives, and have we the right, in their presence, still to call our consciousness a continuous stream?

This objection is based partly on a confusion and partly on a superficial introspective view.

The confusion is between the thoughts themselves, taken as subjective facts, and the things of which they are aware. It is natural to make this confusion, but easy to avoid it when once put on one's guard. The things are discrete and discontinuous; they do pass before us in a train or chain, making often explosive appearances and rending each other in twain. But their comings and goings and contrasts no more break the flow of the thought that thinks them than they break the time and the space in which they lie. A silence may be broken by a thunder-clap, and we may be so stunned and confused for a moment by the shock as to give no instant account to ourselves of what has happened. But that very confusion is a mental state, and a state that passes us straight over from the silence to the sound. The transition between the thought of one object and the thought of another is no more a break in the *thought* than a joint in a bamboo is a break in the wood. It is a part of the *consciousness* as much as the joint is a part of the *bamboo*.

On this gradualness in the changes of our mental content the principles of nerve-action can throw some more light. When studying . . . the summation of nervous activities, we saw that no state of the brain can be supposed instantly to die away. If a new state comes, the inertia of the old state will still be there and modify the result accordingly. Of course we cannot tell, in our ignorance, what in each instance the modifications ought to be. The commonest modifications in sense-perception are known as the phenomena of contrast. In aesthetics they are the feelings of delight or displeasure which certain particular orders in a series of impressions give. In thought, strictly and narrowly so called, they are unquestionably that consciousness of the *whence* and the *whither* that always accompanies its flows. If recently the brain-tract *a* was vividly excited, and then *b*, and now vividly *c*, the total present consciousness is not produced simply by c's excitement, but also by the dying vibrations of a and b as well. If we want to represent the brain-process we must write it thus: $_{ab}c$—three different processes coexisting, and correlated with them a thought which is no one of the three thoughts which they would have produced had each of them occurred alone. But whatever this fourth thought may exactly be, it seems impossible that it should not be something *like* each of the three other thoughts whose tracts are concerned in its production, though in a fast-waning phase. . . .

THOUGHT IS ALWAYS INTERESTED MORE IN ONE PART OF ITS OBJECT THAN IN ANOTHER, AND WELCOMES AND REJECTS, OR CHOOSES, ALL THE WHILE IT THINKS

The phenomena of selective attention and of deliberative will are of course patent examples of this choosing activity. But few of us are aware how incessantly it is at work in operations not ordinarily called by these names. Accentuation and Emphasis are present in every perception we have. We find it quite impossible to disperse our attention impartially over a number of impressions. A monotonous succession of sonorous strokes is broken up into rhythms, now of one sort, now of another, by the different accent which we place on different strokes. The simplest of these rhythms is the double one, tick-tóck, tick-tock, tick-tóck. Dots dispersed on a surface are perceived in rows and groups. Lines separate into diverse figures. The ubiquity of the distinctions, *this* and *that*, *here* and *there*, *now* and *then*, in our minds is the result of our laying the same selective emphasis on parts of place and time.

But we do far more than emphasize things, and unite some, and keep others apart. We actually *ignore* most of the things before us. Let me briefly show how this goes on.

To begin at the bottom, what are our very senses themselves but organs of selection? Out of the infinite chaos of movements, of which physics teaches us that the outer world consists, each sense-organ picks out those which fall within certain limits of velocity. To these it responds, but ignores the rest as completely as if they did not exist. It thus accentuates particular movements in a manner for which objectively there seems no valid ground; for, as Lange says, there is no reason whatever to think that the gap in Nature between the highest sound-waves and the lowest heat-waves is an abrupt break like that of our sensations; or that the difference between violet and ultraviolet rays has anything like the objective importance subjectively represented by that between light and darkness. Out of what is in itself an undistinguishable, swarming *continuum*, devoid of distinction or emphasis, our senses make for us, by attending to this motion and ignoring that, a world full of contrasts, of sharp accents, of abrupt changes, of picturesque light and shade.

If the sensations we receive from a given organ have their causes thus picked out for us by the conformation of the organ's termination, Attention, on the other hand, out of all the sensations yielded, picks out certain ones as worthy of its notice and suppresses all the rest. . . . We do not even know without special training on which of our eyes an image falls. So habitually ignorant are most men of this that one may be blind for years of a single eye and never know the fact.

Helmholtz says that we notice only those sensations which are signs to us of *things*. But what are things? Nothing, as we shall abundantly see, but special groups of sensible qualities, which happen practically or aesthetically to interest us, to which we therefore give substantive names, and which we exalt to this exclusive status of independence and dignity. But in itself, apart from my interest, a particular dust-wreath on a windy day is just as much of an individual thing, and just as much or as little deserves an individual name, as my own body does.

And then, among the sensations we get from each separate thing, what happens? The mind selects again. It chooses certain of the sensations to represent the thing most *truly*, and considers the rest as its appearances, modified by the conditions of the moment. Thus my table-top is named *square*, after but one of an infinite number of retinal sensations which it yields, the rest of them being sensations of two acute and two obtuse angles; but I call the latter *perspective* views, and the four right angles the *true* form of the table, and erect the attribute squareness into the table's essence, for aesthetic reasons of my own. In like manner, the real form of the circle is deemed to be the sensation it gives when the line of vision is perpendicular to its centre—all its other sensations are signs of this sensation. The real sound of the cannon is the sensation it makes when the ear is close by. The real color of the brick is the sensation it gives when the eye looks squarely at it from a near point, out of the sunshine and yet not in the gloom; under other circumstances it gives us other color-sensations which are but signs of this—we then see it looks pinker or blacker than it really is. The reader knows no object which he does not represent to himself by preference as in some typical attitude, of some normal size, at some characteristic distance, of some standard tint, etc., etc. But all these essential characteristics, which together form for us the genuine objectivity of the thing and are contrasted with what we call the subjective sensations it may yield us at a given moment, are mere sensations like the latter. The mind chooses to suit itself, and decides what particular sensation shall be held more real and valid than all the rest.

Thus perception involves a twofold choice. Out of all present sensations, we notice mainly such as are significant of absent ones; and out of all the absent associates which these suggest, we again pick out a very few to stand for the objective reality *par excellence*. We could have no more exquisite example of selective industry.

That industry goes on to deal with the things thus given in perception. A man's empirical thought depends on the things he has experienced, but what these shall be is to a large extent determined by his habits of attention. A thing may be present to him a thousand times, but if he persistently fails to notice it, it cannot be said to enter into his experience. We are all seeing flies, moths, and beetles by the thousand, but to whom, save an entomologist, do they say anything distinct? On the other hand, a thing met only once in a lifetime may leave an indelible experience in the memory. Let four men take a tour in Europe. One will bring home only picturesque impressions—costumes and colors, parks and views and works of architecture, pictures and statues. To another all this will be non-existent; and distances and prices, populations and drainage-arrangements, door- and window-fastenings, and other useful statistics will take their place. A third will give a rich account of the theatres, restaurants, and public balls, and naught beside; whilst the fourth will perhaps have been so wrapped in his own subjective broodings as to tell little more than a few names of places through which he passed. Each has selected, out of the same mass of presented objects, those which suited his private interest and has made his experience thereby. . . .

If now we pass to its aesthetic department, our law is still more obvious. The artist notoriously selects his items, rejecting all tones, colors, shapes, which do not harmonize with each other and with the main purpose of his work. That unity, harmony, "convergence of characters," as M. Taine calls it which gives to works of art their superiority over works of nature, is wholly due to *elimination*. Any natural subject will do, if the artist has wit enough to pounce upon some one feature of it as characteristic, and suppress all merely accidental items which do not harmonize with this. . . .

Looking back, then, over this review, we see that the mind is at every stage a theatre of simultaneous possibilities. Consciousness consists in the comparison of these with each other, the selection of some, and the suppression of the rest by the reinforcing and inhibiting agency of attention. The highest and most elaborated mental products are filtered from the data chosen by the faculty next beneath, out of the mass offered by the faculty below that, which mass in turn was sifted from a still larger amount of yet simpler material, and so on. The mind, in short, works on the data it receives very much as a sculptor works on his block of stone. In a sense the statue stood there from eternity. But there were a thousand different ones beside it, and the sculptor alone is to thank for having extricated this one from the rest. Just so the world of each of us, howsoever different our several views of it may be, all lay embedded in the primordial chaos of sensations, which gave the mere *matter* to the thought of all of us indifferently. We may, if we like, by our reasonings unwind things back to that black and jointless continuity of space and moving clouds of swarming atoms which science calls the only real world. But all the while the world *we* feel and live in will be that which our ancestors and we, by slowly cumulative strokes of choice, have extricated out of this, like sculptors, by simply rejecting certain portions of the given stuff. Other sculptors, other statues from the same stone! Other minds, other worlds from the same monotonous and inexpressive chaos! My world is but one in a million alike embedded, alike real to those who may abstract them. How different must be the worlds in the consciousness of ant, cuttle-fish, or crab!

But in my mind and your mind the rejected portions and the selected portions of the original world-stuff are to a great extent the same. The human race as a whole largely agrees as to what it shall notice and name, and what not. And among the noticed parts we select in much the same way for accentuation and preference or subordination and dislike. There is, however, one entirely extraordinary case in which no two men ever are known to choose alike. One great splitting of the whole universe into two halves is made by each of us; and for each of us almost all of the interest attaches to one of the halves; but we all draw the line of division between them in a different place. When I say that we all call the two halves by the same names, and that those names are "*me*" and "*not-me*" respectively, it will at once be seen what I mean. The altogether unique kind of interest which each human mind feels in those parts of creation which it can call *me* or *mine* may be a moral riddle, but it is a fundamental psychological fact. No mind can take the same interest in his neighbor's *me* as in his own. The neighbor's me falls together with all the rest of things in one foreign mass, against which his own *me* stands out in startling relief. Even the trodden worm, as Lotze somewhere says, contrasts his own suffering self with the whole remaining universe, though he have no clear conception either of himself or of what the universe may be. He is for me a mere part of the world; for him it is I who am the mere part. Each of us dichotomizes the Kosmos in a different place.

*The ancient tradition that the world will be consumed in fire at the
end of six thousand years is true, as I have heard from Hell.*

*For the cherub with his flaming sword is hereby commanded to leave his
guard at the tree of life; and when he does, the whole creation will be
consumed and appear infinite and holy, whereas it now appears
finite & corrupt.*

This will come to pass by an improvement of sensual enjoyment....

*If the doors of perception were cleansed every thing would appear to
man as it is, infinite.*

*For man has closed himself up, till he sees all things thro' narrow
chinks of his cavern.*

How do you know but ev'ry Bird that cuts the airy way,
Is an immense world of delight, clos'd by your senses five?

From William Blake,
The Marriage of Heaven and Hell

13.

The Doors of Perception

Aldous Huxley

Reflecting on my experience, I find myself agreeing with the eminent
Cambridge philosopher, Dr. C. D. Broad, "that we should do well to
consider much more seriously than we have hitherto been inclined to do

Reprinted from Aldous Huxley, *The Doors of Perception* (Copyright © 1954 by Aldous
Huxley), pp. 22–26, by permission of Harper & Row, Publishers, Inc., Mrs. Laura
Huxley, and Chatto & Windus, Ltd.

the type of theory which Bergson put forward in connection with memory and sense perception. The suggestion is that the function of the brain and nervous system and sense organs is in the main *eliminative* and not productive. Each person is at each moment capable of remembering all that has ever happened to him and of perceiving everything that is happening everywhere in the universe. The function of the brain and nervous system is to protect us from being overwhelmed and confused by this mass of largely useless and irrelevant knowledge, by shutting out most of what we should otherwise perceive or remember at any moment, and leaving only that very small and special selection which is likely to be practically useful." According to such a theory, each one of us is potentially Mind at Large. But in so far as we are animals, our business is at all costs to survive. To make biological survival possible, Mind at Large has to be funneled through the reducing valve of the brain and nervous system. What comes out at the other end is a measly trickle of the kind of consciousness which will help us to stay alive on the surface of this particular planet. To formulate and express the contents of this reduced awareness, man has invented and endlessly elaborated those symbol-systems and implicit philosophies which we call languages. Every individual is at once the beneficiary and the victim of the linguistic tradition into which he has been born—the beneficiary inasmuch as language gives access to the accumulated record of other people's experience, the victim in so far as it confirms him in the belief that reduced awareness is the only awareness and as it bedevils his sense of reality, so that he is all too apt to take his concepts for data, his words for actual things. That which, in the language of religion, is called "this world" is the universe of reduced awareness, expressed, and, as it were, petrified by language. The various "other worlds" with which human beings erratically make contact are so many elements in the totality of the awareness belonging to Mind at Large. Most people, most of the time, know only what comes through the reducing valve and is consecrated as genuinely real by the local language. Certain persons, however, seem to be born with a kind of by-pass that circumvents the reducing valve. In others temporary by-passes may be acquired either spontaneously, or as the result of deliberate "spiritual exercises," or through hypnosis, or by means of drugs. Through these permanent or temporary by-passes there flows, not indeed the perception "of everything that is happening everywhere in the universe" (for the by-pass does not abolish the reducing valve, which still excludes the total content of Mind at Large), but something more than, and above all something different from, the carefully selected utilitarian material which our narrowed, individual minds regard as a complete, or at least sufficient, picture of reality.

The brain is provided with a number of enzyme systems which serve to co-ordinate its workings. Some of these enzymes regulate the supply of glucose to the brain cells. Mescalin inhibits the production of these enzymes and thus lowers the amount of glucose available to an organ that is in constant need of sugar. When mescalin reduces the brain's normal ration of sugar what happens? Too few cases have been observed, therefore a comprehensive answer cannot yet be given. But what happens to the majority of the few who have taken mescalin under supervision can be summarized as follows.

1. The ability to remember and to "think straight" is little if at all reduced. (Listening to the recordings of my conversation under the influence of the drug, I cannot discover that I was then any stupider than I am at ordinary times.)

2. Visual impressions are greatly intensified and the eye recovers some of the perceptual innocence of childhood, when the sensum was not immediately and automatically subordinated to the concept. Interest in space is diminished and interest in time falls almost to zero.

3. Though the intellect remains unimpaired and thought perception is enormously improved, the will suffers a profound change for the worse. The mescalin taker sees no reason for doing anything in particular and finds most of the causes for which, at ordinary times, he was prepared to act and suffer, profoundly uninteresting. He can't be bothered with them, for the good reason that he has better things to think about.

4. These better things may be experienced (as I experienced them) "out there," or "in here," or in both worlds, the inner and the outer, simultaneously or successively. That they *are* better seems to be self-evident to all mescalin takers who come to the drug with a sound liver and an untroubled mind.

These effects of mescalin are the sort of effects you could expect to follow the administration of a drug having the power to impair the efficiency of the cerebral reducing valve. When the brain runs out of sugar, the undernourished ego grows weak, can't be bothered to undertake the necessary chores, and loses all interest in those spatial and temporal relationships which mean so much to an organism bent on getting on in the world. As Mind at Large seeps past the no longer watertight valve, all kinds of biologically useless things start to happen. In some cases there may be extra-sensory perceptions. Other persons discover a world of visionary beauty. To others again is revealed the glory, the infinite value and meaningfulness of naked existence, of the given, unconceptualized event. In the final stage of egolessness there is an "obscure knowledge" that All is in all—that All is actually each. This is as near, I take it, as a finite mind can ever come to "perceiving everything that is happening everywhere in the universe."

14.

Experiments in Perception

W. H. Ittelson and F. P. Kilpatrick

What is perception? Why do we see what we see, feel what we feel, hear what we hear? We act in terms of what we perceive; our acts lead to new perceptions; these lead to new acts, and so on in the incredibly complex process that constitutes life. Clearly, then, an understanding of the process by which man becomes aware of himself and his world is basic to any adequate understanding of human behavior. But the problem of explaining how and why we perceive in the way we do is one of the most controversial fields in psychology. We shall describe here some recent experimental work which sheds new light on the problem and points the way to a new theory of perception.

The fact that we see a chair and are then able to go to the place at which we localize it and rest our bodies on a substantial object does not seem particularly amazing or difficult to explain—until we try to explain it. If we accept the prevailing current view that we can never be aware of the world as such, but only of the nervous impulses arising from the impingement of physical forces on sensory receptors, we immediately face the necessity of explaining the correspondence between what we perceive and whatever it is that is there.

An extremely logical, unbeatable—and scientifically useless—answer is simply to say there is no real world, that everything exists in the mind alone. Another approach is to postulate the existence of an external world, to grant that there is some general correspondence between that world and what we perceive and to seek some understandable and useful explanation of why that should be. Most of the prominent theories about perception have grown out of the latter approach. These theories generally agree that even though much of the correspondence may be due to learning, at some basic level there exists an absolute correspondence between what is "out there" and what is in the "mind." But there is a great deal of disagreement concerning the level at which such innately determined correspondence occurs. At one extreme are theorists who believe that the correspondence occurs at the level of simple sensations, such as color, brightness, weight, hardness, and so on, and that out of these sensations are compounded more complex awarenesses, such as the recognition of a pencil or a book. At the other extreme are Gestalt psychologists who feel that complex perceptions such as the form of an object are the result of an inherent relationship between the properties of the thing perceived and the properties of the brain. All these schools seem to agree, however, that there is some perceptual level at which exists absolute objectivity; that is, a one-to-one correspondence between experience and reality.

This belief is basic to current thinking in many fields. It underlies most theorizing concerning the nature of science, including Percy W. Bridgman's attempt to reach final scientific objectivity in the "observable operation." In psychology one is hard put to find an approach to human behavior which departs from this basic premise. But it leads to dichotomies such as organism vs. environment, subjective vs. objective. Stimuli or stimulus patterns are treated as though they exist apart from the perceiving organism. Psychologists seek to find mechanical relationships or interactions between the organism and an "objectively defined" environment. They often rule out purposes and values as not belonging in a strictly scientific psychology.

The experiments to be described here arose from a widespread and growing feeling that such dichotomies are false, and that in practice it is impossible to leave values and purposes out of consideration in scientific observation. The experiments were designed to re-examine some of the basic ideas from which these problems stem.

During the past few years Adelbert Ames, Jr., of the Institute for Associated Research in Hanover, N. H., has designed some new ways of studying visual perception. They have resulted in a new conception of the nature of knowing and of observation. This theory neither denies the existence of objects nor proposes that they exist in a given form independently, that is, apart from the perceiving organism. Instead, it suggests that the world each of us knows is a world created in dealing with the environment.

Let us illustrate this in specific terms through some of the demonstrations. In one of them the subject sits in a dark room in which he can see only two star points of light. Both are equidistant from the observer, but one is brighter than the other. If the observer closes one eye and keeps his head still, the brighter point of light looks nearer than the dimmer one. Such apparent differences are related not only to brightness but also to direction from the observer. If two points of light of equal brightness are situated near the floor, one about a foot above the other, the upper one will generally be perceived as farther away than the lower one; if they are near the ceiling, the lower one will appear farther away.

A somewhat more complex experiment uses two partly inflated balloons illuminated from a concealed source. The balloons are in fixed positions about one foot apart. Their relative sizes can be varied by means of a lever control connected to a bellows, and another lever controls their relative brightness. When the size and brightness of both balloons are the same, an observer looking at them with one eye from 10 feet or more sees them as two glowing spheres at equal distances from him. If the brightnesses are left the same and the relative sizes are changed, the larger balloon appears to nearly all observers somewhat nearer. If the size lever is moved continuously, causing continuous variation in the relative size of the balloons, they appear to move dramatically back and forth through space, even when the observer watches with both eyes open. The result is similar when the sizes are kept equal and the relative brightness is varied.

With the same apparatus the effects of size and brightness may be combined so that they supplement or conflict with each other. When they supplement each other, the variation in apparent distance is much greater than when either size or brightness alone is varied. When conflict is introduced by varying size and brightness in opposition to each

Left balloon appears closer because it is larger and brighter than the balloon at the right. Both balloons, however, are at same distance.

other, the relative change in distance is considerably less than when they act in combination or alone. Most people, however, give more weight to relative size than they give to brightness in judging distance.

These phenomena cannot be explained by referring to "reality," be-

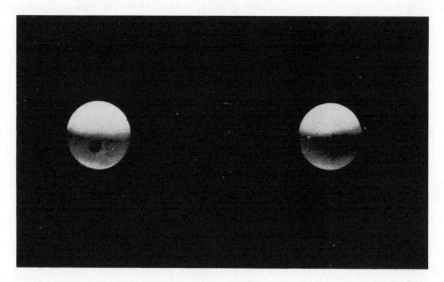

Balloons appear equidistant when they are the same size and brightness. The qualities are manipulated with levers in the demonstration.

Right balloon appears closer when it is larger and brighter. The demonstration shows that size and brightness are cues for distance.

cause "reality" and perception do not correspond. They cannot be explained by reference to the pattern in the retina of the eye, because for any given retinal pattern there are an infinite number of brightness-size-distance combinations to which that pattern might be related. When faced with such a situation, in which an unlimited number of possibilities can be related to a given retinal pattern, the organism apparently calls upon its previous experiences and assumes that what has been most probable in the past is most probable in the immediate occasion. When presented with two star-points of different brightness, a person unconsciously "bets" or "assumes" that the two points, being similar, are probably identical (*i. e.*, of equal brightness), and therefore that the one which seems brighter must be nearer. Similarly the observed facts in the case of two star-points placed vertically one above the other suggest that when we look down we assume, on the basis of past experience, that objects in the lower part of the visual field are nearer than objects in the upper part; when we look up, we assume the opposite to be true. An analogous explanation can be made of the role of relative size as an indication of relative distance.

Why do the differences in distance seem so much greater when the relative size of two objects is varied continuously than when the size difference is fixed? This phenomenon, too, apparently is based on experience. It is a fairly common experience, though not usual, to find that two similar objects of different sizes are actually the same distance away from us. But it is rare indeed to see two stationary objects at the same distance, one growing larger and the other smaller; almost always in everyday life when we see two identical or nearly identical objects change relative size they are in motion in relation to each other. Hence under the experimental conditions we are much more likely to assume distance differences in the objects of changing size than in those of fixed size. In other words, apparently we make use of a weighted average of our past experience in interpreting what we see. It seems that the subject relates to the stimulus pattern a complex, probability-like integration of his past experience with such patterns. Were it not for such integrations, which have been labeled assumptions, the particular perceptual phenomenon would not occur. It follows from this that the resulting perceptions are not absolute revelations of "what is out there" but are in the nature of probabilities or predictions based on past experience. These predictions are not always reliable, as the demonstrations make clear.

Visual perception involves an impression not only of *where* an object is but of *what* it is. From the demonstrations already described we may guess that there is a very strong relationship between localization in space ("thereness") and the assignment of objective properties ("that-ness"). This relationship can be demonstrated by a cube experiment.

Two solid white cubes are suspended on wires that are painted black so as to be invisible against a black background. One cube is about 3

Left cards appear closer than those at the center and right in each of the three rows in this picture. The illusion is revealed on opposite page.

Right cards are closer in the rows at the center and right. Here the cues are size and the fact that the cards appear to overlap.

feet from the observer and the other about 12 feet. The observer's head is in a headrest so positioned that the cubes are almost in line with each other but he can see both, the nearer cube being slightly to the right. A tiny metal shield is then placed a few inches in front of the left eye. It is just big enough to cut off the view of the far cube from the left eye. The result is that the near cube is seen with both eyes and the far cube with just the right eye. Under these conditions the observer can fix the position of the near cube very well, because he has available all the cues that come from the use of the two eyes. But in the case of the far cube seen with only one eye, localization is much more difficult and uncertain.

Now since the two cubes are almost in line visually, a slight movement of the head to the right will cause the inside vertical edges of the cubes to coincide. Such coincidence of edge is strongly related to an assumption of "togetherness." Hence when the subject moves his head in this way, the uncertainly located distant cube appears to have moved forward to a position even with the nearer cube. Under these conditions not only does the mislocated cube appear smaller, but it appears different in shape, that is, no longer cubical, even though the pattern cast by the cube on the retina of the eye has not changed at all.

The same point can be illustrated most dramatically by experiments in which the subject wears a pair of glasses fitted with so-called aniseikonic lenses, which are ground in such a way that they give images of different size and shape to the two retinas. This produces very marked distortions of any objects which the subject visualizes mainly through the use of two-eyed stereoscopic vision. In an ordinary environment there are generally enough one-eye cues, such as shadow, overlay, familiar objects of known size, and so on, to suppress the binocular cues and hold the visual world "in shape." But in an environment poor in one-eye cues the observer is forced to rely on binocular cues, and under these circumstances, the distortion is enhanced for anyone wearing such glasses. It has been found that if an ordinary square room is lined with tree leaves, which reduce monocular cues to a minimum by covering the flat wall spaces, most observers looking through aniseikonic lenses perceive a great deal of distortion of the room and the leaves. To an observer looking at the room as a whole through certain glasses of this type the walls appear to slant inward from floor to ceiling, the ceiling seems much lower than it is and its leaves look very small. The floor, which is the object of interest in this particular analysis, appears to be much farther away than its true position, and the leaves covering it look huge. Now, if the observer wearing the same glasses looks at just the floor instead of the room in general, the floor changes markedly in appearance. It appears to be much nearer than before, and instead of being level it seems to rise from front to back at a pitch of about 45 degrees. The leaves, however, now look more nearly normal in size.

These perceptions can be explained in terms of the geometry of stereoscopic vision. The stimulus patterns on the retinas of the eyes are the geometric projections of an external surface. But identical projections may be produced by surfaces of different kinds. In this case a distant surface that is nearly horizontal, a closer surface that is slightly tipped and a very near surface that is sharply tipped all produce the same stereoscopic stimulus patterns. When the observer looks at the whole room, he "chooses" the nearly horizontal faraway floor surface as the focus of perception, probably because he cannot make a room out of the pattern if the floor is sharply tipped up. When he limits his gaze to the floor, he no longer needs to make a room of what he is looking at, and he sees the floor sharply tipped, perhaps because the leaves now appear more nearly the size he assumes them to be.

In the everyday environment outside the laboratory the wearing of these glasses produces similarly interesting illusions. For example, a large body of water such as a lake appears horizontal and farther away than its real position, but a large expanse of level lawn looks tipped and nearer than its real position. Presumably this happens because the observer brings to these occasions the assumptions, based on past experience, that the probability of a lake surface being other than horizontal is almost zero, while the probability of a grass surface being a slope is fairly high.

The most reasonable explanation of these visual phenomena seems to be that an observer unconsciously relates to the stimulus pattern some sort of weighted average of the past consequences of acting with respect to that pattern. The particular perception "chosen" is the one that has the best predictive value, on the basis of previous experience, for action in carrying out the purposes of the organism. From this one may make two rather crucial deductions: (1) an unfamiliar external configuration which yields the same retinal pattern as one the observer is accustomed to deal with will be perceived as the familiar configuration; (2) when the observer acts on his interpretation of the unfamiliar configuration and finds that he is wrong, his perception will change even though the retinal pattern is unchanged.

Let us illustrate with some actual demonstrations. If an observer in a dark room looks with one eye at two lines of light which are at the same distance and elevation but of different lengths, the longer line will look nearer than the shorter one. Apparently he assumes that the lines are identical and translates the difference in length into a difference in position. If the observer takes a wand with a luminous tip and tries to touch first one line and then the other, he will be unable to do so at first. After repeated practice, however, he can learn to touch the two lines quickly and accurately. At this point he no longer sees the lines as at different distances; they now look, as they are, the same distance from him. He originally assumed that the two lines were the same length because that seemed the best bet under the circumstances. After he had tested this assumption by purposive action, he shifted to the assumption, less probable in terms of past experience but still possible, that the lines were at the same distance but of different lengths. As his assumption changed, perception did also.

There is another experiment that demonstrates these points even more convincingly. It uses a distorted room in which the floor slopes up to the right of the observer, the rear wall recedes from right to left and the windows are of different sizes and trapezoidal in shape. When an observer looks at this room with one eye from a certain point, the room appears completely normal, as if the floor were level, the rear wall at right angles to the line of sight and the windows rectangular and of the same size. Presumably the observer chooses this particular appearance instead of some other because of the assumptions he brings to the occasion.

Figures are distorted when they are placed in a specially constructed room. The woman at left appears much smaller than the one at right because the mind "bets" that the opposite surfaces of the room are parallel.

Heads are distorted by the same process. The head of the man at the left appears to be much smaller than the head of the man at the right because the mind assumes that all the windows are the same height.

If he now takes a long stick and tries to touch the various parts of the room, he will be unsuccessful, even though he has gone into the situation knowing the true shape of the room. With practice, however, he becomes more and more successful in touching what he wants to touch with the stick. More important, he sees the room more and more in its true shape, even though the stimulus pattern on his retina has remained unchanged.

By means of a piece of apparatus called the "rotating trapezoidal window" it has been possible to extend the investigation to complex perceptual situations involving movement. This device consists of a trapezoidal surface with panes cut in it and shadows painted on it to give the appearance of a window. It is mounted on a rod connected to a motor so that it rotates at a slow constant speed in an upright position about its

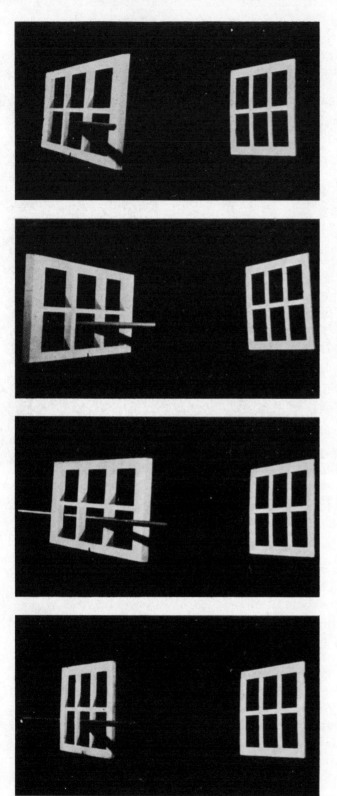

Perception of moving objects was investigated with a rotating window. At the right in each of the eight pictures on these two pages is a rectangular window; at the left in each picture is a trapezoid painted to look like a rectangular window seen in perspective. When the trapezoid rotates, the assumption that it is rectangular causes a straight tube to do strange things.

own axis. When an observer views the rotating surface with one eye from about 10 feet or more or with both eyes from about 25 feet or more, he sees not a rotating trapezoid but an oscillating rectangle. Its speed of movement and its shape appear to vary markedly as it turns. If a small cube is attached by a short rod to the upper part of the short side of the trapezoid, it seems to become detached, sail freely around the front of the trapezoid and attach itself again as the apparatus rotates.

All these experiments, and many more that have been made, suggest strongly that perception is never a sure thing, never an absolute revelation of "what is." Rather, what we see is a prediction—our own personal construction designed to give us the best possible bet for carrying out our purposes in action. We make these bets on the basis of our past experience. When we have a great deal of relevant and consistent experience to relate to stimulus patterns, the probability of success of our prediction (perception) as a guide to action is extremely high, and we tend to have a feeling of surety. When our experience is limited or inconsistent, the reverse holds true. According to the new theory of perception developed from the demonstrations we have described, perception is a functional affair based on action, experience, and probability. The thing perceived is an inseparable part of the function of perceiving, which in turn includes all aspects of the total process of living. This view differs from the old rival theories: the thing perceived is neither just a figment of the mind nor an innately determined absolute revelation of a reality postulated to exist apart from the perceiving organism. Object and percept are part and parcel of the same thing.

This conclusion of course has far-reaching implications for many areas of study, for some assumption as to what perception is must underly any philosophy or comprehensive theory of psychology, of science, or of knowledge in general. Although the particular investigations involved here are restricted to visual perception, this is only a vehicle which carries us into a basic inquiry of much wider significance.

15.

They Saw a Game: A Case Study

Albert H. Hastorf and Hadley Cantril

On a brisk Saturday afternoon, November 23, 1951, the Dartmouth football team played Princeton in Princeton's Palmer Stadium. It was the last game of the season for both teams and of rather special significance because the Princeton team had won all its games so far and one of its players, Kazmaier, was receiving All-American mention and had just appeared as the cover man on *Time* magazine, and was playing his last game.

A few minutes after the opening kick-off, it became apparent that the game was going to be a rough one. The referees were kept busy blowing their whistles and penalizing both sides. In the second quarter, Princeton's star left the game with a broken nose. In the third quarter, a Dartmouth player was taken off the field with a broken leg. Tempers flared both during and after the game. The official statistics of the game, which

Reprinted by permission from *J. Abn. Soc. Psych.*, 49 (Jan. 1954), 129–134. Copyright © 1954 by the American Psychological Association.

Princeton won, showed that Dartmouth was penalized 70 yards, Princeton 25, not counting more than a few plays in which both sides were penalized.

Needless to say, accusations soon began to fly. The game immediately became a matter of concern to players, students, coaches, and the administrative officials of the two institutions, as well as to alumni and the general public who had not seen the game but had become sensitive to the problem of big-time football through the recent exposures of subsidized players, commercialism, etc. Discussion of the game continued for several weeks.

One of the contributing factors to the extended discussion of the game was the extensive space given to it by both campus and metropolitan newspapers. An indication of the fervor with which the discussions were carried on is shown by a few excerpts from the campus dailies.

For example, on November 27 (four days after the game) the *Daily Princetonian* (Princeton's student newspaper) said:

> This observer has never seen quite such a disgusting exhibition of so-called "sport." Both teams were guilty but the blame must be laid primarily on Dartmouth's doorstep. Princeton, obviously the better team, had no reason to rough up Dartmouth. Looking at the situation rationally, we don't see why the Indians should make a deliberate attempt to cripple Dick Kazmaier or any other Princeton player. The Dartmouth psychology, however, is not rational itself.

The November 30th edition of the *Princeton Alumni Weekly* said:

> But certain memories of what occurred will not be easily erased. Into the record books will go in indelible fashion the fact that the last game of Dick Kazmaier's career was cut short by more than half when he was forced out with a broken nose and a mild concussion, sustained from a tackle that came well after he had thrown a pass.
>
> This second-period development was followed by a third quarter outbreak of of roughness that was climaxed when a Dartmouth player deliberately kicked Brad Glass in the ribs while the latter was on his back. Throughout the often unpleasant afternoon, there was undeniable evidence that the losers' tactics were the result of an actual style of play, and reports on other games they have played this season substantiate this.

Dartmouth students were "seeing" an entirely different version of the game through the editorial eyes of the *Dartmouth* (Dartmouth's undergraduate newspaper). For example, on November 27 the *Dartmouth* said:

> However, the Dartmouth-Princeton game set the stage for the other type of dirty football. A type which may be termed as an unjustifiable accusation.
>
> Dick Kazmaier was injured early in the game. Kazmaier was the star, an All-American. Other stars have been injured before, but Kazmaier had been built to represent a Princeton idol. When an idol is hurt there is only one recourse—the

tag of dirty football. So what did the Tiger Coach Charley Caldwell do? He announced to the world that the Big Green had been out to extinguish the Princeton star. His purpose was achieved.

After this incident, Caldwell instilled the old see-what-they-did-go-get-them attitude into his players. His talk got results. Gene Howard and Jim Miller were both injured. Both had dropped back to pass, had passed, and were standing unprotected in the backfield. Result: one bad leg and one leg broken.

The game was rough and did get a bit out of hand in the third quarter. Yet most of the roughing penalties were called against Princeton while Dartmouth received more of the illegal-use-of-the-hands variety.

On November 28 the *Dartmouth* said:

> Dick Kazmaier of Princeton admittedly is an unusually able football player. Many Dartmouth men traveled to Princeton, not expecting to win—only hoping to see an All-American in action. Dick Kazmaier was hurt in the second period, and played only a token part in the remainder of the game. For this, spectators were sorry.
>
> But there were no such feelings for Dick Kazmaier's health. Medical authorities have confirmed that as a relatively unprotected passing and running star in a contact sport, he is quite liable to injury. Also, his particular injuries—a broken nose and a slight concussion—were no more serious than is experienced almost any day in any football practice, where there is no more serious stake than playing the following Saturday. Up to the Princeton game, Dartmouth players suffered about 10 known nose fractures and face injuries, not to mention several slight concussions.
>
> Did Princeton players feel so badly about losing their star? They shouldn't have. During the past undefeated campaign they stopped several individual stars by a concentrated effort, including such mainstays as Frank Hauff of Navy, Glenn Adams of Pennsylvania and Rocco Calvo of Cornell.
>
> In other words, the same brand of football condemned by the *Prince*—that of stopping the big man—is practiced quite successfully by the Tigers.

Basically, then, there was disagreement as to what had happened during the "game." Hence we took the opportunity presented by the occasion to make a "real life" study of a perceptual problem.*

PROCEDURE

Two steps were involved in gathering data. The first consisted of answers to a questionnaire designed to get reactions to the game and to learn something of the climate of opinion in each institution. This questionnaire was administered a week after the game to both Dartmouth and

---

*We are not concerned here with the problem of guilt or responsibility for infractions, and nothing here implies any judgment as to who was to blame.

Princeton undergraduates who were taking introductory and intermediate psychology courses.

The second step consisted of showing the same motion picture of the game to a sample of undergraduates in each school and having them check on another questionnaire, as they watched the film, any infraction of the rules they saw and whether these infractions were "mild" or "flagrant." † At Dartmouth, members of two fraternities were asked to view the film on December 7; at Princeton, members of two undergraduate clubs saw the film early in January.

The answers to both questionnaires were carefully coded and transferred to punch cards.

RESULTS

Table 15.1 shows the questions which received different replies from the two student populations on the first questionnaire.

Questions asking if the students had friends on the team, if they had ever played football themselves, if they felt they knew the rules of the game well, etc., showed no differences in either school and no relation to answers given to other questions. This is not surprising since the students in both schools come from essentially the same type of educational, economic, and ethnic background.

Summarizing the data of Tables 15.1 and 15.2, we find a marked contrast between the two student groups.

Nearly all *Princeton* students judged the game as "rough and dirty"—not one of them thought it "clean and fair." And almost nine-tenths of them thought the other side started the rough play. By and large they felt that the charges they understood were being made were true; most of them felt the charges were made in order to avoid similar situations in the future.

When Princeton students looked at the movie of the game, they saw the Dartmouth team make over twice as many infractions as their own team made. And they saw the Dartmouth team make over twice as many infractions as were seen by Dartmouth students. When Princeton students judged these infractions as "flagrant" or "mild," the ratio was

---

†The film shown was kindly loaned for the purpose of the experiment by the Dartmouth College Athletic Council. It should be pointed out that a movie of a football game follows the ball, is thus selective, and omits a good deal of the total action on the field. Also, of course, in viewing only a film of a game, the possibilities of participation as spectator are greatly limited.

TABLE 15.1

Data from First Questionnaire

Question	Dartmouth students ($N = 163$) %	Princeton students ($N = 161$) %	Question	Dartmouth students ($N = 163$) %	Princeton students ($N = 161$) %
1. Did you happen to see the actual game between Dartmouth and Princeton in Palmer Stadium this year?			the first questions.) From what you have heard and read about the game, do you feel it was clean and fairly played, or that it was unnecessarily rough and dirty?		
Yes	33	71			
No	67	29			
			Clean and fair	7	0
2. Have you seen a movie of the game or seen it on television?			Rough and dirty	18	24
			Rough and fair*	14	1
			Don't know	6	4
Yes, movie	33	2	No answer	55	71
Yes, television	0	1			
No, neither	67	97	(Combined answers to questions 3 and 4 above)		
3. (Asked of those who answered "yes" to either or both of above questions.) From your observations of what went on at the game, do you believe the game was clean and fairly played, or that it was unnecessarily rough and dirty?			Clean and fair	13	0
			Rough and dirty	42	93
			Rough and fair*	39	3
			Don't know	6	4
			5. From what you saw in the game or the movies, or from what you have read, which team do you feel started the rough play?		
Clean and fair	6	0			
Rough and dirty	24	69	Dartmouth started it	36	86
Rough and fair*	25	2	Princeton started it	2	0
No answer	45	29	Both started it	53	11
4. (Asked of those who answered "no" on both of			Neither	6	1
			No answer	3	2

This answer was not included on the checklist but was written in by the percentage of students indicated.

TABLE 15.1 *(continued)*
Data from First Questionnaire

Question	Dartmouth students ($N = 163$) %	Princeton students ($N = 161$) %	Question	Dartmouth students ($N = 163$) %	Princeton students ($N = 161$) %
6. What is your understanding of the charges being made?**			is any truth to these charges?		
			Yes	10	55
			No	57	4
Dartmouth tried to get Kazmaier	71	47	Partly	29	35
			Don't know	4	6
Dartmouth intentionally dirty	52	44	8. Why do you think the charges were made?		
Dartmouth unnecessarily rough	8	35	Injury to Princeton star	70	23
			To prevent repetition	2	46
7. Do you feel there			No answer	28	31

**Replies do not add to 100% since more than one charge could be given.

TABLE 15.2
Data from Second Questionnaire Checked While Seeing Film

Group	N	Total number of infractions checked against			
		Dartmouth team		Princeton team	
		Mean	SD	Mean	SD
Dartmouth students	48	4.3*	2.7	4.4	2.8
Princton students	49	9.8*	5.7	4.2	3.5

Significant at the .01 level.

about two "flagrant" to one "mild" on the Dartmouth team, and about one "flagrant" to three "mild" on the Princeton team.

As for the *Dartmouth* students, while the plurality of answers fell in the "rough and dirty" category, over one-tenth thought the game was "clean and fair" and over a third introduced their own category of "rough and fair" to describe the action. Although a third of the Dartmouth students felt that Dartmouth was to blame for starting the rough play, the majority of Dartmouth students thought both sides were to blame. By and large, Dartmouth men felt that the charges they understood were being made were not true, and most of them thought the reason for the charges was Princeton's concern for its football star.

When Dartmouth students looked at the movie of the game, they saw both teams make about the same number of infractions. And they saw their own team make only half the number of infractions the Princeton students saw them make. The ratio of "flagrant" to "mild" infractions was about one to one when Dartmouth students judged the Dartmouth team, and about one "flagrant" to two "mild" when Dartmouth students judged infractions made by the Princeton team.

It should be noted that Dartmouth and Princeton students were thinking of different charges in judging their validity and in assigning reasons as to why the charges were made. It should also be noted that whether or not students were spectators of the game in the stadium made little difference in their responses.

INTERPRETATION: THE NATURE OF A SOCIAL EVENT*

It seems clear that the "game" actually was many different games and that each version of the events that transpired was just as "real" to a particular person as other versions were to other people. A consideration of the experiential phenomena that constitute a "football game" for the spectator may help us both to account for the results obtained and illustrate something of the nature of any social event.

Like any other complex social occurrence, a "football game" consists of a whole host of happenings. Many different events are occurring simultaneously. Furthermore, each happening is a link in a chain of happenings, so that one follows another in sequence. The "football game," as well as other complex social situations, consists of a whole matrix of events. In the game situation, this matrix of events consists of the actions of all the players, together with the behavior of the referees and linesmen, the action on the sidelines, in the grandstands, over the loud-speaker, etc.

Of crucial importance is the fact that an "occurrence" on the football

---

*The interpretation of the nature of a social event sketched here is in part based on discussions with Adelbert Ames, Jr., and is being elaborated in more detail elsewhere.

field or in any other social situation does not become an experiential "event" unless and until some significance is given to it: an "occurrence" becomes an "*event*" only when the happening has significance. And a happening generally has significance only if it reactivates learned significances already registered in what we have called a person's assumptive form-world (Cantril, 1950).

Hence the particular occurrences that different people experienced in the football game were a limited series of events from the total matrix of events *potentially* available to them. People experienced those occurrences that reactivated significances they brought to the occasion; they failed to experience those occurrences which did not reactivate past significances. We do not need to introduce "attention" as an "intervening third" (to paraphrase James on memory) to account for the selectivity of the experiential process.

In this particular study, one of the most interesting examples of this phenomenon was a telegram sent to an officer of Dartmouth College by a member of a Dartmouth alumni group in the Midwest. He had viewed the film which had been shipped to his alumni group from Princeton after its use with Princeton students, who saw, as we noted, an average of over nine infractions by Dartmouth players during the game. The alumnus, who couldn't see the infractions he had heard publicized, wired:

> Preview of Princeton movies indicates considerable cutting of important part please wire explanation and possibly air mail missing part before showing scheduled for January 25 we have splicing equipment.

The "same" sensory impingements emanating from the football field, transmitted through the visual mechanism to the brain, also obviously gave rise to different experiences in different people. The significances assumed by different happenings for different people depend in large part on the purposes people bring to the occasion and the assumptions they have of the purposes and probable behavior of other people involved. This was amusingly pointed out by the New York *Herald Tribune's* sports columnist, Red Smith, in describing a prize fight between Chico Vejar and Carmine Fiore in his column of December 21, 1951. Among other things, he wrote:

> You see, Steve Ellis is the proprietor of Chico Vejar, who is a highly desirable tract of Stamford, Conn., welterweight. Steve is also a radio announcer. Ordinarily there is no conflict between Ellis the Brain and Ellis the Voice because Steve is an uncommonly substantial lump of meat who can support both halves of a split personality and give away weight on each end without missing it.
> This time, though, the two Ellises met head-on, with a sickening, rending

crash. Steve the Manager sat at ringside in the guise of Steve the Announcer broadcasting a dispassionate, unbiased, objective report of Chico's adventures in the ring. . . .

Clear as mountain water, his words came through, winning big for Chico. Winning? Hell, Steve was slaughtering poor Fiore.

Watching and listening, you could see what a valiant effort the reporter was making to remain cool and detached. At the same time you had an illustration of the old, established truth that when anybody with a preference watches a fight, he sees only what he prefers to see.

That is always so. That is why, after any fight that doesn't end in a clean knockout, there always are at least a few hoots when the decision is announced. A guy from, say, Bill Graham's neighborhood goes to see Billy fight and he watches Graham all the time. He sees all the punches Billy throws, and hardly any of the punches Billy catches. So it was with Steve.

"Fiore feints with a left,"he would say, honestly believing that Fiore hadn't caught Chico full on the chops."Fiore's knees buckle,"he said,"and Chico backs away."Steve didn't see the hook that had driven Chico back.

In brief, the data here indicate that there is no such "thing" as a "game" existing "out there" in its own right which people merely "observe." The "game" "exists" for a person and is experienced by him only in so far as certain happenings have significances in terms of his purpose. Out of all the occurrences going on in the environment, a person selects those that have some significance for him from his own egocentric position in the total matrix.

Obviously in the case of a football game, the value of the experience of watching the game is enhanced if the purpose of "your" team is accomplished, that is, if the happening of the desired consequence is experienced—i.e., if your team wins. But the value attribute of the experience can, of course, be spoiled if the desire to win crowds out behavior we value and have come to call sportsmanlike.

The sharing of significances provides the links except for which a "social" event would not be experienced and would not exist for anyone.

A "football game" would be impossible except for the rules of the game which we bring to the situation and which enable us to share with others the significances of various happenings. These rules make possible a certain repeatability of events such as first downs, touchdowns, etc. If a person is unfamiliar with the rules of the game, the behavior he sees lacks repeatability and consistent significance and hence "doesn't make sense."

And only because there is the possibility of repetition is there the possibility that a happening has a significance. For example, the balls used in games are designed to give a high degree of repeatability. While a football is about the only ball used in games which is not a sphere, the shape of the modern football has apparently evolved in order to achieve a higher degree of accuracy and speed in forward passing than would be obtained with a spherical ball, thus increasing the repeatability of an important phase of the game.

The rules of a football game, like laws, rituals, customs, and mores, are registered and preserved forms of sequential significances enabling people to share the significances of occurrences. The sharing of sequential significances which have value for us provides the links that operationally make social events possible. They are analogous to the forces of attraction that hold parts of an atom together, keeping each part from following its individual, independent course.

From this point of view it is inaccurate and misleading to say that different people have different "attitudes" concerning the same "thing." For the "thing" simply is *not* the same for different people whether the "thing" is a football game, a presidential candidate, Communism, or spinach. We do not simply "react to" a happening or to some impingement from the environment in a determined way (except in behavior that has become reflexive or habitual). We behave according to what we bring to the occasion, and what each of us brings to the occasion is more or less unique. And except for these significances which we bring to the occasion, the happenings around us would be meaningless occurrences, would be "inconsequential."

From the transactional view, an attitude is not a predisposition to react in a certain way to an occurrence or stimulus "out there" that exists in its own right with certain fixed characteristics which we "color" according to our predisposition (Kilpatrick, 1952). That is, a subject does not simply "react to" an "object." An attitude would rather seem to be a complex of registered significances reactivated by some stimulus which assumes its own particular significance for us in terms of our purposes. That is, the object as experienced would not exist for us except for the reactivated aspects of the form-world which provide particular significance to the hieroglyphics of sensory impingements.

16.

The Processes of Vision

Ulric Neisser

It was Johannes Kepler who first compared the eye to a "camera" (a darkened chamber) with an image in focus on its rear surface. "Vision is brought about by pictures of the thing seen being formed on the white concave surface of the retina," he wrote in 1604. A generation later René Descartes tried to clinch this argument by direct observation. In a hole in a window shutter he set the eye of an ox, just in the position it would have had if the ox had been peering out. Looking at the back of the eye (which he had scraped to make it transparent), he could see a small inverted image of the scene outside the window.

Since the 17th century the analogy between eye and camera has been elaborated in numerous textbooks. As an account of functional anatomy the analogy is not bad, but it carries some unfortunate implications for the study of vision. It suggests all too readily that the perceiver is in the position of Descartes and is in effect looking through the back of his own

Reprinted by permission from *Scientific American*, 219, no. 3 (Sept. 1968), 204–214. (Scientific American Offprint 519) Copyright © 1968 by Scientific American, Inc. All rights reserved.

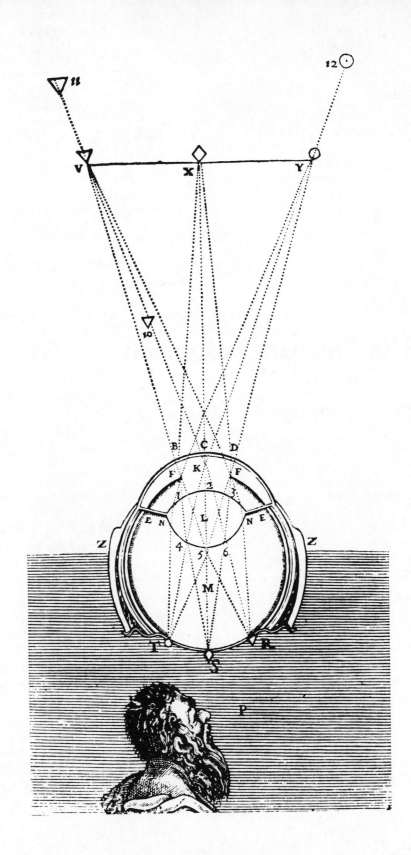

retina at the pictures that appear there. We use the same word—"image"—for both the optical pattern thrown on the retina by an object and the mental experience of seeing the object. It has been all too easy to treat this inner image as a copy of the outer one, to think of perceptual experiences as images formed by the nervous system acting as an optical instrument of extraordinarily ingenious design. Although this theory encounters insurmountable difficulties as soon as it is seriously considered, it has dominated philosophy and psychology for many years.

Not only perception but also memory has often been explained in terms of an image theory. Having looked at the retinal picture, the perceiver supposedly files it away somehow, as one might put a photograph in an album. Later, if he is lucky, he can take it out again in the form of a "memory image" and look at it a second time. The widespread notion that some people have a "photographic memory" reflects this analogy in a particularly literal way, but in a weaker form it is usually applied even to ordinary remembering. The analogy suggests that the mechanism of visual memory is a natural extension of the mechanisms of vision. Although there is some truth to this proposition, as we shall see below, it is not because both perception and memory are copying processes. Rather it is because *neither* perception *nor* memory is a copying process.

The fact is that one does not see the retinal image; one sees with the aid of the retinal image. The incoming pattern of light provides information that the nervous system is well adapted to pick up. This information is used by the perceiver to guide his movements, to anticipate events, and to construct the internal representations of objects and of space called "conscious experience." These internal representations are not, however, at all like the corresponding optical images on the back of the eye. The retinal images of specific objects are at the mercy of every irrelevant change of position; their size, shape, and location are hardly constant for a moment. Nevertheless, perception is usually accurate; real objects appear rigid and stable and appropriately located in three-dimensional space.

The first problem in the study of visual perception is therefore the discovery of the stimulus. What properties of the incoming optic array are informative for vision? In the entire distribution of light, over the retina and over a period of time, what determines the way things look? (Actually the light is distributed over two retinas, but the binocularity of vision has no relevance to the variables considered here. Although depth per-

---

Optical analysis by Descartes included an experiment in which he removed the eye of an ox, scraped the back of the eye to make it transparent and observed on the retina the inverted image of a scene. The illustration is from Descarte's essay *La Dioptrique*.

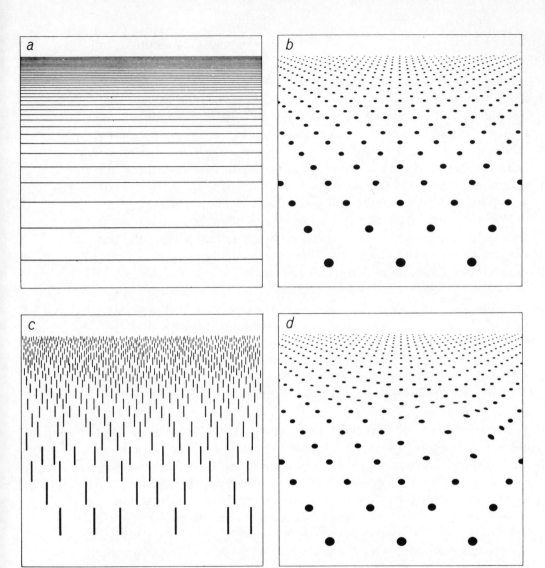

Density gradients convey an impression of depth. Depending on the size, shape and spacing of its textural elements, the gradient may create the impression of a smooth flat surface (a, b), a rough flat surface (c) or a surface broken by an elevation and a depression (d). Like the gradients depicted, the textured surfaces of the visual world (by structuring the light that falls on the retina) convey information concerning the orientation of the surface. Textured surfaces also provide a scale for gauging the size of objects.

ception is more accurate with two eyes than with one, it is not fundamentally different. The world looks much the same with one eye closed as it does with both open; congenitally monocular people have more or less the same visual experiences as the rest of us.)

As a first step we can consider the patterns of reflected light that are formed when real objects and surfaces are illuminated in the ordinary

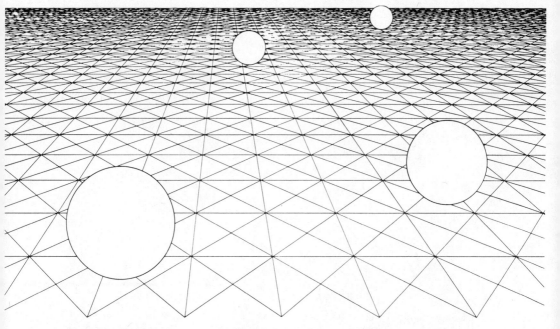

Perception of size relies heavily on cues provided by a textured surface. These four disks, if seen alone, would appear to lie in one plane and be of different sizes. Against this apparently receding surface, however, they seem to lie in four different planes. Since each disk masks the same amount of surface texture, there is a tendency to see them as being equal in size.

way by sunshine or lamplight. J. J. Gibson of Cornell University, who has contributed much to our understanding of perception, calls this inquiry "ecological optics." It is an optics in which point sources, homogeneous fields, and the other basic elements of classical optics rarely appear. Instead the world we ordinarily look at consists mostly of *surfaces*, at various angles and in various relations to one another. This has significant consequences for the visual input.

One of these consequences (the only one we shall examine here) is to give the visual field a microstructure. Most surfaces have some kind of texture, such as the grain in wood, the individual stalks of grass in a field, or the weave in a fabric. These textures structure the light reaching the eye in a way that carries vital information about the layout of environmental objects. In accordance with the principles of perspective the texture elements of more distant surfaces are represented closer to one another on the retina than the elements of surfaces nearby. Thus the microstructure of a surface that slants away from the observer is represented on the retina as a gradient of density—a gradient that carries information about the orientation of the surface.

Consider now an ordinary scene in which discrete figures are superposed on textured surfaces. The gradient of increasing texture density

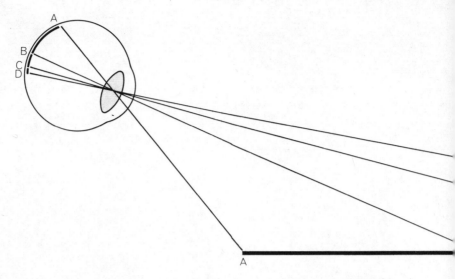

Contraction of image takes place as the distance between the viewer and the object in view increases. The texture elements of a distant surface are also projected closer together than similar elements nearby. Thus a textured surface slanting away from the viewer is represented optically as a density gradient.

on the retina, corresponding to increasing distance from the observer, gives a kind of "scale" for object sizes. In the ideal case when the texture units are identical, two figures of the same real size will always occlude the same number of texture units, regardless of how far away either one may be. That is, the relation between the retinal texture-size and the dimensions of the object's retinal image is invariant, in spite of changes of distance. This relation is a potentially valuable source of information about the real size of the object—more valuable than the retinal image of the object considered alone. That image, of course, changes in dimension whenever the distance between the object and the observer is altered.

Psychologists have long been interested in what is called "size constancy": the fact that the sizes of real objects are almost always perceived accurately in spite of the linear dependence of retinal-image size on distance. It must not be supposed that this phenomenon is fully explained by the scaling of size with respect to texture elements. There are a great many other sources of relevant information: binocular parallax, shifts of retinal position as the observer moves, relative position in the visual field, linear perspective, and so on. It was once traditional to regard these sources of information as "cues" secondary to the size of the object's own retinal image. That is, they were thought to help the observer "correct" the size of the retinal image in the direction of accuracy.

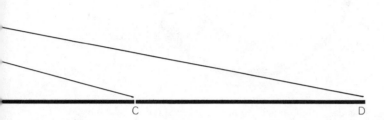

C   D

Perhaps this is not a bad description of Descartes's situation as he looked at the image on the back of the ox's eye: he may have tried to "correct" his perception of the size of the objects revealed to him on the ox's retina. Since one does not see one's own retina, however, nothing similar need be involved in normal perceiving. Instead the apparent size of an object is determined by information from the entire incoming light pattern, particularly by certain properties of the input that remain invariant with changes of the object's location.

The interrelation of textures, distances, and relative retinal sizes is only one example of ecological optics. The example may be a misleadingly simple one, because it assumes a stationary eye, an eye fixed in space and stably oriented in a particular direction. This is by no means a characteristic of human vision. In normal use the eyes are rarely still for long. Apart from small tremors, their most common movement is the flick from one position to another called a "saccade." Saccades usually take less than a twentieth of a second, but they happen several times each second in reading and may be just as frequent when a picture or an actual scene is being inspected. This means that there is a new retinal image every few hundred milliseconds.

Such eye movements are necessary because the area of clear vision available to the stationary eye is severely limited. To see this for oneself it is only necessary to fixate on a point in some unfamiliar picture or on an unread printed page. Only a small region around the fixation point will be clear. Most of the page is seen peripherally, which means that it is hazily visible at best. Only in the fovea, the small central part of the

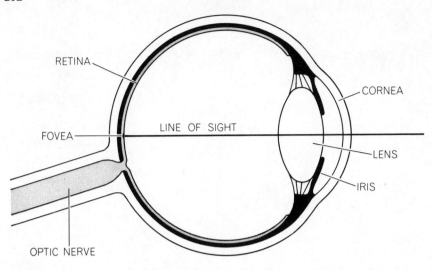

RETINA

CORNEA

FOVEA

LINE OF SIGHT

LENS

IRIS

OPTIC NERVE

Site of optical image is the retina, which contains the terminations of the optic nerve. In the tiny retinal depression known as the fovea the cone nerve endings are clustered. Their organization and dense packing make possible a high degree of visual acuity.

retina, are the receptor cells packed close enough together (and appropriately organized) to make a high degree of visual acuity possible. This is the reason one must turn one's eyes (or head) to look directly at objects in which one is particularly interested. (Animals with nonfoveated eyes, such as the horse, do not find this necessary.) It is also the reason why the eye must make several fixations on each line in reading, and why it roves widely over pictures.

Although it is easy to understand the function of saccadic movements, it is difficult or impossible to reconcile them with an image theory of perception. As long as we think of the perceiver as a homunculus looking at his retinal image, we must expect his experience to be one of almost constant interruption and change. Clearly this is not the case; one sees the page or the scene as a whole without any apparent discontinuity in space or time. Most people are either unaware of their own eye movements or have erroneous notions about them. Far from being a copy of the retinal display, the visual world is somehow *constructed* on the basis of information taken in during many different fixations.

The same conclusion follows, perhaps even more compellingly, if we consider the motions of external objects rather than the motions of the eyes. If the analogy between eye and camera were valid, the thing one looked at would have to hold still like a photographer's model in order to be seen clearly. The opposite is true: far from obscuring the shapes and

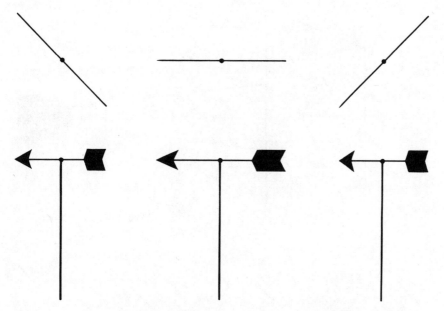

Ambiguous visual input can arise from a stationary weather vane. The weather vane in three different orientations is shown as it would be seen from above (top) and in side view (bottom). If the vane begins to rotate, its real length will become apparent.

spatial relations of things, movement generally clarifies them. Consider the visual problem presented by a distant arrow-shaped weather vane. As long as the weather vane and the observer remain motionless, there is no way to tell whether it is a short arrow oriented at right angles to the line of sight or a longer arrow slanting toward (or away from) the observer. Let it begin to turn in the wind, however, and its true shape and orientation will become visible immediately. The reason lies in the systematic distortions of the retinal image produced by the object's rotation. Such distortions provide information that the nervous system can use. On the basis of a fluidly changing retinal pattern the perceiver comes to experience a rigid object. (An interesting aspect of this example is that the input information is ambiguous. The same retinal changes could be produced by either a clockwise or a counterclockwise rotation of the weather vane. As a result the perceiver may alternate between two perceptual experiences, one of which is illusory.)

Some years ago Hans Wallach and D. N. O'Connell of Swarthmore College showed (1953) that such motion-produced changes in the input are indeed used as a source of information in perceiving; in fact this kind of information seems to be a more potent determiner of what we see than

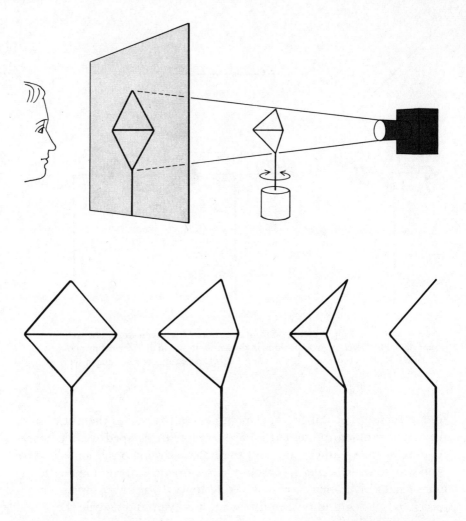

Kinetic depth effect shows how movement can endow perceived objects with three-dimensional shape. The shadow of a bent wire form (shown at bottom in four different orientations) looks as flat as the screen on which it is cast so long as the form remains stationary. When it is swiveled back and forth, the changing shadow is seen as a rigid rotating object with the appropriate three-dimensionality. The direction of rotation remains ambiguous, just as it does for the weather vane.

the traditionally emphasized cues for depth are. In their experiment the subject watched the shadow of a wire form cast on a translucent screen. He could not see the object itself. So long as the object remained stationary the subject saw only a two-dimensional shadow on a two-dimensional screen, as might be expected. The form was mounted in such a way, however, that it could be swiveled back and forth by a small electric motor.

When the motor was turned on, the true three-dimensional shape of the form appeared at once, even though the only stimulation reaching the subject's eyes came from a distorting shadow on a flat screen. Here the kinetic depth effect, as it has been called, overrode binocular stereoscopic information that continued to indicate that all the movement was taking place in a flat plane.

In the kinetic depth effect the constructive nature of perception is particularly apparent. What one sees is somehow a composite based on information accumulated over a period of time. The same is true in reading or in any instance where eye movements are involved: information from past fixations is used together with information from the present fixation to determine what is seen. But if perception is a temporally extended act, some storage of information, some kind of memory, must be involved in it. How shall we conceive of this storage? How is it organized? How long does it last? What other functions might it serve?

With questions like these, we have moved beyond the problem of specifying the visual stimulus. In addition to identifying the sources of information for vision, we want to know how that information is processed. In the long run, perhaps, questions about processes should be answered in neurological terms. However, no such answers can be given at present. The neurophysiology of vision has recently made great strides, but it is still not ready to deal with the constructive processes that are central to perception. We shall have to be content with a relatively abstract account, one that does not specify the neural locus of the implicated mechanisms.

Although seeing requires storage of information, this memory cannot be thought of as a sequence of superposed retinal images. Superposition would give rise only to a sort of smear in which all detail is lost. Nor can we assume that the perceiver keeps careful track of his eye movements and thus is able to set each new retinal image in just the right place in relation to the older stored ones. Such an alignment would require a much finer monitoring of eye motion than is actually available. Moreover, the similar synthesis of information that is involved in the kinetic depth effect could not possibly be explained that way. It seems, therefore, that perceiving involves a memory that is not representational but schematic. During a series of fixations the perceiver synthesizes a model or schema of the scene before him, using information from each successive fixation to add detail or to extend the construction. This constructed whole is what guides his movements (including further eye movements in many cases) and it is what he describes when he is being introspective. In short, it is what he sees.

Interestingly enough, although the memory involved in visual synthesis cannot consist simply of stored retinal afterimages, recent experiments indicate that storage of this kind does exist under certain circumstances. After a momentary exposure (too short for eye movement) that is followed by a blank field the viewer preserves an iconic image of the input pattern for some fraction of a second. George Sperling of the Bell Telephone Laboratories has shown that a signal given during this postexposure period can serve to direct a viewer's attention to any arbitrary part of the field, just as if it were still present.

The displays used in Sperling's experiments consisted of several rows of letters—too many to be reported from a single glance. Nevertheless, subjects were able to report any *single row*, indicated by the postexposure signal, rather well. Such a signal must come quickly; letters to which the observer does not attend before the brief iconic memory has faded are lost. That is why the observer cannot report the entire display: the icon disappears before he can read it all.

Even under these unusual conditions, then, people display selectivity in their use of the information that reaches the eye. The selection is made from material presented in a single brief exposure, but only because the experimental arrangements precluded a second glance. Normally selection and construction take place over a series of glances; no iconic memory for individual "snapshots" can survive. Indeed, the presentation of a second stimulus figure shortly after the first in a brief-exposure experiment tends to destroy the iconic replica. The viewer may see a fusion of the two figures, only the second, or an apparent motion of the figures, depending on their temporal and spatial relations. He does not see them separately.

So far we have considered two kinds of short-term memory for visual information: the iconic replica of a brief and isolated stimulus, and the cumulative schema of the visible world that is constructed in the course of ordinary perception. Both of these processes (which may well be different manifestations of a single underlying mechanism) involve the storage of information over a period of time. Neither of them, however, is what the average man has in mind when he speaks of memory. Everyday experience testifies that visual information can be stored over long periods. Things seen yesterday can be recalled today; for that matter they may conceivably be recalled 20 years from now. Such recall may take many forms, but perhaps the most interesting is the phenomenon called visual imagery. In a certain sense one can see again what one has seen before. Are these mental images like optical ones? Are they revived copies of earlier stimulation? Indeed, does it make any sense at all to speak of "seeing" things that are not present? Can there be visual experience when there is no stimulation by light?

To deal with these problems effectively we must distinguish two issues: first, the degree to which the mechanisms involved in visual memory are like those involved in visual perception and, second, the degree to which the perceiver is willing to say his images look real, that is, like external things seen. Although the first issue is perhaps the more fundamental—and the most relevant here—the second has always attracted the most attention.

One reason for the perennial interest in the "realness" of images is the wide range of differences in imaging capacity from person to person and from time to time. When Francis Galton conducted the first empirical study of mental imagery (published in 1883), he found some of his associates skeptical of the very existence of imagery. They assumed that only poetic fancy allowed one to speak of "seeing" in connection with what one remembered; remembering consisted simply in a knowledge of facts. Other people, however, were quite ready to describe their mental imagery in terms normally applied to perception. Asked in the afternoon about their breakfast table, they said they could see it clearly, with colors bright (although perhaps a little dimmer than in the original experience) and objects suitably arranged.

These differences seem to matter less when one is asleep; many people who report little or no lifelike imagery while awake may have visual dreams and believe in the reality of what they see. On the other hand, some psychopathological states can endow images with such a compelling quality that they dominate the patient's experience. Students of perception have often disregarded dreams and phantasms, considering them "hallucinatory" and thus irrelevant to normal seeing. However, this is a difficult position to defend either logically or empirically. Logically a sharp distinction between perception and hallucination would be easy enough if perceptions were copies of the retinal image; hallucinations would then be experiences that do *not* copy that image. But since perception does more than mirror the stimulus (and since hallucinations often incorporate stimulus information), this distinction is not clear-cut. Moreover, a number of recent findings seem to point up very specific relations between the processes of seeing and imagining.

Perhaps the most unexpected of these findings has emerged from studies of sleep and dreams. The dreaming phase of sleep, which occurs several times each night, is regularly accompanied by bursts of rapid eye movements. In several studies William C. Dement and his collaborators have awakened experimental subjects immediately after a period of eye motion and asked them to report their just-preceding dream. Later the eye-movement records were compared with a transcript of the dream report to see if any relation between the two could be detected. Of course this was not possible in every case. (Indeed, we can be fairly sure that many of the eye movements of sleep have no visual significance; similar motions occur in the sleep of newborn babies, decorticated cats, and congenitally blind adults.) Nevertheless, there was appreciably more correspondence between the two kinds of record than could be attributed to chance. The parallel between the eye movements of the dreamer and the content of the dream was sometimes striking. In one case five distinct upward deflections of the eyes were recorded just before the subject awoke and reported a dream of climbing five steps!

Another recent line of research has also implicated eye movements in the processes of visual memory. Ralph Norman Haber and his co-workers at Yale University reopened the study of eidetic imagery, which for a generation had remained untouched by psychological research. An eidetic image is an imaginative production that seems to be external to the viewer and to have a location in perceived space; it has a clarity comparable to that of genuinely perceived objects; it can be examined by the "*Eidetiker*," who may report details that he did not notice in the original presentation of the stimulus. Most *Eidetikers* are children, but the developmental course of this rather rare ability is not well understood. What is most interesting about these images for the present argument is that the *Eidetiker* scans them with his eyes. Asked about a detail in one or another corner of the image, he moves his eyes to look at the appropriate part of the blank wall on which he has "projected" it. That is, he does just what anyone would do who was really looking at something.

Are these esoteric phenomena really relevant to the study of vision? It might be argued that they do not provide a safe basis for inference; dreaming is a very special physiological state and eidetic imagery is restricted to very special types of people. It is not difficult, however, to show that similar processes occur in persons who do not have vivid visual imagery at all. A simple demonstration suggested by Julian Hochberg of New York University helps to make this point: Try to remember how many windows there are in your own house or apartment.

If you have never considered this question before, it will be hard to find the answer without actively looking and counting. However, you will probably not need to look at the windows themselves. Most people, even those who say they have no visual imagery, can easily form and scan an *internal representation* of the walls, counting off the windows as they appear in them. This process evidently uses stored visual information.

It seems to involve mechanisms much like those used for seeing and counting real windows.

We can draw three conclusions from this demonstration. First, seeing and imagining employ similar—perhaps the same—mechanisms. Second, images can be useful, even when they are not vivid or lifelike, even for people who do not have "good imagery." Third, mental images are constructs and not copies. This last point may have been obvious in any case—you might just as well have been asked to imagine a gryphon and to count its claws—but it bears further emphasis. All the windows could not have been optically imaged on the retina simultaneously, and they may not even have appeared there in rapid succession. The image (or series of images) developed in solving this problem is new; it is not a replica of any previous stimulus.

The first two of these points have received additional confirmation in a recent experiment by Lee R. Brooks of McMaster University, whose method puts imagery and visual perception in direct competition. In one of his studies the subjects were shown a large block F and told to remember what it looked like. After the F was removed from view they were asked to describe the succession of corner points that would be encountered as one moved around it, responding "Yes" for each point that was either on the extreme top or the bottom of the F, and "No" for each point in between. This visual-memory task proved to be more difficult when the responses were made by *pointing* to a printed series of yeses and noes than when a spoken "Yes" or "No" was allowed. However, the difficulty was not intrinsic to the act of pointing; it resulted from the conflict between pointing and simultaneously visualizing the F. In another of Brooks's tasks the subjects had to respond "Yes" for each noun and "No" for each non-noun in a memorized sentence. In this case they tended to rely on verbal-auditory memory rather than visual memory. As a result spoken response was the more difficult of the two.

We would not have been surprised to find a conflict between visually guided pointing and corner-counting on an F the viewer was *looking at*. After all, he could not be expected to look in two places at once. Even if the F had appeared on the same sheet of paper with the yeses and noes, interference would have been easy to understand: the succession of glances required to examine the corners of the F would have conflicted with the visual organization needed to point at the right succession of responses. What Brooks has shown, rather surprisingly, is that this conflict exists even when the F is merely imagined. Visual images are apparently produced by the same integrative processes that make ordinary perception possible.

In short, the reaction of the nervous system to stimulation by light is far from passive. The eye and brain do not act as a camera or a recording instrument. Neither in perceiving nor in remembering is there any enduring copy of the optical input. In perceiving, complex patterns are extracted from that input and fed into the constructive processes of vision, so that the movements and the inner experience of the perceiver are usually in good correspondence with his environment. Visual memory differs from perception because it is based primarily on stored rather than on current information, but it involves the same kind of synthesis. Although the eyes have been called the windows of the soul, they are not so much peepholes as entry ports, supplying raw material for the constructive activity of the visual system.

IV.

THE TRADITIONAL "ESOTERIC" PSYCHOLOGIES

Introduction

We associate "Psychology" with people in laboratories, performing experiments with quantitative methods. Many of the writers in this book have challenged the usefulness of a purely quantitative science, arguing that an entire dimension of man's nature is omitted in such an attempt. To the completely orthodox mind, nothing could be further from "Psychology" than strange men repeating "magic" words over and over, or Yoga masters in unusual postures, or a dervish spinning, or a Zen monk puzzling over a seemingly unanswerable question such as "What is the size of the Real You?"

Yet there *are* two major modes of knowing, and in the cultures of Japan, the Middle East, India, people who were concerned with the central questions of psychology—consciousness—studied their local system of psychology, Buddhism, Sufism, Yoga, among others. These are inwardly directed systems, focused on a personal rather than an intellectual knowledge, concerned with intuition, if you will, rather than verbal intellectuality. Only within the past few years have scientists begun to

recognize that this inward, personal knowledge is an essential complement to normal intellection. These traditional, "esoteric" psychologies
begin from a conception of science advanced by Cantril *et al.*, one
grounded in everyday experience. But these disciplines are more practical even than Cantril's ideal. They consist of technique, not theory, of
exercises and rituals for extending consciousness.

There are many points of agreement between the two major psychologies. They both recognize that consciousness is a personal construction.
The esoteric characterization of this process is quite negative. The Sufis
hold that man is "asleep" or "blind," the Christians that he is "fallen."
But where modern psychology proceeds to a fine analysis of the *process*
of this "illusion" (as in the articles by Neisser and by Hastorf and Cantril), the esoteric systems attempt to develop techniques for the destruc-
turing of the illusion. It is what Arthur Deikman terms a "deautomatization" of the normal process of consciousness.

Deikman here attempts to analyze the "mystic" experience in terms
of contemporary psychology, and in so doing forms an essential bridge
for the study of human consciousness. No survey of human consciousness
can be complete without the inclusion of these "mystic" states, but they
are extremely difficult to study within a linear and scientific mode; so
the temptation has been to ignore them. Deikman uses an analysis similar
to those of James, Hastorf, and Neisser, and examines the mystical experiences as a development of the second mode of consciousness, a holistic
perception of unity in lieu of the normal sequence of separate objects. It
is a superb paper, and one which has given much impetus to the field of
the psychology of consciousness as a whole.

In juxtaposition, in both style and length, there follows a brief article
by Lama Angakarika Govinda, a long-time student of Tibetan Buddhism. His brief extract lays out the differences in intent between the
two types of psychology, one linear, rational, and intellectual, the other
personal and involved with the development of perspective.

Since the traditional esoteric techniques are personal systems, it is
useful here to include three descriptions of meditation exercises from
different traditions. Kapleau is a student of Zen, Rahula of Buddhism,
and Spiegelberg of Yoga. They are juxtaposed so that the essential similarity of the exercises can be observed. In each the practitioner is asked
to focus his consciousness on one source of stimulation, be it breath, a
word, a strange question, or a naturally occurring scene. Meditation (of
the concentrative form) is an exercise which employs repetition to turn
off the active mode of consciousness, and allows a "bypass" to be developed into the quiescent, receptive mode.

Meditation has been studied physiologically of late. Many reports find that it leads to an increase in the alpha rhythm of the brain and to other changes associated with relaxation. There follows a report on "Transcendental Meditation" by Robert Keith Wallace and Herbert Benson of Harvard. This is a technique which employs a specially chosen word as the focus of awareness. Its physiological effects are reported in this study from *Scientific American*. It is followed by a summary of research carried out in Japan on Zen by Kasamatsu and Hirai.

It is useful to study these techniques and effects, but, most importantly, as Lama Govinda states, the effect of these esoteric psychologies is beyond techniques. In large part they serve to open up the restrictions on inquiry in western thought, and to provide a clear glimpse of the possibilities of man which have been "forgotten" in science. We are at the beginnings of a new synthesis of these two psychologies. It arises from a broadened concept of what is possible from Man in the traditional, "esoteric" psychologies and in the technological and methodological sophistication of western science.

17.

Deautomatization and
the Mystic Experience

Arthur J. Deikman

To study the mystic experience one must turn initially to material that appears unscientific, is couched in religious terms, and seems completely subjective. Yet these religious writings are data and not to be dismissed as something divorced from the reality with which psychological science is concerned. The following passage from *The Cloud of Unknowing*, a fourteenth-century religious treatise, describes a procedure to be followed in order to attain an intuitive knowledge of God. Such an intuitive experience is called mystical because it is considered beyond the scope of language to convey. However, a careful reading will show that these

Reprinted from *Psychiatry*, 29 (1966), 324–338, by permission of The William Alanson White Psychiatric Foundation, Inc. This research was supported by Research Grant MH-07683, from the National Institute of Mental Health, USPHS; and by the Austen Riggs Center.

instructions contain within their religious idiom psychological ideas pertinent to the study and understanding of a wide range of phenomena not necessarily connected with theological issues:

> Forget all the creatures that ever God made and the works of them, so that thy thought or thy desire be not directed or stretched to any of them, neither in general nor in special. . . . At the first time when thou dost it, thou findst but a darkness and as it were a kind of unknowing, thou knowest not what, saving that thou feelest in thy will a naked intent unto God . . . thou mayest neither see him clearly by light of understanding in thy reason, nor feel him in sweetness of love in thy affection . . . if ever thou shalt see him or feel him as it may be here, it must always be in this cloud and in this darkness. . . . Smite upon that thick cloud of unknowing with a sharp dart of longing love   (Knowles, 1961, p. 77).

Specific questions are raised by this subjective account: What constitutes a state of consciousness whose content is not rational thought ("understanding in thy reason"), affective ("sweetness of love"), or sensate ("darkness," "cloud of unknowing")? By what means do both an active "forgetting" and an objectless "longing" bring about such a state? A comparison of this passage with others in the classical mystic literature indicates that the author is referring to the activities of renunciation and contemplative meditation. This paper will present a psychological model of the mystic experience based on the assumptions that meditation and renunciation are primary techniques for producing it, and that the process can be conceptualized as one of deautomatization. . . .

BASIC MYSTIC TECHNIQUES

How is the mystic experience produced? To answer this question I will examine the two basic techniques involved in mystical exercises: contemplation and renunciation.

Contemplation is, ideally, a nonanalytic apprehension of an object or idea—nonanalytic because discursive thought is banished and the attempt is made to empty the mind of everything except the percept of the object in question. Thought is conceived of as an interference with the direct contact that yields essential knowledge through perception alone. The renunciation of worldly goals and pleasures, both physical and psychological, is an extension of the same principle of freeing oneself from distractions that interfere with the perception of higher realisms or more beautiful aspects of existence. The renunciation prescribed is most thorough and quite explicit in all texts. The passage that begins this paper instructs, "Forget all the creatures that ever God made . . . so that thy thought . . . be not directed . . . to any of them." In the Lankavatra Scripture one reads, "he must seek to annihilate all vagrant thoughts and notions belonging to the externality of things, and all ideas of individuality and generality, of suffering and impermanence, and cultivate the noblest ideas of egolessness and emptiness and imagelessness" (Goddard, 1938, p. 323). Meister Eckhart promises: "If we keep ourselves free from the things that are outside us, God will give us in exchange everything that is in heaven, . . . itself with all its powers" (Clark and Skinner, 1958, p. 104). In Hilton one reads, "Therefore if you desire to discover your soul, withdraw your thoughts from outward and material things, forgetting if possible your own body and its five senses" (Hilton, 1953, p. 205). St. John calls for the explicit banishment of memory:

> Of all these forms and manners of knowledge the soul must strip and void itself, and it must strive to lose the imaginary apprehension of them, so that there may be left in it no kind of impression of knowledge, nor trace of aught soever, but rather the soul must remain barren and bare, as if these forms had never passed through it and in total oblivion and suspension. And this cannot happen unless the memory be annihilated as to all its forms, if it is to be united with God (St. John of the Cross, 1953, p. 227).

In most Western and Eastern mystic practice, renunciation also extends to the actual life situation of the mystic. Poverty, chastity, and the solitary way are regarded as essential to the attainment of mystic union. Zen Buddhism, however, sees the ordinary life as a proper vehicle for "satori" as long as the "worldly" passions and desires are given up, and with them the intellectual approach to experience. "When I am in my isness, thoroughly purged of all intellectual sediments, I have my freedom in its primary sense . . . free from intellectual complexities and moralistic attachments" (Suzuki, 1959, p. 19).

Instructions for performing contemplative meditation indicate that a very active effort is made to exclude outer and inner stimuli, to devalue and banish them, and at the same time to focus attention on the meditative object. In this active phase of contemplation the concentration of attention upon particular objects, ideas, physical movements, or breathing exercises is advised as an aid to diverting attention from its usual channels and restricting it to a monotonous focus.* Patanjali comments,

> Binding the mind-stuff to a place is fixed-attention. . . . Focusedness of the presented idea on that place is contemplation. . . . This same [contemplation] shining forth [in consciousness] as the intended object and nothing more, and, as

---

*Breathing exercises can also affect the carbon-dioxide content of the blood and thus alter the state of consciousness chemically.

it were, emptied of itself, is concentration. . . . The three in one àre constraint. . . . Even these [three] are indirect aids to seedless [concentration] (Woods, 1914, pp. 203–208).

Elaborate instructions are found in Yoga for the selection of objects for contemplation and for the proper utilization of posture and breathing to create optimal conditions for concentration. Such techniques are not usually found in the Western religious literature except in the form of the injunction to keep the self oriented toward God and to fight the distractions which are seen as coming from the devil. [*The Spiritual Exercises of St. Ignatius* (Puhl, 1962) is a possible exception.]

The active phase of contemplative meditation is a preliminary to the stage of full contemplation, in which the subject is caught up and absorbed in a process he initiated but which now seems autonomous, requiring no effort. Instead, passivity—self-surrender—is called for, an open receptivity amidst the "darkness" resulting from the banishment of thoughts and sensations and the renunciation of goals and desires directed toward the world.

> When this active effort of mental concentration is successful, it is followed by a more passive, receptive state of samadhi in which the earnest disciple will enter into the blissful abode of noble wisdom   (Goddard, 1938, p. 323).
>
> For if such a soul should desire to make any effort of its own with its interior faculties, this means that it will hinder and lose the blessings which . . . God is instilling into it and impressing upon it   (Hilton, 1953, p. 380).

It should not be forgotten that the techniques of contemplation and renunciation are exercised within the structure of some sort of theological schema. This schema is used to interpret and organize the experiences that occur. However, mere doctrine is usually not enough. The Eastern texts insist on the necessity for being guided by a guru (an experienced teacher), for safety's sake as well as in order to attain the spiritual goal. In Western religion, a "spiritual advisor" serves as guide and teacher. The presence of a motivating and organizing conceptual structure and the support and encouragement of a teacher are undoubtedly important in helping a person to persist in the meditation exercises and to achieve the marked personality changes that can occur through success in this endeavor. Enduring personality change is made more likely by the emphasis on adapting behavior to the values and insights associated both with the doctrinal structure and with the stages of mystical experience.

How can one explain the phenomena and their relation to these techniques? Most explanations in the psychological and psychoanalytic literature have been general statements emphasizing a regression to the early infant-mother symbiotic relationship. These statements range from an extreme position, such as Alexander's (1931), where Buddhist training is described as a withdrawal of libido from the world to be reinvested in the ego until an intra-uterine narcissism is achieved—"the pure narcissism of the sperm"—to the basic statement of Freud's (1961, XXI, 64–73) that "oceanic feeling" is a memory of a relatively undifferentiated infantile ego state. Lewin (1950, pp. 149–155) in particular has developed this concept. In recent years hypotheses have been advanced uniting the concepts of regression and of active adaptation. The works of Kris (1952, p. 302), Fingarette (1963), and Prince and Savage (1965) illustrate this approach to the mystic experience. This paper will attempt an explanation of mystic phenomena from a different point of view, that of attentional mechanisms in perception and cognition.

DEAUTOMATIZATION

In earlier studies of experimental meditation, I hypothesized that mystic phenomena were a consequence of a *deautomatization* of the psychological structures that organize, limit, select, and interpret perceptual stimuli. I suggested the hypotheses of sensory translation, reality transfer, and perceptual expansion to explain certain unusual perceptions of the meditation subjects (Deikman, 1966b). At this point I will try to present an integrated formulation that relates these concepts to the classical mystic techniques of renunciation and contemplation.

Deautomatization is a concept stemming from Hartmann's (1958, pp. 88–91) discussion of the automatization of motor behavior:

> In well-established achievements [motor apparatuses] function automatically: the integration of the somatic systems involved in the action is automatized, and so is the integration of the individual mental acts involved in it. With increasing exercise of the action its intermediate steps disappear from consciousness . . . not only motor behavior but perception and thinking, too, show automatization. . . .
> It is obvious that automatization may have economic advantages, in saving attention cathexis in particular and simple cathexis of consciousness in general. . . . Here, as in most adaptation processes, we have a purposive provision for the average expectable range of tasks.

Gill and Brennan (1959, p. 178) developed the concept of deautomatization:

> Deautomatization is an undoing of the automatizations of apparatuses—both means and goal structures—directed toward the environment. Deautomatization is, as it were, a shake-up which can be followed by an advance or a retreat in the level of organization. . . . Some manipulation of the attention directed toward the functioning of an apparatus is necessary if it is to be deautomatized.

Thus, deautomatization may be conceptualized as the undoing of auto-matization, presumably by *reinvesting actions and percepts with attention*.

The concept of psychological *structures* follows the definition by Rapa-port and Gill (1959, pp. 157–158):

> *Structures are configurations of a low rate of change . . . within which, between which, and by means of which mental processes take place. . . . Structures are hierarchically ordered. . . .* This assumption . . . is significant because it is the foundation for the psycho-analytic propositions concerning differentiation (whether resulting in discrete structures which are then co-ordinated, or in the increased internal articulation of structures), and because it implies that the quality of a process depends upon the level of the structural hierarchy on which it takes place.

The deautomatization of a structure may result in a shift to a structure lower in the hierarchy, rather than a complete cessation of the particular function involved.

Contemplative Meditation

In reflecting on the technique of contemplative meditation, one can see that it seems to constitute just such a manipulation of attention as is re-quired to produce deautomatization. The percept receives intense atten-tion while the use of attention for abstract categorization and thought is explicitly prohibited. Since automatization normally accomplishes the transfer of attention *from* a percept or action to abstract thought activity, the meditation procedure exerts a force in the reverse direction. Cog-nition is inhibited in favor of perception; the active intellectual style is replaced by a receptive perceptual mode.

Automatization is a hierarchically organized developmental process, so one would expect deautomatization to result in a shift toward a per-ceptual and cognitive organization characterized as "primitive," that is, an organization preceding the analytic, abstract, intellectual mode typical of present-day adult thought. The perceptual and cognitive func-tioning of children and of people of primitive cultures have been studied by Werner, who described primitive imagery and thought as (a) rela-tively more vivid and sensuous, (b) syncretic, (c) physiognomic and ani-mated, (d) dedifferentiated with respect to the distinctions between self and object and between objects, and (e) characterized by a dedifferen-tiation and fusion of sense modalities. In a statement based on studies of eidetic imagery in children as well as on broader studies of perceptual development, Werner (1957, p. 152) states:

> The image . . . gradually changed in functional character. It becomes essentially subject to the exigencies of abstract thought. Once the image changes in function and becomes an instrument in reflective thought, its structure will also change. It is only through such structural change that the image can serve as an instrument of expression in abstract mental activity. This is why, of necessity, the sensuousness, fullness of detail, the color and vivacity of the image must fade.

Theoretically, deautomatization should reverse this development in the direction of primitive thought, and it is striking to note that classical accounts of mystic experience emphasize the phenomenon of Unity. Unity can be viewed as a dedifferentiation that merges all boundaries until the self is no longer experienced as a separate object and customary perceptual and cognitive distinctions are no longer applicable. In this respect, the mystic literature is consistent with the deautomatization hypothesis. If one searches for evidence of changes in the mystic's experience of the external world, the classical literature is of less help, because the mystic's orientation is inward rather than outward and he tends to write about God rather than nature. However, in certain accounts of untrained-sensate experience there is evidence of a gain in sensory richness and vividness. James (1929, pp. 243–244), in describing the conversion experience, states: "A third peculiarity of the assurance state is the objective change which the world often appears to undergo, 'An appearance of newness beautifies every object.' " He quotes Billy Bray: "I shouted for joy, I praised God with my whole heart . . . I remember this, that everything looked new to me, the people, the fields, the cattle, the trees. I was like a new man in a new world." Another example, this one from a woman, "I pled for mercy and had a vivid realization of forgiveness and renewal of my nature. When rising from my knees I exclaimed, 'Old things have passed away, all things have become new.' It was like entering another world, a new state of existence. Natural objects were glorified. My spiritual vision was so clarified that I saw beauty in every material object in the universe." Again, "The appearance of everything was altered, there seemed to be as it were a calm, a sweet cast or appearance of divine glory in almost everything."

Such a change in a person's perception of the world has been called by Underhill (1955, p. 235), "clarity of vision, a heightening of physical perception," and she quotes Blake's phrase, "cleanse the doors of perception." It is hard to document this perceptual alteration because the autobiographical accounts that Underhill, James, and others cite are a blend of the mystic's spiritual feeling and his actual perception, with the result that the spiritual content dominates the description the mystic gives of the physical world. However, these accounts do suggest that a "new vision" takes place, colored by an inner exaltation. Their authors report perceiving a new brilliance to the world, of seeing everything as if for the first time, of noticing beauty which for the most part they may have previously passed by without seeing. Although such descriptions do not prove a change in sensory perception, they strongly imply it. These particular phenomena appear quite variable and are not mentioned in many mystic accounts. However, direct evidence was obtained on this point in the meditation experiments already cited (Deikman, 1963, 1966b). There, it was possible to ask questions and to analyze the subjects' reports to obtain information on their perceptual experiences. The phenomena the subjects reported fulfilled Werner's criteria completely, although the extent of change varied from one subject to the next. They described their reactions to the percept, a blue vase, as follows: (a) an increased vividness and richness of the percept—"more vivid," "luminous"; (b) animation in the vase, which seemed to move with a life of its own; (c) a marked decrease in self-object distinction, occurring in those subjects who continued longest in the experiments: "I really began to feel, you know, almost as though the blue and I were perhaps merging, or that vase and I were. . . . It was as though everything was sort of merging"; (d) syncretic thought and a fusing and alteration of normal perceptual modes: "I began to feel this light going back and forth," "When the vase changes shape I feel this in my body," "I'm still not sure, though, whether it's the motion in the rings or if it's the rings [concentric rings of light between the subject and the vase]. But in a certain way it is real . . . it's not real in the sense that you can see it, touch it, taste it, smell it or anything but it certainly is real in the sense that you can experience it happening." The perceptual and cognitive changes that did occur in the subjects were consistently in the direction of a more "primitive" organization.

Thus, the available evidence supports the hypothesis that a deautomatization is produced by contemplative meditation. One might be tempted to call this deautomatization a regression to the perceptual and cognitive state of the child or infant. However, such a concept rests on assumptions as to the child's experience of the world that cannot yet be verified. In an oft-quoted passage, Wordsworth (1904, p. 353) writes:

> There was a time when meadow, grove, and stream,
> The earth, and every common sight,
> To me did seem
> Apparelled in celestial light,
> The glory and the freshness of a dream.

However, he may be confusing childhood with what is actually a reconstruction based on an interaction of adult associative capacities with the *memory* of the more direct sensory contact of the child. "Glory" is probably an adult product. Rather than speaking of a return to childhood, it is more accurate to say that the undoing of automatic perceptual and cognitive structures permits a gain in sensory intensity and richness at the expense of abstract categorization and differentiation. One might call the direction regressive in a developmental sense, but the actual experience is probably not within the psychological scope of any child. It is a deautomatization occurring in an adult mind, and the experience gains its richness from adult memories and functions now subject to a different mode of consciousness.

Renunciation

The deautomatization produced by contemplative meditation is enhanced and aided by the adoption of renunciation as a goal and a life style, a renunciation not confined to the brief meditative period alone. Poverty, chastity, isolation, and silence are traditional techniques prescribed for pursuing the mystic path: To experience God, keep your thoughts turned to God and away from the world and the body that binds one to the world. The meditative strategy is carried over into all segments of the subject's life. The mystic strives to banish from awareness the objects of the world and the desires directed toward them. To the extent that perceptual and cognitive structures require the "nutriment" of their accustomed stimuli for adequate functioning, renunciation would be expected to weaken and even disrupt these structures, thus tending to produce an unusual experience (Rapaport, 1951). Such an isolation from nutritive stimuli probably occurs internally as well. The subjects of the meditation experiment quoted earlier reported that a decrease in responsiveness to distracting stimuli took place as they became more practiced. They became more effective, with less effort, in barring unwanted stimuli from awareness. These reports suggest that psychological barrier structures were established as the subjects became more adept (Deikman, 1963, p. 338). EEG studies of Zen monks yielded similar results. The effect of a distracting stimulus, as measured by the disappearance of alpha rhythm, was most prominent in the novices, less prominent in those of intermediate training, and almost absent in the master (Kasamatsu & Hirai, 1963). It may be that the intensive long-term practice of meditation creates temporary stimulus barriers producing a functional state of sensory isolation.* On the basis of sensory isolation experiments it would be expected that long-term deprivation

---

*It has been postulated by McReynolds (1960, p. 269) that a related stimulus barrier system may be operative in schizophrenia.

(or decreased variability) of a particular class of stimulus "nutriment" would cause an alteration in those functions previously established to deal with that class of stimuli (Schultz, 1965, pp. 95–97; Solomon *et al.*, 1961, pp. 226–237). These alterations seem to be a type of deautomatization, as defined earlier—for example, the reported increased brightness of colors and the impairment of perceptual skills such as color discrimination (Zubeck *et al.*, 1961). Thus, renunciation alone can be viewed as producing deautomatization. When combined with contemplative meditation, it produces a very powerful effect.

Finally, the more renunciation is achieved, the more the mystic is committed to his goal of Union or Enlightenment. His motivation necessarily increases, for having abandoned the world, he has no other hope of sustenance.

PRINCIPAL FEATURES OF THE MYSTIC EXPERIENCE

Granted that deautomatization takes place, it is necessary to explain five principal features of the mystic experience: (a) intense realness, (b) unusual sensations, (c) unity, (d) ineffability, and (e) trans-sensate phenomena.

Realness

It is assumed by those who have had a mystic experience, whether induced by years of meditation or by a single dose of LSD, that the truthfulness of the experience is attested to by its sense of realness. The criticism of skeptics is often met with the statement, "You have to experience it yourself and then you will understand." This means that if one has the actual experience he will be convinced by its intense *feeling of reality*. "I know it was real because it was more real than my talking to you now." But "realness" is not evidence. Indeed, there are many clinical examples of variability in the intensity of the feeling of realness that is not correlated with corresponding variability in the reality. A dream may be so "real" as to carry conviction into the waking state, although its content may be bizarre beyond correspondence to this world or to any other. Psychosis is often preceded or accompanied by a sense that the world is *less real* than normally, sometimes that it is more real, or has a different reality. The phenomenon of depersonalization demonstrates the potential for an alteration in the sense of the realness of one's own person, although one's evidential self undergoes no change whatsoever. However, in the case of depersonalization, or of derealization, the distinction between what is external and what is internal is still clear. What changes is the quality of realness attached to those object representations. Thus it appears that (a) the *feeling* of realness represents a function distinct from that of reality *judgment*, although they usually operate in synchrony; (b) the feeling of realness is not inherent in sensations, per se; and (c) realness can be considered a quantity function capable of displacement and therefore, of intensification, reduction, and transfer affecting all varieties of ideational and sensorial contents.*

From a developmental point of view, it is clear that biological survival depends on a clear sense of what is palpable and what is not. The sense of reality necessarily becomes fused with the object world. When one considers that meditation combined with renunciation brings about a profound disruption of the subject's normal psychological relationship to the world, it becomes plausible that the practice of such mystic techniques would be associated with a significant alteration of the feeling of reality. The quality of reality formerly attached to objects becomes attached to the particular sensations and ideas that enter awareness during periods of perceptual and cognitive deautomatization. Stimuli of the inner world become invested with the feeling of reality ordinarily bestowed on objects. Through what might be termed "reality transfer," *thoughts and images become real* (Deikman, 1966, pp. 109–111).

Unusual Percepts

The sensations and ideation occurring during mystic deautomatization are often very unusual; they do not seem part of the continuum of everyday consciousness. "All at once, without warning of any kind, he found himself wrapped around as it were by a flame colored cloud" (Bucke, 1961, p. 8). Perceptions of encompassing light, infinite energy, ineffable visions, and incommunicable knowledge are remarkable in their seeming distinction from perceptions of the phenomena of the "natural world." According to mystics, these experiences are different because they pertain to a higher transcendent reality. What is perceived is said to come from another world, or at least another dimension. Although such a possibility cannot be ruled out, many of the phenomena can be understood as representing *an unusual mode of perception*, rather than an unusual external stimulus.

---

*Paul Federn's (1955, pp. 241–260) idea that the normal feeling of reality requires an adequate investment of energy (libido) in the ego boundary, points toward the notion of a quantity of "realness." Avery Weisman (1958) has developed and extended this idea, but prefers the more encompassing concept of "libidinal fields" to that of ego boundaries.

In the studies of experimental meditation already mentioned, two long-term subjects reported vivid experiences of light and force. For example:

> Shortly I began to sense motion and shifting of light and dark as this became stronger and stronger. Now when this happens it's happening not only in my vision but it's happening or it feels like a physical kind of thing. It's connected with feelings of attraction, expansion, absorption and suddenly my vision pinpointed on a particular place and . . . I was in the grip of a very powerful sensation and this became the center [Deikman, 1966 b, p. 109].

This report suggests that the perception of motion and shifting light and darkness may have been the perception of the *movement* of attention among various psychic contents (whatever such "movement" might actually be). "Attraction," "expansion," "absorption," would thus reflect the dynamics of the effort to focus attention—successful focusing is experienced as being "in the grip of" a powerful force. Another example: "when the vase changes shape . . . I feel this in my body and particularly in my eyes . . . there is an actual kind of physical sensation as though something is moving there which recreates the shape of the vase" (Deikman, 1966b, p. 109). In this instance, the subject might have experienced the perception of a resynthesis taking place following deautomatization of the normal percept; that is, the percept of the vase was being reconstructed outside of normal awareness and the *process* of reconstruction was perceived as a physical sensation. I have termed this hypothetical perceptual mode *"sensory translation,"* defining it as the perception of psychic *action* (conflict, repression, problem solving, attentiveness, and so forth) via the relatively unstructured sensations of light, color, movement, force, sound, smell, or taste (Kris, 1952; Deikman, 1966b, pp. 108–109). This concept is related to Silberer's (1951) concept of hypnagogic phenomena but differs in its referents and genesis. In the hypnagogic state and in dreaming, a *symbolic* translation of psychic activity and ideas occurs. Although light, force, and movement may play a part in hypnagogic and dream constructions, the predominant percepts are complex visual, verbal, conceptual, and activity images. "Sensory translation" refers to the experience of nonverbal, simple, concrete perceptual equivalents of psychic action.*

The concept of sensory translation offers an intriguing explanation for the ubiquitous use of light as a metaphor for mystic experience. It may

---

*Somewhat related concepts, although extreme in scope, are those advanced by Michaux (1963, pp. 7–9), who suggests that the frequent experience of waves or vibrations in hallucinogenic drug states is the result of direct perception of the "brain waves" measured by the EEG; and by Leary (1964, pp. 330–339), who suggests that hallucinogenic drugs permit a "direct awareness of the processes which physicists and biochemists and neurologists measure," for example, electrons in orbit or the interaction of cells.

not be just a metaphor. "Illumination" may be derived from an actual sensory experience occurring when in the cognitive act of unification, a liberation of energy takes place, or when a resolution of unconscious conflict occurs, permitting the experience of "peace," "presence," and the like. Liberated energy experienced as light may be the core sensory experience of mysticism.

If the hypothesis of sensory translation is correct, it presents the problem of why sensory translation comes into operation in any particular instance.

In general, it appears that sensory translation may occur when (a) heightened attention is directed to the sensory pathways, (b) controlled analytic thought is absent, and (c) the subject's attitude is one of receptivity to stimuli (openness instead of defensiveness or suspiciousness). Training in contemplative meditation is specifically directed toward attaining a state with those characteristics. Laski (1961) reports that spontaneous mystic experiences may occur during such diverse activities as childbirth, viewing landscapes, listening to music, or having sexual intercourse. Although her subjects gave little description of their thought processes preceding the ecstasies, they were all involved at the time in intense sensory activities in which the three conditions listed above would tend to prevail. Those conditions seem also to apply to the mystical experiences associated with LSD. The state of mind induced by hallucinogenic drugs is reported to be one of increased sensory attention accompanied by an impairment or loss of different intellectual functions (Crochet et al., 1963; Watts, 1962; Michaux, 1963). With regard to the criterion of receptivity, if paranoid reactions occur during the drug state they are inimical to an ecstatic experience. On the other hand, when drug subjects lose their defensiveness and suspiciousness so that they "accept" rather than fight their situation, the "transcendent" experience often ensues (Sherwood et al., 1962). Thus, the general psychological context may be described as *perceptual concentration*. In this special state of consciousness the subject becomes aware of certain intra-psychic processes ordinarily excluded from or beyond the scope of awareness. The vehicle for this perception appears to be amorphous sensation, made real by a displacement of reality feeling "(reality transfer") and thus misinterpreted as being of external origin.

Unity

Experiencing one's self as one with the universe or with God is the hallmark of the mystic experience, regardless of its cultural context. As James (1929, p. 410) puts it,

"This overcoming of all the usual barriers between the individual and the Absolute is the great mystic achievement. In mystic states we both become one with the Absolute and we become aware of our oneness. This is the everlasting and triumphant mystical tradition, hardly altered by differences of clime or creed. In Hinduism, in Neoplatonism, in Sufism, in Christian mysticism, in Whitmanism, we find the same recurring note, so that there is about mystical utterance an eternal unanimity which ought to make a critic stop and think, and which brings it about that the mystical classics have, as has been said, neither birthday nor native land. Perpetually telling of the unity of man with God, their speech antedates languages, and they do not grow old."

I have already referred to explanations of this phenomenon in terms of regression. Two additional hypotheses should be considered: On the one hand, the perception of unity may be the perception of one's own psychic structure; on the other hand, the experience may be a perception of the real structure of the world.

It is a commonplace fact that we do not experience the world directly. Instead, we have an experience of sensation and associated memories from which we infer the nature of the stimulating object. As far as anyone can tell, the actual *substance* of the perception is the electrochemical activity that constitutes perception and thinking. From this point of view, the contents of awareness are homogeneous. They are variations of the same substance. If awareness were turned back upon itself, as postulated for sensory translation, this fundamental homogeneity (unity) of perceived reality—the electrochemical activity—might itself be experienced as a truth about the outer world, rather than the inner one. Unity, the idea and the experience that we are one with the world and with God, would thus constitute a valid perception insofar as it pertained to the nature of the thought process, but need not in itself be a correct perception of the external world.

Logically, there is also the possibility that the perception of unity does correctly evaluate the external world. As described earlier, deautomatization is an undoing of a psychic structure permitting the experience of increased detail and sensation at the price of requiring more attention. With such attention, it is possible that deautomatization may permit the awareness of new dimensions of the total stimulus array—a process of *"perceptual expansion."* The studies of Werner (1957), Von Senden (1960), and Shapiro (1960) suggest that development from infancy to adulthood is accompanied by an organization of the perceptual and cognitive world that has as its price the selection of some stimuli and stimulus qualities to the exclusion of others. If the automatization underlying that organization is reversed, or temporarily suspended, aspects of reality that were formerly unavailable might then enter awareness. Unity may in fact be a property of the real world that becomes perceptible via the techniques of meditation and renunciation, or under the special conditions, as yet unknown, that create the spontaneous, brief mystic experience of untrained persons.

Ineffability

Mystic experiences are ineffable, incapable of being expressed to another person. Although mystics sometimes write long accounts, they maintain that the experience cannot be communicated by words or by reference to similar experiences from ordinary life. They feel at a loss for appropriate words to communicate the intense realness, the unusual sensations, and the unity cognition already mentioned. However, a careful examination of mystic phenomena indicates that there are at least several types of experiences, all of which are "indescribable" but each of which differs substantially in content and formal characteristics. Error and confusion result when these several states of consciousness are lumped together as "the mystic experience" on the basis of their common characteristic of ineffability.

To begin with, one type of mystic experience cannot be communicated in words because it is probably based on primitive memories and related to fantasies of a preverbal (infantile) or nonverbal sensory experience. * Certain mystical reports that speak of being blissfully enfolded, comforted, and bathed in the love of God are very suggestive of the prototypical "undifferentiated state," the union of infant and breast, emphasized by psychoanalytic explanations of mystical phenomena. Indeed, it seems highly plausible that such early memories and fantasies might be reexperienced as a consequence of (a) the regression in thought processes brought about by renunciation and contemplative meditation, and (b) the activation of infantile longings by the guiding religious promise— that is, "that a benign deity would reward childlike surrender with permanent euphoria" (Moller, 1965, p. 127). In addition, the conditions of functional sensory isolation associated with mystic training may contribute to an increase in recall and vividness of such memories (Suraci, 1964).

A second type of mystical experience is equally ineffable but strikingly different—namely, a revelation too complex to be verbalized. Such

---

*Schachtel (1959, p. 284) regards early childhood, beyond infancy, as unrememberable for structural reasons: "It is not merely the repression of a specific content, such as early sexual experience, that accounts for the general childhood amnesia; the biologically, culturally, and socially influenced process of memory organization results in the formation of categories (schemata) of memory which are not suitable vehicles to receive and reproduce experiences of the quality and intensity typical of early childhood." It would follow that verbal structures would likewise be "unsuitable."

experiences are reported frequently by those who have drug-induced mystical experiences. In such states the subject has a revelation of the significance and interrelationships of many dimensions of life; he becomes aware of many levels of meaning simultaneously and "understands" the totality of existence. The question of whether such knowledge is actual or an illusion remains unanswered; however, if such a multi-leveled comprehension were to occur, it would be difficult—perhaps impossible—to express verbally. Ordinary language is structured to follow the logical development of one idea at a time and it might be quite inadequate to express an experience encompassing a large number of concepts simultaneously. William James suggested that "states of mystical intuition may be only very sudden and great extensions of the ordinary 'field of consciousness.' " He used the image of the vast reaches of a tidal flat exposed by the lowering of the water level (James, 1920, pp. 500–513). However, mystic revelation may be ineffable, not only because of the sudden broadening of consciousness that James suggests, but also because of a new "vertical" organization of concepts.* For example, for a short while after reading *The Decline and Fall of the Roman Empire*, one may be aware of the immense vista of a civilization's history as Gibbon recreated it. That experience can hardly be conveyed except through the medium of the book itself, and to that extent it is ineffable, and a minor version of James's widened consciousness. Suppose one then read *War and Peace* and acquired Tolstoy's perspective of historical events and their determination by chance factors. Again, this is an experience hard to express without returning to the novel. Now suppose one could "see" not only each of these world views individually but also their parallel relationships to each other, and the cross connections between the individual conceptual structures. And then suppose one added to these conceptual strata the biochemical perspective expressed by *The Fitness of the Environment* (Henderson, 1958), a work which deals, among other things, with the unique and vital properties of the water molecule. Then the *vertical* interrelationships of all these extensive schemata might, indeed, be beyond verbal expression, beyond ordinary conceptual capacities—in other words, they would approach the ineffable.

Trans-sensate Phenomena

A third type of ineffable experience is that which I have described earlier as the "trained-transcendent" mystical experience. The author

---

*A similar distinction concerning "vertical" listening to music is made by Ehrenzweig (1964, pp. 385–387).

of *The Cloud of Unknowing*, St. John of the Cross, Walter Hilton, and others are very specific in describing a new perceptual experience that does not include feelings of warmth, sweetness, visions, or any other elements of familiar sensory or intellectual experience. They emphasize that the experience *goes beyond* the customary sensory pathways, ideas and memories. As I have shown, they describe the state as definitely not blank or empty but as filled with intense, profound, vivid perception which they regard as the ultimate goal of the mystic path.* If one accepts their descriptions as phenomenologically accurate, one is presented with the problem of explaining the nature of such a state and the process by which it occurs. Following the hypotheses presented earlier in this paper, I would like to suggest that such experiences are the result of the operation of a new perceptual capacity responsive to dimensions of the stimulus array previously ignored or blocked from awareness. For such mystics, renunciation has weakened and temporarily removed the ordinary objects of consciousness as a focus of awareness. Contemplative meditation has undone the logical organization of consciousness. At the same time, the mystic is intensely *motivated* to perceive something. If undeveloped or unutilized perceptual capacities do exist, it seems likely that they would be mobilized and come into operation under such conditions. The perceptual experience that would then take place would be one outside of customary verbal or sensory reference. It would be *unidentifiable*, hence indescribable. The high value, the meaningfulness, and the intensity reported of such experiences suggest that the perception has a different scope from that of normal consciousness. The loss of "self" characteristic of the trans-sensate experience indicates that the new perceptual mode is not associated with reflective awareness—the "I" of normal consciousness is in abeyance.

CONCLUSION

A mystic experience is the production of an unusual state of consciousness. This state is brought about by a deautomatization of hierarchically ordered structures that ordinarily conserve attentional energy for maxi-

---

*Ehrenzweig (1964, p. 382) proposes that mystic "blankness" is due to a structural limitation: "the true mystic orison becomes empty yet filled with intense experience. . . . This full emptiness . . . is the direct result of our conscious failure to grasp imagery formed on more primitive levels of differentiation. . . . Owing to their incompatible shapes, [these images] cancelled each other out on the way up to consciousness and so produce in our surface experience a blank 'abstract' image still replete with unconscious fantasy."

mum efficiency in achieving the basic goals of the individual: biological survival as an organism and psychological survival as a personality. Perceptual selection and cognitive patterning are in the service of these goals. Under special conditions of dysfunction, such as in acute psychosis or in LSD states, or under special goal conditions such as exist in religious mystics, the pragmatic systems of automatic selection are set aside or break down, in favor of alternate modes of consciousness whose stimulus processing may be less efficient from a biological point of view but whose very inefficiency may permit the experience of aspects of the real world formerly excluded or ignored. The extent to which such a shift takes place is a function of the motivation of the individual, his particular neurophysiological state, and the environmental conditions encouraging or discouraging such a change.

A final comment should be made. The content of the mystic experience reflects not only its unusual mode of consciousness but also the particular stimuli being processed through that mode. The mystic experience can be beatific, satanic, revelatory, or psychotic, depending on the stimuli predominant in each case. Such an explanation says nothing conclusive about the source of "transcendent" stimuli. God or the Unconscious share equal possibilities here and one's interpretation will reflect one's presuppositions and beliefs. The mystic vision is one of unity, and modern physics lends some support to this perception when it asserts that the world and its living forms are variations of the same elements. However, there is no evidence that separateness and differences are illusions (as affirmed by Vedanta) or that God or a transcendent reality exists (as affirmed by Western religions). The available scientific evidence tends to support the view that the mystic experience is one of internal perception, an experience that can be ecstatic, profound, or therapeutic for purely internal reasons. Yet for psychological science, the problem of understanding such internal processes is hardly less complex than the theological problem of understanding God. Indeed, regardless of one's direction in the search to know what reality is, a feeling of awe, beauty, reverence, and humility seems to be the product of one's efforts. Since these emotions are characteristic of the mystic experience, itself, the question of the epistemological validity of that experience may have less importance than was initially supposed.

18.

The Two Types of Psychology

Lama Govinda

Psychology can be studied and dealt with in two ways: either for its own sake alone, i.e., as pure science, which leaves entirely out of account the usefulness or non-usefulness of its results—or else for the sake of some definite object, that is, with a view to practical application which necessitates from the outset certain direct lines of advance. In the former case we get a description of all perceptible and logically deducible ("thinkable") phenomena of the inner life of human beings and their relationship with the outer world. (In this most people see explanation, since they confound description with explanation!) In the latter case it is a question of a selection out of the wealth of inner experiences in view of their application in a given direction. Psychology, as "pure science," also takes the facts of experience as its starting point but arrives at its results by the path of logical development, thus going beyond the given data and building up a system dependent upon logical operations and abstract

Reprinted by permission from Lama Govinda, *The Psychological Attitude in Early Buddhist Philosophy* (Rider & Co., 1961), pp. 35–37.

principles. Practical psychology remains within the boundary lines of the given, in doing which, logic only has to serve for the shaping and arrangement of the material.

The amplitude of "the boundary lines of the given" is the determining factor as to the value of any such psychology. In the case of Buddhism, whose psychology belongs to the latter category, these boundary lines are extraordinarily wide-stretching, since they embrace not only the experiences of the average man but also the planes of the highest experiences, which no science of the West as yet has ventured to approach.

While the results of purely scientific ("theoretical") psychology, which have been attained mainly upon the path of logic, remain more or less hypothetical and stand in need of proof, it may be said that not only the elements but the very aims of Buddhist psychology are based on experience. The method of this psychology is comparable to that of a man who from a high mountain watch-tower looks out over the landscape at his feet and now proceeds in regular order to extricate from the total picture of the landscape the distinguishing marks of his route, and describes them in their corresponding order. His description lays no claim to be a description of the whole landscape but only of those portions of the landscape which are of importance for his route. What he explains about the landscape is what is objectively given. The selection of his route, the arrangement of the distinguishing marks (logic), the manner of his description (composition), these are what is subjectively formed. The straight path corresponds to the laws of simple logic. Since, however, there are obstacles which are more easily gone around than climbed over, it may come about that actuality and logic do not always agree with one another. Looked at from above, also, many things will seem harmonious which, seen from below or from the same level, will appear incompatible. "Hence the rejection of all speculation, hence the declaration that the deepest secrets of the world and of man are inaccessible to abstract, philosophical thinking. It is not logical thinking but only a higher consciousness (bodhi) which resolves the contradictions in which the lower thought, bound up with the life of the senses, is hopelessly involved. Kant demonstrates theoretically where, within the given consciousness, lie the boundary lines of cognition; the Buddha teaches the practice, the way, in which that given form of consciousness may be overpassed. While thus Kant demonstrates how within the confines of thought that is bound up with the life of the senses, pure reason, the cognition of what is real in the higher sense of the word, is unattainable, the Buddha seeks through the surmounting of thought that is bound up with the life of the senses, to rise to the higher cognition." (Beckh, 1938, I, 120f.)

From this it is clear that in Buddhism psychology and philosophy, as the process of knowing (cognition) and the formulation of the known, are indivisibly bound up with each other. The training of consciousness is the indispensable antecedent condition of higher knowledge, because consciousness is the vessel upon whose capacity depends the *extent* of what is to be received. Knowledge on the other hand is the antecedent condition required for the *selection* of the material to be received, and for the *direction* of the course to be pursued for its mastery. Without the presence of a tradition, in which the experiences and knowledge of former generations are formulated (philosophy), every individual would be compelled to master the entire domain of the psychic, and only a few favoured ones would attain the goal of knowledge. Just as little adequate, however, would be the mere acceptance or intellectual recognition of the results laid down as philosophy to the pioneer truth-seeker. Every individual must himself tread the path of realization, for only the knowledge that is won by experience has living, i.e., life-giving, value. It is here that the philosophy of Buddhism is distinguished from the intellectual philosophies of our times, which exhaust themselves in abstract thinking without exercising any influence on man. The same is the case with the purely scientific systems of psychology, especially when they have lost their spiritual background. It is the close interweaving of philosophy and psychology which protects Buddhism from stagnation.

19.

Zen Meditation

Philip Kapleau

In the broad sense zazen embraces more than just correct sitting. To enter fully into every action with total attention and clear awareness is no less zazen. The prescription for accomplishing this was given by the Buddha himself in an early sutra: "In what is seen there must be just the seen: in what is heard there must be just the heard; in what is sensed (as smell, taste or touch) there must be just what is sensed; in what is thought there must be just the thought."

The importance of single-mindedness, of bare attention, is illustrated in the following anecdote:

One day a man of the people said to Zen Master Ikkyu: "Master, will you please write for me some maxims of the highest wisdom?"

Ikkyu immediately took his brush and wrote the word "Attention."

"Is that all?" asked the man. "Will you not add something more?"

Ikkyu then wrote twice running: "Attention. Attention."

Reprinted by permission from Philip Kapleau, ed., *The Three Pillars of Zen* (John Weatherhill, Inc., 1965), pp. 10–15.

"Well," remarked the man rather irritably, "I really don't see much depth or subtlety in what you have just written."

Then Ikkyu wrote the same word three times running: "Attention. Attention. Attention."

Half-angered, the man demanded: "What does that word 'Attention' mean anyway?"

And Ikkyu answered gently: "Attention means attention."

For the ordinary man, whose mind is a checkerboard of crisscrossing reflections, opinions, and prejudices, bare attention is virtually impossible; his life is thus centered not in reality itself but in his *ideas* of it. By focusing the mind wholly on each object and every action, zazen strips it of extraneous thoughts and allows us to enter into a full rapport with life.

Sitting zazen and mobile zazen are two functions equally dynamic and mutually reinforcing. One who sits devotedly in zazen every day, his mind free of discriminating thoughts, finds it easier to relate himself wholeheartedly to his daily tasks, and one who performs every act with total attention and clear awareness finds it less difficult to achieve emptiness of mind during sitting periods.

Zazen practice for the student begins with his counting the inhalations and exhalations of his breath while he is in the motionless zazen posture. This is the first step in the process of stilling the bodily functions, quieting discursive thought, and strengthening concentration. It is given as the first step because in counting the in and out breaths, in natural rhythm and without strain, the mind has a scaffolding to support it, as it were. When concentration on the breathing becomes such that awareness of the counting is clear and the count is not lost, the next step, a slightly more difficult type of zazen, is assigned, namely, following the inhalations and exhalations of the breath with the mind's eye only, again in natural rhythm. The blissful state which flows from concentration on the breath and the value of breathing in terms of spiritual development are lucidly set forth by Lama Govinda: "From this state of perfect mental and physical equilibrium and its resulting inner harmony grows that serenity and happiness which fills the whole body with a feeling of supreme bliss like the refreshing coolness of a spring that penetrates the entire water of a mountain lake. . . . Thus breathing becomes a vehicle of spiritual experience, the mediator between body and mind. It is the first step towards the transformation of the body from the state of a more or less passively and unconsciously functioning physical organ into a vehicle or tool of a perfectly developed and enlightened mind, as demonstrated by the radiance and perfection of the Buddha's body. . . . The most important result of the practice of 'mindfulness with regard to breathing' is the realization that the process of breathing is the connecting link between conscious and subconscious, gross-material and fine-material, volitional and non-volitional functions, and therefore the most perfect expression of the nature of all life."

Until now we have been speaking of zazen with no koan. Koan zazen involves both motionless sitting, wherein the mind intensely seeks to penetrate the koan, and mobile zazen, in which absorption in the koan continues while one is at work, at play, or even asleep. Through intense self-inquiry—for example, questioning "What is Mu?"—the mind gradually becomes denuded of its delusive ideas, which in the beginning hamper its effort to become one with the koan. As these abstract notions fall away, concentration on the koan strengthens.

Now, it may be asked: "How can one question oneself devotedly about a koan and simultaneously focus the mind on work of an exacting nature?" In practice what actually happens is that once the koan grips the heart and mind—and its power to take hold is in proportion to the strength of the urge toward liberation—the inquiry goes on ceaselessly in the subconsciousness. So long as the mind is occupied with a particular task, the question fades from consciousness, surfacing naturally as soon as the action is over, not unlike a moving stream which now and again disappears underground only to reappear and resume its open course without interrupting its onward flow.

Zazen must not be confused with meditation. Meditation, in the beginning at least, involves fixing one's mind on an idea or an object. In some types of Buddhist meditation the meditator envisions or contemplates or analyzes certain elementary shapes, holding them in his mind to the exclusion of everything else. Or he may concentrate in a state of adoration upon his own created image of a Buddha or a Bodhisattva, or meditate on such abstract qualities as loving-kindness and compassion. In tantric Buddhist systems of meditation, mandala containing various seed syllables of the Sanskrit alphabet are visualized and dwelt upon in a prescribed manner. Also employed for meditational purposes are mandala consisting of special arrangements of Buddhas, Bodhisattvas, and other figures.

The uniqueness of zazen lies in this: that the mind is freed from bondage to *all* thought-forms, visions, objects, and imaginings, however sacred or elevating, and brought to a state of absolute emptiness, from which alone it may one day perceive its own true nature, or the nature of the universe.

Such initial exercises as counting or following the breath cannot, strictly speaking, be called meditation since they do not involve visualization of an object or reflection upon an idea. For the same reasons koan zazen cannot be called meditation. Whether one is striving to achieve unity with his koan or, for instance, intensely asking "What is Mu?" he is not meditating in the technical sense of this word.

Zazen that leads to Self-realization is neither idle reverie nor vacant inaction but an intense inner struggle to gain control over the mind and then to use it, like a silent missile, to penetrate the barrier of the five senses and the discursive intellect (i.e., the sixth sense). It demands determination, courage, and energy. Yasutani-roshi calls it " a battle between the opposing forces of delusion and bodhi." This state of mind has been vividly described in these words, said to have been uttered by the Buddha as he sat beneath the Bo tree making his supreme effort, and often quoted in the *zendo* during *sesshin:* "Though only my skin, sinews, and bones remain and my blood and flesh dry up and wither away, yet never from this seat will I stir until I have attained full enlightenment."

The drive toward enlightenment is powered on the one hand by a painfully felt inner bondage—a frustration with life, a fear of death, or both—and on the other by the conviction that through satori one can gain liberation. But it is in zazen that the body-mind's force and vigor are enlarged and mobilized for the breakthrough into this new world of freedom. Energies which formerly were squandered in compulsive drives and purposeless actions are preserved and channeled into a unity through correct Zen sitting; and to the degree that the mind attains one-pointedness through zazen it no longer disperses its force in the uncontrolled proliferation of idle thoughts. The entire nervous system is relaxed and soothed, inner tensions eliminated, and the tone of all organs strengthened. In short, by realigning the physical, mental, and psychic energies through proper breathing, concentration, and sitting, zazen establishes a new body-mind equilibrium with its center of gravity in the vital *hara*.

With the body and mind consolidated, focused, and energized, the emotions respond with increased sensitivity and purity, and volition exerts itself with greater strength of purpose. No longer are we dominated by intellect at the expense of feeling, nor driven by the emotions unchecked by reason or will. Eventually zazen leads to a transformation of personality and character. Dryness, rigidity, and self-centeredness give way to flowing warmth, resiliency, and compassion, while self-indulgence and fear are transmuted into self-mastery and courage.

Because they know from centuries of experience this transforming power of zazen, the Japanese masters have always placed greater reliance on zazen to foster moral conduct in their disciples than upon the mere imposition of the precepts from the outside. Actually, the precepts and zazen, both grounded in the identical Buddha-nature, which is the source of all purity and goodness, are mutually reinforcing. The strongest resolution to keep the precepts will at best be only sporadically successful if it is not supported by zazen; and zazen divorced from the disciplined life which grows out of a sincere effort to observe the precepts cannot but be weak and uncertain. In any case, contrary to what the Hinayana teachings suggest, the precepts are not just simple moral commandments which anyone can easily understand and keep if he has the will to. In reality their relative-absolute sense cannot be grasped as living truth except after long and dedicated zazen. This is why Zen students are normally not given the book of problems called *Jujukinkai*, which deals with the ten cardinal precepts from the standpoints of the Hinayana doctrines, the Mahayana, the Buddha-nature itself, Bodhidharma's view, and Dogen's view, until the very end of their training, when their enlightenment and zazen power have deepened and matured. Indeed, the Japanese masters stress that only upon full enlightenment can one truly know good from evil and, through the power of zazen, translate this wisdom into one's everyday actions.

That a strong sense of moral responsibility is inherent in the spiritual freedom of the [man who has achieved *satori*, enlightenment] was made clear by Yasutani-roshi in response to a question addressed to him in America by a group of university students. "If, as 'beat Zen' has led us to believe," they asked, "satori reveals the unreality of the past and the future, is one not free to live as one likes here and now, without reference to the past and without thought of the future?"

In reply Yasutani-roshi made a dot on the blackboard and explained that this isolated dot represented their conception of "here and now." To show the incompleteness of this view, he placed another dot on the board, through which he drew a horizontal line and a vertical one. He then explained that the horizontal line stood for time from the beginningless past to the endless future and the vertical for limitless space. The "present moment" of the enlightened man, who stands at this intersection, embraces all these dimensions of time and space, he emphasized.

Accordingly, the satori-realization that one is the focus of past and future time and space unavoidably carries with it a sense of fellowship and responsibility to one's family and society as a whole, alike to those who came before and those who will follow one. The freedom of the liberated Zen man is a far cry from the "freedom" of the Zen beatnik, driven as the latter is by his uncontrolled selfish desires. The inseparable bond with his fellow men which the truly enlightened feels precludes any such self-centered behavior as the beatnik's.

20.

"Meditation" or Mental Culture

Walpola Rahula

The Buddha's teaching, particularly his way of "meditation," aims at producing a state of perfect mental health, equilibrium and tranquility. It is unfortunate that hardly any other section of the Buddha's teaching is so much misunderstood as "meditation," both by Buddhists and non-Buddhists. The moment the word "meditation" is mentioned, one thinks of an escape from the daily activities of life; assuming a particular posture, like a statue in some cave or cell in a monastery, in some remote place cut off from society; and musing on, or being absorbed in, some kind of mystic or mysterious thought or trance. True Buddhist "meditation" does not mean this kind of escape at all. The Buddha's teaching on this subject was so wrongly, or so little understood, that in later times the way of "meditation" deteriorated and degenerated into a kind of ritual or ceremony almost technical in its routine.

Most people are interested in meditation or *yoga* in order to gain some spiritual or mystic powers like the "third eye," which others do not possess. There was some time ago a Buddhist nun in India who was trying to develop a power to see through her ears, while she was still in the possession of the "power" of perfect eyesight! This kind of idea is nothing but "spiritual perversion." It is always a question of desire, "thirst" for power.

The word meditation is a very poor substitute for the original term *bhavana*, which means "culture" or "development," i.e., mental culture or mental development. The Buddhist *bhavana*, properly speaking, is mental culture in the full sense of the term. It aims at cleansing the mind of impurities and disturbances, such as lustful desires, hatred, ill-will, indolence, worries and restlessness, sceptical doubts, and cultivating such qualities as concentration, awareness, intelligence, will, energy, the analytical faculty, confidence, joy, tranquility, leading finally to the attainment of highest wisdom which sees the nature of things as they are, and realizes the Ultimate Truth, Nirvana.

There are two forms of meditation. One is the development of mental concentration (*samatha* or *samadhi*), of one-pointedness of mind (*cittekaggata*, Skt. *cittaikagrata*), by various methods prescribed in the texts, leading up to the highest mystic states such as "the Sphere of Nothingness" or "the Sphere of Neither-Perception-nor-Non-Perception." All these mystic states, according to the Buddha, are mind-created, mind-produced, conditioned (*samkhata*). They have nothing to do with Reality, Truth, Nirvana. This form of meditation existed before the Buddha. Hence it is not purely Buddhist, but it is not excluded from the field of Buddhist meditation. However, it is not essential for the realization of Nirvana. The Buddha himself, before his Enlightenment, studied these yogic practices under different teachers and attained to the highest mystic states; but he was not satisfied with them, because they did not give complete liberation, they did not give insight into the Ultimate Reality. He considered these mystic states only as "happy living in this existence" (*ditthadhammasukhavihara*), or "peaceful living" (*santavihara*), and nothing more.

He therefore discovered the other form of "meditation" known as *vipassana* (Skt. *vipasyana* or *vidarsana*), "Insight" into the nature of things, leading to the complete liberation of mind, to the realization of the Ultimate Truth, Nirvana. This is essentially Buddhist "meditation," Buddhist mental culture. It is an analytical method based on mindfulness, awareness, vigilance, observation.

It is impossible to do justice to such a vast subject in a few pages.

However an attempt is made here to give a very brief and rough idea of the true Buddhist "meditation," mental culture or mental development, in a practical way.

The most important discourse ever given by the Buddha on mental development ("meditation") is called the *Satipatthana-sutta* "The Setting-up of Mindfulness" (No. 22 of the *Digha-nikaya*, or No. 10 of the *Majjhima-nikaya*). This discourse is so highly venerated in tradition that it is regularly recited not only in Buddhist monasteries, but also in Buddhist homes with members of the family sitting round and listening with deep devotion. Very often bhikkhus recite this *sutta* by the bed-side of a dying man to purify his last thoughts.

The ways of "meditation" given in this discourse are not cut off from life, nor do they avoid life; on the contrary, they are all connected with our life, our daily activities, our sorrows and joys, our words and thoughts, our moral and intellectual occupations.

The discourse is divided into four main sections: the first section deals with our body (*kaya*), the second with our feelings and sensations (*vedana*), the third with the mind (*citta*), and the fourth with various moral and intellectual subjects (*dhamma*).

It should be clearly borne in mind that whatever the form of "meditation" may be, the essential thing is mindfulness or awareness (*sati*), attention or observation (*anupassana*).

One of the most well-known, popular, and practical examples of "meditation" connected with the body is called "The Mindfulness or Awareness of in-and-out breathing" (*anapanasati*). It is for this "meditation" only that a particular and definite posture is prescribed in the text. For other forms of "meditation" given in this *sutta*, you may sit, stand, walk, or lie down, as you like. But, for cultivating mindfulness of in-and-out breathing, one should sit, according to the text, "cross-legged, keeping the body erect and mindfulness alert." But sitting cross-legged is not practical and easy for people of all countries, particularly for Westerners. Therefore, those who find it difficult to sit cross-legged may sit on a chair, "keeping the body erect and mindfulness alert." It is very necessary for this exercise that the meditator should sit erect, but not stiff; his hands placed comfortably on his lap. Thus seated, you may close your eyes, or you may gaze at the tip of your nose, as it may be convenient to you.

You breathe in and out all day and night, but you are never mindful of it, you never for a second concentrate your mind on it. Now you are going to do just this. Breathe in and out as usual, without any effort or strain. Now, bring your mind to concentrate on your breathing-in and breathing-out; let your mind watch and observe your breathing in and out; let your mind be aware and vigilant of your breathing in and out. When you breathe, you sometimes take deep breaths, sometimes not. This does not matter at all. Breathe normally and naturally. The only thing is that when you take deep breaths you should be aware that they are deep breaths, and so on. In other words, your mind should be so fully concentrated on your breathing that you are aware of its movements and changes. Forget all other things, your surroundings, your environment; do not raise your eyes and look at anything. Try to do this for five or ten minutes.

At the beginning you will find it extremely difficult to bring your mind to concentrate on your breathing. You will be astonished how your mind runs away. It does not stay. You begin to think of various things. You hear sounds outside. Your mind is disturbed and distracted. You may be dismayed and disappointed. But if you continue to practise this exercise twice daily, morning and evening, for about five or ten minutes at a time, you will gradually, by and by, begin to concentrate your mind on your breathing. After a certain period, you will experience just that split second when your mind is fully concentrated on your breathing, when you will not hear even sounds nearby, when no external world exists for you. This slight moment is such a tremendous experience for you, full of joy, happiness and tranquility, that you would like to continue it. But still you cannot. Yet if you go on practising this regularly, you may repeat the experience again and again for longer and longer periods. That is the moment when you lose yourself completely in your mindfulness of breathing. As long as you are conscious of yourself you can never concentrate on anything.

This exercise of mindfulness of breathing, which is one of the simplest and easiest practices, is meant to develop concentration leading up to very high mystic attainments (*dhyana*). Besides, the power of concentration is essential for any kind of deep understanding, penetration, insight into the nature of things, including the realization of Nirvana.

Apart from all this, this exercise on breathing gives you immediate results. It is good for your physical health, for relaxation, [for] sound sleep, and for efficiency in your daily work. It makes you calm and tranquil. Even at moments when you are nervous or excited, if you practise this for a couple of minutes, you will see for yourself that you become immediately quiet and at peace. You feel as if you have awakened after a good rest.

Another very important, practical, and useful form of "meditation" (mental development) is to be aware and mindful of whatever you do, physically or verbally, during the daily routine of work in your life, private, public, or professional. Whether you walk, stand, sit, lie down, or sleep, whether you stretch or bend your limbs, whether you look around, whether you put on your clothes, whether you talk or keep silence, whether you eat or drink, even whether you answer the calls of nature—in these and other activities, you should be fully aware and mindful of the act you perform at the moment. That is to say, that you should live in the present moment, in the present action. This does not mean that you should not think of the past or the future at all. On the contrary, you think of them in relation to the present moment, the present action, when and where it is relevant.

People do not generally live in their actions, in the present moment. They live in the past or in the future. Though they seem to be doing something now, here, they live somewhere else in their thoughts, in their imaginary problems and worries, usually in the memories of the past or in desires and speculations about the future. Therefore they do not live in, nor do they enjoy, what they do at the moment. So they are unhappy and discontented with the present moment, with the work at hand, and naturally they cannot give themselves fully to what they appear to be doing.

Sometimes you see a man in a restaurant reading while eating—a very common sight. He gives you the impression of being a very busy man, with no time even for eating. You wonder whether he eats or reads. One may say that he does both. In fact, he does neither, he enjoys neither. He is strained, and disturbed in mind, and he does not enjoy what he does at the moment, does not live his life in the present moment, but unconsciously and foolishly tries to escape from life. (This does not mean, however, that one should not talk with a friend while having lunch or dinner.)

You cannot escape life however you may try. As long as you live, whether in a town or in a cave, you have to face it and live it. Real life is the present moment—not the memories of the past which is dead and gone, nor the dreams of the future which is not yet born. One who lives in the present moment lives the real life, and he is happiest.

When asked why his disciples, who lived a simple and quiet life with only one meal a day, were so radiant, the Buddha replied: "They do not repent the past, nor do they brood over the future. They live in the present. Therefore they are radiant. By brooding over the future and repenting the past, fools dry up like green reeds cut down (in the sun)."

Mindfulness, or awareness, does not mean that you should think and be conscious "I am doing this" or "I am doing that." No. Just the contrary. The moment you think "I am doing this," you become self-conscious, and then you do not live in the action, but you live in the idea "I am," and consequently your work too is spoilt. You should forget yourself completely, and lose yourself in what you do. The moment a speaker becomes self-conscious and thinks "I am addressing an audience," his speech is disturbed and his trend of thought broken. But when he forgets himself in his speech, in his subject, then he is at his best, he speaks well and explains things clearly. All great work—artistic, poetic, intellectual or spiritual—is produced at those moments when its creators are lost completely in their actions, when they forget themselves altogether, and are free from self-consciousness.

This mindfulness or awareness with regard to our activities, taught by the Buddha, is to live in the present moment, to live in the present action. (This is also the Zen way which is based primarily on this teaching.) Here in this form of meditation, you haven't got to perform any particular action in order to develop mindfulness, but you have only to be mindful and aware of whatever you may do. You haven't got to spend one second of your precious time on this particular "meditation"; you have only to cultivate mindfulness and awareness always, day and night, with regard to all activities in your usual daily life. These two forms of "meditation" discussed above are connected with our body.

Then there is a way of practising mental development ("meditation") with regard to all our sensations or feelings, whether happy, unhappy or neutral. Let us take only one example. You experience an unhappy, sorrowful sensation. In this state your mind is cloudy, hazy, not clear, it is depressed. In some cases, you do not even see clearly why you have that unhappy feeling. First of all, you should learn not to be unhappy about your unhappy feeling, not to be worried about your worries. But try to see clearly why there is a sensation or a feeling of unhappiness, or worry, or sorrow. Try to examine how it arises, its cause, how it disappears, its cessation. Try to examine it as if you are observing it from outside, without any subjective reaction, as a scientist observes some object. Here, too, you should not look at it as "my feeling" or "my sensation" subjectively, but only look at it as "a feeling" or "a sensation" objectively. You should forget again the false idea of "I." When you see its nature, how it arises and disappears, your mind grows dispassionate towards that sensation, and becomes detached and free. It is the same with regard to all sensations or feelings.

Now let us discuss the form of "meditation" with regard to our minds. You should be fully aware of the fact whenever your mind is passionate or detached, whenever it is overpowered by hatred, ill-will, jealousy, or is full of love, compassion, whenever it is deluded or has a clear and right understanding, and so on and so forth. We must admit that very often we are afraid or ashamed to look at our own minds. So we prefer to avoid it. One should be bold and sincere and look at one's own mind as one looks at one's face in a mirror.

Here is no attitude of criticizing or judging, or discriminating between right and wrong, or good and bad. It is simply observing, watching, examining. You are not a judge, but a scientist. When you observe your mind, and see its true nature clearly, you become dispassionate with regard to its emotions, sentiments, and states. Thus you became detached and free, so that you may see things as they are.

Let us take one example. Say you are really angry, overpowered by anger, ill-will, hatred. It is curious, and paradoxical, that the man who is in anger is not really aware, not mindful, that he is angry. The moment he becomes aware and mindful of that state of his mind, the moment he sees his anger, it becomes, as if it were, shy and ashamed, and begins to subside. You should examine its nature, how it arises, how it disappears. Here again it should be remembered that you should not think "I am angry," or of "my anger." You should only be aware and mindful of the state of an angry mind. You are only observing and examining an angry mind objectively. This should be the attitude with regard to all sentiments, emotions, and states of mind.

Then there is a form of "meditation" on ethical, spiritual, and intellectual subjects. All our studies, reading, discussions, conversation, and deliberations on such subjects are included in this "meditation." To read this book, and to think deeply about the subjects discussed in it, is a form of meditation.

21.

The Kasina Exercises: Dharana

Frederic Spiegelberg

Dharana means "fixation"—the concentrating and fixing of the mind on a definite object. In order to arrive at this stage of lofty spiritual meditation the yogi has to undertake a series of exercises which are connected with the subjugation of his sentient nature. These are the Kasina exercises; they are quite unknown here in the West, and a few of them will be described in this chapter.

Without possessing a certain degree of Dharana a person would hardly be able to live at all, and certainly could not work properly. Hence, without being aware of it, everyone is continually practicing Kasina exercises by which his energies are directed towards a single goal. Every rhythmic activity—the common habit of rapping out tunes on the table, or humming under one's breath, often with endless repetition of the same motif, or playing with the corners of the table-cloth, a practice which is

Reprinted by permission from Frederic Spiegelberg, *Spiritual Practices of India* (The Citadel Press, 1962), pp. 42–49.

much like the old habit of twirling the ends of the moustache—is an exercise of the Kasina type, unconsciously undertaken, for the fixation of one's impulses to action. Furthermore, in many instances people have deliberately evolved expedients to help them direct their consciousness towards a single point. This proceeding begins already with the child in the cradle, when a rubber nipple is put in his mouth to quiet him, and he sucks on it for hours without any apparent purpose or result. Older children have a wide variety of practices, largely unrecognized by adults and kept hidden from them, which serve to fasten their attention on some particular performance of their own. As an instance, while walking along the street children will try to step inside of the squares of the pavement, carefully avoiding the grooves between them.

Adults, too, cling tightly to practices of this nature, which are manifestly of the most vital importance to life. In smoking, for instance, it is this aspect of the matter which is more important than the comparatively slight effect of the nicotine, which could be obtained much more easily by other means. What is of real significance is the actual activity of smoking itself. From the standpoint of the goal to be attained through yoga, therefore, it makes no sense whatsoever to break anyone of the habit of smoking. On the contrary, one should simply open the eyes of the inveterate smoker to the real significance of what he is doing. By thus making him aware of its meaning one will transform his smoking from a vice that is thoughtlessly indulged in, into a thoughtful exercise of concentration.

Whenever in his activities a person transcends that which is imperative or vitally necessary at the moment, or goes beyond what is immediately pleasurable, he comes in harmony with the Kasina exercises. When he brings his daily activities into precise order and adheres strictly to such an arrangement, and when he lets the same tidiness and precision govern the arrangement of the objects on his writing table, and the laying out of his clothes on a chair at night, he is in each instance giving expression to this need for Dharana. Such arranging of things, however, must never become an end in itself or turn into pedantry; for then one falls only too readily into ritualism, which is a symptom of psychic illness. In ritualism all the beneficial effect of Kasina exercises is excluded by the constraint to which one has unconsciously, and in an intensely personal way, subjected himself.

It is the same in all tending of plants and animals that is done at home, and in the arrangement of collections of stones, butterflies, postage stamps, or even one's mental furniture. Habits of this kind are directly helpful to concentration so long as they are consciously pursued in this light; but they can divert one from a loftier unfoldment when they over-whelm him with the mania for collecting, and master him instead of serving him.

As a help at this stage of yoga Buddhism has developed particularly the Kasina practices, of which ten different ones are to be distinguished. One of these, the Earth Kasina, will now be described more closely with respect to performance and effect, following the description given in the book called "The Path of Purity."

After choosing a proper place, and practicing the aforementioned pos-tures and breathing exercises, the student should erect a sort of low table in his place of meditation by fixing four stakes in the ground and stretching a cloth or mat across them. On this he should then lay some light brown loam and spread it out with a perfectly smooth stone into a round, level disk. This should be the size of a sieve or a plate, about twenty-eight centimetres in diameter. People who are inclined to selfish-ness, obstinacy, and obsessively fixed ideas will do well to make the disk a little larger in circumference, whereas those who are inclined to be absent-minded and whose thoughts are easily scattered should make the disk smaller. The loam that is used for this purpose must be thoroughly kneaded, and all grass, roots, sand, and gravel removed from it. Next, the place should be carefully cleaned; and then [he] should go away and purify himself as well. Returning, he should sit down about two metres away, on a low chair. The Kasina disk must not be so far away that it cannot be perceived distinctly; but at the same time it must not be so close that the unavoidable little unevennesses of its surface are visible. One's sitting posture must be comfortable, just as the Asana exercises prescribe; his knees should not ache, even if he stays in one position for a fairly long time, and his neck is not to be bent. He should be seated, filled with confidence and faith in the efficacy of the exercise, and begin to practice Pratyahara, letting no disturbing thoughts interrupt his meditation.

The aim now is to evolve the "spiritual image" of the Kasina disk. To do this [he] must contemplate the disk continuously over a long period of time, seated in an attitude of serene, motionless concentration. [He] will find that it is no waste of time repeatedly to give up hours, even, of his leisure to this contemplation. His eyes should be kept only partly open, and he should gaze at the disk in a calm, relaxed manner, some-what as though he were looking at his face in a mirror. If he stares with his eyes and opens them too wide, they tire too readily, and the details of the disk become so distinct as to be disturbing; if, on the other hand, his eyes are not sufficiently wide open, the disk is not seen clearly enough, and [his] spirit droops and grows weary. Moreover, in order to strengthen his concentration, he may repeat softly to himself the various names and designations for earth and all its essential characteristics, such as "Broad Extending One," "Mighty One," "Fruitful One," "The One That is," "Treasure Bestower," "Treasure Concealer," . . . When [he] thus turns his attention away from all other thoughts, the objects outside the disk soon become wholly imperceptible to his senses. After a while he may begin to open and close his eyes, for a hundred times or a thousand, until the spiritual image of the disk rises within him. This image will then appear to him just as distinctly when his eyes are closed as when they are open.

At this point [he] may experiment by leaving the place of meditation for a little while in order to see whether the image will remain fixed within him even when he is in another place. If it does not remain he must return and resume his contemplation. Through this exercise he finally succeeds in unfolding the "Counterpart," which exists entirely within him, and in which, consequently, there no longer appear any of the imperfections of the disk that is being meditated on. It is free from earth and all other material atttibutes, and is pure and luminous as the disk of the moon. [He] should bear this image within him henceforth as a jewel, guarding it tirelessly as the "Embryo of a World Conqueror." It is the Golden Germ, to the attainment of which the Chinese Taoists aspired with the same zeal as the alchemists of the Middle Ages.

A somewhat similar experience was undergone by Jakob Boehme, the mystic, who gazed so long on the spot of sunlight in his cobbler's crystal that an enduring image of it remained impressed on his eye. Wherever he looked afterwards he beheld that divine light in all objects, as something strangely radiant streaming forth from them and shining, as it were, from another plane of reality. What took place in Boehme partly as a result of a blinding of his vision, the yogi on the path of meditation brings forth wholly in spirit.

The point of primary importance is that [he] should really create such a meditation-image to accompany him continuously; only as a secondary consideration does it matter what this particular image may be, that is, through which one of the Kasina exercises it has been produced. Instead of contemplating a disk of earth, for example, [he] may meditate on an evenly ploughed field seen from a distance. In the Water Kasina the yogi concentrates either on the circular surface of water in a jar, or on a lake seen from a mountain. So, too, the fire on the hearth, the flame of a candle, the wind that sways the crests of the trees, may all be used as Kasina. The exercise of Colour Kasina makes use of round coloured disks, and even of bright-coloured flags and flowers. In Space Kasina one meditates on a circular window opening, the attention in this case being directed primarily to the dimensional proportions of the opening.

Every image that remains permanently in one's consciousness, and every enduring mood, can be a help to this fixation of one's consciousness. As a matter of fact, every hallucination, every unappeasable hatred, every amorous attachment provides a certain power of concentration to him who cherishes it, and helps him direct the forces of his being towards a single goal. This is of course much more the case with a man who has achieved self-control and freedom from the passions, and who, after having mastered his sense-impulses, succeeds in giving to his consciousness a definite turn of his own choosing.

In the Tibetan "Stories of the Eighty-Four Magicians" the analogous Dharana exercises are for the most part associated with the daily occupation of the student. The streetcleaner has to take his task of sweeping as the starting-point for meditation; so likewise must the potter take his task of producing clay utensils on his potter's wheel, and the cobbler his handicraft. Here again, therefore, it is evident that [he] may do what he will, so long as he is clearly aware of what he is doing. Every activity is of equal value as a basis for a Dharana exercise. The modern Japanese Buddhism of the Zen sect carries such notions still further. According to this sect there is really no profession nor way of life in which a man who has awakened to clear vision may not achieve the perfection of an enlightened saint, of a bodhisattva. Perhaps the greatest sages of our time, the liberated ones who have overcome the world, are sitting as humble clerks, unrecognized, at a bank-counter, or in some other office; and they themselves have not the least idea of their own real worth and grandeur, simply because they do not direct their attention towards unprofitable contemplation of themselves.

As a starting-point for Dharana meditation the contemplation of plants or parts of plants has proved to be especially efficacious. He who understands how to draw his consciousness forth, so to speak, from his own body, and place it within the luminous interior of a flower—the cup of a tulip, for example, will experience marvel upon marvel in what he beholds. Furthermore, with his eyes closed [he] may produce the exact image of a leaf, and then, in the light of Goethe's doctrine of plants, proceed to unfold out of this leaf, in the manner of an original creation, blossoms, fruit, stalk, root, and all the remaining parts of the plant. Through such transference of his self from his own body into some other body [he] can attain a clear comprehension, such as he never anticipated having, of many kinds of existence. In this way, indeed, he can experience inwardly the life-sensations of other creatures, simultaneously living along with them, and thus penetrate directly into the feeling-realm of other human beings, of animals, or plants.

One's consciousness of self has no fixed, definite dimensions. It is not just the same size as one's body. At any moment one can enlarge it to gigantic proportions, letting it transcend mountains, valleys, and ocean. So, likewise, one can make it smaller, letting it contract in dimension until it reaches the vanishing point. Just as in his fancy [the student] can roam with seven-league boots across the broad expanses of distant lands, so, too, is it possible, by completely immersing [him] self in the world of little things, to forget his human body to such an extent that he finds himself wandering through the realm—of moss and grasses, for example —which he is contemplating. In order to betake [him] self out of the everyday world it is by no means necessary to make tedious and expensive journeys to transport the body to far-off countries. In many instances, diminishing the sense of self, in [his] feeling nature, suffices to carry him into a real, enchanted world, in which with childlike delight he can travel through unknown regions.

As a preliminary meditation at the beginning of the day the following contemplation may be recommended. First of all, decrease your consciousness of self, both dimensionally and with respect to its importance, to such an extent that in relation to the infinite Whole you feel yourself to be a very tiny creature, a microbe of the utmost insignificance which, along with the entire solar system, may at any moment dissolve into nothingness by the breath of a deity. As soon as you have done this, however, follow it with the inverse meditation, in which you have the sensation of being like a god, gigantic in contrast to the world of microscopic atoms existing in every cell of your body. The outcome and significance of exercising one's thoughts in this manner in the early morning is that one is set free, for the whole day ahead, from the folly of evaluating events in life from a purely quantitative standpoint. What, after all, is, in the final analysis, either great or small in the presence of eternal Truth?

Great and manifold is the world of possibilities on which [the student] can fix his thought in the practice of Dharana. The moment, however, that [he] proceeds to re-fashion this world magically by himself, to alter it in its fundamental forms, he has already entered upon the practice of another group of exercises.

22.

The Physiology of Meditation

Robert Keith Wallace and Herbert Benson

How capable is the human organism of adjusting to psychologically disturbing changes in the environment? Our technological age is probably testing this capacity more severely than it was ever tested in the past. The impact of the rapid changes—unprecedented in scale, complexity and novelty—that technology is bringing about in our world seems to be having a deleterious effect on the mental and physical health of modern man. Some of the common disorders of our age, notably "nervous stomach" and high blood pressure, may well be attributable in part to the uncertainties that are burgeoning in our environment and daily lives. Since the environment is not likely to grow less complex or more predictable, it seems only prudent to devote some investigative attention to the human body's resources for coping with the vicissitudes of the environment.

There are in fact several ways in which an individual can control his physiological reactions to psychological events. Among the claims for such control the most notable have come from practitioners of meditation systems of the East: yoga and Zen Buddhism. This article will review and discuss recent studies of the effects of meditation that have been made by ourselves and by other investigators.

Yogis in India have long been reputed to perform phenomenal feats such as voluntarily stopping the heartbeat or surviving for extended periods in an "air-tight" pit or in extreme cold without food or in a distorted physical posture. One of the first investigators to look into these claims in an objective way was a French cardiologist, Thérèse Brosse, who went to India in 1935 equipped with a portable electrocardiograph so that she could monitor the activity of the heart. Brosse concluded from her tests that one of her subjects actually was able to stop his heart. In 1957 two American physiologists, M. A. Wenger of the University of California at Los Angeles and B. K. Bagchi of the University of Michigan Medical School, conducted a more extensive investigation in collaboration with B. K. Anand of the All-India Institute of Medical Sciences in New Delhi. None of the yogis they studied, with more elaborate equipment than Brosse had used, showed a capability for stopping the heart. Wenger and Bagchi concluded that the disappearance of the signal of heart activity in Brosse's electrocardiogram was probably an artifact, since the heart impulse is sometimes obscured by electrical signals from contracting muscles of the thorax. (In attempting to stop the heart the yogis usually performed what is called the Valsalva maneuver, which increases the pressure within the chest; it can be done by holding one's breath and straining downward.) Wenger, Bagchi and Anand did find, however, that some of the yogis could slow both heartbeat and respiration rate.

Reports of a number of other investigations by researchers in the 1950's and 1960's indicated that meditation as practiced by yoga or Zen meditators could produce a variety of physiological effects. One of the demonstrated effects was reduction of the rate of metabolism. Examining Zen monks in Japan who had had many years of experience in the practice of deep meditation, Y. Sugi and K. Akutsu found that during meditation the subjects decreased their consumption of oxygen by about 20 percent and reduced their output of carbon dioxide. These signs of course constitute evidence of a slowing of metabolism. In New Delhi, Anand and two collaborators, G. S. Chhina and Baldeu Singh (1961) made a similar finding in examination of a yoga practitioner; confined in a sealed metal box, the meditating yogi markedly reduced his oxygen consumption and carbon dioxide elimination.

These tests strongly indicated that meditation produced the effects through control of an "involuntary" mechanism in the body, presumably the autonomic nervous system. The reduction of carbon dioxide elimination might have been accounted for by a recognizably voluntary action of the subject—slowing the breathing—but such action should not markedly affect the uptake of oxygen by the body tissues. Consequently it was a reasonable supposition that the drop in oxygen consumption, reflecting a decrease in the need for inhaled oxygen, must be due to modification of a process not subject to manipulation in the usual sense.

Explorations with the electroencephalograph showed further that meditation produced changes in the electrical activity of the brain. In studies of Zen monks A. Kasamatsu and T. Hirai of the University of Tokyo found that during meditation with their eyes half-open the monks developed a predominance of alpha waves—the waves that ordinarily become prominent when a person is thoroughly relaxed with his eyes closed. In the meditating monks the alpha waves increased in amplitude and regularity, particularly in the frontal and central regions of the brain. Subjects with a great deal of experience in meditation showed other changes: the alpha waves slowed from the usual frequency of nine to 12 cycles per second to seven or eight cycles per second, and rhythmical theta waves at six to seven cycles per second appeared. Anand and other investigators in India found that yogis, like the Zen monks, also showed a heightening of alpha activity during meditation. N. N. Das and H. Gastaut, in an electroencephalographic examination of seven yogis, observed that as the meditation progressed the alpha waves gave way to fast-wave activity at the rate of 40 to 45 cycles per second and these waves in turn subsided with a return of the slow alpha and theta waves.

Another physiological response tested by the early investigators was the resistance of the skin to an electric current. This measure is thought by some to reflect the level of "anxiety": a decrease in skin resistance representing greater anxiety; a rise in resistance, greater relaxation. It turns out that meditation increases the skin resistance in yogis and somewhat stabilizes the resistance in Zen meditators.

We decided to undertake a systematic study of the physiological "effects," or, as we prefer to say, the physiological correlates, of meditation. In our review of the literature we found a bewildering range of variation in the cases and results of the different studies. The subjects varied greatly in their meditation techniques, their expertise and their performance. This was not so true of the Zen practitioners, all of whom employ the same technique, but it was quite characteristic of the practice of yoga, which has many more adherents. The state called yoga (meaning "union") has a generally agreed definition: a "higher" consciousness achieved through a fully rested and relaxed body and a fully awake and relaxed mind. In the endeavor to arrive at this state, however, the practitioners in India use a variety of approaches. Some seek the goal through strenuous physical exercise; others concentrate on controlling a particular overt function, such as the respiratory rate; others focus on purely mental processes, based on some device for concentration or contemplation. The difference in technique may produce a dichotomy of physiological effects; for instance, whereas those who use contemplation show a decrease in oxygen consumption, those who use physical exercise to achieve yoga show an oxygen-consumption increase. Moreover, since most of the techniques require rigorous discipline and long training, the range in abilities is wide, and it is difficult to know who is an "expert" or how expert he may be. Obviously all these complications made the problem of selecting suitable subjects for our systematic study a formidable one.

Fortunately one widely practiced yoga technique is so well standardized that it enabled us to carry out large-scale studies under reasonably uniform conditions. This technique, called "transcendental meditation," was developed by Maharishi Mahesh Yogi and is taught by an organization of instructors whom he personally qualifies. The technique does not require intense concentration or any form of rigorous mental or physical control, and it is easily learned, so that all subjects who have been through a relatively short period of training are "experts." The training does not involve devotion to any specific beliefs or life-style. It consists simply in two daily sessions of practice, each for 15 to 20 minutes.

The practitioner sits in a comfortable position with eyes closed. By a systematic method that he has been taught, he perceives a "suitable" sound or thought. Without attempting to concentrate specifically on this cue, he allows his mind to experience it freely, and his thinking, as the practitioners themselves report, rises to a "finer and more creative level in an easy and natural manner." More than 90,000 men and women in the U.S. are said to have received instruction in transcendental meditation by the organization teaching it. Hence large numbers of uniformly trained subjects were available for our studies.

What follows is a report of the detailed measurements made on a group of 36 subjects. Some were observed at the Thorndike Memorial Laboratory, a part of the Harvard Medical Unit at the Boston City Hospital. The others were observed at the University of California at Irvine. Twenty-eight were males and eight were females; they ranged in age from 17 to 41. Their experience in meditation ranged from less than a month to nine years, with the majority having had two to three years of experience.

During each test the subject served as his own control, spending part of the session in meditation and part in a normal, nonmeditative state. Devices for continuous measurement of blood pressure, heart rate, rectal temperature, skin resistance and electroencephalographic events were attached to the subject, and during the period of measurement samples were taken by 10-minute intervals for analysis of oxygen consumption, carbon dioxide elimination and other parameters. The subject sat in a chair. After a 30-minute period of habituation, measurements were started and continued for three periods: 20 to 30 minutes of a quiet, premeditative state, then 20 to 30 minutes of meditation, and finally 20 to 30 minutes after the subject was asked to stop meditating.

The measurements of oxygen consumption and carbon dioxide elimination confirmed in precise detail what had been reported earlier. Oxygen consumption fell sharply from 251 cubic centimeters per minute in

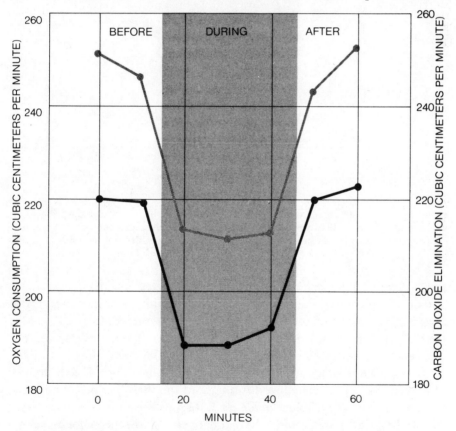

Effect of meditation on the subjects' oxygen consumption (black) and carbon-dioxide elimination (gray) was recorded in 20 and 15 cases, respectively. After the subjects were invited to meditate, both rates decreased markedly (light-gray area). Consumption and elimination returned to the premeditation level soon after the subjects stopped meditating.

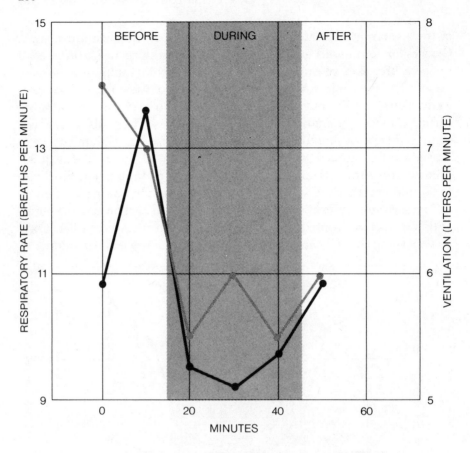

Both respiratory rate (gray) and volume of air breathed (black) decreased during meditation. The ratio between carbon dioxide expired and oxygen consumed, however, continued unchanged and in the normal range during the entire test period.

the premeditation period to 211 cubic centimeters during meditation, and in the postmeditation period it rose gradually to 242 cubic centimeters. Similarly, carbon dioxide elimination decreased, from 219 centimeters per minute beforehand to 187 cubic centimeters during meditation, and then returned to about the premeditation level afterward. The ratio of carbon dioxide elimination to oxygen consumption (in volume) remained essentially unchanged throughout the three periods, which indicates that the controlling factor for both was the rate of metabolism. The reduction in metabolic rate (and hence in the need for oxygen) during meditation was reflected in a decrease, essentially involuntary, in the rate of respiration (off two breaths per minute) and in the volume of air breathed (one liter less per minute).

For the measurement of arterial blood pressure and the taking of blood samples we used a catheter, which was inserted in the brachial artery and hidden with a curtain so that the subject would not be exposed to possible psychological trauma from witnessing the drawing of blood. Since local anesthesia was used at the site of the catheter insertion in the forearm, the subject felt no sensation when blood samples were taken. The blood pressure was measured continuously by means of a measuring device connected to the catheter.

We found that the subjects' arterial blood pressure remained at a rather low level throughout the examination; it fell to this level during the quiet premeditation period and did not change significantly during meditation or afterward. On the average the systolic pressure was equal to

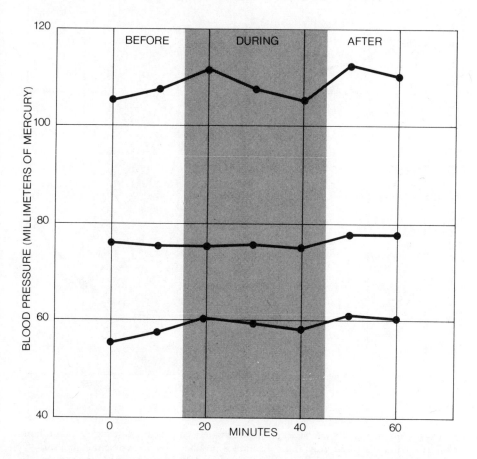

No significant change was observed in nine subjects whose arterial blood pressure was recorded before, during, and after meditation. Systolic pressure (top), mean pressure (middle), and diastolic pressure (bottom), however, stayed relatively low throughout.

106 millimeters of mercury, the diastolic pressure to 57 and the mean pressure to 75. The partial pressures of carbon dioxide and oxygen in the arterial blood also remained essentially unchanged during meditation. There was a slight increase in the acidity of the blood, indicating a slight metabolic acidosis, during meditation, but the acidity was within the normal range of variation.

Measurements of the lactate concentration in the blood (an indication of anaerobic metabolism, or metabolism in the absence of free oxygen) showed that during meditation the subjects' lactate level declined precipitously. During the first 10 minutes of meditation the lactate level in the subjects' arterial blood decreased at the rate of 10.26 milligrams per

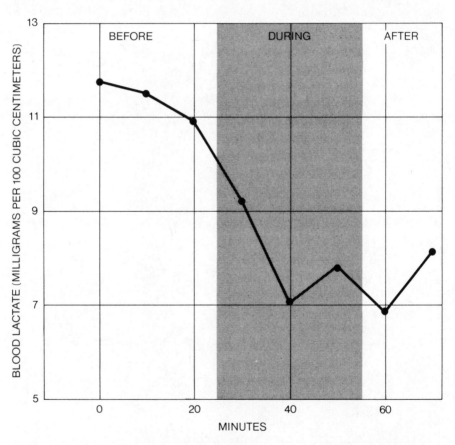

Rapid decline in the concentration of blood lactate is apparent following the invitation to start meditating (light-gray area). Lactate is produced by anaerobic metabolism, mainly in muscle tissue. Its concentration normally falls in a subject at rest, but the rate of decline during meditation proved to be more than three times faster than the normal rate.

100 cubic centimeters per hour, nearly four times faster than the rate of decrease in people normally resting in a supine position or in the subjects themselves during their premeditation period. After the subjects ceased meditating the lactate level continued to fall for a few minutes and then began to rise, but at the end of the postmeditation period it was still considerably below the premeditation level. The mean level during the premeditation period was 11.4 milligrams per 100 cubic centimeters, during meditation 8.0 milligrams and during postmeditation 7.3 milligrams.

How could one account for the fact that lactate production, which reflects anaerobic metabolism, was reduced so much during meditation? New experiments furnished a possible answer. These had to do with the rate of blood flow in meditating subjects; the explanation they suggest appears significant with respect to the psychological benefits that can be obtained from meditation.

In studies H. Rieckert conducted at the University of Tübingen, he reported that during transcendental meditation his subjects showed a 300 percent increase in the flow of blood in the forearm. In similar measurements on our subjects we found the increase in forearm blood flow to be much less: 32 percent. Still, this increase was interesting, and it offered an explanation of the relatively large decrease in blood-lactate concentration. The main site of lactate production in the body is the skeletal muscle tissue. Presumably the observed acceleration of blood flow to the forearm muscles during meditation speeds up the delivery of oxygen to the muscles. The resulting gain in oxidative metabolism may substitute for anaerobic metabolism, and this would explain the sharp drop in the production of lactate that accompanies meditation.

The intriguing consequence of this view is that it brings the autonomic nervous system further into the picture. In a situation of constant blood pressure (which is the case during meditation) the rate of blood flow is controlled basically by dilation or constriction of the blood vessels. The autonomic nervous system, in turn, controls this blood-vessel behavior. One element in this system, a part of the sympathetic nerve network, sometimes gives rise to the secretion of acetylcholine through special fibers and thereby stimulates the blood vessels to dilate. Conversely, the major part of the sympathetic nerve network stimulates the secretion of norepinephrine and thus causes constriction of the blood vessels. Rieckert's finding of a large increase in blood flow during meditation suggested that meditation increased the activity of the sympathetic nerve network that secretes the dilating substance. Our own finding of a much more modest enhancement of blood flow indicated a different view: that meditation reduces the activity of the major part of the sympathetic nerve network, so that its constriction of the blood vessels is absent. This interpretation also helps to account for the great decrease in the production of lactate during meditation; norepinephrine is known to stimulate lactate production, and a reduction in the secretion of norepinephrine, through inhibition of the major sympathetic network, should be expected to diminish the output of lactate.

Whatever the explanation of the fall in the blood-lactate level, it is clear that this could have a beneficial psychological effect. Patients with anxiety neurosis show a large rise in blood lactate when they are placed under stress [see Pitts, 1969]. Indeed, Pitts and J. N. McClure, Jr., a co-worker of Pitts's at the Washington University School of Medicine, showed experimentally that an infusion of lactate could bring on attacks

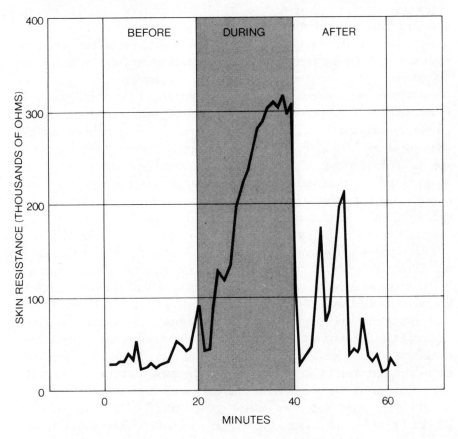

Rapid rise in the electrical resistance of the skin accompanied meditation (light-gray area) in a representative subject. The 15 subjects tested showed a rise of about 140,000 ohms in 20 minutes. In sleep, skin resistance normally rises, but not so much or at such a rate.

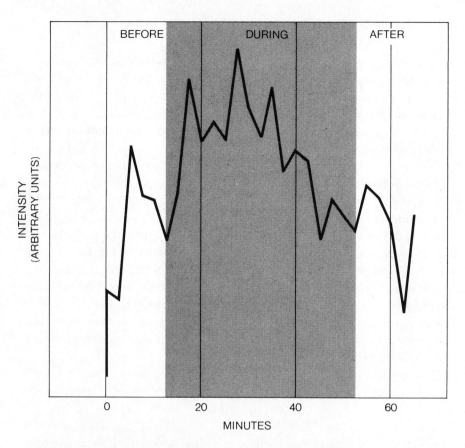

BEFORE   DURING   AFTER

INTENSITY (ARBITRARY UNITS)

0   20   40   60

MINUTES

Increase in intensity of "slow" alpha waves, at eight to nine cycles per second, was evident during meditation (light-gray area) in electroencephalograph readings of the subjects' frontal and central brain regions. This is a representative subject's frontal reading. Before meditation, most subjects' frontal readings showed alpha waves of lower intensity.

of anxiety in such patients and could even produce anxiety symptoms in normal subjects. Furthermore, it is significant that patients with hypertension (essential and renal) show higher blood-lactate levels in a resting state than patients without hypertension, whereas in contrast the low lactate level in transcendental meditators is associated with low blood pressure. All in all, it is reasonable to hypothesize that the low level of lactate found in subjects during and after transcendental meditation may be responsible in part for the meditators' thoroughly relaxed state.

Other measurements on the meditators confirmed the picture of a highly relaxed, although wakeful, condition. During meditation their skin resistance to an electric current increased markedly, in some cases more than fourfold. Their heart rate slowed by about three beats per minute on the average. Electroencephalographic recordings disclosed a marked intensification of alpha waves in all the subjects. We recorded the waves from seven main areas of the brain on magnetic tape and then analyzed the patterns with a computer. Typically there was an increase in intensity of slow alpha waves at eight or nine cycles per second in the frontal and central regions of the brain during meditation. In several subjects this change was also accompanied by prominent theta waves in the frontal area.

To sum up, our subjects during the practice of transcendental meditation manifested the physiological signs of what we describe as a "wakeful, hypometabolic" state: reductions in oxygen consumption, carbon dioxide elimination and the rate and volume of respiration; a slight increase in the acidity of the arterial blood; a marked decrease in the blood-lactate level; a slowing of the heartbeat; a considerable increase in skin resistance; and an electroencephalogram pattern of intensification of slow alpha waves with occasional theta-wave activity. These physiological modifications, in people who were practicing the easily learned technique of transcendental meditation, were very similar to those that have been observed in highly trained experts in yoga and in Zen monks who have had 15 to 20 years of experience in meditation.

How do the physiological changes during meditation compare with those in other relaxed states, such as sleep and hypnosis? There is little resemblance. Whereas oxygen consumption drops rapidly within the first five or 10 minutes of transcendental meditation, hypnosis produces no noticeable change in this metabolic index, and during sleep the consumption of oxygen decreases appreciably only after several hours. During sleep the concentration of carbon dioxide in the blood increases significantly, indicating a reduction in respiration. There is a slight increase in the acidity of the blood; this is clearly due to the decrease in ventilation and not to a change in metabolism such as occurs during meditation. Skin resistance commonly increases during sleep, but the rate and amount of this increase are on a much smaller scale than they are in transcendental meditation. The electroencephalogram patterns characteristic of sleep are different; they consist predominantly of high-voltage (strong) activity of slow waves at 12 to 14 cycles per second and a mixture of weaker waves at various frequencies—a pattern that does not occur during transcendental meditation. The patterns during hypnosis have no relation to those of the meditative state; in a hypnotized subject the brain-wave activity takes the form characteristic of the mental state that has been suggested to the subject. The same is true of changes in heart rate, blood pressure, skin resistance and respiration; all these visceral adjustments in a hypnotized person merely reflect the suggested state.

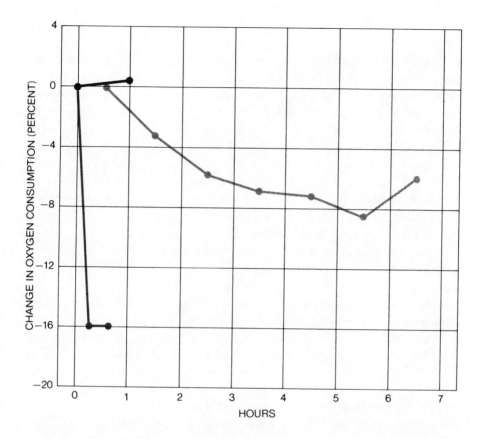

Consumption of oxygen is compared in three different circumstances: during hypnosis (dark gray), sleep (black), and meditation (light gray). No significant change occurs under hypnosis. One study shows that oxygen consumption is reduced by about 8 per cent after five hours' sleep. Meditation brings twice the reduction in a fraction of the time.

It is interesting to compare the effects obtained through meditation with those that can be established by means of operant conditioning. By such conditioning animals and people have been trained to increase or decrease their heart rate, blood pressure, urine formation and certain other autonomic functions [see selection 33, by DiCara, here]. Through the use of rewards that act as reinforcers a subject is taught to make a specific visceral response to a given stimulus. This procedure and the result are quite different, however, from what occurs in transcendental meditation. Whereas operant conditioning is limited to producing specific responses and depends on a stimulus and feedback of a reinforcer, meditation is independent of such assistance and produces not a single specific response but a complex of responses that marks a highly relaxed state.

The pattern of changes suggests that meditation generates an integrated response, or reflex, that is mediated by the central nervous system. A well-known reflex of such a nature was described many years ago by the noted Harvard physiologist Walter B. Cannon; it is called the "fight or flight" or "defense alarm" reaction. The aroused sympathetic nervous system mobilizes a set of physiological responses marked by increases in the blood pressure, heart rate, blood flow to the muscles, and oxygen consumption. The hypometabolic state produced by meditation is of course opposite to this in almost all respects. It looks very much like a counterpart of the fight-or-flight reaction.

During man's early history the defense-alarm reaction may well have had high survival value and thus have become strongly established in his genetic makeup. It continues to be aroused in all its visceral aspects when the individual feels threatened. Yet in the environment of our time the reaction is often an anachronism. Although the defense-alarm reaction is generally no longer appropriate, the visceral response is evoked with considerable frequency by the rapid and unsettling changes that are buffeting modern society. There is good reason to believe the changing environment's incessant stimulations of the sympathetic nervous system are largely responsible for the high incidence of hypertension and similar serious diseases that are prevalent in our society.

In these circumstances the hypometabolic state, representing quiescence rather than hyperactivation of the sympathetic nervous system, may indicate a guidepost to better health. It should be well worthwhile to investigate the possibilities for clinical application of this state of wakeful rest and relaxation.

23.

An Electroencephalographic Study on the Zen Meditation (Zazen)

Akira Kasamatsu and Tomio Hirai

SUMMARY

Zen meditation (Zazen) is a spiritual exercise held in the Zen sect of Buddhism. Apart from its religious significance, the training of Zen meditation produces changes not only in the mind but also in the body— these influences are of interest to scientific studies, from the standpoint of psychology and physiology.

In the present study the EEG changes accompanied with Zen meditation have been revealed and described in detail. The authors discussed further these electrographic changes in relation to the consciousness with its underlying neurophysiological background, compared with that of the hypnotic trance and sleep.

In our study, 48 priests and disciples of Zen sects of Buddhism were

Reprinted by permission from *Folio Psychiat. & Neurolog. Japonica*, 20 (1966), 315–336.

selected as the subjects and their EEGs were continuously recorded before, during, and after Zen meditation. The following results were obtained:

1. The appearance of alpha waves were observed, without regard to opened eyes, within 50 seconds after the beginning of Zen meditation. These alpha waves continued to appear, and their amplitudes increased. And as Zen meditation progressed, the decrease of the alpha frequency was gradually manifested at the later stage. Further, the rhythmical theta train with the amplitude modulated alpha-background was observed in some records of the priests. These EEG changes could be classified into 4 stages: the appearance of alpha waves (Stage I), an increase of alpha amplitude (Stage II), a decrease of alpha frequency (Stage III), and the appearance of rhythmical theta train (Stage IV).

2. These 4 stages of EEG changes were parallel with the disciples' mental states, which were evaluated by a Zen master, and disciples' years spent in Zen training.

3. These electrographic changes were also compared with that of the hypnotic trance and sleep. From the electroencephalographic point of view, the changes of States I, II and III could not be clearly differentiated from those seen in hypnagogic state or the hypnotic sleep, though the changes during Zen meditation were more persistent and did not turn into a deeper sleep pattern. The rhythmical theta train is suppressed by click stimulation and turns into a desynchronized pattern, whereas the drowsy pattern turns into alpha waves (the alpha arousal reaction).

4. The alpha blocking to the repeated click stimuli with regular intervals was also examined in Zen meditation with opened eyes and the ordinary conditions of control subjects with closed eyes. The former showed a fairly constant blocking time (3–5 seconds) to every stimuli repeated 20 times and the habituation was not recognized. On the other hand, in control subjects the habituation of alpha waves occurred very quickly. This alpha blocking, which is less susceptible to habituation, is of importance in considering the neurophysiological basis of the mental state during Zen meditation.

These electroencephalographic findings lead to the following conclusions: In Zen meditation, the slowing of the EEG pattern is confirmed on the one hand, and the dehabituation of the alpha blocking on the other. These indicate the specific change of consciousness. The authors further discussed the state of mind during Zen meditation from the psychophysiological point of view.

V.

CONTEMPORARY SUFISM

Introduction

Although we may be able to study and comprehend them more clearly than ever, the procedures of the "esoteric" traditions remain esoteric, deeply hidden from us. These procedures were for the most part developed for people in other countries at other times, and so their exercises and techniques are doubly strange to us. Sometimes, paradoxically, we may become attracted to the superficial dimensions of these systems merely because they are exotic.

The current need, therefore, is to take the essence of this esoteric knowledge and to transplant it into contemporary terms, rather as one can carry a seed from a long-dormant stock and plant it anew in fresh-tilled soil. The product will differ from previously grown plants, and from everything else. The work of Idries Shah and his associates is such an endeavor. It is an attempt to freshly transplant the essence of an esoteric tradition into modern terms and modern methods.

Shah's books make material available which has not been seen in the west for a thousand years. It is stripped of local coloration and of the accretions both of time and of translations of translations of translations. It is, then, a manifestation of the *living* traditional psychology, readily available to be investigated by those seriously interested in studying the psychology of consciousness.

The first selection is from Shah's *The Sufis*, and is a preface both to that book and to the study of the Sufi work as a whole. The next selection, from that same book, stresses the difficulties of a purely descriptive-intellectual, outside view of "esoteric" phenomena. It recalls Hastorf and Cantril's demonstration on how our biases can predetermine what we "see."

Later, we encounter Nasrudin, a Middle Eastern joke figure. There are many purposes in these quite innocent-appearing Nasrudin stories. They can hold up a moment of action as a template, so that the reader can observe his consciousness more clearly in himself. Often one may read a story, and on later encountering a similar life situation, find oneself prepared for it. In addition, these stories can be considered "word pictures," which can create visual symbolic situations. They embody a most sophisticated use of language to pass beyond intellectual understanding to develop intuition. Indeed, the stories are illustrated to aid in their visualization. "The Legend of Nasrudin" introduces him and describes the conflict between the two modes of consciousness.

The story-teller is a person who has largely gone out of our culture. Yet in the cultures of the Middle East and Central Asia, he remains in a special place. When we read, we usually do it silently and visually; but when a story is read aloud, other possibilities emerge. We have more time to imagine the events, and this imagining is aided by the fact that our eyes and visual system are not involved in the printed page. These stories are intended to provide "food" for both intellect and intuition. In this, like the Nasrudin stories from the same source, they employ specially designed situations to make an "end run" around our usual intellectual filtering apparatus and to "connect with a part of the individual which cannot be reached by any other convention." "The Teaching Story" is an article by Shah which introduces these concepts. It is followed by a long story and by two shorter ones. These stories are best read aloud after having been read to oneself. Both *Caravan of Dreams* and *Tales of the Dervishes* provide additional, similar materials. The "meditations of Rumi" are intended as material for thought, ideas to be turned over in the mind.

24.

The Sufis

Idries Shah

Sufism . . . cannot be appreciated beyond a certain point except within the real teaching situation, which requires the physical presence of a Sufi teacher. For the Sufi, it is no accident that the "secret doctrine" whose existence has for uncounted time been suspected and sought proves so elusive to the seeker. If, say, communism is a religion without a god, academic study of Sufism without being to any extent a "working Sufi" is Sufism without its essential factor. If this assertion militates against the rational tradition that an individual can find truth merely through the exercise of the faculties with which he finds himself endowed, there is only one answer. Sufism, the "secret tradition," is not available on the basis of assumptions which belong to another world, the world of intellect. If it is felt that truth about extraphysical fact must be sought only through a certain way of thinking, the rational and "scientific" one, there can be no contact between the Sufi and the supposedly objective seeker.

Sufi literature and preparatory teaching is designed to help to bridge the gap between these two worlds of thought. Were it not possible to provide any bridge at all, this book [*The Sufis*] would be worthless, and should not have been attempted.

Sufism, considered as a nutrient for society, is not intended to subsist within society in an unaltered form. That is to say, the Sufis do not erect systems as one would build an edifice, for succeeding generations to examine and learn from. Sufism is transmitted by means of the human exemplar, the teacher. Because he is an unfamiliar figure to the world at large, or because he has imitators, does not mean that he does not exist.

We find traces of Sufism in derelict organizations from which this element of human transmission of *baraka* has ceased; where the form alone remains. Since it is this outer shell which is most easily perceptible to the ordinary man, we have to use it to point to something deeper. Unlike him, we cannot say that such and such a ritual, such and such a book, incarnates Sufism. We start with human, social, literary material that is both incomplete (because now unaccompanied by the impact of the living exemplar, the teacher) and secondary, in that it is only partially absorbed. Historical facts, such as religious and social organization, when they persist, are secondary, external phenomena which depend upon organization, emotion and outward show for their survival. These factors, so essential for the continuation of familiar systems, are, Sufistically speaking, only the substitute for the vitality of organism, as distinct from appearance and sentiment.

A Sufi school comes into being, like any other natural factor, in order to flourish and disappear, not to leave traces in mechanical ritual, or anthropologically interesting survivals. The function of a nutrient is to become transmuted, not to leave unaltered traces.

The great Sufi teacher Jami refers to this tendency when he says that if the beard is allowed to grow too bushy, it will vie with the hair of the head in its claim for attention of prominence.

It will easily be understood that both the "organic" and "human exemplar" claims of Sufism remove it immediately from the purview of conventional study.

There is, however, some value in paying attention to Sufi influences upon human culture. In the first place, we can observe attempts to bridge the gap between ordinary thinking and Sufi experience, contained in poetic, literary and other media, which have been designed to lead the ordinary, attenuated or embryonic human consciousness into a greater perception and realization. Secondly, it is maintained by Sufis that even in cultures where authoritarian and mechanical thinking have choked comprehensive understanding, human individuality will have to assert itself, somewhere, even if this be only through the primitive sense that life must have more meaning than the officially propagated one. . . .

Sufism, it should be remembered, is Eastern thought only insofar as it retains beliefs—such as the human exemplar—which have fallen into abeyance in the West. It is occult and mystical inasmuch as it follows a path other than that which has been represented as the true one by authoritarian and dogmatic organization. Sufism claims that the latter attitude constitutes only a part, only a phase, in the human story. Claiming a "real" source of knowledge, Sufism cannot accept the pretensions of the temporary phase which, viewed from within itself, is currently considered to be the "logical" one.

A great deal of the material presented here is incomplete because it is not possible to increase the amount of formal literature about Sufism without the balance of Sufic practice. Much of it, nevertheless, is unknown outside traditional Sufic circles. It is not intended to influence traditional scholasticism, with which it has only the most superficial connection; and one which cannot be carried far without distortion.

Sufism is known by means of itself.

It is interesting to note the difference between science as we know it today, and as it was seen by one of its pioneers. Roger Bacon, considered to be the wonder of the middle ages and one of humanity's greatest thinkers, was the pioneer of the method of knowledge gained through experience. This Franciscan monk learned from the Sufis of the illuminist school that there is a difference between the collection of information and the knowing of things through actual experiment. In his *Opus Maius*, in which he quotes Sufi authority, he says:

> There are two modes of knowledge, through argument and experience. Argument brings conclusions and compels us to concede them, but it does not cause certainty nor remove doubts in order that the mind may remain at rest in truth, unless this is provided in experience.

Thus Sufi doctrine is known in the West as the scientific method of inductive proceeding, and subsequent Western science is largely based upon it.

Modern science, however, instead of accepting the idea that experience was necessary in all branches of human thought, took the word in its sense of "experiment," in which the experimenter remained as far as possible outside the experience.

From the Sufi point of view, therefore, Bacon, when he wrote these words in 1268, both launched modern science and also transmitted only a portion of the wisdom upon which it could have been based.

"Scientific" thinking has worked continuously and heroically with this partial tradition ever since. In spite of its roots in the work of the Sufis, the impairment of the tradition has prevented the scientific researcher from approaching knowledge by means of itself—by "experience," not merely "experiment."

In an instant, rise from time and space. Set the world aside and become a world within yourself.

Shabistari, Secret Garden

25.

Mysteries in the West: Strange Rites

Idries Shah

It is the night of Saturday, especially consecrated to a ritual which is awesome to us, faithfully followed by the devotees of a certain cult.

Two groups of twelve, dressed in colorful costumes, carry out complicated movements within an enclosed space. They at times respond to musical stimuli applied through a primitive instrument by a man of seeming authority who, with a few assistants, supervises their activity. Entirely surrounding the area devoted to the ritual, a congregation gives its responses. At times the people sing, sometimes they shout, sometimes they are silent. Some wield an instrument which gives forth a strange sound.

Much care has evidently gone into the planning of the geometrically designed arena. Around it are colorful insignia, flags, banners, decorations probably designed to raise the emotional pitch of the individual and the group. The atmosphere is eerie partly because of the abrupt changes in emotion. Their reaction to the ecstatogenic processes being enacted in their midst is so explosive at times that one wonders why they do not

Reprinted by permission from Idries Shah, *The Sufis*, pp. 232–234 (Doubleday & Co., Inc., and W. H. Allen & Co., Ltd.). Copyright © 1964 by Idries Shah.

spill over into the sacred enclosure. Both joy and sorrow are manifested among the votaries.

We are observers at a floodlit association football game. What is missing from the observer's account is a knowledge of what is actually happening, and why. If we have this knowledge, we can identify the players, crowd, referee, the use of the chalked lines. If we do not, we continue: Here a man writhes on the ground, another grimaces, sweat pouring from his face. One of the audience strokes himself, another his neighbor. The totem rises into the air, and is hailed by an awesome roar from the assembly. . . . Then we see that blood has been shed.

Other forms of ritual are subject to a similar approach by those who have not been through the experiences which precede their staging. Even more important, very many rituals of one kind or another have undergone alteration throughout the ages, the original intention or force being lost. When this happens, there is a mechanical or associative substitution of other factors. The ritual is distorted, even though there may be apparent reasons for its every aspect. This development is what we can call the dereliction of cult behavior.

Here, now, is an externalist account of a dervish ritual, in which events are described from the point of view of the observer alone. The author is the Reverend John Subhan, of the Methodist Episcopal Church, who was present at this event in India:

> Tonight is Thursday night, the night which is specially sacred to the Sufi. Come, let us visit some shrines and see for ourselves what strange religious rites are practiced almost at our very doors.
>
> We enter a dimly lighted room where a number of men are gathered. As we do so a signal is given by a man who appears to be the leader of the assembly, and the doors are shut. There is a hush as twelve men form into two parallel lines in the center of the room. The glimmer of a solitary hurricane lamp falls on dark faces in which only the eyes seem to live. The rest of us fall back to the sides of the room. The Dhikr is about to begin.
>
> With a startling clap of the hands the leader starts swaying from right to left. Very slowly he begins, and the men fall into the rhythm of his swaying. Every time they sway to the left they call "Hu!" in chorus, "Hu . . . Hu . . . Hu."

The dervish ritual is not of the same nature of the football game—far from it. Since, however, it is not symbolic but concerned with an interior activity, the advantages of describing such an event in this out-of-context manner are few.

26.

The Legend of Nasrudin

Idries Shah

A certain crafty villain was entrusted with the education of a number of
orphans. Observing that children have certain strengths and weaknesses,
he decided to take advantage of this knowledge. Instead of teaching them
how to acquire a skill in learning, he told them that they already possessed it. Then he insisted upon their doing some things and refraining
from others, and thus kept most of them blindly subject to his direction.
He never revealed that his original commission had been to teach them
to teach themselves.

When these children grew up, he noticed that some had detached
themselves from his authority, despite all his efforts, while others remained bound to it.

Reprinted by permission from Idries Shah, *Thinkers of the East* (Jonathan Cape, Ltd.,
and Penguin Books, Inc., for Collins-Knowlton-Wing, Inc.), pp. 191–195. Copyright ©
1971 by Idries Shah.

He was then entrusted with a second school of orphans. From these he did not directly demand obedience and respect. Instead, he enslaved them to his will by telling them that mental culture was the sole aim of education and by appealing to their self-pride. "The mind," he told them, "will give you universal understanding."

"This must be true," thought the children. "After all, why should we not be able to solve all problems by ourselves?"

He supported the doctrine by demonstrations. "This man," he said, "is enslaved by his emotions. What a disastrous case! Only the intellect can control the emotions. That other man, however, is ruled by his intellect. How much happier he is, how free from emotional frenzy!"

He never let the children guess that there was an alternative to the choice between emotions and intellect, namely intuition, which could, however, be overcome or blurred by either of these, and always dismissed its appearance as irrelevant coincidence or guesswork. There are two kinds of "habit": one derived from mere repetition, the other from intuition harnessed both to the emotions and to the intellect. But since intuitive habit is associated with true reality, this villainous old man simply abolished it in favour of repetitive habit.

Some of the children, nevertheless, suspected that certain miraculous aspects of life did not fit into its fragmentary pattern, and asked him whether there was not, perhaps, something else undisclosed, some secret power. He told one group of questioners, "Certainly not! Such a notion is superstitious, and due to faulty mental processes. Do not put any value on coincidence. 'Coincidence' means no more than accident, which, though perhaps of emotional interest, lacks all intellectual significance."

To another group he said, "Yes, there is more in life than you will ever know; because it cannot be acquired by honest extension of the scientific information which I gave you, or which you manage to collect under my direction."

But he took care that the two groups did not compare notes and so realize that he had given two contradictory answers. Now, from time to time, when the children reported inexplicable events to him, he consigned these to oblivion as having no scientific relevance.

He knew that, without taking stock of intuition, the children would never escape from the invisible net in which he had bound them, and that the intuitive knowledge of secrets excluded from their education could be won only when they were in a certain harmony of mind with the emotions. So he taught them to ignore variations in their mental condition; for once they discovered that powers of apprehension vary from hour to hour, they might guess how much he had concealed from them. His training confused their memory of such intuitions as they had been granted and they were willing to think along the logical lines he had prepared for them.

The children whom this villain had mistaught in his first school were now grown up, and since he had let them come nearer to understanding the true nature of life, certain casual remarks that they made to members of the second school disturbed their faith in scientific truth. So he hastily gathered those of the first school who still remained loyal to him and sent them out to preach incomprehensible doctrines purporting to explain the hidden mechanism of life. Then he directed the attention of the second school to these teachers, saying, "Listen carefully, but never fail to use your intellect."

The intellectual children soon found that there was nothing to be learned from these doctrines and said, "They contradict logic. Only with logic are we on firm ground."

Yet some members of the first school who had broken away from the old villain's teaching reproached them, saying, "We, too, reject these doctrines, but that they fail to explain the secret mechanism of life of which you are in search does not deny its existence." They answered, "Can you, then, put the secret in logical terms?" but were told that to do so would be to deny its truth.

So they protested, "Nothing is true that cannot face the cold light of reason." A few, however, cried out, "We are ready to believe everything you tell us. We think you are wonderful." But they were as hopelessly lost as the intellectual children and the teachers of the incomprehensible doctrine, because they trusted only to a slavish credulity, not to the habit of intuition.

A state of educative chaos supervened. So many different ways of thought were current that it was often said, "I cannot trust anyone, I must find out for myself by the exercise of my supreme will."

The old villain who had bred this confusion thrived on it like a madman rejoicing in deeds of violence. Especially this cult of the intellect encouraged egotism and discord. And to those who still felt an inner uncertainty, a sense of incompleteness, or a hankering for something whole and true, he said, "Distract your minds by ambition!" He taught them to covet honours, money, possessions, sexual conquests, to compete with their neighbours, to immerse themselves in hobbies and diversions.

It is said that when a horse cannot find grass, it will accept hay. For want of the green grass of Truth they accepted the dry hay with which he filled their mangers.

The old man devised more and more distractions for them: vogues, crazes, lotteries, fashions in art, music, and literature, sporting competitions and all kinds of achievements which offered them temporary relief from this sense of lack. They were like a patient who accepts palliatives from his physician because he assures him that his disease is incurable. Or they were like the monkey and the crab-apple: he clutched the crab-apple inside a bottle, but the neck was too narrow for him to withdraw his hand and the crab-apple too. Unable to escape because hampered by the bottle, he was soon captured and put into a sack. But he proudly cried, "I still have the apple."

The fragmentary view of life forced on mankind by the old villain was now accepted; and the few people who tried to point out where Truth really lay were thought insane and readily refuted by the old argument, "If what you say is true, then prove it to us logically!"

False coin is accepted only because true coin exists, and deep in their hearts many people knew this. But they were like children born in a house from which they had never been allowed to stray, doomed to walk from one room to another without knowing that there could be another house, elsewhere, with different furnishings and a different view from its windows.

Nevertheless the tradition that true coins exist, that there is another house, and that some horses eat grass, not hay, survived in a book which was not a book, delivered by direct succession from an ancient sage to one of his descendants named Hussein. Hussein searched the world until he found the man who through craft and guile would give the teaching of this book fit expression: namely, the incomparable Mulla Nasrudin. Thereupon this book which was not a book was interpreted by the actions of a Mulla who was no Mulla; who was both wise and a fool; who was both a man and many men. And the teaching was thus brought to the attention of the children who had been misled.

Mulla Nasrudin broke out of the net which had been cast by the old villain. For how can one burn a book which is not a book? How can one name a fool who is no fool? How can one punish a man who is a multitude? How can one strike a man who is oneself?

Study the adventures of Mulla Nasrudin, plumb the depth of the subtleties! He is like a tree which has nourishment in its roots and an edible sap; whose leaves are pot-herbs, whose flowers, fruit, branches and seeds are all variously the same!

Can a tree be a man, or a man a tree?

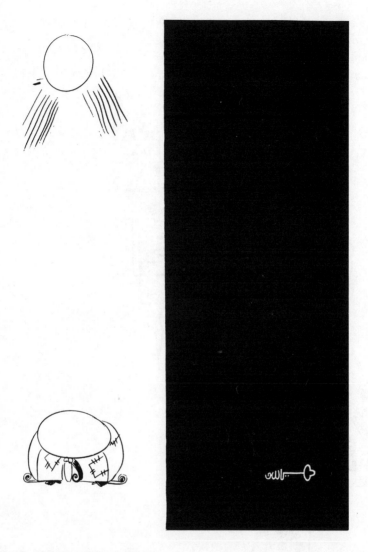

THERE IS MORE LIGHT HERE*

Someone saw Nasrudin searching for something on the ground.

"What have you lost, Mulla?" he asked.

"My key," said the Mulla. So they both went down on their knees and looked for it.

---

*This and the next two stories about Nasrudin are reprinted by permission from Idries Shah, *The Exploits of the Incomparable Mulla Nasrudin* (Jonathan Cape, Ltd., and Simon and Schuster, Inc., for Collins-Knowlton-Wing, Inc.). Copyright © 1966 by Mulla Nasrudin Enterprises.

After a time the other man asked: "Where exactly did you drop it?"
"In my own house."
"Then why are you looking here?"
"There is more light here than inside my own house."

THE VALUE OF THE PAST

Nasrudin was sent by the King to investigate the lore of various kinds of
Eastern mystical teachers. They all recounted to him tales of the miracles
and the sayings of the founders and great teachers, all long dead, of their
schools.

When he returned home, he submitted his report, which contained the single word "Carrots."

He was called upon to explain himself. Nasrudin told the King: "The best part is buried; few know—except the farmer—by the green that there is orange underground; if you don't work for it, it will deteriorate; there are a great many donkeys associated with it."

MOMENT IN TIME

"What is Fate?" Nasrudin was asked by a scholar.

"An endless succession of intertwined events, each influencing the other."

"That is hardly a satisfactory answer. I believe in cause and effect."

"Very well," said the Mulla, "look at that." He pointed to a procession passing in the street. "That man is being taken to be hanged. Is that because someone gave him a silver piece and enabled him to buy the knife with which he committed the murder; or because someone saw him do it; or because nobody stopped him?"

27.

The Teaching Story: Observations on the Folklore of Our "Modern" Thought

Idries Shah

There is no nation, no community, without its stories. Children are brought up on fairy tales, cults and religions depend upon them for moral instruction: they are used for entertainment and for training. They are usually catalogued as myths, as humorous tales, as semi-historical fact, and so on, in accordance with what people believe to be their origin and function.

But what a story can be used for is often what it was originally intended to be used for. The fables of all nations provide a really remarkable example of this, because, if you can understand them at a technical

Reprinted by permission from *Point*, Number 4 (Winter 1968–69), pp. 4–9.

level, they provide the most striking evidence of the persistence of a consistent teaching, preserved sometimes through mere repetition, yet handed down and prized simply because they give a stimulus to the imagination or entertainment for the people at large.

There are very few people nowadays who are able to make the necessary use of stories. Those who know about the higher level of being represented by stories can learn something from them, but very little. Those who can experience this level can teach the use of stories. But first of all we must allow the working hypothesis that there may be such a level operative in stories. We must approach them from the point of view that they may on that level be documents of technical value: an ancient yet still irreplaceable method of arranging and transmitting a knowledge which can not be put in any other way.

In this sense such stories (because *all* stories are not technical literature), such stories may be regarded as part of a curriculum, and as valid a representation of fact as, for instance, any mathematical formula or scientific textbook.

Like any scientific textbook or mathematical formula, however, stories depend for their higher power upon someone to understand them at the higher level, someone who can establish their validity in a course of study, people who are prepared to study and use them, and so on.

At this point we can see quite easily that our conditioning (which trains us to use stories for amusement purposes) is generally in itself sufficient to prevent us from making any serious study of stories as a vehicle for higher teaching. This tendency, the human tendency to regard anything as of use to man on a lower level than it could operate, runs through much of our studies, and has to be marked well.

Yet traditions about stories do in fact linger here and there. People say that certain stories, if repeated, will provide some sort of "good luck"; or that tales have meanings which have been forgotten, and the like. But what would be called in contemporary speech the "security aspect" of stories is almost complete in the case of the genre which we call "teaching-stories" because of another factor.

This factor is the operation of the law that a story, like a scientific industrial formula, say, can have its developmental or teaching effect only upon a person correctly prepared for its understanding. This is why we must use stories in a manner which will enable us to harvest their value for us in a given situation.

There is another problem which has to be appreciated when dealing with stories. Unlike scientific formulae, they have a whole series of developmental effects. In accordance with the degree of preparation of an

individual and a group, so will the successive "layers" of the story become apparent. Outside of a proper school where the method and content of stories is understood, there is almost no chance of an arbitrary
study of stories yielding much.

But we have to go back to an even earlier stage in order to ground
ourselves, prepare ourselves, for the value of the story. This is the stage
at which we can familiarise ourselves with the story and regard it as a
consistent and productive parallel or allegory of certain states of mind.
Its symbols are the characters in the story. The way in which they move
conveys to the mind the way in which the human mind can work. In
grasping this in terms of men and women, animals and places, movement and manipulation of a tale, we can put ourselves into a relationship with the higher faculties possible. to the mind, by working on a
lower level, the level of visualisation.

Let us examine a story or two from the foregoing points of view. First,
take a story of the Elephant in the Dark.* This has actually been published as a children's book. It appears in the books of Rumi and Sanai.
We have made it the subject of a commercial film, *The Dermis Probe*.
This story, on the lowest possible level, makes fun of the scientists and
academics who try to explain things through the evidence which they
can evaluate, and none other. In another direction, on the same level, it
is humorous in as much as it makes us laugh at the stupidity of people
who work on such little evidence. As a philosophical teaching it says that
man is blind and is trying to assess something too great for assessment by
means of inadequate tools. In the religious field it says that God is everywhere and everything, and man gives different names to what seem to
him to be separate things, but which are in fact only parts of some
greater whole which he cannot perceive because "he is blind" or "there
is no light."

The interpretations are far and high as anyone can go. Because of
this, people address themselves to this story in one or more of these
interpretations. They then accept or reject them. Now they can feel
happy; they have arrived at an opinion about the matter. According to
their conditioning they produce the answer. Now look at their answers.
Some will say that this is a fascinating and touching allegory of the presence of God. Others will say that it is showing people how stupid mankind can be. Some say it is anti-scholastic. Others that it is just a tale

---

*A number of blind people, or sighted people in a dark house, grope and find an
elephant. Each touches only a part; each gives to his friends outside a different account
of what he has experienced. Some think that it was a fan (the ears of the animal); another
takes the legs for pillars; a third the tail for a rope, and so on.

copied by Rumi from Sanai—and so on. Because none of these people can taste an inner content, none will even begin to imagine that one exists. As I say these words the ordinary mind will easily be able to dispose of them by thinking that this is just someone who has provided a sophisticated explanation for something which cannot be checked.

But we are not here to justify ourselves. We are here to open the door of the mind to the possibility that stories might be technical documents. We are here to say that there is a method of making use of these documents. Especially we are here to say that the most ancient and most important knowledge available to man is in part contained in these documents. And that this form, however primitive or old-fashioned it may seem, is in fact almost the only form in which certain teachings can be captured, preserved and transmitted. And, too, that these stories are conscious works of art, devised by people who knew exactly what they were doing, for the use of other people who knew exactly what could be done with them.

It may take a conventional thinker some time to understand that if he is looking for truth and a hidden teaching, it may be concealed in a form which would be the last, perhaps, which he would consider to be applicable to his search.

But, in order to possess himself of this knowledge, he must take it from where it *really is*, not from where he imagines it might be.

There is plenty of evidence of the working of this method, that of the story deliberately concocted and passed down, in all cultures. We do not have to confine ourselves to Eastern fables. But it is in stories of Eastern origin that we find the most complete and least deteriorated forms of the tradition. We therefore start with them. They lead us, naturally, to the significant documents in the Western and other branches of the tradition.

In approaching the study of stories, then, we have to make sure that we reclaim the information that stories contain, shall we say, a message. In this sense we are like people whose technology has fallen into disuse, rediscovering the devices used by our ancestors as we become fitted for it. Then we have to realise that we have to familiarise ourselves with certain stories, so that we can hold them in our minds, like memorising a formula. In this use, the teaching story resembles the mnemonic or formula which we trot out to help us calculate something: like saying: "one kilo equals 2.2 pounds in weight"; or even "thirty days hath September."

Now we have to realise that, since we are dealing with a form of knowledge which is specific in as much as it is planned to act in a certain way under certain conditions, those conditions must be present if we are to be able to use the story coherently. By coherently I mean here, if the story is to be the guide whereby we work through the various stages of consciousness open to us.

This means that we must not only get to know certain tales; we must study them, or even just familiarise ourselves with them, in a certain order. This idea tends to find opposition among literate people who are accustomed to doing their own reading, having been led to believe that the more you read the more likely you are to know more. But this quantitative approach is absurd when you are dealing with specific material. If you went to the British Museum library and decided to read everything in it in order to educate yourself, you would not get very far. It is only the ignorant, even in the formal sense, who cannot understand the need for particular kinds of specialisation. This is well exemplified by the club porter who once said to me, in all seriousness "You are a college man, Sir, please explain football pool permutations to me."

It is in order to get some possibility of right study that I continually say things like "Let us get down out of the trees and start to build."

So far, however, we have not been saying much more than this:

1. A special, effective and surpassingly important teaching is contained in certain materials. In this case the materials are stories.
2. We must accept the possibility before we can begin to approach the study of this knowledge.
3. Having accepted, even as a working hypothesis, the foregoing contentions, we have to set about the study in an efficient manner. In the case of the tales, the efficient manner means to approach the right stories, in the right manner, under the right conditions.

Failure to adhere to these principles will make it impossible for us to function on the high level needed. If, for example, we settle for merely knowing a lot of stories, we may become mere raconteurs or consumers. If we settle for the moral or social teaching of the story, we simply duplicate the activities of people working in that domain. If we compare stories to try to see where the higher level is, we will not find it, because we do not know unless guided which are the ones to compare with each other, under what conditions, what to look for, whether we can perceive the secret content, in what order to approach the matter.

So the story remains a tool as much as anything else. Only the expert can use the tool, or produce anything worthwhile with it.

Having heard and accepted the above assertions, people always feel impatience. They want to get on with the job. But, not knowing that "everything takes a minimum time," or at any rate not applying this fact, they destroy the possibility of progress in a real sense.

Having established in a certain order the above facts, we have to follow through with a curriculum of study which will enable us to profit by the existence of this wonderful range of material. If you start to study what you take to be teaching-stories indiscriminately, you are more than likely to get only a small result, even with the facts already set out. Why is this?

Not only because you do not know the conditions under which the study must take place, but because the conditions themselves contain requirements of self-collection which seem to have no relationship to the necessities for familiarising oneself with a literary form.

We must, therefore, work on the mind to enable it to make use of the story, as well as presenting it with the story. This "work" on the mind is correctly possible only in the living situation, when certain people are grouped together in a certain manner, and develop a certain form of rapport. This, and no other, is the purpose of having meetings at which people are physically present.

If read hurriedly, or with one or other of the customary biases which are common among intellectuals but not other kinds of thinkers, the foregoing two paragraphs will be supposed to contain exclusivistic claims which are not in fact there.

This is itself one of the interesting—and encouraging—symptoms of the present phase of human intellectual folklore. If a tendency can readily be seen manifesting itself, whether in physics, scholasticism or metaphysics, one may be approaching its solution. What is this tendency?

The tendency is to demand a justification of what are taken to be certain claims *in the language in which the demand is made*. My stressing, for instance, that meetings at which people are present who have been grouped in a certain manner, may easily (and incorrectly) be supposed to state that the kind of learning to which I am referring can take place in no other manner. The intention of the paragraph, however, was simply to refer to one concrete manner in which what I have called "a living situation" can come about. A meeting of a number of people in a room is the only form of such a situation familiar to any extent to an average reader of such materials as this.

I have used the word "folklore" to refer to a state of mind of modern man closely similar to that of less developed communities. But there is a great difference between the two folklores. In what we regard as in- genuous folklore, the individual may believe that certain objects have magical or special characteristics, and he is more or less aware of what these are claimed to be.

In modern man's folklore, he believes that certain contentions must be absurd, and holds on to other assumptions, without being aware that he is doing so. He is motivated, in fact, by almost completely hidden prejudices.

To illustrate the working of such preconceptions, it is often necessary to provide a "shock" stimulus.

Such a stimulus occurs both in the present series of contentions about the teaching-story (because, and only because, certain information about it is lost to the community being addressed) and exists equally strongly within the frameworks of such stories themselves, when one can view them in a structural manner.

This train of thought itself produces an illustration of the relative fragmentation of contemporary minds. Here it is:

Although it is a matter of the everyday experience of almost everyone on this planet, irrespective of his stage of culture or his community, that any one thing may have a multiplicity of uses, functions and meanings, man does not apply this experience to cases which—for some occult reason—he regards as insusceptible to such attention. In other words, a person may admit that an orange has colour, aroma, food value, shape, texture and so on; and he will readily concede that an orange may be many different things according to what function is desired, observed or being fulfilled. But if you venture to suggest that, say, a story has an equal range of possible functions, his folkloric evaluating mechanism will make him say: "No, a story is for entertainment," or else something almost as byzantine: "Yes, of course. Now, are you talking about the psychological, social, anthropological or philosophical uses?"

Nobody has told him that there are, or might be, categories of effective function of a story in ranges which he has not yet experienced, perhaps not yet heard of, perhaps even cannot perceive or even coherently discuss, until a certain basic information process has taken place in his mind.

And to this kind of statement the answer is pat and hard to combat. It is: "You are trying to be clever." This, you may recall is only the "yaa-boo" reaction of the schoolchild who has come up against something which it cannot, at least at that moment, rationalise away or fully understand.

o   o   o

THE MAGIC HORSE

This tale is of great importance because it belongs to an instructional corpus of mystical materials with inner content but—beyond entertainment value—without immediate external significance.

The teaching-story was brought to perfection as a communication instrument many thousands of years ago. The fact that it has not developed greatly since then has caused people obsessed by some theories of our current civilisations to regard it as the product of a less enlightened time. They feel that it must surely be little more than a literary curiosity, something fit for children, the projection, perhaps, of infantile desires, a means of enacting a wish-fulfilment.

Hardly anything could be further from the truth of such pseudo-philosophical, certainly unscientific, imaginings. Many teaching-stories *are* entertaining to children and to naive peasants. Many of them in the forms in which they are viewed by conditioned theorists have been so processed by unregenerate amateurs that their effective content is distorted. Some apply only to certain communities, depending upon special circumstances for their correct unfolding: circumstances whose absence effectively prevents the action of which they are capable.

So little is known to the academics, the scholars, and the intellectuals of this world about these materials, that there is no word in modern languages which has been set aside to describe them.

But the teaching-story exists, nevertheless. It is a part of the most priceless heritage of mankind.

Real teaching-stories are not to be confused with parables; which are adequate enough in their intention, but still on a lower level of material, generally confined to the inculcation of moralistic principles, not the assistance of interior movement of the human mind. What we often take on the lower level of parable, however, can sometimes be seen by real specialists as teaching-stories; especially when experienced under the correct conditions.

Unlike the parable, the meaning of the teaching-story cannot be unravelled by ordinary intellectual methods alone. Its action is direct and certain, upon the innermost part of the human being, an action incapable of manifestation by means of the emotional or intellectual apparatus.

The closest that we can come to describing its effect is to say that it connects with a part of the individual which cannot be reached by any other convention, and that it establishes in him or in her a means of communication with a non-verbalised truth beyond the customary limitations of our familiar dimensions.

Some teaching-stories cannot now be reclaimed because of the literary and traditionalistic, even ideological, processing to which they have been subjected. The worst of such processes is the historicising one, where a community comes to believe that one of their former teaching-stories represents literal historical truth.

This tale is given here in a form which is innocent of this and other kinds of maltreatment.

Once upon a time—not so very long ago—there was a realm in which the people were exceedingly prosperous. All kinds of discoveries had been made by them, in the growing of plants, in harvesting and preserving fruits, and in making objects for sale to other countries: and in many other practical arts.

Their ruler was unusually enlightened, and he encouraged new discoveries and activities, because he knew of their advantages for his people.

He had a son named Hoshyar, who was expert in using strange contrivances, and another—called Tambal—a dreamer, who seemed interested only in things which were of little value in the eyes of the citizens.

From time to time the king, who was named King Mumkin, circulated announcements to this effect:

"Let all those who have notable devices and useful artifacts present them to the palace for examination, so that they may be appropriately rewarded."

Now there were two men of that country—an ironsmith and a woodworker—who were great rivals in most things, and each delighted in making strange contraptions. When they heard this announcement one day, they agreed to compete for an award, so that their relative merits could be decided once and for all, by their sovereign, and publicly recognized.

Accordingly, the smith worked day and night on a mighty engine, employing a multitude of talented specialists, and surrounding his workshop with high walls so that his devices and methods should not become known.

At the same time the woodworker took his simple tools and went into a forest where, after long and solitary reflection, he prepared his own masterpiece.

News of the rivalry spread, and people thought that the smith must easily win, for his cunning works had been seen before, and while the woodworker's products were generally admired, they were of occasional and undramatic use.

When both were ready, the king received them in open court.

The smith produced an immense metallic fish which could, he said,

---

swim in and under the water. It could carry large quantities of freight over the land. It could burrow into the earth; and it could even fly slowly through the air. At first the court found it hard to believe that there could be such a wonder made by man: but when the smith and his assistants demonstrated it, the king was overjoyed and declared the smith among the most honoured in the land, with a special rank and the title of "Benefactor of the Community."

Prince Hoshyar was placed in charge of the making of the wondrous fishes, and the services of this new device became available to all mankind.

Everyone blessed the smith and Hoshyar, as well as the benign and sagacious monarch whom they loved so much.

In the excitement, the self-effacing carpenter had been all but forgotten. Then, one day, someone said: "But what about the contest? Where is the entry of the woodworker? We all know him to be an ingenious man. Perhaps he has produced something useful."

"How could anything possibly be as useful as the Wondrous Fishes?" asked Hoshyar. And many of the courtiers and the people agreed with him.

But one day the king was bored. He had become accustomed to the novelty of the fishes and the reports of the wonders which they so regularly performed. He said: "Call the woodcarver, for I would now like to see what he has made."

The simple woodcarver came into the throne-room, carrying a parcel, wrapped in coarse cloth. As the whole court craned forward to see what he had, he took off the covering to reveal—a wooden horse. It was well enough carved, and it had some intricate patterning chiselled into it, as well as being decorated with coloured paints but it was only . . . "A mere plaything!" snapped the king.

"But, Father," said Prince Tambal, "let us ask the man what is is for . . ."

"Very well," said the king, "what is it for?"

"Your majesty," stammered the woodcarver, "it is a magic horse. It does not look impressive, but it has, as it were, its own inner senses. Unlike the fish, which has to be directed, this horse can interpret the desires of the rider, and carry him wherever he needs to go."

"Such stupidity is fit only for Tambal," murmured the chief minister at the king's elbow; "it cannot have any real advantage when measured against the wondrous fish."

The woodcarver was preparing sadly to depart when Tambal said: "Father, let me have the wooden horse."

"All right," said the king, "give it to him. Take the woodcarver away and tie him on a tree somewhere, so that he will realise that our time is valuable. Let him contemplate the prosperity which the wondrous fish has brought us, and perhaps after some time we shall let him go free, to practise whatever he may have learned of real industriousness, through true reflection."

The woodcarver was taken away, and Prince Tambal left the court carrying the magic horse.

Tambal took the horse to his quarters, where he discovered that it had several knobs, cunningly concealed in the carved designs. When these were turned in a certain manner, the horse—together with anyone mounted on it—rose into the air and sped to whatever place was in the mind of the person who moved the knobs.

In this way, day after day, Tambal flew to places which he had never visited before. By this process he came to know a great many things. He took the horse everywhere with him.

One day he met Hoshyar, who said to him: "Carrying a wooden horse is a fit occupation for such as you. As for me, I am working for the good of all, towards my heart's desire!"

Tambal thought: "I wish I knew what was the good of all. And I wish I could know what my heart's desire is."

When he was next in his room, he sat upon the horse and thought: "I would like to find my heart's desire." At the same time he moved some of the knobs on the horse's neck.

Swifter than light the horse rose into the air and carried the prince a thousand days' ordinary journey away, to a far kingdom, ruled by a magician-king.

The king, whose name was Kahana, had a beautiful daughter called Precious Pearl, Durri-Karima. In order to protect her, he had imprisoned her in a circling palace, which wheeled in the sky, higher than any mortal could reach. As he was approaching the magic land, Tambal saw the glittering palace in the heavens, and alighted there.

The princess and the young horseman met and fell in love.

"My father will never allow us to marry," she said; "for he has ordained that I become the wife of the son of another magician-king who lives across the cold desert to the east of our homeland. He has vowed that when I am old enough I shall cement the unity of the two kingdoms by this marriage. His will has never been successfully opposed."

"I will go and try to reason with him" answered Tambal, as he mounted the magic horse again.

But when he descended into the magic land there were so many new and exciting things to see that he did not hurry to the palace. When at length he approached it, the drum at the gate, indicating the absence of the king, was already beating.

"He has gone to visit his daughter in the Whirling Palace," said a passer-by when Tambal asked him when the king might be back; "and he usually spends several hours at a time with her."

Tambal went to a quiet place where he willed the horse to carry him to the king's own apartment. "I will approach him at his own home," he thought to himself, "for if I go to the Whirling Palace without his permission he may be angry."

He hid behind some curtains in the palace when he got there, and lay down to sleep.

Meanwhile, unable to keep her secret, the princess Precious Pearl had confessed to her father that she had been visited by a man on a flying horse, and that he wanted to marry her. Kahana was furious.

He placed sentries around the Whirling Palace, and returned to his own apartment to think things over. As soon as he entered his bed-chamber, one of the tongueless magic servants guarding it pointed to the wooden horse lying in a corner. "Aha!" exclaimed the magician-king. "Now I have him. Let us look at this horse and see what manner of thing it may be."

As he and his servants were examining the horse, the prince managed to slip away and conceal himself in another part of the palace.

After twisting the knobs, tapping the horse and generally trying to understand how it worked, the king was baffled. "Take that thing away. It has no virtue now, even if it ever had any," he said. "It is just a trifle, fit for children."

The horse was put into a store-cupboard.

Now King Kahana thought that he should make arrangements for his daughter's wedding without delay, in case the fugitive might have other powers or devices with which to try to win her. So he called her to his own palace and sent a message to the other magician-king, asking that the prince who was to marry her be sent to claim his bride.

Meanwhile Prince Tambal, escaping from the palace by night when some guards were asleep, decided that he must try to return to his own country. His quest for his heart's desire now seemed almost hopeless. "If it takes me the rest of my life," he said to himself, "I shall come back here, bringing troops to take this kingdom by force. I can only do that by convincing my father that I must have his help to attain my heart's desire."

So saying, he set off. Never was a man worse equipped for such a journey. An alien, travelling on foot, without any kind of provisions, facing pitiless heat and freezing nights interspersed with sandstorms, he soon became hopelessly lost in the desert.

Now, in his delirium, Tambal started to blame himself, his father, the magician-king, the woodcarver, even the princess and the magic horse itself. Sometimes he thought he saw water ahead of him, sometimes fair cities, sometimes he felt elated, sometimes incomparably sad. Sometimes he even thought that he had companions in his difficulties, but when he shook himself he saw that he was quite alone.

He seemed to have been travelling for an eternity. Suddenly, when he had given up and started again several times, he saw something directly in front of him. It looked like a mirage: a garden, full of delicious fruits, sparkling and almost, as it were, beckoning him towards them.

Tambal did not at first take much notice of this, but soon, as he walked, he saw that he was indeed passing through such a garden. He gathered some of the fruits and tasted them cautiously. They were delicious. They took away his fear as well as his hunger and thirst. When he was full, he lay down in the shade of a huge and welcoming tree and fell asleep.

When he woke up he felt well enough, but something seemed to be wrong. Running to a nearby pool, he looked at his reflection in the water. Staring up at him was a horrible apparition. It had a long beard, curved horns, ears a foot long. He looked down at his hands. They were covered with fur.

Was it a nightmare? He tried to wake himself, but all the pinching and pummelling had no effect. Now, almost bereft of his senses, beside himself with fear and horror, thrown into transports of screaming, racked with sobs, he threw himself on the ground. "Whether I live or die," he thought, "these accursed fruits have finally ruined me. Even with the greatest army of all time, conquest will not help me. Nobody would marry me now, much less the Princess Precious Pearl. And I cannot imagine the beast who would not be terrified at the sight of me—let alone my heart's desire!" And he lost consciousness.

When he woke again, it was dark and a light was approaching through the groves of silent trees. Fear and hope struggled in him. As it came closer he saw that the light was from a lamp enclosed in a brilliant star-like shape, and it was carried by a bearded man, who walked in the pool of brightness which it cast around.

The man saw him. "My son," he said, "you have been affected by the influences of this place. If I had not come past, you would have remained just another beast of this enchanted grove, for there are many more like you. But I can help you."

Tambal wondered whether this man was a fiend in disguise, perhaps the very owner of the evil trees. But, as his sense came back he realised that he had nothing to lose.

"Help me, father," he said to the sage.

"If you really want your heart's desire," said the other man, "you have only to fix this desire firmly in your mind, not thinking of the fruit. You then have to take up some of the dried fruits, not the fresh, delicious ones, lying at the foot of all these trees, and eat them. Then follow your destiny."

So saying, he walked away.

While the sage's light disappeared into the darkness, Tambal saw that the moon was rising, and in its rays he could see that there were indeed piles of dried fruits under every tree.

He gathered some and ate them as quickly as he could.

Slowly, as he watched, the fur disappeared from his hands and arms. The horns first shrank, then vanished. The beard fell away. He was himself again. By now it was first light, and in the dawn he heard the tinkling of camel bells. A procession was coming through the enchanted forest.

It was undoubtedly the cavalcade of some important personage, on a long journey. As Tambal stood there, two outriders detached themselves from the glittering escort and galloped up to him.

"In the name of the Prince, our lord, we demand some of your fruit. His celestial Highness is thirsty and has indicated a desire for some of these strange apricots," said an officer.

Still Tambal did not move, such was his numbed condition after his recent experiences. Now the Prince himself came down from his palanquin and said:

"I am Jadugarzada, son of the magician-king of the East. Here is a bag of gold, oaf. I am having some of your fruit, because I am desirous of it. I am in a hurry, hastening to claim my bride, Princess Precious Pearl, daughter of Kahana, magician-king of the West."

At these words Tambal's heart turned over. But, realising that this must be his destiny which the sage had told him to follow, he offered the Prince as much of the fruit as he could eat.

When he had eaten, the Prince began to fall asleep. As he did so, horns, fur and huge ears started to grow out of him. The soldiers shook him, and the Prince began to behave in a strange way. He claimed that *he* was normal, and that *they* were deformed.

The councillors who accompanied the party restrained the prince and held a hurried debate. Tambal claimed that all would have been well if the prince had not fallen asleep. Eventually it was decided to put Tambal in the palanquin to play the part of the prince. The horned Jadugarzada was tied to a horse with a veil thrown over his face, disguised as a serving-woman.

"He may recover his wits eventually," said the councillors, "and in any case he is still our Prince. Tambal shall marry the girl. Then, as soon as possible, we shall carry them all back to our own country for our king to unravel the problem."

Tambal, biding his time and following his destiny, agreed to his own part in the masquerade.

When the party arrived at the capital of the West, the king himself came out to meet them. Tambal was taken to the princess as her bride-groom, and she was so astonished that she nearly fainted. But Tambal managed to whisper to her rapidly what had happened, and they were duly married, amid great jubilations.

In the meantime the horned prince had half recovered his wits, but not his human form, and his escort still kept him under cover. As soon as the feasting was over, the chief of the horned prince's party (who had been keeping Tambal and the princess under a very close watch) presented himself to the court. He said: "O just and glorious monarch, fountain of wisdom; the time has now come, according to the pronouncements of our astrologers and soothsayers, to conduct the bridal pair back to our own land, so that they may be established in their new home under the most felicitous circumstances and influences."

The princess turned to Tambal in alarm, for she knew that Jadugarzada would claim her as soon as they were on the open road—and make an end of Tambal into the bargain.

Tambal whispered to her, "Fear nothing. We must act as best we can, following our destiny. Agree to go, making only the condition that you will not travel without the wooden horse."

At first the magician-king was annoyed at this foible of his daughter's. He realised that she wanted the horse because it was connected with her first suitor. But the chief minister of the horned prince said: "Majesty, I cannot see that this is anything worse than a whim for a toy, such as any young girl might have. I hope that you will allow her to have her plaything, so that we may make haste homeward."

So the magician-king agreed, and soon the cavalcade was resplendently on its way. After the king's escort had withdrawn, and before the time of the first night-halt, the hideous Jadugarzada threw off his veil and cried out to Tambal:

"Miserable author of my misfortunes! I now intend to bind you hand and foot, to take you captive back to my own land. If, when we arrive there, you do not tell me how to remove this enchantment, I will have you flayed alive, inch by inch. Now, give me the Princess Precious Pearl."

Tambal ran to the princess and, in front of the astonished party, rose into the sky on the wooden horse with Precious Pearl mounted behind him.

Within a matter of minutes the couple alighted at the palace of King Mumkin. They related everything that had happened to them, and the king was almost overcome with delight at their safe return. He at once gave orders for the hapless woodcarver to be released, recompensed and applauded by the entire populace.

When the king was gathered to his fathers, Princess Precious Pearl and Prince Tambal succeeded him. Prince Hoshyar was quite pleased, too, because he was still entranced by the wondrous fish.

"I am glad for your own sakes, if you are happy," he used to say to them, "but, for my own part, nothing is more rewarding than concerning myself with the wondrous fish."

And this history is the origin of a strange saying current among the people of that land, yet whose beginnings have now been forgotten. The saying is: "Those who want fish can achieve much through fish, and those who do not know their heart's desire may first have to hear the story of the wooden horse."

THE STORY OF TEA

In ancient times, tea was not known outside China. Rumours of its existence had reached the wise and the unwise of other countries, and each tried to find out what it was in accordance with what he wanted or what he thought it should be.

The King of Inja ("here") sent an embassy to China, and they were given tea by the Chinese Emperor. But, since they saw that the peasants drank it too, they concluded that it was not fit for their royal master: and, furthermore, that the Chinese Emperor was trying to deceive them, passing off some other substance for the celestial drink.

The greatest philosopher of Anja ("there") collected all the information he could about tea, and concluded that it must be a substance which existed but rarely, and was of another order than anything then known. For was it not referred to as being a herb, a water, green, black, sometimes bitter, sometimes sweet?

In the countries of Koshish and Bebinem, for centuries the people tested all the herbs they could find. Many were poisoned, all were disappointed. For nobody had brought the tea-plant to their lands, and thus they could not find it. They also drank all the liquids which they could find, but to no avail.

In the territory of Mazhab ("Sectarianism") a small bag of tea was carried in procession before the people as they went on their religious observances. Nobody thought of tasting it: indeed, nobody knew how. All were convinced that the tea itself had a magical quality. A wise man said: "Pour upon it boiling water, ye ignorant ones!" They hanged him and nailed him up, because to do this, according to their belief, would mean the destruction of their tea. This showed that he was an enemy of their religion.

Before he died, he had told his secret to a few, and they managed to obtain some tea and drink it secretly. When anyone said: "What are you doing?" they answered: "It is but medicine which we take for a certain disease."

And so it was throughout the world. Tea had actually been seen growing by some, who did not recognize it. It had been given to others to drink, but they thought it the beverage of the common people. It had been in the possession of others, and they worshipped it. Outside China, only a few people actually drank it, and those covertly.

Then came a man of knowledge, who said to the merchants of tea, and the drinkers of tea, and to others: "He who tastes, knows. He who tastes not, knows not. Instead of talking about the celestial beverage, say nothing, but offer it at your banquets. Those who like it will ask for more. Those who do not, will show that they are not fitted to be tea-drinkers. Close the shop of argument and mystery. Open the teahouse of experience."

The tea was brought from one stage to another along the Silk Road, and whenever a merchant carrying jade or gems or silk would pause to rest, he would make tea, and offer it to such people as were near him, whether they were aware of the repute of tea or not. This was the beginning of the Chaikhanas, the teahouses which were established all the way from Peking to Bokhara and Samarkand. And those who tasted, knew.

At first, mark well, it was only the great and the pretended men of wisdom who sought the celestial drink and who also exclaimed: "But this is only dried leaves!" or: "Why do you boil water, stranger, when all I want is the celestial drink?" or yet again: "How do I know what this is? Prove it to me. Besides the colour of the liquid is not golden, but ochre!"

When the truth was known, and when the tea was brought for all who would taste, the roles were reversed, and the only people who said things like the great and intelligent had said were the absolute fools. And such is the case to this day.

o   o   o

Drinks of all kinds have been used by almost all peoples as allegories connected with the search for higher knowledge.

Coffee, the most recent of social drinks, was discovered by the dervish sheikh Abu el-Hasan Shadhili, at Mocha in Arabia.

Although the Sufis and others often clearly state that "magical drinks" (wine, the water of life) are an analogy of a certain experience, literalist students tend to believe that the origin of these myths dates from the discovery of some hallucinogenic or inebriative quality in potations. According to the dervishes, such an idea is a reflection of the investigator's incapacity to understand that they are speaking in parallels.

This tale is from the teachings of the Master Hamadani (died 1140), teacher of the great Yasavi of Turkestan.

o   o   o

THE TALE OF THE SANDS

A stream, from its source in far-off mountains, passing through every kind and description of countryside, at last reached the sands of the desert. Just as it had crossed every other barrier, the stream tried to cross this one, but it found that as fast as it ran into the sand, its waters disappeared.

It was convinced, however, that its destiny was to cross this desert, and yet there was no way. Now a hidden voice, coming from the desert itself, whispered: "The Wind crosses the desert, and so can the stream."

The stream objected that it was dashing itself against the sand, and only getting absorbed: that the wind could fly, and this was why it could cross a desert.

"By hurtling in your own accustomed way you cannot get across. You will either disappear or become a marsh. You must allow the wind to carry you over, to your destination."

But how could this happen? "By allowing yourself to be absorbed in the wind."

Reprinted by permisssion from Idries Shah, *Tales of the Dervishes* (E. P. Dutton & Co., Inc., 1970, and Jonathan Cape, Ltd.), pp. 23–24. Copyright © 1967 by Idries Shah.

This idea was not acceptable to the stream. After all, it had never been absorbed before. It did not want to lose its individuality. And, once having lost it, how was one to know that it could ever be regained?

"The wind," said the sand, "performs this function. It takes up water, carries it over the desert, and then lets it fall again. Falling as rain, the water again becomes a river."

"How can I know that this is true?"

"It is so, and if you do not believe it, you cannot become more than a quagmire, and even that could take many, many years; and it certainly is not the same as a stream."

"But can I not remain the same stream that I am today?"

"You cannot in either case remain so," the whisper said. "Your essential part is carried away and forms a stream again. You are called what you are even today because you do not know which part of you is the essential one."

When he heard this, certain echoes began to arise in the thoughts of the stream. Dimly, he remembered a state in which he—or some part of him, was it?—had been held in the arms of a wind. He also remembered—or did he?—that this was the real thing, not necessarily the obvious thing, to do.

And the stream raised his vapour into the welcoming arms of the wind, which gently and easily bore it upwards and along, letting it fall softly as soon as they reached the roof of a mountain, many, many miles away. And because he had had his doubts, the stream was able to remember and record more strongly in his mind the details of the experience. He reflected, "Yes, now I have learned my true identity."

The stream was learning. But the sands whispered: "We know, because we see it happen day after day: and because we, the sands, extend from the riverside all the way to the mountain."

And that is why it is said that the way in which the Stream of Life is to continue on its journey is written in the Sands.

o   o   o

This beautiful story is current in verbal tradition in many languages, almost always circulating among dervishes and their pupils.

It was used in Sir Fairfax Cartwright's *Mystic Rose from the Garden of the King*, published in Britain in 1899.

The present version is from Awad Afifi the Tunisian, who died in 1870.

28.

Meditations of Rumi

There is no cause for fear. It is imagination, blocking you as a wooden bolt holds the door. Burn that bar . . .

Every thought has a parallel action.

Every prayer has a sound and a physical form.

The man of God is not an expert made by books.

First you were mineral, then vegetable, then man. You will be an angel, and you will pass beyond that too.

There are a thousand forms of mind.

If the sea-water did not rise into the sky, where would the garden get its life?

A totally wise man would cease to exist in the ordinary sense.

Reprinted by permission from Idries Shah, *Caravan of Dreams* (Penguin Books, Inc., 1972), pp. 79–80. Copyright © 1968 by Idries Shah.

You make no spark by striking earth on a flint.

The worker is hidden in the workshop.

To the ignorant, a pearl seems a mere stone.

If a tree could move on foot or feather, it would not suffer the agony of the saw nor the wounds of the blade.

What bread looks like depends upon whether you are hungry or not.

You may seek a furnace, but it would burn you. Perhaps you need only the weaker flame of a lamp.

Counterfeiters exist because there is such a thing as real gold.

Whoever says everything is true is a fool, whoever says all is untrue is a liar.

A great obstacle in the Path is fame.

God's mirror: the front is the heart, its back the world.

The infinite universe lies beyond this world.

They say: "He cannot be found" . . . Something that cannot be "found" is what I desire.

To make wine, you must ferment the grape juice.

Water does not run uphill.

You have two "heads." The original, which is concealed, the derivative, which is the visible one.

The moment you entered this world of form, an escape ladder was put out for you.

Wool only becomes a carpet because knowledge is available.

To boil water you need an intermediary—the vessel.

VI.

AN EXTENDED CONCEPT OF MAN

Introduction

With the shift in cultural emphasis, the appearance of the esoteric traditions, and the emergence of new research tools, a new consensus is
forming within the scientific community. It largely rests on the idea that
our conception of what is possible for people has been radically too low
in contemporary culture and especially within contemporary science.
The new synthesis in contemporary science results from a merging of this
extended idea of the possible with the technological developments of
the past century.

We have begun to understand that our consciousness is not single but
dual, that we exist both in linear time and outside of this particular construction. Some of the articles in this section introduce the idea that man
is, or rather can be trained to be, sensitive to quite subtle sources of information, sources often overlooked in our personal world. These sources
exist within ourselves (the part of the nervous system which we have considered "involuntary"). They exist on earth as subtle geophysical forces,
such as the negative ionization of the air, the rhythmic shifts in the earth,

and the constant, invisible force of gravity. These energies can be sensed in other people in a form of communication termed "paranormal."

Yet all these phenomena have often been relegated to the realm of the "paranormal" simply because our conception of what is *normal* and possible with man has been radically too low. The new consensus in psychology is at its merest beginning; so a selection at this time must be quite diverse, ranging from articles on the nature of consciousness itself to pieces on psychotherapy and on ESP. Yet each reflects a newly extended concept of human capacities.

The first two papers are by men who have found it necessary to work in both areas of knowledge, the esoteric and the modern. These are theoretical papers, one on consciousness and one on language. The first is by Arthur Deikman, who considers one of the most difficult philosophical and scientific questions: What is the nature of consciousness *itself*, divorced from the contents of consciousness? It is a question many feel quite diffident to tackle, but one which must be met and faced. It requires considerable scientific training and a personal knowledge of the area involved. This is probably one of the most thought-provoking papers yet written on consciousness.

The second article is from a man remembered most as an adjective— "The Whorfian Hypothesis." This idea has been merely encoded as "language can affect consciousness" and hardly explored, even in 'its most attenuated form. But Benjamin Lee Whorf himself, insurance man, linguist, and student of consciousness, was far more developed than his image as an adjective. In this selection it is clear that his unusual intellectual development was wedded to a profound personal knowledge of the possible development of consciousness.

Any event, training, or specialty, if followed with an open and sensitive mind, can lead to a more unified understanding of consciousness. This can be through Yoga, in making a rug, in an analysis of a football game, or here, by the analysis of language. Whorf's writings and those of Idries Shah, among others, are first-order examples of the use of language to transcend itself. Whorf is a rich and challenging writer, and deserves careful reading.

Following these two theoretical articles are two on psychotherapy. Psychosynthesis and Gestalt therapy are two modern therapies which have been developed around the idea of consciousness change. The very name Psychosynthesis is in complement to Psychoanalysis. It is a system developed by the Italian psychiatrist Roberto Assagioli to integrate the therapeutic and esoteric dimensions of psychology. His book *Psychosynthesis*, from which this selection is taken, consists of a series of practical therapeutic techniques for cultivation and integration of capacities left fallow for the most part. His comments on the underdeveloped intuition of most western intellectuals recall the writings of Polanyi and Blackburn, and even Mulla Nasrudin.

Claudio Naranjo, the author of the article on Gestalt therapy, is a practitioner of therapy, and a student of meditation and of the nature of religious experience. In the sense of this book, he is a psychologist of both modes. Here he allows his experiences in both Gestalt and meditation to guide us to their communality, which is to enable an experience of a total present-centeredness.

If Psychosynthesis and Gestalt allow the therapist to bring out previously uncultivated faculties in man, the technique of biofeedback may allow many people to perform similar learning independent of others. It is a striking example of the new synthesis, one which combines the esoteric suggestion that man has a far greater degree of self-mastery than is usually considered, with modern technological monitoring devices for sensing minute variations in internal states.

The only fully definitive research in this area has been with animals, notably in the work of Neal Miller and Leo DiCara. They have trained their research animals to voluntarily alter such "autonomous" functions as heart activity and the activity of the glands and of other internal organs. These experiments lead to a "new" view of the nature of the nervous system, one much more akin to the esoteric.

There has been a lot of hoopla recently about the advent of "alpha" training, but as yet little of any practical import. This research remains for specialized investigators who are currently attempting to correlate differences in brain activity with EEG states. The article by Nowlis and Kamiya is an example of an early research report on alpha training in people. The article by Ralph Ezios focuses on the implications of such biofeedback training.

Just as we can become capable of sensing minute changes in internal physiology, we can in addition become aware of processes, subtle and constant, which occur on Earth, but which are too weak for usual notice. Human beings have evolved, for millions of years, to function maximally within our particular geophysical environment. Consciousness and physiology are continually affected by these geophysical variations, yet these forces are rarely considered as "relevant variables" in psychology.

Our consciousness is in a body with a specifically evolved structure; yet the influence of body states on consciousness is rarely considered in academic circles, as if the brain were a disembodied computer. Nevertheless, each person knows that consciousness can vary with physical state. Consider pain, for example, which radically alters consciousness.

If we could speak fish-talk and could ask an intelligent and learned fish to discourse on water, we might find that he had never noticed it at all. We are in the same position regarding the influence of our own "invisible ocean," including gravity. In an article prepared especially for this book, David Sobel writes on Structural Integration, a system (hardly researched as yet) which does consider gravity a major influence on man and links body states to consciousness.

Similarly, Dr. A. P. Krueger directs our awareness to a neglected subtle source of physical energy in the air—its ionization. When schools of esoteric psychology were set up, the microclimate was always considered. Often the settings were on mountaintops, near waterfalls, or next to the ocean. These sites share an abundance of negative ions, which do seem to produce physiological effects, though subtle ones.

Gay Luce's work on biological rhythms brings out another unnoticed source of influence on ourselves—the turning of the earth and the light-dark cycles. Our body and awareness and capabilities are changing from moment to moment and season to season. And all these articles also note that we are far more sensitive to subtle sources of energy than we are usually considered to be.

As we become more aware that consciousness is malleable by the exercises of the esoteric traditions, we can consider that man can attune himself to more subtle sources of force than are usually perceptible to him; we note also that quite weak energies can affect life processes; we become more receptive to the idea that "paranormal" faculties exist.

In a theoretical article, the Swiss psychiatrist Jung links such rhythmic considerations as are expressed by Luce with the concept of a time outside the normal linear mode of science, one more akin to the "time" of the right hemisphere. He also recalls a concept of the limits of scientific inquiry which some of the earlier selections in this book exemplify. We must establish, Jung says, "an age of large views which do not cry halt and think that the limits of nature have been reached just where the scientific roadbuilders had come to a temporary stop." He also points to the possibility that science can consider *exceptions* as useful data (which has occurred in modern physics). This article has been extensively edited (with the generous assistance of Ms. Lynn Lumbard) for this book.

LeShan's article is a further attempt to give theoretical perspective to the question of paranormal phenomena. LeShan himself is a psychotherapist who has spent the last decade investigating this area. The final article, by Charles Tart, covering current research into the data of paranormal communication, was prepared especially for this book.

29.

The Meaning of Everything

Arthur J. Deikman

When I once told a friend it was my intention to explain consciousness, he exclaimed, "But consciousness is everything!" After thinking about it, I agreed with him. Thus, my title, for I will present a model of consciousness that explains what pure awareness is, what the self is, and the "I" feeling, and the mystical experience, and meditation, and other phenomena as well. It is a serious attempt because this is what truly interests me. By its nature, it is also grandiose, for it is hard to see how one man can accomplish it all. However, I can make the attempt, and other people can complete the job.

AWARENESS

Upon reflection you will find that thoughts can cease for a brief while, that there can be silence and darkness and the temporary absence of

Printed by permission of the author.

images or memory patterns—any one component of our mental life can disappear, but awareness, itself, remains. Awareness is the ground of our conscious life, the background or field in which these elements exist. It is not the same thing as thoughts, sensations, or images. To experience this, try an experiment now. Look straight ahead and be aware of your conscious experience—then close your eyes. Awareness remains. "Behind" your thoughts and images is awareness. The distinction between awareness and the contents of awareness is crucial to the discussion that follows.

THE BIOSYSTEM

All around us is a world of structure. Brilliant, various, complex, the forms of our life surround us, and through them and in them we live. Most of these forms appear to be abiding structures or objects, like our bones, that are formed or are born, and disintegrate or die. We ourselves seem to be objects, and we think using a language that defines and creates relationships between objects. However, as we examine ourselves and other "objects" more closely, we begin to see them differently. Gardner Murphy (1956) has pointed out that our concept of biological boundaries is a function of the particular time and size scale employed. Apparent boundaries are sensory phenomena in terms of those scales; they are not absolutes. For example, we are in constant exchange with the surrounding environment through respiration, eating, and elimination. Radioisotope studies have established the fact that our bodies are in a state of continual turnover of materials; we are not the same collection of atoms that we were a year ago. Bertalanffy (1952) summarizes, "As a result of its metabolism, which is characteristic of every living organism, its components are not the same from one moment to the next. Living forms are not in being, they are happening" (p. 124). Bones and muscles are reinterpreted: "What are called structures are slow processes of long duration, functions are quick processes of short duration. If we say that a function, such as the contraction of a muscle, is performed by a structure, it means that a quick and short process wave is superimposed on a long-lasting and slowly running wave" (p. 134). Activity, change, process—these are the "substance" of our bodies, of our world, of the universe. Gradients, not boundaries, determine form.

Furthermore, our individual organisms exist within a meshwork of higher levels of organization that ultimately includes all individual life forms and our planet itself. A swarm of bees furnishes an example of two levels of organization—each bee is an individual, but the swarm functions together as an organism in its own right. Its individual members cooperate in fulfilling a function possible only for the swarm, but at the same time necessary to the members. That swarm is part of a larger biosystem unity that includes the flowering plants that the bees pollinate. As you begin to picture the dazzling spectrum of organizational hierarchies that make up our biosystem and the cosmic system of which it is a part, it is not hard to perceive that we are part of one system that extends throughout the universe. In this view the biosystem is a whole, and the distinction between what is usually called biological (organic) and the inorganic is neither necessary nor basic. In what follows I shall use the term biosystem to refer to the entire range of world components that we apprehend through our sensory apparatus.

AWARENESS AND ORGANIZATION

As I noted earlier, a major problem in thinking about consciousness has been the mixing together of awareness with mind functions, such as calculating, sensations, memory, perception, and symbol formation. It is plausible to assume that mind functions are performed in the brain, which is the thinking organ. On the other hand, I would like to suggest that awareness, as distinct from the contents of awareness, is not a special form of sensation, with a particular receptor organ or some other neurological system responsible, nor is it any kind of neural response at all. Rather than being the product of a particular neural circuit, awareness is the *organization* of the biosystem; that is, awareness *is* the "complementary" aspect of that organization, its psychological equivalent.

COMPLEMENTARITY

Niels Bohr (1958) introduced the term "complementarity" to account for the fact that two different conditions of observation yielded conclusions that were conceptually incompatible, i.e., light behaved like a particle on one occasion and like a wave on another. He suggested that there is no intrinsic incompatibility because the two aspects were functions of different conditions of observation, and no experiment could be devised that could demonstrate both aspects in a single observational condition. Similarly, the special characteristic of mental life, e.g., freedom from space considerations, is in apparent contradiction with the space characteristics of physical objects. The two realms of the mental and the biological are separate spheres of observation, and may be said to represent complementary aspects of the biological system that constitutes an individual. The conditions of observation of the physical world are those of the sensory apparatus (vision, hearing, touch, smell, taste), whereas the mental is "observed" by the non-sensory (memory, thought, imagery, and "intuitive" processes).

ORGANIZATION

Questions that arise immediately are: "What is meant by organization?" and "If awareness or consciousness is the complementary aspect of organization, what is it that is organized?" Let us say that an organism is "any thing or structure composed of distinct parts and so constituted that the functioning of the parts and their relation to one another is governed by their relation to the whole" (Webster's 2nd, unabridged, 1961, p. 1719). Relation is "any aspect or quality that can be predicted only if two or more things are taken together" (*ibid.*, p. 2102). Thus, we are talking about elements that are mutually interdependent. In this connection, Bertalanffy (1952) has specifically defined the characteristics of the biological organism: (1) the organism is a complex of elements in mutual interaction; (2) the behavior of an individual element is influenced by the state of the whole organism; (3) the whole exhibits properties absent from its isolated parts; and (4) a biological organism is a basically active system—it has an autonomous activity, and is not basically reflexive or basically reactive.

Are the elements that are organized mental or physical? This question is dualistic and assumes a separation of mind and matter. In terms of the hypothesis I am presenting, the answer would be that the elements organized are both mental and physical, because the mental and the physical are hypothesized as being "complementary" aspects of the biological system.

On the biological side, the elements of the person system range from such low-level elements as chemical entities to the higher-order, more strictly biological elements of muscles, nerves, bones, and skin, and to the still higher-level components of respiratory, digestive, vascular, and motor systems. On the psychological side, ideas, affects, and sensations are at one level, and memories, thinking, and self-concepts are at a higher level. On the biological side, the organization of these elements is life; on the psychological side, the organization is awareness.

Thus, when I state that awareness *is* organization, I do not mean that consciousness is the "experience" of organization. The latter phrase implies a separate system that senses consciousness, the way we see light and smell odors. Rather, I mean to say that awareness is the complementary aspect of organization—it is organization, itself, in its mental dimension.

LOCALIZATION

The biosystem is a totality embracing our entire planet and the solar system. Awareness is the organization of that continuous system. It follows that awareness is not localized. The awareness that each individual believes to be his own is, in fact, an awareness that extends throughout existence, for it is the organization of reality. Since our thought contents are localized by the particular groups of perceptual and cognitive systems that constitute individual persons, we have taken for granted that the awareness that underlies our mental processes is localized as well. For example, our visual activity is usually experienced as being identical with awareness. However, if you close your eyes, you will recognize that your awareness and your visual field are not the same. Try it now. Once again, close your eyes and ask yourself what constitutes your awareness. With your eyes closed, you will tend to identify awareness with sounds and body sensations. If next you imagine these sounds and sensations to be absent, you will appreciate the fact that awareness is something other than sensations or thoughts. The sense that my awareness is my own is due to mixing the sensations and thoughts, which are indeed personal, with awareness itself, which is universal. Expressed in the more abstract terms I used earlier, the conclusion is that our individual centers of organizing activity are located within the general field of organization that is awareness.

ACTIVE ENERGY

Let us now go a step further and consider a departure from traditional assumptions concerning matter and energy. It is a basic axiom of contemporary physics that energy has no direction nor structural tendency of its own. Toulmin (1967) has discussed the historical development of this concept of inert or passive matter, and has shown it to be an assumption. Continuing from his discussion, I propose that matter is intrinsically active in the direction of increasing organization. By this I mean that progressive organization is a basic characteristic of matter, like mass. As a corollary, increasing organization is the intrinsic aim of energy.

Such a concept is not compatible with our ordinary assumption that matter is purposeless, inert, and passive. Since the seventeenth century, we have looked at the elements of reality and expected to find that events are the product of pre-existing vectoral forces, acting on inert entities. Only man seems to have prefigured goals toward which his actions tend. We regard it as erroneous and primitive to give to inanimate or lower animate forms the characteristics of our own mental life. However, we have not really been able to avoid doing so, because our analysis of the physical world is based on the psychological. For example, the concept of force is derived from our experience of our own willed action. At the same time, because we associate aim and direction with our own will and desires, the notion that energy might have an intrinsic aim (as postulated by Freud for mental energy) appears very strange, for that would make energy "human."

Likewise, our belief in the passivity of matter and the directionless nature of energy resides in our experience with inanimate objects: a stone does not move unless we push it. This assumption of inertness works well for analyzing problems within a particular spatial class and a particular time span. Because of these temporal and spatial limits, we may not be in a position to observe the "activities" of inanimate objects. However, if we increase our time scale and widen our spatial scale, it might appear that inanimate matter moves towards a goal similar to the animate. For example, from a long-term time scale we are aware of what appears to be a direction of change that produces life forms. Increasing diversity and increasingly complex organization appear to be a trend that is discernable biologically, sociologically, and psychologically. We have given the name "evolution" to the phenomenon. That this phenomenon has been apparent to man for a long time is witnessed by the ancient Vedanta and Buddhist texts, as well as by the more recent conceptual efforts of Darwin, Erikson (1950), Bertalanffy (1952), Piaget (1954), Polanyi (1958), Chardin (1959), and Spitz (1959).

VARIABLE AWARENESS

If awareness is organization and thus extends throughout the universe, present in varying degrees everywhere, why is it that sometimes awareness is vivid and total (as in phases of meditation), but at other times is absent, for example, when we are intent on an intellectual calculation or absorbed in a conversation or a movie? Traditionally, psychologists have tended to handle such problems by falling back on the searchlight model. The field of our attention is likened to the field of a searchlight that illuminates one area after the other. But if awareness is the searchlight and we can be aware of being aware, what illuminates the searchlight?

The problem can be solved if we define mind functions as organizing activities. Thus, perceptual processes organize stimulus inputs into series of gestalts, and thinking activity organizes events in terms of meanings of different kinds—philosophical, arithmetic, and symbolic. Let us now compare the biosystem to a pond of water. When the system is quiet, not occupied with the organizing activities of various mental functions, the surface of the pond is smooth, still, and reflective. At such times we exist in pure awareness, in a state of relationships, of organization. When the organizing activity of thought functions takes place, the surface of the pond becomes transformed into patterns of ripples, as if a stone had been thrown into the quiet water. When the activity ceases, the surface of the pond is smooth and reflecting once again. We do not have to postulate a super-observer of both awareness and thoughts if we recognize that awareness depends on the state of the pond, or biosystem; thought functions are the organization's activity. There is no experiencing agency; the "experience" *is* the state or the activity, as the case may be.

One may ask, "If awareness is coextensive with everything, why is it that we can lose consciousness?" The answer is that when we lose consciousness, the individual receptor-organizing region ceases to function. Awareness, itself, does not cease, but the thought organization, including memory, of the individual person ceases to operate. When that happens, there can be no local (individual) articulation or memory of awareness. At such times, awareness cannot be known in that location. To put it in slightly different terms, the individual person is the means whereby reality articulates itself.

Mystics have stated that through mankind, God is able to know himself. Perhaps what basically has blocked our understanding of such pronouncements has been our automatic assumption that the feeling of awareness is as localized as our personal perceptual system. However, once we discriminate between the general awareness and local mental contents, the puzzling concepts of mystics become more clear.

It should be noted that, in terms of this model, the awareness of a tree is not different from our own, but continuous with it, because awareness is the organization of the entire system. Awareness probably cannot be *known* or articulated in the system of the tree, but the awareness of the tree is not less intense or less rich than our own. We are not *more* aware because we are more complex; awareness is not a quantitative function, not a mind-stuff that accumulates as forms become more complex. Rather, awareness is the mental aspect of the organization of the entire biosystem. It is "known" only in those locales whose systems of organization permit "knowledge" of awareness.

Ordinarily, we do not recognize "our" awareness for what it is. The awakening to the true nature of this awareness constitutes the Enlightenment of a host of mystic disciplines. As illustrated by the Zen monastery, these disciplines all feature techniques, attitudes, and living conditions designed to bring about a subsidence of the thinking activities that take the place of awareness (Deikman, 1971). These thinking activities are individual, in that they are the activity of the individual center of organization of each individual person. Insofar as the person is activated to individual goals, thought activity persists and is dominant. However, the cultivation of selflessness can decrease the goal activity of the individual. Individual activity then subsides relative to the general field of organization—awareness itself.

The classical meditation disciplines were developed as a means of heightening awareness by subduing thought activity. Meditation, properly done, facilitates a shift from individual-centered activity to the general field of organization. Here, too, giving up individual striving (e.g., for spiritual advancement) can be a special problem. Furthermore, although it is not too hard to fill one's mind completely with a particular percept, such as breathing sensations, it is hard to have that perception and not work at it, not apply the mind to it, not be exercising the mind muscle, as it were, on that percept. When this active attention or concentrating can cease, then the sense of personal boundary that is associated with the individual's organizing activity fades away, and limitless awareness grows clear, vivid, and dominant. It is this limitless awareness that constitutes the unity experience of the higher mystical states.

THE "I" FEELING AND THE SELF

The self is that collection of attributes that identifies me as a particular human being. "Myself" is my body, my memories, my personality, my fears, my assets—all the things that constitute who I am in the eyes of others and of myself. We can understand the self as being a particular field of organization for the individual. The limits of the self are the experienced limits of the individual; those based on sensory perception, language, and the space-time of the object world. The self is all those things that I consciously include in the zone of my personal organization.

But what shall we make of the "I" feeling? Is it just another sensation, some spurious illusion based on a synthesis of sensory impressions? Try and locate the feeling or sensation inside yourself that corresponds to the word "I." For example, if you say such phrases to yourself as "I am going to go on reading this paper" or "I want a new car," the referent to the word "I" is the feeling of intention, of will, of urge, or of desire. This "I" of "I want" is a tension along a particular axis, a force impelling in a particular direction, the intensity of which varies, but the basic quality of which remains the same. The "I want" feeling is the organizing force, itself, acting in the specific locus or node of an individual organism. Each of us is a circumscribed area of organizing activity, expressing the same organizing tendency or force that I have hypothesized to be a basic attribute of mass/energy. Awareness is the organization of the system but the organizing force, itself, specifically active in our own local region, is what we experience as the "I" or "I want."

However, there is another type of "I" that we can notice. This "I" emerges in periods when our urges do not dominate our awareness. Then "I" feels like an abiding, resting awareness, featureless and unchanging, a central something that is witness to all events, exterior and interior. It is the "I" of "I am." This "I" is identical with awareness. In most cases it is awareness circumscribed by the beliefs and assumptions that form actual barriers separating local awareness (local organization) from universal awareness (universal organization).

Beliefs and assumptions act as barriers because they are mental activities, action currents transforming the still water of awareness into waves and eddies. To extend the metaphor even further, it would seem that some type of spatial correspondence exists such that the belief that one is part of all mankind locates the delimiting barrier at a "wider" periphery than the belief that one is totally separate from other persons. This effect of a belief occurs because the psychological event is an event in the biosystem, not an event isolated in a "mental" world. Thus, a belief has a substantial existence, although that existence is not to be defined as physical. The physical and the mental are both aspects of the biosystem; they are a translation or manifestation of an entity that is basic to both. Reality is neither one nor the other.

OVERVIEW

Organizing activity takes place continuously and throughout the universe because it is a basic characteristic of mass/energy. Each person is a manifestation of that same activity, as if he were an eddy in a river. The organization of the entire system is awareness. We confuse our local mind-functions with the general awareness and believe we are separate selves. To the extent that we separate ourselves conceptually from other people, we perform an action that actually delimits our awareness by forming a biosystem barrier that interferes with the experience of oneness. Caught in the illusion of separateness, we engage in actions that bring suffering to ourselves and others.

In those cases in which, by means of an arduous discipline, a powerful drug, or an extreme life crisis, the delimiting barriers are temporarily dissolved, the individual awareness becomes the general awareness. These events of barrier dissolution constitute the phenomena of mystical experiences, provide the basis for religious metaphysics, and introduce into our lives the reality of the transpersonal.

30.

Language, Mind, and Reality

Benjamin Lee Whorf

It needs but half an eye to see in these latter days that science, the Grand Revelator of modern Western culture, has reached, without having intended to, a frontier. Either it must bury its dead, close its ranks, and go forward into a landscape of increasing strangeness, replete with things shocking to a culture-trammeled understanding, or it must become, in Claude Houghton's expressive phrase, the plagiarist of its own past. The frontier was foreseen in principle very long ago, and given a name that has descended to our day clouded with myth. That name is Babel. For science's long and heroic effort to be strictly factual has at last brought it into entanglement with the unsuspected facts of the linguistic order. These facts the older classical science had never admitted, confronted, or

Reprinted by permission from J. B. Carroll, ed., *Language, Thought and Reality: Selected Writings of Benjamin Lee Whorf* (Cambridge, Mass.: The MIT Press, 1956), pp. 246–254, where it was reprinted by permission of the Theosophical Society from *Theosophist* (Madras, India), January and April issues, 1942.

understood as facts. Instead they had entered its house by the back door and had been taken for the substance of Reason itself.

What we call "scientific thought" is a specialization of the western Indo-European type of language, which has developed not only a set of different dialectics, but actually a set of different dialects. THESE DIALECTS ARE NOW BECOMING MUTUALLY UNINTELLIGIBLE. The term "space," for instance, does not and CANNOT mean the same thing to a psychologist as to a physicist. Even if psychologists should firmly resolve, come hell or high water, to use "space" only with the physicist's meaning, they could not do so, any more than Englishmen could use in English the word "sentiment" in the meanings which the similarly spelled but functionally different French utterance *le sentiment* has in its native French.

Now this does not simply breed confusions of mere detail that an expert translator could perhaps resolve. It does something much more perplexing. Every language and every well-knit technical sublanguage incorporates certain points of view and certain patterned resistances to widely divergent points of view. This is especially so if language is not surveyed as a planetary phenomenon, but is as usual taken for granted, and the local, parochial species of it used by the individual thinker is taken to be its full sum. These resistances not only isolate artificially the particular sciences from each other; they also restrain the scientific spirit as a whole from taking the next great step in development—a step which entails viewpoints unprecedented in science and a complete severance from traditions. For certain linguistic patterns rigidified in the dialectics of the sciences—often also embedded in the matrix of European culture from which those sciences have sprung, and long worshiped as pure Reason *per se*—have been worked to death. Even science senses that they are somehow out of focus for observing what may be very significant aspects of reality, upon the due observation of which all further progress in understanding the universe may hinge.

Thus one of the important coming steps for Western knowledge is a re-examination of the linguistic backgrounds of its thinking, and for that matter of all thinking. My purpose in developing this subject before a Theosophical audience is not to confirm or affirm any Theosophical doctrines. It is rather that, of all groups of people with whom I have come in contact, Theosophical people seem the most capable of becoming excited about ideas—new ideas. And my task is to explain an idea to all those who, if Western culture survives the present welter of barbarism, may be pushed by events to leadership in reorganizing the whole human future.

This idea is one too drastic to be penned up in a catch phrase. I would rather leave it unnamed. It is the view that a noumenal world—a world of hyperspace, of higher dimensions—awaits discovery by all the sciences, which it will unite and unify, awaits discovery under its first aspect of a realm of PATTERNED RELATIONS, inconceivably manifold and yet bearing a recognizable affinity to the rich and systematic organization of LANGUAGE, including *au fond* mathematics and music, which are ultimately of the same kindred as language. The idea is older than Plato, and at the same time as new as our most revolutionary thinkers. It is implied in Whitehead's world of prehensive aspects, and in relativity physics with its four-dimensional continuum and its Riemann-Christoffel tensor that sums up the PROPERTIES OF THE WORLD at any point-moment; while one of the most thought-provoking of all modern presentations, and I think the most original, is the *Tertium Organum* of Ouspensky. All that I have to say on the subject that may be new is of the PREMONITION IN LANGUAGE of the unknown, vaster world—that world of which the physical is but a surface or skin, and yet which we ARE IN, and BELONG TO. For the approach to reality through mathematics, which modern knowledge is beginning to make, is merely the approach through one special case of this relation to language.

This view implies that what I have called patterns are basic in a really cosmic sense, and that patterns form wholes, akin to the Gestalten of psychology, which are embraced in larger wholes in continual progression. Thus the cosmic picture has a serial or hierarchical character, that of a progression of planes or levels. Lacking recognition of such serial order, different sciences chop segments, as it were, out of the world, segments which perhaps cut across the direction of the natural levels, or stop short when, upon reaching a major change of level, the phenomena become of quite different type, or pass out of the ken of the older observational methods.

But in the science of linguistics, the facts of the linguistic domain compel recognition of serial planes, each explicitly given by an order of patterning observed. It is as if, looking at a wall covered with fine tracery of lacelike design, we found that this tracery served as the ground for a bolder pattern, yet still delicate, of tiny flowers, and that upon becoming aware of this floral expanse we saw that multitudes of gaps in it made another pattern like scrollwork, and that groups of scrolls made letters, the letters if followed in a proper sequence made words, the words were aligned in columns which listed and classified entities, and so on in continual cross-patterning until we found this wall to be—a great book of wisdom!

First, the plane "below" the strictly linguistic phenomena is a physical, acoustic one, phenomena wrought of sound waves; then comes a level of patterning in rippling muscles and speech organs, the physiological-phonetic plane; then the phonemic plane, patterning that makes a systematic set of consonants, vowels, accents, tones, etc., for each language; then the morphophonemic plane in which the "phonemes" of the previous level appear combined into "morphemes" (words and subwords like suffixes, etc.); then the plane of morphology; then that of the intricate, largely unconscious patterning that goes by the meaningless name of syntax; then onto further planes still, the full import of which may some day strike and stagger us.

Speech is the best show man puts on. It is his own "act" on the stage of evolution, in which he comes before the cosmic backdrop and really "does his stuff." But we suspect the watching Gods perceive that the order in which his amazing set of tricks builds up to a great climax has been stolen—from the Universe!

The idea, entirely unfamiliar to the modern world, that nature and language are inwardly akin, was for ages well known to various high cultures whose historical continuity on the earth has been enormously longer than that of Western European culture. In India, one aspect of it has been the idea of the MANTRAM and of a MANTRIC ART. On the simplest cultural level, a mantram is merely an incantation of primitive magic, such as the crudest cultures have. In the high culture it may have a different, a very intellectual meaning, dealing with the inner affinity of language and the cosmic order. At a still higher level, it becomes "Mantra Yoga." Therein the mantram becomes a manifold of conscious patterns, contrived to assist the consciousness into the noumenal pattern world—whereupon it is "in the driver's seat." It can then SET the human organism to transmit, control, and amplify a thousandfold forces which that organism normally transmits only at unobservably low intensities.

Somewhat analogously, the mathematical formula that enables a physicist to adjust some coils of wire, tinfoil plates, diaphragms, and other quite inert and innocent gadgets into a configuration in which they can project music to a far country puts the physicist's consciousness on to a level strange to the untrained man, and makes feasible an adjustment of matter to a very strategic configuration, one which makes possible an unusual manifestation of force. Other formulas make possible the strategic arrangement of magnets and wires in the powerhouse so that, when the magnets (or rather the field of subtle forces, in and around the magnets) are set in motion, force is manifested in the way we call an electric current. We do not think of the designing of a radio station or a power plant as a linguistic process, but it is one nonetheless. The necessary mathematics is a linguistic apparatus, and, without its correct specification of essential patterning, the assembled gadgets would be out of proportion and adjustment, and would remain inert. But the mathematics used in such a case is a SPECIALIZED formula-language, contrived for making available a specialized type of force manifestation through metallic bodies only, namely, ELECTRICITY as we today define what we call by that name. The mantric formula-language is specialized in a different way, in order to make available a different type of force manifestation, by repatterning states in the nervous system and glands—or again rather in the subtle "electronic" or "etheric" forces in and around those physical bodies. Those parts of the organism, until such strategic patterning has been effected, are merely "innocent gadgets," as incapable of dynamic power as loose magnets and loose wires, but IN THE PROPER PATTERN they are something else again—not to be understood from the properties of the unpatterned parts, and able to amplify and activate latent forces.

In this way I would link the subtle Eastern ideas of the mantric and yogic use of language with the configurative or pattern aspect which is so basic in language. But this brings me to the most important part of my discussion. We must find out more about language! Already we know enough about it to know it is not what the great majority of men, lay or scientific, think it is. The fact that we talk almost effortlessly, unaware of the exceedingly complex mechanism we are using, creates an illusion. We think we know how it is done, that there is no mystery; we have all the answers. Alas, what wrong answers! It is like the way a man's uncorrected sense impressions give him a picture of the universe that is simple, sensible, and satisfying, but very wide of the truth.

Consider how the world appears to any man, however wise and experienced in human life, who has never heard one word of what science has discovered about the Cosmos. To him the earth is flat; the sun and moon are shining objects of small size that pop up daily above an eastern rim, move through the upper air, and sink below a western edge; obviously they spend the night somewhere underground. The sky is an inverted bowl made of some blue material. The stars, tiny and rather near objects, seem as if they might be alive, for they "come out" from the sky at evening like rabbits or rattlesnakes from their burrows, and slip back again at dawn. "Solar system" has no meaning to him, and the concept of a "law of gravitation" is quite unintelligible—nay, even nonsensical. For him bodies do not fall because of a law of gravitation, but rather "because there is nothing to hold them up"—i.e., because he cannot imagine their doing anything else. He cannot conceive space without an "up" and "down" or even without an "east" and "west" in it. For him the blood does not circulate; nor does the heart pump blood; he thinks it is a place where love, kindness, and thoughts are kept. Cooling is not a removal of heat but an addition of "cold"; leaves are green not from the chemical substance chlorophyll in them, but from the "greenness" in them. It will be impossible to reason him out of these beliefs. He will assert them as plain, hard-headed common sense; which means that they satisfy him because they are completely adequate as a SYSTEM OF COMMUNICATION between him and his fellow men. That is, they are adequate LINGUISTICALLY to his social needs, and will remain so until an additional group of needs is felt and is worked out in language.

But as this man is in conception of the physical universe, of whose scope and order he has not the faintest inkling, so all of us, from rude savage to learned scholar, are in conception of language. Only the science of linguistics has begun to penetrate a little into this realm, its findings still largely unknown to the other disciplines. Natural man, whether simpleton or scientist, knows no more of the linguistic forces that bear upon him than the savage knows of gravitational forces. He supposes that talking is an activity in which he is free and untrammeled. He finds it a simple, transparent activity, for which he has the necessary explanations. But these explanations turn out to be nothing but statements of the NEEDS THAT IMPEL HIM TO COMMUNICATE. They are not germane to the process by which he communicates. Thus he will say that he thinks something, and supplies words for the thoughts "as they come." But his explanation of why he should have such and such thoughts before he came to utter them again turns out to be merely the story of his social needs at that moment. It is a dusty answer that throws no light. But then he supposes that there need be no light thrown on this talking process, since he can manipulate it anyhow quite well for his social needs. Thus he implies, wrongly, that thinking is an OBVIOUS, straightforward activity, the same for all rational beings, of which language is the straightforward expression.

Actually, thinking is most mysterious, and by far the greatest light upon it that we have is thrown by the study of language. This study shows that the forms of a person's thoughts are controlled by inexorable laws of pattern of which he is unconscious. These patterns are the unperceived intricate systematizations of his own language—shown readily enough by a candid comparison and contrast with other languages, especially those of a different linguistic family. His thinking itself is in a language—in English, in Sanskrit, in Chinese.* And every language is a vast pattern-system, different from others, in which are culturally ordained the forms and categories by which the personality not only communicates, but also analyzes nature, notices or neglects types of relationship and phenomena, channels his reasoning, and builds the house of his consciousness.

This doctrine is new to Western science, but it stands on unimpeachable evidence. Moreover, it is known, or something like it is known, to the philosophies of India and to modern Theosophy. This is masked by the fact that the philosophical Sanskrit terms do not supply the exact equivalent of my term "language" in the broad sense of the linguistic order. The linguistic order embraces all symbolism, all symbolic processes, all processes of reference and of logic. Terms like *Nāma* refer rather to subgrades of this order—the lexical level, the phonetic level. The nearest equivalent is probably *Manas*, to which our vague word "mind" hardly does justice. *Manas* in a broad sense is a major hierarchical grade in the world-structure—a "manasic plane" as it is indeed explicitly called. Here again "mental plane" is apt to be misleading to an English-speaking person. English "mental" is an unfortunate word, a word whose function in our culture is often only to stand in lieu of an intelligent explanation, and which connotes rather a foggy limbo than a cosmic structural order characterized by patterning. Sometimes *Manas* is used to mean, however, simply the personal psyche; this according to Mr. Fritz Kunz is the case in the famous saying of *The Voice of the Silence:* "The mind is the great slayer of the real."

It is said that in the plane of *Manas* there are two great levels, called the *Rūpa* and *Arūpa* levels. The lower is the realm of "name and form," *Nāma* and *Rūpa*. Here "form" means organization in space ("our" three-dimensional space). This is far from being coextensive with pattern in a universal sense. And *Nāma*, "name," is not language or the linguistic order, but only one level in it, the level of the process of "lexation" or of giving words (names) to parts of the whole manifold of experience, parts which are thereby made to stand out in a semifictitious isolation.

---

*To anticipate the text, "thinking in a language" does not necessarily have to use WORDS. An uncultivated Choctaw can as easily as the most skilled litterateur contrast the tenses or the genders of two experiences, though he has never heard of any WORDS like "tense" or "gender" for such contrasts. Much thinking never brings in words at all, but manipulates whole paradigms, word-classes, and such grammatical orders "behind" or "above" the focus of personal consciousness.

Thus a word like "sky," which in English can be treated like "board" (the sky, a sky, skies, some skies, piece of sky, etc.), leads us to think of a mere optical apparition in ways appropriate only to relatively isolated solid bodies. "Hill" and "swamp" persuade us to regard local variations in altitude or soil composition of the ground as distinct THINGS almost like tables and chairs. Each language performs this artificial chopping up of the continuous spread and flow of existence in a different way. Words and speech are not the same thing. As we shall see, the patterns of sentence structure that guide words are more important than the words.

Thus the level of *Rūpa* and *Nāma*—shape-segmentation and vocabulary—is part of the linguistic order, but a somewhat rudimentary and not self-sufficient part. It depends upon a higher level of organization, the level at which its COMBINATORY SCHEME appears. This is the *Arūpa* level—the pattern world par excellence. *Arūpa*, "formless," does not mean without linguistic form or organization, but without reference to spatial, visual shape, marking out in space, which as we saw in the "hill" and "swamp" is an important feature of reference on the lexical level. *Arūpa* is a realm of patterns that can be "actualized" in space and time in the materials of lower planes, but are themselves indifferent to space and time. Such patterns are not like the meanings of words, but they are somewhat like the way meaning appears in sentences. They are not like individual sentences but like SCHEMES of sentences and designs of sentence structure. Our personal conscious "minds" can understand such patterns in a limited way by using mathematical or grammatical FORMULAS into which words, values, quantities, etc., can be substituted. A rather simple instance will be given presently.

It is within the possibilities of the "culture of consciousness" that the *Arūpa* level of the "mental" plane may be contacted directly in an expansion of consciousness. In Ouspensky's book, *A New Model of the Universe*, there are arresting glimpses of extraordinary mental states which that philosopher attained—adumbrations only, for these completely "nonlexical" vistas cannot be well put into words. He speaks of realms of "moving hieroglyphs" composed entirely of "mathematical relations," and of the expansion and ramification of such a "hieroglyph" till it covered a whole aspect of the universe. Ouspensky's mathematical predilections and his study of such things as non-Euclidean geometries, hyperspace, and the relation between time and consciousness may have led him to stress mathematical analogies. Mathematics is a special kind of language, expanded out of special sentences containing the numeral words, 1, 2, 3, 4, . . . *x*, *y*, *z*, etc. But every other type of sentence of every language is also the potential nucleus of a far-reaching system. To very few is it granted to attain such consciousness as a durable state; yet many mathematicians and scientific linguists must have had the experience of "seeing," in one fugitive flash, a whole system of relationships never before suspected of forming a unity. The harmony and scientific beauty in the whole vast system momently overwhelms one in a flood of aesthetic delight. To "see," for instance, how all the English elementary sounds ("phonemes") and their groupings are coordinated by an intricate yet systematic law into all possible forms of English monosyllabic words, meaningful or nonsensical, existent or still unthought of, excluding all other forms as inevitably as the chemical formula of a solution precludes all but certain shapes of crystals from emerging—this might be a distinct experience.

31.

Psychosynthesis: A Technique for the Use of Intuition

Roberto Assagioli

In this discussion we assume that intuition exists as an independent and specific psychological function. It was called by Jung an irrational function, to use his own words: "this term does not denote something contrary to *reason*, but something outside the province of reason" (Jung, 1933, p. 569).

We will consider intuition mainly in its cognitive function, i.e., as a [mental] organ or means to apprehend reality. It is a synthetic function, in the sense that it apprehends the totality of a given situation or psychological reality. It does not work from the part to the whole—as the analytical mind does—but apprehends a totality directly in its living existence. [Since] it is a normal function of the human psyche, its activation is

Reprinted by permission from Roberto Assagioli, *Psychosynthesis: A Manual of Principles and Techniques* (Hobbs, Dorman, and Co., Inc., 1971), pp. 217–223.

produced chiefly by eliminating the various obstacles preventing its activity.

Intuition is one of the least recognized and least appreciated, and therefore one of the repressed, functions. It is repressed by a mechanism similar to that of the repression of unconscious drives, but generally the motivation is different. Repression of intuition is produced by non-recognition, devaluation, neglect, and lack of its connection with the other psychological functions. Regarding this last point, [for intuition to be] a true cognitive process implies not only the functioning of intuition alone, but also its intelligent apprehension, interpretation, and inclusion in the existing body of knowledge.

It is necessary to make a definite distinction between so-called day-by-day intuition and real spiritual intuition. For instance, intuition as described by Bergson is predominantly on the personal levels, while intuition according to Plotinus is purely spiritual. Intuition according to Jung is on both of these two levels; and for our present practical and therefore limited purposes we will take the Jungian attitude and speak of intuition fundamentally as a function which can be active on different levels, and can therefore assume different aspects but remain fundamentally the same.

PURPOSE

The purpose of activating the intuition is that of putting at the disposal of the individual a precious function which generally remains latent and unused, thereby leaving the individual incomplete in his or her development. Another purpose is that of offering to the individual an instrument of cognition and of approach to reality, and a means of interpersonal relationships through the intuitive understanding of other human beings. A further purpose is to help him to discriminate between genuine intuitions and false or supposed intuitions which are really either sentimental generalizations or imaginative notions with no foundation in reality.

Rationale

As with every other function, intuition is a psychological experience. Anyone who feels has emotions; he experiences as an immediate content of his consciousness the emotion or feeling, and looks not for any demonstration of its existence or reality. The same is true for the function of thinking; there are people of low psychological development who really never think in the proper sense of the word, and it would be hopeless to try to demonstrate to them the existence of thought and the working of the thinking function; and yet, thinking does exist. The same reasoning is true for intuition. Anyone who is intuitive, who spontaneously and naturally uses the intuition, experiences what it is without any need of explanation or demonstration.

The essential distinction between cognition by way of intuition and cognition by way of the thinking or feeling functions is that intuition has the following characteristics: it is immediate and direct, not mediate and progressive as is thinking; it is synthetic or holistic, i.e., it is an immediate apprehension of a whole, one could say of a Gestalt, and not of different parts later put together to form a whole. Intuition in its purest manifestation is devoid of feeling in the ordinary and right meaning of the nature of emotion, of a warm reaction of the personality—generally either positive or negative toward the object apprehended. Intuition, as well as the other psychological functions, can be activated, following the general law that attention and interest foster their manifestation. It has been said that attention has feeding power; it has also a focusing power. One could even say that it has an evocative power, and attention really implies appreciation and therefore valuation.

PROCEDURE

The first step is of a negative character—the temporary checking or elimination from the field of consciousness of other functions which generally have a spontaneous and uninterrupted activity. Constantly sensations from the outer world or from the body intrude into the field of consciousness; emotional reactions do the same, and often the mind is over-active and undisciplined. All this obstructs, fills the field of consciousness, and makes either the entrance or the recognition of intuitions impossible or difficult. Therefore, it is necessary to carry out what we might call a psychological cleaning of the field of consciousness; metaphorically, to ensure that the projection screen is clear and white. This permits in the subject a sympathetic opening of the consciousness towards, or a reaching actively for, that truth or section of reality with which he seeks to come into contact for the solution of a human or an impersonal cognitive problem.

The second stage is then possible, in which he quietly waits for the result of the approach, this nearing, which in successful cases becomes a contact with and even an identification of the subject with the looked-for experience of reality or truth.

In this process we emphasize the necessary cooperation of the will (in every technique there is the god behind the machine—"deus ex machina"—which is the will). Just as in the first part of the procedure, of the stilling or cleansing of consciousness, there is a conscious and active action of the will, so also in the second part, that of relaxation and quiet waiting, the will continues to function, although in a subtler way and, as it were, remaining in the background. This is so because in order to maintain an attitude of relaxation and quietness—and one which is not purely passive—the will is still required, to act, metaphorically, as the watchman at the door of consciousness to exclude intruders.

To further clarify the difference between the action of the will in the first and second stages, we could say that in the former the will actively ejects the occupants of the "room of consciousness" and in the second stage the will merely watches at the door so that no unwanted intruder can enter.

A characteristic of intuitions is that they are fleeting and, curiously, very easily forgotten, in spite of the fact that at the time they enter the field of consciousness they are very vivid and the subject does not think he can or will forget them easily. Such intuitions can be likened to a stray bird entering a room, circling swiftly around it, and then after a few seconds flying out of the window. The practical deduction from this "fleeting" characteristic is to write down immediately any intuitions we may have—more particularly when we recall the distorting effect of time on all our recollections. Also, of course, it is correct scientific procedure to write down immediately and with precision the supposed intuition for its necessary checking later.

Preparatory to utilizing the technique with patients, the first requirement is the assessment, in which we ask the patient if he has ever had intuitions and, if so, if he found them reliable or not; or what his reaction is to his intuitions, i.e., does he overvalue them or feel superior because of his supposed intuitive ability? According to the patient's reactions the approach is correspondingly changed. In the first case—where the fact or possibility of intuition is questioned—the value of intuition has to be emphasized and examples given; and in the second case—of overvaluation—the difference between intuition and "hunches" or imaginative flights has to be explained and emphasized.

If the patient at an early stage of the therapy recounts intuitive experiences, then that clearly indicates the opportunity to take up the subject with him there and then. If, on the contrary, the patient does not show evidence of intuitive activity it is better to postpone dealing with this rather subtle and difficult subject until the treatment requires it—generally at a rather late stage.

INDICATIONS AND APPLICATIONS

The general application is for cases where the patient is seeking the attainment of understanding in its fullest psychological sense. Only intuition gives true psychological understanding both of oneself and of others. Whenever one wants to reach a true understanding of the essence of the specific quality of a human being, of a group, or of human relationships, the use of intuition is indicated and even necessary.

A general field of application is in *valuation*, for sound valuation is often the outcome of an intuitive perception of the essence or purpose of a person, [of] an activity, or of a situation. Then, as with every other intuition, this valuation has to be checked and examined through other functions, such as that of critical analysis; but one can say that the intuition is the specific organ of psychological function for achieving understanding and true valuation.

Another large field of application is that of the sciences. There also it can be used to reach the truth in a synthetic way, a truth which has a universal or general value—such as a principle, a law, or a general method of procedure, even if applied to a specific problem.

Concerning specific indications there is first the psychotherapist himself. We cannot conceive a true and successful therapist who has not developed and [does not use] the intuition. For this reason, this technique should be given special attention in every didactic psychosynthesis. And of course this applies also to educators certainly no less than to therapists. Regarding education, children and adolescents often have a very active intuition, because it is not checked and interfered with by overactivity of other functions. Therefore, in education, intuition should be dealt with at an early stage.

The greatest need for intuition is in intellectual or overintellectualized people; i.e., for those who have an active or overactive mind, but specifically for those who identify themselves with their mind and are proud of their intelligence. Such intellectuals often have a very lopsided development and are in great need of psychosynthesis in general, and of the activation of the other functions, which, as we mentioned earlier, very often remain undeveloped. Even the sensation function can be warped by intellectualism, and the feeling nature is sometimes shamefully suppressed, with the will practically nonexistent—but they share this last deficiency with the majority of human beings.

In contrast, we have cases—especially among women—where the intuition is active but in a "rough" undiscriminating way; in a technical sense "impure." In such cases the indication would be to refine, to purify it, to separate it from heterogeneous elements.

LIMITATIONS AND CONTRA-INDICATIONS

The limitation—which also applies to all other techniques and the use of all other functions, but which has to be reiterated—is that the separative use of any function can give only limited, one-sided results. It is in the cooperation and synthetic use of all human functions that success—either in cognition or in action—can be achieved. Therefore, however valuable intuition may be, it should be used concomitantly with the other psychological functions.

The contra-indications arise in the case of certain types who are too prone to be affected and impressed by hunches, by imaginative ways of pretended knowledge, and who have not enough mental capacity to exercise the necessary discrimination and to develop the fine ability to distinguish between true and false intuitions. In such cases, the development of intuition should be postponed to the stage in which the other complementary and supplementary functions have been cultivated. Here, of course, comes in the need to be able to check the validity of an intuition and to know how this can be done.

COMBINATION WITH OTHER TECHNIQUES

The most important combination is that with a controlled mental activity and mental discrimination. To use an analogy, it is a necessary and difficult marriage. Often it is a stormy marriage which sometimes ends in divorce. [Many] do not even contemplate such a marriage. They are content to use either only the intuition or only the intellect. Even when this attempt at matrimony is begun, there are various difficulties: in some cases one of the partners is too imperative and devaluates and keeps in subjection the other—and it can be either one that makes this mistake, with all the drawbacks of repression, of overt or covert rebellion. In other cases there is an oscillation, a fight between the two in which temporarily the one or the other predominates.

Many intellectuals are to a certain extent afraid when an intuition intrudes into their thought processes; they are diffident and treat it very gingerly; consciously or unconsciously, in most cases they repress it.

To speak more directly, and without metaphor, of the true relationship between intuition and intellect, intuition is the creative advance towards reality. Intellect [needs, first, to perform] the valuable and necessary function of interpreting, i.e., of translating, verbalizing in acceptable mental terms, the results of the intuition; second, to check its validity; and third, to coordinate and to include it into the body of already accepted knowledge. These functions are the rightful activity of the intellect, without its trying to assume functions which are not its province. A really fine and harmonious interplay between the two can work perfectly in a successive rhythm: intuitional insight, interpretation, further insight and its interpretation, and so on.

32.

Present-Centeredness in Gestalt Therapy

Claudio Naranjo

If we want to list the implicit moral injunctions of Gestalt therapy, the list may be longer or shorter according to the level of generality or particularity of our analysis. Without claiming to be systematic or thorough, here are some that may give an impressionistic notion of the style of life entailed:

1. Live now. Be concerned with the present rather than with past or future.

2. Live here. Deal with what is present rather than with what is absent.

3. Stop imagining. Experience the real.

4. Stop unnecessary thinking. Rather, taste and see.

Reprinted by permission from Joen Fagan and Irma Lee Shepherd, eds., *Gestalt Therapy Now* (Science and Behavior Books, Inc., 1970), pp. 47–69.

5. Express rather than manipulate, explain, justify, or judge.
6. Give in to unpleasantness and pain just as to pleasure. Do not restrict your awareness.
7. Accept no *should* or *ought* other than your own. Adore no graven image.
8. Take full responsibility for your actions, feelings, and thoughts.
9. Surrender to being as you are.

The paradox that such injunctions may be part of a moral philosophy that precisely recommends giving up injunctions may be resolved if we look at them as statements of truth rather than duty. Responsibility, for instance, is not a *must*, but an unavoidable fact: we *are* the responsible doers of whatever we do. Our only alternatives are to acknowledge such responsibility or deny it. All that Gestalt therapy is saying is that by accepting the truth (which amounts to a non-undoing rather than a doing) we are better off—awareness cures. Of course, it cures us of our lies.

I think that the specific injunctions of Gestalt therapy may in turn be subsumed under more general principles. I would propose the following three:

1. Valuation of actuality: temporal (present versus past or future), spatial (present versus absent), and substantial (act versus symbol).
2. Valuation of awareness and the acceptance of experience.
3. Valuation of wholeness, or responsibility. . . .

In the following pages I will consider in some detail one of the aspects of actuality, in itself one aspect of the philosophy of life of Gestalt therapy. In choosing *living-in-the-moment* as a theme, I am not implying that this is more important than the issues of consciousness or responsibility, but only limiting the scope of this paper to the subject on which I feel most inclined to write at the moment. I think, too, that whatever the point of departure, the content will be somewhat similar, for the three issues are only superficially distinct. On close examination we may discover, for instance, that the question of actuality is not only related to the valuation of present tense and present locus, but also to the valuing of concrete reality, sensing and feeling rather than thinking and imagining, to awareness, and to self-determination. More specifically, I hope that the following pages will show that the willingness to live in the moment is inseparable from the question of openness to experience, trust in the workings of reality, discrimination between reality and fantasy, surrender of control and acceptance of potential frustration, a hedonistic outlook, and awareness of potential death. All these issues are facets of a single experience of being-in-the-world, and looking at such an experience from the perspective of present-centeredness rather than other conceptual vantage points amounts to an arbitrary choice. . . .

PRESENT-CENTEREDNESS AS TECHNIQUE

There are at least two ways in which present-centeredness is reflected in the technical repertoire of Gestalt therapy. One is the outspoken request to the patient to attend to and express what enters his present field of awareness. This will most often be coupled with the instruction to suspend reasoning in favor of pure self-observation. The second is the *presentification* of the past or future (or fantasy in general). This may take the form of an inward attempt to identify with or relive past events or, most often, a reenacting of the scenes with gestural and postural participation as well as verbal exchanges, as in psychodrama.

Both techniques have antecedents in spiritual disciplines older than psychotherapy, and it could not be otherwise, given their importance. Presentification is found in the history of drama, magic, and ritual, and in the enacting of dreams among some primitive people. Dwelling in the present is the cornerstone of some forms of meditation. Yet both presentification and dwelling in the present find in Gestalt therapy a distinctive embodiment and form of utilization that deserve discussion at length. In the following pages I will concentrate on the approach called *the exercise of the continuum of awareness*. Since it is very much like a meditation translated into words, and its role in Gestalt therapy is comparable to that of free-association in psychoanalysis, I will deal with it mostly in comparative terms.

Gestalt Therapy and Meditation

The practice of attention to present experience has had a place in several traditions of spiritual discipline. In Buddhism it is a corollary of "right-mindfulness," one of the factors in the "Noble Eightfold Path." An aspect of right-mindfulness is the practice of "bare attention":

> Bare Attention is concerned only with the *present*. It teaches what so many have forgotten: to live with full awareness in the Here and Now. It teaches us to *face* the present without trying to escape into thoughts about the past or the future. Past and future are, for average consciousness, not objects of observation, but of

reflection. And, in ordinary life, the past and the future are taken but rarely as objects of truly *wise* reflection, but are mostly just objects of day-dreaming and vain imaginings which are the main foes of Right Mindfulness, Right Understanding and Right Action as well. Bare Attention, keeping faithfully to its post of observation, watches calmly and without attachment the unceasing march of time; it waits quietly for the things of the future to appear before its eyes, thus to turn into present objects and to vanish again into the past. How much energy has been wasted by useless thoughts of the past: by longing idly for bygone days, by vain regrets and repentance, and by the senseless and garrulous repetition, in word or thought, of all the banalities of the past! Of equal futility is much of the thought given to the future: vain hopes, fantastic plans and empty dreams, ungrounded fears and useless worries. All this is again a cause of avoidable sorrow and disappointment which can be eliminated by Bare Attention (Nyaponika Thera, 1962, p. 41).

Past and future do not qualify as "bare objects" in that they are in the nature of imagining, but are also to be avoided because dwelling in them entails a loss of freedom: illusion ensnares us in its recurrence. As Nyaponika Thera (1962, p. 41) says:

Right Mindfulness recovers for man the lost pearl of his freedom, snatching it from the jaws of the dragon Time. Right Mindfulness cuts man loose from the fetters of the past which he foolishly tries even to re-inforce by looking back to it too frequently, with eyes of longing, resentment or regret. Right Mindfulness stops man from chaining himself even now, through the imaginations of his fears and hopes, to anticipated events of the future. Thus Right Mindfulness restores to man a freedom that is to be found only in the present.

The most important practice related to the view in the quotation above is that form of meditation the Chinese call *we-hsin* (or idealessness), which consists, as Watts (1950, p. 176) puts it, in the ability to retain one's normal and everyday consciousness and at the same time let go of it.

That is to say, one begins to take an objective view of the stream of thoughts, impressions, feelings, and experiences which constantly flows through the mind. Instead of trying to control and interfere with it, once simply lets it flow as it pleases. But whereas consciousness normally lets itself be carried away by the flow, in this case the important thing is to *watch* the flow without being carried away ... one simply accepts experiences as they come without interfering with them on the one hand or identifying oneself with them on the other. One does not judge them, form theories about them, try to control them, or attempt to change their nature in any way; one lets them be free to be just exactly what they are. "The perfect man," said Chuang-tzu, "employs his mind as a mirror; it grasps nothing, it refuses nothing, it receives but does not keep." This must be quite clearly distinguished from mere empty-mindedness on the one hand, and from ordinary undisciplined mind-wandering on the other.

The practice of attention to the present in the context of Gestalt therapy is very much like verbalized meditation. Moreover it is a meditation carried into the interpersonal situation as an act of self-disclosure. This permits a monitoring of the exercise by the therapist (which may be indispensable to the inexperienced) and may also add significance to the contents of awareness.

I would not doubt that the search for words and the act of reporting can interfere with certain states of mind; yet the act of expression also adds to the exercise in awareness, beyond its being merely a means of information for the therapist's intervention. At least the following advantages of communicated awareness over silent meditation may be listed:

1. The act of expression is a challenge to the sharpness of awareness. It is not quite true to say that we know something but cannot put it into words. Of course, words are mere words and we can never *put* anything into words; yet, within limits, clarity of perception goes together with the ability to express, an artist being a master in awareness rather than a skilled patternmaker. And in art, as in psychotherapy, the task of having to communicate something involves having to really look at it rather than dreaming about looking.

2. The presence of a witness usually entails an enhancement both of attention and of the meaningfulness of that which is observed. I think too that the more aware an observer is, the more our own attention is sharpened by his mere presence, as if consciousness were contagious or one person could not as easily avoid seeing what is exposed to the gaze of another.

3. The contents of consciousness in an interpersonal setting will naturally tend to be that of the interpersonal relationship, whereas the solitary meditator focused on the here and now will systematically fail to find such contents in his field of awareness. Since it is mainly the patterns of relating and the self-image in the process of relating that are disturbed in psychopathological conditions, this factor looms large in making the here-and-now exercise a therapy when in the I-thou setting.

4. The interpersonal situation makes present-centeredness more difficult, for it elicits projection, avoidance, and self-delusion in general. For instance, what for the solitary meditator may be a series of observations of physical states may, in the context of communication, become embedded in a feeling of anxiety about the therapist's eventual boredom, or in an assumption that such observations are trivial, or that they show the patient's essential barrenness. The elicitation of such feelings and fantasies is important.

a. If present-centeredness is a desirable way of living which is usually marred by the vicissitudes of interpersonal relationships, the challenge of contact entails the ideal *training* situation. I would like to invite the thought that the practice of living in the moment is truly an *exercise* and not merely an occasion for self-insight. Just as in behavior therapy, this is a process of desensitization in the course of which a person becomes free of the central conditioning of avoiding experience, and he learns that there is nothing to fear.

b. Related to the above is the fact that it is precisely the awareness of the difficulties in present-centeredness that can provide the first step toward overcoming them. Experiencing the compulsive quality of brooding or planning may be inseparable from an appreciation of the alternative to them, and of a true understanding of the distinction between these states of mind and present-centeredness.

5. The therapeutic context allows for a monitoring of the process of self-observation, whereby the therapist brings the patient back to the present when he has been distracted from it (that is, from himself). There are two main ways of doing this. The simplest (aside from merely reminding him of the task) is to call his attention to what he is doing unawares, by directing his attention to aspects of his behavior that seem to be automatic response patterns or to clash with his intentional actions. Simply being mirror to him may serve to bring into focus his relationship to himself and his actions in general:

P.: I don't know what to say now. . . .
T.: I notice that you are looking away from me.
P.: (Giggle.)
T.: And now you cover up your face.
P.: You make me feel so awful!
T.: And now you cover up your face with both hands.
P.: Stop! This is unbearable!
T.: What do you feel now?
P.: I feel so embarrassed! Don't look at me!
T.: Please stay with that embarrassment.
P.: I have been living with it all my life! I am ashamed of everything I do! It is as if I don't even feel that I have the right to exist!

An alternative to this process of simply reflecting the patient's behavior is that of regarding the occasions of failure in present-centeredness as cues to the patient's difficulties (or rather, living samples thereof), just as in psychoanalysis the failure to free-associate is the target of interpretation. Instead of interpretation, in Gestalt therapy we have explicitation: the request that the patient himself become aware of and express the experience underlying his present-avoiding behavior. One of the assumptions in Gestalt therapy is that *present-centeredness is natural*: at depth, living in the moment is what we want most, and therefore deviations from the present are in the nature of an avoidance or a compulsive sacrifice rather than random alternatives. Even if this assumption were not true of human communication in general, it is made true in Gestalt therapy by the request that the patient stay in the present. Under such a structure, deviations may be understood as failures, as a sabotaging of the intent, or as distrust in the whole approach and/or the psychotherapist.

In practice, therefore, the therapist will not only coach the patient into persistent attention to his ongoing experience, but will especially encourage him to become aware and to express his experience at the point of failing at the task. . . .

The Continuum of Awareness and Asceticism

It may be a psychological truth that a person can hardly attain present-centeredness while remembering, before having known the taste of it in the easier situation of reminiscence-deprivation. The same may be parenthetically said on the matter of contacting one's experience while thinking. Ordinarily, thinking dispels the awareness of the self-in-the-activity-as-thinker and the feelings constituting the ground of the thinking-motivation, just as the sun during the daytime prevents our seeing the stars. The experience of thinking and not being lost in thought (that is, caught up in the exclusive awareness of the figure in the totality of figure-ground) is a condition that can be brought about most easily by contacting such experience-ground in moments of thoughtlessness. In this the Gestalt therapy techniques of suspending reminiscence, anticipation, and thinking fall in with the implicit philosophy of asceticism in general: certain deprivations are undergone in order to contact what is currently hidden by the psychological activity involved in the renounced situations. This deprivation of sleep, talking, social communication, comfort, food, or sex is supposed to facilitate the access to unusual states of consciousness but is not an end or ideal in itself.

The practice of attention to the stream of life relates to asceticism in that it not only entails a voluntary suspension of ego-gratification, but also presents the person with the difficulty of functioning in a way that runs counter to habit. Since the only action allowed by the exercise is that of communicating the contents of awareness, this precludes the operation of "character" (that is, the organization of copying mechanisms) and even *doing* as such. . . .

PRESENT-CENTEREDNESS AS PRESCRIPTION

Not all that is of value as a psychological exercise need automatically be a good prescription for living. Free association may be a useful exercise, but not necessarily the best approach to conversation, just as the headstand in Hatha Yoga need not be the best posture to be in most of the time. To a greater or lesser extent, techniques have a potential for being carried into ordinary life, thus making of life the occasion for a growth endeavor. Yet it is not only the specific value of a certain approach that makes it appropriate as a prescription, but its compatibility with other desirable purposes in life; the degree of clash that it will bring about with the existing social structure and, especially, its compatibility with a conception of the good society. Thus the abreaction of hostility in a situation of no constraints can be of value in psychotherapy, but is this approach the one that would maximize sanity and well-being in a community? I think that opinions on the matter would be divided. They would be divided even on the question of truth. Whereas aggression tends to be socially reproved and the commandment states, "Thou shalt not kill," truth is commonly regarded as virtue, and lying a sin. One might therefore expect that the technique of self-disclosure, valuable in the context of psychotherapy, would be immediately applicable to life. Given the ordinary condition of humanity, though, truth has been and may continue to be not only uncomfortable or inconvenient but dangerous. The example of Socrates, Jesus Christ, or the heretics at the time of the Inquisition, point out that an unconditional embracing of truth may mean the acceptance of martyrdom, for which I am sure the average human being is not ready. The desire to turn feelings into prescriptions in cases where society did not make such a project feasible has been one of the implicit or explicit rationales in the creation of special communities among those who share the goal of living for the inner quest. In such groups, sometimes veiled by secrecy, man has sought to live according to principles not compatible with other than a monastic, therapeutic, or otherwise special setting.

Humanistic Hedonism

Living in the moment, in contrast to other techniques, seems a perfectly appropriate prescription for life. Moreover, it appears to be more in the nature of a technicalization of a life formula than the prescribing of a technique. The idea of prescription may evoke images such as that of the bad-smelling tonic that children were frequently compelled to take "for their own good," before the time of gelatin capsules and flavor chemistry. This is part of a dualistic frame of mind in which "the good things" seem different from the "things for our good," and the goal of self-perfecting seems something other than "merely living."

This is not what the classic injunctions of present-centeredness convey. Take, for instance, King Solomon's "A man hath no better thing under the sun, than to eat, and to drink, and to be merry [Eccles. 15]." The character of this quotation, like that of most statements that stress the value of actuality, is hedonistic. And it could not be otherwise, for if the value of the present is *not* going to be for a future, it must be *intrinsic*: the present must contain its own reward.

In our times the hedonistic outlook seems to be divorced from and to run counter to religious feeling (just as to "prescription orientation" in general). Insofar as "body" and "mind" are regarded as incompatible sources of value, idealism and spirituality tend to be associated with a grim asceticism, while the defense of pleasure is most often undertaken by the cynically practical, tough-minded, and hard-nosed "realists." This does not seem to have always been so, and we know that there was a time when religious feasts were real festivals. So, when we read Solomon's words in the Old Testament, we should not superimpose on them our present body-mind split, or the tough-mindedness with which those words are often repeated. Behind them was an outlook according to which living life and living it now was a holy action, a way in accordance with God's will.

Rarely do we find this balance of transcendence and immanence in Western thought, with the exception of remarkable individuals that seem to be marginal to the spirit of the times—heretics to the religious, or madmen to the common folk. William Blake, for instance, was such a man in claiming that "eternity is in love with the productions of time."

Even in psychoanalysis, which in practice has done much for mankind's *id*, the "pleasure principle" is looked upon as a childishness and a nuisance that the "mature," reality-oriented ego must hold in check.

Contrariwise, Gestalt therapy sees a much stronger link between pleasure and goodness, so that its philosophy may be called hedonistic in the same sense as the good old hedonisms before the Christian era. I would like to suggest the notion of humanistic hedonism, which does not necessarily entail a theistic outlook and yet seems to distinguish this approach from the egoistic hedonism of Hobbes, the utilitarian hedonism of J. S. Mill, and that of the ordinary pleasure seeker. (If at this point the reader wonders how Gestalt therapy can be called ascetic and hedonistic at the same time, let him remember that in Epicurus's view the most pleasurable life was one devoted to philosophical reflection while on a simple diet of bread, milk, and cheese.) . . .

PRESENT-CENTEREDNESS AS IDEAL

> *Der den Augenblick ergreift/Das ist der rechte Mann.*
> He who seizes the moment is the right man.
>
> Goethe

The word *ideal* needs clarification. Ideals are frequently understood with a connotation of duty and/or intrinsic goodness that is foreign to the philosophy of Gestalt therapy. If we deprive an ideal of its quality of *should* or *ought*, it remains as either a statement of the desirable way to an end—that is, a prescription—or else a "rightness." By this I mean an *expression* of goodness rather than a means or an injunction: a sign or symptom of an optimal condition of life. This is the sense in which we may speak of ideals in Taoism, for instance, in spite of its being a philosophy of nonseeking. In spite of its noninjunctional style, the Tao Te Ching is always elaborating on the qualities of the sage: "For this reason the sage is concerned with the belly and not the eyes. . . . The sage is free from the disease because he recognizes the disease to be disease. . . . The sage knows without going about . . . accomplishes without any action," and so on. In the same sense, present-centeredness is regarded as an ideal in statements such as: "*Now* is the watchword of the wise."

Some recipes for better living are means to an end that differ from such an end in quality, but this is not true of present-centeredness. Here, as in Gestalt therapy in general, *the means to an end is a shifting to the end state right away*: the way to happiness is that of starting to be happy right away; the way to wisdom that of relinquishing foolishness at this very moment—just as the way to swim is the practice of swimming. The prescription of living in the now is the consequence of the fact that we *are* living in the now; this is something that the sane person *knows*, but the neurotic does not realize while enmeshed in a dreamlike pseudo-existence.

In Buddhism the now is not merely a spiritual exercise but the condition of the wise. In a passage of the *Pali Canon*, Buddha first utters the prescription:

> Do not hark back to things that passed,
> And for the future cherish no fond hopes:
> The past was left behind by thee,
> The future state has not yet come.

and then the ideal:

> But who with vision clear can see
> The present which is here and now
> Such wise one should aspire to win
> What never can be lost nor shaken.

Whereas the Buddhist version of the *now* injunction stresses the illusoriness of the alternatives, the Christian view stresses the trust and surrender entailed by present-centeredness. When Jesus says, "Take, therefore, no thought of the morrow, for the morrow shall take thought of the things of itself," giving the example of the lilies of the fields [Matt. 6], he is not only saying, "Don't act upon catastrophic expectations," but more positively, "Trust!" While the Christian version is framed in a theistic map of the universe, and trust means trust in the heavenly Father, the attitude is the same as that regarded as the ideal in Gestalt therapy, which may be rendered as trust in one's own capacities for coping with the now as it comes. The ideal of present-centeredness is one of experiencing rather than manipulating, of being open to and accepting experience rather than dwelling in, and being defensive in the face of, possibility. Such attitudes bespeak two basic assumptions in the *Weltanschauung* of Gestalt therapy: *things at this moment are the only way that they can be;* and *behold, the world is very good!*

If the present cannot be other than it is, the wise will surrender to it. Furthermore if the world is good, why not, as Seneca puts it, "gladly take the gifts of the present hour and leave vexing thoughts." To say of anything that *it* is good is, of course, a statement alien to Gestalt therapy, which holds that things can only be good to *us*. Whether they are depends on us and what we do with our circumstances.

Our current perception of existence is full of pain, helplessness, and victimization. As Edmund Burke remarked over two centuries ago: "To complain of the age we live in, to murmur of the present possessors of power, to lament the past, to conceive of extravagant hopes of the future are the common disposition of the greatest part of mankind." In the view of Gestalt therapy, however, such complaints and lamentations are no more than a bad game we play with ourselves—one more aspect of rejecting the potential bliss of now. At depth, we are where we want to be, we are doing what we want to do, even when it amounts to apparent tragedy. If we can discover our freedom within our slavery, we can also discover our essential joy under the cover of victimization.

The whole process of estrangement from reality, as reality is given in the eternal now, may be conceived as one of *not trusting* the goodness of the outcome, of *imagining* a catastrophic experience or, at best, an emptiness for which we compensate by creating a paradise of ideals, future expectations, or past glories. From such "idols" we keep looking down on present reality, which never quite matches our constructs and therefore never looks perfect enough. This is how the question of present-centeredness ties in with accepting experience rather than being judgmental.

As Emerson said,

> These roses under my window make no reference to former roses or to better ones; they are for what they are; they exist with God today. There is not time to them. There is simply the rose; it is perfect in every moment of its existence . . . but man postpones and remembers. He cannot be happy and strong until he, too, lives with nature in the present, above time.

Searching for the ideal rose, we don't see that each rose is the utmost perfection of itself. For fear of not finding the rose we seek, we hang on to the concept of "rose" and never learn that "a rose is a rose is a rose." Our greed and impatience do not permit us to let go of the substitute through which we enjoy the reflection of reality in the form of promise or possibility, and by which we are at the same time cut off from present enjoyment. The intuition of Paradise Lost and the Promised Land is better than total anesthesia, but short of the realization that they are right here. Omar Khayyám knew well:

> Here with a loaf of bread beneath the bough,
> A flask of wine, a book of verse—and thou
> Beside me singing in the wilderness—
> And wilderness is Paradise enow.
>
> "How sweet is mortal sovereignty!" think some;
> Others, "How blest the Paradise to come!"
> Ah, take the cash in hand and waive the rest;
> Nor heed the music of a *distant* drum!
>
> *Rubáiyát*

33.

Learning in the Autonomic Nervous System

Leo V. DiCara

The heart beats and the stomach digests food without any obvious training, effort, or even attention. That may be the basis of a curious prejudice against the visceral responses—the responses of glands, of cardiac
muscle, and of the smooth muscle of the alimentary canal and blood
vessels—and against the autonomic nervous system, which controls them.
Such responses are assumed to be quite different from, and somehow inferior to, the highly coordinated voluntary responses of skeletal muscles
and the cerebrospinal nervous system that controls them. A corollary of
this attitude has been the assumption that visceral responses can be "conditioned" but cannot be learned in the same way as skeletal responses. It
turns out that these long-standing assumptions are not valid. There is

Reprinted by permission from *Scientific American*, 222, no. 1 (Jan. 1970), pp. 30–39.
(Scientific American Offprint 525.) Copyright © 1970 by Scientific American, Inc. All
rights reserved.

apparently only one kind of learning; supposedly involuntary responses can be genuinely learned. These findings, which have profound significance for theories of learning and the biological basis of learning, should lead to better understanding of the cause and cure of psychosomatic disorders and of the mechanisms whereby the body maintains homeostasis, or a stable internal environment.

Learning theorists distinguish between two types of learning. One type, which is thought to be involuntary and therefore inferior, is classical, or Pavlovian, conditioning. In this process a conditioned stimulus (a signal of some kind) is presented along with an innate unconditioned stimulus

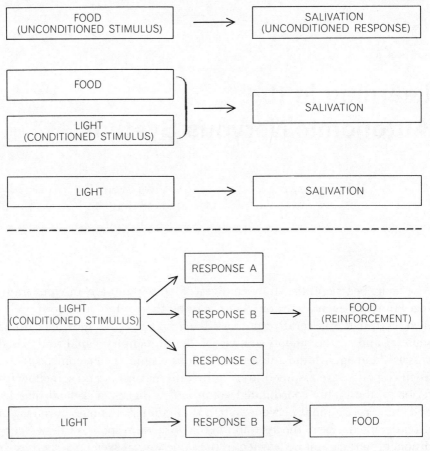

Two types of learning are classical conditioning and instrumental learning. Classical conditioning (top) begins with an unconditioned stimulus. The conditioned stimulus that is paired with it comes to substitute for it in producing the unconditioned response. In instrumental learning (bottom), a conditioned stimulus is presented along with an opportunity to respond in various ways. The correct response is reinforced, or rewarded. After several reinforcements the stimulus serves as a signal to perform the learned response.

(such as food) that normally elicits a certain innate unconditioned response (such as salivation); after a time the conditioned stimulus elicits the same response. The other type of learning—clearly subject to voluntary control and therefore considered superior—is instrumental, or trial-and-error, learning, also called operant conditioning. In this process a reinforcement, or reward, is given whenever the desired conditioned response is elicited by a conditioned stimulus (such as a certain signal). The possibilities of learning are limited in classical conditioning, because the stimulus and response must have a natural relationship to begin with. In instrumental learning, on the other hand, the reinforcement strengthens any immediately preceding response; a given response can be reinforced by a variety of rewards and a given reward can reinforce a variety of responses.

Differences in the conditions under which learning occurs through classical conditioning and through instrumental learning have been cited to show that the two processes are two distinct phenomena that operate through different neurophysiological mechanisms. The traditional belief has been that the involuntary and inferior visceral responses can be modified only by the correspondingly inferior type of learning—classical conditioning—and not by the superior and voluntary instrumental learning, which has been thought to modify only voluntary, skeletal responses.

Not all learning theorists accepted this distinction. For many years Neal E. Miller of Rockefeller University has held that classical conditioning and instrumental learning are not two basically different phenomena but rather two manifestations of the same phenomenon under different conditions—that there is, in fact, only one kind of learning. To support such a position he had to show that instrumental training procedures can produce learning of any visceral responses that can be acquired through classical conditioning, and the demonstration had to be very clear and convincing in the face of the ingrained belief that such learning is simply not possible.

Research on the instrumental modification of visceral responses comes up against a basic problem: most such responses can be affected by voluntary activities, such as the tensing of muscles or changes in the rate or pattern of breathing. It is therefore hard to rule out completely the possibility that the experimental subject has not directly learned to control a visceral response through the autonomic system but rather has learned to execute some subtle and undetectable skeletal response that in turn modifies the visceral behavior. (A skilled disciple of yoga, for example, can stop his heart sounds by controlling his rib cage and diaphragm muscles so that pressure within the chest is increased to the point where the venous return of blood to the heart is considerably retarded.)

To guard against the contamination of experimental results by such "cheating," careful controls and detailed statistical analysis of data are required. The primary control Miller and I apply in our animal experiments is paralysis of the subject's skeletal muscles. This is accomplished by administering a drug of the curare family (such as *d*-tubocurarine) that blocks acetylcholine, the chemical transmitter by which cerebrospinal nerve impulses are delivered to skeletal muscles, but does not interfere with consciousness or with the transmitters that mediate autonomic responses. A curarized animal cannot breathe and must therefore be maintained on a mechanical respirator. Moreover, it cannot eat or drink, and so the possibilities of rewarding it are limited. We rely on two methods of reinforcement. One is electrical stimulation of a "pleasure center" in the brain, the medial forebrain bundle in the hypothalamus, and the other is the avoidance of or escape from a mildly unpleasant electric shock.

Utilizing these techniques, we have shown that animals can learn visceral responses in the same way that they learn skeletal responses. Spe-

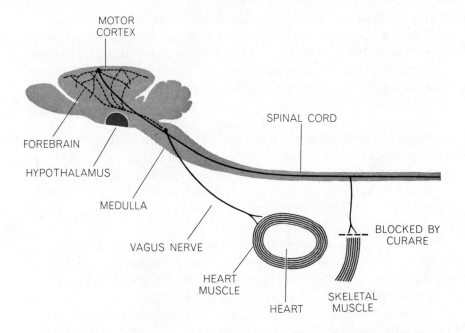

Curare paralyzes skeletal muscles. It ensures, for example, that a change in heart rate has been controlled by autonomic impulses from the vagus nerve and not by cerebrospinal impulses to skeletal muscles. The two nervous systems are not completely separate: visceral reponses have representation at higher brain centers in the cortex (broken lines).

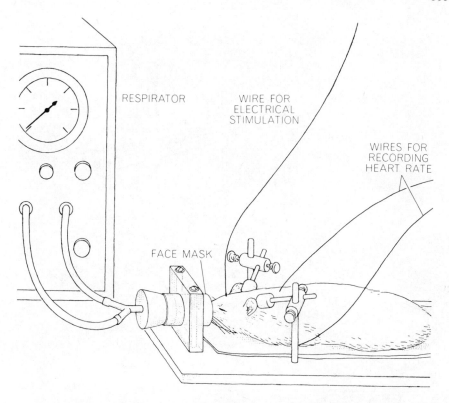

RESPIRATOR

WIRE FOR
ELECTRICAL
STIMULATION

WIRES FOR
RECORDING
HEART RATE

FACE MASK

Curarized rats cannot breathe and must be fitted with a face mask connected to a respirator. Such usual instrumental-learning rewards as food and water cannot be used.

cifically, we have produced, through instrumental training, increases and decreases in heart rate, blood pressure, intestinal contractions, control of blood-vessel diameter and rate of formation of urine. Other investigators have demonstrated significant instrumental learning of heart-rate and blood-pressure control by human beings and have begun to apply the powerful techniques developed in animal experiments to the actual treatment of human cardiovascular disorders.

After Miller and his colleagues Jay Trowill and Alfredo Carmona had achieved promising preliminary results (including the instrumental learning of salivation in dogs, the classical response of classical conditioning), he and I undertook in 1965 to show that there are no real differences between the two kinds of learning: that the laws of learning observed in the instrumental training of skeletal responses all apply also to the instrumental training of visceral responses. We worked with curarized rats, which we trained to increase or to decrease their heart rate in order to

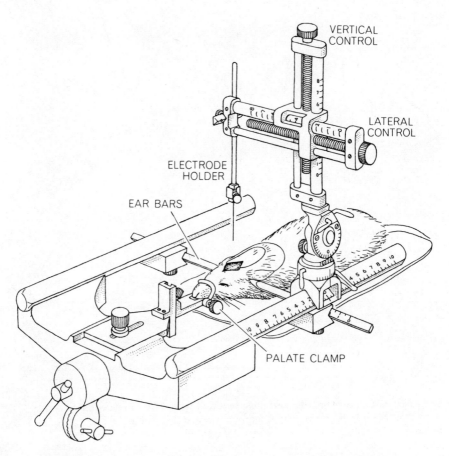

VERTICAL
CONTROL

LATERAL
CONTROL

ELECTRODE
HOLDER

EAR BARS

PALATE CLAMP

Reward for visceral learning is either electrical stimulation of the brain or avoidance of electric shock. For brain stimulation, an electrode is implanted in the brain of an anesthetized rat, guided to a "pleasure center" in the hypothalamus with the aid of a stereotactic device.

obtain pleasurable brain stimulation. First we rewarded small changes in the desired direction that occurred during "time in" periods, that is, during the presentation of light and tone signals that indicated when the reward was available. Then we set the criterion (the level required to obtain a reward) at progressively higher levels and thus "shaped" the rats to learn increases or decreases in heart rate of about 20 percent in the course of a 90-minute training period.

These changes were largely over-all increases or decreases in the "base line" heart rate. We were anxious to demonstrate something more: that heart rate, like skeletal responses, could be brought under the control of a discriminative stimulus, which is to say that the rats could learn to

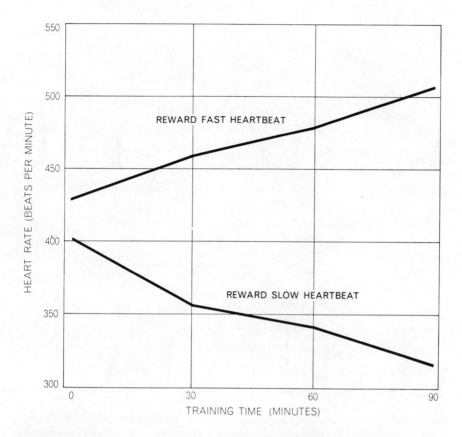

Heart-rate changes are shown for rats rewarded for increasing the rate (gray) and for decreasing it (black). Animals were curarized and rewarded with brain stimulation.

respond specifically to the light and tone stimuli that indicated when a reward was available and not to respond during "time out" periods when they would not be rewarded. To this end we trained rats for another 45 minutes at the highest criterion level. When we began discrimination training, it took the rats some time after the beginning of each stimulus period to meet the criterion and get the reward; by the end of the training they were changing their heart rate in the rewarded direction almost immediately after the time-in period began.

In skeletal instrumental training discrimination is also learned between a positive stimulus, response to which is rewarded, and a negative stimulus, response to which is not rewarded. Our animals learned to respond with the proper visceral behavior to one stimulus (such as a light) and not to respond to another (such as a tone). Moreover, once an animal

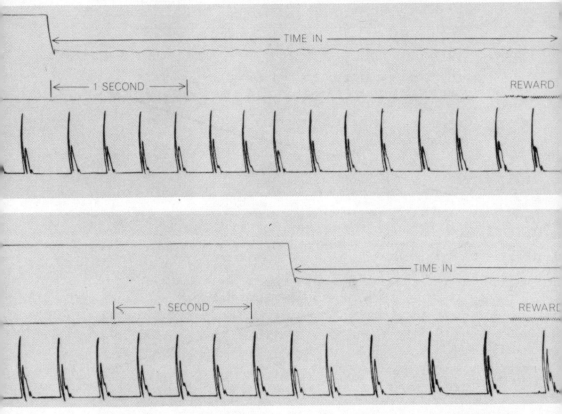

Electrocardiograms made at the beginning and at the end of an extra period of training demonstrate discrimination. At first the rat takes some time after the onset of stimulus ("time in") to respond (by slowing its heartbeat) and earn a reward (top). After 45 minutes of discrimination training the rat responds more directly: it slows its heartbeat soon after time-in period begins (bottom).

has learned to discriminate between positive and negative cues for a given skeletal response, it is easier for it to respond similarly with a different response for the same reward. We found that this phenomenon of transfer also appeared in visceral training: rats that showed the best discrimination between a positive and a negative stimulus for a skeletal response (pressing a bar) also showed the best discrimination when the same stimuli were used for increased or decreased heart rate.

Two other properties of instrumental training are retention and extinction. To test for retention we gave rats a single training session and then returned them to their home cages for three months. When they were again curarized and tested, without being reinforced, rats in both the increase group and the decrease group showed good retention by exhibiting reliable changes in the direction for which they had been rewarded three months earlier. Although learned skeletal responses are remembered well, they can be progressively weakened, or experimentally extinguished, by prolonged trials without reward. We have observed this phenomenon of extinction in visceral learning also. To sum up, all the phenomena of instrumental training that we have tested to date have turned out to be characteristic of visceral as well as skeletal responses.

The experiments I have described relied on electrical stimulation of the brain as a reinforcement. In order to be sure that there was nothing unique about brain stimulation as a reward for visceral learning, Miller and I did an experiment with electric-shock avoidance, the other of the two commonly used rewards that can conveniently be administered to paralyzed rats. A shock signal was presented to the curarized rats. After it had been on for five seconds it was accompanied by brief pulses of mild shock delivered to the rat's tail. During the first five seconds the animal could turn off the shock signal and avoid the shock by making the correct heart-rate response; failing that, it could escape the shock by making the correct reponse and thus turning off both the signal and the shock.

In the course of a training session we mixed shock trials with "safe" trials and "blank" trials at random. During a safe trial we presented a different signal and did not administer a shock; during a blank trial there was no signal or shock. For half of the rats the shock signal was a tone and the safe signal a flashing light; for the other half the stimuli were reversed. The rats that were rewarded for increasing their heart rate learned to increase it and those that were rewarded for decreasing the rate learned to decrease it. In part the learning represented a general change in base line, as indicated by the trend of the heart rate during blank trials. Beyond this, however, the rats clearly learned to discriminate. As their training progressed, the shock signal began to elicit a greater change in the rewarded direction than the blank trials did. Conversely, the safe signal elicited a trend in the opposite direction—toward the base line represented by the data for the blank trials.

At this point we had shown that instrumental learning of visceral responses follows the laws of skeletal instrumental training and that it is not limited to a particular kind of reward. We also showed that the response itself is not limited: we trained rats to raise and lower their systolic blood pressure in much the same way. These results were all obtained, however, with animals that were paralyzed. Would normal, active animals also learn a visceral response? If so, could that response be shown to be independent of skeletal activity? We designed a special experimental cage and the necessary equipment to make possible the recording of various responses of active rats, and we established that heart-rate and blood-

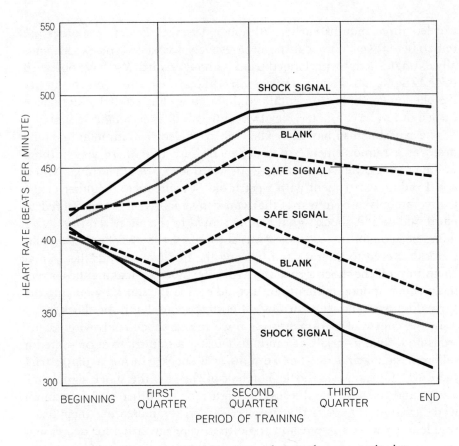

Discrimination is demonstrated by these curves for rats that were trained to increase (top three lines) and decrease (bottom three) heart rate and were rewarded by avoidance of shock. The results for blank trials (no signal or shock) show "base line" learning. The results for shock-signal and safe-signal trials show discriminating responses to more specific stimuli.

pressure changes could be learned by noncurarized animals. The heart-rate learning persisted in subsequent tests during which the same animals were paralyzed by curare, indicating that it had not been due to the indirect effects of overt skeletal responses. This conclusion was strengthened when, on being retrained without curare, the two groups of animals displayed increasing differences in heart rate, whereas any differences in respiration and general level of activity continued to decrease.

We noted with interest that initial learning in the noncurarized state was slower and less effective than it had been in the previous experiments under curare. Moreover, a single training session under curare facilitated later learning in the noncurarized state. It seems likely that

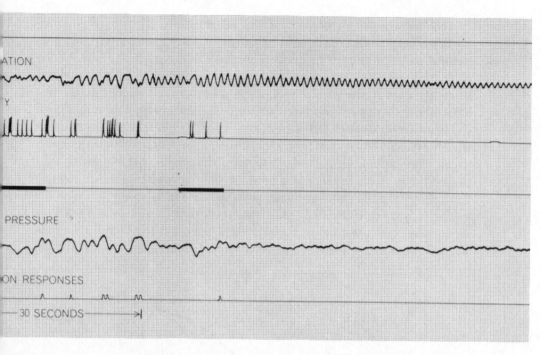

Polygraph record, a small portion of which is reproduced, records a free-moving rat's respiration, activity, and systolic blood pressure. It also shows when trials took place, whether the blood-pressure increase met the criterion, and whether, not having met the criterion, the animal received an electric shock. This record was made by an animal being tested as in the illustration on page 360.

paralysis eliminated "noise" (the confusing effects of changes in heart action and blood-vessel tone caused by skeletal activity) and perhaps also made it possible for the animal to concentrate on and sense the small changes accomplished directly by the autonomic system.

In all these studies the fact that the same reward could produce changes in opposite directions ruled out the possibility that the visceral learning was caused by some innate, unconditioned effect of the reward. Furthermore, the fact that the curarized rats were completely paralyzed, which was confirmed by electromyographic traces that would have recorded any activity of the skeletal muscles, ruled out any obvious effect of the voluntary responses. It was still possible, however, that we were somehow inducing a general pattern of arousal or were training the animals to initiate impulses from the higher brain centers that would have produced skeletal movements were it not for the curare, and that it was the innate effect of these central commands to struggle and relax that were in turn changing the heart rate. Such possibilities made it desirable to discover whether or not changes in heart rate could be learned independently of changes in other autonomic responses that would occur as natural concomitants of arousal.

To this end Miller and Ali Banuazizi compared the instrumental learning of heart rate with that of intestinal contraction in curarized rats. They chose these two responses because the vagus nerve innervates both the heart and the gut, and the effect of vagal activation on both organs is well established. In order to record intestinal motility they inserted a water-filled balloon in the large intestine. Movement of the intestine wall caused fluctuations in the water pressure that were changed into electric voltages by a pressure transducer attached to the balloon.

The results were clear-cut. The rats rewarded (by brain stimulation) for increases in intestinal contraction learned an increase and those rewarded for decreases learned a decrease, but neither group showed an

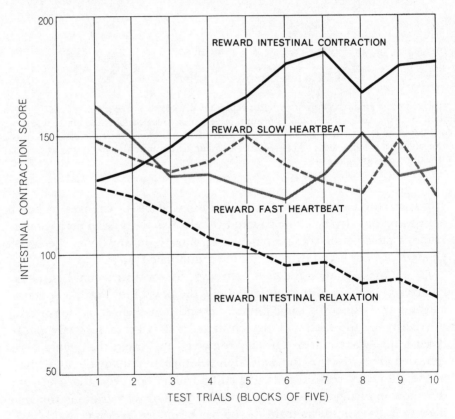

Intestinal contraction is learned independently of heart-rate changes. Contractions are increased by rats rewarded for increases (black line) and decreased by rats rewarded for decreases (broken black line). The intestinal-contraction score does not change appreciably, however, in rats rewarded for increasing or decreasing heart rate (gray).

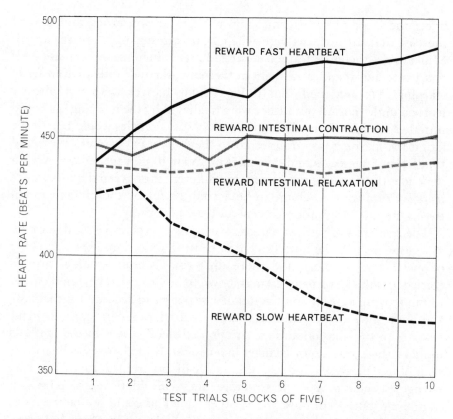

Specificity of learning is shown by both this graph and the one on p. 366. Here the results for heart rate rather than intestinal contraction are shown for the same animals. Rats rewarded for changing their heart rate change it in the appropriate direction (black lines). Rats rewarded for intestinal changes do not change heart rate (gray lines).

appreciable change in heart rate. The group that was rewarded for increases in heart rate learned an increase and the group rewarded for decreases learned a decrease, but neither heart-rate group showed an increase in intestinal contraction. Moreover, the heart-rate and intestinal learning were negatively correlated: the better the response being rewarded was learned, the less change there was in the unrewarded response. These results showed that the instrumental learning of two visceral responses can occur independently of each other and that what is learned is specifically the rewarded response. They ruled out the possibility that the learning was mediated by a general reaction such as arousal.

There was still a remote possibility to be eliminated: The central impulses I mentioned might be initiated selectively toward muscles that affect the intestines when intestinal changes are rewarded and toward muscles that affect heart rate when heart-rate changes are rewarded. Miller and I therefore trained curarized rats to increase or decrease their heart rate and then tested them in the noncurarized state for transfer of learning. We reasoned that if heart-rate changes were not directly learned under curare but rather were mediated by the learning of central impulses to skeletal muscles, movement of such muscles would betray the fact if the learning was transferred to the noncurarized state. We found that learned increases and decreases of about 10 percent did transfer independently of muscle movement: the differences between the two groups in heart rate were too large to be accounted for by the differences between them in respiration or general level of activity.

The strongest argument against attempts to explain visceral learning as a response to skeletal movement or central motor impulses is this kind of specificity. As more and more different visceral responses are recorded and the learning of them is shown to be specific, it becomes harder to think of enough different voluntary responses to account for them all. We have shown, for example, that curarized rats can learn to make changes in the dilation and constriction of blood vessels in the skin and to make these vasomotor changes independently of changes in heart rate and blood pressure. Indeed, the rats can be trained to make these changes specific to a single structure: they can dilate the blood vessels in one ear more than those in the other ear! This could not be the result of heart-rate or blood-pressure changes, which would affect both ears equally. We also obtained instrumental learning in the rate of urine formation by the kidneys, independent of blood pressure or heart rate. The increases and decreases in the amount of urine produced were achieved by specific changes in the arteries of the kidneys that resulted in an increase or decrease in the blood flow through the kidneys.

In addition to buttressing the case for instrumental learning of visceral responses, these striking results suggest that vasomotor responses, which are mediated by the sympathetic division of the autonomic nervous system, are capable of much greater specificity than was believed possible. This specificity is compatible with an increasing body of evidence that various visceral responses have specific representation at the cerebral cortex, that is, that they have neural connections of some kind to higher brain centers.

Some recent experiments indicate that not only visceral behavior but also the electrical activity of these higher brain centers themselves can be modified by direct reinforcement of changes in brain activity. Miller and Carmona trained noncurarized cats and curarized rats to change the character of their electroencephalogram, raising or lowering the voltage of the brain waves. A. H. Black of McMaster University in Canada trained dogs to alter the activity of one kind of brain wave, the theta wave. More recently Stephen S. Fox of the University of Iowa used instrumental techniques to modify, both in animals and in human subjects, the amplitude of an electrical event in the cortex that is ordinarily evoked as a visual response.

We are now trying to apply similar techniques to modify the electrical activity of the vagus nerve at its nucleus in the lowermost portion of the brain. Preliminary results suggest that this is possible. The next step will be to investigate the visceral consequences of such modification. This kind of work may open up possibilities for modifying the activity of specific parts of the brain and the functions they control and thereby learning more about the functions of different parts of the brain.

Controlled manipulation of visceral responses by instrumental training also makes it possible to investigate the mechanisms that underlie visceral learning. We have made a beginning in this direction by considering the biochemical consequences of heart-rate training and specifically the role of the catecholamines, substances such as epinephrine and norepinephrine that are synthesized in the brain and in sympathetic-nerve tissues. Norepinephrine serves as a nerve-impulse transmitter in the central nervous system. Both substances play roles in the coordination of neural and glandular activity, influencing the blood vessels, the heart, and several other organs. Alterations in heart rate produced by increased sympathetic-nerve activity in the heart, for example, are accompanied by changes in the synthesis, uptake, and utilization of catecholamines in the heart, suggesting that it may be possible to influence cardiac catecholamine metabolism through instrumental learning of heart-rate responses. This would be important in view of the possible role of norepinephrine in essential hypertension (high blood pressure) and congestive heart failure; it might also help to establish the role of learning and experience in the development of certain psychosomatic disorders.

Eric Stone and I found that the level of catecholamines in the heart varies with heart-rate training. After three hours of training under curare, rats trained to increase their heart rate have a significantly higher concentration of cardiac catecholamines than rats trained to decrease their heart rate. Experiments are now under way to determine how long such biochemical differences between the two groups persist after training and whether the heart-rate conditioning has long-range effects on the heart and on the excitability of the sympathetic nerves. When we examined the brains of rats in the two groups we found a similar biochemical difference: the animals trained to increase their heart rate had a significantly higher level of norepinephrine in the brain stem than rats trained to decrease heart rate. Brain norepinephrine helps to determine the excitability of the central nervous system and is involved in emotional behavior. We have therefore started experiments to see whether or not changes in sympathetic excitability obtained by cardiovascular instrumental training are related to changes in the metabolism of norepinephrine and, if so, in which areas of the brain these metabolic changes are most apparent.

Is the capacity for instrumental learning of autonomic responses just a useless by-product of the capacity for cerebrospinal, skeletal-muscle learning? Or does it have a significant adaptive function in helping to maintain homeostasis, a stable internal environment? Skeletal responses operate on the external environment; there is obvious survival value in the ability to learn a response that brings a reward such as food, water, or escape from pain. The responses mediated by the autonomic system, on the other hand, do not have such direct effects on the external environment. That was one of the reasons for the persistent belief that they are not subject to instrumental learning. Yet the experiments I have described demonstrate that visceral responses are indeed subject to instrumental training. This forces us to think of the internal behavior of the visceral organs in the same way we think of the external, observable behavior of the skeletal muscles, and therefore to consider its adaptive value to homeostasis.

In a recent experiment George Wolf, Miller and I found that the correction of a deviation from homeostasis by an internal, glandular response (rather than by an external response such as eating or drinking) can serve as a reward to reinforce learning. We injected albino rats with an antidiuretic hormone (ADH) if they chose one arm of a T-shaped maze and with a control solution (a minute amount of isotonic saline solution) if they chose the other arm. Before running the maze each rat had been given an excess of water through a tube placed in the stomach, so that the antidiuretic hormone was maladaptive: it interfered with the kidney response that was necessary to get rid of the excess water and restore homeostasis, whereas the control solution did not interfere. The rats learned to select the side of the maze that insured an injection of saline solution, so that their own glandular response to the excess water could restore homeostasis. Then we did the same experiment with rats that suffered from diabetes insipidus, a disorder in which too much urine is passed and it is insufficiently concentrated. These rats had been tube-

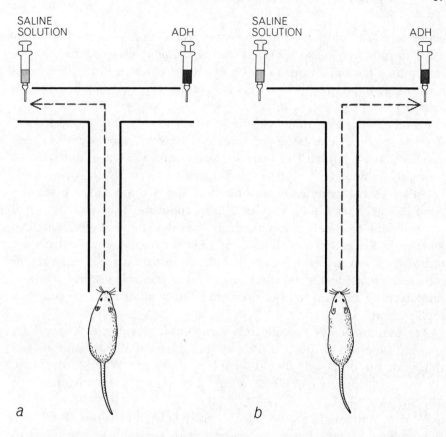

Visceral response that adjusts the internal environment can serve as a reward to reinforce learning. Rats "loaded" with water (a) learned to choose the side of a T-maze that resulted in an injection of a control solution rather than one of antidiuretic hormone (ADH), which would interfere with water excretion. (The arms associated with each reward were changed at random.) Rats loaded with salt (b), on the other hand, for whom the hormone would induce the proper kidney response, learned to pick the ADH-associated arm.

fed an excess of a highly concentrated salt solution. Now the homeostatic effects of the two injections were reversed: the ADH was adaptive, tending to concentrate the urine and thereby get rid of the excess salt, whereas the control solution had no such effect. This time the rats selected the ADH side of the maze. As a control we tested normal rats that were given neither water nor concentrated saline solution, and we found they did not learn to choose either side of the maze in order to obtain or avoid the antidiuretic hormone.

In many experiments a deficit in water or in salt has been shown to serve as a drive to motivate learning; the external response of drinking water or saline solution—thus correcting the deficit—functions as a reward to reinforce learning. What our experiment showed was that the return to a normal balance can be effected by action that achieves an internal, glandular response rather than by the external response of drinking.

Consider this result along with those demonstrating that glandular and visceral responses can be instrumentally learned. Taken together, they suggest that an animal can learn glandular and visceral responses that promptly restore a deviation from homeostasis to the proper level. Whether such theoretically possible learning actually takes place depends on whether innate homeostatic mechanisms control the internal environment so closely and effectively that deviations large enough to serve as a drive are not allowed. It may be that innate controls are ordinarily accurate enough to do just that, but that if abnormal circumstances such as disease interfere with innate control, visceral learning reinforced by a return to homeostasis may be available as an emergency replacement.

Are human beings capable of instrumental learning of visceral responses? One would think so. People are smarter than rats, and so anything rats can do people should be able to do better. Whether they can, however, is still not completely clear. The reason is largely that it is difficult to subject human beings to the rigorous controls that can be applied to animals (including deep paralysis by means of curare) and thus to be sure that changes in visceral responses represent true instrumental learning of such responses.

One recent experiment conducted by David Shapiro and his colleagues at the Harvard Medical School indicated that human subjects can be trained through feedback and reinforcement to modify their blood pressure. Each success (a rise in pressure for some volunteers and a decrease for others) was indicated by a flashing light. The reward, after 20 flashes, was a glimpse of a nude pinup picture. (The volunteers were of course male.) Most subjects said later they were not aware of having any control over the flashing light and did not in fact know what physiological function was being measured, and so they presumably had not exerted any voluntary effort (at least not consciously and deliberately) to modify the response.

Whatever is actually being learned by such subjects, the extent of learning is clearly less than can be achieved in animals. In one of our experiments the average difference in blood pressure between the two groups of curarized rats was 58 millimeters of mercury. Shapiro's two

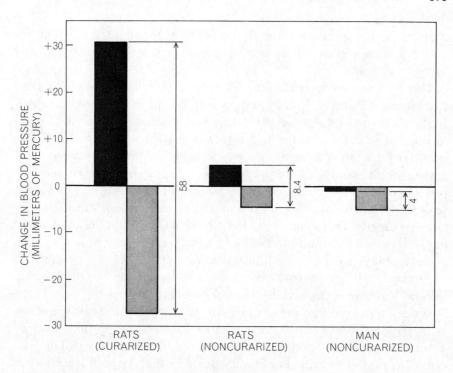

Comparison of blood-pressure learning in rats and humans rewarded for increasing (dark gray bars) and for decreasing (light gray) blood pressure shows that the difference between curarized and noncurarized subjects is greater than the difference between species.

human groups, in contrast, yielded a comparable difference of about four millimeters. Clearly curarized rats do better than noncurarized people, but that is not really surprising. The difference between the non-curarized rats and the noncurarized human subjects is much smaller.

The curare effect here is in line with what is seen in experiments with a single species. What does it mean? I mentioned above that initial training under curare facilitated further training in the noncurarized state. Perhaps the curare keeps the animal from being confused (as it may be in the noncurarized state) when a small change in the correct direction that is produced by direct control of the visceral response is obscured by a larger change in the opposite direction that is accomplished through skeletal activity and is therefore not rewarded. It is also possible that the curare helps to eliminate variability in the stimulus and to shift the ani-mal's attention from distracting skeletal activity to the relevant visceral activity. It may be possible to facilitate visceral learning in humans by

training people (perhaps through hypnosis) to breathe regularly, to relax, and to concentrate in an attempt to mimic the conditions produced
by curarization.

The evidence for instrumental learning of visceral responses suggests
that psychosomatic symptoms may be learned. John I. Lacey of the Fels
Research Institute has shown that there is a tendency for each individual
to respond to stress with his own rather consistent sequence of such visceral responses as headache, queasy stomach, palpitation, or faintness.
Instrumental learning might produce such a hierarchy. It is theoretically
possible that such learning could be carried far enough to create an actual psychosomatic symptom. Presumably genetic and constitutional differences among individuals would affect the susceptibility of the various
organ systems. So would the extent to which reinforcement is available.
(Does a child's mother keep him home from school when he complains
of headache? When he looks pale?) So also would the extent to which
visceral learning is effective in the various organ systems.

We are now trying to see just how far we can push the learning of visceral responses—whether it can be carried far enough in noncurarized
animals to produce physical damage. We also want to see if there is a
critical period in the animal's infancy during which visceral learning has
particularly intense and long-lasting effects. Some earlier experiments
bear on such questions. For example, during training under curare seven
rats in a group of 43 being rewarded for slowing their heart rate died,
whereas none of 41 being rewarded for an increase in heart rate died.
This statistically reliable difference might mean one of two things.
Either training to speed the heart rate helps a rat to resist the stress of
curare or the reward for slowing the heart rate is strong enough to overcome innate regulatory mechanisms and induce cardiac arrest.

If visceral responses can be modified by instrumental learning, it may
be possible in effect to "train" people with certain disorders to get well.
Such therapeutic learning should be worth trying on any symptom that
is under neural control, that can be continuously monitored, and for
which a certain direction of change is clearly advisable from a medical
point of view. For several years Bernard Engel and his colleagues at the
Gerontology Research Center in Baltimore have been treating cardiac
arrhythmias (disorders of heartbeat rhythm) through instrumental training. Heart function has been significantly improved in several of their
patients. Miller and his colleagues at the Cornell University Medical
College treated a patient with long-standing tachycardia (rapid heartbeat). For two weeks the patient made almost no progress, but in the

third week his learning improved; since then he has been able to practice on his own and maintain his slower heart rate for several months. Clark T. Randt and his colleagues at the New York University School of Medicine have had some success in training epileptic patients to suppress paroxysmal spikes, an abnormal brain wave.

It is far too early to promise any cures. There is no doubt, however, that the exciting possibility of applying these powerful new techniques to therapeutic education should be investigated vigorously at the clinical as well as the experimental level.

34.

Implications of Physiological Feedback Training

Ralph Ezios

In a much-cited passage, Weston LaBarre (1954, p. 90) explicates his idea of *evolution-by-prosthesis* in the following way:

> With human hands, the old-style evolution by body adaptation is obsolete. All previous animals had been subject to the *autoplastic* evolution of their self-substance, committing their bodies to experimental adaptations in a blind genetic gamble for survival. The stakes in this game were high: life or death. Man's evolution, on the other hand, is through *alloplastic* experiments with objects outside his own body and is concerned only with the products of his hands, brains, and eyes—and not with his body itself.

Printed by permission. The author acknowledges the invaluable assistance of Barbara B. Brown, Eleanor Criswell, Lester Fehmi, Elmer Green, Joseph Hart, Joe Kamiya, Hugh MacDonald, David Nowlis, and Robert Ornstein. [This note appeared in the original printing. Ed.]

As LaBarre implies, man's technological evolution so far has allowed him to gain better and better discrimination of, control over, and ability to communicate about all manner of events and processes in his environment.

Included in the ever-increasing comprehension of the environment, with concomitant ability to manipulate it, through science man has come to learn more about all organisms' internal events and processes. However, man's ability to discriminate, control, and communicate about his own personal internal events and processes has never been markedly aided by technological development, and thus the prosthetic evolution has primarily had its effect on man's external environment and only indirectly has it affected him internally. Men have dreamed however of prosthetic devices which would expand their awareness and facility with their interiors. For example, in *Mr. Tomkins Inside Himself* (Gamow and Ycas, 1967) the central character has the technological capacity to shrink himself to the size of a blood cell and then inject himself into his own body, so that he can observe various phenomena of modern biology going on inside his heart, cortex, sexual organs, and so on.

Physiological feedback training is exciting in this context because it is a small beginning in expanding and changing the direction of *evolution-by-prosthesis* and for the first time making it possible for an individual man to use technology to come to know himself better. The basic mechanism employed in feedback training is an electronic system which amplifies and informs the person as to the on-going activity of a selected physiological process, thereby aiding the person in discriminating the presence of events or stages in the process, thereby enabling him to gain some degree of voluntary control over this process, and also allowing him to develop a degree of sophistication in communicating about the process previously out of his scope. Although it could be argued that the mirror and the bathroom scale are considerably earlier instruments designed to give personal feedback on intrapersonal processes, the type of feedback is useful primarily in monitoring internal processes only indirectly as they effect externally apparent aspects of a person using them.

Now that the basic technique has been pioneered by Kamiya (1962) and Brown (1968), a number of psychologists have independently taken up the study of physiological feedback training. In discussions with each other we have been surprised at how many times various potential applications of the basic technique have occurred to us separately in our various laboratories. Consequently we have gathered together the following list of potential applications of the technique, in the hopes that these ideas will stimulate further research interest in the basic technique, that our report will be helpful for students in learning more about it, and that we may prove helpful in providing some sort of jumping-off place for others to go further with our ideas. Thus we list below some of our ideas about potential applications of the technique to basic research, therapy, entertainment, and education.

BASIC RESEARCH IN PSYCHOLOGY

Recently mathematical techniques have been developed for describing internal representations, and the relationship between these internal representations and their corresponding external objects (Shepard and Chipman, 1969). So far the technique has only been applied to internal representations of external objects, but there would seem to be no barrier to using the technique to study internal representations of internal events. It is hoped, for example, that Shepard's technique (see also Shepard, 1962) could be applied to scaled reports on the mental activity associated with EEG alpha generation or alpha suppression (Nowlis and MacDonald, 1969a). Perhaps even more promising would be the possibility of applying the Shepard and Chipman procedure to subjective reports on a number of concurrent physiological processes. Green (1969), for example, now has a technique for simultaneously giving EEG, EMG, and skin temperature feedback. And MacDonald, at Stanford, has developed a feedback system capable of giving wave-analog, envelope-analog, or on-off auditory feedback that has been used successfully in teaching discrimination and control over heart rate, skin temperature, EMG, EEG, vasodilation, and GSR. Using such electronic systems in a laboratory, the mathematical model to be derived could be of the relations between the internal representations of the processes in question, and the isomorphism could be studied with the relations between the processes themselves as recorded on the polygraph. For example, rather than be asked to describe the experience of EEG alpha per se, a subject could be asked whether it was more similar to lowering EMG or lowering skin temperature. With many physiological parameters, a model could be built up of the subjective proximities of the various parameters, and it certainly would be interesting to compare such a subjective model with an objectively derived model of actual tendencies for the various parameters to vary conjointly or independently.

The above considerations point to a need for a more adequate theory of the relationship between awareness and internal somatic events. We have definitely felt this need. Three alternatives are currently vying for our favor, and hopefully some of the basic and applied research problems that we will enumerate here, plus others using feedback training as an investigatory tool, will lead to a selection between, or, more likely, a synthesis of, the various points of view. One perspective, implicitly advanced in the paper on feedback training by Stoyva and Kamiya (1968) is that awareness and the physiological processes are overlapping and to some extent identical. That is, a person generating regular alpha is, while the alpha is present, in an "alpha state," strongly predisposing him to certain subjective feelings (e.g., pleasure and relaxation) and certain behaviors (e.g., wanting to generate more alpha). The second perspective, advanced by Shepard and Chipman for the study of internal representations of external events and revised by us only slightly so as to be applicable to internal events, posits that the internal events themselves are not identical or even isomorphic with internal representations of them, but that the internal representations can best be brought to the fore and made the object of research by looking into their relations with each other. Finally there is a third perspective, best described as the *evolution-by-prosthesis* argument turned inward, which assumes that awareness and internal physiological processes are basically separate, although affected by one another, and that feedback training can simply be a tool of awareness, for developing the same skills in discrimination, control, and verbalization of one's somatic world that earlier technological advancement has led to for one's external environment. The first position lends itself to model building based on subjective report concerning single physiological processes, the second to the Shepard proximity-analysis technique, and the third to standard psychophysical scaling techniques, designed to study the threshold and just noticeable differences in the awareness of one's own physiological processes. Whatever theoretical position wins the day, a positive result will be reconceptualization of the presently unsatisfactory term *introspection.* . . .

Clearly some of the basic research applications of the feedback technique are closely tied to problems in diagnosis and treatment. The dividing line is not clear, but let us now move on to some applications that are still researchable, but more straightforwardly oriented toward the therapeutic.

THERAPEUTIC APPLICATIONS: BIOMEDICAL AND PSYCHOLOGICAL

Hart (1967) points out that feedback training tends to obscure somewhat the normal expert-patient relationship in therapy. Feedback devices allow a patient to know himself better, while allowing him to develop his own attitudes about what he finds out.

The development of inexpensive and portable devices to give feedback opens up a number of therapeutic possibilities. One may begin by considering some applications in the field of psychosomatic medicine. For example, Shapiro *et al.* (1969) have shown that people can learn to lower their blood pressure. Thus patients with high blood pressure could be given small portable devices for checking themselves regularly against high blood pressure. If the blood pressure were unusually high, they could then employ techniques that they had previously learned to lower it, and could make sure that they had succeeded by checking themselves against the portable device. This procedure either could be used at bedside in the hospital, or the device could be rented or purchased to be used in the patients' regular daily life. Thus the physiological consequences of states of mind engendered by environments or actions which the patient would be likely to encounter could be better comprehended, thereby allowing the patient to get insight into the psychological component of his particular illness, and even providing an opportunity to learn to control the symptomatology after developing this insight. While the patient should not be led to overly high expectations during his illness, the ability to use such devices could well be morale-boosting to the patient who otherwise feels he has no hand in combating his own illness, and that his fate is in the hands of the experts alone.

Many variations on the theme exist. A portable device for |monitoring psychogalvanic skin response is already in production. Similarly a device that has been built by Hugh MacDonald with integrated circuitry capable of giving feedback on EEG, EMG, heart rate, skin temperature, vasoconstriction, and GSR could be mass-produced for sale at very low prices. Patients with irregular EEGs predisposing to epilepsy, who get headaches or backaches from tense muscles, who have irregular heart beats at times, or who have any relevant physiological irregularities which vary with their psychological state might find these devices helpful. It would even seem in the realm of possibility to build small, inexpensive devices for feed-back concerning stomach acidity, of potential use to patients with ulcers. Or feedback devices could be developed to allow a patient to listen to his intestinal functioning, to aid in proper digestive actions. Miller (1969) has shown that control over intestinal and digestive functioning can be developed very rapidly in animals.

A number of alternatives exist as to the type of feedback that would be given in these portable devices. In one potential type, most useful as a portable constant monitor, a physiological process would be monitored and the patient would receive a signal only if the process should cross a criterion indicating it was moving in an unfavorable direction (blood pressure too high, stomach acidity too high, heart becoming irregular, etc.). In another approach, most useful as a portable means for learning or regaining control, the feedback would be more analogous to the full process. Tiny variations in the physiological parameter would be brought to the attention of the patient and the patient could then engage in mental activities which would help to bring out desirable functioning.

In the area of psychiatry and clinical psychology such devices could also possibly be used with patients who had no specific somatic complaints. Because it is now possible to simultaneously monitor overt behavior, covert moods, and physiological processes in the natural setting (Nowlis and Cohen, 1968), procedures could be developed whereby both patient and therapist could develop more understanding of the covert moods and physiological patterns of behavior accompanying exposure to various aspects of the patients' environment. Then the patient could choose internal events which he would like to have occur more regularly, or more voluntarily, in his daily life and could begin a program of training, first at some training facility, then attempting to produce the pattern in the desired situation in his natural setting. Such procedures could increase the number of patients that a therapist could see, decrease the cost of psychotherapy, and decrease the problems associated with therapists' perceiving and dealing with patients from a single value system. In this type of therapy program, patients would have an unusual degree of freedom to choose their own goals, experiment with implementing and modifying the goals as they progressed in therapy, and test the results of the therapy in a very direct way against their actual life situation.

More basic research needs to be done on understanding physiological relaxation. Most of the physiological processes which have been successfully conditioned in our various laboratories are apparently influenceable by relaxation; that is, subjects learning to generate more alpha rhythm in their electroencephalogram, or lower muscle tension in their electromyogram, or lower heart rate, or warmer skin temperature, or larger vasodilation, or lower galvanic skin responsivity all tend to say that there is an element of relaxation involved in moving the process in that direction. Interestingly, our early findings also tend to agree that a subject who, through relaxation, has learned to influence one of these processes is not necessarily making any change in the other processes apparently influenceable by relaxation—for which the subject has not been given feedback. In fact, the processes appear to be remarkably independent in spite of the similar reports of relaxation. However, because relaxation is clearly involved in some way in the learning of each, one wonders if feedback training could in any way be used as a substitute for relaxant and tranquilizing drugs with patients suffering from anxiety symptoms, especially if the patients were trained to relax by multiple physiological criteria.

In our laboratories we know of at least one case of anxiety that has been treated with EMG and EEG feedback. Doctors had prescribed doses of tranquilizing drugs so heavy that the patient could barely operate in her normal setting. The patient now has successfully learned to keep her EMG low and the alpha component of her EEG high, even while sitting in postures similar to the ones she must sit in during her normal daily routine. Anxiety and tension have been reduced markedly enough, so that the patient now uses much lower amounts of tranquilizers, as recommended by her independent physician. EMG may be a particularly promising process to work with for such therapeutic benefits (see also Stoyva, 1969), but it may be that several processes monitored simultaneously could give the most effective relaxation training of all.

Those of us who have had experience in teaching relaxation to subjects through hypnosis, autogenic training, the Jacobson relaxation method, or other systems all feel that subjects can learn the same degree of deep relaxation which otherwise might take months of training after only a few sessions, perhaps two or three hours, of feedback training.

More directly in the area of psychopharmacology, another clinical use could be in the area of studying the interaction of various levels of a given physiological process with the effects of pharmacological agents. For example, pharmacological research could be aided by human or animal subjects who had learned to shift to many different levels of functioning so that the effects of the drug could be evaluated more precisely at specific levels over fairly long periods of time. This would be preferable to the present method of letting subjects simply fluctuate without controlling their physiological processes in any way. It could become easier to identify certain dangers in the way in which a drug could interact with a person's physiological changes. Also, it might be that certain desirable drug effects could be potentiated by administering them to a subject who would then keep himself in a certain state. For example, a psychoactive drug might have a particularly positive effect in a subject maintaining a high amount of alpha in his EEG. Or a pain-reducing drug might be especially effective when a patient also was showing vasodilation. Thus smaller doses of drugs might be used, and their effects predicted more carefully, in suitable patients who had learned to control appropriate physiological processes. . . .

EDUCATION

In most of our laboratories the most easily obtained subjects have been college students. We have all been impressed with the intense enthusiasm that some of these subjects have developed for feedback training. Some have offered to shave off their hair if it would be helpful in attaching the electrodes (a totally unnecessary step, incidentally); others have asked if we would be willing to continue running them as subjects if they would pay us to do it.

The remarkable interest in feedback training, unprecedented in the other kinds of psychological research that we have done, has also been apparent among professional people in psychology, particularly in the younger members of the field. Plans to form a "feedback society" of people in the field were met with unusual enthusiasm, and there are now over 100 professionals on a potential society mailing list (a marked increase over the six on the list last year), many of them planning to attend the first meetings of the proposed society in September [1960, Ed.].

What explains this interest? Part of it is that very meaningful questions are being asked about human beings, questions which are fascinating to layman and professional, and to people from eastern and western cultural backgrounds alike. Part of it is the pleasure both experimenter and subject can feel in research which does not need to include deceit or manipulation on the part of the experimenter. And part of the interest may be because of an increasing desire on the part of young people to explore and come to know the internal world as well as the external.

We ourselves have felt this interest in exploring our own internal process. Thus one of us, like his subjects, has learned to control to at least some extent his EEG, EMG, vasodilation, GSR, heart rate, and skin temperature. The most fascinating and pleasurable experience for this experimenter was in the brief time he spent working on the skin temperature of his hands. Within ten minutes the person could warm or cool his hands, deliberately altering the direction on command when another of us signalled with a click from a nearby instrument room, the click signaling "go in the opposite direction." The experimenter could alternately cool and warm his hands even when the clicks came as rapidly as one a second. The process involved was one the experimenter had lived with all his life but had never had any insight into or voluntary control over until the ten-minute feedback practice period. It was almost like discovering a new frontier, still needing to be charted and explored although close to us for millennia.

Some feel that oriental meditators are among the very few people who have developed sophisticated perceptual skills for internal processes. Such considerations might be useful in explaining why one aspect of the feedback training technique has been of particular fascination to many lay people (e.g., Luce and Segal, 1966) and professionals alike. This aspect is the potential application of feedback training to the western practice of eastern meditation. A number of independent studies done in India and Japan (e.g., Anand, Chhina, and Singh, 1961a; Kasamatsu and Hirai, 1962) agree that there are physiological patterns which are strongly related to deep meditation, particularly in the EEG, and EMG. The alpha rhythm is markedly increased in both yogic and zen meditation, and is generated over areas of the cortex normally not involved in alpha production. Meanwhile, the EMG tends to fall to very low levels.

By this time some yogis and zen monks have actually had the opportunity to try feedback training, and to listen to themselves as they meditate. They have tended to agree with westerners' speculations that such devices might be useful in teaching people the elementaries of meditation. In other words, westerners could overcome handicaps of cross-cultural translations and busy schedules in imitating the physiological patterns of expert meditators, thereby perhaps learning the basic state of mind for at least the beginning stages of meditation. Subjects can learn to control their EEG to a measurable extent after only a brief period of practice (Nowlis and Kamiya, 1968; Nowlis and MacDonald, 1969). EMG control, depending on the muscle used, is also not difficult to achieve. Thus a student with either a portable feedback device similar to that designed by MacDonald, or with a central training facility available, for example at his college health service, could learn to meditate in a state of mind similar to that of a zen monk or a yogi.

Thus feedback devices and feedback training may be helpful in providing people with a chance to explore the internal processes, and in a socially constructive way. Perhaps because western society and western education are so oriented to discrimination and control of external events, the opposite abilities, perhaps providing some relief from practice of the others, are highly prized among the younger generation. Certainly feedback training is less dangerous and more constructive than drug use, or "dropping out," alternatives which attract large numbers of bright and potentially highly valuable young members of our society (H. H. Nowlis, 1968).

Thus, our first hope is that feedback training will be valuable in education because through it students could learn to discriminate internal processes potentially affecting their physical health and psychological well-being, and, in addition, would be provided with a meaningful alternative to taking drugs or dropping out of school to "expand" their internal awareness.

Other applications to education are possible. For example, educational psychologists might want to determine if certain controllable physiological states lead to maximum receptivity in learning. If so, probably depending on the type of learning task, a student could deliberately bring out a favorable internal state before involving himself with his work. Particularly, on days of high academic stress, a student could imitate the covert behavior patterns, during studying and/or breaks, of students who had shown themselves especially capable of handling such stressful days (Nowlis and Cohen, 1968).

WHERE DO WE STAND?

Although results on feedback training have so far consistently yielded encouraging results, we have no idea at present of what the limits are. Results with animals have demonstrated some particularly complex processes can be rapidly brought under control, such as blood flow in one ear lobe, blood flow in the stomach lining, peristalsis, and kidney functioning (see review by Miller, 1969). There is no doubt that EEG activity can be controlled by animals and humans (Kamiya, 1962, Olds, 1963; Bundzen, 1965; Dewan, 1966; Mulholland, 1967; Hart, 1967; Sterman and Wyrwicka, 1967; Carmona, 1967; Sterman and Howe, 1969; Fox, 1969). Heart rate can clearly be controlled by humans (see review by Murray and Katkin, 1968), and blood pressure can be lowered (Shapiro et al., 1969). Similarly, with humans, GSR, EMG, skin temperature, and vasodilation are controllable (Green, 1969; Stoyva, 1969).

In one experiment, subjects were allowed to gain insight into the effect of various types of mental activity on their EEG for a practice period of 15 minutes, observing the effects on a feedback tone keyed to their EEG alpha. After this short practice period, 16 out of 16 were able to show some ability to control the feedback tone, that is, when instructed to keep the tone on for 2 minutes they did so more than when instructed to keep the tone off for the same period of time (Nowlis & Kamiya, 1969). In another similar experiment, 28 out of 32 subjects were able to show evidence of control after only seven minutes practice and 31 out of 32 showed control after 12 minutes of practice (Nowlis and MacDonald, 1969a). The subjects used in these experiments knew nothing about EEG alpha beforehand and were not aware of the reports of other subjects as to mental activity associated with control.

LIMITATIONS

Although there is clearly promise in the area, the dynamics of the types of control acquired are poorly understood; there are many thorny theoretical problems to be solved; and there are important issues of methodology, especially with human subjects, involving experimental control procedures, baseline recordings, and other things which have not been well worked out. . . .

A good deal of basic research and theory building still needs to be done. Hopefully, the proposed feedback society will be helpful in encouraging communication and areas of specialization in the field.

CONCLUDING REMARKS

The feedback training technique lends itself easily to speculation, and we are sure there are many applications beyond what we have mentioned here. When inexpensive portable feedback devices are commercially available, for example, we are sure people will think of many creative uses. We have only mentioned our more straightforward and practical ideas. Much more speculative thinking has gone along the lines of (1) could a feedback device be built to cue a woman as to her time of ovulation, (2) could feedback devices be used to get two or more people into very similar states, thus allowing demonstration of mental telepathy and other phenomena of parapsychology, (3) could feedback devices be helpful in the training of creative artists, training the artists to bring out internal states appropriate to various types of aesthetic productions, (4) could such devices be used in controlling artificial limbs, so that voluntary physiological changes would change the position of the limb, (5) could awareness of various muscle activities through EMG feedback be useful to athletes, etc. It is hard to stop thinking of uses once you begin trying it.

35.

The Control of Electroencephalographic Alpha Rhythms Through Auditory Feedback and the Associated Mental Activity

David P. Nowlis and Joe Kamiya

Attempts have been made for some time to modify the appearance of the blocking of the alpha rhythm in the human EEG through classical conditioning paradigms (e.g., Stern *et al.*, 1961; Jasper and Shagass, 1941; see review in Carmona, 1967). More recently, evidence has been accumulating that EEG responses in men and animals, including the alpha

---

Reprinted by permission from *Psychophysiology*, 6, no. 4 (1970), 476–484. Copyright ©1970 by The Society for Psychophysiological Research.

rhythm in the human, can be modified through instrumental or operant conditioning.

With humans, Kamiya (1962, 1968), Bundzen (1965), Dewan (1966), Mulholland (1967), Hart (1968), and others have demonstrated that subjects can learn to control the appearance of their alpha rhythm in the EEG record through an auditory feedback loop keyed to the alpha, letting the subject know when he is having the desired pattern. Kamiya (1962, 1967, 1968) has shown that subjects can learn to control both the amplitude and the frequency of alpha, depending on how the feedback apparatus is set up. Bundzen has reviewed parallel work by himself and others in Russia. Dewan was able to learn to control the presence or absence [of alpha] in his own EEG record so well that he could use his EEG to send messages to a computer in Morse code. Hart has shown that subjects given both two-minute totals and immediate feedback for presence of alpha learn faster than those who just receive immediate feedback.

Mulholland (1967) has hypothesized that, in some subjects at least, alpha rhythm is related to position of the eye. He feels alpha increases when the eyes are moving to an extreme side or up position, particularly the latter. However, a study of 16 subjects by Fenwick (1966) found that alpha was not significantly related to the eye positions suggested by Mulholland, although a few of the subjects did show the hypothesized effect. Furthermore, Kamiya (1967) states that his subjects could learn to control alpha with their eyes in up or down position. Thus, although the Mulholland effect has not been ruled out for all subjects, it does not seem to be widespread. Mulholland himself (1967) recognizes that the hypothesized relationship is not characteristic of all subjects.

With animals, Olds and Olds (1961) and Olds (1963) were able to show that single cortical cells in lightly anesthetized rats could be brought to increase their rate of firing through instrumental conditioning. Electrical stimulation of the medial forebrain bundle, centered in the lateral hypothalamus, was used for positive reinforcement. Single unit responses could be reinforced when derived from micro-electrodes placed in numerous paleocortical areas (sensory and motor).

Sterman and Wyrwicka (1967) have shown that cats can learn to control two EEG patterns through instrumental conditioning with food as a reinforcer.

Carmona (1967) also demonstrated that cats can learn to increase the amount of voltage in their EEG; he used electrical stimulation of the lateral hypothalamus as reward. The findings were then replicated with rats that were paralyzed throughout the experimental periods with injections of curare. The rats were kept at a point where they showed no signs of breathing; artificial respiration was used to keep them alive. In spite of total paralysis of all voluntary skeletal muscles, the rats were able to learn to both increase and decrease the voltage in their EEG in order to receive reinforcing electrostimulation.

The study reported here was undertaken to again confirm that human subjects can learn to control the percent-time alpha in their EEG. In the previous work subjects were given training trials with instructions to increase, or decrease, percent-time alpha. In this study, the question was whether subjects could learn to control their alpha without such requirements throughout the session, using practice sessions in which the subjects were left free to learn control in any manner they chose before the timed trials to test their performance. Also, we wanted preliminary evidence concerning the subjective states associated with control of the tone.

METHOD

Apparatus

Equipment used in the system included a Grass Model 7 8-channel polygraph, with 3 P5 and 5 P1 preamplifiers, a Krohn-Hite Model 330 bandpass filter set at 8 and 13 Hz, an electronic counter, audio oscillator and amplifier, and a timer.

The signal from the subject was first amplified by the polygraph, then filtered, rectified, and integrated, and then amplified again in a separate channel of the polygraph, this time as a DC voltage. The resulting signal was used to drive the counter, the audio-feedback loop, and a signal marker on the recording paper of the polygraph via a Schmitt trigger and relay.* EEG activity of 8 to 13 Hz activated the trigger and relay, provided that the amplitude was sufficient to cause a pen deflection of at least two-thirds of a centimeter. Regular 35-microvolt alpha rhythms met these requirements and were adequate to create auditory feedback when using a sensitivity of 50 microvolts/cm. The auditory signal was a 520 Hz tone. Loudness was 50–56 db, re .0002 dynes/cm². Ambient noise level was 43 db, re .0002 dynes/cm².

---

*Diagrams of the apparatus and further description of its operation are available in Hawthorne House Research Memorandum No. 78 by the author at the Laboratory of Hypnosis Research [Stanford University], March 29, 1968, available upon request.

Subjects

Twenty-six young men and women of the local university community served as subjects. The age range was about 21 to 30.

Subjects were solicited with an offer of two dollars for their participation in an "experiment on learning how to control brain waves." Most subjects had participated in earlier experiments in hypnosis. All subjects who volunteered were used in the experiment, except one who had no discernible alpha in her EEG.

Procedure

Subjects were seated in a large reclining chair in a sound-deadened room adjacent to the recording room. Three Grass cup electrodes and one Grass ear electrode were used for each subject after careful cleaning of the appropriate areas with acetone. The electrodes were all placed on the right side (Liske, Hughes, & Stowe, 1967; Hill & Parr, 1963, p. 238), over the occipital, central, and frontal areas of the scalp, and on the right ear for ground. After the electrodes were placed on the subject, the experimental room was moderately darkened and the experimenter left the room to operate the polygraph. All further communication between subject and experimenter was via intercom.

Two EEG channels were recorded: occipital-frontal and occipital-central. Both channels were initially recorded at sensitivities of 50 microvolts/cm. If the pen deflections for alpha in the two channels were similar, the central-occipital channel was used to drive the feedback system. If alpha registration was distinctly superior in the frontal-occipital channel, it was used instead. It turned out that the central-occipital channel was used in 15 of the 28 cases, the frontal-occipital channel in the other 13. The sensitivity of each channel was adjusted if alpha amplitude was less than 35 microvolts until the deviation caused by alpha was approximately equal to two-thirds of a centimeter. This resulted in providing a minimum input for the rest of the system, and in clear records of alpha activity on both EEG channels.

In all cases we attempted to give subjects feedback for all rhythmic activity in the 8 to 13 Hz range that measured at least 20 microvolts. Because of this there was considerable variation in the percent of time that various subjects tended to hear the tone during their trials.

After the feedback system was connected, the subject was given approximately two minutes to get used to the tone coming on and off. He was then given a two-minute baseline trial, with his eyes closed and the instruction to remain still, and with the tone appearing with alpha. After this baseline test, subjects were instructed to try to figure out what made the tone come on and what made it go off. They were told to inform the experimenter when they felt that they had some insight into the problem, and he would then proceed to give them another two-minute trial during which they should try to keep the tone on as much as possible. The experimenter then allowed the subject up to 15 minutes to experiment with the tone.

This relaxed period of experimentation was given the subjects before they ran their test trials because it was thought that a period of relative relaxation would be helpful in bringing out the alpha state. If the subject did not request a trial after 15 minutes, the experimenter then initiated the first trial. After the trial for keeping the tone on, a second trial was run for keeping the tone off. Further trials were run only if time allowed. The procedure was devised to take one hour of time including the initial preparation of the subject and final removal of electrodes. The experimenter never directly suggested the use of any tactics, besides warning against vigorous movement of the eyes or body.

If more than one trial was given for either tone-on or tone-off, the last relevant trial of the session was always used for comparison with the baseline score, since by this time maximum learning should have occurred.

Ten subjects with a very high initial baseline for alpha with eyes closed were given a second baseline with eyes open prior to experiencing feedback. These subjects were then requested to develop some insight into control of the tone with eyes open, and then were given tone-on and tone-off trials with open eyes.

All subjects were given an open-ended post-session interview. They were asked to describe their methods of turning the tone off and on. This phase of the research was done to provide a basis for standardized scales that could be used with later subjects going through similar procedures. Every effort was made to gather and score the reports as objectively as possible. Subjects' reports were recorded verbatim and scored later as a group. It is recognized, of course, that such a procedure does not rule out all sources of inadvertent experimenter bias.

RESULTS

The results are sufficiently self-consistent to permit some generalizations both on the degree of control achieved over alpha and on the methods used by the subjects in keeping alpha on and off.

Control of Alpha

The degree of control over alpha can be quantified by comparing the number of seconds out of 120 that the tone indicative of alpha was sounding under the three conditions of (a) a relaxed baseline, (b) the last trial on which the attempt was being made to keep alpha on, and (c) the last trial on which the attempt was being made to keep alpha off. These results, by subject, are given in Tables 35.1 and 35.2. The following results are noteworthy.

1. Every subject (26 of 26) succeeded in having more alpha during the final "on" trial than during the final "off" trial.
2. For 21 of the 26 subjects, the amount of alpha in the "on" condition was increased over that in the relaxed baseline period; for 19 of the 26 subjects, the amount in the "off" condition was decreased below

TABLE 35.1
Effectiveness of Experience in Controlling EEG Alpha, Eyes Closed Condition

Subject	Number of seconds tone on in 120 seconds		
	Baseline	Last "on" trial	Last "off" trial
M.P.	46	79	10
K.K.	24	50	12
R.J.	27	41	16
R.S.	26	35	13
A.D.	22	33	11
J.F.	8	8	6
E.S.	69	68	14
S.C.	110	103	61
D.D.	79	70	60
T.G.	26	30	29
F.J.	10	50	19
M.K.	6	69	14
W.M.	14	42	20
P.I.	7	30	17
D.A.	65	99	91
L.F.	15	37	28
Mean (N = 16)	35	53	26
Standard deviation	30.6	26.3	23.7

TABLE 35.2

Effectiveness of Experience in Controlling EEG Alpha, Eyes Open Condition

Subject	Number of seconds tone on in 120 seconds		
	Baseline	Last "on" trial	Last "off" trial
J.H.	80	106	30
J.C.	91	111	0
J.P.	83	93	0
A.R.	49	84	2
L.B.	70	83	32
J.N.	50	95	47
N.N.	41	57	13
J.R.	20	41	17
D.P.	26	39	18
V.N.	60	58	0
Mean (N = 10)	57	77	16
Standard deviation	24.1	26.1	16.3

the baseline condition. Using the sign test, the tendency toward change in the "on" trial relative to baseline is significant at the .01 level and in the "off" trial relative to baseline at the .05 level.

3. An over-all picture of the degree of control in both directions (on and off) is better provided by examining the tendency of subjects to change in the appropriate direction from baseline for both the generation and the suppression trial. The eyes open and eyes closed results are analyzed separately. In the eyes closed condition, five of the 16 subjects showed appropriate change for *both* trials. Seven subjects showed increases for both trials, while four showed decreases for both. No subjects showed inappropriate change for both trials. Using the small sample version of the McNemar test for the significance of changes (Siegel, 1956, pp. 66–67), the tendency for appropriate change in the two trials as compared to baseline is significant at the .06 level for the eyes closed condition. For eyes open, nine of the 10 subjects showed the appropriate changes for both trials, one decreased in both, and no subjects increased on both or showed inappropriate change for both. Using the McNemar test again, the change in the two trials is significant at the .005 level. Thus, there is evidence of a tendency toward learning in both eye conditions.

4. The subjects who had high initial alpha, i.e., those who controlled their alpha with eyes open, achieved somewhat greater success than those who did so with their eyes closed. Whether subject differences or differences in eye condition are more important in determining this result cannot be determined by these data; also, the eyes open subjects had two more minutes of baseline, during which time they could hear the tone.

Sex of subject and whether or not the central-occipital or frontal-occipital comparison was used in the feedback system were both examined in relationship to degree of control achieved. There was no evidence that either of these factors had any influence on success at the task. In addition, five subjects who had particular success in learning control in the first session were given additional practice sessions until they had excellent control over alpha. They then were asked to increase and decrease alpha while their heart rate, blood pressure, breathing, and in some cases galvanic skin response were being monitored. No striking relationships were found between alpha and these other measures.

Post-Session Verbal Reports

When asked at the end to describe what they did in trying to keep the tone "on" or "off," the subjects described what they did in many ways. It was not very difficult, however, to code their remarks. The results of such coding are listed in Table 35.3.

The subjects found it difficult in many cases to state clearly what they were doing. As can be seen in the table, while the direction of differences is consistent, they do not fully concur on the most effective methods for doing the task. The only situation in which there is some unanimity of report is in eyes open, alpha "off." Here every subject indicated that attentiveness was especially helpful in keeping the tone off, and nine out of ten agreed that it was visual attentiveness that was most effective. The general agreement on how to effectively approach this situation may fit with the comparative ease of success found in the eyes open condition, and especially with the dramatic reductions that most of the subjects were able to show when requested to reduce alpha with eyes open. The reports are also in harmony with earlier research on EEG alpha and visual attentiveness (as reviewed by Walter and Yeager, 1956).

It is perhaps noteworthy, in light of Mulholland's findings, that there was no report of eye position as an effective means of alpha control.

The results, taken together with other studies done on the problem,

TABLE 35.3

How Subjects Reported They Controlled EEG Alpha; A Coding of Their
Spontaneous Remarks*

For keeping alpha on		For keeping alpha off	
PART I—SUBJECTS IN THE EYES CLOSED CONDITION			
Method	Number of reports (possible for each category: 16)	Method	Number of Reports (possible for each category: 16)
Relaxation	7	Being alert and vigilant	6
Awareness of inhalations and exhalations	4	Tension, agitation	4
Letting go	3	Attitude of "holding on"	2
Floating	3	Imagining seeing the room	2
Feeling of pleasure, security	3	No idea	4
Sensual warmth	3		
Not focusing	2		
Awareness "in back"	2		
No idea	4		
PART II—SUBJECTS IN THE EYES OPEN CONDITION			
Method	Number of reports (possible for each category: 10)	Method	Number of reports (possible for each category: 10)
Relaxation	5	Not trying hard	2
Not focusing (visual)	5	Letting mind wander	2
Letting go	3	Visual attentiveness	9

*Reports listed only if given by two or more; isolated remarks omitted. No more than one report per subject in each category, however subjects could contribute to more than one category.

indicate that human subjects, as well as cats and rats, can learn to control those high-amplitude, regular EEG rhythms normally associated with resting in an awake condition, in a short amount of time. Caution is clearly necessary in interpreting the verbal reports concerning control techniques however. Interviewing and scoring techniques were not as fully standardized as will be possible in a later study; more consistency of self-report was obtained in the eyes open condition, especially for alpha suppression; and intermediary processes involved in the process of attaining control are not as well understood as we hope they will be someday. However, the evidence at present is strongly toward associated differences in the verbal reports of mental activities for the various conditions. Because of this, the method holds promise for experimenters wishing to explore the relationship between physiological and behavioral measures. These two classes of observations, in studies of the kind here reported, should be useful in providing converging indicators of the hypothetical mental processes (Stoyva and Kamiya, 1968).

Fishes, asking what water was, went to a wise fish.
He told them that it was all around them, yet they still
thought that they were thirsty. (Shah, 1964, p. 401)

36.

Gravity and
Structural Integration

David S. Sobel

We are like fishes in a sea of gravity: because gravity is so ubiquitous, so constant, we tend to be unaware of its effect and its importance. Experimental psychology has established that the human nervous system screens out constancies, "habituates," and no longer responds to unchanging stimuli. However, whether man is aware of it or not, he is influenced by subtle geophysical forces such as light, negative air ions, geomagnetic forces, the seasonal changes, the cycles of the moon, and certainly the gravitational field of the Earth.

Following Newton's discovery of gravity as a physical law, the effect of gravity on man became an accepted area of study. However, as the mechanical consideration of man yielded to the physiochemical approach, gravity and man's relationship to it were not primary areas of concern. Today, gravity is being studied almost exclusively in terms of man's adaptation to the low gravitational forces involved in space travel.

My special appreciation to Ida Rolf, who introduced me to the concepts of Structural Integration and aided me in my own integration.

Printed by permission of the author.

Nevertheless, to understand man as a whole in his total environment, we should begin to consider the effect of the environmental force of gravity on man's internal environment and his well-being. I will begin to explore this relationship by discussing the system of Structural Integration, also known as "Rolfing."

Structural Integration, developed by Ida P. Rolf, is both a theory and a technique which deals with the alignment of an individual's body in the gravitational field. Structural Integration rests on two basic assumptions: first, bodies are material objects in a three-dimensional world and are subject to the laws of mechanics; second, bodies are plastic and capable of being changed. Man evolved in the gravitational field of the Earth and developed a structure, a muscular system, and a physiology to relate to this energy field. All movement, all behavior, takes place against a background of gravity. The physical body may be viewed as the materialization of an individual energy field existing within the greater energy field of the Earth. The Earth's field, experienced as gravity, interacts with the localized field, and the laws of mechanics describe the behavior of such a material body in the gravitational field. The results of this interaction may greatly influence the vitality and well-being of the man.

> "Certain considerations become self-evident if we return to a basic architectural awareness of the mechanics involved. First, we must recognize the overwhelming gravity component and the importance of its role in the life process of man. This force which unites us to the Earth is so much with us that we are of necessity unconscious of it. As a result we give a vague assent to the idea that gravity is important, that gravity is ubiquitous, that gravity tears a body down. But the critical evaluation of gravity as a supporting and uplifting force in the life of man has received little consideration . . . In this formulation it is the concept of *relation* that needs to be stressed. For man is an energy field, as the earth and its outward envelope of forces is an energy field. How well a man can exist and function depends on whether the field which is himself, his psychological and physical personality, is reinforced or disorganised by the field of gravity. Looked at from this angle gravity not only upholds a man, it feeds him.
>
> "In a real and material world, this supporting energy can be supplied only if certain conditions are met. Gravity as a force acts as if it operated through a vertical, straight line at right angles to the Earth. Therefore, to profit from this flow, a man must be so organized that he operates as though he existed symmetrically around such a gravity line." (Rolf, 1963, p. 12.)

Thus if a physical structure is not properly aligned in relationship to gravity, then this force may function entropically, disordering and breaking down a body. However, the structure may be organized so that gravity supports, reinforces, and upholds the body.

Another basic premise of Structural Integration is that bodies are plastic structures capable of dramatic change and reorganization. We might consider the body as a dynamic process phenomenon, constantly changing from the molecular and cellular level to the gross physical level. The potential for change of the physical body may be conceptualized as the result of the segmentation and the chemical nature of the connective tissue. The physical structure can be seen as an aggregate of structural segments, each corresponding to the major weight segments: the head, the thorax, the pelvis, and the legs. These major weight blocks may exist in a myriad of interrelationships, but only one arrangement yields a stable stacking: when the centers of gravity of the segments are aligned vertically. Deviations may be visualized as lateral or anterior-posterior displacements and as rotations of the segments. A deviation in any one segment will upset the balance of the entire system and set off a series of compensations. These compensatory adjustments result in strains which are transmitted throughout the body by the connective tissue. This fundamental structural interdependence makes it necessary to align the total structure, the whole man, not just work locally on an apparent distortion. I should add that the concept of segmental stacking is a dynamic one, which requires freedom to adjust continuously during movement. But what allows these segments to be shifted and reorganized in the work of Structural Integration? The relationships of the muscles, bones, organs, and segments are determined by the connective tissue, or fascia, which is the organ of shape and structure. Unfortunately, little is known about fascia, but it is postulated that the chemical and physical nature of the collagen fibers in fascia allow the elasticity and resilience of the connective tissue to be changed by application of mechanical energy (manipulation). This stretching process frees the segments and permits their relationships to be changed. Thus, the goal of Structural Integration: to realign the plastic structure of the body so that the energy field of gravity can act to support the energy field of man.

As one observes individual bodies, one notices a great variety of body types and characteristic patterns. Some reflect previous physical trauma; others dramatize chronic emotional sets; still others result from improper learning of muscular use. Physical accidents, common to all of us, often cause slight displacements, for instance, a knee injury. In response to such an injury, the growth of connective tissue is stimulated; fascial structures may become chronically shortened, and joint mobility may be restricted. Displaced muscles may be unable to return to normal position because of the fusion of fascial envelopes which surround the muscles. A knee accident can thus result in a permanent outward rotation of the leg, which necessitates a series of compensations, such as a rotation of the pelvis and spine, and perhaps a forward displacement of the head and neck to balance the structure.

Such structural aberrations can also have an emotional origin. Feldenkrais observed in his pioneering work entitled *The Body and Mature Behavior* (1949, p. 93) that "to every emotional state corresponds a personal conditioned pattern of muscular contraction without which it has no existence." Ida Rolf (1963, pp. 9–10) further comments:

> An individual experiencing temporary fear, grief, or anger all too often carries his body in an attitude which the world recognizes as the outward manifestation of that particular emotion. If he persists in this dramatization or consistently re-establishes it, thus forming what is ordinarily referred to as a 'habit pattern,' the muscular arrangement becomes set. Materially speaking, some muscles shorten and thicken, others are invaded by connective tissue, still others become immobilised by consolidation of the tissue involved. Once this has happened the physical attitude is invariable; it is involuntary; it can no longer be changed basically by taking thought, or even mental suggestion. Such setting of a physical response also establishes an emotional pattern. Since it is not possible to express free flow through the physical flesh, the subjective emotional tone becomes progressively more limited and tends to remain in a restricted and closely defined area. Now, what the individual feels is no longer an emotion, a single response to an immediate situation; henceforth he lives, moves and has his being in an attitude.

In man most muscular patterns are learned. A child must learn to control and direct his movements, and often in this process learns inefficient muscular patterns. For instance, when a child first stands, he may associate the success of standing with an imperfect muscular configuration, and thereby reinforce this pattern. Through repeated approval, these habitual ways of moving become the only ones which feel "right," whereas the most efficient patterns feel incorrect and strained. Feldenkrais says that the average body needs a reeducation of the kinesthetic sense. F. Matthias Alexander spoke of the unreliable sensory appreciation of what feels "right" or "wrong." Structural Integration works to change the structure, repattern the muscles, and thereby develop an efficient use of the body.

Relying on the segmentation and the plasticity of the body, the process of Structural Integration consists of aligning the total structure of the individual in the gravitational field. It is a manipulative technique in which mechanical energy is applied to release the connective tissue, reorganize the muscle relationships, and balance the body according to an anatomical norm. The work itself is a series of ten one-hour processings which sequentially unwind and free the muscles, decompensate previous compensations, and integrate the total structure. The body is treated as a whole, with emphasis on integrating and relating the segments, rather than on treating localized symptoms or complaints. It is understood, to give an example, that the pain in a lower back region cannot be relieved permanently without changing the relationship and support of the feet, the legs and the pelvis, and so on. The body is also viewed dynamically in terms of motion and continual adjusting in response to gravity. Normal alignment is approximated, and a dynamic process of change is initiated, allowing further spontaneous change and adjustment to take place as the body seeks to establish the structures of least strain.

But let's examine more closely this concept of structure. The meaning of structure lies in *relationship*: the dynamic relationship of segmented units creates the total energy pattern of that system. Within the structure of the human body, there are endless possibilities for the relationship in space of the body segments. There are also scores of theoretical models for the "ideal" or "normal" body structure, each emphasizing different principles, each based on different premises. Structural Integration has one such model of the anatomically normal structure which is fundamentally based on the alignment of the body with respect to the gravitational field. This alignment permits gravity to act through the segments to support the total structure. But what are the characteristics of this normal structure which Structural Integration approximates?

> Normal body alignment is for the purpose of attaining these results: (1) movement is performed with minimum work, that is, minimum expenditure of energy; (2) motion can be initiated in any direction with maximum ease and speed; (3) movement can start anywhere with minimum preliminary adjustment of the body; (4) structure is appropriate to the most adequate functional position of internal organs and nervous system; . . . and, (5) there is minimum 'wear and tear' on the parts of the body. (Schutz, 1967, p. 31.)

This structure is energetically the most efficient pattern and requires the minimum muscle tone to support and maintain the system. This distinguishes normal structure from good posture which can be maintained at considerable cost in muscle tension. Subjectively, proper alignment is experienced as "lighter," "more at ease," and effortless.

How does this efficient muscular patterning represent itself structurally? First of all, one would see a body capable of full, upright extension in which one could draw a straight line through the ear, the shoulder, the hip bone, the knee, and the external malleolus of the ankle. In order to achieve this alignment of the centers of gravity of the segments, one needs to approach a symmetric balance in the body. This balance in tone, length, and position applies to the left and right sides, the front and the back, the flexors and extensors, the intrinsic and extrinsic musculature, as well as the upper and lower parts of the body. When the agonist-antagonist muscle balance is established, the extensors will fully relax and extend as the flexors flex. The metaphor of a tent may be useful in understanding the importance of this balance. A tent is not actually upheld by the tent poles, but rather the left and right sides are stretched out and secured and thereby balance and uphold each other. The tent poles maintain the relationship between the two sides, much as the bones of the body maintain the balance and direction of tension in the musculature. The relationship of balanced structure in the human body is visually evident in the appearance of horizontal structure and functioning. For instance, the horizontalization of the pelvis, both frontally and laterally, is the keystone of a balanced structure. Horizontals also represent efficiency in movement. For the hinge joint in the knee, horizontal functioning means that motion is only in the direction of movement, which is straight forward and straight back. Rotations, the result of an imbalance, would show up as an inefficient lateral motion in the hinge joint. Another characteristic of the integrated body is the full extension of the spine, with the head moving upward and the lumbar vertebrae brought back. The result of this patterning and organization is seen as a lift, a gracefulness in movement. According to Rolf (1963, p. 10), "an integrated man might be defined as a person capable of free flow, free exchange, free movement (which we feel as resilience), both in physical body and in emotional expression."

I will now venture a look at the physical and psychological changes which result from Structural Integration. This area, in terms of empirical research, is virtually unexplored, although it is quite fertile and promising. Most of what can be said about results is based on theoretical considerations, subjective reports, and clinical observation. Nevertheless, in a field so young, speculation can be of some value if it stimulates interest and perhaps directs more energy into researching the importance of body structure and extending our knowledge of how to change that structure.

The basic premise of Structural Integration is that physical and psychological problems indicate the failure of a structure to integrate with its three-dimensional environment, with the gravitational field. Therefore, to enhance the functioning and well-being of an individual, work is done on changing his structure. Of course, structure and function are not really separable, as Bertalanffy (1952, p. 134) points out:

> Actually, this separation between a pre-established structure and processes occurring in this structure does not apply to the living organism. For the organism

is the expression of an everlasting, orderly process, though, on the other hand, this process is sustained by underlying structures and organized forms. What is described in morphology as organic forms and structures, is in reality a momentary cross-section through a spatio-temporal pattern. What are called structures are slow processes of long duration, functions are quick processes of short duration. If we say that a function, such as the contraction of a muscle, is performed by a structure, it means that a quick and short process wave is superimposed on a long-lasting and slowly running wave.

Furthermore, structure, itself a process, determines functioning, and functioning feeds back to create structure. Since structure is the materialization of the forces at work in a energy system, if one changes that organization, then one changes the functioning of the system. A partial parallel can be seen in physical chemistry, where the three-dimensional structure of a molecule is the major determinant of its chemical behavior and its properties. Any impurities in the substance can disorder a crystal structure and change its properties. Thus, on a chemical level, structure determines behavior. In Structural Integration, it is believed that by changing and aligning the physical structure the physiological functioning of the person can be improved.

In dealing with the physiology of man, one must consider both the internal and external environment. The forces of the external environment, such as light, sound, gravity, radiation, have an effect on the internal homeostatic environment. For instance, it has been observed that physical light can affect the pineal gland. Gravity is certainly one of the most powerful forces in the external environment, and it is suggested that by changing the relationship of the body in the gravitational field, the internal chemistry of the body can be altered. It is the goal of Structural Integration to potentiate the physiological functioning of the whole man, not just treat symptoms. Physiological malfunctioning is viewed as the functional level of a structural blockage of circulation, resulting in fluid stasis and the build up of toxins and wastes. By relieving the structural blockage, flow is enhanced and functioning improved. Once the body is aligned with gravity, it is then free to make its own corrective, homeostatic adjustments. Studies are now underway to explore changes in blood and urine chemistry, as well as shifts in the electroencephalographic (EEG) and electromyographic (EMG) recordings in response to ten hours of Structural Integration processing. Right now the field is open to speculation. By freeing the intercostal muscles of the chest wall and thereby changing the pattern and quality of respiration, one might expect changes in oxygenation of the blood and blood chemistry. Or by improving the circulation to the autonomic nervous system plexi, one might expect a wide range of changes in organ function and glandular secretion. Such potential alterations of the homeostatic environment could also have far-reaching effects on the emotional patterns and consciousness of man.

The whole area of the effects of body states on consciousness is one in which most of the data is experiential. One of the most important relationships to explore is that between mental processes and the motor system. The neurophysiologist Roger Sperry proposes (1964b, p. 410),

> An analysis of our current thinking will show that it tends to suffer generally from a failure to view mental activities in their proper relation, or even in any relation, to motor behavior . . . In order to achieve this insight, our present one-sided preoccupation with the sensory avenues to the study of mental processes will need to be supplemented by increased attention to the motor patterns, and especially to what can be inferred from these regarding the nature of the associative and sensory functions. In a machine, the output is usually more revealing of the internal organization than is the input. Similarly in the case of our thinking apparatus, an examination of its terminal operations and finished products may be more enlightening than any amount of analysis of the transport of raw materials into it.

Margaret Washburn (1916) proposed that all consciousness is directly related to movement. Sperry maintains that the primary function of the brain is to produce patterns of motor output and that consciousness consists of an implicit preparation-to-respond to a stimulus. It is this motor output, the patterns of muscular activity, which is altered in Structural Integration, and the effect of this on perception and consciousness has not yet been tested.

In addition to the importance of motor output, one should also note that "the bulk of stimuli arriving at the nervous system is from muscular activity constantly affected by gravity" and that all perception and sensation takes place on a background of muscular activity (Feldenkrais, 1949, p. 36). Subjective reports indicate an increased sensitivity and awareness of the internal and external environment after Structural Integration. Some light may be shed on these reports by considering the Weber-Fechner Law.

> The general principle at work is as follows. All sensations are related to the stimuli producing them in a fixed manner. For example, if you hold a 20-lb. weight in your hand and you shut your eyes, and if, noiselessly, a certain weight were added on to the weight you already carry, you will not become aware of it unless the additional weight is big enough to produce the least detectable difference in sensation. . . . In simple words, the Weber-Fechner law means that the smaller the weight you are holding, the smaller is the added or subtracted portion that you will be able to notice . . . All sensations in which muscular activity is involved are largely dependent on the smallest amount of tonus persistent in the musculature. When the tonus is the smallest possible, you sense the finest increase in effort.

> Easy and smooth action is obtained when the aim is achieved by the smallest amount of exertion, which, in turn, is obtained with the minimum tonus present. The smaller the stimulus present, the smaller is the change that we perceive, or are capable of detecting . . . People with a fine kinaesthetic sense tend to a low tonic contraction, and are not satisfied until they find the way of doing which involves the smallest amount of exertion; also, the limit to which the unnecessary effort is eliminated is closer to the ideal minimum.   (Feldenkrais, 1949, p. 108–109)

Also it has been demonstrated in rats that when the muscle activity is inhibited by curare, learning in the autonomic nervous system takes place more easily. Perhaps turning down the extraneous background muscle noise and tension aids in learning and perceiving. Lower muscle tension is also a physiological characteristic of the "receptive mode of consciousness" described by Deikman as an increase in perceptive and sensory appreciation at the expense of abstraction and as a lessening of the self-others dichotomy.

The process of Structural Integration decreases wasteful muscle tension in the body and reeducates the kinaesthetic sense. By decompensating previous compensations in the body, it may perhaps bring a person more into the here and now, free from the inefficient muscle patterns and emotional sets conditioned in the past.

Another important aspect of Structural Integration is the belief that the body should function without conscious control; once a body is properly organized structurally, the natural rhythms and self-regulating mechanisms will operate so as to make conscious control undesirable. Feldenkrais (1949, p. 94) also shares this perspective.

> Conscious control, when properly directed, often improves certain details here and there, but intellect is no substitute for vitality . . . The conscious control is paramount in integrating all the functions fitting the immediate circumstances. The internal mechanisms enabling him to succeed, should be left to the self-regulating nervous co-ordination. At least in the present state of our knowledge of the nervous system, we can do no better than follow the best adjusted and mature specimens, and they do not abuse the conscious control.

Rolf maintains that the physical body *is* the personality, not just its expression. Therefore if the physical structure is integrated, then the psyche is also integrated. One of the most profound experiences in Structural Integration is the realization of the literalness of body metaphors. Phrases like "feet on the ground," "head on straight," "loosening of attachments," or "inspiration" take on a physical and psychological reality. The premise of the relationship between structure and consciousness finds resonance, if not evidence, in many areas outside of Structural Integration.

Deikman (in selection 29 here) postulates that consciousness is the psychological manifestation of organization, while structure is the biological manifestation of organization. This formulation presents physical structure and consciousness as complementary aspects of organization. Thus, structure and consciousness may be viewed as levels of manifestation of an organizing principle. A change on the physical or structural level will manifest in some way as a change on the psychological level, and vice versa.

This concept of form influencing consciousness appears in many disciplines. In physical chemistry the structure of a substance determines its properties, its interaction. "Structure, here, means relationship in space. And structure (relationship in space) on another plane, in another dimension, is behavior" (Rolf, 1963, p. 7). It may be that the structure and organization specify what energies can be received and used by a system. Benjamin Lee Whorf, the brilliant psycholinguist, compares the construction of a radio receiver with the structuring and patterning of the nervous system by mantram, specialized sounds repeated in meditation exercises (Carroll, 1956, pp. 249-250):

> The mantram becomes a manifold of conscious patterns, contrived to assist the consciousness into the noumenal pattern world—whereupon it is 'in the driver's seat.' It can then *set* the human organism to transmit, control, and amplify a thousandfold forces which that organism normally transmits only at unobservably low intensities.
>
> Somewhat analogously, the mathematical formula that enables a physicist to adjust some coils of wire, tinfoil plates, diaphragms, and other quite inert and innocent gadgets into a configuration by which they can project music to a far country puts the physicist's consciousness on a level strange to the untrained man, and makes feasible an adjustment of matter to a very strategic configuration, one which makes possible an unusual manifestation of force. . . . The mantric formula language is specialized in a different way, in order to make available a different type of force manifestation, by repatterning states in the nervous system and glands—or again rather in the subtle 'electronic' or 'etheric' forces in and around those physical bodies. Those parts of the organism, until such strategic patterning has been effected, are merely 'innocent gadgets,' as incapable of dynamic power as loose magnets and loose wires, but *in the proper pattern* they are something else again—not to be understood from the properties of the unpatterned parts, and able to amplify and activate latent forces.

It is conceivable that Structural Integration works in a similar manner to repattern and reorganize the structure to make it more sensitive and receptive to subtle energies. Form and consciousness have long been related in architecture; note the inspiring, uplifting influence of high Gothic cathedrals or the curious effect of the shape of the pyramids. It has been reported that the shape of the pyramid serves to somehow focus energy which can affect biological processes as well as crystal structure (Ostrander and Schroeder, 1970). Within the system of Hatha Yoga, specific mudras (gestures) and asanas (postures) are used to induce different states of consciousness. Here again we encounter the complementarity of structure and consciousness. Any process which organizes and patterns the nervous system and the body, whether it be mantram, mandalas, rhythmic breathing exercises, stroboscopes, dervish dancing, yogic postures, or Structural Integration, is likely to affect the consciousness of man. Ida Rolf (1963, p. 19) comments:

> Meanwhile, can we, or need we, measure psychic being? Many students have felt that its most realistic index lies in the sensitivity of the individual, his awareness of the forces surrounding him. They feel that the secret of 'intuition' lies in the ability to perceive that which is too fine for the average perception. On such a premise, it would seem unlikely that random, makeshift instruments can offer adequate expression of an evolving psychic force. Rather it would seem logical that a more potent energy would be unable to function until finer, more perceptive instruments are available, both as tools and as housing. . . . Ancient mystery schools apparently understood this relation. There seems to be evidence that among their teachers were men expert in refining the body for the express purpose of furthering individual psychic progression. In some areas remnants of this still survive, witness the branch of Yoga sometimes misnamed 'Hatha.' Some sort of evocation, a 'calling out' of the forces of the physical body, seems to be a first step in the consistent, conscious effort toward individual kinetic progression. A technique fostering the expansion of the individual, but starting with the material which is peculiarly his at any given point, his body, as it is at that moment in time, seems to be a reasonable point of departure, and a logical progression.

There is also an evolutionary perspective to Structural Integration. Man is evolving from four-legged to a fully upright position. Similarly each individual is born in the position of fetal flexion and the maturing process involves fully extending the spine to reach the upright structure. The Taoist philosophy conceives of man with his feet grounded in the earth, with his head reaching upward for the heavens, in harmony with his environment, and aligned with the energies of the cosmos.

Thus Structural Integration works to align man with the energy field of the earth in order to increase man's well-being and to extend his potential and sensitivity.

37.

Preliminary Consideration of the Biological Significance of Air Ions

A. P. Krueger

The reactions between water, land, and air during the long, slow physical evolution of our planet have greatly affected the course of biological evolution. To a very considerable extent this interplay is responsible for the emergence of man—a singular product of evolution—and man, in an extremely brief span of time, through his genius for blindly manipulating natural resources, has attained the unique capacity to alter his total environment. While we have begun to express serious concern for the grim consequences of our role as spoilers in disturbing ecological balances in general, our interest is most avidly focused upon those facets of man-engendered pollution which pose the most immediate and direct danger to us.

Reprinted by permission from *Scientia*, 104 (Sept.-Oct. 1969), 1–17.

We live in an ocean of air, and each of us is inexorably required to breathe in at least 10,000 liters of air every 24 hours, just to maintain life in our bodies. Since we are utterly dependent upon the physical and chemical properties of this air, it isn't surprising that we now are deeply immersed in exploring all atmospheric parameters. Characteristically, most of our efforts are devoted to the detection and control of those toxic particulates and gases contributed to the ambient air by industry and by the multitude of anthropocentric activities which require the combustion of fuels. Their threat to life is pressing, and it is obvious that measures for their abatement must be developed in the immediate future. Other, more subtle atmospheric changes are in progress which, because they are less conspicuous, tend to be put aside for future consideration. Among these, one would have to list those phenomena involving small air ions.

Very shortly after the existence of atmospheric electricity was demonstrated by Franklin and by d'Alibard in [1752], several natural philosophers ascribed to it a variety of biological effects. For example, Father Giambattista Beccaria in 1775 reported that "it appears manifest that nature makes extensive use of the atmospheric electricity for promoting vegetation." In this he was supported by l'Abbé Nollet (1752) and l'Abbé Bertholon (1783). L'Abbé Bertholon (1780) in addition concluded that the course of various diseases of man was influenced by atmospheric electricity. In 1899, Elster and Geitel proved that atmospheric electricity depends upon the existence of gaseous ions in the air. It then became possible to develop generators for producing air ions and equipment for determining their numbers in the air. Using these technical aids, a vast amount of experimentation was undertaken to define the physical and biological properties of air ions.

Within a short time it was shown that small air ion formation begins when sufficient energy acts on a gaseous molecule to displace an electron. The freed electron promptly attaches to an adjacent molecule which becomes a negative molecular ion, while the original molecule, now carrying a positive charge, becomes a positive molecular ion. . . .

Certain properties of small air ions are pertinent to this discussion. They readily unite: (1) with condensation nuclei to form large or Langevin ions, and (2) with most classes of air pollutants. In both cases the biological activity of the small air ions is lost. This is true also of the combination that occurs between small air ions of opposite charge. Further, ions of like charge (unipolar ions) repel one another and tend to flow to enclosing surfaces where their ionic nature dissipates. Since they are small and carry a charge, they are deflected by electrical fields.

All of these characteristics make it difficult to maintain high ion concentrations during a biological experiment; in practical terms, this means a maximum of 5×10^5 [to] 1×10^6 ions/cm^3.

While the nature of air ions was under investigation by the physicists, vigorous attempts were being made by life scientists to determine their biological effects. Although the amount of work accomplished by the biologists is a tribute to their industry, it must be admitted that the results are less than definitive. Several factors serve to cloak the whole field in an aura of ambiguity. Often experiments were performed with corona discharges as ion sources, neglecting the ozone and oxides of nitrogen inevitably produced along with the ions. Ion densities, temperature and relative humidity were not monitored. Experimental subjects were not grounded; their external surfaces developed high electrostatic charges and in consequence, repelled ions. As a rule, the air was not purified, and combination of ions with air pollutants led to widely fluctuating ion densities. Clinicians, assessing the value of air ions as a therapeutic modality, were perhaps the worst offenders. They usually committed all or some of the errors listed above, and in addition neglected to utilize the double-blind technique for ion administration.

In view of these difficulties, it isn't to be wondered at that most of the data are not adequate for establishing convincing proof that air ions either affect a particular physiological process or are useful in treating a given disease. Nevertheless, there is a rich vein of circumstantial evidence running through the air-ion literature; certainly sufficient to warrant continued interest in the field and to suggest that much of the older work could bear repetition, taking appropriate precautions to avoid experimental pitfalls.

In addition to these elements of uncertainty in experimental procedures, the evaluation of air ions as biologically active agents has been hampered by the widely cultivated belief that the idea is theoretically absurd. There seems to be something about the term, "ion," that provokes incredulity—witness the years that elapsed before universal recognition was accorded the magnificent concept of ions in solution, elaborated by Faraday and Arrhenius. In their case the major obstacle to acceptance was the requirement of the theory that large differences exist in the properties of charged molecules (ions) and uncharged molecules. In the case of air ions there is no disagreement about the disparate physical nature of air ions and nonionized gaseous molecules, but there is considerable reluctance to grant that this diversity is of biological significance.

At any rate, the essence of the argument is this. The maximal ion density one can attain in a closed atmosphere is approximately 1×10^6 ions/cm³ of air. Air contains 2.7×10^{19} nonionized molecules/cm³, so that the ratio of small ions to nonionized molecules is $1:27$ trillion. For the reasons already mentioned above, ions have a very brief life span, and under the conditions ordinarily prevailing, attainable ion densities usually are considerably less than 1×10^6 ions/cm³, making the final dilution in nonionized air greater by one or two orders of magnitude. From this unquestioned fact, the dubious conclusion has been drawn that the very sparseness of air ions places them beyond the range of biological effectiveness. We have pointed out elsewhere that the merit of this inference is more specious than real, since many biological systems respond to extremely minute chemical and physical stimuli. Two examples suffice to bear out this contention: first, the human eye can detect a flash of light when a single active quantum reaches the retina (Pirenne, 1958); and second, the male silkworm reacts to as few as 2600 molecules of the female's sex-attractant pheromone in air containing a concentration of < 200 molecules/cm³ (Bassert and Wilson, 1963).

It is evident then that progress in the field of research devoted to the detection of air-ion effects on living forms has been retarded both by the very real difficulties attending the performance of meaningful experiments, and by the categorical rejection of the whole idea as a matter of principle on the part of many competent scientists. The technical obstacles comprise the major reason that we now are faced with an enormous accumulation of data of very uneven quality. The matter of rejection is not so vital, although it is disconcerting at times to find that some of our peers classify the subject with the occult arts.

On the bright side of the picture is the fact that several investigators have conducted physiological experiments with air ions under rigorously controlled test conditions and have demonstrated measurable responses clearly related to the ion content of the air. Bachman and his colleagues (1966) have accomplished this in their studies of various physiological parameters in the rat. In our own laboratories we have worked for six years on the changes in blood level of 5-hydroxytryptamine (serotonin-5HT) in the mouse during exposure to negative and positive air ions (Krueger, Andriese, and Kotaka, 1968). We selected 5HT as a biological indicator because it is a powerful neurohormone of acknowledged importance, and because elegant spectrofluorometric micro-methods for its assay have been developed by Udenfriend et al. (1955). Our experimental procedures, described here in order to answer the question of air-ion causality, included the following essential elements. (1) Mice of uniform age were acclimatized in cylindrical plexiglas chambers. The design of the exposure units was based on a long series of experiments and insured satisfactory, monitored control of the environment. The units were positioned in cubicles provided with air which had been purified by passage through an electrostatic precipitator, an activated carbon filter, and an absolute filter. An air conditioner downstream from the purifying train kept the cubicles at constant temperature, while humidifiers in the cubicles maintained a constant relative humidity. (2) The mice were held at ground potential in an air mass moving at selected rates varying from 17 to 55 ft/minute. Vacuum pans for collecting excreta were positioned at the bottom of the cylinders and served the purpose of minimizing back-diffusion of water vapor or ammonia. Prior to and after acclimitization, blood levels of 5HT were determined and a population was selected having an acceptably uniform mean 5 HT level with a minimal variance. The mice were exposed in groups of 10 to a chamber, an adequate number for statistical analysis of the data, and they were provided with a suitable diet and water supply. While each experiment served as its own control, through the initial 5HT level of the test population, we also included additional control groups exposed to nonionized air and maintained under the same conditions with and without identical electrical fields. (3) Tritium-powered ion generators were mounted at the top of the exposure chambers and were equipped with a rectifying circuit operating at 90–900 volts for selection of ion charge. The tritium, contained in sealed foils, is a low-energy β emitter with a range of <2 cm, so direct radiation effects do not enter into the experiments. Each generator produced about 1×10^9 ions/second. The generators did not contribute detectable quantities of ozone or other pollutants to the air stream.

With this equipment and these procedures, we undertook a thorough study of the effects of unipolar air of either charge on the blood level of 5 HT in mice. When the air ion densities were between 4 [and] 5×10^5 negative ions/cm^3, blood 5 HT decreased. With equal concentrations of positive ions, blood 5 HT rose. These reactions were readily reproducible and were statistically significant at the 95 per cent confidence level. . . .

Although these experiments are not yet complete, the results obtained so far are compatible with physical theory. Thus there are systems, such as the one just described, in which the conclusion that specific physiological reactions are due to small air ions, is logical and is consistent with modern concepts of ion structure. Many other studies have been conducted without imposing such detailed control of the micro-environment. While on careful inspection most of them will not meet the requirement that air-ion concentration be the only variable to which the experimental subject is exposed, they supply strong inferential evidence that air ions are biologically active. Both categories of experiments have yielded data amenable to a rudimentary classification which, together with examples, is given below.

1. *Charge-related effects.* These are exemplified by three reactions.
   a. The 5HT phenomenon described above.
   b. Worden's experiments (1961) at the cellular level, in which he demonstrated that Girardi's human heart cells, exposed for 14 days to unipolar ionized atmospheres and then transplanted into nonionized atmospheres for an additional 14 days, showed adversely affected growth characteristics and rate of proliferation with positively ionized air; growth was normal with negatively ionized air. Using Earle's strain of L. mouse fibroblasts MCTC clone 929, he obtained statistically significant evidence that negative ions increase and positive ions decrease the rate of proliferation. Furthermore when the fibroblasts were removed to a nonionized atmosphere, the cells previously exposed to negative ions continued to divide at an increased rate, while the cells treated with positive ions recovered slowly and eventually attained the normal rate of growth.
   c. Guillerm *et al.* (1967) observed the effects of air ions on the terminal tidal air of humans and found that negative ions increased the partial pressure of oxygen and decreased the partial pressure of carbon dioxide; positive ions had the reverse effect.

2. *Reactions occurring only during exposure to positive ions.* In Edwards' work (1960), unipolar positively ionized air augmented the flight activity of the blowfly. Dr. H. Levine and I (1967) found that treatment with positive ions shortened the time of onset and increased the mortality rate in coccidioidomycosis. In both instances negative ions produced no observable effect.

3. *Stimulation of biological processes by ions of either charge.* When higher plants were grown in chemically defined substrates in the presence of high concentrations of positive or negative air ions, growth was regularly accelerated, the differences between treated and untreated plants at 20–30 days being of the order of 50–75 per cent (Krueger, Kotaka, and Andriese, 1963).

   With the cooperation of our Japanese colleagues, we were able to conduct a series of experiments at Ibaraki University on the effects of air ions on the silkworm. Ions of either charge accelerated the germination of silkworm eggs and markedly stimulated the rate of growth of the developing larvae (Krueger *et al.*, 1966).

4. *Random effects produced by ions of either charge.* Knoll and his coworkers (1964) conducted extensive studies on the effects of air ions on simple visual reaction time in humans. They found that the elapsed time was randomly increased or decreased by exposure to positive or negative ions.

5. *Stimulation of a biological process by increasing concentrations of ions of one charge or decreasing concentrations of ions of opposite charge.* Haine *et al.* (1964) observed that a significant increase in the molting of aphids is brought about by either a sharp drop in positive air ion concentration or an abrupt increase in negative ion concentration.

If it is granted that abnormally high concentrations of air ions elicit physiological changes, the question naturally arises as to what will happen when ion densities are reduced to the lowest possible level. Ion depletion can be accomplished by a number of means but no matter how efficient the procedure, some ion pairs always will be generated in the test chamber by cosmic rays. The best we have been able to do in this regard is to maintain the total ion count at ca. 60 ions/cm^3 of air. Under these conditions, barley seedlings grown in a chemically defined medium for 30 days displayed a statistically significant reduction in integral elongation, fresh weight, and dry weight (Krueger, Kotaka, and Andriese, 1965). There was no observable interference with chlorophyll production, but the plants had very soft leaves and lacked normal rigidity. These findings are consonant with the results obtained by several investigators who grew plants in Faraday cages and noted a striking reduction in growth. The general function of the Faraday cage is to conduct atmospheric electricity to earth and accordingly the ion content of the ambient air is reduced.

Physicians and environmental engineers have long suspected that the inimical effects of "dead air" in crowded rooms are due to ion depletion. Kimura and others (1939) actually measured the ion densities under these conditions and found that discomfort occurred when light air-ion concentrations were drastically reduced, even though temperature, relative humidity, and carbon-dioxide levels were within ranges ordinarily considered suitable for human comfort. When normal ion densities were restored by the use of ion generators, the symptoms were promptly relieved. Tchijevsky (1933), the eminent Russian pioneer in air ion research, together with his confreres, tried to maintain groups of small animals in air that was nearly ion-free. The animals sickened and died. We have in progress a series of similar experiments with mice. Our most interesting results to date related to two groups of 10 mice each which have been observed nearly one year under the following conditions: Group 1 lives in air containing <80 ions/cm^3. This deionized air from Chamber No. 1 passes over a tritium-powered ion generator and is reconstituted to contain ca. 1200 positive ions and 1000 negative ions/cm^3; it then enters Chamber No. 2. The rate of air flow is so large that the carbon dioxide concentration in each chamber is essentially identical. The two groups of animals therefore live in precisely the same air except for the ion content. To date, the only observable difference is that the mice in Group No. 1 have not grown as fast as those in Group No. 2. The average body weight at 10 months in Group 1 is 45.8 grams, compared with 52.2 grams in Group 2. The animals in both chambers have shown no signs of illness or discomfort. On the first anniversary date, we plan to determine the blood and brain 5 HT levels, the organ weights, and to do complete blood counts and histopathological studies. In similar experiments conducted for periods of 1 to 3 months, no consistent or significant pathological changes developed among ion-deprived mice.

Perhaps it is redundant to state again that an objective analysis of experiments relating air ions to living forms reveals a distressing lack of solid information, but it is nevertheless a necessary admission if we are to obtain a valid picture of the present status of the subject. Although the essential nature of small air ions as they exist in the earth's atmosphere is now fairly well defined, we know very little about such areas as:

1. What happens when air ions make contact with the tissues of the test organism. Our ignorance extends from the interface between the atmosphere and the cell wall to include the cellular organelles, their component enzyme systems, and almost all the tissues and organs of living forms.

2. What dosages of air ions are required to elicit biological responses. This is a practical point, for if extremely high ion densities are demanded, there is little likelihood of air ions playing a significant role in nature and the whole topic becomes academic, or at best is limited to therapeutic applications. If, on the other hand, biological effects are associated with such displacements of ion densities or charge ratios as are known to occur in the troposphere, or even with the relatively small shifts in ion concentration that can be effected by ion depletion or artificial ionization in ordinary living and working quarters, the subject acquires great interest and importance. Here again, information is scanty. . . .

Turning next to the matter of ion dosage, we are confronted with several interesting phenomena. The work done in our laboratories is subject to the serious limitation that for the most part we have employed very high ion dosages (3 to 5 $\times$ 10^5 positive or negative ions/cm^3). Because we were looking for any evidence of air-ion-induced physiological changes in bacteria, protozoa, higher plants, insects, and animals, we felt that this procedure was justified, even though it entailed ion concentrations 300–500 (l.c.) those found in nature. In the course of our work on higher plants, we observed that the growth stimulation appearing during exposure to positively or negatively ionized air paralleled ion density and was accompanied by a proportional change in the flow of current from plant to ground. Unfortunately we have not had an opportunity to extend these experiments to lower ranges of ion concentrations. This has been done, however, by Knoll and his collaborators in their experiments on the effects of ions on simple visual reaction time in humans (1964). Ion densities of only 2 $\times$ 10^3 ions/cm^3 produced a remarkable decrease in reaction time; the deviation from normal values compared favorably with that obtained when the dosage of ions was 1 $\times$ 10^6 ions/cm^3. Also, Deleanu and his colleagues (Cupcea, Deleanu, and Frits, 1959) found that relatively small ion dosages, e.g., 5 [to] 15 $\times$ 10^3/cm^3 of air, effectively influenced the development of gastric ulcers in the starving rat.

A somewhat different type of dosage relationship has been uncovered by Bachman's group at Syracuse University (1966). They studied the influence of air ions on the spontaneous activity of rats and noted a curious zonal response. That is, with increasing concentrations of negative ions, activity declined to a minimum at ca. 15 $\times$ 10^4 ions/cm^3. Beyond this point a gradual rise in activity occurred, reaching a peak well above control values at ca. 75 $\times$ 10^4 ions/cm^3. Activity then gradually dropped in higher ranges of ion concentration. Increasing concentrations of positive ions up to ca. 2 $\times$ 10^4 ions/cm^3 elicited a sharp drop in activity. As ion dosage was raised beyond this level, activity slowly rose until finally at very high ion densities it returned to normal.

It can be deduced from the foregoing section that the air ion densities normally found in the ambient atmosphere possibly may suffice for detectable physiological changes. This has been suspected since the eighteenth century, when Nollet, Beccaria and Bertholon speculated about the biological influence of fair-weather atmospheric electricity. With the passage of time, the suspicion has grown into a formidable folklore, and ultimately has been linked with another legend common to nearly every country in the world. The latter tradition has to do with the winds of ill-repute, e.g., the Foehn, Sirocco, Zonda, Santa Ana, Khamsin, and Mistral. Wherever they prevail, their victims attribute to them the ability to induce respiratory distress of various sorts, nervousness, headache, and a multitude of other ills. So malign is their influence that when they blow, judges deal leniently with crimes of passion, surgeons postpone elective surgery, and teachers expect more than the usual fractiousness from their students. Czermak (1901) was the first to postulate a positive correlation between the adverse effects of these winds and the presence of excessive concentrations of positive ions in the air.

Meteorological evidence provides a modicum of support for this correlation, in that high concentrations of positive ions actually have been detected accompanying the winds. Recently, Robinson and Dirnfeld (1963) studied the Khamsin, a weather complex afflicting the Near East and characterized by a persistent wind, a rapid rise in temperature, and a fall in relative humidity. They measured solar radiation, temperature, relative humidity, wind velocity and direction, and the electrical state of the atmosphere before, during, and after the Khamsin and found that the ratio of positive ion concentration to negative ion concentration, normally about 830:700, shifted to approximately 1510:1140, ten to twelve hours before their meteorological instruments recorded the typical Khamsin features. This coincided with the onset of nervous and physical symptoms among weather-sensitive people. They concluded that the early change in air-ion values is responsible for the discomfort associated with the Khamsin.

A great deal of work has been done in France, Germany, Italy, and the U.S.S.R. on the ionic environment of spas, particularly those situated near waterfalls. The consensus seems to be that the air in many such locales, for a variety of reasons, contains a high concentration of small air ions with the ratio of negative to positive ions being considerably greater than normal. Bioclimatologists are inclined to attribute to this fact some of the "vis mediatrix" of these resorts. This is an attractive hypothesis, but one that is difficult to prove, since many curative modalities are brought to bear on the patient simultaneously. At any rate, espousal of air ions in this capacity meets the requirement of that ancient and admirable medical admonition, "primum non nocere" ["first, do no harm"].

At this point, a penultimate statement seems in order; viz., this brief account of the biological effects of air ions is very incomplete—several aspects of the subject have not been mentioned at all, nor has it been possible to pay tribute to the individual investigators who are actively working in this area. Finally, I am certain that the reader will have asked the questions: "Do air-ion-induced biological phenomena occur outside the laboratory? And if so, is there reason to believe that they bear a meaningful relationship to life processes and the art of living?" The answer to both questions, I think, is a qualified and speculative affirmative. We now can assert with assurance that air ions elicit biological responses under well-controlled conditions, and in addition there is a plethora of presumptive evidence suggesting their implication in biological reactions studied under a great variety of imperfectly controlled conditions.

The latter group includes situations in nature not yet upset by the incursion of human activities, such as the large-scale weather-linked changes in air-ion concentrations and charge ratios, as well as others already detrimentally affected by man. The ratio between these categories is constantly shifting because the more the population grows, the more widespread air pollution becomes and the further we are removed from those conditions which permit natural air-ion balance to prevail. The fundamental reaction is disarmingly simple: man $\longrightarrow$ atmospheric pollutants; atmospheric pollutants $+$ small air ions $\longrightarrow$ air-ion depletion.

That this progression has attained significant magnitude is evidenced by the fact that small air-ion levels far at sea—normally very constant— are becoming appreciably lower with time, as air pollutants drift out from land.

Thus while very few of our activities add small ions to the air, much of what we do culminates in ion loss. The question then amounts to this: Will the smogs, hazes and invisible pollutants we generate with a lavish hand so reduce the small-ion content of the atmosphere that plants, animals, and man must suffer harmful consequences? Although the early results of ion depletion very likely will be unimpressive compared to the immediate and dramatic action of known toxic components of polluted air, this alone should furnish little solace. We have every reason to be aware from past experience that adverse effects may follow continued exposure to a small amount of a minor irritant (e.g., organic solvents) or the long-term deprivation of an essential metabolic requirement (e.g., trace elements or vitamins). The ultimate dimensions of biological changes produced by air-ion loss conceivably may prove to be as disenchanting as some revealed by Rachel Carson in *The Silent Spring*.

So much for the potential role of an air-ion-depleted environment in man's future. There remains the question what portents exist for the actual use of air ions in that unpromising tomorrow. Certainly the available data provide an infirm base from which to prognosticate, but if pressed I would hazard a guess that small air ions will be used in the following applications.

1. *The control of the individual's microenvironment in living and working quarters.*

Eventually air-ion standards for comfort will be established, just as we now have set limits for temperature, relative humidity, air turnover, etc. The goal then will be to maintain air-ion concentrations and ratios at levels approximating those existing in nature; this should be especially valuable in ensuring an optimal environment for personnel inhabiting space vehicles, submersibles, and deep submergence chambers for long periods of time. Difficulties can be anticipated from air-ion loss due to reactions with pollutants such as tobacco smoke, but there is no reason to doubt the ability of the environmental engineers to mount effective countermeasures, e.g., laminar airflow.

2. *The treatment of disease.* Air ions already are used as therapeutic agents in allergic conditions of the respiratory tract, burns, aphthous stomatitis, and gastric ulcer, but their use is limited. Some applications are not without rationale. For example, burned patients present increased levels of 5HT in damaged tissues and in the blood. We have shown that inhalation of negative ions increases the rate of conversion of 5HT to 5-hydroxyindoleacetic acid (a physiologically inactive metabolite), thus decreasing tissue and blood concentrations of 5HT. Since 5HT causes pain under some circumstances, perhaps this reaction has something to do with the relief of pain reportedly experienced by patients treated with negative ions (David, Minehart, and Kornbluth, 1960). Another instance of laboratory observations coinciding with clinical usage is to be found in our work at the University of California, and that of Palti, Denour, and Abramov (1966) at Hadassah Medical School in Jerusalem. Smith and I (1959) noted that the inhalation of positively ionized air by small animals contracted the smooth muscle of the tracheo-bronchial tree and decreased the operational efficiency of the mucus escalator; negative ions had the opposite effect. Palti *et al.* produced tachypnea and bronchospasm in infants by exposing them to positively ionized air. Negatively ionized air reduced the tachypnea and relieved bronchospasm. They were able to apply negative air-ion treatment for spastic bronchitis with excellent results. As the essential physical procedures for handling air ions become better known and as more is learned about the basic biological properties of air ions, their clinical applications should become more acceptable and numerous.

Recently, Dr. A. P. Wehner of the Battelle Institute reported in *Scientia* (1968) on a closely related modality: electro-aerosols. His excellent work and that of others in this field provide convincing evidence that the acquisition of multiple electrical charges by aerosol droplets materially extends the borders of aerosol therapy.

3. *The promotion of agricultural production.* To examine this subject with a clairvoyant eye requires the retrieval of a bit of generally forgotten history. Experiments by Blackman *et al.* (1924) dating back to the post World War I period in Britain, involved extensive tests of the effects of electrical discharges on plant growth. The early work dealt with pot cultures of wheat, barley, and maize exposed to overhead wire networks carrying currents of ca. 1×10^{-11} amp/plant at 16,000 volts. Dry-weight yields were increased from 18 to 27 per cent. In larger-scale experiments with field crops of oats, wheat, and barley, thin wires were strung seven feet above the soil with an applied voltage of 40,000 to 80,000 volts and a current of 0.5 to 1 milliamperes/acre. Eighty per cent of these experiments resulted in increased crop yields ranging from 10 to 30 per cent. We know now that under these circumstances, the wires served as air-ion generators, and there is little doubt that the growth stimulation was due to the ions so produced. In view of the growing worldwide food crisis and the continuing decline in the cost of electricity, it may not be too farfetched to suggest that practical means will be found to enhance production of food crops by the widescale application of air ions.

It is possible also that economically successful use of air ions will be made in aviculture and related fields, areas already pioneered by A. L. Tchijevsky and his colleagues in the U.S.S.R.

Based upon the evidence reviewed in this paper, it appears that air-ion investigations constitute a legitimate and even promising branch of biological research. As more information is acquired about the mechanisms underlying the reactions between air ions and living forms, we should be able to evaluate more clearly than at present the importance of air ions in nature and to assess their potential for practical applications in the areas described above.

There is a season for everything
And a time for every purpose under the heaven:
A time to be born, and a time to die;
A time to plant and a time to reap. . . .

Ecclesiastes

38.

Biological Rhythms

Gay Luce

Invisible rhythms underlie most of what we assume to be constant in ourselves and the world around us. Life is in continual flux, but the change is not chaotic. The rhythmic nature of earth life is, perhaps, its most usual yet overlooked property. Though we can neither see nor feel them, we are nevertheless surrounded by rhythms of gravity, electromagnetic fields, light waves, air pressure, and sound. Each day, as earth turns on its axis, we experience the alternation of light and darkness. The moon's revolution, too, pulls our atmosphere into a cycle of change.

Night follows day. Seasons change. The tides ebb and flow. These various rhythms are also seen in animals and man. We, too, change, growing sleepy at night and restlessly active by day. We, too, exhibit the rhythmic undulations of our planet.

Reprinted from Gay Luce, *Biological Rhythms in Psychiatry and Medicine* (National Institute of Mental Health, 1970), by permission of the author.

CIRCADIAN RHYTHMS

In concert with the turning earth, plants and animals exhibit a very pronounced daily rhythm. Often external cues synchronize living organisms into an exact tempo. However, when men or animals are isolated from their usual time cues, they do not keep to a precise solar day (24 hours) nor even a precise lunar cycle (24.8 hours). Nonetheless, isolated creatures do show rhythms that do not deviate very much from the 24 hours. This daily rhythm is denoted by the popular term "circadian." It means "about a day," from the Latin, *circa dies*.

Mollusks, fish, cats, marigolds, baboons, men—indeed, most living organisms show a circadian rhythm of activity and rest. Time-lapse photography has captured the circadian dance of plant life, showing how leaves lift and drop, open and close every 24 hours. Man, no exception to this daily ebb and flow, may be unaware that his body temperature, blood pressure, and pulse, respiration, blood sugar, hemoglobin levels, and amino acid levels are changing in a circadian rhythm. So, too, do the levels of adrenal hormones in his blood and concentrations of essential biochemicals throughout his nervous system. Urine also shows the influence of the circadian cycle. We excrete rhythmically, not merely according to the time of liquid intake. As a decade of laboratory researches has disclosed, there is a rhythmic fluctuation in the contents of the urine, along with almost every physiological function, from the deposition of fat or sugar in the liver to the rate at which cells are dividing.

In health we have an appearance of stability that cloaks a host of rhythms, hormonal tides, intermeshed with surges of enzyme activity, production of blood cells, and other multitudinous necessities for life. Our smoothness of function seems to rest upon a high degree of integration among these circadian production lines, and they in turn may act as timekeepers for us, guiding us in our periods of energetic endeavor, or rest, acting as distributors of our dreams and the tidal motions underlying our ever-shifting moods. Although we appear constant from the outside, we can feel inside that we are not really the same from one hour of the day to the next.

The corollary of all this circadian change is very dramatic, for a creature's strength and weakness also vary, depending upon biological time of day. Life and death may hang on the balance of timing. Mortality has been decided, experimentally, not by the amount, but by the time of day that a rodent received X-rays or was injected with pneumonia virus, bacteria, or drugs. Exposure to loud noise affects a rodent little during his period of rest, but may hurtle him into a frenzy, into convulsions, and even death if it occurs during his activity period. A volume of anecdotal literature attests that man, too, must be different at different biological times of day. Now, these casual observations are being researched. People do perform differently on psychological and physiological tests at different hours. We may soon learn why more pregnant women go into labor during the night or early morning hours than afternoon, and why doctors receive so many of their calls from patients with coronaries during these same hours. Deaths and symptoms of diseases do not seem to be distributed evenly around the clock. The pain of glaucoma and symptoms of certain allergies or of asthma seem to occur mostly at certain hours. As we should expect, drugs also affect us differently according to biological time of day. Biological time of day does not necessarily jibe with the local clock time. For example, a person who works at night and sleeps by day is likely to be 180 degrees out of phase with the daytime workers of the world. He sleeps when they are awake. His temperature is falling as theirs is rising. His adrenal steroid levels are low when theirs are high. The positions of various body functions indicate "time of day" in the body—biological time of day.

Subjectively, people do notice that they are changing during the 24 hours of the day. Some people express this by their preference for afternoon or morning work, or may notice that they are emotionally resilient at certain hours and irritable at others. Like mechanical clocks, we synchronize our activity with the imperatives of society around us, and squeeze ourselves into the 24-hour schedule of modern life. But unlike mechanical clocks, our bodies will not instantly adjust. Jet travel has forced many of us to realize that internal time must be respected. A person is not the same at 4 a.m. as at 4 p.m., a fact that is unpleasantly palpable to the traveler who flies from Moscow to New York and finds himself trying to make mid-afternoon conversation in an office, while his body feels that it is not quite dawn. Two weeks later, long after he feels adjusted to local time, his body may be showing signs that adjustment is still not complete.

RELEVANCE TO RESEARCH

The fluctuations that continuously transform us each day are small, and superficially some of them may seem random. Nonetheless, biological cycles are pertinent to experimentation in many fields of psychology, pharmacology, and medicine. In the past, experimenters in these fields have made delicate manipulations to hold the experimental conditions constant but have not realized that their animal or human subjects were changing right under their hands. More sophisticated researchers may carefully take their measurements at the same time each day, but unless they have controlled many aspects of their subjects' environment this precaution may be futile. Time, indeed, may be a factor in some of the embrangled debates that arise when one scientist cannot replicate the experiment of another. Was something amiss with the initial study, or did the second scientist fail to take precisely the same steps? Even if the replication were conducted at precisely the same clock hours, this does not mean that animals or volunteers had all been synchronized to exactly the same schedule and were at the same biological time of day. The experiment may not reproduce the original findings because the subjects were at different points on their cycle.

MONTHLY, SEASONAL, ANNUAL CYCLES

Although the day is our most important social unit, there are other cycles that alter a person. A woman differs at the various points of her menstrual cycle, before, during, and after. These monthly hormonal tides influence not only her physiology, but her emotional responses, performance, and as some slight evidence suggests, even the content of her nightly dreams. Psychological ramifications of the monthly cycle are most visible in women with premenstrual tension, a common yet often overlooked symptomatology now being studied by Dr. Oscar Janiger, at the University of California in Irvine, and by a team of National Institute of Mental Health grantees, at Stanford University Medical School. Men also exhibit a few signs of monthly change. Sanctorious, a seventeenth-century doctor, used a fine scale to weigh healthy men over long periods of time and he reported that normal men underwent a monthly weight change of about one or two pounds.

Dr. Christian Hamburger, a renowned Danish endocrinologist, kept daily records of his urinary hormones (a group known as the 17-keto-steroids) for some 16 years. When the daily hormonal fluctuations were later analyzed by Dr. Franz Halberg, at the University of Minnesota Medical School, they showed a roughly 30-day rhythm in addition to a pronounced daily rhythm. Because few physicians are cycle conscious, and few individuals have the patience to accumulate serial records of their own changes, such rhythms are often caught only obliquely. A 28-day rhythm was observed in the drifting bedtime of a physicist during a year's research in Antarctica. He would go to bed later and later for 28 days, and then revert to his original time of retiring, a pattern dis-

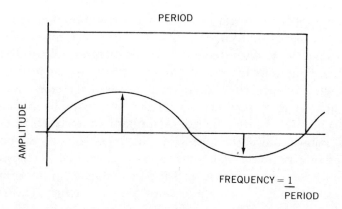

covered by Drs. Jay Shurley, at the University of Oklahoma Medical School, and Chester Pierce, at Harvard Medical School.

Advances in data analysis will probably reveal many slow rhythms in man, cycles with long periods that have not yet been documented. Even known seasonal and annual rhythms are difficult to study. We secrete something known as "summer-hormone," a thyroid product that helps to reduce body heat, but we still know little about it and how its secretion is triggered so as to anticipate the hot summer months. Presumably, there are other subtle changes in our metabolism, consonant with seasonal change.

Annual changes in tissue have been observed in laboratory animals kept under standardized conditions of food, temperature, and humidity, as reported by Dr. H. von Mayersbach and his colleagues, at the University of Hannover, Germany. They found changes in the structure of liver cells and in the amount of a sugar, known as glycogen, that makes energy available to the animal. The seasonal changes were enough to make experimental results seem unstable.

Recently, an even more startling and controlled study has been performed by Drs. Erhard Haus and Franz Halberg. Their mice lived in a controlled environment where lighting was standardized, so as to exclude the major cues to seasonal change. Nonetheless, these inbred, antiseptically treated laboratory animals showed annual cycles in their blood levels of an adrenal hormone, corticosterone. Even without cues, their bodies registered an annual rhythm.

Man's own annual rhythms were largely a matter of anecdotal reports, or very sketchy statistics, until the last several years. Rhythms in the number of suicides and suicide attempts and in deaths from arteriosclerosis do seem to exist. Dr. Halberg has analyzed statistics from the Minnesota Department of Health and has seen that, at least, in the temperate zone, there are several distinguishable rhythms. There is a peak in the number of deaths from arteriosclerosis around January, a peak in suicides around May, and accidental deaths peak in July and August. Some of these rhythms may relate to social customs, such as summer vacations, while others, indeed, may relate to seasonal changes within us, and may help us to explain certain medical and psychiatric disorders.

Very recently, a venturesome researcher has found what may be clues to the well-known, but mysterious winter madness, the "arctic hysteria" reported among Eskimos. This sudden experience, like psychosis, may last for a few hours or days in winter. Dr. Joseph Bohlen, at the University of Wisconsin, has found that there is an annual physiological rhythm among Eskimos living at Wainwright, Alaska. Aided by his wife, Bohlen studied ten individuals around the clock for ten days during each of the four seasons.

It took something of a heroic effort, for the Bohlens had to visit their subjects' houses every two hours to gather urine samples and record oral temperature, blood pressure, pulse, and make tests of hand-grip and eye-hand coordination. They found that the Eskimos' body temperature and the amount of potassium excreted in urine were rising and falling in precisely 24-hour cycles, although they had no circadian cardiac rhythm. The urinary calcium excretion cycle was of greatest interest. Calcium, like other electrically-charged elements in the body, has a profound influence upon the functioning of the nervous system since it appears to be necessary in the transmission of nervous messages. Every Eskimo in Bohlen's study showed a striking annual rhythm in calcium excretion. They excreted eight to ten times as much calcium in winter as they did in summer.

Eskimos seem to suffer from an unusual amount of emotional illness, and it has been postulated that their symptoms are a kind of periodic illness. In Dr. Bohlen's study, we can see that some of the keys to mysterious disorders, such as arctic winter madness, may lie buried in the time cycles of man's physiology. Studies of these cycles may begin to offer explanations for certain social customs and strange human talents.

TIME SENSE

People who can "set" themselves for a night's sleep or a 20-minute nap and awaken "on time" are envied by all. Yet, many creatures measure time as accurately as if they contained a timer. We have recently learned about the marvelous time sense of bees. In one experiment bees were placed in a salt mine in constant light and temperature, where they learned to feed at certain dishes only at certain times of day, despite the fact that there were no time cues from the sun. In another experiment, bees were trained to collect sugar water from 8 a.m. to 10:15 a.m. in France. The hive was flown to the Eastern United States. Now the bees arrived for feeding at 3 a.m., which was precisely 24 hours later. It would have been the correct time in France. Bees in similar experiments have adjusted to local time within a period of about a week.

Ants have learned to show up for food at various intervals, as precisely as if carrying a watch, and the eyes of crayfish turn light every 12 hours, even in constant darkness.

Migrating fish, mammals, and birds orient themselves in part by relying on their inner time sense. They maintain a particular angle to the sun (or to polarized light when the sun is not visible). Their problem is analogous to that of a person who is dropped, blind-folded, into the Sahara Desert and told to walk east. One would need to know whether it was 10 a.m. or 2 p.m. to know from the sun's position which direction was east. In studies of time sense, birds, bees, crabs, and flies have been flown around the world and exposed to many experimental situations. Few such studies have been done with man. Indeed, the physiological bases for human time sense are only beginning to be researched.

When a person awakens at the precise time he has elected beforehand, it almost seems as if he is responding to biological signals inside. Perhaps there are subtle signals, of which most of us remain unaware, signals that function as a delicate stimulus to give a person time information. During the last several years experiments with animals have demonstrated a kind of "trainable" yet unconscious time sense. Experimental creatures have exhibited abnormal symptoms that might be called "psychosomatic" at the precise time of day they had previously experienced unpleasant experimental manipulations. Can time of day become a conditioned stimulus? Perhaps within the "clock" of the brain remain echoes of past events in the glands and circulatory system. Is this how certain illnesses evolve? Are there periodic symptoms at the hour of a trauma, out of awareness but remembered by the body? Perhaps this could illuminate the so-called "anniversary symptoms" seen by psychiatrists. Such questions multiply from new studies of man's rhythms that promise a dramatic departure from traditional research on time sense.

SUBJECTIVE TIME SENSE

The experience of time and the personal evolution of time sense have been more explored by philosophers, anthropologists, and historians than by physiologists and other medical scientists. Time sense and rhythm develop before language. Before a baby speaks he will drum on his crib and show a love of music and rhythm. Some infants rock rhythmically. Psychiatrists have speculated that the newborn infant loves to be cradled and rocked partly because it orients him in the way his mother's heartbeat may have oriented him in the womb. Out of an environment of heartbeat and protection, one is born into seeming chaos. Maybe rhythms do serve to comfort and reorient babies after the lonely confusion of being born. Surely young children show greed for dance, poetry, marching, and rhythmic repetition. However, some of our earliest time measures are not like heartbeat, but mark off stages of growth or other intervals.

There seem to be critical periods in the life cycle. There are critical moments in which a microsecond of light in a constantly darkened experimental room will pull an entire population of larval flies into synchrony to be born. There are critical periods for humans, during which a malnourished baby may incur permanent mental retardation. Many researchers think there are critical periods for learning language.

The passage of time also seems to be experienced differently by the child than by the adult. Drs. Jean Piaget and Paul Fraisse have explored this difference in their psychological studies. Until about age eight, time generally feels very expanded or seems to pass slowly. Most parents have heard their children make such statements as, "If I ever live to be nine . . ." in tones implying that it would take about a century.

Through repeated experience, adults have learned to measure units in estimating time and to apply reasoning. In young children, each day is its own universe. Tomorrow is a barely comprehensible concept. Moreover, until a certain age children do not seem to have a sense of the ordering of events or classification of order, even after adults have tried to teach them about it. Piaget reports one typical instance:

> "How old are you?"
> "Seven years old."
> "Do you have a friend who is older than you?"
> "Yes, this one next to me is eight years old."
> "Very good. Which one of you was born first?"
> "I don't know. I don't know when his birthday is."
> "But come on, think a little. You told me that you are seven years old and that he is eight, now which of you was born first?"
> "You'll have to ask his mother. I can't tell you."

Children do not seem to be able to comprehend certain concepts when they are young and are often notoriously subjective in their perceptions of things. In their feelings about the duration of time, or at least, the reason for their subjectivity, may be a physiological system that functions at a rate different from that of the adult.

The speed of the transactions of neurons in our brains and bodies must be calibrated to the rhythms of the physical world we perceive. Our brains must respond at a certain rate to hear sounds of certain frequencies. We do not have receptors to respond as fast as those of the dog, for instance, which means that our pets can hear ultra high sound but we cannot. We can see certain colors, but others are beyond our vision. We can see discrete movement, until it becomes so fast that our brains no longer separate the frames of a moving picture and instead, see continuous motion, or flashes of light occurring so rapidly that we perceive only a beam.

The role of physiological speed in perception has fascinated many scientists.

> The relativity of our reference point (writes Roland Fischer in *The Voices of Time*) can be demonstrated by taking a moving picture of a plant at one frame a minute, and then speeding it up to thirty frames a second. The plant will appear to behave like an animal, clearly perceiving stimuli and reacting to them. Why then, do we call it unconscious? To organisms that react 1800 times as quickly as we react we might appear to be unconscious. They would in fact be justified in calling us unconscious since we would not normally be conscious of their behavior.
>
> Our restricted range of consciousness can be demonstrated by exposing a man to a sequence of similar or nearly similar stimuli, such as a succession of frames on television. If the frequency of these stimuli is increased to about fifteen cycles per second, previously distinct images cease to be separated and a spatialization or fusion of events takes place.

We all know that time interval perception is relative. Albert Einstein once wrote, "When you sit with a nice girl for two hours you think it's only a minute. But when you sit on a hot stove for a minute you think it's two hours. That's relativity."

A RHYTHM IN TIME ESTIMATION

A considerable literature on time estimation by psychologists shows how variously people have explored the questions asked by Hoagland. In 1962, the French speleologist, Michel Siffre, lived two months in a cave, isolated from all normal time cues. Several times during each waking period he estimated two minutes, counting to 120 via telephone to a base-camp operator above ground. These data were later analyzed by Drs. M. Engeli and Franz Halberg, at the University of Minnesota, and showed that he fluctuated—counting too fast or too slowly—in a rhyth-mic manner. That same year Dr. D. H. Thor predicted that time esti-mation and time perception both would depend on time of day, varying according to a person's period of maximal alertness. Thor was working at the Johnstone Training and Research Center in Bordentown, New Jersey.

Thor and his associates asked 450 people to tell them the time of day without looking at a clock. They asked the question at six different points between 8 A.M. and 6 P.M., and averaged the estimates at each time. The subjects were most accurate between 8 A.M. and 10 A.M., and again around 4 P.M. During midday, people typically misjudged the time, thinking it earlier; while at the end of the day they assumed the hour was later than it was in actuality. There was no doubt that their subjective sense of the clock hour varied in a predictable way, following a diurnal rhythm.

In 1968, Dr. Donald Pfaff, at Rockefeller University, showed that the estimation of short time intervals varied in a way that correlated with body temperature. Pfaff's subjects were consistent and when asked to denote a five- or eight-second interval, they made the interval smaller when their body temperatures were at their peak and longer when tem-perature was lower—much as Hoagland would have predicted. Thus, studies of time sense must, themselves, encompass a reference for physio-logical time of day if they are to be precise.

If Michel Siffre instigated interest in the circadian fluctuations of indi-vidual subjective time perception, he also exemplified one of the strange misperceptions of time that seems to occur during isolation. He spent 60 days in a cave, and emerged thinking he had been there only 35 days. Many factors influence the perception of both long and short time intervals.

ALTERED MENTAL STATES AND DRUGS

Under hypnotic time regression, some extremely susceptible subjects re-live past experiences, and grown men act like infants, capable of poking an inquisitive finger into a flame, unable to handle matches.

People demonstrably change their sense of time when they are under the influence of such hallucinogenic and excitatory drugs as LSD or psilocybin. If asked to tap on a Morse key at a self-chosen rate and in-structed to tap as evenly as possible, they will tap fastest at the peak of the drug state, says Roland Fischer in *Interdisciplinary Perspectives of Time*. At the time of increased tapping rate, they experience "a flood of inner sensations" or time contraction. In such states, people arrive too early for appointments if they do not consult their watches. At the same time they experience an expansion of nearby space, and this is evident in their enlarged handwriting. An opposite effect occurs under tranquilizers, which are used as antidotes for hallucinogenics, and under these drugs people are often late for appointments and their handwriting shrinks in size.

Distortions of time sense are reported among many psychotic patients, and the bleak distortions of many schizophrenics have invited tests that might define them operationally. Testing psychiatric patients in hope of finding some unique distortion of time estimation that would correlate with a diagnosis has proven exceedingly difficult. In their studies of schizophrenic patients and normals, Dr. William T. Lhamon, at the New York Medical College, and Dr. Sanford Goldstone found that methods and sensory modality influenced the results: it mattered greatly whether one asked patients to estimate the duration of a sound or a visual display.

Drs. F. T. Melges and C. E. Fougerousse, Jr., have been studying psychiatric patients at the University of Rochester School of Medicine. Recently, they studied a sizeable group of patients when they first entered the hospital, and again when they had improved and felt better. When asked to produce a specified short-time interval, patients in unhappy emotional states gave inaccurately brief intervals, as if their nervous systems were running at an accelerated pace. Patients in pleasanter states gave more accurate intervals. Psychotic patients seemed to have a more distorted time sense than depressed or neurotic patients, and their time judgments became more accurate as they improved.

Dr. Robert Ornstein, at the Langley Porter Neuropsychiatric Institute in San Francisco, has reviewed the literature on time experience in his book, *On the Experience of Time*. He concludes that our sense of duration cannot be correlated with any physiological "clock." Time sense, as he sees it, is more psychological than biological. Time durations seem long to us if we are conscious of a great deal of information. Ornstein performed nine ingenious experiments that demonstrated a role of awareness and memory in time experience. Subjects reported feeling the assigned intervals as increased in length when the amount and complexity of the stimuli within the measured interval were increased. People judged intervals as comparatively longer when they recalled the contents than when they did not, suggesting that our sense of duration may be related to memory as well as to information processing. A variety of experiments and studies of people under hallucinogenic drugs has begun to reveal that subjective time experience must be related to the elusive phenomenon we call "conscious awareness."

CULTURAL CONCEPTS OF TIME

If neural firing rates and altered biochemistry may lie behind some of the time distortions observed in psychiatric illness, environment also must play a role. What we consider healthy or abnormal in the general perception of time is probably modulated by cultural attitudes. Temporal attitudes pervade a culture to such an extent that they are almost invisible. Probably they are more influential than we like to imagine. In subtle but powerful ways, cultural concepts of time have helped to mold the history of civilizations. Ancient Egyptian culture was exceedingly involved in natural cycles of the sun and the moon, for instance. However, dedication to a philosophy involving eternal life gave Egyptian existence dimensions that had been absent among their African predecessors, who were also guided by moon cycles.

Time concepts may help to explain the accuracy of early Chinese histories. These are unrivalled. Not only did the Chinese document events from earliest antiquity, but they expressed an orderly respect for family tradition and rules of human conduct, qualities that appear to have been generated by a philosophy embodying respect for time cycles of considerable magnitude. Naturalists and astronomers saw that the cycles of the sun and moon were reflected in life, and this in turn influenced their philosophy: "The sun at noon is the sun declining; the creature born is the creature dying." Ancient Taoism was cycle-oriented. Time was divided into seasons and eras, considered part of an infinite chain of duration—past, present, and future.

The calendar was an inevitable focus of interest in an agrarian society, and there was almost no Chinese mathematician or astronomer who did not work on calendars. Between 370 B.C. and A.D. 1742, there were about a hundred different calendars, each one embodying astronomical events with ever greater accuracy. Early in Chinese history, astronomers belonged to the history department of the ruler. The Chinese were so historically oriented that they meticulously dated all objects and inscriptions. Twenty-five dynastic histories (beginning about 90 B.C.) offer a wealth of material on science, government, and customs.

In the first century A.D., Buddhism and a philosophy of continual metamorphosis spread through China. Naturalists and philosophers observed evolutionary transformations in living organisms. Some sixteen centuries before Darwin they expressed a kind of evolutionary naturalism that embodied a succession of phylogenetic unfoldings rather than the concept of a single train of evolution with which Western science began. The complex concepts of time held by the Chinese led to remarkably sophisticated theories that included accurate perception of astronomical change, views on the nature of fossils, and explanations of the unity of these vast time cycles in the development and personal history of each man. In the Chinese view, man's place was a humble and appropriate part of the time cycle. Morally and biologically, he fit into the expanse of nature and history. Thus, he saw his world and his future very differently than does any modern Westerner.

In the thirteenth century, the Chinese *Book of Changes* gave an estimate of phases in the evolution of life covering about 130,000 years. At that time the Chinese were calculating astronomical periods in millions of years. Western attitudes of that era are primitive by contrast. Judeo-Christian perception of time was linear. The flow of time was believed to begin with some specific point in space time. Indeed, in seventeenth-century Europe, people piously followed Bishop Usher's calculation of the date of the creation of the universe—as October 6, 4004 B.C. After all, time had to begin with some significant event.

This simple linearity dictated much of Western thought, custom, and philosophical egotism. It encouraged a self-centered concept of our place in the universe, our hustling individuality, and our philosophies of cause and effect. These notions have indeed been instrumental in the development of Western science.

If time were linear, one could ask ultimate questions about "the beginning," but other cultures with different concepts of time have shown them in their development.

Westerners measure time by action. How different are the Hindustani. For instance, India has never produced a written history. After all, why would people trouble to make detailed chronological records of their national development if they lived in a time domain characterized by a changeless sense of everbecoming? By contrast with Westerners, Indians may seem lacking in urgency. Their universe, world, and social order are eternal; personal life is only a sample of a succession of lives, repeating themselves endlessly. Transmigration of souls and perpetual rebirth make meaningless any quantitative view of a particular period of time. Life, infinitely recycled, makes history less significant, and an individual's biography is merely a transient moment in the process.

The Japanese Buddhist concept of the transience of the physical world has very different consequences: it has led to intuitive, sensitive admonitions that if all things are transient, one must appreciate but not cling to them. "Time flies more swiftly than an arrow and life is more transient than dew." Thus, the ultimate reality is what one sees and experiences. The urgency of Western action is a new phenomenon in Japan.

In Japanese sensibility, time is not an absolute, nor an objective set of categories, but a process. It is the change of nature. Man is part of that change and able to appreciate it, feeling transience to be part of the eternal loveliness of the universe rather than a threat to the ego (as Western man sees mortality).

Even in a brief and oversimplified sketch, it is apparent that cultural concepts of time have a pervasive influence upon individuals and upon major social developments. In medicine, for instance, one can see why ancient peoples might have accepted notions of biological rhythmicity, connecting human life with natural cycles—and why there might be resistance to such ideas within our own culture. . . .

THE HEART AND LUNGS: INTEGRATION OF RHYTHMS

We are often aware of the rhythm of the heart. It works hard, pumping about 70 barrels of blood a day, alternating rhythmically between dilation (diastole) and contraction (systole). Listening to the beat of one's own heart through the pressure changes at the wrist, one hears roughly 60–80 beats per minute. Heart and lungs must operate rhythmically together. When a person is at rest, his respiration is four times slower than his pulse, about 15–20 breaths per minute. The pulse rate and respiration rate have a circadian rhythm, rising to a peak by day and falling to a low point during sleep. . . .

The circulatory system is a complicated, closed, hydraulic system. A number of German scientists have searched for relationships between heart rate and athletic activity for causes of arrhythmia. Dr. Hildebrandt has observed that people who do not feel well, but whose electrocardiograms appear "normal," often have exhibited abnormal ratios of pulse and respiration or other signs of internal discoordination during late sleep. One way in which internal rhythmicity has been studied is by stressing a person with heat, cold, or exercise and examining aspects of heart function.

At another level, the laboratory has been studying blood flow through muscle tissue. A rhythmic decline and rise in flow volume that suddenly doubled its wavelength was observed when a drop of adrenaline (epinephrine) was injected. Many aspects of long and short rhythms of the body are being assayed for new criteria in judging health and illness, new measures of physiological efficiency that may prove useful in diagnosis and treatment.

Some of these body rhythms are rarely noticed. For instance, skin temperature, particularly the temperature of the hands and feet, changes in a circadian rhythm. Ordinarily, during sleep, temperature is higher on the left side of the body, and during the day, slightly higher on the right. This alternation in skin temperature has gone as unremarked as the alternation we experience in breathing. Anyone who has suffered with a bad head cold will surmise that we do not breathe evenly through both nostrils at once: we alternate. The yogic masters have long known about these alternations. A normal man will breathe mainly through one nostril for three hours, while the tissues of the other are slightly engorged. Then, in a three-hour exchange he will breathe predominantly through the other nostril.

Alternating functions, ftom left to right, and a rise in body temperature that corresponds with a cooling of extremities, are relatively unstudied. By looking at these rhythms will we understand certain asymmetries in a body that is thought to be predominantly symmetrical? Do we, indeed, alternate in the use of our "duplicate" organs, our double-sided brain?

Quite a few scientists now suspect that the long and short biological cycles probably have an over-all integration. Certain rhythms are clearly determined by a creature's physiological characteristics. For instance, heart rate depends upon an animal's size, his surface-to-volume ratio, and circulatory efficiency. But whether the rhythm is as rapid as a discharge of nerve cells, or as slow as the menstrual cycle, various types of rhythmic phenomena are bound to interact and to influence one another. They are also bound to be influenced by a person's habits, as Hippocrates remarked so long ago.

A healthy person lives in harmony with his environment. Only when he takes a jet trip across time zones and feels uncomfortable for a day or a week does he become aware of interior schedules. Now he is sleepy and hungry at "inappropriate times." What occurs inside might be likened to a major production-line adjustment within the world's most complex factory. The analogy of a factory may indicate how important rhythmicity may be for our health.

No factory could produce an item as simple as a shoe unless each step were part of an orderly, well-timed sequence. Parts must be ready before they are needed on the assembly line, yet they cannot be overstocked so as to burden storage facilities. Analogously, man's infinitely more complicated system must rely upon an orderly sequencing of millions of events so that a person functions smoothly. When production is well meshed, the clockwork is scarcely perceptible, but when it runs amuck, the result may be illness.

In 1960, Dr. Erwin Bünning, of the University of Tübingen, Germany, opened a symposium in Cold Spring Harbor by suggesting that there must be a rhythmic harmony between cell behavior and the whole organism in health, probably organized around the unit of a day. When a person travels across several time zones, his internal rhythms adjust to the new local time, each at its own rate. Therefore, some functions of the body have adjusted within three days, but others have not adjusted at the end of a week. This may mean internal cacophony. As Bünning stated, "a glandular tissue may be in the phase of hormone production while another organ, being in another phase, cannot make use of the hormone; or an enzyme may be very active in a particular tissue at a time when its substrate is not available. Every transatlantic air traveler knows the physiological discomforts that may arise from such a lack of cooperation. More important, however, are graver illnesses, even cancer, which may be shown to be evidence for this."

At the level of the cell, disordered rhythms in division and multiplication may be symptomatic of malignancy. Studies by Dr. Franz Halberg and his many associates have begun to find a contrast in the rhythms of healthy and cancerous tissue. Halberg has also shown that disordered rhythms of cell behavior are reflected, on occasion, in abnormality of gross rhythms. The daily body temperature rhythms of certain cancer patients have proven to be extraordinarily disordered, obviously differing from those of other sick patients.

As electronic techniques have been developed that enable us to trace a variety of human physiological functions for hours at a time, researchers have become aware of rhythmicity as an aspect of "normalcy." In sleep laboratories, where healthy adults exhibit predictable rhythms of cyclic change in nightly sleep, a deviation in rhythm (from fever, mental illness, or drugs) is often the first warning signal of the symptoms to follow. Many abnormal rhythms are known by the names of illness. A common name for a disordered sleep rhythm, for instance, is insomnia.

It is abundantly clear that healthy living things are not only internally rhythmic; they are also synchronized with their environment. Is environmental change the source of a creature's circadian rhythms? Some have suggested that they are genetic, reflecting an inbuilt rhythmicity that evolved some 180 million years ago as an adaptation to this turning earth. Others think they are imprinted upon the organism early in life by the external periodicities of environment and parents. Still other theorists speculate that rhythms are caused by geophysical events to which living things constantly respond anew. We could, after all, be very sensitive cosmic receivers, acting in accord with rhythmic changes not only on light and temperature but in cosmic rays, barometric pressure, ionization, magnetic fields. The most generally accepted theory suggests that inherited oscillators allow creatures to respond to recurrent geophysical stimuli.

Research on biological rhythms began in earnest in eighteenth-century botany. Leaves and flowers were observed to show circadian movement, which continued even when plants were isolated from time cues, as in caves. The suspicion that such a rhythm might be inherited was stated and bolstered by the work of Dr. Erwin Bünning. Experiments with plants in a constant laboratory environment showed that their circadian rhythm was not precisely 24 hours, yet never more than about three hours shorter or longer. Moreover, each plant species showed a typical circadian period in isolation. One plant might show a 24.2-hour cycle while another would have a 25.6-hour rhythm. Hybrids were found to have intermediate periods, strongly suggesting that the rhythm had a genetic basis.

As zoologists entered the field, experiments with unicellular organisms, insects, and mammals began to delineate the complexity of endogenous rhythms. Dr. Colin Pittendrigh, now at Stanford University, has experimented with a variety of organisms, from flagellates and fruit flies to mammals. He concluded that the circadian rhythm must originate in some basic molecular mechanism—a clocklike mechanism with a periodicity of 23 to 25 hours that shows a sustained oscillation in the absence of external synchronizers. Dr. Pittendrigh feels that this inheritance is an evolutionary adaptation to a strongly rhythmic planet, in which sun and moon create periodicities of 24 to 25 hours.

As physiologists experimented with birds, mammals, and man, the importance of environmental influences suggested that circadian rhythms might be to some extent acquired. Living things seem to use time cues to orient themselves. Dr. Jürgen Ashoff, and his associates, have been working on the problem of time cues at the Max-Planck Institut für Verhaltensphysiologie in Erling-Andechs, Germany. They have shown, with birds and man, that light is a most prominent synchronizer in the hierarchy of time cues, but that a hungry animal would adapt his activity and rest to the timetable of available food.

For rodents, as Dr. Franz Halberg amply demonstrated, light and darkness are the most important synchronizers of the rhythm of activity, and of physiological rhythms, such as the level of adrenal hormones. If the light schedule were shifted a few hours, the adrenal rhythm would follow, adjusting to the new schedule within about four days. If the light schedule were inverted, the adrenal rhythm might need nine days to adjust. If mice were blinded, however, their adrenal hormone rhythms would begin to deviate from the precise 24-hour day, so that they showed rhythms with a period between 23 and 25 hours.

Developmental studies with mammals have suggested that circadian rhythms might be acquired. Both the social and physical environment may play a major role in the evolution of these rhythms. Human infants, for instance, only slowly develop circadian rhythms of sleep and waking, of urinary excretion, and other functions. Of course, the fact that patterns do not appear at the start does not necessarily mean they are not inherited. Certain genetic illnesses, such as Huntington's Chorea, are inherited but do not appear until late in life. There are other evidences suggesting that inherited propensities must be very much influenced by environment.

Dr. Mary Lobban, working at the National Institute for Medical Research in Hampstead, London, has found that urinary excretion rhythms in Arctic Eskimos differ from those of people in temperate zones. Eskimo excretion patterns, nonetheless, exhibited some circadian rhythmicity despite the lack of a pronounced day-night difference during most of the year.

It is now probably fair to say that many of the scientists now studying biological rhythms believe that inherited mechanisms give earth organisms the propensity to synchronize themselves with certain periodicities in the environment. A roughly 24-hour oscillator within living cells may help the creature to survive by acting in tune with its changing environment.

In attempting to understand the rhythmicity of life forms, there are some scientists who propose that creatures could be a kind of cosmic receiving station, responding to a continuous inpouring of information from rhythmic geophysical changes of the environment. Dr. Frank Brown, of Northwestern University in Evanston, Illinois, has been the most active proponent of the cosmic theory, suggesting that an independent internal timing system for rhythms is not necessary to life since the environment is always generating rhythmic signals. These include variations in terrestrial magnetism, electric fields, and background radiation and other signal sources, such as gravitation, from which no creature on earth can be completely isolated. Only experiments in space can isolate life from these cycles. If animals and plants comprise a multiplicity of very sensitive receivers, they could utilize this continuous influx of information from external pacemaker signals.

Using a variety of life forms in which he has ascertained rhythmic changes, Dr. Brown has sought geophysical periodicities that might account for them. His point of view is worth expression for it underscores what we do not yet know about biological rhythms and suggests that man may be a more diversely sensitive creature, more subject to the invisible influences of the surrounding universe than Western science usually considers him.

THE COSMIC RECEIVER

Many forms of earth life exhibit both solar and lunar rhythms. Fiddler crabs, for instance, show a rhythm of color change, darkening and lightening each day in exactly solar 24-hour rhythm, even in isolation. On the other hand, they show an activity cycle that is the length of a lunar day, 24.8 hours.

In studying daily cycles of metabolism in crabs, Dr. Brown fortuitously found they were the mirror image of average daily fluctuations in cosmic radiation. Dr. Brown's contact with physicists in the mid-1950's was fortunate, indeed. At the time, cosmic-radiation cycles underwent unusual modifications of form, including cycle inversion. The oxygen-consumption cycles of potatoes, carrots, shellfish, and rats also varied with the cosmic-ray changes so as to suggest that living organisms might be responsive to cosmic radiation and, perhaps, also to geomagnetic influences.

Actually, our atmosphere, and especially its magnetic field, protects us from primary cosmic rays. These must enter the ionosphere, one of earth's protective layers, which is composed of electrically charged particles (ions) of gaseous matter. The ionosphere is held close to earth by the geomagnetic field, shielding us from harmful rays from outer space. However, the ionosphere is not steady. It attenuates at night as it draws away from earth and increases in density by day, when it draws close to earth.

In his laboratory, Dr. Brown interfered with the normal activity of cosmic rays by manipulating lead shields. He created a cascade, or serial flow, of the rays so that fiddler crabs could be exposed to intensified cosmic ray showers every other 12 hours. In doing so, he saw that he amplified a normal 24-hour solar rhythm—the darkening and lightening of their surface color, which occurs every solar day—24 hours.

The amount of primary cosmic rays entering earth's atmosphere is the inverse of the geomagnetic strength. Since geomagnetic strength is a factor that also fluctuates, Brown wondered if living creatures were sensitive to earth's magnetic field as well. To investigate geomagnetic influences, Brown performed experiments with planaria (worms) and mud snails. He used as his experimental focus the direction in which the creature veered. Worms and snails tend to veer in given compass directions at certain times of day, month, and year. By simply rotating a bar-magnet beneath the experimental grid on which the creatures rested, he could change their tendency to take a certain compass orientation. They reoriented themselves according to very weak changes in magnetic field. Using essentially the same kind of test, he showed that these organisms were very responsive to the natural ambient electrostatic fields in the atmosphere. When tested with weak gamma fields, they also responded both to the strength and direction. Clearly, if organisms could sense these geophysical properties, there was no such thing as placing a creature in "constant" conditions. Even in the deepest, most shielded underground chamber, such factors as tides of neutrinos, or rhythms of geomagnetism, would continue to convey some of the periodicity of the cosmos.

Geomagnetism, Brown conjectured, might be an important kind of compass cue. Other cues might be related to earth's electrostatic and electromagnetic fields. At any moment in time, the geophysical field varies with geographic direction, and for any geographic direction or location, there is a continuous variation of earth's field in time. The same cues that might offer directional information could also be used to sense time. Worms, for instance, were given an easterly light source, to which they repeatedly responded with a characteristic veering, when they were directed north. Even later when the worm had been turned south with a light source from the west, it appeared to recall the formerly easterly light source. Memory for light appeared to be associated with the directional magnetic fields at the time. If one assumed great geophysical sensitivity, as Brown reports, one could also account for distortions in daily cycles that occur in supposedly isolated subjects in supposedly constant conditions, distortions that Brown has correlated with weather changes in some instances.

Brown believes that all living organisms gain information about time and orientation in space from weak electromagnetic fields in the environment. In his terms, these fields are used by the central nervous system and provide a kind of medium enabling the bioelectric activity of the brain. Presumably, the full use of the atmospheric media could give man unusual "sense" information, including abilities to detect weather changes. Animal lore is rich in this respect. Fiddler crabs have been reported to disappear into inland burrows two days before an oncoming hurricane. Foresters in the Pacific Northwest sometimes predict snow by the behavior of the elk, which begin to gather in the shelter of trees two to three days before a blizzard.

The question remains—Is man sensitive to magnetic field changes? No one has produced experimental demonstration that man responds to magnetic changes comparable to those of the environment. Some people have suggested that the discomfort of crossing time zones may be generated by crossing bands of magnetic force. The earth is a huge magnet, layered from north to south like an onion, with bands of magnetic force, whose lines of changing field strength lie between the North and South Poles.

During the last few years there has been some evidence that human beings may be sensitive to very strong electric fields. In one of the Max-Planck laboratories near Munich, a research team led by Drs. Jürgen Aschoff and Rutger Wever has been studying human volunteers in underground bunkers, one of which is heavily shielded against ordinary electromagnetic fields. By introducing artificial electric fields into the bunker, the experimenters influenced the circadian rhythms of volunteers, shortening the period of their cycles. A number of experiments, described in another section, showed that slight effects could be observed after using very strong fields, but these do not prove that human beings would respond significantly to the corresponding natural fields. Although electromagnetic sensitivity is not one of the receptor modalities man customarily enumerates among his senses, it may be that certain individuals are unusually sensitive to exceedingly small changes in magnetic field strength. In attempting to explain the mysterious capability of the "dowser," the person who can divine underground water, the French physicist, Dr. Y. Rocard, at the Universite de Paris, Paris, followed dowsers on their sensing missions. They would hold their arms straight and taut, balancing before them a long hickory stick. Rocard followed with a magnetometer, and found that they were responding to tiny (3–5 milligauss) changes in the earth's magnetic field strength. Since they held their arms with a certain degree of muscle tension, he reasoned that the small changes affected bioelectric transmission in their arms. He then planted electric coils underground to create changes in magnetic strength similar to those of nature. By reinforcing people as they went over the test ground, he was able to condition the ability to detect .3–1.0 milligauss changes in magnetic field.

Dr. Brown suggests that variations in earth's magnetic field may form a space-and-time-grid for living creatures, and that even man may unconsciously use a variety of subtle cosmic cues rather than depending upon inherited clocks for his physiological rhythms. Perhaps a major value of this point of view is that it suggests the posibility of overlooked inputs into man's nervous system, inputs relevant to understanding human behavior.

SUNSPOTS AND BEHAVIOR

Periodically, in mental hospital wards, aggressive patients show intense surges of activity: individuals become hostile, excitable, even violent. Such outbursts occur only sporadically but are striking enough to have invited study. At Douglas Hospital in Montreal, continuous, round-the-clock observation studies of patients over periods of several months did, indeed, show a picture of such periodic outbursts. Correlations between increased aggression and staff on duty, changes in menu, medication, or visiting days were too weak to explain the group behavior. Barometric pressure, temperature, humidity, and other environmental factors were juxtaposed against the hospital calendar of aggressive behavior. When no explanation could be found, Dr. Heinz Lehmann compared his hospital data against data from the U.S. Space Disturbance Forecast Center in Boulder, Colorado. There appeared to be a correlation between solar flare activity (sun spots), geomagnetic disturbances, and excitement on the ward. It seemed unlikely but the study continues. Since sun flares are bursts of gaseous material, high energy particles that influence the ionosphere, causing changes in magnetic fields on earth, a relationship is not impossible. Sun storms sometimes cause a noticeable deflection in a compass needle. Perhaps, since the brain is at least as sensitive as a fine compass, it also responds to large magnetic disturbances.

We know that rats are sensitive to X-rays, which act as aversive stimulation. The human brain may also respond to such inputs. The possibility of an expanded "sensory" range has been raised by studies of biological rhythms.

TIME STRUCTURE

Timing in the heart, in muscle contractions, and nerve cell transactions has been an issue for research for some time. Until recently, however, nobody considered the possibility that the entire body and brain might depend upon an integrated time structure. The human being is often treated as if he were—or should be—a constant system with homeostatic balance, capable of great flexibility in dealing with exigencies outside.

There is growing evidence that all mammals are predictably changing from one hour of the day to another. Until the last decade, it was possible to imagine that these changes were random fluctuations. Now, when a fluctuation is called "random," it often means that its variation in time has not been carefully studied. Over the years experimenters have searched the anatomy for the origin of circadian rhythmicity. They have removed stomachs, yet the animal's activity rhythms remained. They have removed adrenals, but the circadian rhythms persisted. Mice born without pituitary glands are rhythmic, as are rodents from which the thyroid has been removed. Isolated organs also beat with circadian rhythmicity. Dr. Erwin Bünning once removed sections of hamster intestine, and their contractions sustained a circadian rhythm for three days. Dr. G. Edgar Folk, Jr., and his associates took isolated hearts and adrenals from hamsters, and the hearts continued to beat with a circadian rhythm and the adrenals continued to secrete steroids in a circadian rhythm.

Since light and darkness perform such an important role in synchronizing mammal activity rhythms, animals have been blinded, or left in constant light or darkness; but their rhythms of activity have deviated only a little from the precise 24-hour schedule. Indeed, as Dr. D. H. Thor and his associates have shown, when rats are given control over their own lighting they choose the stimulation of darkness and light in a circadian rhythm. Attempts to deflect animals from a circadian activity, or temperature pattern, have involved brain lesions, stress with drugs, scheduled lighting changes, changes in feeding, and physical injury. These many experiments have reinforced the notion that the circadian rhythm is persistent and that different body systems may exhibit this rhythmicity independently of each other. Perhaps one definition of health is a state in which these rhythms are integrated in certain phase relationships. Surely, as the experiments of Dr. Franz Halberg and his associates demonstrate, timing is an inescapable part of our structure, and essential to well-being.

If human beings and animals change as they follow multitudinous cycles each day and night, subtle diagnostic tests (psychiatric, endocrine, etc.) will evoke different responses at different points on the person's daily cycle. As psychiatric experiments now demonstrate, the relation between rhythmicity and mental health is not coincidental. Experiments at the Institute of Living indicate that biological time influences learning, memory, and the rate at which an animal can unlearn fear. Stress has been followed by psychotic and neurotic behavioral reactions, accompanied by characteristic changes in circadian physiological rhythms.

The study of biological rhythms offers a first step toward deciphering the time structure of other living creatures and of ourselves. Temporal structure, like the structure of matter, must be an important aspect of the anatomical and functional ability of organisms. Without temporal structure, indeed, we could not exist. . . .

Not knowing that one has a time structure is like not knowing one has a heart or lungs. In every aspect of our physiology and lives, it becomes clear that we are made of the order we call time. As we look deeper into this dimension of our being, we may find that we, too, are like the plant that flowers if given a little light at the right time every 72 hours. There may be in man a combination lock to his activity and rest, his moods, illnesses, and productiveness. Moreover, by cultivation, he may learn to utilize his subjective sense of time.

39.

Synchronicity: An Acausal Connecting Principle

Carl G. Jung

FOREWORD

In writing this paper I have, so to speak, made good a promise which for many years I lacked the courage to fulfill. The difficulties of the problem and its presentation seemed to me too great; too great the intellectual responsibility without which such a subject cannot be tackled; too inadequate, in the long run, my scientific training. If I have now conquered my hesitation and at last come to grips with my theme, it is chiefly because my experiences of the phenomenon of synchronicity have multiplied themselves over the decades, while on the other hand my researches

Reprinted from W. Pauli and C. C. Jung, eds., *The Interpretation of Nature and the Psyche*, translated from the German by R. F. C. Hull, Bollingen Series LI (copyright © 1955 by Bollingen Foundation), by permission of Princeton University Press and Routledge & Kegan Paul, Ltd.

into the history of symbols, and of the fish symbol in particular, brought the problem ever closer to me, and finally because I have been alluding to the existence of this phenomenon on and off in my writings for twenty years without discussing it any further. I would like to put a temporary end to this unsatisfactory state of affairs by trying to give a consistent account of everything I have to say on this subject. I hope it will not be construed as presumption on my part if I make uncommon demands on the open-mindedness and goodwill of the reader. Not only is he expected to plunge into regions of human experience which are dark, dubious, and hedged about with prejudice, but the intellectual difficulties are such as the treatment and elucidation of so abstract a subject must inevitably entail. As anyone can see for himself after reading a few pages, there can be no question of a complete description and explanation of these complicated phenomena, but only an attempt to broach the problem in such a way as to reveal some of its manifold aspects and connections, and to open up a very obscure field which is philosophically of the greatest importance. As a psychiatrist and psychotherapist I have often come up against the phenomena in question and could convince myself how much these inner experiences meant to my patients. In most cases they were things which people do not talk about for fear of exposing themselves to thoughtless ridicule. I was amazed to see how many people have had experiences of this kind and how carefully the secret was guarded. So my interest in this problem has a human as well as a scientific foundation. . . .

EXPOSITION

The discoveries of modern physics have, as we know, brought about a significant change in our scientific picture of the world, in that they have shattered the absolute validity of natural law and made it relative. Natural laws are *statistical* truths, which means that they are completely valid only when we are dealing with macrophysical quantities. In the realm of very small quantities *prediction* becomes uncertain, if not impossible, because very small quantities no longer behave in accordance with the known natural laws.

The philosophical principle that underlies our conception of natural law is *causality*. But if the connection between cause and effect turns out to be only statistically valid and only relatively true, then the causal principle is only of relative use for explaining natural processes and therefore presupposes the existence of one or more other factors which would be necessary for an explanation. This is as much as to say that the connection of events may in certain circumstances be other than causal, and requires another principle of explanation.*

Now, there is in our experience an immeasurably wide field whose extent forms, as it were, the counterbalance to the domain of causality. This is the world of chance, where a chance event seems causally unconnected with the coinciding fact. So we shall have to examine the nature and the whole idea of chance a little more closely. Chance, we say, must obviously be susceptible of some causal explanation and is only called "chance" or "coincidence" because its causality has not yet been discovered. Since we have an inveterate conviction of the absolute validity of causal law, we regard this explanation of chance as being quite adequate. But if the causal principle is only relatively valid, then it follows that even though in the vast majority of cases an apparently chance series can be causally explained, there must still remain a number of cases which do not show causal connection. We are therefore faced with the task of sifting events and separating the acausal ones from those that can be causally explained. It stands to reason that the number of causally explicable events will far exceed those suspected of acausality, for which reason a superficial or prejudiced observer may easily overlook the relatively rare acausal phenomena. As soon as we come to deal with the problem of chance the need for a statistical evaluation of the events in question forces itself upon us.

It is not possible to sift the empirical material without a criterion of distinction. How are we to recognize acausal combinations of events, since it is obviously impossible to examine all chance happenings for their causality? The answer to this is that acausal events may be expected most readily where, on closer reflection, a causal connection appears to be inconceivable. As an example I would cite the "duplication of cases" which is a phenomenon well known to every doctor. Occasionally there is a trebling or even more, so that Kammerer can speak of a "law of series," of which he gives a number of excellent examples. In the majority of such cases there is not even the remotest probability of a causal connection between the coinciding events. When for instance I am faced with the fact that my tram ticket bears the same number as the theatre ticket which I buy immediately afterwards, and I receive that same evening a telephone call during which the same number is mentioned again as a telephone number, then a causal connection between them seems to me

---

*[Other than, or supplementary to, the laws of chance.—Eds.]

improbable in the extreme, although it is obvious that each event must have its own causality. I know, on the other hand, that chance happenings have a tendency to fall into aperiodic groupings—necessarily so, because otherwise there would be only a periodic or regular arrangement of events which would by definition exclude chance. . . .

Decisive evidence for the existence of acausal combinations of events has been furnished, with adequate scientific safeguards, only very recently, mainly through the experiments of J. B. Rhine and his fellow-workers, who have not, however, recognized the far-reaching conclusions that must be drawn from their findings. Up to the present no critical argument that cannot be refuted has been brought against these experiments. The experiment consists, in principle, in an experimenter turning up, one after another, a series of numbered cards bearing simple geometrical patterns. At the same time the subject, separated by a screen from the experimenter, is given the task of guessing the signs as they are turned up. A pack of twenty-five cards is used, each five of which carry the same sign. Five cards are marked with a star, five with a square, five with a circle, five with wavy lines, and five with a cross. The experimenter naturally does not know the order in which the pack is arranged, nor has the subject any opportunity of seeing the cards. Many of the experiments were negative, since the result did not exceed the probability of five chance hits. In the case of certain subjects, however, some results were distinctly above probability. The first series of experiments consisted in each subject trying to guess the cards 800 times. The average result showed 6.5 hits for 25 cards, which is 1.5 more than the chance probability of 5 hits. The probability of there being a chance deviation of 1.5 from the number 5 works out at $1:250,000$. This proportion shows that the probability of a chance deviation is not exactly high, since it is to be expected only once in 250,000 cases. The results vary according to the specific gift of the individual subject. One young man, who in numerous experiments scored an average of 10 hits for every 25 cards (double the probable number), once guessed all 25 cards correctly, which gives a probability of $1:298,023,223,876,953,125$. The possibility of the pack being shuffled in some arbitrary way is guarded against by an apparatus which shuffles the cards automatically, independently of the experimenter.

After the first series of experiments the spatial distance between the experimenter and the subject was increased, in one case to 250 miles. The average result of numerous experiments amounted here to 10.1 hits for 25 cards. In another series of experiments, when experimenter and subject were in the same room, the score was 11.4 for 25; when the subject was in the next room, 9.7 for 25; when two rooms away, 12.0 for 25. Rhine mentions the experiments of F. L. Usher and E. L. Burt, which were conducted with positive results over a distance of 960 miles. With the aid of synchronized watches experiments were also conducted between Durham, North Carolina, and Zagreb, Yugoslavia, about 4000 miles, with equally positive results.

The fact that distance has no effect in principle shows that the thing in question cannot be a phenomenon of force or energy, for otherwise the distance to be overcome and the diffusion in space would cause a diminution of the effect, and it is more than probable that the score would fall proportionately to the square of the distance. Since this is obviously not the case, we have no alternative but to assume that distance is [psychologically] variable, and may in certain circumstances be reduced to vanishing point by a [psychological] condition.

Even more remarkable is the fact that *time* is not in principle a prohibiting factor either; that is to say, the reading of a series of cards to be turned up in the future produces a score that exceeds chance probability. The results of Rhine's time experiment show a probability of 1:400,000, which means a considerable probability of there being some factor independent of time. They point, in other words, to a [mental] relativity of time, since the experiment was concerned with perceptions of events which had not yet occurred. In these circumstances the time factor seems to have been eliminated by a [mental] function or [psychological] condition which is also capable of abolishing the spatial factor. If, in the spatial experiments, we were obliged to admit that energy does not decrease with distance, then the time experiments make it completely impossible for us even to think of there being any energy relationship between the perception and the future event. We must give up at the outset all explanations in terms of energy, which amounts to saying that events of this kind cannot be considered from the point of view of causality, for causality presupposes the existence of space and time in so far as all observations are ultimately based upon bodies in motion.

As is only to be expected, every conceivable kind of attempt has been made to explain away these results, which seem to border on the miraculous and frankly impossible. But all such attempts come to grief on the facts, and the facts refuse so far to be argued out of existence. Rhine's experiments confront us with the fact that there are events which are related to one another experimentally, and in this case *meaningfully*, without there being any possibility of proving that this relation is a causal one, since the "transmission" exhibits none of the known properties of energy. There is therefore good reason to doubt whether it is a question of transmission at all. The time experiments rule out any such thing in principle, for it would be absurd to suppose that a situation which does not yet exist and will only occur in the future could transmit itself as a phenomenon of energy to a receiver in the present. It seems more likely that scientific explanation will have to begin with a criticism of our concepts of space and time on the one hand, and with the unconscious on the other. As I have said, it is impossible, with our present resources, to explain ESP, or the fact of meaningful coincidence, as a phenomenon of energy. This makes an end of the causal explanation as well, for "effect" cannot be understood as anything except a phenomenon of energy. Therefore it cannot be a question of cause and effect, but of a falling together in time, a kind of simultaneity. Because of this quality of simultaneity, I have picked on the term "synchronicity" to designate a hypothetical factor equal in rank to causality as a principle of explanation. In my essay "The Spirit of Psychology" I defined synchronicity as a [psychologically] conditioned relativity of space and time. Rhine's experiments show that in relation to the psyche space and time are, so to speak, "elastic" and can apparently be reduced almost to [the] vanishing point, as though they were dependent on [psychological] conditions and did not exist in themselves but were only "postulated" by the conscious mind. In man's original view of the world, as we find it among primitives, space and time have a very precarious existence. They became "fixed" concepts only in the course of his mental development, thanks largely to the introduction of measurement. In themselves, space and time consist of *nothing*. They are hypostatized concepts born of the discriminating activity of the conscious mind, and they form the indispensable co-ordinate for describing the behavior of bodies in motion. They are, therefore, essentially [mental] in origin, which is probably the reason that impelled Kant to regard them as *a priori* categories. But if space and time are only apparently properties of bodies in motion and are created by the intellectual needs of the observer, then their relativization by [psychological] conditions is no longer a matter for astonishment but is brought within the bounds of possibility. This possibility presents itself when the psyche observes, not external bodies, but *itself*. That is precisely what happens in Rhine's experiments: the subject's answer is not the result of his observing the physical cards, it is a product of pure imagination, of "chance" ideas which reveal the structure of that which produces them, namely the unconscious. Here I will only point out that it is the decisive factors in the unconscious psyche, the archetypes, which constitute the structure of the collective unconscious. The latter represents a psyche that is identical with itself in all individuals. It cannot be directly perceived or "represented," in contrast to the perceptible [mental] phenomena, and on account of its "irrepresentable" nature I have called it "psychoid." . . .

Here I would like to call attention to a possible misunderstanding which may be occasioned by the term "synchronicity." I chose this term because the simultaneous occurrence of two meaningfully but not causally connected events seemed to me an essential criterion. I am therefore using the general concept of synchronicity in the special sense of a coincidence in time of two or more causally unrelated events which have the same or a similar meaning, in contrast to "synchronism," which simply means the simultaneous occurrence of two events.

Synchronicity therefore means the simultaneous occurrence of a certain [mental] state with one or more external events which appear as meaningful parallels to the momentary subjective state—and, in certain cases, vice versa. [To give an example!] An acquaintance of mine saw and experienced in a dream the sudden death of a friend, with all the characteristic details. The dreamer was in Europe at the time and the friend in America. The death was confirmed next morning by telegram, and ten days later a letter confirmed the details. Comparison of European time with American time showed that the death occurred at least an hour before the dream. The dreamer had gone to bed late and not slept until about one o'clock. The dream occurred at approximately two in the morning. The dream experience is *not synchronous* with the death. Experiences of this kind frequently take place a little before or after the critical event. . . .

Synchronistic events rest on the *simultaneous occurrence of two different [psychological] states*. One of them is the normal, probable state (i.e., the one that is causally explicable), and the other, the critical experience, is the one that cannot be derived causally from the first . . . and whose objective existence can only be verified afterwards. This definition must be borne in mind particularly when it is a question of future events. They are evidently not *synchronous* but are *synchronistic*, since they are experienced as [mental] images *in the present*, as though the objective event already existed. An unexpected content which is directly or indirectly connected with some objective external event coincides with the ordinary [mental] state: this is what I call synchronicity, and I maintain that we are dealing with exactly the same category of events whether their objectivity appears separated from my consciousness in space or in time. This view is confirmed by Rhine's results in so far as they were not influenced by changes in space or time. Space and time, the conceptual coordinates of bodies in motion, are probably at bottom one and the same (which is why we speak of a long or short "space of time"), and Philo Judaeus said long ago that "the extension of heavenly motion is time." Synchronicity in space can equally well be conceived as perception in time, but remarkably enough it is not so easy to understand synchronicity in time as spatial, for we cannot imagine any space in which future events are objectively present and could be experienced as such through a reduction of this spatial distance. But since experience has shown that under certain conditions space and time can be reduced almost to zero, causality disappears along with them, because causality is bound up with the existence of space and time and physical changes, and consists essentially in the succession of cause and effect. For this reason synchronistic phenomena cannot in principle be associated with any conceptions of causality. Hence the interconnection of meaningfully coincident factors must necessarily be thought of as acausal.

In view of this complicated situation it may be worth while to recapitulate the argument discussed above, and this can best be done with the aid of our examples. In Rhine's experiment I made the assumption that, owing to the tense expectation or emotional state of the subject, an already existing, correct, but unconscious image of the result enables his conscious mind to score a more than chance number of hits. . . . Similarly, the almost simultaneous dream of the violent death of the friend arose from an already existing unconscious knowledge of it.

In all these cases and others like them there seems to be an *a priori*, causally inexplicable knowledge of a situation which is at the time unknowable. Synchronicity therefore consists of two factors: (a) An unconscious image comes into consciousness either directly (i.e., literally) or indirectly (symbolized or suggested) in the form of a dream, idea, or premonition. (b) An objective situation coincides with this content. The one is as puzzling as the other. How does the unconscious image arise, and how the coincidence? I understand only too well why people prefer to doubt the reality of these things. Here I will only pose the question. Later in the course of this study I will try to give an answer. . . .

I am only too conscious that synchronicity is a highly abstract and "irrepresentable" quantity. It ascribes to the moving body a certain psychoid property which, like space, time, and causality, forms a criterion of its behavior. We must completely give up the idea of the psyche's being somehow connected with the brain, and remember instead the "meaningful" and "intelligent" behavior of the lower organisms, which are without a brain. Here we find ourselves much closer to the formal factor which, as I have said, has nothing to do with brain activity.

If that is so, then we must ask ourselves whether the relation of soul and body can be considered from this angle, that is to say whether the co-ordination of [mental] and physical processes in a living organism can be understood as a synchronistic phenomenon rather than as a causal relation. Both Geulincx and Leibnitz regarded the co-ordination of the [mental] and the physical as an act of God, of some principle standing outside empirical nature. The assumption of a causal relation between psyche and physis leads on the other hand to conclusions which it is difficult to square with experience: either there are physical processes which cause [mental] happenings, or there is a pre-existent psyche which organizes matter. In the first case it is hard to see how chemical processes can ever produce [mental] processes, and in the second case one wonders how an immaterial psyche could ever set matter in motion. It is not necessary to think of Leibnitz's preestablished harmony or anything of that kind, which would have to be absolute and would manifest itself in a universal correspondence and sympathy, rather like the meaningful coincidence of time-points lying on the same degree of latitude in Schopenhauer. The synchronicity principle possesses properties that may help to clear up the body-soul problem. Above all it is the fact of causeless order, or rather, of meaningful orderedness, that may throw light on psychophysical parallelism. The "absolute knowledge" which is characteristic of synchronistic phenomena, a knowledge not mediated by the sense organs, supports the hypothesis of a self-subsistent meaning, or even expresses its existence. Such a form of existence can only be transcendental, since, as the knowledge of future or spatially distant events shows, it is contained in a [psychologically] relative space and time, that is today in an irrepresentable space-time continuum. . . .

Synchronicity is not a philosophical view but an empirical concept which postulates an intellectually necessary principle. This cannot be called either materialism or metaphysics. No serious investigator would assert that the nature of what is observed to exist, and of that which observes, namely the psyche, are known and recognized quantities. If the latest conclusions of science are coming nearer and nearer to a unitary idea of being, characterized by space and time on the one hand and by causality and synchronicity on the other, that has nothing to do with materialism. Rather it seems to show that there is some possibility of getting rid of the incommensurability between the observed and the observer. The result, in that case, would be a unity of being which would have to be expressed in terms of a new conceptual language—a "neutral language," as W. Pauli once called it.

Space, time, and causality, the triad of classical physics, would then be supplemented by the synchronicity factor and become a tetrad, a *quaternio* which makes possible a whole judgment:

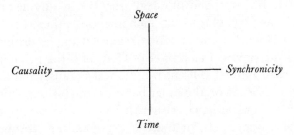

Here synchronicity is to the three other principles as the one-dimensionality of time is to the three-dimensionality of space, or as the recalcitrant "Fourth" in the *Timaeus*, which, Plato says, can only be added "by force" to the other three. Just as the introduction of time as the fourth dimension in modern physics postulates an irrepresentable space-time continuum, so the idea of synchronicity with its inherent quality of meaning produces a picture of the world so irrepresentable as to be quite baffling. The advantage, however, of adding this concept is that it makes possible a view which includes the psychoid factor in our description and knowledge of nature—an *a priori* meaning or "equivalence." The problem that runs like a red thread through the speculations of alchemists for fifteen hundred years thus repeats and solves itself, the so-called axiom of Maria the Jewess (or Copt): "Out of the Third comes the One as the Fourth." This cryptic observation confirms . . . that in principle new points of view are not as a rule discovered in territory that is already known, but in out-of-the-way places that may even be avoided because of their bad name. The old dream of the alchemists, the transmutation of chemical elements, this much-derided idea, has become a reality in our own day, and its symbolism, which was no less an object of ridicule, has turned out to be a veritable goldmine for the psychology of the unconscious. . . .

The revolution brought about by the discovery of radioactivity has considerably modified the classical views of physics. So great is the change of standpoint that we have to revise the classical schema I made use of above. As I was able, thanks to the friendly interest which Professor Pauli evinced in my work, to discuss these questions of principle with a professional physicist who could at the same time appreciate my psychological arguments, I am in a position to put forward a suggestion that takes modern physics into account. Pauli suggested replacing the opposition of space and time in the classical schema by (conservation of) energy and the space-time continuum. This suggestion led me to a closer

definition of the other pair of opposites—causality and synchronicity—
with a view of establishing some kind of connection between these two
heterogeneous concepts. We finally agreed on the following *quaternio:*

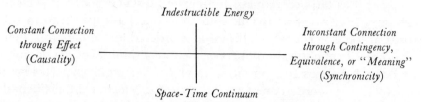

This schema satisfies on the one hand the postulates of modern physics,
and on the other hand those of psychology. The psychological point of
view needs clarifying. A causalistic explanation of synchronicity seems
out of the question for the reasons given above. It consists essentially of
"chance" equivalences. . . . The meaningful coincidence or equivalence
of a psychic and a physical state that have no causal relationship to one
another means, in general terms, that it is a modality without a cause, an
"acausal orderedness." The question now arises whether our definition of
synchronicity with reference to the equivalence of [mental] and physical
processes . . . requires expansion. This requirement seems to force itself
on us when we consider the above, wider conception of synchronicity as
an "acausal orderedness." Into this category come all "acts of creation,"
a priori factors such as the properties of natural numbers, the discontinuities of modern physics, etc. Consequently we would have to include constant and experimentally reproducible phenomena within the scope of
our expanded concept, though this does not seem to accord with the
nature of the phenomena included in synchronicity narrowly understood. The latter are most individual cases which cannot be repeated
experimentally. This is not of course altogether true, as Rhine's experiments show and numerous other experiences with clairvoyant individuals. These facts prove that even in individual cases which have no
common measure there are certain regularities and therefore constant
factors, from which we must conclude that our narrower conception of
synchronicity is probably too narrow and really needs expanding. I in-
cline in fact to the view that synchronicity in the narrower sense is only
a particular instance of general acausal orderedness—that, namely, of
the equivalence of [mental] and physical processes where the observer
is in the fortunate position of being able to recognize the *tertium compara-
tionis.* But as soon as he perceives the archetypal background he is
tempted to trace the mutual assimilation of independent and physical
processes back to a (causal) effect of the archetype, and thus to overlook
the fact that they are merely contingent. This danger is avoided if one

regards synchronicity as a special instance of general acausal orderedness. In this way we also avoid multiplying our principles of explanation illegitimately, for the archetype *is* the introspectively recognizable form of *a priori* [mental] orderedness. If an external synchronistic process now associates itself with it, it falls into the same basic pattern—in other words, it too is "ordered." This form of orderedness differs from that of the properties of natural numbers or the discontinuities of physics in that the latter have existed from eternity and occur regularly, whereas the forms of [mental] orderedness are *acts of creation in time*. That, incidentally, is precisely why I have stressed the element of time as being characteristic of these phenomena and called them *synchronistic*. . . .

Synchronicity is no more baffling or mysterious than the discontinuities of physics. It is only the ingrained belief in the sovereign power of causality that creates intellectual difficulties and makes it appear unthinkable that causeless events exist or could ever occur. But if they do, then we must regard them as *creative acts*, as the continuous creation of a pattern that exists from all eternity, repeats itself sporadically, and is not derivable from any known antecedents. We must of course guard against thinking of every event whose cause is unknown as "causeless." This, as I have already stressed, is admissible only when a cause is not even thinkable. But thinkability is itself an idea that needs the most rigorous criticism. Had the atom corresponded to the original philosophical conception of it, its fissionability would be unthinkable. But once it proves to be a measurable quantity, its non-fissionability becomes unthinkable. Meaningful coincidences are thinkable as pure chance. But the more they multiply and the greater and more exact the correspondence is, the more their probability sinks and their unthinkability increases, until they can no longer be regarded as pure chance but, for lack of a causal explanation, have to be thought of as meaningful arrangements. As I have already said, however, their "inexplicability" is not due to the fact that the cause is unknown, but to the fact that a cause is not even thinkable in intellectual terms. This is necessarily the case when space and time lose their meaning or have become relative, for under those circumstances a causality which presupposes space and time for its continuance can no longer be said to exist and becomes altogether unthinkable.

For these reasons it seems to me necessary to introduce, alongside space, time, and causality, a category which not only enables us to understand synchronistic phenomena as a special class of natural events, but also takes the contingent partly as a universal factor existing from all eternity, and partly as the sum of countless individual acts of creation occurring in time. . . .

RÉSUMÉ

I have been informed that many readers find it difficult to follow my argument. Acausality and the idea of synchronicity as such, seem to present especial difficulties to their understanding, and for this reason I should like to make a few additional remarks in order to sum.

1. ACAUSALITY. If natural law were an absolute truth, then of course there could not possibly be any processes that deviate from it. But since causality is a *statistical* truth, it holds good only on average and thus leaves room for *exceptions* which must somehow be experienceable, that is to say, *real*. I try to regard synchronistic events as acausal exceptions of this kind. They prove to be relatively independent of space and time; they relativize space and time in so far as space presents in principle no obstacle to their passage and the sequence of events in time is inverted, so that it looks as if an event which has not yet occurred were causing a perception in the present. But if space and time are relative, then causality too loses its validity, since the sequence of cause and effect is either relativized or abolished.

2. SYNCHRONICITY. Despite my express warning I see that this concept has already been confused by the critics with *synchronism*. By synchronicity I mean the occurrence of a *meaningful coincidence in time*. It can take three forms:
   a. The coincidence of a certain [mental] content with a corresponding objective process which is perceived to take place simultaneously.
   b. The coincidence of a subjective [mental] state with a phantasm (dream or vision) which later turns out to be a more or less faithful reflection of a "synchronistic," objective event that took place more or less simultaneously, but at a distance.
   c. The same, except that the event perceived takes place in the future and is represented in the present only by a phantasm that corresponds to it.

Whereas in the first case an objective event coincides with a subjective content, the synchronicity in the other two cases can only be verified subsequently, though the synchronistic event as such is formed by the coincidence of a neutral [mental] state with a phantasm (dream or vision).

"We are still so far from understanding all the agents in nature and their different modes of action that it would display very little of the spirit of philosophy to deny the existence of phenomena only because they are inexplicable in the actual conditions of our knowledge."
Laplace (quoted in Tweedale, 1925, p. 338).

40.

What Is Important About The Paranormal?

Lawrence LeShan

Psychical research, whether one calls it "parapsychology," "Psi," "the study of the paranormal," or "ESP research," is far more than it appears to be on first glance. In the most profound sense, it is the study of the basic nature of man.

To demonstrate this, and its meaning for us today, let us start with examining our present concept in this culture of what man "is." We might begin with a quotation from James Branch Cabell . . .

> What is man that his welfare be considered? An ape who chatters of kinship with the archangels while he very filthily digs for groundnuts. And yet I perceive that this same man is a maimed God. He is condemned under penalty to measure eternity with an hourglass and infinity with a yardstick, and what is more he nearly does it.

We ask, "What is man?" In this anti-metaphysical age we regard the question as of little importance. It is, however, the most crucial question of all. How we answer it determines how we treat other men and how we treat ourselves. If we believe that man is basically good, we treat him as if he were, and—as Goethe pointed out long ago—thereby tend to make him a little better. If we believe that man is basically evil, we treat him as such, and thereby not only make him worse, but also, since we know ourselves to be part of humanity, tend to stifle our own inner being and, in consequence, lose our joy, spontaneity, and zest.

A change in our concept of man leads to changes in behavior. For example, the new understanding that Freud gave us in the last half-century changed one part of our concept. Knowing that man has an unconscious, that it often very strongly influences him, has led to considerable changes in education, medicine, art, child-raising practices, law, and a host of other fields.

When we look at our present cultural picture of what man is, we see that we can describe it as "rational" and "sensible." Man is made up of flesh, bone, and nerve. He is the material of earth in an unusually complex form, and that is all he is.

In the same way that we perceive one bicycle as being separate from another, we perceive ourselves as cut off from the world and from other men by our skin limits. (This, by the way, itself strongly influences how we treat one another. If I see you as separate and different from myself, I am likely to treat you differently from myself. If I perceive you and me as a part of one another, I am likely to treat you the same way I treat myself.) It is obvious just from our behavior, as reflected in our newspapers, that we regard each man as alone, isolated: only in moments of love, compassion, religious awe, ecstasy, laughter, dedication, are we able to bridge the gap and become a part of one another. Each man is separate, although made up of the same type of atoms, molecules, and physical structure. "If you prick me, do I not bleed?" asks Shylock. Of similar structure we may be, but we see each man as basically locked in his skin, knowing the world only through the narrow windows of his senses, touching another only through these.

We live in a world, and have a science, that supports this view. The facts we know seem to point directly to the validity of this viewpoint, that man is understandable in terms of essentially the same basic, everyday, physical concepts we use to understand cars and computers. There are, we all agree, more details to understand, but we know the outlines, the major conceptual tools we need, and they are of this familiar type and order.

Do *all* the facts we know support this view—or is it *almost all*? If we look carefully and honestly, we find it is *almost all*. There are some that do not. *There are facts that do not fit in.*

Parapsychology is the scientific study of what Charles Fort used to call "The Damned Facts": the facts that do not fit in, the facts that cannot be reconciled with the concepts we ordinarily use to explain man and his world. However, if we have learned one thing from science, it is that the atypical case, the unusual incident, the one fact that does *not* fit in with the rest, is the one which—if we look seriously at it—teaches us about all the others.

It is the *one* substance in Madame Curie's workshop that glows in the dark which teaches us about the basic structure of all the others that do not. It is the *one* petri dish in Fleming's laboratory in which the bacteria die unexpectedly that leads us to the discovery of the antibiotics. It is the one set of flasks in Pasteur's experiments in which life does *not* appear that teaches us the source of life in the others. It is the atypical paralysis in which neurology *cannot* find the lesion that leads Freud to the discovery of the unconscious. It is the one problem in physics (the "addition of velocities problem") that can *not* be solved in the usual way that leads to an Einsteinian revolution and teaches us a deeper understanding of the problems we have not been able to solve in the old way.

In our picture of man that *almost* all the facts agree with, there *are* exceptions. There are facts that do not fit in with our neat ideas of our each being so separate from each other, or of our just being ordinary matter like rocks and airplanes and computers. There are facts we cannot reconcile with all our preconceived ideas.

About three years ago, a physician in a town over 1,000 miles from New York, where I was living, went to a medical meeting several states away from his home. It was a five-day meeting. He checked into the hotel at nine in the morning, checked out at five the same afternoon, and vanished. I had never met or spoken to the man, or to any member of his family. Several weeks later there was still no trace of him, and he was on the police "Missing Persons" list from coast to coast. Through a rather complex chain of connections, the man's wife heard that I was doing research with Eileen Garrett, one of the most gifted and dedicated clairvoyants of all time. She wrote me, asking if I could help her locate her husband, and enclosing a two-inch square from a shirt he had worn the day before he left for the meeting. The morning I got the letter, I phoned Mrs. Garrett asking for an appointment. She told me to come in at two that afternoon. When I came into her office, we went into the seance room without saying one word about the problem. There, after she was in trance, I told her two sentences: "A man has disappeared; his wife is very worried. Can you help?" Mrs. Garrett fingered the scrap of cloth, and presently said, "He is in La Jolla. He went there due to a psychic wound he suffered when he was 14 years old and his father disappeared."

That evening I telephoned the wife and asked her, "Did anything happen to your husband between the ages of 13 and 15?" She replied, "When he was 14 his father deserted the family and was not heard of again for 25 years." Three weeks later, when the physician was located, it turned out he had been in La Jolla on the date of the seance.

Here is a fact that does not fit into our picture of man and his relations with each other. Nor does it fit into any science based on the idea of separateness of individuals in the usual sense of the term.

"But," we say, as we try to save our nice, accustomed, materialistic picture of man and his world, "perhaps it is something like radio waves. He gave them off, she received them, perhaps tuned in somehow by the piece of his shirt. It would simply be a case of her receiving his broadcasts. A radio station and a radio set are separate, and neither has to know where the other is for one to receive signals from the other. What is the problem?"

It just won't work that way. To show why such an explanation is not at all adequate, let us take one of the older cases in the literature of psychical research. (I will present a more modern, laboratory-type use shortly, but one of the older examples may be helpful in getting more of the "flavor" of this field.)

Mrs. Verrall (a very talented and carefully studied clairvoyant) recorded on Dec. 11, 1911, the following (Fodor, 1966, p. 296).

> The cold was intense and a single candle gave poor light. He was lying on the sofa or on a bed and was reading Marmontel by the light of a single candle. . . . The book was lent to him, it did not belong to him. [On Dec. 17 she continued the message.] The name Marmontel is correct. . . . A French book, I think his memoirs. The name Passy may help him to remember. Passy or Fleury. The book was bound in two volumes, the binding was old and the book was lent to him. The name Marmontel is not on the cover.

On March 1, Mrs. Verrall was told by a friend, Mr. Marsh, that he had read the memoirs of Marmontel on a bitterly cold night in Paris on February 20 [1912] by the light of a candle. At one time he was reading in bed, at another he reclined on two chairs. He had borrowed the book, it had three volumes, and on February 21, he had read the chapter in which the finding of a picture, painted at Passy, is described by Marmontel, the discovery being associated with Mr. Fleury.

Now, you can work all you wish with radio waves and all the other concepts of our everyday world and everday science, but you *cannot* get the radio waves to go ahead in time and be received *before* they are sent. To explain "Damned Facts" like this one, you need a new concept: a new definition of man, and of his relationship to the cosmos. (I should also remark that, for every example of "psi" or "the paranormal" I refer to here, many dozens of others, just as good or better, have been published by serious people.)

There are four major sources of our "Damned Facts." We might term these *Laboratory experiments*, *Spontaneous incidents*, *Mediumistic cases*, and *Psychotherapy cases*. Let us look at a fairly typical example from each.

1. LABORATORY EXPERIMENTS

Dr. Gertrude Schmeidler; a psychologist, has repeated the following basic experiments many times and with many modifications. A group of subjects (such as a class of college students) is asked, "Do you believe or not in the possibility of ESP existing?" After they have written their answers, she gives each of them a form with spaces to record a great many guesses. They are then told that on the following day a pack of special cards will be thoroughly shuffled, and the order they fall into will be written on a similar form. They are to "guess" the order the cards will fall into tomorrow, and to record their guesses now. After everyone has recorded his guesses, the forms are collected and put away safely. The next day the cards are shuffled, and their final order compared to the guesses. The group of students who stated that they believed in the possibility that ESP could exist can be scientifically demonstrated to have guessed more accurately than the group who stated that they did not believe in such a possibility.

Such precognition experiments, which are among the easiest parapsychological experiments to do, not only provide scientific demonstration of the existence of psi, but are also valuable in helping us develop our beginning understanding of the relationship of ESP and personality. There are hundreds of serious laboratory demonstrations of precognition in the literature.

They also show (as do many other studies) that psi cannot be reconciled with the usual concepts and explanations given in our culture of how-the-world-works. As J. B. Rhine and Gaither Pratt, two of the leading scientists in this field, have stated (1962, p. 66):

> In order to be considered as parapsychological, the phenomena must be demonstrably non-physical. That is, they must occur under conditions which clearly

eliminate the types of operation known as physical. . . . The question of whether or not the operation of psi shows any relation to known physical law is not a matter of interpretation. It has been brought into experimental focus and is now only a question of the facts themselves.

2. SPONTANEOUS CASES

A child was one day playing under observation in a field out of sight or sound of her house. Suddenly she left her play, dashed to the road, and ran down it to the nearby doctor's home. She told him to come quickly, that her mother had fallen down in the sewing room of the house and did not move. The physician, believing the child had come from the house and had seen this, went immediately with her and found the mother lying unconscious on the floor in the "sewing room" (a room very rarely entered by anyone in the family), having had a stroke. The child was unable to explain how she knew, saying she "just knew."

3. MEDIUMISTIC CASES

The two cases described previously, the "Vanished Man" and the "Marmontel" cases, are fairly typical of this type.

4. PSYCHOTHERAPY CASES

Several years before the following incident happened, I had worked with a patient named "Marla." She was an artist and an expert on modern art. Obviously, as a psychotherapist, one never mentions one patient's name to another.

At the time the incident happened, I was working with a fairly new patient. She was an amateur painter, and one day brought in a painting of hers to show me. We talked about it for a while, and I told her I did not know much about this type of art and, thinking about getting Marla's opinion, asked if I might show it to a friend of mine who did and get an opinion on it. The patient replied, "Of course," and then, for a moment, looked curiously blank. She then asked me, "Tell me, did anyone named 'Marla' ever sit in this chair?" When I—quite startled—asked her why she had asked, she could only reply that she just felt she had to ask. She, herself, knew no one by that name, she said.

These are the four major sources of our evidence for the existence of the "paranormal." In order to give a better picture of our present experimental approach to the subject. I will describe briefly one research program now underway.

At Maimonides Hospital in New York, under the leadership of Drs. Stanley Krippner and Montague Ullman, a long-term study of the paranormal is being conducted. The general design of the research is as follows.

The subject ("percipient" or "receiver") goes to sleep at night in a special room in which he is monitored by instruments that can tell when he is dreaming. (This is known as "REM Technique.") *After* the subject is asleep, one of the experimenters ("agent" or "sender") goes to a room a good distance away. There he chooses, from a large file of envelopes, one by a random procedure. In the envelope are 12 pictures, of which he chooses one at random; all night the experimenter (the only person who knows which envelope or picture he has chosen) concentrates on this picture.

Another experimenter watches the instruments which indicate the subject's sleep state. As soon as they show he has finished a dream, he is awakened and tells his dream into a tape recorder. He then goes back to sleep.

In the morning, the tapes of his dreams are typed, and together with all 12 pictures in the original envelope go to a panel of judges. Their job is to try to tell *from the dreams of the "receiver"* which of the 12 pictures the "sender" concentrated on. Generally speaking, the judges do not have too much trouble doing this.

This type of study not only clearly demonstrates scientifically the existence of telepathy, but also is extremely valuable in studying various important aspects of it, such as the question of "What relationships between 'sender' and 'receiver' make it most likely to occur?" "Is it better if they like each other, know each other well, etc.?" "What types of subject matter are most likely to be transmitted: calm, peaceful, exciting, depressing, etc.?"

Many hundreds of carefully studied cases and precise laboratory experiments, published in the professional literature of this field, have now established that ESP (telepathy, clairvoyance, precognition, etc.) exists— but what does all this mean? Primarily that there is far more to man than we have known. We have the data, and they are strong and clear. But *they could not exist* if man were only what we have believed him to be. If he were only flesh and bone, if he worked on the same type of principle as a machine, if he were really as separate from all others as we have thought, it would be impossible for him to do the things we know he sometimes does. A new concept of man, a new way of looking at others and ourselves, a *knowledge* that there is more to man than our old concepts allow, is scientifically demonstrated in these facts. And *that* is the real importance of ESP.

When the concept of the unconscious was clarified by Freud and accepted by our culture, it led to to major changes in our behavior toward others and toward ourselves. Understanding a little more about his own nature helped man to act a little less like a wolf to other men and to himself.

The changes in viewpoint implied by these "Damned Facts" is many times greater than that implied by Freud's concepts. And we must not underestimate how terribly we need a new concept of man. The philosophical legacy of the seventeenth century, which Western civilization has been living on, is used up. The materialistic metaphysics which gave us the Industrial Revolution is now destroying us. Our institutions are foundering one after the other: our way of life is becoming unworkable. Our techniques of relating to each other are driving our species toward extinction and making our only planet an unlivable garbage dump.

In the *New York Post* (May 15, 1969, p. 47) U Thant stated:

> "I do not wish to seem overdramatic, but I can only conclude from the information that is available to me as Secretary General [of the United Nations] that the members of the United Nations have perhaps 10 years left in which to subordinate their ancient quarrels and launch a global partnership to end the arms race, to improve the human environment, to defuse the population explosion, and to supply the required momentum to world development efforts. If such a global partnership is not forged within the next decade, then I very much fear that the problems I have mentioned will have reached such staggering proportions that they will be beyond our capacity to control."

Most ecologists, and most students of the effect of population pressure on behavior, give us between 10 and 30 years to make major changes before it is too late to save the species of man. From the time this is written, the crucial dates fall between A.D. 1979 and 1999. That is a terribly short time to change our long-standing ways of acting and reacting as much as we must to save ourselves.

One thing is perfectly clear: *we cannot hope to change our ways of relating to ourselves and others without a major change in how we perceive ourselves and others; we must have a new and more complete concept of what-man-is than we have now, or we perish.*

Psychical research has given us the clues and clear signposts to a new concept, a more accurate picture based on deeper understanding. This new picture is hard to see as yet. It flies in the face of all our preconceptions and of what we think of as our experience. Consider:

The Earth goes around the sun. "Ridiculous; who has not seen the sun rise, circle the heavens, and set?"
The Earth is round, not *flat.* "Idiotic; those on the bottom would fall off."
Emotions can contribute to the cause of an ulcer. "Nonsense; everyone knows the mind is one thing, the body another."

These preconceptions are broken now, and new concepts accepted. But the old ideas were very strong, and were accepted as "obvious common sense" at the time the new ideas came in.

Because they go against all our preconceptions, it is very hard for most of us to evaluate objectively the "impossible facts" of ESP, the facts that cannot happen, but do. As Dr. Gardner Murphy, past president of the American Psychological Association, has observed: "If there were one-tenth of the evidence in any other field of science that there is in parapsychology, it would be accepted beyond question."

Why, then, is it so difficult for psi to be accepted? Partly because of the theoretical bind it seems to lead us to. The "impossible facts" seem to put us into a logically impossible, even insane, position. This position might be stated as follows:

1. If what we *generally* know about how the world works is basically true, then certain things—such as seeing ahead in time—are impossible.

2. What we know about how the world works *is, generally speaking, true.* We function far too effectively in our everyday life to make it possible for us to be operating on a set of false assumptions.

3. But psi events *do* happen.

Stated this way, which is the way it has generally been formulated, it *is* an illogical position, and a reasonable mind can only assume (in spite of the overwhelming evidence) that statement 3 is *not* true: that these things do *not* happen. Most individuals (and most scientists) shy away from the whole contradictory mind-bending mess by simply not looking at the data, and thus are able to ignore the problem completely.

There is, however, another answer, one that fits the evidence and that seems clearly indicated if the problem is approached scientifically: what we know *is* true, but there is *more* to man, *more* to him and his relationship to the cosmos than we have accepted; further, this *more* is of a different kind and order than the parts we know about. This answer flies in the face of only one preconception—that we really know *all that is important to know* about man. And this preconception no scientist and no rational mind would consciously accept on *any* subject if it were stated clearly. Yet this is the preconception that we have unconsciously accepted, and that has seemed to make so hopeless our attempts to keep the human race from following the path of the dinosaurs. The evidence is clear that it is not a valid conception. If we have the courage, we can follow the clues we have to new, fresh answers.

Coleridge wrote somewhere: "What if you slept? And what if in your sleep, you dreamed? And what if in your dream you went to heaven and there plucked a strange and beautiful flower? And what if, when you woke, you had the flower in your hand? Ah! What then?"

The human race *has* dreamed. We have dreamed of men like angels, and have awakened with the long, gold-tipped feathers of angels' wings in our hands. The "impossible facts" of ESP are these feathers. They tell us of a part of man, long hidden in the mists of legend, art, dream, myth, and mysticism, which our explorers of reality in the last 90 years have demonstrated to be scientifically valid, to be real. At the least, we have learned that man is far more than he seems to be, more than the materialist philosopher has ever conceived of, that he can and does touch others and the universe in a way we do not yet understand, but a way obeying quite different laws than do his senses, that his separation from others and his loneliness in the world are, at least partly, illusion.

Psychical research offers a new and deeper understanding of the ancient crucial question, "What is Man?" This understanding awaits us beyond the next horizon. Let us try to reach it in time.

41.

Preliminary Notes on the Nature of Psi Processes

Charles T. Tart

One of the more frequent and interesting classes of phenomena reported by experiencers of many altered states of consciousness are *paranormal* or *psi* phenomena, experiences in which the mind seemingly transcends the ordinary laws of time and space. For example, 47 per cent of a sample of experienced marijuana users reported that they had personally experienced mind-to-mind contact with others while intoxicated; some had experienced their minds leaving their physical body, etc. (Tart, 1971). The conventional Western world view indicates that such phenomena are, *a priori*, impossible. Therefore reports of such phenomena may be studied as examples of the arbitrary, nonsensical, and unusual ways the human biocomputer may be temporarily reprogrammed in altered states, but they are not to be taken seriously as indicating anything about the nature of the real world or the ultimate nature of man.

If, on the other hand, some of these phenomena may sometimes repre-

Printed by permission of the author.

sent more than an arbitrary reprogramming of the biocomputer, they not only have vast implications for our view of the universe, but also call for a much wider approach to the study of altered states of consciousness. Although generally neglected, there exists a solid body of scientific evidence indicating that such phenomena are indeed sometimes "real." This paper will review the more basic findings of modern parapsychology.

The careful research of parapsychologists over the last half-century has solidly established the existence of several types of paranormal (psi) effects, viz., telepathy (mind-to-mind communication), clairvoyance (direct mental perception of a state of physical affairs), precognition (foretelling the future), and psychokinesis (the direct influence of mind on matter). Telepathy, clairvoyance, and precognition are generally referred to collectively as extrasensory *perception* (ESP), while psychokinesis (PK) is a sort of paranormal motor action. The term psi includes both sorts of processes. In each case, no known physical energy can act as the carrier of the information or force.

Many scientists do not accept the reality of these phenomena—because of an *a priori* rejection of the possibility of psi phenomena, and a consequent ignorance of the experimental evidence: since those things *can't* really exist, why should I waste my time reading evidence that must be flawed? Price (1955), in the last serious attack on ESP to appear in a major scientific journal, epitomized this attitude, arguing that no matter how good the experimental evidence for ESP was, he would not accept it because it was incompatible with contemporary physical knowledge of the universe.

Such an attitude is illustrative of what Kuhn (1962) has called "paradigm clash": the psychology of human scientists is such that commitment to a generally successful and wide-ranging theory of how things work (the paradigm) narrows their perception; so data that do not fit into the paradigmatic view are overlooked or considered inherently invalid. One cannot argue on a scientific level with someone who says (1) your findings are *a priori* impossible, and (2) your insistence that you have such findings means that you are stupid, a charlatan, or both. Thus I shall make no attempt to "prove" the existence of various psi phenomena: the reader interested in the large mass of experimental evidence supporting the existence of psi phenomena may consult the rebuttals to Price's article (Meehl and Scriven, 1956; Rhine, 1956; Soal, 1956) or some good general review books* (Broad, 1962; Gudas, 1961; Heywood,

---

*Knowledge about psi phenomena is greatly confused by the immense popular interest in the subject, which has resulted in a flood of books by nonscientists. Too many of these books present data that fall far short of the standards of evidence used in scientific parapsychology. The books listed above are ones that are scientifically sound.

1955; Murphy and Dale, 1961; Pratt, 1966; Pratt *et al.*, 1966; Rao, 1966; Rhine, 1964; Schmeidler, 1969; Smythies, 1967; Soal and Bateman, 1954).

Aside from the effects of paradigm clash, psi phenomena are difficult to accept because there is no comprehensive theory for understanding them, although there are some decent small-scale theories about particular phenomena. This paper will present some general models of four major psi phenomena (telepathy, clairvoyance, precognition, and psychokinesis) which will put major empirical findings into general relationship. The emphasis will be primarily psychological, since psychological variables are the only ones that clearly influence the operation of psi. Note that this presentation is of *models*, not a general theory: models are useful for putting data together in a convenient and comprehensible way, but are not required to have the predictive power required of a theory. * Further, I shall try to indicate where significant gaps exist in our knowledge and where we badly need testable theories.

MODEL I: CLAIRVOYANCE (AND PRECOGNITION)

Clairvoyance is defined as the extrasensory perception of physical objects or events, without any possibility of there being knowledge of such objects or events in another person's mind (i.e., telepathy) as an intervening factor. The classic experimental form that has established the reality of clairvoyance is this: a deck of cards is thoroughly shuffled to randomize their order; and a subject then guesses what this order is before any human being looks at the cards and learns their order. Scores significantly beyond chance expectation indicate the operation of clairvoyance: in some fashion, the subject becomes aware of at least some of the cards when no sensory cues exist to give this information. Variations on the basic experimental design have been discussed by Rao (1966).

I have sketched a model of clairvoyance in Figure 41.1. The rectangular blocks in this figure and in subsequent figures indicate "processes" or "mechanisms" of some sort where information is transformed or used. The arrows indicate the direction of information flow within the model. I will discuss this model in considerable detail, since many points relevant to it will also apply to later models.

---

*Many other possible psi phenomena are not touched on in this paper, because they have not been researched as much as telepathy, clairvoyance, precognition, and PK have. They are covered in the general reference books mentioned above.

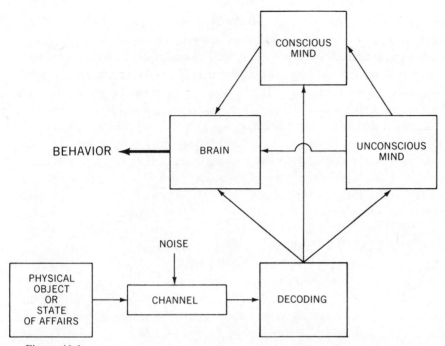

Figure 41.1
Model I: Clairvoyance. Reprinted from the *International Journal of Neuropsychiatry*,
2, no. 5 (1966), 491. Copyright 1966 by Research in Organic Psychiatry, Inc.

The model as a whole describes the following steps. We begin with a
physical event or state of affairs from which information reaches the subject via a channel of transmission. After reaching the subject, the information is decoded and eventuates in some sort of observable behavior
from which we infer that the information about the object or state of
affairs has reached the subject in the first place. Now let us look at these
various steps and processes in some detail.

The Target

We may begin with the physical object or state of affairs, the "target"
about which we wish to acquire information. Any object has a certain
set of physical properties which constitute its nature, its uniqueness. The
ruler on my desk, for instance, has a set of physical properties, such as
mass, elasticity, the ability to reflect certain wavelengths of light (color),
which make it a particular ruler.

In addition to these physical properties, we should also allow for the possibility that an object may possess "psychical" properties, properties which would be very convenient in understanding some of the more curious parapsychological phenomena. For example, Pratt has reported a "focusing effect" on certain target cards in the research he and Ryzl have done (Ryzl and Pratt, 1963). Physically these target cards were identical objects (unless you go to an extremely fine level of measurement, beyond that of the unaided senses), green and white pieces of cardboard; yet there was significantly higher ESP scoring with some of these target cards than with others. So we may postulate that these particular cards have psychical properties of some sort which make them more distinctive to the clairvoyant process. A large number of studies have been carried out on the physical and psychological nature of this focusing effect (Keil, 1971; Keil and Pratt, 1969; Pratt, 1967; Pratt and Jacobson, 1969; Pratt and Keil, 1969; Pratt, Keil and Stevenson, 1970; Pratt and Roll, 1968; Pratt *et al.*, 1968; Pratt *et al.*, 1969).

We must also distinguish between *active* properties and *passive* properties, for both the physical and the postulated psychical properties. By an *active* property, I mean one where some sort of information is "emitted" by the object's intrinsic nature or state of being. My desk lamp has an active property, that of emitting light rays. My ruler, on the other hand, is a passive object in this respect: if no light impinged on it from the outside to be reflected back, I would not be able to see it.

In Figure 41.2 I have sketched the different classes of object in clairvoyance tests. The object may have active properties, either physical or psychical, which are picked up or detected simply because they are constantly being "radiated" from the object or event. (I use "radiated" in the broadest sense here, without meaning to imply electromagnetic radiation.) On the other hand, the object might have only passive properties as far as the clairvoyance process is concerned, and may only be clairvoyantly detectable because some sort of activating "energy" is impinging on it and being "reflected." This "energy" might specifically result from a process within the subject, analogous to the way a radar set sends out a scanning beam of electromagnetic energy, or it might be a general background, activating energy that does not specifically depend on human subjects for its origin, analogous to the way most objects are visible during the day because of the background radiation of sunlight.

It is here, at this first step in the clairvoyance process, that we need some models and theories, and very much need the assistance of physicists in constructing them. Before we can begin to theorize, we must answer certain basic questions, all concerned with the nature of the information that is detected in the process of clairvoyance. What prop-

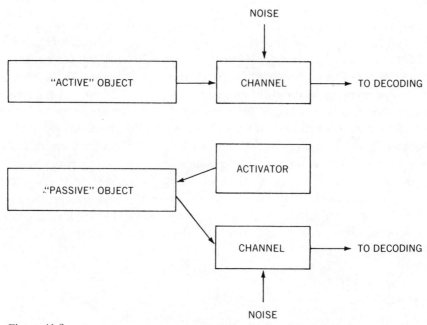

Figure 41.2

The Target Object. Reprinted from the *International Journal of Neuropsychiatry*, 2, no. 5 (1966), 178. Copyright 1966 by Research in Organic Psychiatry, Inc.

erties of an object or event are psychically detectable? We do not know whether *every* known physical property of an object is detectable by clairvoyance; it might be, for instance, that clairvoyance can detect surface patterns on an object, but not be able to tell us anything about its internal molecular structure. Physical variations in target objects that have been investigated to date, such as size, shape, color, and form, seem to be of no relevance (Rao, 1966). We need to know what sorts of *psychical* properties there are, whether they interact with physical properties, whether there are passive psychical properties that can be activated by some form of external "energy," and whether they can be deactivated by some method. Is there any kind of process which might destroy the clairvoyant detectability of an object? We have so many unanswered questions here that general theorizing is virtually impossible now.

On a more positive note, let me give you an example of a small-scale, testable theory in parapsychology. One concerning the nature of psychically detectable objects was originated by W. G. Roll of the Psychical Research Foundation (Roll, 1957–64). The theory postulates that physical objects have some sort of *psychical* properties associated with them by virtue of their history, by virtue of what they have been in spatial proximity to, and, of course, that these psychical properties are psychically detectable (albeit quite imperfectly at present) by human subjects. This leads to a testable prediction. If you systematically vary the associational history of an object, you should make it more or less psychically detectable in proportion to the differences in its history. That is, if I have one object that has been carried for years in the pocket of a very colorful person, a real adventurer, and another, physically identical object that has simply sat in a drawer for the same length of time, a psychically gifted person should be more successful in discriminating these objects by some form of clairvoyance than in clairvoyantly discriminating two identical physical objects that have both sat in the same drawer for their whole history. An initial test of whether the postulated psychical properties of an object can be clairvoyantly detected gave promising results (Roll and Tart, 1965).

The Channel

We now have some information available for the clairvoyance process to detect. Because the object or state of events and the subject are in two different places, we must postulate some sort of channel over which the information "travels" to the subject. There is no *known* physical channel, because we rule that out by the definition of ESP. We have no idea what the nature of this channel is. There is a "cosmological" theory here that says the concepts of "space" and "time" are illusory productions of our own minds rather than conditions in the real world. If you accept this, you need ask no questions about the nature of the channel, as there is nothing for a channel to bridge. This sort of theory seems to be a good description of the *psychological* concepts of many psychics and mystics (LeShan, 1969), but until someone tells us how to translate this idea into testable predictions, we cannot consider it a scientific theory; so we shall stick with the idea of a channel.

All channels have two important properties, those of noise and loss: information conveyed over a channel is subject to distortion by noise, and to attentuation of the energy conveying the information. We may consider attenuation a form of noise in this discussion. In some channels, the noise is negligible compared to the amount of information transferred and we can ignore it; other channels may be very noisy. Noise may vary from time to time in a channel, but as long as the ratio of information energy (signal) to noise energy is high, the channel is useful for transmitting information.

Given that we need a channel for the clairvoyant information, again certain basic and unanswered questions arise as a prelude to parapsychological theorizing. What is the nature of the channel? Does it, for instance, depend simply on space existing between object and subject, or do you need a known physical medium between object and subject? For all we know, clairvoyance might be impossible if there is no air between subject and object, or be more reliable if there is water between subject and object. Can you interfere with information flow over the channel, and can you distinguish between interference at the source of the information and interference at later stages in the process? Does physical distance attenuate clairvoyance? Some preliminary work by Osis and his colleagues (Osis, 1965; Osis and Turner, 1968; Osis, Turner, and Carlson, 1971) with a general ESP experiment (where telepathy and clairvoyance cannot be distinguished) suggest that distance may produce some attenuation, on the order of .7 to 1.7 units of information per thousand miles. There are many spontaneous instances, however, of verifiable telepathy or clairvoyance half-way around the Earth.

Can clairvoyant transmission through the channel be blocked by shielding of any sort? Both Russian (Vasiliev, 1963) and American (Puharich, 1962) studies suggest that not only does thorough electromagnetic shielding *not* block ESP (telepathy has mainly been tested), but it may actually enhance ESP in gifted subjects. We know nothing about possible noise in the channel, even whether there is appreciable noise: do people in the vicinity of the subject create a "mental noise" on the channel which interferes with information flow? Can we increase or reduce the channel noise? We do not know. Again, modeling and theorizing are difficult here for sheer lack of basic data. Also, in investigating particular stages in the clairvoyance process, such as the channel, we may find it difficult experimentally to differentiate where the procedure we apply has its effect in the process. For example, scores in clairvoyance tests may decline with distance but because of the beliefs of the subjects (*or* the experimenter), not because of anything in the nature of the channel (Osis, Turner, and Carlson, 1971).

Decoding

We now have information originating at an object or event and flowing through a channel. Now it goes into a block in Figure 41.1 I have labeled *decoding*. We can be rather sure that the information impinging on the subject is not in a form suitable for directly affecting him: It does not consist of known physical energies or of neural impulses that could stimulate the nervous system; so we must have a process to transform or decode the information, from whatever unknown form it is in, into a form that can be handled in the internal information-processing circuits of the human subject.* We can think of the outcome of this decoding process as a series of neural impulses, or, if you are more mentalistically inclined, as mental images or thoughts or feelings: since both points of view can lead to testable propositions, I feel no need to join one side or the other of the mind-body controversy, or speculate about which is more "basic."

Notice that you are using a decoding mechanism right now: It is called the eye, and it enables you to see this page. It takes light rays, which in themselves can not stimulate the nervous system, and turns them into (decodes into) sequences of neural impulses, which in turn are somewhere turned (decoded) into your mental experience of seeing the page.

What sorts of questions must we ask at this point before we can theorize? What is the nature of the decoding process? Does it have a specific locus, or is it a function of the whole central nervous system? To answer these questions, we need help from psychologists and biologists, as well as from physicists. Our known senses have specific receptor organs (decoders): is there a specific "organ" for detecting clairvoyant information? As another way of asking the question, is there a specific mental structure for decoding?

A decoder not only transforms information from a nonuseful to a useful form, but has a *limited* capacity for decoding information. Your eyes, for instance, with which you see this page, decode light rays into useful, neural impulses, but they are also limiting organs; you cannot see infrared light or the ultraviolet. Thus, decoders limit information, and give it particular characteristics. The sensation of "red" is made possible by the operation of a decoding mechanism, your eye, but this decoder also makes it impossible for you to experience the sensation we might call "ultra-red," which would arise from "seeing" infrared radiation.

The decoding process must therefore be *selective*: there may be untold millions of "clairvoyant impulses" reaching us at any given time; how do we select the right one? Present knowledge is of little help here.

From this point on we are "inside" the human subject, and now have several possible routes of information flow.

---

*This is based on the assumption that the brain and nervous system are the generators of consciousness: if they are merely the *transmitters* of consciousness, we do not need a decoding process of the sort described here, only a *selection* process.

Decoder to Brain

The first possible route is where information flows directly from the *decoder* to the *brain*, and eventuates in overt *behavior*. As an everyday example of this route, if someone behind you suddenly fired a pistol, you would jump out of your chair. We could then talk about the decoding of the intense sound waves into a barrage of neural impulses in the ear, and their direct effect on various startle-reflex mechanisms within the nervous system, resulting in your behavior of jumping from your chair.

Modeling this particular route of information flow has two advantages in parapsychology. The first is that it is a purely behavioristic or physiological approach, and so can be a way of approaching the problem for those who do not like the mentalistic concepts of consciousness and the like. More important, however, is that we have observations in some spontaneous cases which suggest that this was the route taken by the extrasensory information; i.e., the subject's behavior suggests ESP of some sort, but the subject reports no conscious experience of any sort accompanying this behavior. An analogous laboratory observation occurred in an experiment I carried out some years ago, in which each subject was sitting in a sound-proof chamber (normally used for sensory deprivation work) while his physiological reactions (brain waves, skin resistance, and heart rate) were being continuously recorded. Down the hall, in another soundproof chamber, an agent (sender) was electrically shocked at random intervals, and I .analyzed the subject's physiological reactions during the times the agent was being shocked. The subjects showed significantly greater reactions, indicative of activation, while the agent was being shocked than during control periods; yet their *conscious* guesses of when they thought something was happening bore no relation to the shock periods (Tart, 1963). Thus we have a form of behavior, internal activation of the central nervous system, suggesting the operation of ESP, but with no indication of conscious mental participation, a flow of ESP information directly from decoding mechanism to brain.

Given the possibility of this route, we have many questions to answer before we can adequately model it. What is the neural pathway from the decoding mechanism to the eventual behavior? This, of course, is a very general question for psychophysiology, but we can make it more specific: is this the same neural pathway that is used in non-paranormal processes? What sorts of general brain conditions can affect this decoder-to-behavior pathway? For example, is a high level of activation favorable to information flow along this route, or a state of relaxation? Almost a dozen studies, e.g., summarized by Honorton, Davidson, and Bindler (1971), have investigated the possibility that EEG states characterized by high alpha rhythms are more favorable to the operation of ESP.

A similar behavioristic approach to modeling was undertaken independently by Christopher Scott (1961) in England and by Remi Cadoret (1961) in Canada. They postulate four ways in which ESP can occur. In the first, you have continuous transmission of ESP information, which consists of all relevant facts about the target material. In the second, the transmission is also continuous, but the information itself is not comprehensive; i.e., all the information you want is not being encoded into the transmission. In the third, the information transmission is discontinuous, but when it does occur all the relevant aspects of the target are transmitted. In the fourth, the information flow is both discontinuous and incomplete. Both investigators have proposed statistical techniques for deciding which of these models is correct; although the models have not been tested yet, they do illustrate a purely behavioral approach to explaining ESP which may be fruitful.

Decoder to Conscious Mind

Another possible route of information flow is from *decoder* to *conscious mind* to *brain* to *behavior*. Here I will emphasize questions about the decoder to consciousness link, since the consciousness to brain to behavior link is a general psychological problem. We need to postulate this route because in many spontaneous cases of ESP the subject has a conscious experience, such as a vision or a feeling, which contains the ESP information, and which he then tells about (the overt behavior).

One question we can ask about the nature of the linkage between the decoding process and consciousness is "What sorts of conscious mental attitudes and characteristics affect the flow of ESP information?" The concept of personality characteristics is included in the system of consciousness here, and personality characteristics generally show more relationship to ESP functioning than do any other class of variables. Foremost among these is belief in the existence of psi phenomena. Schmeidler has shown repeatedly that subjects who believe in ESP tend to score *above* chance expectation in card-guessing tests, thus confirming their belief, whereas subjects who disbelieve in ESP tend to score *below* chance expectation, thus confirming their beliefs (Schmeidler and McConnell, 1958). The latter fact reveals that unconscious personality factors can affect psi, for a subject cannot score significantly *below* chance unless he is using psi on an unconscious level to correctly identify *some* targets and then altering that information as it reaches consciousness in order to make more errors than we would expect by chance. Unconscious processes may distort psi operation in numerous ways, but the subject is too complex to go into here; the interested reader should see Eisenbud's recent volume (1970).

Although many personality characteristics have been shown to affect psi operation in various studies (see Rao, 1966, and Schmeidler and McConnell, 1958, for literature reviews), all the correlations are of very small magnitude, in spite of being statistically significant. They are frequently obtainable in large groups of subjects, but are almost never large enough to be predictive for individuals.

The state of consciousness of the subject is also important in influencing the operation of psi, although our knowledge is rudimentary here. Hypnotic states have sometimes facilitated psi operation (Honorton and Krippner, 1969; Ryzl, 1962; van de Castle, 1969), and states induced by meditation (Osis and Bokert, 1971) or psychedelic drugs (Tart, 1971) have potentials. There are very complex methodological problems here, however, which I have discussed elsewhere (Tart, 1968). The interested reader should also see White's (1964) excellent article on the mental states of some of the highly talented ESP subjects of the past.

Many questions still remain about conscious attitudes and psi. What sorts of conscious acts can aid information flow from decoder to consciousness? Mental relaxation? An attitude of expectancy? Free play of imagery? Occult exercises? If there is an activating mechanism within the subject needed to pick up information by clairvoyance from passive objects, what sorts of conscious acts make this mechanism or process function? We have no lack of questions to answer before we can theorize about this route.

Decoder to Unconscious

A third possible route that can be modeled is from *decoder* to *unconscious mind* to *brain* to *behavior*. By unconscious mind I refer to the conventional concept of a dynamic area of the mind which significantly influences our behavior and feelings, but which is generally inaccessible to conscious inspection. Call it a Freudian or Jungian unconscious if you will. The basic observations which require us to postulate such a route consist of cases where a subject's behavior suggests that ESP is operating, where this behavior seems to be affected by unconscious drives or affects, but where there is no conscious representation of the behavior sequence.

As an analogue, consider a subject who has been hypnotized and told that he will not hear the experimenter's voice after awakening, but that whenever the experimenter says some key word the subject will twitch his hand. After awakening the subject, the experimenter says the key word. The subject's hand twitches, yet on being questioned he swears he did not know his hand twitched and did not hear the experimenter say anything. We might also observe that the hand twitch took the form of a thumbs-down gesture, congruent with an unconscious resentment by the subject over being manipulated in this manner.

In the parapsychological area, the phenomenon of *psi-missing* suggests such an information route. Psi-missing refers to the observation that some subjects score significantly *lower* than chance expectancy. Although Schmeidler's work (Schmeidler and McConnell, 1958) shows that conscious belief accounts for some psi-missing, it only accounts for a small part. (Again, see Eisenbud's excellent 1970 monograph for a discussion of unconscious dynamics and psi.)

All sorts of questions arise over the functioning of this information-flow route. How does the unconscious affect behavior in general, and ESP information in particular? Is there enough regularity in the way ESP information is transformed and distorted that we might learn to "decode" or translate the final output and get back to the original message?

One attempt at theorizing about this route is Carl Jung's theory of Synchronicity [see selection], which postulates an essential connection between potent archetypal constellations in the unconscious mind and ESP events (Jung and Pauli, 1955). But Jung's theory has not yet been developed enough that one could make *a priori* predictions based on it.

Decoder to Unconscious Mind to Conscious Mind

The fourth possible information-flow route is from *decoder* to *unconscious mind* to *conscious mind* to *brain* to *behavior*. The basic observation here is that many conscious representations which contain ESP information also show signs that the information has been distorted in ways congruent with what we know of unconscious dynamics. Dreams which convey ESP information illustrate this clearly. Some dreams that subjects report are straightforward pictures of a situation apparently perceived by ESP; others are a symbolic representation that the subject "translates," thereby obtaining the information.

An excellent example of psi operation (telepathy and clairvoyance cannot be distinguished in this particular experiment) showing unconscious distorting factors before the psi material enters consciousness (stage 1 REM dreaming consciousness, in this case) is provided in a study by

Ullman, Krippner, and Feldstein (1966). The target that a sender was attempting to transmit telepathically to a sleeping subject was a reproduction of the Dali painting, "The Sacrament of the Last Supper," which portrays Christ at the center of a table surrounded by his twelve disciples. A glass of wine and a loaf of bread are on the table, while a body of water and a fishing boat can be seen in the distant background. Relevant excerpts from the subject's dreams, obtained by an experimenter awakening him from each stage 1 REM dream period of the night, are as follows.

S's first dream: "There was one scene of an ocean . . . It had a strange beauty about it and a strange formation."

S's second dream: "I haven't any reason to say this, but somehow boats come to mind. Fishing boats. Small-size fishing boats . . . There was a picture in the Sea Fare Restaurant that came to mind as I was describing it. It's a very large painting. Enormous. It shows, oh, I'd say about a dozen or so men pulling a fishing boat ashore right after having returned from a catch."

S's third dream: "I was looking at a catalog . . . a Christmas catalog. Christmas season."

S's fourth dream: "I had some sort of a brief dream about an M.D. . . . I was talking to someone and . . . the discussion had to do with why . . . a doctor becomes a doctor because he's supposed to be an M.D., or something of that nature."

S's fifth dream: "It had to do with doctors again . . . The picture . . . that I'm thinking of now is the doctor sitting beside a child that is ill . . . It's one of those classical ones . . . It's called 'The Physician'. "

S's sixth dream: "I was in this office—a doctor's office again . . . We were talking about Preston . . . He's a psychiatrist. A supervisor I had. Before he became a psychiatrist he was a pathologist."

S's seventh dream: "The only part that comes to mind is the part where I'm in a kitchen, and there is a restaurant that I was planning to go to."

S's eighth dream: "I was sampling these different articles that looked like spices. Herbs. Grocery store. Place to eat. Food of different types."

From S's associations: "The fisherman dream makes me think of the Mediterranean area, perhaps even some sort of Biblical time. Right now my associations are of the fish and the loaf, or even the feeding of the multitudes . . . Once again I think of Christmas . . . Having to do with the ocean—water, fishermen, something in this area."

Those familiar with psychoanalytic theories of the unconscious can see the very typical sorts of distortions here that keep the target picture from being *directly* represented in dreaming consciousness, even though it is clearly influencing the dream.*

---

*That the target picture is clearly influencing the dream is not simply a subjective evaluation of correspondences, but is based on the objective, statistical-matching evaluation procedure used by blind judges in all the extensive work on dreams and telepathy carried out by Ullman and Krippner's group. Their extensive work has recently been summarized in monograph form (Ullman and Krippner, 1970).

Numerous questions arise about this information route, not only the general psychological one of how information passes from the unconscious mind to the conscious mind, but also the more specific one of how ESP information thus passes and whether it passes differently from other kinds of information. What sorts of conditions in the conscious mind facilitate the flow of information from the unconscious? What sorts of conscious conditions minimize the distortion that seems to occur as information passes from one level to another?

General Comments on Model I

We have looked at four discrete pathways that information might flow through after reaching the subject's decoding process. In the typical spontaneous case of ESP, probably several of these pathways are simultaneously active, thus complicating our task of understanding what happens.

Let me point out several other features of this model before we leave it and move on to the next. I have introduced it as a model of clairvoyance, but in many ways it is far more general. For instance, it is a model of ordinary visual perception. My ruler is a passive object that emits information by virtue of the background radiation of light in the room. The channel of space between us conveys the information in the form of light waves to a specific decoding mechanism, my eye. The neural impulses from the eye somewhere eventuate in the conscious experience of seeing a very specific thing, a *ruler*.

It can also be a model of precognition, if you "simply" allow the channel to extend through time as well as space, or of telepathy, if you think of telepathy as being the clairvoyant perception of the state of someone else's brain.

MODEL II: PSYCHOKINESIS

Let us now turn our attention to the phenomenon of psychokinesis or PK, for which the model is, in many ways, the reverse of the clairvoyance model. The basic observation behind it is that some subjects seem able to significantly influence the outcome of physical events by paranormal means, simply by wishing that they happen in such and such a way. The typical PK experiment involves throwing dice by hand or machine, and willing that certain selected laboratory faces come up more frequently than would be expected by chance. The laboratory evidence that there really is such an effect here is not overwhelming (whereas that for the existence of clairvoyance and telepathy is), but it is, in conjunction with occasional spontaneous cases, quite convincing (Rao, 1966).

The modern laboratory experiments which have established the existence of PK have generally used falling dice as the target, and the subjects have tried to mentally cause certain faces to come up on given trials. As with most ESP effects, the deviations from chance expectation are quite small in absolute value, even though they may reach enormous levels of statistical significance. PK studies have been extended to more or less successful attempts to influence radioactive decay (Bionetto, 1968; Beloff and Evans, 1961; Wadhams and Farrelley, 1968), enzyme activity (Smith, 1968), fungus growth (Barry, 1968), photographic development (Eisenbud, 1967; Stevenson and Pratt, 1968), electromechanical systems (Cox, 1965), protozoan movement (Randall, 1970), spinning silver coins (Tart, in press), and plant growth (Grad, 1965 and 1967).

I have modeled PK in Figure 41.3. We start with an external stimulus or item of information, typically the experimenter's request to the subject to make a particular die face come up as frequently as possible. This information is processed internally by brain, conscious mind, and unconscious mind, and ends up in a process I have called the converter or

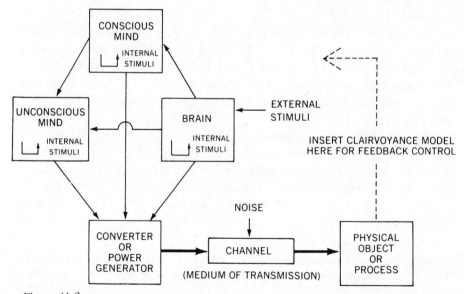

Figure 41.3.
Model II: Psychokinesis. Reprinted from the *International Journal of Neuropsychiatry*, 2, no. 5 (1966), 179. Copyright 1966 by Research in Organic Psychiatry, Inc.

power generator. From this point on the heavy arrows indicate that some sort of "power" flows over a channel and finally affects a physical object or process. We shall now consider this model in detail.

Operational Routes

Within the subject, that is, between the initiating information and the output of the power generator, we can conceive of four possible routes of information flow, as well as the possibility of simultaneous operation and interaction among the routes, just as we did for the clairvoyance model in getting information from the decoder to overt behavior. Starting with the external stimulus in every case, the first route is directly from *brain* to *power generator*: this is a behavioristic or physiological approach. It is more than just a theoretical possibility, because two recent studies (Levy and André, 1970; Schmidt, 1970) suggest that lower animals (cats, cockroaches, and chickens) can exercise some PK, and we would not ordinarily attribute consciousness to these organisms.

The second possible route of information flow is from *brain* to *conscious mind* to *power generator*. This route is ostensibly followed in everyday PK experiments: the subject is consciously aware that the experimenter has requested that he exercise PK, and he consciously tries to operate whatever mechanism does the job. This mechanism is mysterious in that no subject has ever been able to say that whenever he does conscious operation X he invariably gets a PK effect. * Thus *something* intervenes between the conscious desire to produce a PK effect and the effect; however, since such intervening may not necessarily happen in all conceivable instances, we can conceptualize a direct effect of the conscious mind on the power generator.

The third route, then, takes into account the mysterious *something* that intervenes, for the route is *brain* to *conscious mind* to *unconscious mind* to *power generator*. The fourth possible route is from *brain* to *unconscious mind* to *power generator*, with no conscious involvement. This final route is again largely a theoretical possibility, and I cannot produce a clearcut example to illustrate it.

---

*We may lack this kind of information for both ESP and PK processes because subjects have seldom been put in experimental situations where talented subjects might *learn* to use ESP or PK more effectively. I have discussed the application of learning procedures to psi processes elsewhere (Tart, 1966). This theory that people can be taught to to use ESP is beginning to receive experimental support (Dagle, 1968; Dagle and Puryear, 1969; Honorton, 1970, 1971; Targ and Hurt, 1971).

All the questions that we raised about the interaction among these possible routes for the clairvoyance model also apply here—but here I shall simply remind you of the vast number of fundamental questions that stand in the way of adequate theorizing and modeling.

Just to complicate things a little more, or, more accurately, to reflect the complexity that undoubtedly exists in reality, I have drawn an arrow labeled "internal stimuli" within each information-processing area of the organism (conscious mind, unconscious mind, brain) to reflect the fact that more events are operating than the experimenter's request to influence the dice. For example, there may be some spontaneous discharge or "noise" within the brain that interferes with information flow to the power generator. Or you may consciously dislike the experimenter, so that when he tells you to make the dice come up fours, you mentally say, "Nuts to you," even while trying to do so because of the obligation imposed on you by virtue of participating in the experiment. Or you may be consciously cooperative, but on an unconscious level the experimenter may remind you of someone you dislike; so that the unconscious mind alters or interferes with the flow of information designed to set the power generator into action. You can imagine a complex situation, with all sorts of such factors working, in which you score on the dice, but the machine that throws the dice mysteriously breaks down! Thus you may have complied with the request to exercise PK (the machine breaking), and have expressed your hostility toward the experimenter, without being consciously aware that you were anything but a cooperative experimental subject. These "internal stimuli" problems also apply to Model I, even though they were not drawn in there for the sake of simplicity.

Most of our experimental problems at this stage are ones for psychologists and neurophysiologists, and focus on how to activate the power generator, given the complex nature of human beings.

The Power Generator

For the mysterious process that I have been calling the power generator, we need to hypothesize some sort of new process or mechanism, simply because the known electromagnetic or chemical energies of the brain cannot influence external events of any magnitude except via muscular intervention. The electrical field of your brain is the only thing that really gets through the skull at all, and it is just too impossibly weak to influence the course of a falling die ten feet away, even if it could somehow be focused. Thus we need a power generator, a process of converting the informational command to influence a die into some form of power that is capable of influencing that die.

I use the word "power" here in the broadest sense of the word, to simply designate something that can do work, that can change the state of things or processes. I do not refer to any known form of energy, and I do not feel it is fruitful to argue whether this is a "physical" or "non-physical" form of power, whether it is "spiritual" or "material"; rather, the relevant questions are what is the nature of this power, how does it operate, what things affect its operation?

Notice that I am using a power generator right now: the nerve impulses conveying the information I want to get across to you are activating a particular form of power generator called a muscle, in fact, a whole set of muscles, which enable me to write this page, and eventually to bridge the space between us and activate your decoder mechanism, your eye, producing neural impulses in your nervous system, which somewhere end up as the conscious registration and understanding of what I am writing. This normal process is, if you think about it, actually fantastically complex, and not understood in many of its most important aspects; but since it is so familiar, who ever thinks of it as a mystery? Going back to our PK power generator, we have many fundamental questions to answer about its nature. Is there a special brain center for it? Is it some form of "mental" energy (whatever mental energy is in the first place)? Does it consist of specific electrical or chemical operations? What is the nature of the power generated by it? Are known forms of physical energy generated in conjunction with (or as an aspect of) the PK power?

To this last question, there must be a yes answer in some form. No matter how unknown the basic form of PK energy is, at its point of application it affects physical objects, and so must have some sort of physical energy component. But since we are totally ignorant of the nature of both the PK force and the generator, obviously our theorizing and modeling here can lead only to negligible results.

To illustrate how we *might* develop some fruitful theories, though, let me indicate the substance of some discussions I had with Mr. Edward Cox of the Parapsychology Laboratory at Duke University several years ago. He has invented some new types of machines for testing PK. These machines involve the subject's attempting to influence a very large number of moving particles, such as drops of falling water, or ions moving through a solution between two electrodes, and he has been getting some statistically significant results from these devices. I felt that his devices offered a chance to test two alternative formulations of the nature of the psychokinetic force. One formulation would be that PK is a spatially discrete "push" or "jab"; the other that PK is uniformly spread out over a fairly wide volume of space, rather than spatially discrete. If the former view is correct, we would expect maximum success in PK tests involving single objects. If the latter, many objects moving through this wider field would allow the PK force to be used more effectively and thus would give greater success. Neither formulation is a formal theory as yet, but an illustration of how a small-scale theory might be developed *and* tested.

The PK Channel

What is the nature of the channel, the medium through which the power is transmitted from the point of generation to the point of application? If I lift my ruler, the molecules of the skin of my hand serve as the channel or medium of transmission whereby the power from my muscles is applied to the ruler. Some energies, such as radio waves or light, require only space as a channel; others require a physical medium, as, e.g., sound waves require air to travel.

Another feature of a channel I have labeled noise, to maintain comparability with the clairvoyance model. You could think of this noise as loss, distortion, or "slippage." In shooting an arrow at a target, e.g., any wind blowing across the range constitutes noise, for it deflects the power in the arrow from being applied at the point you intended.

Given these characteristics of the channel, we may ask many questions about the nature of the channel in PK. Is it just space, or must there exist a physical medium between subject and PK target? Can PK operate through a vacuum, or under water? Is any kind of shielding possible? Is there any loss of PK force with distance? Can PK operate forward and/or backward in time, or only in the present? Does the nature of the channel limit the amount of PK force that can be transmitted through it? Here we are asking questions that we must have the assistance of physicists (paraphysicists?) to answer.

The PK Target

At last we arrive at the object to be affected, usually a die spinning through the air. We can immediately ask what physical (or psychical) properties an object must possess in order to be affected by PK. We have long worked with an implicit assumption that almost any convenient object will do for PK tests, but, aside from some early exploratory work on dice size, there has been little exploration of how various properties of objects correlate with PK effects. Perhaps metals, e.g., cannot be affected by PK, while ceramics can. Can such psychical properties be altered by physical manipulations? If objects may have *psychical* properties, as we postulated in the clairvoyance model, perhaps they have specific psychical properties that allow PK to operate on them.

General Comments on Model II

As a final complication to this PK model, I have drawn in a dotted line from the object back to the human subject. If you think about it, how can you possibly influence a falling, tumbling, spinning die to land with a given face up just by exerting a momentary or continuous push on it? Obviously you have to know exactly where the die is and all the components of its velocity, linear and angular, at the moment you are ready to "push," so that you can push with just the right amount of force in just the right direction. Thus, for falling dice, we have to insert the whole clairvoyance model to provide informational feedback between dice and subject in order to make it a workable system! I will not even attempt to point out the way that this multiplies the possible interactions within the subject, but is it any wonder that the results of PK tests have generally been slight?

Finally, notice that we also have here a model of normal action, if you think of muscles as the power generator, and of telepathy, if you conceive of telepathy as psychokinetic action on someone else's brain.

MODEL III: TELEPATHY

The basic laboratory experiment used to establish the reality of telepathy is similar to the card-guessing clairvoyance experiment, except that another human being, the "agent" or "sender," looks at each card in the deck at fixed time intervals. Thus each time the receiver makes a guess at a card, that information exists in the sender's mind.* Telepathy and

---

*The astute reader will note that in this experimental situation the subject could be *clairvoyantly* perceiving the target cards rather than the state of mind of the sender. Thus experiments of this type are referred to as GESP (general ESP) in the parapsychological literature. Studies have been carried out which show that one can have "pure" telepathy in the sense that no objective record is ever made that could be "read" by contemporaneous or precognitive clairvoyance (McMahon, 1946; Soal and Bateman, 1954).

clairvoyance experiments are about equally successful, and there are many such experiments in the literature (see Rao, 1966, for summaries).

An over-all model of telepathy is presented in Figure 41.4. You will notice immediately that it is a combination of the clairvoyance and PK models. All the previously mentioned considerations about getting information to activate the power generator in the PK model apply here to the problem of getting the information to be transmitted into the encoding mechanisms, the mechanism or process whereby neural or mental information is turned into a form suitable for telepathic transmission. Then all the problems that arise between decoding and the final overt behavior occur in the person acting as receiver, as in the clairvoyance model. Then, too, that the diagrams look the same does not necessarily imply that the identical mechanisms or processes are used here as in the PK or clairvoyance processes, but only that similar functions must be performed.

Mental Radio

The most popular "theory" of telepathy, the idea that telepathy is a form of mental *radio*, is actually a model, not a theory at all. Basically,

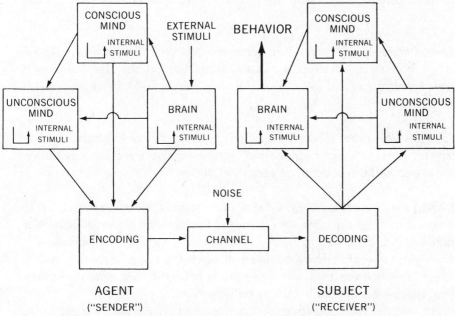

Figure 41.4.

Model III: Telepathy. Reprinted from the *International Journal of Neuropsychiatry*, 2, no. 5 (1966), 179. Copyright 1966 by Research in Organic Psychiatry, Inc.

the idea of mental radio postulates that the encoding mechanism is an electrical network in the brain which functions like a radio transmitter, feeding the human body as an antenna, just as commercial radio stations broadcast. The channel of transmission is then ordinary space. The decoder is an electrical network in the brain which functions like a receiver, again using the subject's body as an antenna. This conception "explains" (or makes us feel comfortable with) all sorts of observations about telepathy—it forms analogies with them, some of which are as follows.

Warmup. Observation: subjects have to get in the mood, "warm up" sometimes, before they can do well in telepathy tests. "Explanation": both transmitters and receivers have to heat up, and circuits have to stabilize before they function well.

Selective Transmission. Observation: some pairs of subjects are good in telepathy experiments; others are not. "Explanation": only transmitters and receivers that happened to be tuned to the same frequency will transmit information.

Incomplete Transmission. Observation: only parts of the target material are sometimes received. "Explanation": radio transmissions are subject to atmospheric static and attenuation that washes out part of the message.

Agent Differences. Observation: some subjects are much more successful as agents (senders) in telepathy experiments than others. "Explanation": some transmitters are more powerful than others and can send on more frequencies.

Subject Differences. Observation: some people are better subjects (receivers) than others. "Explanation": some receivers are more sensitive and cover wider frequency ranges than others.

Training for Telepathic Ability. Observation: some subjects seem to be able to sort out telepathic messages from the background noise of their own minds better than others, and improve with practice. "Explanation": some radio operators learn to listen through the noise of radio sets and receive much more of a message than others. Further, some receivers have special circuits built in that reduce noise.

The mental-radio position also performs one function of a scientific theory, in suggesting where we might look for observations that are important. For instance, we might see if a higher antenna helps (raising the subject high above the earth), if some people act like directional antennas (they do well on telepathy tests if the other person is in a particular direction from them), whether a good ground connection helps (connect the subject to earth), and whether reducing the noise from nearby sources improves reception (get your subject away from the mental noise generated by nearby people).

The mental-radio position, then, is a good model. It makes the unfamiliar facts about telepathy analogous with the familiar ones about radio, and even suggests other things to look for. It fails as a scientific theory, however. As I stated earlier, a scientific theory must *always* make correct predictions, and the mental-radio position fails miserably on three important predictions. First, it would predict an inverse-square-law, a falling off of telepathic effect with distance, which has not been observed (Osis, 1965). Second, it would predict that electromagnetic shielding of either agent (sender) or subject (receiver) should reduce or eliminate telepathic effects, but this has never been observed—indeed, there is some suggestion that shielding enhances the effect (Puharich, 1962; Vasiliev, 1963). Third, the known radiation of electromagnetic energy from the human body (primarily the brain waves or electroencephalogram) is so weak compared to the ambient noise level that exists on Earth that it would be well-nigh impossible to conceive of an electronic instrument that could detect this radiation even a few inches from the head, much less at a distance of miles. Thus the idea of mental radio is a good and intriguing model, but indefensible as a scientific theory.

SUMMARY

I have discussed where we have the most pressing needs for, and greatest difficulties in constructing, models and theories for the basic parapsychological phenomena of precognition, clairvoyance, PK, and telepathy, and have briefly mentioned some of the models and theories that have been proposed in this area.

What are our prospects here? As I mentioned at the beginning, many scientists have difficulties in accepting ESP because the phenomena make no sense in terms of current theories about the nature of the world. For many people, whom Carl Jung called the introverted intellectual type (which covers many scientists), having a comprehensive view of things, an all-inclusive theory, is vitally important; and if the facts do not fit the theory, so much the worse for the facts! Thus we badly need some theories in this area for that reason. A further need is for theories and models to organize the data of parapsychology: there are so many scattered observations and literature that the investigator cannot hope to digest it all.

Yet how can we hope to construct adequate theories and models if the data we work with are so unreliable? How can you theorize, e.g., about the nature of the energy involved in PK, when you do not know if there is a distance effect, whether it can be shielded, etc.? How can you test the manner in which various factors affect telepathy and clairvoyance if you are dealing with such a small-scale and unreliable effect that you have to put in tremendous amounts of experimental time to check out even one factor? On the other hand, how can you train subjects to produce the phenomena at a higher rate, making its study easier, when you do not have models or theories to guide you in this endeavor? We are caught in a vicious circle of not having enough ideas of how it works to make it work well enough so that so we can get some idea of how it works!

I do not like to end on a pessimistic note, especially after spending my time "modeling" ignorance, but we *are* in a bad position. What we need in parapsychology are small-scale theories, testable theories. We are not ready to tackle the big questions of spiritual versus material and the like. The total amount of research in parapsychology is small compared to that in almost any other field of science; so this situation is not surprising. But if we have the opportunity to expand our research efforts, we can at least take the more optimistic position that, in view of our tremendous ignorance, we have the opportunity to make really significant and revolutionary discoveries!

Bibliography

Adorno, T. W., E. Frenkel-Brunswik, D. J. Levinson, and N. Sanford. 1950. *The Authoritarian Personality.* New York: Harper.

Akhilananda. 1946. *Hindu Psychology: Its Meaning for the West.* New York: Harper.

Akishige, Yoshihara. 1968. "A historical survey of psychological studies on Zen." In Y. Akishige, ed., *Psychological Studies on Zen*, I (*Kyushu psychol. Studies*, no. 5), 1–56.

Alajouanine, T. 1948. "Aphasia and artistic realization." *Brain*, 71, 229–241.

Alajouanine, T., and F. Lhermitte. 1964. "Aphasia and physiology of speech." *Res. Pub. Assn. Res. nerv. ment. Dis.*, 42, 204–219.

Alexander, F. 1931. "Buddhistic training as an artificial catatonia (the biological meaning of psychic occurrence)." *Psychoanal.*, 19, 129–145.

Alexander, Frederick M. 1969. *The Resurrection of the Body.* Ed. by Edward Maisel. New York: University Books.

Anand, B. K., G. S. Chhina, and Baldeve Singh. 1961a. "Some aspects of electroencephalographic studies in Yogis." *EEG clin. Neurophysiol.* 13, 452–456.

Anand, B. K., G. S. Chhina, and Baldev Singh. 1961b. "Studies on Shri Ramanand Yogi during his stay in an air-tight box." *Indian J. med. Res.*, 49, no. 1 (Jan. 1961), 82–89.

Bachman, C. H., R. D. McDonald, and T. J. Lorenz. 1966. "Some effects of air ions on the activity of rats." *Int. J. Biometeor.*, 10, 39–46.

Bagchi, B., and M. Wenger. 1957. "Electrophysiological correlates of some Yogic exercises." *EEG clin. Neurophysiol.* 7, 132–149.

Barnouw, Victor. 1963. *Culture and Personality.* Homewood, Ill.: Dorsey Press.

Barry, J. 1968. "General and comparative study of the psychokinetic effect on a fungus culture." *J. Parapsychol.*, 32, 237–243.

Bartemeier, L. H. 1965. "Psychoanalysis and religion." *Bull. Menninger Clinic*, 29, 237–244.

Basmajian, J. V. 1963. "Control and training of individual motor units." *Science*, 141, 440–441.

Basser, L. S. 1962. "Hemiplegia of early onset and the faculty of speech with special reference to the effects of hemispherectomy." *Brain*, 85, 427–460.

Bateson, G., and D. D. Jackson. 1964. "Some varieties of pathogenic organization." *Res. Pub. Assn. Res. nerv. ment. Dis.*, 42, 270–283.

Bay, E. 1964. "Aphasia and intelligence." *Int. J. Neurol.*, 4, 252–264.

Beccaria, G. 1775. *Della Elettricita Terrestre Atmosferica a Cielo Sereno.* Torino.

Beckh, Hermann. 1938. *Buddhismus.*

Beidleman, T. O. 1964. "Pig (Guluwe): An essay on Ngulu sexual symbolism and ceremony." *Southwestern J. Anthropol.*, 20, 359–392.

Bell, E., and L. J. Karnosh. 1949. "Cerebral hemispherectomy: Report of a case ten years after operation." *J. Neurosurg.*, 6, 285–293.

Beloff, J., and L. Evans. 1961. "A radioactivity test of psychokinesis." *J. Soc. psychical Res.*, 41, 41–54.

Benedict, Laura W. 1953. "People who have two souls." In M. Mead and N. Calas, eds., *Primitive Heritage* (New York: Random House, 1953), pp. 577–583.

Bentley, A. F. 1941. "The factual space and time of behavior." *J. Philos.*, 38, no. 18 (Aug. 28, 1941), 477–485.

Benton, A. L., and R. J. Joynt. 1960. "Early descriptions of aphasia." *Arch. Neurol.*, 3, 205–222.

Berkeley-Hill, Owen. 1921. "The anal-erotic factor in the religion, philosophy, and character of the Hindus." *Int. J. Psychoanal.*, 2, 317–319.

Berlucchi, G., M. S. Gazzaniga, and G. Rizzolati. 1972. "Microelectrode analysis of transfer of visual information by the corpus callosum." *Arch. Ital. Biol.*, in press.

Bertalanffy, Ludwig von. 1952. *Problems of Life.* New York: Wiley.

Bertholon, L'Abbé P. 1780. *De L'Electricite du corps humain dans l'etat de sante el de maladie.* Lyon: Bernuset.

Bertholon, L'Abbé P. 1783. *De L'Electricité des végétaux.* Paris.

Bionetto, B. 1968. "PK with a radioactive compound, cesium 137." Paper, Parapsychological Association, Freiburg, West Germany.

Blackburn, Thomas. 1971. "Sensuous-intellectual complementarity in science." *Science*, 174 (June 4, 1971), 1003–1007. Selection 4 in this book.

Blackman, V. H. 1924. "Field experiments in electro-culture." *J. agric. Sci.*, 14, 24–267.

Blyth, R. H. 1960. *Zen and Zen Classics*, vol. I. Japan: Hokuseido Press.

Bogen, J. E. 1969. "The other side of the brain, II: An appositional mind," *Bull. Los Angeles neurol. Soc.*, 34, 135–162.

Bogen, J. E., and G. M. Bogen. 1969. "The other side of the brain, III: The corpus callosum and creativity." *Bull. Los Angeles neurol. Soc.*, 34, 191–220.

Bogen, J. E., E. D. Fisher, and P. J. Vogel. 1965. "Cerebral Commissurotomy." *J. Amer. Med. Assn.*, 194, no. 12 (December 20, 1965), 1328–1329.

Bogen, J. E., and M. S. Gazzaniga. 1965. "Cerebral commissurotomy in man: Minor hemisphere dominance for certain visuospatial functions." *J. Neurosurg.*, 23, 394–399.

Bogen, J. E., R. W. Sperry, and P. J. Vogel. 1969. "Commissural Section and the Propagation of Seizures." In H. H. Jasper, A. A. Ward, and A. Pope, eds. *Basic Mechanisms of the Epilepsus.* Boston: Little, Brown, 1969.

Bohr, Niels. 1958. *Atomic Physics and Human Knowledge.* New York: Wiley.

Bohr, Niels. 1963. *Essays, 1958–1962, on Atomic Physics and Human Knowledge.* New York: Wiley.

Bossert, W. H., and E. O. Wilson. 1963. "The Analysis of Olfactory Communication among Animals." *J. theoret. Biol.*, 5, 443–469.

Bowers, M. B. 1968. "Pathogenesis of acute schizophrenic psychosis." *Arch. gen. Psychiat.*, 19, 348–355.

Bowers, M. B., and D. X. Freedman. 1966. "Psychedelic experiences in acute psychoses." *Arch. gen. Psychiat.*, 15, 240–248.

Brain, W. R. 1941. "Visual disorientation with special reference to lesions of the right cerebral hemisphere." *Brain*, 64, 244–272.

Brain, W. R. 1962. *Diseases of the Nervous System.* London: Oxford Univ. Press, 6th ed.

Brener, J., R. A. Kleinman, and W. J. Goeslin. 1969. "The effects of different exposures to augmented sensory feedback on the control of heart rate." *Psychophysiol.*, 5, 510–516.

Broad, C. 1962. *Lectures on Psychical Research.* New York: Humanities Press.

Bronowski, J. 1956. *Science and Human Values.* New York: Harper.

Brown, B. B. 1968. "Awareness of EEG-subjective activity relationships detected within a closed feedback system." Presented to the Society for Psychophysiological Research, October 1968.

Brown, B. B. 1970. "Recognition of aspects of consciousness through association with EEG alpha activity represented by a light signal." *Psychophysiol.*, 6, 442–452.

Brown, N. O. 1959. *Life Against Death: The Psychoanalytical Meaning of History.* Middletown, Conn.: Wesleyan Univ. Press.

Bruell, J. H., and G. W. Albee. 1962. "Higher intellectual functions in a patient with hemispherectomy for tumors." *J. consult. Psychol.*, 26, 90–98.

Bruner, Jerome. 1962. *On Knowing: Essays for the Left Hand.* Cambridge, Mass.: Harvard Univ. Press.

Brunswik, E. 1949. *Proc. Berkeley Symp. Math. Statistics and Probability.* Berkeley: Univ. of Calif. Press.

Buber, Martin. 1958. *I and Thou.* New York: Charles Scribner's Sons.

The Bulletin of Structural Integration, The Guild for Structural Integration, 1874 Fell St., San Francisco, Ca. 94117.

Bundzen, P. V. 1965. "Autoregulation of functional state of the brain: An investigation using photostimulation with feedback." *Fiziolog. Zh. SSSR imeni I. M. Sechenova*, 51, 936ff. Republished in *Federation Proc. Trans. Supp.*, 1966, 25, T551–T554.

Cadoret, R. 1961. "Some applications of information theory to card-calling performance in ESP." *J. general Psychol.*, 65, 89–107.

Cantril, Hadley. 1949. *J. Psychol.*, 27, 363.

Cantril, Hadley. 1950. *The "Why" of Man's Experience.* New York: Macmillan.

Carmona, A. B. 1967. "Trial and error learning of the voltage of the cortical EEG activity." Yale University, doctoral dissertation.

Carr, H. A. 1935. *An Introduction to Space Perception.* New York: Longmans, Green.

Carroll, J. B., ed. 1956. *Language, Thought, and Reality: Selected Writings of Benjamin Lee Whorf.* Cambridge, Mass.: The MIT Press.

Carson, Rachel. 1962. *The Silent Spring.* Boston, Mass.: Houghton-Mifflin.

Cavanna, R., and M. Ullman, eds. 1968. *Psi and Altered States of Consciousness.* New York: Garrett Press.

Chadwick, J., and W. N. Mann. 1950. *The Medical Works of Hippocrates.* Oxford: Blackwell.

Chase, R. A. 1966. "The effect of temporal lobe lesions on some auditory information processing tasks in man." In Darley, 1966.

Clark, J., and J. Skinner. 1958. *Treatises and Sermons of Meister Eckhart*. New York: Harper.

Conant, J. B. 1947. *On Understanding Science*. New Haven, Conn.: Yale Univ. Press.

Cox, W. 1965. "The effect of PK on electromechanical systems." *J. Parapsychol.*, 29, 165–175.

Critchley, M. 1953; 1966. *The Parietal Lobes*. London: E. Arnold, 1953. New York: 1966 reprint.

Crochet, R., R. Sandison, and A. Walk, eds. 1963. *Hallucinogenic Drugs and Their Psychotherapeutic Use*. Springfield, Ill.: Thomas.

Cupcea, S., M. Deleanu, and T. Frits. 1959. "Experimentelle Untersuchungen über den Einfuss der Luftionisation auf pathologische Veranderungen der Magenschleimhaut." *Act. Biol. Med. Germ.* 3, 407–416.

Czermak, P. 1901. "Uber Electrizitätszerstreuung bei Foehn." *Anz. Akad. Wiss. Wien. Math. Natur. Kl.*, 38, 310–316.

Dagle, L. 1968. "The effect of immediate reinforcement in a two-choice ESP test." Unpublished M.A. thesis, Trinity University.

Dagle, L., and H. Puryear. 1969. "The effects of immediate reinforcement in a two-choice GESP test." *J. Parapsychol.*, 33, 339.

D'Alibard, T. F. 1752. Letter to Acad. de Sci., vol. 3.

Dandy, W. E. 1928. "Removal of right cerebral hemisphere for certain tumors with hemiplegia." *J. Amer. med. Assoc.*, 90, 823–825.

Darley, F. L., ed. 1966. *Brain Mechanisms Underlying Speech and Language*. New York: Grune and Stratton.

David, T. A., J. R. Minehart, and I. H. Kornbluth. 1960. "Polarized air as an adjunct in the treatment of burns." *Amer. J. phys. Med.*, 39, 111–113.

Deikman, Arthur J. 1963. "Experimental meditation." *J. nerv. ment. Dis.*, 136, no. 4, 329–343.

Deikman, Arthur J. 1966a. "Deautomatization and the mystic experience." *Psychiat.*, 29, no. 4, 324–338.

Deikman, Arthur J. 1966b. "Implications of experimentally induced contemplative meditation." *J. nerv. mental Disease*, 142, no. 2, 101–116.

Deikman, A. 1971. "Bimodal consciousness." *Arch. gen. Psychiat.*, 45, 481–489. Selection 6 in this book.

Deikman, A. 1973. "The meaning of everything." Selection 29 in this book.

Delafresnaye, J. F., ed. 1954; 1961. *Brain Mechanisms and Consciousness*. Springfield, Ill.: Thomas. 2d ed., 1961.

Dement, William, and Edward A. Wolpert. 1958. "The relation of eye movements, body mobility, and external stimuli to dream content." *J. exper. Psychol.*, 55, no. 6, 543–553.

Denny-Brown, D. 1962. (Untitled discussion on hemispheric diversity.) In Mountcastle, 1962, pp. 244–252.

De Reuck, A. V. S., and Maeve O'Connor, eds. 1964. *Disorders of Language*. Boston: Little, Brown.

Devereux, George. 1951. "Cultural and characterological traits of the Mohave related to the anal stage of psychosexual development." *Psychoanal. Q.*, 20, 398–422.

Dewan, E. 1966. "Communication by voluntary control of the electroencephalogram." *Proc. Symp. biomed. Engineering*, Marquette University, June, 1966.

Dewey, J. 1946. *Problems of Men*. New York: Philosophical Library.

Dewey, John. 1948. "Common sense and science: Their respective frames of reference." *J. Philos.*, 45, 197–208.

Dewey, John, and A. F. Bentley. 1945, 1946. [A series of articles on epistemology.] *J. Philos.*: 42, 5–6, 225–247, 645–622, 701–712; 43, 505–517, 533–551, 645–663.

DiCara, Leo V., and Neal E. Miller. 1968. "Instrumental learning of vasomotor responses by rats: Learning to respond differentially in the two ears." *Science*, 159, 1485–1486.

Dide, M. 1938. "Diagnostic anatoma-clinique de désorientations temporospatiales." *Rev. Neurol.*, 69, 720–723.

Domhoff, G. W. 1969. "But why did they sit on the king's right in the first place?" *Psychoanal. Rev.*, 56, 586–596. Selection 11 in this book.

Edwards, D. K. 1960. "Effects of experimentally altered unipolar air-ion density upon the amount of activity of the blowfly, *Calliphora vicina R.D.*" *Canad. J. Zool.*, 38, 1079–1091.

Ehrenzweig, A. 1964. "The undifferentiated matrix of artistic imagination." In Neusterberger and Axelrod, 1964, 373–398.

Eisenbud, J. 1967. *The World of Ted Serios*. New York: Morrow.

Eisenbud, J. 1970. *Psi and Psychoanalysis*. New York: Grune and Stratton.

Elster, J., and H. Geitel. 1899. "Über die existenz elektrischer Ionen in der Atmosphäre." *Terrestr. Magazin.*, vol. 4.

Engel, B. T., and R. A. Chism. 1967. "Operant conditioning of heart-rate speeding." *Psychophysiol.*, 3, 418–426.

Engel, B. T., and S. P. Hansen. 1966. "Operant conditioning of heart-rate slowing." *Psycholophysiol.*, 3, 176–187.

Erikson, E. 1950. *Childhood and society*. New York: Norton.

Ettlinger, E. G., A. V. S. Reuck, and R. Porter, eds. 1965. *Functions of the Corpus Callosum*. Boston, Mass.: Little, Brown.

Federn, P. 1955. *Ego Psychology and the Psychoses*. New York: Basic Books.

Fehmi, L., chmn. *Autoregulation of Electrophysiological processes*. Symposium presented at the Second Annual Winter Conference on Brain Research, Snowmass-at-Aspen, Colorado, January, 1969.

Feldenkrais, M. 1949. *The Body and Mature Behavior*. New York: International Universities Press.

Fenichel, O. 1945. *The Psychoanalytic Theory of Neurosis*. New York: Norton.

Fenwick, P. B. C. 1966. "The effects of eye movement on alpha rhythm." *EEG clin. Neurophysiol.*, 21, 618.

Ferrier, D. 1886. *The Functions of the Brain*. New York: Putnam's, 2d ed.

Fetz, E. E. 1969. "Operant conditioning of cortical unit activity." *Science*, 163, 955–958.

Fingarette, H. 1963. *The Self in Transformation: Psychoanalysis, Philosophy, and the Life of the Spirit*. New York: Basic Books.

Fox, S. S., and A. P. Rudell. 1968. "Operant-controlled neural event: Formal and systematic approach to electrical coding of behavior in brain." *Science*, 162, 1299–1302.

Franklin, B. 1752. *Roy. Soc. London Philos. Trans.*, 47, 289.

Freud, Sigmund. 1946. *Collected Papers, Vol. IV*. London: Hogarth Press.

Freud, Sigmund. 1961. *Standard Edition of the Complete Psychological Works*. London: Hogarth.

Frolov, Y. P. 1937. *Pavlov and His School*. New York: Oxford Univ. Press.

Fromm, E. 1968. "The present crisis in psychoanalysis." In M. L. Simmel, ed. *The Reach of Mind*. New York: Springer, 1968.

Gamow, G., and M. Ycas. 1967. *Mr. Tompkins Inside Himself: Adventures in the New Biology*. New York: Viking.

Gazzaniga, M. 1970. *The Bisected Brain*. New York: Appleton-Century-Crofts.

Gazzaniga, M. S., J. E. Bogen, and R. W. Sperry. 1965. "Observations on visual perception after disconnexion of the cerebral hemispheres in Man." *Brain*, 88, part 2, 221–236.

Gazzaniga, M. S., and R. W. Sperry. 1967. "Language after section of the cerebral commissures." *Brain*, 90, part 1, 131–148.

Gazzaniga, M. S., and E. D. Young. 1967. "Effects of commissurotomy on the processing of increasing visual information." *Exper. Brain Res.*, 3, 368–371.

Ghiselin, Brewster. 1952. *The Creative Process*. New York: New American Library.

Gibson, James J. 1966. *The Senses considered as Perceptual Systems*. New York: Houghton Mifflin.

Gill, M., and M. Brennan. 1959. *Hypnosis and Related States*. New York: International Universities Press.

Glees, P. 1961. *Experimental Neurology*. London: Oxford Univ. Press.

Goddard, Dwight. 1938. *A Buddhist Bible*. Thetford, Vt.: Dwight Goddard, 2d ed.

Goldstein, K. 1960. "Thinking and speaking." *Ann. N. Y. Acad. Sci.*, 91, 38–51.

Goltz, F. 1960. "On the functions of the hemispheres." In von Bonin, 1960.

Grad, B. 1965. "Some biological effects of the 'laying on of hands': A review of experiments with animals and plants." *J. Amer. Soc. psychical Res.*, 59, 95–129.

Grad, B. 1967. "The 'laying on of hands': Implications for psychotherapy, gentling, and the placebo effect." *J. Amer. Soc. psychical Res.*, 61, 286–305.

Green, Elmer E. 1969. "Autoregulation of electrophysiological processes." In Fehmi, 1969.

Green, Elmer E., Alyce M. Green, and E. Dale Walters. 1970. "Voluntary control of internal states: Psychological and physiological." *J. transpersonal Psychol.*, 2, no. 1, pp. 1–26.

Green, Elmer E., E. D. Walters, Alyce M. Green, and Gardner Murphy. 1969. "Feedback technique for deep relaxation." *Psychophysiol.*, 5, 371–377.

Griaule, M. 1950. *Folk Art of Black Africa*. New York: Tudor.

Grinker, R. R., P. C. Bucy, and A. L. Sahs. 1959. *Neurology*. Springfield, Ill.: Thomas, 5th ed.

Gudas, F., ed. 1961. *Extrasensory Perception*. New York: Scribners.

Guillerm, R., R. Badre, J. J. Vogt, and J. Hee. 1967. "Effects physiologiques et psychophysiologiques chez l'homme d'un séjour de 24 heurs en atmosphere chargée en ions positifs ou négatifs." *Int. J. Biometeor.*, suppl. to vol. 11, p. 319.

Haine, E., H. L. Konig, and H. Schmeer. 1964. "Aphid moulting under controlled electrical conditions." *Int. J. Biometeor.*, 7, 265–275.

Halpern, L. 1963. *Problems of Dynamic Neurology*. Jerusalem: Hebrew Univ. Hadassah Medical School.

Harman, W. W., R. H. McKim, R. E. Mogar, J. Fadiman, and M. J. Stolaroff. 1966. "Psychedelic agents in creative problem solving: A pilot study." *Psychol. Rep.*, 19, 211–227. Also in Tart, 1969, pp. 445–461.

Hart, J. T. 1967. "Autocontrol of EEG alpha." Paper delivered to the Society for Psychological Research, San Diego, October, 1967. Abstract in *Psychophysiol.*, 1968, 4, 506.

Hart, J. T. 1970. "Beyond psychotherapy: A programmatic essay on the applied psychology of the future." In Hart and Tomlinson, 1970, Chapter 34.

Hart, J. T., and T. M. Tomlinson, eds. 1970. *New Directions in Client-Centered Psychotherapy*. New York: Houghton-Mifflin.

Hartmann, H. 1958. *Ego Psychology and the Problem of Adaptation*. New York: International Universities Press.

Hayes, K. J. 1962. "Genes, drives, and intellect." *Psychol. Rep.*, 10, 299–342.

Head, H. 1926. *Aphasia and Kindred Disorders of Speech*, vol. I. New York: Hafner, 1963 reprint.

Hebb, D. O. 1954. "The problem of consciousness and introspection." In Delafresnaye, 1954.

Hécaen, H. 1962. "Clinical symptomatology in right and left hemispheric lesions." In Mountcastle, 1962.

Hécaen, H., and R. Angelergues. 1963. *La Cecite Psychique; Etude Critique de la Notion d'Agnosie*. Paris: Masson.

Hécaen, H., J. de Ajuriaguerra, and R. Angelergues. 1963. "Apraxia and its various aspects." In Halpern, 1963.

Heisenberg, Werner. 1952. *Philosophic Problems of Nuclear Science*. New York: Pantheon.

Heisenberg, Werner. 1967. "Quantum theory and its interpretation." In Rozental, 1967.

Henderson, L. 1958. *The Fitness of the Environment: An Inquiry into the Biological Significance of the Properties of Matter*. Boston: Beacon Press.

Henschen, S. E. 1926. "On the function of the right hemisphere of the brain in relation to the left in speech, music, and calculation." *Brain*, 49, 110–123.

Herrick, C. J. 1949. *George Ellett Coghill*. Chicago, Ill.: Univ. of Chicago Press.

Hertz, Robert. 1960. *Death and the Right Hand*. Glencoe, Ill.: Free Press.

Heywood, R. 1955. *Beyond the Reach of Sense: An Inquiry into Extrasensory Perception*. New York: Dutton.

Hildreth, Gertrude. 1949. "The development and training of hand dominance." *J. genet. Psychol.*, 75, 197–275.

Hill, D., and G. Parr. 1963. *Electroencephalography*. New York: Macmillan.

Hilton, W. 1953. *The Scale of Perfection*. London: Burnes & Coates.

Hobsbawn, E. 1970. "Is science evil?" *New York Rev. Books*, November, 19, 1970.

Holt, J. 1967. *How Children Learn*. New York: Pitman.

Honorton, C. 1970. "Effects of feedback on discrimination between correct and incorrect ESP responses." *J. Amer. Soc. psychical. Res.*, 64, 404–410.

Honorton, C. 1971. "Effects of feedback on discrimination between correct and incorrect ESP responses: A replication study." *J. Amer. Soc. psychical Res.*, 65, 155–161.

Honorton, C., R. Davidson, and P. Bindler. 1971. "Feedback-augmented EEG alpha, shifts in subjective state, and ESP card-guessing performance." *J. Amer. Soc. psychical Res.*, 65, 308–323.

Honorton, C., and S. Krippner. 1969. "Hypnosis and ESP performance: A review of the experimental literature." *J. Amer. Soc. psychical Res.*, 63, 214–252.

Humphrey, M. E., and O. L. Zangwill. 1951. "Cessation of dreaming after brain injury." *J. neurol. neurosurg. Psychiat.*, 14, 322–325.

Hunt, J. McV., ed. 1944. *Personality and the Behavior Disorders*. New York: Ronald Press.

Hurlock, Elizabeth. 1964. *Child Development*. New York: McGraw-Hill, 4th ed.

Isaacson, Robert. 1964. *Basic Readings in Neuropsychology*. New York: Harper & Row.

Jackson, D., ed. 1960. *The Etiology of Schizophrenia*. New York: Basic Books.

Jacobson, E., ed. 1967. *Tension in Medicine*. Springfield, Ill.: Thomas.

James, William. 1890. *The Principles of Psychology*. New York: Henry Holt.

James, William. 1902. *The Varieties of Religious Experience*. New York: Modern Library, 1929.

Jasper, H., and C. Shagass. 1941. "Conditioning the occipital alpha rhythm in man." *J. exper. Psychol.*, 26, 373–379.

St. John of the Cross. 1953. *The Complete Works of Saint John of the Cross*. Westminster: Newman Press.

Joint Committee on Atmospheric Electricity of the Union Geodesique et Geophysique Internationale. 1967. Announcement at the discussion on Mobility of Atmospheric Ions. Symposium at Lucerne, Switzerland, October 2, 1967.

Jones, R., ed. 1967. *Contemporary Educational Psychology: Selected Readings*. New York: Harper.

Jung, C. G. 1933. *Psychological Types*. New York: Harcourt.

Jung, C., and W. Pauli. 1955. *The Interpretation of Nature and the Psyche: Synchronicity; and the Influence of Archetypal Ideas on the Scientific Ideas of Kepler*. New York: Pantheon.

Kamiya, J. 1962. "Conditional discrimination of the EEG alpha rhythm in humans." Paper presented at the Western Psychological Association, San Francisco, April 1962.

Kamiya, J. 1967. "EEG operant conditioning and the study of states of consciousness." In D. X. Freedman, chm., *Laboratory Studies of Altered Psychological States*. Symposium presented at the American Psychological Association, Washington, D.C., September 1967.

Kamiya, J. 1968. "Conscious control of brain waves." *Psychol. Today*, 1, 57–60.

Kamiya, J. 1969. "Operant control of the EEG alpha rhythm and some of its reported effects on consciousness." In Tart, 1969, pp. 507–517.

Kasamatsu, A., and T. Hirai. 1963. "Science of Zazen." *Psychologia*, 6, 86–91.

Kasamatsu, A., and T. Hirai. 1966. "An electroencephalographic study on the Zen meditation (Zazen)." *Folia Psychiat. Neurol.*, 20, 315–336.

Keil, H., 1971. "A wider conceptual framework for the Stepanek focusing effect." *J. Amer. Soc. psychical Res.*, 65, 75–82.

Keil, H., and J. Pratt. 1969. "Further ESP tests with Pavel Stepanek in Charlottesville dealing with the focusing effect." *J. Amer. Soc. psychical Res.*, 63, 253–272.

Kennard, M. 1965. "The EEG in schizophrenia." In Wilson, 1965, pp. 168–184.

Kilpatrick, F. P., ed. 1952. *Human Behavior from the Transactional Point of View*. Hanover, N.H.: Institute for Associated Research.

Kimura, D. 1964. "Left-right differences in the perception of melodies." *Q. J. exper. Psychol.*, 16, 355–358.

Kimura, S., M. Ashiba, and I. Matsushima. 1939. "Influences of the air lacking in light ions and the effect of its artificial ionization upon human beings in occupied rooms." *Japan. J. med. Sci.*, 7, 1–12.

Kinsbourne, Marcel. 1971. "The minor cerebral hemisphere as a source of aphasic speech." *Arch. Neurol.*, 25, 302–306.

Kleinsorge, H., and G. Klumbies. 1964. *Techniques of Relaxation*. Bristol: John Wright.

Kluckhohn, C., and H. A. Murray, eds. 1959. *Personality in Nature, Society, and Culture*. New York: Knopf, rev. ed.

Kluckhohn, F. R. 1959. "Dominant and variant value orientations." In Kluckhohn and Murray, 1959, pp. 342–357.

Knoll, M., J. Eichmeier, and R. W. Schon. 1964. "Properties, measurement, and bioclimatic action of small multimolecular atmospheric ions." *Adv. electr. Electron Phys.*, 19, 177–254.

Knowles, D. 1961. *The English Mystical Tradition*. London: Burnes & Oates.

Kotaka, S., and A. P. Krueger. 1967. "Studies on air ion-induced growth increase in higher plants." *Advancing Frontiers of Plant Sci.*, 20, 115–208.

Kris, E. 1952. *Psychoanalytic Explorations in Art*. New York: International Universities Press.

Krueger, A. P., P. C. Andriese, and S. Kotaka. 1968. "Small air ions: Their effect on blood levels of serotonin in terms of modern physical theory." *Int. J. Biometeor.*, 12, no. 3, 225–239.

Krueger, A. P., S. Kotaka, and P. C. Andriese. 1963. "A study of the mechanism of air ion-induced growth stimulation in *Hordeum vulgaris*." *Int. J. Biometeor.*, 7, 17–25.

Krueger, A. P., S. Kotaka, and P. C. Andriese. 1965. "The effect of abnormally low concentrations of air ions on the growth of *Hordeum vulgaris*." *Int. J. Biometeor.*, 9, 201–209.

Krueger, A. P., S. Kotaka, K. Nishizawa, Y. Kogure, M. Takenobu, and P. C. Andriese. 1966. "Air-ion effects on the growth of the silk worm (*Bombyx mori L.*)." *Int. J. Biometeor.*, 10, 29–38.

Krueger, A. P., and H. B. Levine. 1967. "The effect of unipolar positively ionized air on the course of Coccidioidomicosis in mice." *Int. J. Biometeor.*, 11, 279–288.

Krynauw, R. A. 1950. "Infantile hemiplegia treated by removing one cerebral hemisphere." *J. neurol. neurosurg. Psychiat.*, 13, 243–267.

Kuhn, T. 1962. *The Structure of Scientific Revolutions.* Chicago, Ill.: Univ. of Chicago Press.

Kuprianovich, L. 1965. "The process of instruction during sleep can be regulated". *Technika-Molodezhi*, no. 11, pp. 26–28. Cited by T. Mulholland in "Feedback electroencephalography." *Activitas Nervosa Superior*, 10 (1968), 410–438.

LaBarre, Weston. 1954. *The Human Animal.* Chicago, Ill.: Univ. of Chicago Press.

Laing, R. D. 1965. *The Divided Self.* Baltimore, Md.: Pelican.

Lashley, K. S. 1958. "Cerebral organization and behavior." *Res. Pub. Assn. Res. nerv. ment. Dis.*, 36, 1–18.

Laski, M. 1961. *Ecstasy: A Study of Some Secular and Religious Experiences.* London: Cresset Press.

Leary, Timothy. 1964. "The religious experience: its production and interpretation." *Psychedelic Rev.*, 1, 324–346.

Lee, Dorothy. 1940. "A primitive system of values." *Philos. Sci.*, 7, 355–378.

Lee, Dorothy. 1949. "Being and value in a primitive culture." *J. Philos.*, 46, 401–415.

Lenneberg, E. H. 1969. "On explaining language." *Science*, 164, 635–643.

LeShan, Lawrence. 1969. "Physicists and mystics: similarities in world view." *J. transpersonal Psychol.* 1, no. 2, 1–20.

Levi-Strauss, Claude. 1965. "Man has never been so savage as he is today." *Réalités*, 175, 48–51.

Levy, W., and E. André. 1970. "Possible PK by young chickens to obtain warmth." *J. Parapsychol.*, 34, 278–279.

Levy-Agresti, J., and R. W. Sperry. 1968. "Differential perceptual capacities in major and minor hemispheres." *Proc. Nat. Acad. Sci. U.S.*, 61, 1151.

Lewin, B. 1950. *The Psychoanalysis of Elation.* New York: Norton.

Lewis, G. N., and M. Randall. 1923. *Thermodynamics and the Free Energy of Chemical Substances.* New York: McGraw-Hill.

Lindsley, D. "Electroencephalography." In Hunt, 1944, pp. 1081–1083.

Liske, E., H. M. Hughes, and D. E. Stowe. 1967. "Cross-correlation of human alpha activity: Normative data." *EEG clin. Neurophysiol.*, 22, 429–436.

Luce, G. G., and J. Segal. 1966. *Sleep.* New York: Lancer.

Luria, A. R. 1966a. *Higher Cortical Functions in Man.* New York: Basic Books.

Luria, A. R. 1966b. *Human Brain and Psychological Processes.* New York: Harper, Row.

Luria, A. R., L. S. Tsvetkova, and D. S. Futer. 1965. "Aphasia in a composer." *J. neurol. Sci.*, 2, 288–292.

Lynd, R. 1939. *Knowledge for What?* Princeton, N. J.: Princeton Univ. Press.

Magoun, H. W. 1958. *The Waking Brain.* Springfield, Ill.: Thomas.

Maher, B. 1964. *Progress in Experimental Personality Research.* New York: Academic Press.

Malinowski, Bronislaw. 1922. *Argonauts of the Western Pacific.* London: London School of Economics.

Malinowski, Bronislaw. 1929. *The Sexual Life of Savages.* London: Routledge and Kegan Paul.

Malinowski, Bronislaw. 1935. *Coral Gardens and their Magic.* New York: American Book Co.

Marechal, J. 1964. *Studies in the Psychology of the Mystics*. Albany, N.Y.: Magi.

Maslow, Abraham. 1957. "Two kinds of cognition and their integration." *Gen. Semantics Bull.*, 20, 17–22.

Maslow, Abraham. 1966. *The Psychology of Science: A Reconnaissance*. New York: Harper & Row.

Masters, R. E. L., and J. Houston. 1967. *The Varieties of Psychedelic Experience*. New York: Dell.

McCleave, P. M. 1959. (Untitled letter). *J. Amer. med. Assn.*, 207, 159.

McCutchen, C. W. 1970. "Surface films compacted by moving water: Demarcation lines reveal film edges." *Science*, 170 (Oct. 2, 1970), 61–64.

McFie, J., and M. F. Piercy. 1952. "Intellectual impairment with localized cerebral lesions." *Brain*, 75, 292–311.

McMahon, E. 1946. "An experiment in pure telepathy." *J. Parapsychol.*, 10, 224–242.

McReynolds, P. 1960. "Anxiety, perception, and schizophrenia." In Jackson, 1960.

Mednick, S. A., and F. Schulsinger. 1970. "Factors related to breakdown in children at high risk for schizophrenia." In Roff and Ricks, 1970, pp. 87–88.

Meehl, P., and M. Scriven. 1956. "Compatability of science and ESP." *Science*, 123, 14–15.

Mensh, I. N., H. G. Schwartz, J. G. Matarazzo, and J. D. Matarazzo. 1952. "Psychological functioning following cerebral hemispherectomy in man." *Arch. Neurol. Psychiat.*, 67, 787–796.

Michaux, H. 1963. *Light through Darkness*. New York: Orion Press.

Miller, Neal E. 1969. "Learning of visceral and glandular responses." *Science*, 163, 434–445.

Miller, Neal E., and Leo DiCara. 1967. "Instrumental learning of heart-rate changes in curarized rats: Shaping, and specificity to descriminative stimulus." *J. compar. physiol. Psychol.*, 63, no. 1, 12–19.

Miller, Neal E., Leo V. DiCara, and George Wolf. 1968. "Homeostasis and reward: T-maze learning induced by manipulating antidiuretic hormone." *Amer. J. Physiol.*, 215, no. 3, 684–686.

Milner, B. 1958. "Psychological defects produced by temporal lobe excision." *Res. Publ. Assn. nerv. ment. Dis.*, 36, 244–257.

Milner, B. 1962. "Laterality effects in audition." In Mountcastle, 1962.

Milner, B. 1971. "Interhemispheric differences in the localization of psychological processes in man." *Brit. med. Bull.*, 27, no. 3, 272–277.

Moller, H. 1965. "Affective mysticism in western civilization." *Psychoanal. Rev.*, 52, 115–130.

Moncrief, Lewis W. 1970. "The cultural basis for our environmental crisis." *Science*, 170 (Oct. 30, 1970), 508–512.

Mountcastle, V. B., ed. 1962. *Interhemispheric Relations and Cerebral Dominance*. Baltimore, Md.: Johns Hopkins Press.

Mulholland, T. 1967. "The concept of attention and the electroencephalographic alpha rhythm." Paper read at National Physical Laboratory on "The concept of attention in neurophysiology," Teddington, England, October, 1967.

Mumford, Lewis. 1970. *The Myth of the Machine: The Pentagon of Power*. New York: Harcourt Brace, Jovanovich.

Murphy, Gardner. 1951. *Historical Introduction to Modern Psychology*. New York: Harcourt Brace.

Murphy, Gardner. 1956. "The boundaries between the person and the world." *Brit. J. Psychol.*, 47, 88–94.

Murphy, Gardner, and L. Dale. 1961. *Challenge of Psychical Research*. New York: Harper & Row.

Murray, H. A., *et al.* 1948. *Assessment of Men.* New York: Rinehart.

Murray, E. N., and E. S. Katkin. 1968. "Comment on two recent reports of operant heart rate conditioning." *Psychophysiol.*, 5, 192–195.

Myers, R. E., 1965. "The neocortical commissures and interhemispheric transmission of information." In Ettlinger, Reuck, and Porter, 1965.

Myers, R. E., and R. W. Sperry. 1953. "Interocular transfer of a visual form discrimination habit in cats after section of the optic chiasma and corpus callosum." *Anat. Record*, 115, 351–352.

Naranjo, Claudio, and Robert E. Ornstein. 1971. *On the Psychology of Meditation.* New York: Viking.

Needleman, Jacob. 1970. *The New Religions.* New York: Doubleday.

Neisser, Ulric. 1967. *Cognitive Psychology.* New York: Appleton-Century-Crofts.

Neusterberger, W., and S. Axelrod, eds. 1964. *The Psychoanalytic Study of Society.* New York: International Universities Press.

Nielsen, J. M. 1937. "Unilateral cerebral dominance as related to mind blindness: Minimal lesion capable of causing agnosia for objects." *Arch. Neurol. Psychiat.*, 38, 108–135.

Nielsen, J. M. 1940. "Dominance of the right occipital lobe." *Bull. Los Angeles neurol. Soc.*, 5, 135–145.

Nielsen, J. M. 1946. *Agnosia, Apraxia, Aphasia.* New York: Hoeber, 2d ed.

Nielsen, J. M., and C. W. Sult. 1939. "Agnosias and the body scheme; five clinical cases." *Bull. Los Angeles neurol. Soc.*, 4, 69–76.

Nollet, L'Abbé. 1752. *Mem. Acad. Roy. Sci.*, Paris.

Nowlis, D. P., and A. Y. Cohen. 1968. "Mood-reports and the college natural setting: A day in the lives of three roommates under academic pressure." *Psychol. Reports*, 23, 551–566.

Nowlis, D. P., and J. Kamiya. 1970. "The control of electroencephalographic alpha rhythms through auditory feedback and the associated mental activity." *Psychophysiol.*, 6, 476–484.

Nowlis, D. P., and H. MacDonald. 1969a. "Progress toward a model of mental activity associated with voluntary control of EEG alpha." In Fehmi, 1969.

Nowlis, D. P., and H. MacDonald. 1969b. "Rapidly developed control of EEG alpha rhythms through feedback training with reports of associated mental activities." Unpublished.

Nowlis, H. H. 1968. *Drugs on the College Campus.* New York: Doubleday.

Nyaponika Thera. 1962. *The Heart of Buddhist Meditation.* London: Rider.

Olds, J. 1963. "Mechanisms of instrumental conditioning." In R. Hernandez-Peon, ed. "The physiological basis of mental activity." *EEG clin. Neurophysiol.*, suppl. 24, pp. 219–234.

Olds, J., and M. E. Olds. 1961. "Interference and learning systems." In Delafresnaye, 1961, pp. 153–187.

Orne, M. 1962. "On the social psychology of the psychological experiment: with particular reference to demand characteristics and their implications." *Amer. Psychol.*, 17, 776–783.

Osgood, Charles, B. J. Suci, and P. H. Tannenbaum. 1957. *The Measurement of Meaning.* Urbana: Univ. of Illinois Press.

Osis, K. 1965. "ESP over distance: A survey of experiments published in English." With an appendix by M. Turner, "A statistical model for examining the relation between ESP and distance." *J. Amer. Soc. psychical Res.*, 59, 22–46.

Osis, K., and E. Bokert. 1971. "ESP and changed states of consciousness induced by meditation." *J. Amer. Soc. psychical Res.*, 65, 17–65.

Osis, K., and M. Turner. 1968. "Distance and ESP: A transcontinental experiment." *Proc. Amer. Soc. psychical Res.*, vol. 27 (whole issue).

Osis, K., M. Turner, and M. Carlson. 1971. "ESP over distance: Research on the

ESP channel." *J. Amer. Soc. psychical Res.*, 65, 245–288.

Ostrander, S., and L. Schroeder. 1970. *Psychic Discoveries Behind the Iron Curtain.* Englewood Cliffs, N. J.: Prentice-Hall.

Paget, S. 1919. *Sir Victor Horsley.* London: Constable.

Palti, Y., E. Denour, and A. Abramov. 1966. "The effect of atmospheric ions on the respiratory system of infants." *Pediat.*, 38, 404–411.

Perls, Frederick S. 1954. "Morality, ego-boundary and aggression." *Complex*, winter issue, 1953–54.

Piaget, Jean. 1954. *The Construction of Reality in the Child.* New York: Basic Books.

Pirenne, M. H. 1958. Photobiology Group Meeting at Oxford University. Quoted in *Office of Naval Res. European sci. Notes*, 12, 11.

Pitts, Ferris N., Jr. 1969. "The Biochemistry of Anxiety." *Scientific American*, 220 (Feb. 1969), 69–75.

Poetzl, O., *et al.* 1960. "Preconscious stimulation in dreams, associations, and images." *Psychol. Issues*, 2, 1–18.

Polanyi, M. 1958. *Personal Knowledge: Towards a Post-critical Philosophy.* Chicago, Ill.: Univ. of Chicago Press.

Poulain, Augustine. 1950. *The Graces of Interior Prayer: A Treatise on Mystical Theology.* St. Louis: Herder.

Pratt, J. 1966. *Parapsychology: An 'Insider's View.* New York: Dutton.

Pratt, J. 1967. "Further significant ESP results from Pavel Stepanek and findings bearing upon the focusing effect." *J. Amer. Soc. psychical Res.*, 61, 95–119.

Pratt, J., and N. Jacobson. 1969. "Prediction of ESP performance on selected focusing effect targets." *J. Amer. Soc. psychical Res.*, 63, 38–56.

Pratt, J., N. Jacobson, J. Blom, and G. Meinsma. 1969. "A transitional period of research on the focusing effect: From confirmation toward explanation." *J. Amer. Soc. psychical Res.*, 63, 21–37.

Pratt, J., and H. Keil. 1969. "The focusing effect as patterned behavior based on habitual object-word associations: A working hypothesis with supporting evidence." *J. Amer. Soc. psychical Res.*, 63, 314–337.

Pratt, J., H. Keil, and I. Stevenson. 1970. "Three-experimenter ESP tests of Pavel Stepanek during his 1968 visit to Charlottesville." *J. Amer. Soc. psychical Res.*, 64, 18–39.

Pratt, J., J. Rhine, B. Smith, C. Stuart, and J. Greenwood. 1966. *Extrasensory Perception After Sixty Years.* Sommerville, Mass.: Bruce Humphries.

Pratt, J., and W. Roll. 1968. "Confirmation of the focusing effect in further ESP research with Pavel Stepanek in Charlottesville," *J. Amer. Soc. psychical Res.*, 62, 225–245.

Pratt, J., I. Stevenson, W. Roll, J. Blom, G. Meinsma, H. Keil, and N. Jacobson. 1968. "Identification of concealed randomized objects through acquired response habits of stimulus and word association." *Nature*, 220, 89–91.

Pribram, K. H. 1962. (Untitled discussion.) In Mountcastle, 1962.

Price, D. K. 1969. "Purists and politicians." *Science*, 163, 25–31.

Price, G. 1955. "Science and the supernatural." *Science*, 122, 359–367.

Prince, R., and C. Savage. 1965. "Mystical states and the concept of regression." Paper read at 1st Annual Meeting of the R. M. Bucke Soc., Montreal, 1965.

Puharich, A. 1962. *Beyond Telepathy.* New York: Doubleday.

Puhl, L., trans. 1963. *The Spiritual Exercises of St. Ignatius.* Westminster, Md.: Newman.

Quarton, G. C., T. Melnechuck, and F. O. Schmitt, eds. 1967. *The Neurosciences: A Study Program.* New York: Rockefeller Univ. Press.

Ramon y Cajal, S. 1960. "Anatomical and physiological considerations about the brain." In von Bonin, 1960.

Randall, J. 1970. "An attempt to detect psi effects with protozoa." *J. Soc. psychical*

Res., 45, 294–296.

Rao, K. 1966. *Experimental Parapsychology: A Review and Interpretation*. Springfield, Ill.: Thomas.

Rapaport, D., ed. 1951. *Organization and Pathology of Thought*. New York: Columbia Univ. Press.

Rapaport, David. 1958. "The theory of ego autonomy: A generalization." *Bull. Menninger Clinic*, 22, no. 1, 13–35.

Rapaport, D., and M. Gill. 1959. "The points of view and assumptions of metapsychology." *Int. J. Psychoanal.*, 40, 153–162.

Rather, L. J. 1965. *Mind and Body in Eighteenth-Century Medicine; A Study Based on Jerome Gaub's De regimine mentis*. Berkeley: Univ. of California Press.

Rhine, J. 1956. "Comments on 'Science and the supernatural'." *Science*, 123, 11–14.

Rhine, J. 1964. *Extrasensory Perception*. Somerville, Mass.: Bruce Humphries.

Rhine, J. B., and J. G. Pratt. 1962. *Parapsychology: Frontier Study of the Mind*. Springfield, Ill.: Thomas.

Rickersman, M., ed. 1960. *Rorschach Psychology*. New York: Wiley.

Robinson, N., and F. S. Dirnfeld. 1963. "The ionization state of the atmosphere as a function of the meteorological elements and the various sources of ions." *Int. J. Biometeor.*, 6, 101–110.

Roff, M., and D. F. Ricks, eds. 1970. *Life History Research in Psychopathology*. Minneapolis: Univ. of Minnesota Press.

Rolf, Ida P. 1963. "Structural Integration: Gravity, an unexplored factor in a more human use of human beings." *Systematics*, vol. I, June 1963.

Rolf, Ida P. 1972. "Structural Integration: A Contribution to the Understanding of Stress." Unpublished manuscript.

Roll, W. 1964. "The psi field." *Proc. parapsychol. Assn.*, 1957–64, no. 1, pp. 32–65.

Roll, W., and C. Tart. 1965. "Exploratory token objects tests with a 'sensitive.'" *J. Amer. Soc. psychical Res.*, 59, 226–236.

Rosadini, G., and G. F. Rossi. 1967. "On the suggested dominance for consciousness." *Brain*, 90, 101–112.

Rosenthal, R. 1966. *Experimenter Effects in Behavioral Research*. New York: Appleton-Century-Crofts.

Roszak, Theodore, 1969. *The Making of a Counter Culture*. Garden City, N.Y.: Doubleday.

Rowe, S. N. 1957. "Mental changes following removal of right cerebral hemisphere for brain tumors." *Amer. J. Psychiat.*, 94, 604–614.

Rozental, S., ed. 1967. *Neils Bohr: His Life and Work as Seen by His Friends and Colleagues*. New York: Wiley.

Ruesch, J., and W. Kees. 1956. *Nonverbal Communication*. Berkeley: Univ. of California Press.

Russell, W. R. 1963. "Some Anatomical Aspects of Aphasia." *Lancet*, June 1, 1963, pp. 1173–1177.

Ryzl, M. 1962. "Training the psi faculty by hypnosis." *J. Soc. psychical Res.*, 41, 234–252.

Ryzl, M., and J. Pratt. 1963. "The focusing of ESP upon particular targets." *J. Parapsychol.*, 27, 227–241.

Salamon, I., and J. Post. 1965. "Alpha blocking and schizophrenia." *Arch. gen. Psychiat.*, 13, 367–374.

Schachtel, E. 1959. *Metamorphosis: On the Development of Affect, Perception, Attention, and Memory*. New York: Basic Books.

Schaller, G. 1965. *The Year of the Gorilla*. New York: Ballantine.

Schlesinger, B. 1962. *Higher Cerebral Functions and Their Clinical Disorders*. New York: Grune and Stratton.

Schmeidler, G., ed. 1969. *Extrasensory Perception*. New York: Atherton.

Schmeidler, G., and R. McConnell. 1958. *ESP and Personality Patterns*. New Haven, Conn.: Yale Univ. Press.

Schmidt, H. 1970. "PK experiments with animals as subjects." *J. Parapsychol.*, 34, 255–261.

Schultz, D. 1965. *Sensory Restriction: Effects on Behavior*. New York: Academic Press.

Schultz, J., and W. Luthe. 1959. *Autogenic Training: A Psychophysiologic Approach in Psychotherapy*. New York: Grune & Stratton.

Schutz, William. 1967. *Joy*. New York: Grove Press.

Scott, C. 1961. "Models for psi." *Proc. Soc. psychical Res.*, 53, 195–225.

Semmes, J. 1968. "Hemispheric specialization: A possible clue to mechanism." *Neuropsychologia*, 6, 11–26.

Semmes, J., S. Weinstein, L. Ghent, and H. L. Teuber. 1960. *Somatosensory Changes after Penetrating Brain Wounds in Man*. Cambridge, Mass.: Harvard Univ. Press.

Shah, Idries. 1971a. *The Pleasantries of the Incredible Mulla Nasrudin*. New York: Dutton.

Shah, Idries. 1971b. *The Sufis*. New York: Doubleday.

Shankweiler, D. 1966. "Effects of temporal lobe damage on perception of dichotically presented melodies." *J. comp. physiol. Psychol.*, 62, 115–119.

Shapiro, D. 1960. "A perceptual understanding of color response." In Rickersman, 1960, pp. 154–201.

Shapiro, D. 1965. *Neurotic Styles*. New York: Basic Books.

Shapiro, D., B. Tursky, E. Gershon, and M. Stern. 1969. "Effects of feedback and reinforcement on the control of human systolic blood pressure." *Science*, 163, 588–590.

Shepard, R. N. 1962. "The analysis of proximities: Multidimensional scaling with an unknown distance function, I & II." *Psychometrika*, 27, 125–140 and 219–246.

Shepard, R. N., and S. Chipman. 1969. "A revised concept of isomorphism and a technique for the study of internal representations." Unpublished manuscript, Stanford and Harvard Universities, April 1969.

Sherrington, C. 1947. *The Integrative Action of the Nervous System*. Cambridge, Eng.: Cambridge Univ. Press.

Sherwood, J., M. Stolaroff, and W. Harman. 1962. "The psychedelic experience: A new concept in psychotherapy." *J. Neuropsychiat.*, 4, 69–80.

Siegel, S. 1956. *Nonparametric Statistics*. New York: McGraw-Hill.

Silberer, H. 1951. "Report on a method of eliciting and observing certain symbolic and hallucination phenomena." In Rapaport, 1951, pp. 195–207.

Silverman, J. 1967. "Variations in cognitive control and psychophysiological defense in the schizophrenias." *Psychosom. Med.*, 29, 225–251.

Silverman, J. 1968. "A paradigm for the study of altered states of consciousness." *Brit. J. Psychiat.*, 114, 1201–1218.

Silverman, J., P. Berg, and R. Kantor. 1965. "Some perceptual correlates of institutionalization." *J. nerv. ment. Dis.*, 141, 656–657.

Smith, A. 1966. "Speech and other functions after left (dominant) hemispherectomy." *J. neurol. neurosurg. Psychiat.*, 29, 467–471.

Smith, A. 1969. "Nondominant hemispherectomy." *Neurology*, 19, 442–445.

Smith, C. S. 1968. "Matter versus materials: A historical view." *Science*, 162, 637–644.

Smith, J. 1968. "Paranormal effects on enzyme activity." Paper, Parapsychological Assn., Freiburg, West Germany.

Smythies, J., ed. 1967. *Science and ESP*. London: Routledge and Kegan Paul.

Snow, C. P. 1959. *The Two Cultures and the Scientific Revolution*. New York: Cambridge Univ. Press.

Soal, S. 1956. "On 'Science and the supernatural,' " *Science*, 123, 9–11.

Soal, S., and F. Bateman. 1954. *Modern Experiments in Telepathy*. London: Faber & Faber.

Solomon, P., P. Kubzansky, P. Leiderman, J. Mendelson, R. Trumbull, and D. Wexler. 1961. *Sensory Deprivation*. Cambridge, Mass.: Harvard Univ. Press.

Sperry, R. W. 1961. "Cerebral organization and behavior." *Science*, 133, 1749–1757.

Sperry, R. W. 1964a. "The Great Cerebral Commissure." *Scientific American*, (Jan. 1964).

Sperry, R. W. 1964b. "Neurology and the mind-brain problem." In Isaacson, 1964.

Sperry, R. W. 1964c. "Problems outstanding in the evolution of brain function." James Arthur Lecture. New York: American Museum of Natural History.

Sperry, R. W. 1967. "Split-brain approach to learning problems." In Quarton, Melnechuck, and Schmitt, 1967.

Sperry, R. W., M. S. Gazzaniga, and J. E. Bogen. 1969. "Role of the neocortical commissures." In Vinken and Bruyn, 1969, vol. IV.

Sperry, R. W., P. J. Vogel, and J. E. Bogen. 1970. "Syndrome of hemispheric deconnection." In P. Bailey and R. E. Fiol, eds. *Proceedings, Second Pan-American Congress of Neurology*. Puerto Rico: Dept. de Instruct.

Spitz, R. A. 1959. *A Genetic Field Theory of Ego Formation*. New York: International Universities Press.

Spreen, O., A. L. Benton, and R. W. Fincham. 1965. "Auditory agnosia without aphasia." *Arch. Neurol.*, 13, 84–92.

Sterman, M. B., and R. Howe, "EEG correlates of behavioral inhibition." In Fehmi, 1969.

Sterman, M. B., and W. Wyrwicka. 1967. "EEG correlates of sleep: Evidence for separate forebrain substrates." *Brain Res.*, 6, 143–163.

Stern, J. A., K. C. Das, J. M. Anderson, R. C. Biddy, and W. Surphlis. 1961. " 'Conditional' alpha desynchronization." *Science*, 134, 388–389.

Stevenson, I., and J. Pratt. 1968. "Exploratory investigations of the psychic photography of Ted Serios." *J. Amer. Soc. psychical Res.*, 62, 103–129.

Stoyva, J. 1969. "Can electrophysiological studies of dreaming be used as a paradigm for other research in psychophysiological relationships?" In E. Hartmann, ed. *Sleep and Dreaming*. Boston, Mass.: Little Brown, 1969.

Stoyva, J., and J. Kamiya. 1968. "Electrophysiological studies of dreaming as the prototype of a new strategy in the study of consciousness." *Psychol. Rev.*, 75, 192–205.

Strong, O. S., and A. Elwyn. 1943. *Human Neuroanatomy*. Baltimore, Md.: Williams and Wilkins.

Suraci, A. 1964. "Environmental stimulus reduction as a technique to effect the reactivation of crucial repressed memories." *J. nerv. ment. Dis.*, 138, 172–180.

Suzuki, Daisetz T. 1959. *The Training of the Zen Buddhist Monk*. New York: University Books.

Suzuki, Shunryu. 1968. Lecture given at Zen Mountain Center, July 1968. *Wind Bell*, 7, nos. 3–4, 26–28.

Targ, R., and D. Hurt. 1971. "Learning clairvoyance and precognition with an extrasensory perception teaching machine." Paper, Parapsychological Assn., Durham, N.C.

Tart, Charles T. 1963. "Physiological correlates of psi cognition." *Int. J. Parapsychol.*, 5, 375–386.

Tart, Charles T. 1966. "Card-guessing tests: Learning paradigm or extinction paradigm?" *J. Amer. Soc. psychical Res.*, 60, 46–55.

Tart, Charles T. 1968. "Hypnosis, psychedelics, and psi: Conceptual models." In Cavanna and Ullman, 1968, pp. 24–41.

Tart, Charles T. 1969. *Altered States of Consciousness: Book of Readings.* New York: Wiley.

Tart, Charles T. 1971. *On Being Stoned: A Psychological Study of Marijuana Intoxication.* Palo Alto, Calif. Science and Behavior Books.

Tart, Charles T. 1972. "Some studies of psychokinesis with a spinning silver coin." *J. Soc. psychical Res.*, in press.

Taylor, G. Rattray. 1954. *Sex in History.* New York: Ballantine.

Taylor, J., ed. 1958. *Selected Writings of John Hughlings Jackson.* New York: Basic Books.

Tchijevsky, A. L. 1933. *Trans. Central Laboratory Sci. Res. Ionification.* Voronej, The Commune: Publication House.

Teilhard de Chardin, Pierre. 1959. *The Phenomenon of Man.* New York: Harper.

Teuber, H. L. 1965. "Postscript: Some needed revisions of the classical views of agnosia." *Neuropsychologia*, 3, 371–378.

Thass-Thienemann, Theodore. 1955. "Left-handed writing: A study in the psychoanalysis of language." *Psychoanal. Rev.*, 42, 239–261.

Tomkins, Sylvan. 1964a. "Left and right: A basic dimension in personality and ideology." In Robert W. White, ed. *The Study of Lives.* New York: Atherton, 1964.

Tomkins, Sylvan. 1964b. "The psychology of knowledge." Invited address to Division 8 of the American Psychological Association, September 1964.

Toulmin, S. 1967. "Neuroscience and human understanding." In Quarton, Melnechuck, and Schmitt, 1967.

Trevarthen, C. B. 1962. "Double visual learning in split-brain monkeys." *Science*, 136, 258–259.

Tweedale, E. I. 1925. *Man's Survival After Death.* London: Grant Richards.

Udenfriend, S., H. Weissbach, and C. T. Clark. 1955. "The estimation of 5-hydroxtryptamine (serotonin) in biological tissues." *J. biol. Chem.*, 215, 337–344.

Ullman, M., and S. Krippner. 1969. "A laboratory approach to the nocturnal dimension of paranormal experience: report of a confirmatory study using the REM monitoring technique." *Biol. Psychiat.*, 1, 259–270.

Ullman, M., and S. Krippner. 1970. *Dream Studies and Telepathy: An Experimental Approach.* New York: Parapsychology Foundation.

Ullman, M., S. Krippner, and S. Feldstein. 1966. "Experimentally-induced telepathic dreams: Two studies using EEG-REM monitoring technique." *Int. J. Neuropsychiat.*, 2, 420–438.

Underhill, Evelyn. 1955. *Mysticism: A Study in the Nature and Development of Man's Spiritual Consciousness.* New York: Meridian.

Van de Castle, R. 1969. "The facilitation of ESP through hypnosis." *Amer. J. clin. Hypnosis*, 12, 37–56.

Vasiliev, L. 1963. *Experiments in Mental Suggestion.* Church Crookham, Hampshire, England: Institute for the Study of Mental Images.

Venables, P. H. 1964. "Input dysfunction in schizophrenia." In Maher, 1964.

Vinken, P. J., and G. W. Bruyn, eds. 1969. *Handbook of Clinical Neurology*, Vol. IV. Amsterdam: North Holland Pub.

Von Bonin, G., trans. 1960. *Some Papers on the Cerebral Cortex.* Springfield, Ill.: Thomas.

Von Senden, M. 1960. *Space and Sight.* Glencoe, Ill.: Free Press.

Wadhams, P., and B. Farrelley. 1968. "The investigation of psychokinesis using beta particles." *J. Soc. psychical Res.*, 44, 736.

Wallace, Robert Keith. 1970. "Physiological effects of Transcendental Meditation." *Science*, 167, 1751–1754.

Wallace, Robert Keith, Herbert Benson, and Archie F. Wilson. 1971. "A wakeful hypometabolic physiologic state." *Amer. J. Physiol.*, 221, no. 3, 795–799.

Wallach, H., and D. N. O'Connell. 1953. "The kinetic depth effect." *J. exper. Psychol.*, 45, no. 4, 205–218.

Walter, R. D., and C. L. Yeager. 1956. "Visual imagery and electroencephalographic changes." *EEG clin. Neurophysiol.*, 8, 193–199.

Warrack, G. 1952. *Julian of Norwich, Revelations of Divine Love.* London: Metheun.

Washburn, Margaret. 1916. *Movement and Mental Imagery.* New York and Boston: Houghton Mifflin.

Watson, James. 1968. *The Double Helix.* New York: Atheneum.

Watts, Alan W. 1950. *The Supreme Identity.* New York: Pantheon.

Watts, Alan W. 1962. *The Joyous Cosmology: Adventures in the Chemistry of Consciousness.* New York: Pantheon.

Wehner, A. P. 1968. "The biological significance of electroaerosols." *Scientia*, 103, 1–15.

Weisenberg, T., and K. E. McBride. 1935. *Aphasia: A Clinical and Psychological Study.* New York: Commonwealth Fund.

Weisman, A. 1958. "Reality sense and reality testing." *Behav. Sci.*, 3, 228–261.

Werner, H. 1957. *Comparative Psychology of Mental Development.* New York: International Universities Press.

Wertheim, N. 1963. "Disturbances of the musical functions." In Halpern, 1963.

Whatmore, G. 1967. "Tension factors in schizophrenia and depression." In Jacobson, 1967.

White, H. H. 1961. "Cerebral hemispherectomy in the treatment of infantile hemiplegia." *Confin. Neurol.*, 21, 1–50.

White, Lynn, Jr. 1967. "The historical roots of our ecologic crisis." *Science*, 155 (March 10, 1967), 1203–1207.

White, R. 1964. "A comparison of old and new methods of response to targets in ESP experiments." *J. Amer. Soc. psychical Res.*, 58, 21–56.

Whitehead, Alfred North. 1925. *Science and the Modern World.* New York: Macmillan.

Wigan, A. L. 1844. *The Duality of the Mind.* London: Longman.

Wilson, W., ed. 1965. *Applications of Electroencephalography in Psychiatry.* Durham, N.C.: Duke Univ. Press.

Woods, J. 1914. *The Yoga-system of Patanjali.* Cambridge, Mass.: Harvard Univ. Press.

Worden, J. L. 1961. "Proliferation of mammalian cells in ion-controlled environments." *J. Natl. Cancer Inst.*, 26, 801–811.

Wordsworth, W. 1904. "Intimations of Immortality from Recollections of Early Childhood." In *Complete Poetical Works of William Wordsworth.* New York: Houghton Mifflin, Riverside Press.

Wyrwicka, W., and M. B. Sterman. 1968. "Instrumental conditioning of sensorimotor cortex EEG spindles in the waking cat." *Physiol. Behav.*, 3, 703–707.

Young, J. Z. 1962. "Why do we have two brains?" In Mountcastle, 1962.

Zangwill, O. L. 1961. "Asymmetry of cerebral hemisphere function." In H. Garland, ed. *Scientific Aspects of Neurology.* London: E. & S. Livingstone, 1961.

Zangwill, O. L. 1964a. "The current status of cerebral dominance." *Res. Publ. Assn. Res. nerv. ment. Dis.*, 42, 103–113.

Zangwill, O. L. 1964b. "Intelligence in aphasia." In De Reuck and O'Connor, 1964.

Zangwill, O. L. 1967. "Speech and the minor hemisphere." *Acta Neurol. Psychiat. Belgica*, 67, 1013–1020.

Zubeck, J., D. Pushkar, W. Sanson, and J. Gowing. 1961. "Perceptual changes after prolonged sensory isolation (darkness and silence)." *Canad. J. Psychol.*, 15, 83–100.

Index